Praise for Buzz Kill

"*Buzz Kill* describes in riveting detail a disturbing and colossal get-your-friends-rich-quick scheme that exposes political influence-peddling by well-connected commercial forces. DeVillaer provides an insightful, alarming and revealing account of the federal government's feverish drive to commercialize cannabis in Canada and the massive propaganda campaign behind it. Despite ongoing assurances to the contrary, public health has reportedly taken a back seat to profits, privilege and party politics. As DeVillaer reveals, the government's "Reefer Madness" drive to rapidly commercialize cannabis within one election cycle is quickly heading toward re-criminalization as its ill-conceived, industry-driven and overambitious legal supply and marketing structure appears to be collapsing under its own lofty weight. *Buzz Kill* calls for and describes a more thoughtful, rational, apolitical, and public-health-grounded approach to remove crime from cannabis while reducing the potential harm of its misuse."

– Les Hagen, M.S.M.
Adjunct Professor, School of Public Heath, College of Health Sciences, University of Alberta

"Thoughtful and well-researched, this book explores the full breadth of this process from its early conception through to the present-day and draws links between the economic, political and policy components of this drastic policy shift. *Buzz Kill* is a must read for everyone concerned about Canada's drug policies and for those who want to learn lessons from this radical experiment."

– Malcolm G. Bird, PhD
Associate professor, Department of Political Science, University of Winnipeg

T0384222

"*Buzz Kill* is one of those rare books that is meticulously researched but at the same time passionate and easy to read. It is essential reading for those working in the fields of addiction, public health and public policy."

– Meldon Kahan MD CCFP FRCPC
Medical Director, META:PHI
Staff physician, Substance Use Service

"This important book brings needed critical perspective to cannabis legalization as a public health achievement. DeVillaer's exposé of broken promises, corruption, and outsized corporate influence is essential reading for drug policy observers in Canada and jurisdictions seeking to avoid the same mistakes."

– Andy Hathaway
Professor of sociology
University of Guelph

"*Buzz Kill* is a compelling story of how the legalization of cannabis unfolded and how the public good was subverted to corporate interests and those of its government enablers [...] This deeply researched book is a cautionary tale—a must-read for understanding the cannabis industry's troubling record, the dangers going forward, and what can be done to change course with alternatives that prioritize public health.

– Bruce Campbell
Adjunct professor, York University, Faculty of Environmental and Urban Change.

"In *Buzz Kill: The Corporatization of Cannabis*, Michael DeVillaer tells the story of how the Liberal Party of Canada abandoned its commitment to decriminalizing cannabis possession in favour of a system of legalization that comes nowhere close to its purported goals of realizing social justice and protecting public health. As DeVillaer cogently demonstrates, the real and tragic story of cannabis law reform in this country is one of ignoring scientific evidence and best practices, political conflicts of interest, and an over-hyped, under-regulated and corrupt industry fixated on maximizing profits with little to no regard for public interests. A must-read for anyone interested in the evolution of Canada's drug policy and the program of decriminalization that the author concludes is desperately needed to get us out of this mess."

– Steven Bittle
Full Professor/Professeur Titulaire
Department of Criminology/Département de criminologie
University of Ottawa/Université d'Ottawa

"The back story of the legalization of cannabis in Canada unfolds in Mike DeVillaer's book. From the hazards of the legal alcohol, tobacco and pharmaceutical industries, to detailed descriptions of the tensions between public health and a commercial approach, and the outcomes of the first years since the Cannabis Act was proclaimed, DeVillaer has written a well-organized, very readable and extensively researched book. Recommended."

– Jennifer Brasch, MD, FRCPC, FCPA
Lead, Addiction Psychiatry
St. Joseph's Healthcare Hamilton

"In this trenchant analysis of the Trudeau government's decision to open the commercial cannabis market in Canada, Buzz Kill connects the consequences of this action to the historic impacts of the alcohol and tobacco trade. Combining scholarly detail and personal reflections, Mike DeVillaer sets a roadmap towards healthier ways to supply these addictive substances. [...] This book is a must read for all those who care about substance use—and should be required reading for those responsible for regulating such markets."

– Cynthia Callard
Executive Director
Physicians for a Smoke-Free Canada

"We have years of experience in seeing how the tobacco and alcohol industries abused self-regulation to increase the use of their products. [...] The legislation allowing recreational use of cannabis has set free an industry that is focused first and foremost on driving consumption and increasing profits to the detriment of public health concerns. *Buzz Kill* documents how we should have seen the multiple warning signs. DeVillaer did, but people in power ignored him."

– Joel Lexchin MD, CCFP(EM), FCFP
Emergency Physician, Retired
Emergency Department
University Health Network
Toronto

BUZZ KILL

The Corporatization of Cannabis

Michael R. DeVillaer

Montréal · New York · London

Black Rose Books No.WW429

Library and Archives Canada Cataloguing in Publication:
Title: Buzz kill : the corporatization of cannabis / Michael R. DeVillaer.
Names: DeVillaer, Michael R., author.
Description: Includes bibliographical references.
Identifiers: Canadiana (print) 20220469989 | Canadiana (ebook) 20220470014 | ISBN 9781551647975 (hardcover) | ISBN 9781551647951 (softcover) | ISBN 9781551647999 (PDF)
Subjects: LCSH: Marijuana industry—Government policy—Canada. | LCSH: Corporatization—Canada.
Classification: LCC HD9019.M382 C3 2023 | DDC 338.1/73790971—dc23

Cover design by Associés Libres.

C.P. 42002, Succ. Roy
Montréal, QC H2W 2T3
CANADA
blackrosebooks.com

ORDERING INFORMATION

CANADA / USA	UK / INTERNATIONAL
University of Toronto Press	Central Books
5201 Dufferin Street	50 Freshwater Road
Toronto, ON	Chadwell Heath, London
M3H 5T8	RM8 1RX
1-800-565-9523	+44 20 85 25 8800
utpbooks@utpress.utoronto.ca	contactus@centralbooks.com

Table of Contents

*for the
ladder
builders
and the
climbers*

Acknowledgements

I would like to acknowledge the input of individuals who read portions of the manuscript and offered suggestions for improvement. These include Francois Gagnon, Clayton McCann, Robert Simpson, Paula Stanghetta, and Darryl Upfold. I would also like to thank editing coordinator Clara Swan Kennedy at Black Rose Books and the book's copy editor Jesse Chase. Most of all, I want to thank my wife Violet for doing so much so I could do this.

The perspectives and recommendations contained herein are my own and do not necessarily extend to the contributors listed or to any organizations with which I am affiliated.

An earlier version of Chapter 5 was published as DeVillaer, Michael. 2019. "Cannabis Legalization: Lessons from Alcohol, Tobacco, and Pharmaceutical Industries", in *High Time: The Legalization and Regulation of Cannabis in Canada,* edited by Andrew Potter and Daniel Weinstock. Montréal: McGill-Queens University Press, 2019.

Some content in Chapters 6 and 7 was taken from DeVillaer, Michael. 2022. "Cannabis Legalization: *Déjà Vu* All Over Again?" in *The High North: Cannabis in Canada,* edited by Andrew D. Hathaway and Clayton James Smith McCann. Vancouver: University of British Columbia Press, 2022.

Some content in Chapter 6 was taken from DeVillaer, Michael. 2019. "Cannabis Legalization in Canada: The Public Health Approach We Did Not Get." *Canadian Journal of Addictions,* 2019:10(3);51-59.

Introduction

This is the story of one of Canada's least understood drug policy failures that quietly unfolded beneath the cover of two calamitous and loud pandemics: COVID-19 and drug overdoses.

Buzz Kill: The Corporatization of Cannabis tells the story of how the Liberal Party of Canada abandoned a half century of social justice advocacy and expert advice in favour of establishing a lucrative new drug industry. The undisclosed intent was to enrich a small group of Party elites already invested in a cannabis industry for therapeutic (medical) use. They anticipated enormous financial rewards with the expansion into recreational use.

The Liberal Party did not tell us about that part. It told us our children were buying cannabis from dangerous organized crime figures—something the academic research and the government's own intel indicated was not true. They also told us that a legal industry would be strictly regulated to operate within a law-abiding framework to provide safe products. This book tells how that did not go so well. The industry often produced substandard, mislabelled or contaminated products. Regulatory non-compliance was common. Some companies engaged in criminal activity and still retained their production licenses. The Royal Canadian Mounted Police (RCMP) and investigative journalists uncovered evidence that some licensed companies are connected to organized crime. The Canadian Government denies it.

Large cannabis corporations purchased or built some of the world's largest greenhouses—that sat mostly empty. Yet the industry still produced much more cannabis than it could sell. An analysis by *Marijuana Business Daily* found that between 2018 and 2020, Canadian cannabis companies incinerated more product than they sold. Some of the largest licensed production companies have accumulated billions of dollars in debt and have yet to turn an annual profit. Many companies closed multiple growing facilities. Thousands of employees lost their jobs while some of Canada's largest cannabis corporations collected millions of dollars in COVID-19 federal government subsidies—ostensibly to protect those jobs. As stock values plunged and companies declared insolvency the savings and dreams of once-hopeful investors were replaced with debt and despair. But the corporate cannabis executives, including the ones who broke the law, walked away with millions of dollars in salary, bonuses, and guaranteed severances. None have been held legally accountable. In contrast, thousands of people in Canada are still being arrested for petty cannabis infractions. How could anyone think this was a success?

The Cannabis Act requires the Canadian Government to evaluate its legalization of cannabis. In mid-2022, Health Canada was being very guarded about the timeframe for the report's completion. When released, it is unlikely to be more than a meticulously crafted exoneration. *Buzz Kill* was written to provide the disheartening but necessary counterpoint to set the record straight.

Section I
Laying the Foundation

Chapter 1

Playing with Our Body Chemistry: Drugs and Society

DRUGS: A MOSAIC OF CONTRADICTIONS

Legal industries for alcohol, tobacco, and pharmaceutical products are older than any of us. We have known them only as mature, adult industries and must read about their birth and early development. The legalization of cannabis—the creation of a new legal drug industry—is an unprecedented experience for Canadians, and increasingly, for the people of other nations.

For the licensed cannabis industry, we have witnessed, in real time, the courtship, conception and birth. The legalization for therapeutic (medical) use survived an unsteady infancy and childhood. Legalization for recreational use has been a stormy adolescence. The challenges of adulthood await. Its elder drug industry siblings watch with curiosity and knowing opportunism. This is an experiment and not the controlled kind.

To understand a new drug industry, the biggest mistake we could make would be to think about it as a strictly contemporary and solitary phenomenon. If we want to understand the likely results of the legalization and corporatization of cannabis, we must understand how our other legal drug corporations selling alcohol, tobacco and pharmaceutical products, operate within a societal context. And we must understand the forces—commercial, cultural, political and otherwise—that shape that societal context and how that context shapes how we think about and use drugs.

The prevailing societal narratives about various types of drugs, spanning decades and continents, comprise a confusing mosaic of contradictions. Drugs are deified and demonized. Their use is promoted, enabled and rewarded. Drug use is also discouraged, restricted, banned, and punished—sometimes severely.

Drugs calm us and energize us. They bring us together to bond, laugh, celebrate, make love and to worship. Drugs save lives and make many types of discomfort, including stress and trauma, easier to endure. They also injure us, make us sick and disable us—sometimes before we are even born.

We also use drugs to amuse ourselves, usually harmlessly. But some of us gradually amuse ourselves to death. Drugs can also end lives suddenly—by carelessness or hopelessness. They are also used to end lives as a questionable attempt at justice—perhaps more accurately described as societal vengeance. Other times drugs are used to end lives with compassion—but not without controversy.

In the realm of drug policy and politics, provocation, controversy and divisiveness are the norm. This is not new. In 1967 members of the United Kingdom Young Communists League referred to cannabis legalization as "a capitalist plot" (Seddon 2020). A half century later, a Canadian United Conservative Party Member of the Legislative Assembly in Alberta warned that cannabis legalization "could lead to a communist revolution" (Kornik and Ramsay 2017). What might a dispassionate anthropologist in a distant future write about all this?

Beneath the surface mosaic of contradiction is a foundation of evidence that helps to make sense of it all. Some of the evidence is deeply disturbing and challenges our fondest beliefs about who we are as a species and what kind of society we have made. I will not shy away from presenting this evidence and introducing its disquieting implications.

To fully appreciate the longer term implications of the establishment of a new drug industry requires an indispensable understanding of foundational concepts concerning drugs and society. This foundation includes why people use drugs and how we, often deceptively, talk about drugs. It also includes how we use drugs to bond with each other. Then there is the complex matter of why some people develop problems from their use of drugs (while most do not) and what we, as a society, have tried to do about that. Attempted solutions have ranged from evidenced-based and humanitarian to illconceived, exploitive and destructive. We must also consider how drug use affects the economy (and vice-versa). Our legal drug businesses have been allowed, to varying degrees, to promote their products, sometimes to vulnerable populations, in ways that are manipulative, duplicitous and profoundly harmful. At the same time fabrication and hyperbole have been deployed to demonize some unlicensed drug trades and their customers, providing a strategic distraction from the often unethical and sometimes illegal conduct of legal drug businesses.

The world has three long-established, legal, commercial drug industries—alcohol, tobacco, and pharmaceutical; and we have three international public health crises associated with the products of these industries. This is chronically the case for the recreational drugs tobacco and alcohol (Oxford Martin School, n.d.). What are the implications of this for cannabis as it continues to make its historic transformation from an illegal, demonized drug to a glamourous and celebrated, commercialized pastime?

To further broaden your understanding of the place and role of drugs in society, I would recommend a book titled *Drugs and Society*, by Andrew Hathaway, at the University of Guelph's Department of Sociology and Anthropology.

WHAT DOES THIS BOOK HAVE TO OFFER?

Canadian Prime Minister, Justin Trudeau, said "Legalization is not an event, it's a process...and that process will continue." Mr. Trudeau is correct. Four years in, legalization for recreational use continues to evolve in ways that have been mostly predictable, but with a few surprising variants. It is reasonable to expect more surprises to come.

To provide context, parts of this book cover historic information related to other drug industries and a very brief history of cannabis law reform beginning with prohibition. However, for the contemporary cannabis legalization story, the book begins with recreational legalization at sub-national jurisdictions in the United States—specifically with the State of Colorado in 2012. It then moves onto legalization for therapeutic (medical) and recreational use in Canada. It also covers developments in other countries including Uruguay and European nations. I have tried to keep up with major events through the middle of 2022, but, unavoidably, there will be some omissions. Cannabis legalization, in Canada and abroad, continues to be a highly dynamic one. As this book was entering the production phase, new, exciting events continued to happen. It was painful to have to exclude them. By the time you read this book, significant events will have occurred that are not included here. But the book will help you evaluate both the implications and importance of those developments.

This book is not about the cannabis plant or the drug molecules within the plant. There is little about the people who use cannabis, or its effects, including the harms and benefits accrued. It is not principally about the legalization of cannabis for therapeutic (medical) use other than when it has some direct relevance to legalization for recreational use.

The book is primarily about the process of commercial cannabis legalization for recreational use in Canada, how it went seriously wrong, and why. The book also describes alternative approaches to cannabis law reform that were recommended to the Canadian government by both domestic and foreign health policy organizations. And how and why the government ignored that advice.

Finally, this book offers cannabis legalization as a compelling example of how Canada's drug policy, in general, continues to be a domestically tragic and internationally embarrassing failure.

WHAT DOES THIS CHAPTER PROVIDE?

Most of this chapter is about drugs other than cannabis and little of the content refers to cannabis legalization. That is also the case for the next chapter. But these first two chapters provide a critical foundation for understanding cannabis legalization as the focus of the book. Until then, to help keep you connected to the main topic, I will end many sections of this and the next chapter with a paragraph prefaced with Implications for Cannabis Legalization. The questions and comments in the paragraph will prompt you to think about the implications of the preceding content for cannabis legalization. Later chapters will dig into those issues.

The first two chapters, which I think of as the warm, shallow end of the book, are intended to invite you to wade in. They will provide an overview and introduction to many concepts. I save many of the details for what I consider the deep end of the book that comes later. The foundational concepts covered in the first two chapters will provide some supportive buoyancy for when you venture into the deep end.

I am not normally one to drown readers or listeners with what is sometimes derisively referred to as a data tsunami or data dump. But I will make some provocative statements in this first chapter and you are entitled to some substantiation. So prepare yourself for the tsunami. To make the data less overwhelming, I have spread it around throughout the sections of this chapter.

I will use the data to substantiate two main points. The first is that drugs pose a major health and social problem in Canada. It was a major problem long before the current drug overdose crisis caught everyone's attention. Drug problems also contribute significant costs to our economy.

The second point is one that is surprising for most people who do not work in the drug field (and even for some who do). It is our legal drugs that account for most of the drug-related harm and economic costs. The contribution of illegal drugs, by comparison, is small. By some measures, extremely small. This should make us wonder what the war on drugs (the illegal ones) was all about.

While detailed substantiation is beyond the scope of this book, both points apply equally well to most nations worldwide. A glimpse is provided in a compelling graphic posted by the Oxford Martin School (n.d.).

When you have finished reading this chapter you may see drugs and their role in society from a novel, more nuanced and hopefully more fascinating perspective. You will possess a fuller understanding than almost all the Canadian legislators who voted yay or nay (mostly yay) on cannabis legalization. This is also true for the legislators who are now considering the legalization of other currently illegal drugs and the decriminalization of all drugs. You will be able to apply this foundation to understanding the potential benefits and perils of drug law reform, not only in Canada, but also across the globe. The next decade will be an interesting and unprecedented one for world-wide drug policy reform. But that is getting ahead of ourselves. I will return to laying the foundation for this provocative story.

A DRUG BY ANY OTHER NAME

"I am, by calling, a dealer in words; and words are, of course, the most powerful drug used by mankind."

— *Rudyard Kipling*

Whether by calling or not, we are all dealers in words when we talk about drugs. When I talk about drugs, drug products, drug use, drug problems or drug policy I use the word drug with its most inclusive application—to alcohol, tobacco, cannabis, caffeine, pharmaceutical products, and a lot of other substances of illegal or uncertain status. I call all of them drugs because that is what they are. (But please do not ask me if sugar is a drug. I once posed the question to a pharmacologist, an expert on such matters. She winced and quickly changed the subject.)

In ironic contrast to my chosen lexicon, companies that produce and sell recreational drug products will rarely, if ever, explicitly acknowledge publicly that they are in a drug business. In their lexicon, they do not sell drugs, they sell pleasure and belonging.

Beer, wine and spirits producers and retailers never use the words drug, ethanol or alcohol in their advertising and marketing. Promotional content is not concerned so much with the product, as it is with the social benefits, real and imagined, of enjoying the product. Canadian advertising icon Terry O'Reilly has cleverly opined that Molson is not so overtly in the beer business, as it is in the party business.

Words can be fashioned into less appetizing impressions as well. The next time you see an aesthetically seductive ad for an alcohol beverage, consider that alcohol is a product of a fermentation process involving yeast and bacteria. Alcohol is the urine of micro-organisms. This adds a more literal meaning to "getting pissed."

In the days when tobacco companies more publicly advertised cigarettes, they were not inclined to mention nicotine to promote their product. Neither does the new nicotine monger on the market—the e-cigarette (vaping) industry. This industry has been called out by Physicians for a Smoke-Free Canada as "...the highly-transmissible vaping variant of the older tobacco pandemic." You will never see the word nicotine or addiction in public promotions for e-cigarettes either. A Reuters investigation quoted a former executive from e-cigarette company, Juul, who disclosed that the company's sales staff would emphasize "the device's unique addictive power" only when they were talking to retailers (Kirkham 2019).

In his book, Smokescreen, Philip Hilts (1996, 217) tells how language used within the tobacco industry obscured the reality of what they did:

> *Things that cause disease become things that are "biologically active". Nicotine becomes "satisfaction". The rank bitterness that indicates how much nicotine a smoker is getting becomes "its impact". Addiction is just a "habit". Toxic chem-*

icals are merely "controversial compounds". Children are "the youth market".

Neither do cannabis companies ever talk about being a drug company. Interestingly, some cannabis companies will extol elevated levels of delta 9 tetra-hydra cannabinol (THC) in its products. THC is the component most responsible for cannabis' psychoactive effects. In doing so, these companies conflate potency with quality and desirability, or worse yet, with bad-ass machismo, or what a tobacco marketer once called, in the case of women, "female virility." The legal cannabis industry is still immature, and largely testosterone mediated. I expect that it will eventually learn and mature out of its current pubescence.

Even pharmaceutical companies will almost never use the word drug in their public communications. They prefer the unstigmatized "medicine" or "product." The fine art of euphemism has also found its way into the language used by Health Canada in its inspections of licensed cannabis producers. If a licensed producer fails to follow legislative and regulatory requirements, the inspectors do not report an infraction or failure, they report an "observation." When Health Canada requires a producer to issue a recall of a contaminated or improperly labelled product, it is called a "voluntary recall" by the manufacturer.

The murky vernacular often found in industry and government bureaucracy has also infiltrated our daily language customs. Very few people would say they were going to take a drug when they intended to use alcohol, tobacco, cannabis, or caffeine, except satirically. When I worked in The Centre for Addiction and Mental Health's (CAMH) Community Programs Office in Hamilton, Ontario, I would sometimes tell my colleagues that I was going downtown to buy drugs and ask if anyone else wanted to score. They knew I was going on a coffee run. I must confess that I always thought there was something disturbingly Huxleyan about lining up for a drug to help us get through the day. Calling this drug product, a latte, cappuccino, double-double, Frappuccino, or matcha green tea lassi seems so much less dystopian.

Nonetheless, the word drug aptly applies to caffeine, possibly the most popular recreational drug in the world, and one that many of us have already used today. I do not give much attention to caffeine in this book as it is not commonly associated with significant harm. That said, I would not dispute a challenge concerning the ten days of headaches and lethargy that come from caffeine withdrawal when one abruptly curtails long-term daily intake of cappuccinos and flat whites. I re-learned this recently. It was not an enjoyable experience. I am reminded of 18th century English writer Samuel Johnson who wryly confessed to being "...a hardened and shameless tea drinker."

But isn't it interesting how commonplace is the use of the word drug when we talk about the illegal ones? There are the legacy street drugs: heroin, opium, cocaine, crystal meth (methamphetamine), LSD (lysergic acid diethylamide), peyote, psilocybin, MDMA (methylenedioxymethamphetamine), etc. When substances belonging to legal pharmaceutical categories of medicines such as stimulants, sedative-hypnotics, and opioids are diverted from the legal supply to the street, they become illegal. Only at that point, are they commonly called drugs. They are the same substances; only the context has changed. Illegal knockoffs of these substances are forged in clandestine drug labs. A presumption of purity and dosage from these labs is always a gamble that, too often, ends in drug overdoses and drug-related deaths. In addition to the legacy drugs, we also have designer drugs, with new ones emerging from underground labs as you read this.

The stigma attached to the word drugs has led to language changes in our health and social care systems as well, giving rise to the use of the word "substance" as in substance use and substance misuse.

The law enforcement system has not been so quick to likewise respond. The police drug squad carries out drug raids on illicit labs and the homes of those involved in the retail end of the illegal drug trade. The media covers these events with great fanfare as drug busts.

In contrast, no one is smashing down doors in the middle of the night when legal drug companies run afoul of the law. The broader context is that we have two types of drug crime in Canada. One type is committed by people who trade in drugs that are illegal. They are serviced by the drug squads, armed with battering rams and military ordnance. The other type of drug crime is committed by people who have licenses to sell legal drug products but, as we will see in later chapters, often do so illegally. This group receives the polite attention of government ministries or commissions, and only rarely the courts. Battering rams and war weaponry are replaced by legal documents, warning letters, and stay-out-of-jail-free cards. Unlike their unlicensed counterparts, corporate drug law violators almost never go to jail or prison. The inequity of this juxtaposition might be enshrined in social media with hashtags such as:

#DealersInHoodiesVersusDealersInSuits

#CrimeInTheStreetsVersusCrimeInTheSuites.

If there really is such a thing as turning in one's grave, George Orwell must get a great deal of exercise.

Much has been made of the stigmatization of drug use, which is widespread and harmful, as are the harms from indiscriminate drug use. However, stigma represents only one end of a spectrum of attitudes about drugs. At the other end is the valorization of drug use—the disingenuous and perilous promise of an upgraded lifestyle from playing with one's body chemistry. This omnipresent promise has been, in part, the architect of our pandemics of alcohol and tobacco harms. Both extremes of drug attitudes are harmful.

Implication for Cannabis Legalization: How will the language used to describe cannabis and cannabis users change? Will it become less stigmatized? Will commercial interests unrealistically glamourize cannabis? Will we call it a drug? Confronted with stigmatization and glamourization, will we find that elusive sweet spot of informed and non-judgmental acceptance when we talk about cannabis?

WHY DO PEOPLE USE DRUGS, ANYWAY?

So, here's the thing, people want to use drugs, and they take their drugs seriously. Some people's quality of life, and even their lives, depend upon specific drug products from pharmaceutical companies. The recreational use of drugs, such as alcohol, tobacco, caffeine, and cannabis, is not life saving, but their use is still important to people. In Canada, producers, distributors, and retailers of alcohol and cannabis have been widely protected as "essential services" during the COVID-19 pandemic. I recall a discussion on alcohol policy just a few years ago in which Catherine Zahn, CEO of The Centre for Addiction and Mental Health (CAMH), exclaimed "There are no beer emergencies." I agree. Apparently, Canada's provincial governments do not. In 2021, Dr. Zahn stepped down from CAMH to become the Deputy Minister of Health for Ontario. Beer and liquor stores in Ontario remained essential services.

People who use illegal drugs are also very serious about it, and well organized. They have formed not-for-profit organizations with formal memberships. They fund-raise, they stimulate discussion among the public, and lobby the government for legislative reform. Some of these organizations have a President, a Board of directors, and written constitutions and bylaws. They maintain websites where they cite articles from academic journals to support their cause. Consider the Canadian Association of People Who Use Drugs (http://capud.ca/). Then consider The International Network of People Who Use Drugs (https://www.inpud.net/) with dozens of regional and national affiliates. #PWUD has become a widely recognized acronym and hashtag on social media. I admire these organizations. Not because their members use drugs—anyone can do that. It is their untiring, lived experience commitment to a compassionate rather than punitive approach to drug policy that is admirable. This is a concept that continues to elude many leaders in almost all nations. A sad aspect of the plight of these groups raises an interesting contradiction. They resent that government-imposed laws threaten their personal control over their bodies. But those who are drug-dependent, perhaps for reasons beyond their control, have already surrendered control of their bodies to one or more types of drugs. It is also important to recognize that this surrender is cultivated, at least in part, by the people who manufacture and sell them legally and illegally.

So, why do people use drugs? The question is asked by students working on a class project and by academics devoting their careers to the pursuit of the elusive answer. This seemingly simple question has been discussed and disputed, sometimes fiercely, for many decades. It has been addressed in an unimaginable number of books, movies, documentaries, interviews, reports from health authorities, journal articles, lectures, debates, and seminars. The ubiquity of the question continues with its presence on websites, podcasts, blogs, social media posts, as well as in many substance-fueled pub discussions. I will attempt only a summary of the predominant views.

Across centuries and continents, we have used drugs to rid ourselves of illness and other discomforts, or to make them and injuries easier to endure. We use drugs to alleviate or prevent a wide variety of unwanted physical and psychological sensations. Simply put, drugs can make us feel better, or at least less miserable for a while.

We have also shown a persistent curiosity for using drugs to amuse ourselves—essentially, by playing with our body chemistry. This is what we now colloquially call recreational use, and is the focus of this chapter, and most of this book.

To do it justice, the answer to the question of why people use drugs must be broken down into three sequential stages: initial use, occasional use, and daily or almost daily use. The potential for entering a fourth category—high-risk use; and a fifth category– problem use, exists at all three sequential stages. However, the likelihood of engaging in high-risk use or problem use would tend to increase as one moves from initial use to daily use.

Before describing each of these categories of drug use, it is important to appreciate that they are not distinct categories. Rather, they represent sequential stages along a spectrum of drug use, with only vaguely defined separation points. Any attempt to quantifiably distinguish the sequential stages from each other is somewhat arbitrary. The statistical anchors that I offer for each stage are intended to give only a very approximate appreciation for the differences in drug use along the spectrum from initial use, through occasional use, to daily or almost daily use.

Conveying an understanding of these aspects of drug use requires that I draw upon a large body of research—the previously mentioned data tsunami. Given that drug use and associated problems comprise such a complex phenomenon, I will rely upon several data types or indicators:

- *drug use*

- *high-risk drug use*

- *harm from drug use (morbidity)*

- *drug dependence (addiction)*

- *death from drug use (mortality)*

- *drug-related costs to the economy.*

An additional overarching concept is that the transition from use of a drug to higher risk use can be mediated by three aspects of use: frequency of use, quantity of use, and circumstances of use. Using a drug every day (frequency) presents an increased risk for dependence and harm. Using high amounts of a drug (quantity) either at once or continually over time, increases the likelihood of biomedical trauma. Using a drug just before driving is a high-risk circumstance for harm. I will give more attention to each of these aspects as I explore the stages and types of use and harm.

Prevalence of Drug Use

Before looking at specific categories of drug use and problems, we can put them in societal context with prevalence data. Prevalence is a measure of the percentage of the general population that uses a drug within a given period—usually within the past year. Other common time frames include the past 30 days, the past 3 months, or over the person's lifetime.

Statistics on the prevalence of drug use are just that—reflecting only use and not necessarily harm. At an individual level, most people who use drugs do not experience serious harm. However, at the population level, the prevalence of drug use is often directly correlated with the prevalence of drug problems. If aggregate use of a drug increases in the general population, use will also increase in that segment of the population that is vulnerable to drug problems. Thus, there is likely to be an increase in the overall prevalence of problems. Accordingly, one often encounters drug use being used as a proxy for drug problems at the population level.

Statistics Canada's Canadian Tobacco, Alcohol and Drugs Survey (CTADS) is a general population survey of tobacco, alcohol, and other drug use by Canadians aged fifteen and older (Canada 2021). The most recent data were collected in 2017. The results tell us that alcohol was by far the most popular drug among Canadians with 78.2% having used it at least once in the past year. Alcohol was followed distantly by cannabis (illegal for recreational use at the time of the survey) which had been used by 14.8%. Recreational use of any type of drug in the past year, other than alcohol and cannabis, was reported by 15.7%. These other drug types include cocaine/crack, speed, methamphetamine, crystal meth, hallucinogens, ecstasy, and heroin. None of these drugs, alone, was used by more than 2.5% of survey respondents.

Tobacco use is reported by CTADS as use in the past 30 days instead of use in the past year as for the other drug types. The prevalence for any use of tobacco in the past 30 days is 17.8%. This includes cigarettes, cigars, cigarillos, e-cigarettes, pipe, water pipe, and smokeless tobacco.

The inconsistency of period prevents an equitable comparison with the other drug types. However, we can be confident that the prevalence of tobacco use in the past year would be higher than the past 30 day prevalence of 17.8%. Tobacco use would therefore remain higher than the other drug types. But we know from other sources, that it is far below the past year prevalence for alcohol use of 78.2%.

CTADS also reports on the prevalence of use of prescribed medications in the past year. Use of pain relievers (e.g., oxycodone) was reported by 11.8% of respondents, followed by 11.7% for sedatives (e.g., diazepam), and 2.4% for stimulants (e.g., methylphenidate).

Self-report surveys tend to underestimate people's use of drugs. We can expect that the true extent of use is probably higher than estimated by CTADS. Nonetheless, we can safely conclude that alcohol and tobacco appear to be the most popular drugs among Canadians, as they have been for the past half century. Alcohol remains well ahead of the pack. But cannabis is closing in on tobacco, and as we will see with some other indicators, it is surpassing tobacco.

Implication for Cannabis Legalization: Will more people who are not current cannabis users begin, or resume, cannabis use following legalization? Will there be increases in frequency of use and quantity used? Will it be used in high-risk circumstances? What is the potential for a portion of increased use to lead to higher risk use? And what portion?

Initial Use

Initial use is sometimes referred to as onset of use. Short and simple explanations for why people begin to use a drug recreationally include: peer acceptance, a proclamation of maturity, curiosity, boredom, stress, novel experience, pleasure, or escape. Any combination of these reasons can also be at play.

That is all I feel I need to say about why people start to use a drug recreationally. If you are looking for a deeper dive on the topic, there is no shortage of information available elsewhere. Just don't expect everyone, including the experts, to fully agree.

What I will do is present some information on how many Canadians have initiated drug use. Again, I turn to the Canadian Tobacco, Alcohol and Drugs Survey (CTADS) (Canada, 2021). It provides the percentage of Canadians that have ever used various drug types during their lifetime, which also tells us the percentage who have ever initiated use of each drug. We find that 90.3% of Canadians have initiated alcohol use and 40.1% have tried tobacco at some point in their life. Lifetime use of cannabis (illegal at the time of the survey) was 46.6%. Percentages for other illegal drugs drop off significantly: hallucinogens (14.8%), cocaine/crack (10.4%), ecstasy (7.5%), speed/methamphetamine/crystal meth (3.7%), and heroin (0.7%).

CTADS also provides us with the average age for initiation of use for major drug types: sixteen years for tobacco, eighteen for alcohol, and nineteen for cannabis.

Implication for Cannabis Legalization: CTADS data were collected in 2017 before recreational legalization of cannabis. It will be interesting to see if the average age for cannabis initiation will change. Upon legalization, underage users may have easier access through their legal age peers and siblings.

Occasional Use

Now it gets more interesting. This group includes people who go beyond an initial experiment with a recreational drug and continue to use it, even if only occasionally. Use of the drug has not become incorporated into their lives as a daily or near daily pastime. Occasional users include a smaller part of the population than do people who have ever used.

The continued experience of pleasure as well as the security of belonging to a group can be powerful reinforcers for drug use that continues beyond initial use. If the drug experiences continue to be pleasurable and do not become boring, the person will continue to use the drug, at least occasionally, and even alone, separate from their peer group.

It is also possible for social acceptance to be a much more powerful reinforcer than the pleasure factor. Many people who remember their first experience smoking a cigarette at an early age are unlikely to forget the memory of a burning, unpleasant taste in the mouth and throat, a disorienting light-headedness, and the discomfort of nausea. The unpleasant sensations associated with smoking might also apply to a first time of cannabis use. An over-indulgence in the first use of alcohol to the point of vomiting can also be quite memorable—also not in a good way. We might think of these initial experiences, metaphorically, as the evolutionary wisdom of our bodies trying to impart a warning—which many novice users, especially young ones, choose to ignore.

Where is the sensorial pleasure and recreational exhilaration in nausea and vomiting? Why would anyone experiencing such odious initial experiences, want to do it again, and continue to do so—as many do? The value lies mostly within the social cache of achieving acceptance into a group of peers—a rite of passage perhaps. For many young people, this milieu is one that places a premium on rebellion from adult rules while finding an easy proxy for transitional adult-like behaviour. To achieve that social cache, they are even willing to feel physically terrible for a while.

So how many brave or foolish souls soldiered on despite the initial unpleasant experiences? Based on the prevalence data, quite a few.

Implication for Cannabis Legalization: Most cannabis users have traditionally inhaled smoke to get high, and this remains the case. Will legal edible cannabis products make it more likely for first-time users to continue without having to adapt to the unpleasant, and more detectable, practice of smoking?

Daily or Almost Daily (DAD) Use

"...most of the time, what we do is what we do most of the time..."
— David Townsend

For some people, the use of a drug evolves from being an occasional activity to a more routine part of their lifestyle. Use is still very much aligned with social interaction but will also usually involve an increase in solitary use. It is sometimes referred to as habitual use. Such daily or near daily use of a drug by an individual can be an indicator of what is referred to in the public health literature as normalization.

Drug use normalization typically refers to drug use becoming embedded within broader social norms—as alcohol has become a customary

Drug Use Normalization — in an Unlikely Workplace?

I am reminded of a long-gone era (circa late 1970s-early 1980s) when I worked for the Addiction Research Foundation of Ontario. It was not uncommon for generous amounts of free alcohol to be available after educational events. Such a practice, at such an organization, seems bizarre by 2022 standards. But it was the norm of the time, and few questioned the practice. But a few did, and the discussions were fascinating. I was at a junior stage of my career and did not offer much input. But I listened carefully. One argument was that the educational events provided an opportunity to show that alcohol could be introduced into a social event in a civilized manner such that moderation and responsible use could be showcased for all to see. That sounded reasonable. The counterpoint was that a responsible attitude towards alcohol use also meant sending a message that alcohol need not be a part of every social event and should not be so elevated in its societal importance (i.e., normalized). Also, a reasonable point. It was not too many years before the counterpoint prevailed. However, I have always suspected that the change also had something to do with budgetary constraints. Alcohol for sale remains common at many academic conference social events—including ones on drug policy.

part of social events such as weddings, seasonal and anniversary celebrations and, less frequently these days, workplace social events.

Daily or almost daily drug use in an individual is recognized as the stage at which higher risk practices are more likely to be adopted and in some cases can lead to adverse consequences. It can also be an indicator of drug dependence. I will get to higher risk practices, adverse consequences, and dependence shortly.

Drug use is typically measured along two dimensions. The first is how many days a person uses a drug over a period (week, month, or year). This is called frequency. A person's drug use can also be measured in the amount used on a given occasion, usually referred to as quantity or dosage. Use, as defined by frequency and quantity, occurs along a spectrum, ranging from infrequent use of small quantities to frequent use of large quantities. As one moves from the former to the later there can be an increase in risk for moving to the problem stage of drug use. There are considerable individual differences in how people are affected by drugs and under what conditions. These individual differences can affect the movement of a person from increased drug use to higher risk use and to harmful use.

There are also uncommon variants in which a person uses a drug rarely, but in a high concentration when they do. This would include the binge drinker. I recall a former colleague who showed another variant. He was a non-smoker, except when he went to an out-of-town meeting for a couple days. He would buy a pack of cigarettes and smoke the entire pack over the two days he was away. He would then return home and not smoke at all—until the next out-of-town meeting, typically several weeks from then. I once asked him if he ever craved a cigarette when he returned home. He said he did not, also noting this was a good thing because his wife would not tolerate it.

Surveys that measure use patterns of major drug types find that most people's use of drugs is at the low end of frequency and dosage, but with a group that uses drugs such that it places them at increased risk of harm.

The Canadian Tobacco, Alcohol and Drugs Survey (CTADS) (Canada 2021) tells us that, in 2017, 10.8% of Canadians used tobacco daily and that 3.6% used cannabis daily or almost daily. Daily use of other illegal drugs occurs among only a much smaller part of the population.

CTADS does not provide information on daily use of alcohol. Another survey we can draw upon is The Centre for Addiction and Mental Health's CAMH Monitor (Nigatu et al. 2021). The 2020 Monitor found that daily drinking is reported by 9.4% of Ontarians. This survey is based upon interviews with a large sample of Ontario adults aged eighteen and older. For this, and other reasons, the data are not directly comparable to the CTADS which covers all of Canada. Nonetheless, results of this independent survey provide an estimate for daily use of alcohol that fits with a general pattern of alcohol, tobacco, and cannabis being the most used drugs.

Implications for Cannabis Legalization: As we will see in Chapter 2, legal drug industries, along with the media and pop culture, have played a significant role in normalizing drug use. Will legalization lead to the normalization of cannabis use such that daily or almost daily use will increase to that of our other two legal recreational drugs? Will cannabis use become normalized, as is alcohol, as a routine part of social events such as weddings, sports team celebrations, and seasonal or holiday festivities? What about conferences or trade meetings that have a cash bar for social events? Will cannabis edibles also be for sale? At drug policy conferences?

HIGHER RISK DRUG USE

Higher risk drug use places an individual at increased risk for experiencing harm. This could include using a large amount of a drug at one time, using a drug too often, or using it in dangerous circumstances. An important caveat is that engaging in high-risk scenarios does not guarantee that an individual will experience harm—it just increases the likelihood. For example, drinking and driving is a well-known high-risk behaviour. Yet, there are people who become intoxicated and drive, and have the good fortune to navigate their way home without incident.

We would expect to see more types of high-risk use in a person who uses on a daily or almost daily basis. However, higher risk use can also occur in a pattern of occasional use—such as drinking to a point of intoxication on an occasion that led to an injury or a public intoxication charge. This could also happen during a person's initial use of a drug. For example, trying to drive a car during one's first use of magic mushrooms would be considered higher risk circumstances.

As discussed, drug use generally occurs along a spectrum, ranging from negligible risk to substantial risk for experiencing drug problems. An individual's location on the spectrum is not necessarily fixed but can change over time. One major factor is simple maturation. Some older adolescents and young adults will spend time at the higher risk end of the spectrum. As they reach various maturation milestones in their lives—such as graduation, moving into the workforce, building a career, getting married, moving into their own home, having children—most people will move a few steps to-wards the lower risk end. So older adults generally spend more time closer to the lower risk end of the continuum. A change in peers or dramatic life changes can also lead to changes in drug use—in either direction.

Movement along the continuum is not always unidirectional. For a given individual, there may be back and forward movement over the course of their lives. A reunion may provide an opportunity to reconnect with former acquaintances and high-risk behaviours, and some people will move back towards higher risk use, but not permanently. Once the triggering antecedents are no longer in play, the revellers will re-emerge at the lower risk end. Other people, who have experienced serious disruption or trauma in their lives, may engage in increased or less judicious drug use to cope.

Exceeding Low-risk Alcohol Drinking Guidelines

Canada's Low-risk Alcohol Drinking Guidelines (Canadian Centre for Substance Use and Addiction 2013) were developed by a team of alcohol re-searchers in 2011 to provide evidence-based guidance to Canadians on maintaining low-risk alcohol consumption. The research team reviewed the available evidence and identified circumstances for zero consumption (preg-nancy, driving). It also set limits for low-risk consumption. The guidelines specified daily limits of two standard drinks for women and three standard drinks for men. The weekly limits are 10 standard drinks for women and 15 standard drinks for men. A standard drink is defined by an equivalent amount of alcohol by volume: 1.5 oz. of 40% distilled spirits, or 5 oz. of 12% wine, or 12 oz. of 5% beer or cider. Each of these standard drinks has exactly 0.6 oz of absolute or pure alcohol.

Given that the guidelines are based on research that was more than a decade old, The Canadian Centre for Substance Use and Addiction (CCSA) assembled a team of experts to review more recent research and consider the need to revise the guidelines. CCSA also held a public consultation so all Canadians could have input.[1]

The Canadian Tobacco, Alcohol and Drugs Survey (CTADS) used the 2011 guidelines to determine that 16.1% of Canadians exceeded the (chronic) low-risk consumption guidelines in 2017. That means that almost 5 million

---

1. New guidelines were released in January 2023 and were much lower. They can be seen at: https://ccsa.ca/canadas-guidance-alcohol-and-health.

Canadians over the age of fifteen were, at least occasionally, drinking in a manner that placed them at risk for experiencing harm (Canada 2021). Using the new guidelines would significantly increase that number.

Impaired Driving

Data on impaired driving is available for Ontario from the CAMH Monitor (Nigatu et al. 2020). The Monitor defines drinking and driving as having two or more drinks in the hour before driving and having done so in the previous year. In 2020, 4.7% of drivers reported doing so.

Driving after using cannabis is another risk behaviour. It is defined as having used cannabis in the hour before driving and having done so in the previous year. In 2020, 2.7% of drivers reported doing so.

To place these numbers within an interesting context, 25% of the survey's respondents reported texting while driving. The survey did not ask about other potentially distracting practices while driving such as making program selections on media devices, lighting cigarettes, or applying makeup.

Higher Risk Use of Prescribed Medications

CTADS reported on "problematic use" of prescription medications as defined by "use for reasons other than for prescribed therapeutic purposes" (i.e. "to get high"). Such higher risk use of any prescribed medication was reported by 1.2% of respondents (Canada 2021).

Non-fatal Overdoses

Another high-risk behaviour is using high quantities of a drug on a single occasion such that there is a threat to the functioning of major body organs or systems. The drugs most likely involved in overdoses include opioids, barbiturates, amphetamines, and alcohol. Overdoses can result in paramedic responses and hospital admissions.

The Special Advisory Committee on the Epidemic of Opioid Overdoses (2022) at Public Health Agency of Canada releases reports on opioid- and stimulant-related harms. Almost all opioid events involved fentanyl or its analogues. Most stimulant events included cocaine or methamphetamine. The most recent report shows that between January 1, 2016 and December 31, 2021, hospitalizations included 30,860 for opioid overdoses and 13,575 for stimulants. Given the prevalence of poly-substance use, these hospitalization counts are not mutually exclusive. Sometimes people die from their overdoses. The Advisory Committee also reports figures for those deaths. I will get to that shortly.

Implications for Cannabis Legalization: Over the last three decades we have seen major reductions in cigarette use and drinking and driving. These have been hard-earned, major public health achievements. Will cannabis legalization increase cannabis use, the inhalation of smoke, and the associated health hazards? Will cannabis legalization increase impaired driving by cannabis alone and combined with other drugs?

DRUG PROBLEMS: A SPECTRUM OF CONSEQUENCES

A drug problem is a very generic term that can involve not only various kinds of drugs, but also apply to many different scenarios related to a single drug type. A drug problem can be obvious. It can also be subjective and elusive to define.

One of the longest-lived and still unresolved controversies in the drug field is why some people use drugs to the point that it seriously disrupts their lives and continue to do so until it takes their lives. There are many theories covering biological, psychological, sociological, political, economic, and environmental factors. Many clinicians point to trauma or elevated levels of chronic stress as major contributing factors among the people who come to their clinics.

There is no single theory that has emerged to stand above all other theories in explaining harmful drug using behaviour. It is possible that all these explanations have some legitimacy and make some amount of contribution. Just as there can be several roads leading to the same city, there is no reason to believe that there would be only a single path to a drug problem. Individuals may get there via different predisposing and enabling factors and via different paths.

Some of the strongest research support for explaining drug problems comes from the psychology literature for alcohol problems. I will return to that topic later. First, we need some foundational understanding of what drug problems look like.

I want to start by dispelling a popular notion that there are safe and unsafe types of drugs and that drug problems occur when people use the unsafe ones. The reality is that any drug type can be used in ways that are safe and any drug type can be used in a manner that is dangerous. It is more about safe and dangerous decisions that lead to safe and dangerous behaviour and result in safe and dangerous consequences.

Consuming copious amounts of a drug, using drugs often, and in perilous circumstances, are all high-risk factors for experiencing problems. Drug problems become conspicuous when there are specific tangible adverse harms arising from the person's use. An important consideration is whether a person's drug use is interfering with their responsibilities or aspirations in life. Is the drug use interfering with the person's health or daily functioning, their family life, the welfare of their children, and other relationships? Is it harming financial and housing stability, or performance in school or at work? This perspective places an emphasis on being able to maintain control of one's use of the drug when it might interfere with safety, obligations, or aspirations. In other words, who is in control—the drug user or the drug? Tangible evidence of the latter, coupled with specific harms, almost always indicates a problem. The problem may not be the person's fault but it is theirs to solve. And help is available.

Drug problems, like drug use, also occur on a spectrum. At one end the consequences of misuse can be rare incidents that are embarrassing but otherwise benign. There is no shortage of such incidents ("fails") that have been immortalized in video on the internet. (I occasionally ponder my good fortune and gratitude for there being no internet during my early adult years.) At the other end of the continuum, dire consequences can occur daily and disrupt and literally destroy lives. Many people with drug problems will experience consequences between these two extremes.

The critical point to be made is that the world is not so simple that we have only two distinct groups of people, one who's drug use is "normal" and the other made up of people who are often referred to as "alcoholics" or "addicts." The people bearing these labels can be regarded in a very stigmatized manner with the labels being used derisively to add discrimination to their difficult lives. We have all heard descriptors that are equally or even more judgmental and harmful. We should all stop using stigmatizing language directed at people with drug problems and we should encourage others to do likewise.

If we could count them all we would find that there are many people who develop problems from their drug use. However, we should not lose sight of the fact that they are a small portion of people who use drugs. Most drug users lead happy, productive, and fulfilling lives. But some do not. In this next section I look at the nature and extent of the problems.

Methods for Estimating the Extent of Harms

Harm arising from drug use is usually captured by measures of injuries, illness, or other harmful consequences, sometimes referred to as morbidity, and by deaths, sometimes referred to as mortality.

We can gain an appreciation for the extent of harms from drug use, whether as morbidity or mortality, from two types of information. One consists of routinely kept statistical records such as admissions to health services and to drug treatment programs, disruption of the workforce, and crime statistics. The other is general population surveys of randomly selected individuals who are anonymously questioned on their use of drugs and any harms arising.

Statistical Records

There are databases of routinely collected statistics on health information, including drug problems. These statistical records can be accessed at chosen intervals by researchers to provide ongoing summative reports. Such reports can give a comprehensive picture of the extent of harm from drug use.

The Canadian Substance Use Costs and Harms (CSUCH) Scientific Working Group is a collaborative project of the Canadian Institute for Substance Use Research (CISUR) at the University of Victoria and the Canadian Centre for Substance Use and Addiction (CCSA) in Ottawa. The CSUCH Working Group has issued two reports (Canadian Substance Use Costs and Harms 2018; 2020) that provide statistical estimates of drug-related harms and costs for:

Healthcare: inpatient hospitalizations, day surgeries, emergency department visits, specialized treatment for substance use disorders, physician time and prescription drugs.

Lost productivity: substance use-attributable premature deaths, long-term disability, and short-term disability (absenteeism and impaired performance on the job).

Criminal justice: policing, courts, and correctional services (admissions to sentenced custody) attributable to substance use, including costs associated with the enforcement of current drug and impaired-driving laws, as well as the impact of violent and non-violent crimes that would not have occurred without some substance use; and,

A variety of other costs: research and prevention, fire damage, damage to motor vehicles and workplace costs not already covered in lost productivity, which would include employee assistance programs, drug testing programs and administrative costs associated with workers' compensation.

Much of the data in the CSUCH reports and in its online interactive database (Canadian Substance Use Costs and Harms, n.d.) show the economic costs of drug problems to the Canadian economy. There is also some additional information on the types and extent of harms experienced by Canadians. In this section, I will cover only the harms to people and will turn to the data on costs to the economy later in the chapter.

There are two major limitations to using these statistical records. One is that people who go to hospitals, enter drug treatment programs, or become involved in the criminal justice system are not necessarily representative of the general population. Given the more serious health and social problems of these groups, they make up a biased sample, so to speak. The other limitation is that with aggregate statistics such as hospital admissions, we cannot be certain if we are dealing with a large group of people who were admitted to a hospital only once or twice, or a much smaller number of people, each with many admissions.

General Population Surveys

Statistical records are therefore well complemented by the second type of information, general population surveys. These surveys provide us with an estimate of the number of distinct individuals in the general population who are using drugs and experiencing harm.

Earlier, I used the results from such a survey—The 2017 Canadian Tobacco, Alcohol, and Drug Survey (CTADS) to create an understanding of the prevalence of drug use, use patterns, and high-risk behaviour. (Recall that CTADS surveyed Canadians aged fifteen years and older.) I will also draw upon CTADS for information on harmful consequences of drug use. The assessed consequences included physical health, friendships and social life, financial position, home life or marriage, work, studies, employment opportunities, legal problems, difficulty learning, and housing problems.

Surveys are limited in the amount of information they collect because questionnaires are best kept short to maximize participation. CTADS, with its national scope, did not provide information on adverse consequences from alcohol use. However, we will once again draw upon another survey, the 2019 CAMH Monitor which surveyed adults aged eighteen and older, and only for the province of Ontario.

Harms

The General Population

The CAMH Monitor reported that in 2020, 21.4% of Ontario adults reported hazardous or harmful drinking in the past twelve months. It also reported that 17.2% of Ontario adults identified problems related to their use of cannabis (Nigatu et al. 2021). The cannabis estimate represents a substantial increase from the pre-legalization low of 4.7% in 2012, and 10.2% in the last pre-legalization survey in 2017 as reported in the previous issue of the Monitor (Nigatu et al. 2020). During the same period, estimates of alcohol risk and harm remained relatively stable. CTADS shows that adverse consequences from use of illegal or prescribed drugs were reported by 4.1% of survey respondents (Canada 2021). It bears repeating that these two surveys are not directly comparable given the different geographic scopes and age range of survey respondents, as well as other methodological reasons.

Tobacco use generally does not lead to the kind of personal and social disruption that we see with alcohol and other drugs, so surveys do not assess it. The surveys do assess for indications of dependence on tobacco, and I will explore some data on that shortly.

The Healthcare System

Canadian Substance Use Costs and Harms (CSUCH) (2020) reported alarming numbers of drug-related encounters with Canada's health care system in 2017. A substantial proportion arose from alcohol and tobacco use. Alcohol and tobacco together accounted for:

- *88.9% of 277,060 drug-related inpatient hospitalizations*

- *84% of 1.1 million drug-related visits to the emergency department*

- *98.3% of 63,511 drug-related day surgeries.*

The take-home message is that drug problems pose an enormous burden on Canada's healthcare system, and our legal drug industries, alcohol and tobacco, account for almost all of it—this, in a healthcare system that is struggling with sustainability. Add a pandemic to the mix, and well, I think you get the picture.

The Workplace

There are also statistical records on the role of drugs on lost productivity in the workplace. CSUCH's 2018 report provided an estimate of the number of workplace removals due to drug problems. In 2014, there were 87,908 drug-related removals. Alcohol and tobacco were dominant, accounting for 85.9% of all drug-related removals.

The Criminal Justice System

We also have routinely kept information on drug-related offences from the criminal justice system. CSUCH's 2020 report showed that drugs played a significant role in this system as well. 42% of all crimes in Canada were committed by people under the influence of, or while seeking, drugs including alcohol. This excludes impaired driving and crimes defined under the Controlled Drugs and Substances Act.

The data for the criminal justice system paint quite a different picture than do the indicators for the health care system and the workforce. The il-

---

A Story About Health Warning Labels on Alcohol Products

Canada's Globe and Mail (Wilt 2018) reported on an interesting turn of events for a 2017 study to assess the impact of including health warning labels on alcohol bottles in Whitehorse, Yukon. The labels provided information on lower risk drinking practices and the link between alcohol and cancer. The study was disrupted when the labels on cancer were banned by the Yukon Liquor Corporation. The details only became public when The Globe and Mail accessed them through an Access to Information request. The documents supplied details of communications between the Yukon Liquor Corporation and alcohol industry lobby organizations: Beer Canada, Spirits Canada, and the Canadian Vintners Association. The lobbyists claimed the content of the labels was "false" and "alarmist." One described the study as "fatally flawed (in both design and execution)", while another questioned the objectivity of the research team.

The research project was designed by a team of alcohol research experts from Canada and the United States and was led by researchers at the Canadian Institute for Substance Use Research (CISUR) at The University of Victoria. The study had the support of several public health authorities in Canada. The link between alcohol and six distinct types of cancer has international verification from the World Health Organization, the International Agency for Research on Cancer, and the American Society of Clinical Oncologists.

The study was reinstated only when the labels linking alcohol and cancer were removed. The president of the Yukon Liquor Corporation said the government's decision to drop the cancer label was to avoid "protracted litigation" with alcohol manufacturers.

21

legal drugs take on much more prominence and the prominence of tobacco is significantly diminished. But alcohol is still dominant. It accounted for 30.2% of all kinds of criminal justice cases. Almost 20% of violent crimes were associated with alcohol use alone.

Some might think that close to 1 in 3 criminal cases and 1 in 5 violent crimes would call for a sobering warning on the otherwise deceptively benign face of alcohol product labels and alcohol advertisements. Imagine this warning emblazoned upon the label of your favourite alcohol beverage:

> *Warning: indiscriminate use can induce violence and other criminal behaviour.*

That has a sharper point to it than does the customarily timid prompt to "Please use responsibly" that occasionally cowers in a barely legible font in a bottom corner of alcohol print ads.

Addiction Treatment Programs

People who enter addiction treatment programs are not representative of the general population in terms of their drug use and problems. This clinical population shows us drug problems in their most concentrated form. It is also in the clinical population where drugs such as cannabis, cocaine, crack, opioids, and amphetamines become more prominent as problem substances.

Data collected in a Canada-wide study over a two year period in 2016-2018, ranked problem substances named by people entering a treatment program. Overall, alcohol was ranked highest. It was followed in sequence by cocaine, cannabis, opiates, and amphetamines (Konefal et al. 2021).

Ontario has an interagency database for its Ministry of Health funded drug treatment programs. The Centre for Addiction and Mental Health (CAMH) operates The Drug and Alcohol Treatment Information System (DATIS). This database has been collecting data on patients entering addiction treatment programs in Ontario since 1994. It is also able to discern distinct individuals in the system and provides reports with actual numbers of patients. It also included tobacco in the list of problem substances. If you detect a bit of pride in this description, it is because while employed with the Addiction Research Foundation, I developed the prototype of the system in Hamilton, Ontario. That was a time when there was almost no real time program level data available in the province. The pilot project began in 1986 and issued its first full report in 1988 as The Substance Abuse Monitor (SAM). A description of the system was published in the journal Addiction (DeVillaer 1996). SAM ran as a Hamilton-only project through 1994 and was superseded by DATIS as a provincial initiative. DATIS continues operation to this day.

The most recently available reports from DATIS are for calendar year 2021 (Centre for Addiction and Mental Health. Drug and Alcohol Treatment Information System (DATIS) 2022). The results are very similar to those of the national study. Alcohol remains as the most frequently identified problem substance with 26,886 patients identifying it as one of their problem substances. Cannabis is a distant second at 18,532 followed closely by cocaine/crack at 17,076. Opioids/opiates were identified by 14,298 patients and tobacco by 13,789. Benzodiazepines, crystal methamphetamine, hallucinogens, and amphetamines make up a less-often reported third tier. Given the high prevalence of polysubstance use, these counts are not mutually exclusive. It should be noted that the total number of individuals entering treatment and the counts of problems for all drug types have continued to decline during the pandemic relative to pre-pandemic years. Perhaps the pandemic has had some impact on access to treatment programs.

The major drug problem types identified by DATIS are very similar to those identified in the inaugural reports from Hamilton three decades earlier. Some things do not change much—in space or time.

Implications for Cannabis Legalization: Will cannabis become a problem following legalization? Past reports from DATIS show us that it already was a problem before legalization—second only to alcohol. This is still the case. In Ontario, Canada, in most years, there are approximately 20,000 people registered in programs for the treatment of cannabis related problems. That is just one province. The more pertinent question is whether cannabis will become a greater problem. If so, it will not likely happen immediately. A drug problem for an individual person usually has a gestation period. If there is an increase in cannabis-related problems in the general population, it is not likely to manifest as a tsunami crashing upon the shores of our healthcare system. We should expect there to be a dormancy period, followed by a slowly rising tide.

Drug Dependence

"I don't have a drinking problem,
except when I can't get a drink."

— Tom Waits

Drug problems can manifest in a variety of ways. Dependence is one way and is often referred to as addiction. Regardless of what we call it, the essence is a compulsion to continue using a drug in the face of harmful consequences, and an inability and/or an unwillingness to change that. A definition that has been proposed by the World Health Organization introduces another element:

...a cluster of physiological, behavioural, and cognitive
phenomena in which the use of a substance takes on a much
higher priority for a given individual than other behaviours
that once had greater value....

The emphasis on a change in a person's priorities is one that will be sadly appreciated by anyone who has witnessed a family member or close acquaintance on the journey from casual use of a drug to dependence.

Dependence typically arises from daily or near daily use of a drug, and that will certainly increase the risk of health and/or social problems, particularly with drugs like alcohol, tobacco, cannabis, opioids, or stimulants. But daily use and dependence are not necessarily associated with social or health problems. Having a single, small glass of wine with dinner each night is certainly habitual, but it may not be harmful. Someone who uses nicotine patches as a harm reduction alternative to smoking can prevent the health consequences associated with smoking cigarettes. But the person is still very much dependent on nicotine. The advantage of a methadone maintenance program is to allow someone to function safely and productively in their daily lives without impairment. But the person is still very much opioid dependent.

The Slippery Slope of Relapse

At the softer end of the spectrum, there is withdrawal from caffeine dependence—unpleasant, but certainly not life-threatening.

When talking to a class of students about drug problems I sometimes challenged the regular coffee/energy drink users to try a week without it—just to experience a small taste of what breaking a drug habit is like. I warn them that they will feel lethargic for a few days and perhaps have headaches. But it is within the psychological, not the physical, experience of withdrawal where the more interesting lesson resides. What one learns is how easy it is, during the week, to create seemingly compelling reasons for why one should abandon the caffeine abstinence challenge.

I must pull an all-nighter to finish an assignment.

I must stay awake in class.

I must be alert to drive.

My friends will think I am weird.

It is rare that such reasons are truly compelling. There are almost always workarounds available. But while in the throes of caffeine withdrawal, these excuses take on a powerful legitimacy in their imagined necessity for academic performance, personal safety, and peer acceptance.

I find the same dynamic comes into play when I have tried to change my eating habits or stay on a regular exercise regimen. It is quite easy to stray from the routine on a single occasion for what we are convinced is a justifiable and forgivable reason at the time. But the isolated exceptions can gradually occur more frequently and eventually reassume the problematic pattern. This is an example of relapse.

The caffeine abstinence experience provides an important insight into drug dependency. Try it. It just might give you a more empathic perspective on those who struggle with more challenging drug dependencies.

One caveat about problem-free dependence is that if one ever needs to completely curtail use of the drug for any reason, the withdrawal experience can be a very unpleasant one, lasting from days to weeks. In some cases, involving alcohol and opioids, withdrawal can be fatal without monitoring and proper care.

So how common is drug dependence? I return to the general population survey data. The Canadian Tobacco, Alcohol, and Drug Survey (CTADS) helps us to calculate an estimate of how many Canadians are dependent on nicotine. From the CTADS data we know that 10.8% of respondents are daily smokers and that 72.8% of those daily smokers reported having a cigarette within the first hour of waking up in the morning (Canada 2021). Using that criterion we can produce an estimate of 7.9% of Canadians, aged fifteen and over, being dependent on nicotine. The estimate would be a bit higher if sources of nicotine other than cigarettes were included.

Lacking national data on an estimate for alcohol dependence, we again turn to Ontario's CAMH Monitor which reported a population estimate of alcohol dependence of 14.2% among those 18 and over (Nigatu et al. 2021).

The prevalence of use of other drug types is too low to provide statistically reliable estimates for the prevalence of dependence—even for cannabis and opioids.

While the dependence estimates from CTADS and the Monitor are not comparable it is probably safe to conclude that the prevalence of dependence in Canada is highest for alcohol and tobacco.

I want to emphasize that the stages of drug use, higher risk use, and the development of problems do not necessarily occur in a linear, one directional process. The world is not that simple. Once past initial use, people can move back and forth among occasional, daily, high risk, and problem use over time. Even after success in a treatment program relapse to problem use is common. Another complication is that a person who uses multiple drug types can be at a different stage for each one. In an admittedly extreme example, a person could be:

- *dependent upon tobacco and experiencing serious adverse health effects from smoking*

- *a daily user of alcohol, engaging in higher risk drinking, but without having experienced any harms (yet)*

- *a daily or almost daily user of small amounts of cannabis edibles, and not engaging in other higher risk use of cannabis*

- *an occasional psilocybin user*

All those drug use patterns could be in play when the person tries cocaine for the first time (initial use).

Yes, it's complicated. But such complicated cases appear at our specialized addiction treatment programs. Counsellors working in these programs have seen it all.

My Story of Drug Dependence: A Tell-all Disclosure

Before anyone gets too excited, I should tell you that my story of drug dependence will never make it onto the cover pages of the magazines at the checkout counters at the grocery store. This is for two reasons. One is that my history is relatively pedestrian and benign by Hollywood standards. The other is that the magazines do not care about drug dependence in a non-celebrity. Nor do most of their audience.

I recall one of my many attempts to quit smoking as an undergraduate. (There is an old joke: quitting smoking is easy; I've done it many times). But before I tell you about my former nicotine dependence, I will provide you with the backdrop. In those days at the University of Waterloo, we could smoke in class. Many of the desks had one of those flimsy tinfoil ash trays, always part-filled with a layer of ash and several butts. Some students would occasionally roll their own tobacco cigarettes but with a little extra something—just to make a boring drug like nicotine more interesting. When the university brought in the smoke-free classrooms policy it posed a disruption in the lives of smokers and was sometimes ignored by students and faculty alike. I had a political science professor who chain-smoked as he paced and lectured, lighting his next cigarette with the current one before extinguishing it. He was neither a champion nor an early adopter of the new policy. To make things interesting, some of the fanatical pink lunged supporters of the new policy took exception to the continued smoking in the classrooms. Add in a few compliant smokers in a highly impatient and easily irritated state of nicotine withdrawal and things became even more interesting. In one class, harsh words were exchanged between a pro-smoker and an anti-smoker which quickly escalated into a physical brawl, the antagonists rolling about on the floor, exchanging blows, and dislodging desks, chairs, and the hapless students in them. It is difficult to imagine such a scene in today's classrooms—a powerful testimony that social norms can dramatically change—painfully slowly, perhaps—but they do change. What seems impossible in the short-term can be inevitable in the long-term.

Well before the non-smoking policy was enacted at Waterloo, I had been trying to quit and without much success. I tried a harm reduction approach of reducing the number of cigarettes I smoked per class. While this was somewhat successful, it came at a cost. I was directing so much of my attention to clock-watching (in anticipation of my next nicotine dose) I was missing some of the lecture content. My dependence on nicotine was interfering with my learning. This realization supplied some of the motivational fuel for what would become my most successful quit attempt yet (but still not my last; it took the impending birth of my son to achieve that.) The other source of motivation came from an increasing realization that I was under the control of a drug and an industry. That conflicted with my emerging anti-corporate radicalization. Ultimately, I abandoned the harm reduction approach and did it cold turkey, but not without visiting some misery on those people closest to me. Quitting smoking was very difficult, and nicotine replacement products were not available in those days.

My other disclosure comes from life in a student residence where there would occasionally be an extended drought of cannabis. During such droughts there was a noticeable change in people's mood and tolerance of others. Non-users learned to tread carefully in all matters of residence decorum. I had good friends in both camps and occasionally was called upon as peacekeeper. This was not an easy assignment given my own drug adventures which had swirled somewhat out of control in the first semester of that year—during which I earned the worst marks in my academic history. This prompted a bit of soul-searching over the holiday break during which I reacquainted myself with my long-term goals in life. The second semester saw the best academic performance of my life. I emerged all the wiser and fortunately with relatively little personal harm incurred. Except for that first semester Genetics course—what a disaster that was.

These days I maintain a stubborn and unapologetic dependence on dark chocolate.

Implications for Cannabis Legalization: In his book "Smokescreen", Philip Hilts (Hilts 1996), describes how teams of molecular biology researchers employed by tobacco companies worked for decades on engineering the modern cigarette as an optimum nicotine delivery device—designed to create dependence as quickly as possible and to sustain that dependence. Large cannabis companies also employ molecular biology researchers. What might they be getting up to?

Imprudent Decisions: Drug Problems Without Dependence

Dependence is a common type of drug problem. However, it is not as common as many might think it is among people experiencing alcohol problems. A study from Münster, Germany, showed that among 327 alcohol-impaired drivers, only 48% of the drivers could be characterised as alcohol dependent (Brinkmann et al. 2002).

So, what accounts for the other half of harmful incidents? In two words: imprudent decisions. Sometimes people who are not dependent will use a drug to the point of impairment of their vision, reaction time, fine and gross motor co-ordination, and prudent judgment—which can all lead to accidents leading to physical injury to oneself and others. For cases in which those involved are not dependent it is not a case of diminished control over one's consumption of the drug. The harm arises through a single or series of imprudent decisions.

Decisions made while ingesting high doses of a drug can be particularly harmful. Sitting at home having several alcoholic drinks and/or ingesting a large amount of THC is one thing. Doing that and then deciding to drive a car or operate a chainsaw is quite another. Every year, around the world, similarly imprudent decisions, made by non-dependent individuals, lead to many incidents of injury and death.

Implications for Cannabis Legalization: In what ways will imprudent decisions made by cannabis users result in harm to themselves or others? How often will this happen?

Drugs and Mortality

Sometimes people die prematurely from their use of drugs, often referred to as drug related mortality. Some victims die slowly over years, even decades, from the cumulative harm to specific organs or bodily systems. Chronic alcohol consumption and tobacco smoking are prime examples.

Others die more abruptly from acute overdose in which there is profound trauma placed upon specific organs or bodily systems which may already be compromised and vulnerable from earlier drug use and other lifestyle risk factors. There is an elevated risk of fatal overdose with opioids, barbiturates, cocaine, amphetamines and to a lesser extent, alcohol. Fatal overdose from opioids and stimulants has become an international crisis.

Mixing two or more drugs, such as barbiturates and alcohol, also increases the risk of fatal overdose. Fatal poisonings can also be caused by misrepresented contents and strength of a substance that is taken.

Of course drug-related deaths can also arise from accidents, including impaired driving, falls, household fires, and careless use of firearms.

Both acute and chronic incidents of drug-related mortality are increasingly common with horrific effects on the families and friends of the victims. This is a national tragedy in Canada, as it is abroad.

For the numbers I return to the CSUCH Group which reported 74,890 drug related deaths in Canada in 2017—a staggering number (Canadian Substance Use Costs and Harms Scientific Working Group 2020). Can you imagine the public outcry if seventy thousand people died in airline crashes every year? If that were the case, would you continue to fly?

Statistics Canada (Canada 2019) reported 276,689 deaths from all causes in Canada in 2017 (excluding Yukon). So, the drug-related deaths reported by CSUCH accounted for 27.1% of all recorded deaths in Canada—more than 1 in 4. Think about that. It is an astounding statistic.

Then consider another statistic from CSUCH. Our legal drugs, alcohol and tobacco, account for 66,027 or 88.2% of all drug-related deaths in Canada. Tobacco accounts for 47,707 of those deaths. All the other drugs combined account for less than 12% of drug-related deaths. Again, it prompts the question: What was the war on drugs about?

When people die prematurely they are considered to have lost potential years of productive life. For purposes of their report, the CSUCH group counted any years lost to death before the age of sixty-five as a measure of the number of potential years of productive life lost. (That definition means that much of this book was written during the non-productive phase of my life.)

CSUCH reports that, arising from premature deaths in 2017, drugs were responsible for 338,554 potential years of productive life lost. (Stated another way, this is the number of productive years that would have occurred if the deaths had not occurred.) Alcohol and tobacco combined accounted for 51.9% of those lost years. This figure is lower than most other percentages related to the proportional impact of alcohol and tobacco. This reflects the fact that the use of opioids, cocaine, stimulants, and depressants play a greater role in mortality among younger people. That translates into more potential years of productive life lost for deaths involving those drugs. But alcohol and tobacco still account for more lost years than all other drugs combined. Our legal drug industries continue to be dominant in all measures of drug-related harms.

Drug Overdose Crisis: Not Just in Canada, Not Just Opioids

The predominance of the tobacco and alcohol industries in drug-related harm would be difficult to dispute. The pharmaceutical industry is another legal, government-regulated, commercial drug industry. Much of the western world is well into the third decade of a pandemic of opioid-related deaths. A key point is that except for a few hotspots in Canada, for example, the Downtown East Side of Vancouver, opioid dependence was not a major problem. All that changed just before the turn of the century with the aggressive, misleading, and illegal marketing campaigns for opioid medications by several pharmaceutical companies—with Purdue Pharma being the most notorious. Shortly thereafter the illegal trade got involved at which point things really spiralled out of control.

With a statement dated December 10, 2019, Federal Health Minister Patti Hajdu was the fourth consecutive Canadian Minister of Health to acknowledge that opioid overdose deaths are a public health crisis in this country (Hajdu 2019). Public Health Agency of Canada has reported continuing high counts of opioid-related mortality and morbidity. The Agency reports that from the beginning of 2016 through to the end of December in 2021, there were a total of 29,052 opioid-related deaths. 59% of the opioid-related deaths in 2021 also involved a stimulant (Special Advisory Committee on the Epidemic of Opioid Overdoses 2022). Thus the frequently encountered "opioid crisis" is a misnomer. Neither is this crisis restricted to Canada, having reached epidemic proportions in the United States and parts of Europe as well.

Nor is the problem restricted to illegal drug products. A US National Institute on Drug Abuse report (2020, 2) declared "misuse of prescription opioids, CNS depressants, and stimulants is a serious public health problem in the United States." Canada's National Advisory Committee on Prescription Drug Misuse (2013, 1) noted that for prescribed opioids, sedative-hypnotics, and stimulants "the associated harms have become a leading public health and safety concern." In May of 2015, Canada's Minister of Health, Rona Ambrose announced that "prescription drug abuse and addiction is a significant public health concern across Canada" (Canada 2015). Products of the pharmaceutical industry are clearly implicated in our three-industry, multi-decade, pandemic of drug-related harms.

Long-term Trends for Drug Problems

CSUCH data on the extent of harms presented thus far are mostly from 2017. What about longer-term trends that include years before 2017? In its 2020 Report, CSUCH also reported high levels of harm for 2015 and 2016, and that the levels of harms generally increased between 2015 and 2017 (Canadian Substance Use Costs and Harms Scientific Working Group 2020). In its 2018 Report, CSUCH also reported high levels of harm that generally increased from 2007 through 2014 (Canadian Substance Use Costs and Harms Scientific Working Group 2018). From even earlier reports (Rehm et al. 2006; Single et al. 1996, 1998), it appears that high levels of harm have been occurring since at least 1992. Although the different methodologies used across studies make exact comparisons uncertain, drug problems appear to have been on the increase from 1992 to 2017.

These reports also consistently showed that alcohol and tobacco, our two long-term legal recreational drugs, accounted for the very great majority of drug related harm—another finding that has prevailed for three decades, even with the various methodologies used. As this book was entering the production stage, CSUCH released data for 2018-2020 (csuch.ca). While the covid pandemic appears to have had variable effects on some measures, the general picture of rising harms and costs, and the harms and costs being attributable mostly to alcohol and tobacco was maintained.

Implications for Cannabis Legalization: Cannabis is not a threat for overdose so that will keep mortality rates lower than for some other drugs. But often heard claims that there are no cannabis related deaths are unfounded. Cannabis is a threat for impairment leading to fatal accidents and for fatal respiratory illness if combusted over many years. CSUCH reported 1,080 deaths attributable to cannabis use in Canada in 2017. Could that count increase if cannabis use increases after legalization?

IT'S THE ECONOMY

Drugs Giveth to the Economy...

Drugs are a major part of our economy, generating revenues that sustain some of the most financially successful industries worldwide. Alcohol, tobacco, and pharmaceutical industries create many jobs in research, manufacturing, marketing, distribution, and retail. There are also many spinoff industries that manufacture and retail a wide assortment of drug-using accessories, paraphernalia, and swag. Law firms also prosper from their consultative services to drug industries. There are law firms that declare cannabis law as one of their areas of specialization. Law firms also increasingly represent drug companies or plaintiffs when companies face civil and criminal law-suits. Just ask the tobacco and pharmaceutical industries. And let us not ex-clude jobs for industry lobbyists who, like a drug molecule through a fully permeable membrane, move effortlessly between employment in government and industry. Former politicians and government bureaucrats have been el-bowing their way to belly up to the cannabis lobbying trough. I will share some data, stories, and thoughts on cannabis lobbyists later.

A portion of revenue from the sales of products from drug industries goes to the government through taxation. These taxes are used to help fund many public services which include universities, hospitals, and drug treat-ment and prevention programs, all of which employ a lot of people, includ-ing me, for my entire professional career.

The trade in illegal drugs is also big business with estimated annual global revenues of half a trillion dollars (Mavrellis 2017).

Not all these illicit revenues stay in a separate bubble from the legal economy. Illegal drug traders make mortgage and car payments, and buy furniture, groceries, and toys for their children. They frequent restaurants, bars, cafes, frozen yogurt shops, and cinemas. They support local sports teams, live theatre, the symphony, and charitable organizations. They may also buy tacky lawn ornaments and sketchy Paltrow products. More dis-cerning ones may buy books on cannabis legalization. Most of their cus-tomers earn their money through the legal economy.

While people may have misgivings about revenues from illegal drug sales and laundering, much of the revenue begins in, and eventually returns to, the mainstream economy. The unlicensed drug trade keeps only a tem-porary hold on a significant portion of its assets.

It must be acknowledged however that money laundering is a prob-lem in drug and many other illegal trades. (Interestingly, as legal businesses also earn money illegally, they must find ways to launder it as well.)

Of course the existence of an illegal drug trade is not ideal. We should continue to try to contain it as much as possible. But it is more complex than most people imagine and has been going through some interesting transformations.

Those of you who have attended one or more of my presentations, in person or online, might recall that my second slide (after the title slide) is always titled "All-inclusive Disclosure" in which I declare that I have not had funding from any of the following drug industries: alcohol, tobacco, pharmaceutical, cannabis, and illegal drug cartels.

I originally added illegal drug cartels to inject a bit of wry humour at the beginning of what might be an otherwise troubling presentation. Then I came across the work of Dr. Rodrigo Canales with the Yale School of Man-agement. Dr. Canales is not your typical business school academic. He stud-ies the business practices of illegal drug cartels, and his research has surfaced some fascinating findings. He reported that the cartels were trying to counter their reputations for unfettered violence. They were hiring consulting firms to help them with their branding, public relations, and market-ing strategies. The cartels were engaging communities and supporting local charities (Canales 2013). In other words, they were beginning to behave more like legal drug companies. Of course, the more violent cartels still oc-casionally arrange for their competitors or critics to be abducted and trans-ported to a remote location for execution. But the trend is towards outsourcing these less brandable aspects of their mission statements.

So with such transformations afoot perhaps it was not so far-fetched that drug cartels might want to finance drug education initiatives after all. Sometimes life can mimic fiction.

Of course we are horrified by the violent tactics that prevail in some il-legal drug trades. However I want to introduce the subversive idea that we are much more hospitable towards our legal drug industries when they sacrifice lives for profit. Both the tobacco industry and pharma corporations such as Purdue Pharma have branded themselves as laudable organizations and have supported charitable causes while they marketed their cigarettes and opioids in ways that they knew were killing large numbers of people. And they re-peatedly denied what they were doing. No one in either industry has yet to confess guilt, take responsibility, or to issue an apology. The difference between licensed and unlicensed drug trades is not as profound as drug policy orthodoxy has led us to believe. This is also true for the cannabis industry. I cover that unpleasant topic in disturbing detail in Chapter 7.

The sometimes unsettling practices of the illegal drug trade have oc-casionally been used strategically by political parties. Sometimes the stories are exaggerated and even fabricated. This was certainly the case during the Liberal Party of Canada's cannabis legalization campaign. The strategic misrepresentation and demonization of the unlicensed cannabis trade will arise repeatedly in subsequent chapters of this book in which I will provide a more detailed account of the story and of the evidence.

Implication for Cannabis Legalization: As cannabis makes its trans-ition from illegal to legal drug, what are the implications for the type of in-dustry we will have? Will the criminal elements disappear or will different types of criminal conduct appear within the legal industry?

...And Drugs Taketh Away

To mention only the economic revenues from legal and illegal drug trades would be to tell only part of the story. Drug use is also responsible for an enormous economic liability for Canada.

Health economists have devised statistical techniques for estimating the cost of drug problems to the economy and the results of their analysis are shocking.

I turn again to The Canadian Substance Use Costs and Harms Sci-entific Working Group (CSUCH). The Group's 2020 report estimated the total costs of harmful drug use in Canada in 2017 at almost $46 billion. The $46 billion is distributed across four categories in the following proportions:

- *lost productivity 43.5%*
- *healthcare   28.4%*
- *criminal justice 20.1%*
- *other   7.9%*

An important consideration is that these costs represent lost opportunities to assign the funds elsewhere to chronically underfunded health and social services such as residential and homecare for low-income seniors and the disabled, programs to address income disparity, and much needed enhancements for municipal infrastructure.

By drug type, the four highest in costs to the economy are:

- *alcohol 36.2%*

- *tobacco 26.7%*

- *opioids 12.9%*

- *cannabis 7.0%.*

The rest was accounted for by other drug types which included cocaine, central nervous system depressants, central nervous system stimulants, hallucinogens, and inhalants—none of which were higher than cannabis.

A sizable portion of the $46 billion is accounted for by drugs from legal industries. $16.6 billion is accounted for by alcohol and $12.3 billion by tobacco for a total of $28.9 billion. That amounts to 62.9% of all drug-related costs to our economy. An unknown portion of the total costs could also have arisen from use of products from the legal pharmaceutical industry, including opioids, sedative-hypnotics, and stimulants and from the legal therapeutic cannabis industry. Those additional amounts would increase the total costs beyond the known 62.9% from alcohol and tobacco industries. Perhaps far beyond.

We cannot determine how much of the $46 billion is attributable to purely recreational drug use as opposed to therapeutic use. It would certainly be more than the 62.9% figure for alcohol and tobacco alone. Even a conservative guess at the cost of all recreational drug use would place a high price tag on the self-indulgence of playing with our body chemistry.

I have already discussed the long-term trends of drug-related harm. The same long-term trends also prevail for drug-related costs to the economy. The data show high perennial costs with most of the costs arising from our legal drug industries: alcohol and tobacco. The data also suggest that the financial burden of these industries on the economy has been rising for three decades (Single et al. 1996, 1998; Rehm et al. 2006; Canadian Substance Use Costs and Harms Scientific Working Group 2018; Canadian Substance Use Costs and Harms Scientific Working Group 2020). There is no known cause for optimism that this long-term trend of increasing harm and costs will end in the foreseeable future.

The most recent data from CSUCH show that opioids are the third highest in drug-related costs, after alcohol and tobacco. We do not know what portion of the opioid costs is attributable to the legal industry versus the illicit trade. But we are certainly aware of the leading role played by the legal industry in the genesis of the opioid crisis.

Concern about high levels of harm from the products of the alcohol and tobacco industries has been expressed by investigators and public health authorities throughout much of the world for a long time. These concerns are supported by the data on the multi-decade persistence of excessive costs and harms associated with these legal drug products. We now have similar expressions of concern about the pandemic of opioid deaths which was fueled by the purely monetary ambitions of some pharmaceutical companies.

In sum, each of our legal, government-regulated, commercial drug industries, is linked to an international public health crisis involving their respective drug products. In baseball hitting lexicon, that is three for three—a perfect day at the park for the industries. But, for public health, it's three big swings and misses. Baseball enthusiasts know what that means.

We are prompted to consider the potential role played by these businesses in the extent of harms and costs. It cannot be conclusively proven that the model of a legal, commercial drug industry is solely responsible for the high levels of harms and costs observed. However, as we have seen, the harms and costs from legal drug industries by far exceed those attributable to all illegal drugs combined. Perhaps we need to consider alternate approaches to supplying both recreational and therapeutic drugs to people. I will address that in Chapter 9.

This chapter has described both the benefits and liabilities of our legal drug industries. A remaining question is which is greater—the benefits or the liabilities? A paper published by a researcher at the Canadian Institute for Substance Use Research (CISUR) compared Canadian government revenue from alcohol sales in 2014 to the costs, as tallied by CSUCH, for 2014. Statistics Canada reported government revenue of $10.9 billion which was offset by net societal costs of $14.6 billion. Thus government-borne costs exceeded revenues by $3.7 billion (Sherk 2020).

Admittedly there are other less tangible aspects to a full comparison. The various personal benefits enjoyed by people employed in or by our drug industries is not part of that analysis, but then neither is the suffering of people close to those with alcohol problems. Inclusion of such factors would require a much more complex and difficult analysis.

However, at the very least, we know that the taxes collected by the government do not cover the costs incurred by the government. That is something we all pay for—in tangible and intangible ways. We all need to ponder the possibility that the alcohol industry in Canada may be a net economic loss.

WHAT DO WE DO ABOUT DRUG USE AND DRUG PROBLEMS?

Drug problems should not be addressed in isolation, but within a broader framework of healthy living. This must include coordinated approaches of prevention, treatment, harm reduction and advocacy on the social, economic, and political determinants of health.

I have already introduced the idea that drug use and drug harms occur on a dynamic spectrum. It is not realistic to think that we are going to shepherd everyone into the safe end of the spectrum and keep them there. The more feasible public health goal is to do what we can to maximize the amount of time that people spend at the safer end of the spectrum. This is what prevention initiatives try to do. Less time spent by fewer individuals in the high-risk end means less harm to people and lower costs to society. A comprehensive approach to prevention has two indispensable components: demand-side prevention and supply-side prevention.

Demand-Side Prevention

Demand-side prevention is aimed at the public and tries to reduce the demand for drug products. This includes initiatives that foster an evidence-based understanding of drugs and their actions, and facilitate personal awareness, responsibility, resiliency, and self-esteem. These assets can be deployed to encourage any combination of abstinence, moderation, or otherwise safer drug use. The commonality among demand-side interventions is that the onus is placed upon individuals to regulate their personal drug use.

All levels of government also try to regulate drug use by people through the application of drug laws and enforcement. To say that this criminal law approach to illegal drug use has become increasingly controversial over the last half-century would be an understatement. The criminalization of drug use has too often been justified by associating drug use with moral turpitude, sometimes as a guise for parochial economic or political gain. We have seen the construction of complex legislative provisions and expansive, unwieldy bureaucracies to punish those who use drugs that have not been approved by the state for commercial trade. I will have more to say about that in Chapters 4, 6, and 10.

Supply-side Prevention

Apart from overly zealous and oppressive law enforcement, demand-side interventions are worthwhile. But even at their best demand-side approaches are insufficient for a comprehensive drug policy strategy.

A comprehensive approach must also address how society supplies drugs to meet the demand. Supply-side interventions address a variety of considerations such as drug product integrity and safety during manufacturing, safe and accurately labelled packaging, and ultimate availability of

Origin Story

One of the most memorable and influential experiences from my very early career occurred one afternoon in 1979 when I attended a lecture on Canada's drug laws. I was still fresh out of a graduate school program in psychology at the University of Waterloo and recently employed as a drug counsellor and community developer with The Addiction Research Foundation of Ontario. The lecture was held at the Foundation's May Street campus in Toronto's upscale Rosedale neighbourhood. The speaker was Western Ontario University Law Professor, Robert Solomon. I recall that as I waited for the session to begin, the room was abuzz with conversations. Professor Solomon walked into the room and up to the podium. He took a few seconds to organize his speaking notes. Then, with no introduction or fanfare, he looked up from his notes, scanned the room with unapologetic eyes, and froze the conversations by unleashing the commanding and stunning proclamation that Canada's drug laws were founded on racial prejudice. The room fell into a seemingly long dramatic silence before Professor Solomon went ahead to deliver a stirring account of the origin of Canada's Opium and Drug Act (to be followed by the Narcotic Control Act). He talked of how in early years of the twentieth century, such Acts appeared as one means of persecution of Asian populations, some of whom preferred a recreational drug from their own culture—opium, over Canada's more accepted recreational drug—alcohol. Solomon also talked of drug policy gone seriously awry, and how it could be much better. The intent of the Act as a tool of prejudice has been challenged by some academics. However, at the time, Solomon's assertion was a provocative, even subversive, message for the addiction field, the usually genteel Rosedale environs, and probably for almost everywhere else in Canada.

The details of Solomon's account were the prelude to a more contemporary war on drugs that would cost so many people their dignity, freedom, livelihood, and even their lives—all at enormous economic cost to the taxpayers of participating countries—which encompassed almost all western democracies, including Canada.

The story also sounds hauntingly familiar to us as we now, a century later, read accounts of how people of colour are still disproportionately targeted by drug law enforcement, including for cannabis.

I did not realize it at the time but Professor Solomon's talk would eventually change my career plans. I appreciated that, as a drug counsellor, I might be able to help one person at a time with a small part of their struggle with addiction. Clinical work remains an indispensable role in the drug field and one we must generously resource. But Professor Solomon's talk opened other possibilities.

I spent that evening at The Delta Chelsea Hotel. During my restless attempt at sleep, with the backdrop of Yonge and Gerrard and Bay

Street traffic noise, and seemingly perpetual sirens, it occurred to me that policy could change society. An enlightened, well designed, properly implemented policy could prevent the struggle with addiction for many thousands. I saw my future that night, and in a manner of thinking, I started to paint the broad strokes of this book.

the drug through retail outlets. Measures can include restrictions on the appearance of retail outlets as well as a maximum supply in any area and their locations. They can restrict operating hours and who can own or operate them. And finally they can restrict who can be served and the amount sold to each customer.

The methods of product promotion through advertising and marketing or the depictions of drug use in pop culture can also be regulated to control the degree to which normalization and the demand for the drug product is stimulated by drug and entertainment industries.

A supply-side approach must also address how well the government regulates these supply-side aspects through policy and enforcement. The important feature of supply-side prevention is that it extends responsibility beyond the individual person to include responsibilities for the suppliers in drug companies and the promoters in the entertainment industry. The supply-side approach also includes expectations of the government in communicating a public health priority to these industries, reinforcing those communications with policy and law, and consistently enforcing those laws with meaningful consequences for violations when they occur. Thus, there is clearly a role for the courts as well in managing the conduct of the suppliers, be it tobacco and pharmaceutical manufacturers or bars that serve patrons to intoxication.

Later sections of this book will show that industry and government often fail in these roles, and the failure is rooted in systemic neglect. That is a problem that requires political change. I am reminded of the United Kingdom's advocate against child poverty, Sir Michael Marmot, who admonished us all with "...you live in a democracy. This must be the level of child poverty that you want. Otherwise, you'd elect a government that did something different."

As nations waged the now-discredited war on drugs, young people were told to "just say no." It was clearly unfair and unrealistic to place such an onus on young people. This is particularly true given that they were simultaneously encouraged to just say "let's party!" by pop culture icons and by well-resourced, expertly advised, drug industries. As a society we need to do more to protect young people. Simply supplying a shield of knowledge, self esteem, and resiliency to help protect them from a perpetual stream of heat-seeking advertising missiles is insufficient. Someone must also deal with the person launching those missiles. This is neither a new nor radical idea.

A Nagging Feeling, an Unanswered Question, Something Missing...

Inspired by Nader's book, I would sometimes use the following metaphor for animating the importance of supply-side prevention: Imagine that someone is shooting at your children. I mean literally shooting bullets out of a gun at your children. Would you be content to just give your children a shield and hope that it would sufficiently protect them? Or would you also want to do something about the shooter?

On one occasion, it was suggested to me that this is too disturbing of a metaphor. I was considering not using it anymore—until the early summer of 2014 when I stumbled upon something that was receiving scattered media attention in the United States. I found this story unnerving in a way that I am still not able to fully articulate to my satisfaction. But it did fortify my resolve to remain critical of the narrowness of vision of some industries and governments towards important matters of public health and safety.

In the early summer of 2014, a US company called ProTecht was marketing a protective Kevlar blanket which was intended to shield children from airborne building debris during a tornado or from bullets during school shootings. The application to school shootings captured most of the media attention. Given the horrible spectre of school shootings in the US, we can appreciate the potential value of this product, particularly if it were to be used during a school shooting and saving lives. Parents would be forever grateful.

But there is still a nagging feeling when we consider such a product—an unanswered question, something missing. As a society, is a shield really the best we can do? Might we also want to discuss, advance, and implement science-based policy on gun control? Some of the media coverage seemed to have conceded that these larger issues are beyond intervention and that supplying shields truly is the best we can do. But making such a concession just does not sit well, does it? On ProTecht's website, in 2014, there was a poignant lament of the tragedy of school shootings, but again, there was something missing. I wrote to ProTecht, acknowledging their concern for gun violence against children, congratulating them on their innovative product, and asked if they had a concurrent advocacy campaign in place to encourage government legislation on stricter gun control. I never heard back. What was missing on their website was any suggestion that these horrors might, at least partially (and probably most effectively), be addressed through the introduction of a supply-side preventative measure such as improved legislation on gun control. Herein lies the danger. Once such a product generates revenue for a company, there is a financial disincentive to do anything about the problem that creates the market for the product.

Such a troubling story does not inspire optimism. We have much work to do on addressing some of our society's unfathomable, even perverse, priorities. Closer to home, we have much to do to protect our children from the practices of not only various drug industries, but also of those industries targeting young people with the promotion of gambling, unhealthy food, and violent entertainment media. But not all is despair. The harbinger of hope is that policy-enabled supply-side measures have contributed to considerable success in reducing high-risk drug use practices. Just think of how changes in policy and public engagement have changed the way we think about cigarette smoking and drinking and driving over the last few decades.

Over two decades ago consumer advocate, Ralph Nader, co-authored Children First ! A Parent's Guide to Fighting Corporate Predators. Nader is a five-time candidate for the presidency of the United States and was ranked by Time Magazine among the one hundred most influential Americans of the twentieth century. The corporate predators Nader challenges include not only drug industries but also purveyors of unhealthy food.

On the Canadian side of the border there are also acknowledgements of the enormous volume of advertising directed at children. In the April 25, 2015, Canadian Broadcasting Corporation (CBC) broadcast of Under the Influence, host Terry O'Reilly noted that the entire production costs of the children's movie, Smurfs 2 were paid for by product placement within the film. In the activist world, Vancouver-based Adbusters, wields an edgy anti-corporate swagger. Adbusters was the creator of the anti-consumerism meme "the product is you", and catalyst for the Occupy Wall Street and Buy Nothing Day movements. These can be unsettling ideas and tactics to those who would prefer not to confront the darker aspects of the determinants of our health. But confront them we must. I will provide more thoughts on this topic near the end of the book.

When Prevention Fails

If prevention efforts were entirely successful we would have no drug problems and no need for treatment programs. Some people are not immediately successful at navigating the potentially perilous journey of maturation and living in a complex, demanding society. Some of them will resort to drug use to cope. Drug industries and governments chronically fail to operate and regulate in ways that prevent drug problems and they are rarely held accountable. People with drug problems should not be punished for that.

Some people require clinical interventions to help them get their lives back on track. Drug treatment programs act as the first of two safety nets for those who do not receive, or respond favourably to, prevention efforts. The other is harm reduction initiatives.

Drug Treatment Programs

Canadian provinces offer drug treatment programs at no charge to the user. These programs help many people, literally saving lives. But treatment is not a panacea for our societal drug problem. For a variety of reasons, including stigma, people will resist getting help for many years, even in the face of considerable harm to themselves and to those around them. Some data I collected in the early 1990s from addiction treatment programs in Hamilton, Ontario, showed that, on average, twelve years passed between an individual's perceived onset of a problem and their entry into a treatment program. Imagine the harm that can occur during those twelve years.

When people finally try to get help many find the system difficult to access and navigate. Some will face long waiting lists. The same Hamilton data set showed that, within a one year period only 7% of those who might benefit from help received that help from an addiction treatment program. There is limited capacity for follow-up after treatment, and accordingly, substantial risk for relapse—a phenomenon fueled by the same cultural forces that contribute to the onset of problems in the first place. Treatment success rates are inconsistent. Our treatment system will continue to struggle to keep up with the population prevalence of drug problems. Under the prevailing conditions it is a tribute to the people working in our treatment system that they manage to help as many people as they do. It is unreasonable to expect much more from them.

Harm Reduction

If our treatment programs had a 100% success rate no one would be talking about the second safety net—harm reduction. Harm reduction is for individuals struggling with control of their drug use, and for whom treatment programs, for whatever reason, are not attractive or effective. Harm reduction does not try to curtail or even reduce the person's drug use. The intent is to minimize the harm associated with the person's ongoing drug use.

One of the first introductions of a harm reduction approach was a controversial one referred to as "controlled drinking." The controversy arose in the early 1960s—a time when it was widely believed that abstinence was the only viable treatment approach to harmful use of alcohol. However, over the ensuing years, research studies repeatedly supported controlled drinking as a treatment option. Treatment goals other than abstinence are now supported in many out-patient treatment programs.

Another example of harm reduction is naloxone—a medication that can be administered to a person in a state of opioid overdose. It prevents an opioid from attaching to a cell's receptors. This prevents the drug's effects. Naloxone is now carried by many first responders and has been increasing in public availability. This is helping to prevent fatal opioid overdoses.

Safe injection sites provide injection drug users with an uncontaminated needle and a safe place to inject. Some programs dispense uncontaminated supplies of the drugs being used. Others, as in the case of methadone, offer a safer substitute for illegally obtained opioids.

These interventions are not intended to help the person to stop using drugs—only to save them from some, perhaps the worst, of the harm. A quarter century ago I collaborated on a report with the Hamilton Department of Public Health Services to set up needle exchange services (DeVillaer and Smye 1994). The service allowed needle users to exchange damaged and/or potentially contaminated needles for new and sterile ones. Today Public Health advocates are still fighting to have such services established and protected from uninformed and unsympathetic legislators.

At the beginning of this section I mentioned political-economic advocacy. This is a critical necessity to correct the inequities to opportunity and resources that lie at the heart of so many of our social and health chal-

So, Let Me Get This Straight...

The considerable controversy that still surrounds safe injection sites reflects a misunderstanding of public health strategies. Just a few years ago, I remember reading one particularly misinformed inquiry seeking confirmation that a safe injection site was a place where you could inject heroin, but you could not smoke a cigarette. The writer was suggesting that this was an absurd inconsistency. Any seeming inconsistency rests upon three misunderstandings. The first is the belief that heroin is a more dangerous drug than cigarettes. But nicotine is just as addictive as heroin, and cigarettes account for far more deaths than does heroin. The second misunderstanding is that safe injection sites are primarily about offering an opportunity to inject free heroin or other drugs. They are not. They are about lowering the prevalence of drug-related deaths and the spread of infectious disease. The third misunderstanding is the suggestion that the restriction on indoor smoking is frivolous compared to the allowance of heroin injection.

The restriction on smoking is intended to prevent exposure to second-hand smoke which is a well-documented contributor to respiratory illness, various cancers, and premature death. This is especially important for staff who work at safe injection sites who would be exposed to this risk on a long-term daily basis—as would people who work in bars, restaurants, cafes, and proposed cannabis lounges. The policies make perfect sense once you understand the operation of safe injection sites within the appropriate public health framework.

Some cannabis reform advocates have described cannabis lounges as safe consumption sites. They would not be so safe for the staff who worked there and were exposed to daily high levels of smoke and vapor. I've seen the same advocates refer to bars as safe consumption sites. These advocates appear to be unaware of the elevated levels of neighbourhood property damage, impaired driving, and violence, at the bars, surrounding the bars, and at home in the form of domestic violence. Let's also get this straight—bars are not safe consumption sites.

lenges. These problems have become more manifest during the COVID-19 pandemic—not just because the pandemic has created or worsened them but also because the pandemic has shone a spotlight on them. The political-economic challenges are daunting and a full treatment of them is beyond the scope of this book. However, I will provide some ideas in Chapters 9 and 10 that are specifically related to the changes in political-economic thinking that must catalyze a more humanitarian approach to cannabis and other drug policy reform.

Implications for Cannabis Legalization: Cannabis will require the same spectrum of interventions to moderate the potential increase in related public health problems. This being a new industry, there was a unique opportunity to implement supply-side interventions at an early stage—something that was not feasible with our other drug industries. In later chapters, I will reveal how well that went.

SO WHY DID WE LEGALIZE CANNABIS?

The extensive harm to Canadians and the excessive costs to the economy from our legal drug industries has prompted some people to question the wisdom of legalizing yet another drug industry, and a recreational one at that. At this point in the book, you might believe that I am one of them. I am not. I believe that the research evidence and a social justice perspective support cannabis law reform. More specifically, I favour decriminalization and non-commercial legalization of cannabis. I will provide more on what that means in Chapters 4, 9, and 10. But let us talk a little bit about the rationale for reform in general.

I make three arguments in support of cannabis law reform.

1. Prohibition has not reduced cannabis use. From the onset of prohibition, prevalence of use has generally increased. The criminalization that goes with prohibition is also causing harm by giving many (mostly young) people life-long criminal records for a victimless crime. Prohibition and criminalization appear to have done more harm than good. It has also cost inestimable amounts of money. We needed to end it everywhere as soon as possible.

2. We should replace a criminal enforcement approach with a public health approach. Some elements of a public health approach can be seen in the prevailing approach to alcohol policy. As we have seen, alcohol misuse is associated with substantial levels of harm. Yet, in contemporary times, few nations have banned the drug and criminalized its possession or safe use by adults. Rather, policy efforts have been focused on encouraging lower risk conditions of supply and responsible use by individuals. But there remains much to improve in a public health approach to alcohol—particularly addressing its widespread promotion, as has been done with tobacco.

An example of a public health approach familiar to healthcare practitioners is the use of The Compendium of Pharmaceuticals and Specialities. The Compendium lists all monographs for drugs, vaccines, natural health, and medical devices available in Canada along with guidelines for their effective and safe use. One would be hard-pressed to find many entries in the Compendium that did not include contraindications: circumstances in which the product should not be used due to potential adverse (even lethal) impacts on patients. The chosen policy approach was not to use these contraindications as a rationale to ban the products and criminalize their use. Rather, the Compendium provides prescribers with the information they require to prescribe safely and to educate their patients in the safe use of the products. Managing the potential harms of cannabis use could be viewed through a similarly public health-oriented lens.

3. There is also a philosophical consideration. In what kind of a society do we wish to live? If we believe that anything that poses risk to our health and safety should be prohibited, then maybe cannabis should be illegal. But then we would also have to prohibit cigarettes, alcohol (again), gambling, video games, automobiles, most contact sports, and a substantial amount of the products at our food stores. I do not believe that is the world in which most people want to live. The public health approach would have cannabis be available as consumer choices, and subject to efforts to prevent, contain and reduce the harm.

Implications for Cannabis Legalization: Cannabis law reform is needed. Prohibition and criminalization must end but many public health authorities, world-wide, do not believe that commercial legalization is the best choice available. Will a legal commercial cannabis industry behave in the same manner as other legal drug industries? Will it engage in a relentless pursuit of profit while escalating the harms and costs associated with cannabis use? Will we be able to find that elusive legislative sweet spot—an alternative to prohibition and commercial legalization, that will maintain priorities of social justice and public health protection? As Canada's commercial cannabis industry becomes increasingly entrenched, how likely are we to advance significant reforms?

We need a strong commitment to explore humanitarian and evidence-based alternatives. I will explore what this looks like in Chapters 4, 9, and 10. But first, we have much to cover. Next up in Chapter 2—how does society manage to convince significant segments of the population that it is a good idea to consume carcinogens for fun?

SUMMING UP

This chapter lays a solid foundation of evidence to support an essential message of the book—that Canada has high levels of drug problems and costs to its economy. Furthermore, most of these costs and harms do not arise from illegal drugs but from our legal drugs—alcohol and tobacco. Another message introduced here, but revealed more fully in later chapters, is that our existing drug industries (alcohol, tobacco, pharmaceutical) often do not comply with regulations and occasionally break the law in an unfettered pursuit of revenue. That pursuit tragically affects public health and the Canadian economy. The not-so-hip, new kid on the block, corporate cannabis, appears to be adopting the same playbook.

It is critical that we regard the legalization of cannabis within the context of the societal role played by our other legal drug industries: alcohol, tobacco, and pharmaceutical and their respective drug products. This indispensable context is complex. Social messaging and prevailing norms on drugs and their use are varied and often, seemingly, contradictory. Drug use, from initial experimentation, and for some—increasing use, the development of dependence, and in the worst cases, the end of life, is also complicated. This complexity requires a diverse menu of compassionate, evidence-based options including policy, prevention, treatment, and harm reduction. If evidence-based solutions directed at individuals were all that were needed this book would not have to be written. To add to the complexity of drugs in society, drugs are big culture and big business. They add and subtract from a nation's fiscal prosperity. Government regulation is a battleground where public health protection competes against industry's relentless pursuit of revenue. Public health victories are rare. That must change and it can change. That is a major reason this book was written.

Chapter 2

Persuasion and Influence

*"Dishonest advertising fools you with lies.
Honest advertising fools you with the truth."*

—Author unknown

DRUG USE AS SOCIAL BONDING

Congratulations! You have made it through the Chapter 1 data dump. Unfortunately, you do so with the burden of knowing that our three long-established legal drug industries are associated with three international public health crises. You also know the situation appears to be worsening and there is no cause for optimism that it will improve soon. No political party has proposed a workable solution. Might we derive a measure of comfort from some social bonding—a socially distanced, virtual group hug? Maybe. But that is not what this section on social bonding is about. Sorry.

As with the first chapter, most of this chapter is about drugs other than cannabis, most notably our recreational drugs—alcohol and tobacco. Little of it refers to cannabis legalization. But drawing from the swirling, often contradictory mosaic of messages about alcohol and tobacco, this chapter will supply more foundation for understanding the place of drugs in society. It will also ask you to consider the potential trajectory of a new recreational drug industry for cannabis. There is much to learn from the legacy of conduct by alcohol and tobacco corporations. And there is much to learn from how they try to deploy the power of persuasion and influence to make their product central to your identity and your life. It has become clear that the cannabis industry in Canada has detailed plans to do the same.

Beginning with Chapter 3 on the history of cannabis policy in Canada, the book will be much more focused on cannabis legalization. Until then, as in Chapter 1, many sections of this chapter will include a passage prefaced with Implications for Cannabis Legalization. These passages will keep you connected to the main topic of the book. The questions and comments will prompt you to think, in often specific terms, about the implications of the content for cannabis legalization. Subsequent chapters will dig into those issues in more detail.

Our long-lived drug industries continue to not only persist, but to flourish. Drug use, most notably alcohol use, has worked itself deeply into the essence of who we are. Alcohol plays a role in many of our social bonding rituals. Events like weddings, gala fundraisers, trade conventions, and team sports celebrations are almost unimaginable without alcohol.

The successful marketing of cigarettes in the 1960s, even once the harms were known, may very well stand as one of the most unlikely, yet successful, examples of mass persuasion in the history of civilization. It took public health authorities half a century to substantially reverse it—a slow, hard-earned achievement that now teeters precariously with the arrival of vaping technology. Public health authorities worry about what might happen when the cool sheen of vaping devices wears off with a young, fashion-fickle market—a market that will be perilously dependent upon nicotine. Might cigarettes once again become the fashionable choice with all their attendant harms? The tobacco industry, which I have recently taken to calling the "nicotine addiction industry" has been unrelenting in its drive and will in finding ways to survive and prosper. The continued success of two industries selling Class 1 carcinogens as ingestible consumer products seems both inexplicable and remarkable.

The facilitation of social bonding through alcohol and tobacco use is ubiquitous. This could be sharing a bottle of wine over dinner, going for a drink with teammates after a game, going outside with coworkers for a cigarette during a work break, or sharing a hookah. It might also include sharing a prescription with a friend who has similar symptoms. Passing a joint or a pipe (saliva and all) at a concert was iconic in cannabis folklore, but perhaps less so in the era of COVID-19. The practice of snorting cocaine from the naked body of a companion is another intimate form of drug-mediated social intercourse. I have often suspected that this practice is more a product of a sub-genre of Hollywood folklore than an actual widespread practice. Or maybe that just says something about the sheltered existence I have led.

The practice of sharing needles to inject drugs like heroin, fentanyl, or crystal meth also has a social component, so strong that it may take precedence over concern about the collateral risk of also sharing infectious disease.

On the lighter side of drug use, cafes, coffee clubs, coffee breaks, coffee runs, and high tea are all examples of caffeine playing a role as an elixir of social bonding. In some contemporary venues, high tea may now offer other possibilities.

Some of the drug-using behaviours I have described are widely regarded as glamourous, fashionable, or simply cool, while others are more stigmatized. But they all have an important social bonding component.

Society now has a much less tolerant attitude towards cigarette use than it once did. Consider that in Canada it was once legal, and socially acceptable, to smoke in bars, restaurants, most indoor workplaces, buses, planes, trains, automobiles, hockey arenas, and theatres. People also smoked in college and university classrooms, and even hospitals and child day care centres. For the first years of my employment at the Addiction Research

Foundation of Ontario, I smoked in my Hamilton office. None of my co-workers complained—ever. When I visited non-smoking friends at their homes, they would open windows—even during the coldest of Ontario winter days. But none of them ever complained—not once. I still carry some guilt about that. Today, only the exceedingly rare, unfathomably self-absorbed smoker would even contemplate lighting up in a non-smoking home.

Tobacco use is now widely prohibited indoors and in many outdoor public places. Indoor bans on the use of tobacco have displaced smokers and vapers to several meters from the entrance to their workplaces where they huddle in compliant solidarity—a powerful demonstration of the persistence of social bonding that occurs around the use of a drug.

Another example of social bonding with tobacco is the centuries-long use of the hookah, a device that allows a group of smokers to sit together and simultaneously draw the smoke through hoses attached to a glass body. An attached bowl at the top of the device holds the tobacco. Due to concerns about the harmful effects of second-hand smoke, hookah lounges have recently been banned in many places in Canada, but not without push-back and non-compliance. Of course, a hookah can also be used for smoking cannabis.

Social bonding practices can evolve into social niches in which drug use is incorporated and celebrated as a salient aspect of a chosen lifestyle among members of what can be a devoted community. The use of the drug can become iconic for a particular social niche.

The social bonding associated with tobacco and cannabis use is also extended to recent vaping technologies, including electronic cigarettes. A strong vape community maintains an enthusiastic endorsement of vaping as a harm reduction approach to avoiding the health harms associated with tobacco and cannabis combustion. The matter has been controversial for a decade. A recent comprehensive review of the research concluded that e-cigarettes should not be used for any purpose other than quitting smoking, especially for young people, where the risk of addiction and use of combustion, as well as vaping, is high (Banks et al. 2022).

The tobacco industry is apparently in favour of moving smokers to vaping. The home page of the website of Rothmans Benson & Hedges (https://www.rbhinc.ca/), when viewed in April 2022, prominently displayed the proclamation "We want cigarettes gone by 2035." The assertion appeared with a backdrop of revolving images of lithe models engaged in fitness and outdoor activities amidst majestic scenes of nature. The imagery was strikingly reminiscent of the depictions that once adorned industry ads in magazines and on billboards during the heyday of the cigarette.

But the industry would not support the conclusion from the research that recommends vaping as only a temporary strategy towards eventual cessation. The industry's end goal is market expansion and profit from sustained and increasing sales of tobacco products. Having people switch from combustion to vaping has two advantages for the industry. First, the optics of encouraging what is alleged to be a less harmful alternative are better for the industry's image with the public and with legislators. Secondly, if there are even modest preventative advantages of vaping over combustion, vaping may keep their customers alive longer, thus extending the years of tobacco purchases. That means more revenue.

The unfettered enthusiasm for the merits of vaping continues to far exceed the evidence. To see first-hand the passionate devotion of the vape community in social media, one needs only to post the results of a study that suggests caution in our embrace of vaping. I once posted a study's findings of the low social attractiveness of vaping to non-vapers. It prompted a tsunami of criticism. A few respondents offered reasonable counterpoints, but the rest consisted of seemingly random assertions with no connection to anything in the article or to anything I had written. It appeared that the respondents simply did not like to see vaping criticized. A few other responses were outright, completely disconnected, personal attacks. One puzzling *non sequitur* inexplicably accused me of being an anti-Semite. This experience was reminiscent of a previous social media post in which I questioned proposals for cannabis lounges, due to the issue of second-hand emissions. That post also generated some reasonable responses. But it too unleashed several unrelated personal attacks. They included a particularly bizarre one that somehow saw the content of my post as justification for calling me a pedophile. These are the perils of social media—where angels fear to tread, but I sometimes still rush in.

Another quite different type of social bonding among smokers became clear in a 2010-2012 project while I was working for the Centre for Addiction and Mental Health (CAMH). The project involved a partnership with Addictions and Mental Health Ontario (AMHO), the province's association of addiction and mental health programs. The aim of the project was to support drug and mental health treatment programs, and their staff, to routinely address nicotine dependence with clients who had come for help with mental health and drug problems. Drug problems most often included alcohol, cannabis, cocaine, and opioids. Tobacco use was high among this group. CAMH's DATIS database reported smoking in 45.9% of admissions to addiction treatment programs in Ontario (Centre for Addiction and Mental Health. Drug and Alcohol Treatment Information System (DATIS) 2013)—three times the prevalence in the general population at 15.0% (Canada 2013).

A part of the inspiration for this project was a Minnesota study (Hurt et al. 1996) that had shown that 51% of those who entered treatment for a drug problem subsequently died of tobacco-related disease. In other words tobacco was the number one killer of this group. My challenge to Ontario's addiction treatment system was the prospect of saving their clients from the harms of drugs such as alcohol, opioids, and crystal meth, only to have them die from their use of tobacco. I asked if that would be an acceptable legacy for the system? To be clear, I thought at the time, and still do, that Ontario has a highly evolved addiction treatment system, providing compassionate, evidence-based care. But the system also had this one blind spot related to smoking and its eventual impact on people who enter the system for help.

Not too surprisingly, the project encountered some indifference, and even polite resistance, from some addiction counselors who were tobacco smokers. I had once been one of them. Their pushback provided some interesting insights. Some smoking counselors reported that they would go outdoors for "smoke breaks" with their patients, which some specifically referred to as a way of "bonding" with their patients. I always wondered (to myself) if the counselors would meet a patient at a bar for a drink, share a joint, or share a syringe as a way of bonding with them. I assume that none would. So why the exception for smoking tobacco—the number one killer of their clients? I sometimes wondered, perhaps unfairly, if some smoking counselors were not comfortable seeing themselves as drug dependent—making them, in that way, no different from their clients. Is that a subtle form of stigma?

I have focused on tobacco use simply because, more so than for any other type of drug, it has been so profoundly removed from its once powerful pedestal as the ultra cool symbol of social, romantic, and sexual prowess. Despite this fall from greatness, or perhaps because of it, social bonding, and a sense of community among smokers, and vapers, has survived and prevailed.

However, the same dynamics of social bonding within a community of mutual support also prevails for alcohol—fueled by pop culture and industry product promotion. From Canada, there is that classic Old Vienna beer slogan "Our beer around here"—promoting a sense of community built around brand loyalty.

There are also well-organized groups of patients who rally around their access to a certain pharmaceutical product, lobbying the government on behalf of the product's manufacturer that provides financial support to the group. This has been recently documented in Canada by Lexchin et al (2022).

Implications for Cannabis Legalization: Drug industries encourage and help people who use their products to bond into social niches and communities of mutual support around the use of those products. For cannabis, such niches and communities existed long before legalization. Will commercial legalization lead to a proliferation of these cannabis communities? The hashtag #cannabiscommunity is a prominent one on social media.

DEMONIZATION AND DEIFICATION: MIXED MESSAGES ON DRUG USE

Except for sexuality, I am unable to think of another topic that, more so than drugs, exists within such a perplexing kaleidoscope of mixed messages. From an early age, we encounter messages that glamourize and encourage drug use as well as some that demonize and discourage it. Some of the more prominent societal forces include drug education programs, media news stories, pop culture, and product promotion by drug companies.

Drug Education

Decades of drug education programs in schools brandished a "scared straight" approach that trumpeted a "just say no" solution. Generations of students sat through classroom presentations by police officers describing lurid tales of addicts suffering before dying horrible deaths from drugs. Former "addicts" were also invited in to tell their stories of desperation, misery, and recovery—a Jerry Springer motif brought to the classroom for consumption by impressionable young minds. An interesting retrospective on the anti-drug education programs from that era can be found in Carstairs (2022).

It often occurred to me that it might be interesting to bring in people to talk about how they navigated the perilous years of development in adolescence and early adulthood without becoming dependent on a drug. If such programs exist, they have not been given much attention.

School-based drug education programs have evolved to become more evidence- than fear-based over the years. However, even current programs tend to emphasize the potential harms more so than the pleasures.

It also appears that even when the programs provide evidence-based content, they do not have much of an immediate impact on most students. This does not mean we should not do drug education. After all, the only alternative to providing young people with information about drugs is not to provide it. How would we justify that? It may be more about having realistic objectives to achieve within a realistic period. Attitudes about drugs are shaped over years, not weeks or months. As for drug education programs, maybe we should not be taunting the prevailing rebellion that comes with the adolescent years. Perhaps we should emphasize the learning of critical appraisal skills. Young people can apply these skills to the mixed messages about drugs, and other topics that, like heat-seeking missiles, are perpetually coming their way. Such an approach could be used to encourage young people to be more skeptical of tobacco and alcohol industry messaging. The approach makes sense developmentally. If adolescents are inclined to question adult beliefs and behaviour, why not aim those inclinations at adults who are attempting to manipulate them in ways that will be harmful?

Implications for Cannabis Legalization: Chapters 5, 6, and 7 will show how alcohol, tobacco, pharmaceutical and cannabis industries engage in a great deal of regulatory non-compliance and, at least occasionally, criminal conduct. Educational programs for young people should provide information, not only on health risks related to cannabis, but on the conduct of the companies that supply cannabis.

News Media

Drugs, as a news story topic, are enormously pervasive. You would be challenged to look through any daily newspaper from a major population centre, on any day, and not find at least one news story related to drugs. In the past, too many of these stories have been alarmist and based on questionable information. Apparently people love this stuff—the more gore the better. Let's look at a sampling from my archives.

In 2012, there was a major scare about so-called bath salts, a type of synthetic stimulant drug called cathinones, allegedly associated with acts of violence. The most gruesome and publicized was a case of a man chewing the face off another man while allegedly under the influence of bath salts. The headline read "'Bath salts' drug behind Miami face eating attack could be banned in Canada." However, forensic analysis revealed that the only substance detected in the blood stream of the perpetrator was delta 9 tetrahydra cannabinol (THC), the most active ingredient in cannabis. And no - cannabis use is not associated with live cannibalism either.

Around the same time, there was a great deal of media attention given to a drug known as krokodil with headlines such as "KROKODIL: Flesh-Rotting Horror and Coming Plague?" The actual drug name is desomorphine, a strong and fast-acting analgesic, often cut with a variety of toxic substances. Instances of severe skin damage from frequently injecting adulterated desomorphine were embellished in media reports which likened its effects on the skin to the hide of a crocodile (thus, krokodil) and to "flesh-eating" and "zombie-like." This was media attention at its most alarmist. I remember a satirically titled presentation on media alarmism at the annual conference of Addiction Mental Health Ontario: "Krokodil Ate My Crack Baby". Some people were offended, but I think they may have missed the point.

Rohypnol, the much-publicized "date rape drug" also had its media feeding frenzy. Rohypnol is a benzodiazepine sold in tablet form, able to produce a relatively sudden sedative effect. While Rohypnol use is not particularly widespread, this drug did bring to light a particularly disturbing practice associated with the singles bar scene. It had apparently become a drug of choice, in a different sense, for people who enjoy sex with people who are unconscious. Perverse, offensive, and rather sad.

Moving on to another drug, the headline of a 1990 media report of a Toronto incident read: "2 seeking hallucinogen lick toad, go to hospital." The story was about a substance, bufotenin (5-HO-DMT), a tryptamine derivative. The substance is excreted through skin pores as a defence mechanism by the Bufo, or Cane, toad. Apparently, some people can experience hallucinogenic effects from ingesting bufotenin. Less fortunate lickers can get quite ill.

The article also reported that, out of concern for an impending epidemic of toad licking, Queensland Australia had banned the practice. It was unclear whether the frantically hurried legislation was out of concern for human or toad populations. I no longer have the original clipping or reference—only a digital image of the title of the article that I used in presentations to add a moment of levity. I recall one participant asking "Ban it? How do you punish someone who licks toads to get off?"

The licking of toads is unlikely to become a popular choice for getting high and unlikely to result in a widespread societal impact. However, such practices certainly add to the diverse and wondrous mosaic of playing with our body chemistry. You may be thinking that getting high on toad venom is so 1990. In an interesting resurrection of the phenomenon, a recent news story reported on a chemist who synthesized the toad venom compound, 5-MeO-DMT (Bauer 2021). The article lauds the potential impact of using the synthetic product to save the world's toad population from extinction.

To be fair to the news media, the quality of articles on drug issues has improved notably over the last decade. There is a group of journalists in Canada (you know who you are) who write about drug issues as a specialty—the drug beat. They do their homework on the issues involved and write with an admirable balance of healthy skepticism and compassion.

Now we need to do something about the omnipresent, glamourizing drug ads that adorn the same print media dailies for which these journalists contribute news stories. They are ads for the enormously popular drug - alcohol—often known on the street as "booze."

"Imagine if the Media Covered Alcohol Like Other Drugs"

As we saw in Chapter 1, alcohol is one of our most harmful drugs. Yet, it typically gets treated much more favourably than illegal drugs in so many ways—including in the media.

A cleverly written satire—"Imagine if the media covered alcohol like other drugs"—was published in Vox a few years back. Here is a shot glass sample of the article:

"Here in New Orleans, the horror of the drug was particularly prominent in the city's French Quarter, where hundreds of young adults could be seen roiling from the effects of the drug. Some collapsed on the ground, dazed from alcohol's effects. Others could be seen vomiting in public—a common result of drinking alcohol. Many could be seen limping and clumsily walking down the street, showcasing the type of impairment that public health officials warn can lead to accidents, especially when someone is behind the wheel of a car." (Lopez 2018)

Implication for Cannabis Legalization: How well will the media balance its coverage of legalization of the new recreational drug cannabis?

Pop Culture

Messages about drug use are pervasive in pop culture. Running parallel to tales of the bizarre, the gory, and the stigmatized is the way some drug use is glamourized, valorized, and even deified in the entertainment industry. Despite this ball of confusion of drug messaging many people are ultimately mesmerized by the temptations.

People are wise to be concerned about how children might struggle to make sense of it all and make safe decisions. They deserve much better than "just say no." The simple-mindedness of such a paternalistic directive to surrender is no match for the siren song of pop culture with its many wry, seductive, bad-ass, and cleverly satirical celebrations of drug use. A sampling follows.

> *David Auerbach: "In wine there is wisdom, in beer there is strength, in water there is bacteria."*

> *Mark Twain: "I have made it a rule never to smoke more than one cigar at a time."*

> *Dean Martin: "I once shook hands with Pat Boone and my whole right side sobered up."*

> *Snoop Dogg: "The more medicated, the more dedicated."*

> *unknown author: "Laughter is the best medicine, next to Oxycontin, and of course medicinal marijuana."*

> *Robin Williams: "Reality is just a crutch for people who can't cope with drugs."*

> *Henny Youngman: "When I read about the evils of drinking, I gave up reading."*

Youngman's one-liner prompts us to keep in mind that alcohol use (probably more so than any other drug) is deeply ingrained within the culture of 'cool' that prevails in our culture. Even the gentlest attempts by health advocates to encourage moderation can sometimes evoke a defensive reaction among a segment of the public accusing us of being the humourless defenders of the nanny state.

Alcohol's default legitimacy will surface in clinical encounters as well. The unquestioned acceptance of alcohol consumption as a way of life, even in the face of harm, is lampooned in a *Hagar the Horrible* cartoon.

> *What can I do about these bad hangovers I get, Doctor?*
> *You can stop drinking alcoholic beverages.*
> *No, seriously - what can I do?*

Readers, particularly clinicians, familiar with The Transtheoretical (Stages of Change) Model will recognize the patient as being clearly pre-contemplative.

Since at least the middle of the twentieth century, various pop culture eras in North America had their respective drugs around which celebratory mythology was forged and embellished. Alcohol was king among the glitterati of the Hollywood film industry in the late 1950s and the 1960s. The notorious "Rat Pack" of entertainers Frank Sinatra, Dean Martin, and Sammy Davis Jr. personified the glamourous Tinseltown lifestyle of using alcohol as the elixir of playful mischief and success. Alcohol-related harms received little attention, and were either ignored or lampooned, as in the

Youngman quote above. Dean Martin once disclosed, in a candid moment, that his on-stage drinking was mostly an act—the apparent glass of liquor in his hand was typically tea or apple juice. Many film stars of that era also smoked cigarettes, cigars, or pipes—some almost perpetually, while on screen. Their tobacco use was an important part of their onscreen *persona*. These images, broadcast to the world within glamourous context, helped to establish smoking tobacco and drinking alcohol as symbols of success, popularity, sophistication, romance, and seduction.

The same era would also bring, in a different niche, the beatnik coffee house scene and the use of cannabis, aka reefer—a drug that did not enjoy the legal and commercial entitlement that alcohol did at the time. The slang name, reefer, is probably most known today from *Reefer Madness*—a film made in the 1930s intended to spread fear about cannabis's alleged capacity for causing promiscuity, insanity, and death. In later years, the film would develop a cult-following that found amusement in the film's absurd depictions and stern reprimands. In my first year at the University of Waterloo I saw a poster in the Student Campus Centre advertising a screening of the film. The poster read "presented in smell-o-vision"—a playful allusion to the smell of the audience's assured participation. The film provided grim warnings from a dour commentator to "beware the friendly stranger" luring naïve youth into his world of miscreation. I often smile when I go past a cannabis retail store not far from where I live called The Friendly Stranger.

If you have access to original images of the Beatles from the early-mid 1960s, you will notice that they were often photographed holding cigarettes (I Want to Hold Your Brand?). (Posters of those same images sold in the current era almost always have the cigarettes air-brushed out.) Individual members of the Beatles would also go on to acquire a reputation for using cannabis and LSD. Consider the surreal lyrics of their song "Lucy in the Sky with Diamonds" within the context of the acronym formed by the three main words of the song's title.

The 1970's brought an intensification of the counterculture celebration of the so-called psychedelic drugs that had emerged in the late 1960's. Use of these drugs was championed by many rock and roll artists within the context of hippie culture. There are so many examples that it would be entirely arbitrary to pick one, but with apologies, I will. The Moody Blues' song, "Legend of a Mind", was a tribute to Timothy Leary—the American academic psychologist who promoted the use of LSD and other hallucinogens as a means of enhancing personal awareness and development. Leary was eventually fired by Harvard University for the controversy surrounding his research, opinions, and numerous arrests and incarcerations. During the early years of the war on drugs President Richard Nixon once called Leary "the most dangerous man in America."

Hippie culture would give way to the punk movement and associated music scene, perhaps emblemized in a line from The Clash's 1979 song "London Calling": "Phony Beatlemania has bitten the dust." But the celebration of drug use in the music of the time was nowhere near biting the dust.

Drug use as lifestyle was perhaps most blatantly asserted in a song by the punk band Ian Dury and the Blockheads, who sang out "...sex 'n' drugs 'n' rock 'n' roll are all my brain 'n' body need...." So-called alternative radio stations, with demographically sculpted playlists, delighted in broadcasting this anthem of unbridled and unapologetic hedonism.

The sensationalized drug scene of the day, always part reality and part mythology, would continue to morph along with pop culture. Cocaine use became iconic for the disco dance club culture of the late 1970s and 1980s. From the 1990s on, designer drugs have increasingly captured the attention of those wishing to explore the frontiers of playing with their body chemistry. In 2008, a United States band emerged called The Designer Drugs and released a song in 2013 called "Drugs are in Control."

It was not necessarily the case that large numbers of people used all the drugs that became iconic for their respective eras. But the pop culture celebrities, who sometimes trumpeted their own use of these drugs, were larger than life. Their edgy lifestyles and social stature created disproportionate caricatures of reality. The perceived prominence of drug use was proportionately embellished.

At the 2015 Canadian music awards (*The Junos*), held that year in Hamilton, Ontario, musician and host Jacob Hoggard announced to millions of viewers in the live broadcast that both he and Sam Roberts were "so high" that evening. Hoggard also thanked the members of Hamilton's local band, the Arkells, for letting him sleep on their couch and have sex with their girlfriends. We can safely assume that Hoggard was joking—albeit it in the most callous of taste. (Perhaps not so tangentially, in early 2022, Hoggard was in court for charges related to incidents of sexual assault causing bodily harm and sexual interference.)

The point to be made is that the iconic meme of "sex, drugs, and rock and roll" continues to be promoted, to an essentially younger entertainment market, as a cohesive pop culture mythology. The meme lived on for yet another generation.

Satirical references to drug use by entertainers such as screenwriters, comedians, or cartoonists are usually nothing more than attempts to get an audience to laugh, or by pop stars to earn some notoriety that might help them sell their music. The references are not necessarily intended to promote or increase drug use. There may be nothing necessarily wrong with enjoying some clever satire or comedic hyperbole about drug use. Those of us who work in public health must be careful that we do not deserve our reputation as the dour architects of the nanny state.

But we also need to regularly remind society that there are real people with real drug problems—and there are lots of them. We should not shrink from our responsibility to effectively communicate that our pandemics of drug problems arise within a context of a society that is saturated with drug promotion messages. The potential for pop culture to shape attitudes and behaviour, including destructive ones, is just as real.

A United Kingdom study did an analysis of alcohol, tobacco, high fat, sugar, salt (HFSS) food content in randomly selected intervals of eleven original films released by Amazon Prime and Netflix in 2017. Alcohol content appeared in 41.7% of the intervals. Tobacco appeared in 26.9% and HFSS foods in 35.2%. The observed percentages did not vary with film age classification (Alfayad et al. 2021).

You can do your own casual observational study. Whenever you are watching a film or television series, pay attention to how often characters use alcohol—specifically as a way of handling stress. It is fascinating to realize how often it happens once you start watching for it. From my own casual observations, I have noticed that straight liquor is the type of alcohol that is most often used by film characters to handle stress. That makes sense pharmacologically. Straight liquor would typically be about 40% alcohol—compared to wine, typically at 11-14%, and beer at 5-6%. Film characters typically do not measure out standard drinks, so this is all about more alcohol per volume of liquid for quicker and greater stress relief.

There may be nothing wrong with occasionally using a drug to handle the stresses of a tough day. But our personal welfare is best served by having a variety of strategies for healthy stress management—most of which should not involve altering our body chemistry with an exogenous substance. The omnipresence of managing stress with alcohol in film and television could, over time, be a powerful and harmful influence on attitudes about alcohol. This might be particularly perilous for impressionable young minds that begin to drink these messages from an early age.

Using alcohol as a default strategy for coping with stress may be a good example of what sociologists call "cultural mythology." Cultural mythology does not necessarily refer to something that is untrue, but it might. It consists of a set of beliefs that are communicated, starting at an early age for most people, and continue to be communicated over a person's life span. This occurs in such a pervasive, yet subtle, fashion that people may adopt these beliefs without being conscious of doing so. The construct of cultural mythology might provide some insight into the subtle ways by which our attitudes about alcohol are shaped by pop culture and advertising.

Pop culture sometimes more overtly promotes drug products through product placement in television series and movies. This is a strategic form of sponsorship that can be used as part of a marketing strategy to sell more drug products. A drug product can also benefit from an implied endorsement by a famous actor when the actor's character uses the product in a film.

Connections between pop culture celebrities and specific products can be more overt. 1950s film star and singer, Frank Sinatra, routinely promoted Jack Daniels whiskey. On his April 4, 2015, CBC radio program *Under the Influence*, Terry O'Reilly told us that Frank was literally buried with a bottle of Jack. The manufacturers of Jack Daniels recently returned the favour with the release of a Sinatra Select edition of their whiskey with the promotional tag line: "They were inseparable and still are." In another genre of contemporary music, Willie Nelson was an early adopter in the green rush of cannabis branding by celebrities. He was followed by another American performer—Calvin Cordozar Broadus Jr., known professionally as Snoop Dogg. Mr. Broadus Jr. added cannabis to his already established line of cigars. (There is a story there that I will share in Chapter 5.) Many other celebrities would follow—more stories to be told in Chapters 5, 6, and 7.

Implications for Cannabis Legalization: Pop culture changes over time. And so will the celebrities who animate it—as will the messages concerning cannabis and other drugs. What new frontiers of cannabis culture might become iconic in a legalized commercial world?

Drug Product Promotion

Drug Promotion and Drug Laws: Itch, Scratch, and Bleed

Another part of the prevailing mixed messages within our story of drugs and society is how diverse types of drugs are promoted to people in juxtaposition with the legal constraints on their access.

Legal recreational drugs, such as alcohol, tobacco, and (in some jurisdictions) cannabis are seductively marketed to people. However, legislation restricts their availability to government-licensed gatekeepers with designated retail outlets and minimum age requirements. This alluring stimulation of appetite with restricted access is a significant part of the mixed messaging, and there are concerns about its impact on youth. Does the promotion of drug products create an itch and an irresistible urge to scratch it? Does much of the recreational drug use among youth involve a surrender to the allure of the forbidden fruit?

Other drugs are available to us for therapeutic use. However, access to some of the most effective ones is typically controlled by licensed healthcare providers who prescribe and dispense according to evidence-based protocols intended to protect us. Well at least most of them do. Product promotion of therapeutic drugs is directed primarily at prescribers. By law in Canada, ads directed at the public for controlled medicines have only vague information, followed by advice to "talk to your doctor." The laws are quite different elsewhere. I recall being confined to a hotel room due to weather in a city on the Canada-US border. I do not currently subscribe to broadcast television at home so I decided to take advantage of a rare opportunity to watch a US television station for an afternoon. By far the two most often broadcast types of ads were: ads promoting new pharmaceutical products and ads from personal injury law firms looking for plaintiffs for class actions against pharmaceutical companies. Balance is good.

Legislation is also used to outright prohibit the use of some drugs and can carry harsh penalties for those who disregard the law. The penalties become more severe for those who trade in these illegal drugs. This makes traditional product promotion strategies potentially perilous for those entrepreneurs on the unlicensed side of the drug trade. Yet, many drug users find illegal online suppliers who manage to escape enforcement efforts, at least for a time.

What is Drug Product Promotion?

Drug product promotion is quite different from most pop culture references to recreational drug use. Product promotion is always strategic. It is always intended to promote use of the drug and increase its sales to generate revenue.

Product promotion is a generic term that includes marketing campaigns that can include advertising, event sponsorship, and celebrity endorsements. But the major product promotion vehicle that contributes to the mixed messages about drugs is advertising.

I am going to do a deeper dive on advertising. I will cover some theories of advertising and introduce how the theory is used in ads. In a later section I will demonstrate advertising strategies by referencing actual ads designed to sell alcohol and tobacco. And I will have a few things to say about those ads.

Implications for Cannabis Legalization: advertising practices for alcohol and tobacco have profound implications for the cannabis industry. As we will see in Chapters 5, 6, and 7, the cannabis industry's unbridled enthusiasm for market expansion is matched only by its comorbid indifference to public health and the law. If the industry is successful, the alcohol ads that so prominently populate our landscapes now, will have to compete for that space against a newly arrived cannabis industry. Or will the amount of space available for drug advertising be expanded to accommodate the promotional ambitions of both industries?

Product Promotion Objectives: Market Expansion, Market Share, Normalization, Brand Loyalty

Market expansion and increasing market share represent two different and potentially overlapping objectives. Market expansion is usually an objective shared by competing companies to increase the overall size of a product's market—that is, increase the number of people who buy the product, and the amount they buy. Market expansion might also have a specific market segment in mind—based upon sex, age, occupation, income, race, ethnicity, or sexual orientation.

Consider that 78% of Canadians drink alcohol at least once a year, leaving 22% who do not drink (Canada 2021). Any alcohol manufacturer would be delighted to capture even a portion of that untapped market. However, despite omnipresent alcohol advertising, the 78% prevalence has not changed much in recent years so the remaining non-drinkers appear to be intransigent. The potential for overall market expansion appears to be limited.

Then consider that only 15% of Canadians used cannabis at least once per year (Canada 2021). Now that is an opportunity for market expansion! If 78% of Canadians use recreational drug A, why not recreational drug B? That 78% will be the long-term benchmark for success for the cannabis industry. Individual cannabis brands will fight it out for the greater share of that expanding market, just as alcohol brands compete for the share of the 78%.

And that brings us to toilet paper. No, that is not the provocative name of the latest cannabis brand or designer drug. I literally mean the consumer product, toilet paper. This is an example of market saturation in the extreme. After all, who, in Canada, needs to be convinced to buy this product? There is no room for market expansion. Product promotion for toilet paper is all about increasing market share—competing brands trying to convince consumers to switch from a competitor's brand to their own. They are all fighting for a bigger piece of the fixed-size pie.

As a brief aside, Terry O'Reilly, in his podcast *Under the Influence* tells of a print ad for an early brand of toilet paper that featured a strong selling point: "No slivers." Now that's what I call product innovation!

Probably the most famous ad campaign for brand switching was the Pepsi Challenge. It was not competition over a saturated market, but it was a brand switching campaign in its most overt form—pitting two soft drink juggernauts against each other in a taste test cage match.

In contrast to getting more people to buy your product another objective of product promotion is to convince your existing customers to buy more product. For drugs, this is usually done by convincing customers to integrate the drug more fully into their lives by making it a widely accepted part of specific life events such as weddings or outdoor festivals, or even part of a person's daily routine—such as having a drink after work, or "wake 'n' bake" with cannabis. This is called normalization. You may have seen the television ad campaign proclaiming "Eggs aren't just for breakfast anymore." The suggestion is clear: include eggs in any of the daily meals. Of course, normalization can have the highly desirable collateral effect of attracting new customers as well. Normalization is all about market expansion.

Perhaps the holy grail of product promotion is establishing brand loyalty. The objective is to create an emotional connection between brand and customer to achieve a level of devotion through which customers would only buy your brand and not your competitors'. What normalization is to market expansion, brand loyalty is to market share.

Brand loyalties can last lifetimes. Philip Hilts' 1996 book *Smokescreen* has a chapter called "For Starters" that provides a fascinating account of Canadian tobacco manufacturer, Imperial Tobacco, and its code name "Project Sixteen" initiative. In the late 1970s, Imperial brought sixteen- and seventeen-year-olds to high end hotels in Toronto to interview them to figure out the initiators of smoking and the enablers of brand loyalty. This was critical intelligence gathering for the design of ad campaigns for young smokers. The objective was to create brand loyalty for life. Imperial pursued this objective even with the knowledge that the campaign would cause Imperial to lose some of its older customers. Future returns would be greater with the younger customers. Hilts also cites a document from US Tobacco that showed that the company spent half of its promotion budget on youth which made up only 2% of its market (Hilts 1996). Think of the strategy as a long-term investment, rather than a short-term one. There is limited merit in spending promotional resources on a market whose demise is relatively imminent and even hastened by your product.

It is only fair to mention that occasionally a drug company will produce an ad that encourages social responsibility rather than increased consumption. An example is a video ad by Heineken called "Moderate Drinkers Wanted", in which several women are seen leaving their drunken male companions behind in a bar. The music is up-beat, with an assertive female vocalist singing "I need a hero." Near the end of the ad, a guy sitting at the bar wins the flirtatious admiration of a female bartender when he declines her offer of another Heineken. Nice ad—warm fuzzy feeling. Think public relations and brand loyalty. The ad also sends an important message to women—that there is no need to tolerate drunkenness in a male companion. The ad might also help to reduce excessive consumption among men with its message that moderation is more appreciated by women than is drunkenness.

I remember seeing an online image that depicted a rough looking, disheveled, young man, angrily throwing his fist into the air and yelling "Let's drink moderately!" The dissonance makes you linger in your thoughts and enhances retention. Maybe it will affect behaviour.

Despite claims by alcohol and tobacco industries that their advertising is intended only to shift brand preference, and not to stimulate market growth, we have reason to be skeptical of this claim. To varying degrees, there is potential for each of our major drug industries to grow the market by attracting new customers as they come of legal age. As we saw with Project Sixteen, drug companies do not wait until young people come of age to woo them. They begin the courtship process years earlier. Attracting new young customers is particularly important for the tobacco industry for two reasons.

One is that young adolescents are at a vulnerable age at which they seek an easy to achieve symbol for maturity, belonging, and attractiveness to others. Consider these legacy tobacco ad slogans for Camel and Lucky Strike brands:

Camel, where a man belongs

Luckies separate the men from the boys, but not from the girls.

The second reason for attracting new young customers hearkens back to our Chapter 1 data tsunami from which we learned that the tobacco industry loses more than 47,000 customers every year in Canada due to tobacco-related mortality. Someone must replace those departed customers to maintain revenues.

Implications for Cannabis Legalization: If cannabis companies are allowed to advertise as alcohol currently is, there is potentially enormous room for market expansion. With increases in aggregate use will come increases in harm.

Market Segmenting is All About You (Because You Are Important to Us)

The grand template into which the objectives of product promotion fit is a powerful, near-universal approach known as market segmenting.

People have always been curious about psychoactive substances, and they find various kinds of benefits in their physical and mental effects. However, it would be a mistake to see such curiosity and hedonism as arising spontaneously within individuals and as isolated from the broader forces of society. Somehow, along the path of social evolution, it became not only personally enjoyable, but socially fashionable in some circles for members to play with their body chemistry. Among members of these social niches, drug use was incorporated and celebrated as a salient aspect of the niche's culture. I provided several examples in the earlier segment on pop culture to which we could add the indispensable role of wine in the contemporary niche of gourmet foodies. The Liquor Control Board of Ontario's flagship marketing vessel is its *Food & Drink* publication. Produced with an irresistible aesthetic, it is pornography for foodies. No judgment.

The use of some drugs transcends many eras and disparate social niches. But what is pertinent to this discussion is when a specific drug type becomes emblematic or iconic of a specific niche. Some of these niche icons may have arisen spontaneously, while others may have been envisioned and engineered by ad agencies. Some may have been a product of both.

The social niches that have formed around the use of a drug have been successfully exploited by the madmen and madwomen of the advertising industry in promoting the use of drug products. Historically this was tobacco and alcohol and now cannabis in some jurisdictions. But we also saw social niche appeal in magazines, websites, and head shops for cannabis, long before it became legal in some jurisdictions.

Age-old social niche appeal has been reverse-engineered, re-tooled, and modernized as market segmenting. Market segmenting has three components:

- *study a segment of the population in terms of its demographics, its members' likes, dislikes, and aspirations (hopes, fears, and dreams)*

- *design your advertising campaign so your product appeals to people with that profile or (and this is especially important) to people who do not currently have, but desire that lifestyle*

- *design your ads to integrate your product as an important part of that lifestyle.*

We often hear the term "lifestyle advertising." If market segmenting provides the structure, lifestyle provides the aesthetics and adornment. Once a target market segment is defined, lifestyle is what makes using the drug appear attractive and desirable. Lifestyle advertising has been used to sell everything from kitchens to jacuzzis. I am reminded of a classified ad: "For sale: 1 man, 7 women hot tub."

Implications for Cannabis Legalization: What market segments will be used to attract cannabis users? You can think about it now. Some potential answers are coming later in the chapter.

Event Sponsorship and Celebrity Endorsement

In the months leading up to the 2010 Vancouver Winter Olympics, McDonalds ran a series of posters in their Canadian restaurants. The posters depicted members of the Canadian Olympic team holding McDonalds products. The upper front of the athletes' jerseys was designed as a v-neck so the trim of the V would look like a lanyard from which an Olympic medal would hang. The McDonalds products were held by the athletes in the position where the medal would hang. Some may find it offensive that burgers and fries were being associated with the extraordinary level of health and fitness needed to win an Olympic medal.

A company's marketing campaign can include sponsorship of concerts, festivals, sports tournaments, and arts events. In the summer and early autumn of 2018, leading up to the legalization of cannabis in Canada, legal cannabis producers sponsored many concerts and festivals. Every one of those sponsorships was illegal. I will tell that story in Chapter 6.

Marketing campaigns can also include celebrity endorsements (now often called partnerships). Companies love to attach their brands to celebrities—instant fame!

In an episode of his radio podcast, *Under the Influence,* Terry O'Reilly has told of gladiators in ancient Rome endorsing products. More recently, many entertainment celebrities have endorsed drug products. Lucille Ball did print advertisements for Philip Morris cigarettes, and Danny DeVito appeared on the cover of the magazine *Cigar Aficionado.* Alcohol beverages have been endorsed by Jay-Z, Kate Hudson, David Beckham, Drew Barrymore, and Marilyn Manson. And then there was the courageous endorsement of Viagra by major league baseball player Rafael Palmeiro. In Chapters 6 and 7, I will explore the partnerships of Canadian cannabis producers with The Tragically Hip, the Trailer Park Boys, Martha Stewart, and Snoop Dogg.

The purpose of all product promotion strategies is straightforward: to make more people aware of, and feel a connection to, a company's product. They will begin to buy it, continue to buy it, and buy more of it. The company will make more money.

Advertising Works

Advertising is everywhere. And most people despise it, largely because much of it is banal to the point of being irritating. It often reflects a low-brow style of humour with a disputable premise and an equally suspect promise. For years, a homemade sandwich board adorned a sidewalk near

McMaster University displaying an ad for a haircutting business: "If your haircut is sexy, you have more friends."

A pink truck often parked not far from where I live has the words "your hole is my business" emblazoned on its side. We can feel a small amount of relief upon learning that it is not a slogan for a health practitioner but a posthole digging company.

Such pervasive triteness in advertising can cause us to underestimate the power of the art when it is done with judicious thought and inspired finesse. The best people at the best ad agencies are very smart people. I believe they are some of the most creative people on the planet and they are incredibly good at what they do: the engineering of belief and behaviour on a mass scale. When an alcohol, tobacco, pharma, or cannabis company wants a promotional campaign, these are the people they hire—not the guy who made the sandwich board. With only the occasional surrender to camp, alcohol and tobacco promotional campaigns have always been sophisticated and wonderous in concept and meticulous in design and presentation. If only we could convince more of these highly gifted artisans to apply their craft to something that serves the betterment of humanity, rather than just selling us stuff. Even the most aesthetically elevated art can be banal in its purpose.

Implication for Cannabis Legalization: The cannabis industry in Canada continues to lobby hard for the right to advertise with omnipresence. Most independent cannabis retailers will have small budgets and may have to settle for the guy behind the sandwich board. But the corporate producers have deep pockets. They have the resources to hire the people most able to seduce us.

An Incompatible Relationship: Recreational Drug Market Expansion and Public Health Protection

The power of advertising arises from the marriage of the rigors of behavioural science with a finely honed acumen for creative expression. This union has created some of the most powerful tools of persuasion ever conceived in our civilization's history.

The strategies and tools include market segmenting, lifestyle advertising, market expansion, increasing market share, normalization, and brand loyalty. Ad campaigns, including event sponsorships and celebrity endorsements, are designed, and shepherded by people with advanced expertise in social psychology and adolescent development. In my undergraduate and graduate studies in psychology, I had always assumed that what my peers and I were learning would be used, exclusively, to help people. I was naïve to how the same expertise would be used in a manner that might take advantage of people, and even harm them.

The expertise of graduates from academic behavioural science programs gives drug companies extraordinary potential to expand markets, sales, and revenues. (We should acknowledge that taxpayers generously subsidize the academic training of these employees.) Combine that talent with the allure and reach of radio and television, and the ubiquity of the internet, and you have a perfect storm for mass influence.

Market expansion is not a problem if you are expanding a market for benign, or even beneficial, commodities such as organically grown vegetables or sustainable energy sources. That could be a very good thing. However, market expansion comes with a cost when applied to drug products. As we saw in Chapter 1, drugs harbour substantial potential for harm. They are not ordinary commodities. Drugs create quick and reliable pleasure or relief. Immediacy and reliability are critical forces in shaping our behaviour. Drugs are said to be self-reinforcing. Therein lies their power to make us susceptible to harm. The tools of behavioural science can further unleash and strengthen that power. Chapter 1 also showed us that the harm extends beyond individual drug users to include families, communities, and economies.

For alcohol and tobacco, research has shown that advertising is associated with increases in aggregate use in the population. (Yes, advertising works.) The research also tells us that when use of a drug increases in a population, so do problems that are associated with the use of the drug. That relationship has also been demonstrated in the current opioid pandemic. These relationships will be revisited in Chapter 5.

However, these correlations do not tell us much about what is happening inside the opaque box of human consciousness. How does increased marketing contribute to increased use, and how do increases in use at the population level contribute to increased problems in the population? These are complex relationships that will take years of research to elucidate. But the beginning of understanding has been abetted by an established area of research in experimental clinical psychology—one that has not been fully appreciated in the public health arena or in the development of drug policy in Canada and elsewhere.

Reinforcement Expectancies: Beliefs, Drinking Behaviour and Harm

Unless you are an academically oriented psychologist, you read that title and may have thought "re-in what?" That is okay. For many people, it may seem an incomprehensible academic construct wrapped up in the most arcane of disciplinary jargon. But please do not hold that against it. I have found reinforcement expectancies a useful construct that is well-supported by experimental evidence. It also overlays very well with public health analyses of drug product advertising.

Reinforcement expectancies mean that what we believe about a drug will have an important impact on how we use that drug and the consequences of doing so. The supporting research base was begun in the mid-1980s with the work of Sandra Brown at San Diego University. (Sandra received her Ph.D. from the University of Windsor, Canada.)

Several years of research findings can be summarized as follows:

If you believe that alcohol enhances your physical, mental, social, or sexual functioning (positive expectancies), then you are more likely to show certain reinforced behaviours. (See. Not so arcane after all.)

The reinforced behaviours include:

- *heavier drinking*

- *harmful psychosocial consequences from drinking*

- *poor progress in a treatment program*

- *poor outcome one year after treatment.*

These results tell us that what we believe about the benefits of alcohol will have a strong influence on our drinking behaviour and the consequences of that behaviour.

These beliefs that alcohol improves our physical, mental, social, or sexual prowess apparently leads us to engage in higher risk drinking behaviour, and therefore may increase the likelihood of experiencing harmful consequences. It is also interesting that having these beliefs not only gets people into trouble with alcohol, but also makes it more difficult for them to get out of trouble should they try to get help from a treatment program.

The power of our beliefs in determining our drug experiences should be no surprise to anyone who is familiar with the placebo effect. That lesson was acquired most memorably for me, not from papers I have read, but from a research project in which I had subjects staggering and slurring their speech while blowing zeros on the alcohol breathalyzer! I was astounded when the double-blind codes were revealed. That placebo worked beautifully. Reinforcement expectancies!

The question of real interest to me at this point of my career is where do these beliefs about alcohol come from? How has alcohol, so profoundly, become a part of our cultural mythology as the magic elixir of empowered physical, mental, social, and sexual functioning?

This is where drug promotion strategies and reinforcement expectancies form an elucidating partnership. The next section of this chapter will propose credible explanations for where these beliefs come from. More specifically, I will explore how prevailing beliefs about tobacco and alcohol are reinforced among current generations and introduced to the next generation of customers. It is all done through the miracle of advertising.

Implications for Cannabis Legalization: Demonization and deification, or stigmatization and valorization, of drug use are opposite and extreme ends of the same continuum. Both are harmful in different ways. Will we be able to find a middle ground to communicate compassionate and healthy attitudes about cannabis?

ALCOHOL AND TOBACCO ADVERTISING: WHAT'S WRONG WITH THIS PICTURE?

One of the major take home messages from the data dump is that alcohol and tobacco are responsible for a very large proportion of the drug-related harm and costs in Canada. Alcohol and tobacco accounted for more harm and costs than all the illegal drugs combined. This is confirmed by data spanning 1992 to 2017. There is no reason to believe that this was not the case before 1992 or has not continued since 2017.

So why are alcohol and tobacco use and harms so prominent? Many will answer that these are drugs that adults are legally allowed to use. That is a factor. But these are also drugs that we have been encouraged to use. For older Canadians, alcohol and tobacco advertising was pervasive for most of their lives—on tv, radio, newspapers, magazines, and billboards. For most of those years, these drug products somehow, quite arbitrarily, gained a special status for many Canadians as the pathways to social, vocational, and romantic success. In Canada, tobacco has lost its presence in the ad landscape, and simultaneously, its special status as an enhancer of success. Looking at vintage tobacco ads gives us a rear-view mirror perspective on strategies now used by cannabis companies in the United States and, more surreptitiously, in Canada. I will have more to say about that in Chapters 5, 6 and 7.

Alcohol ads remain as prominent as ever in traditional advertising platforms. Despite being mostly self-regulated, the alcohol industry still complains of over-regulation and has embraced the internet with its presumed libertarian, free-market ethos, and lowered capacity for regulatory surveillance. Tobacco and cannabis companies have also enthusiastically staked a claim in the new internet frontier of minimal regulation, and sometimes, in ways that are not entirely legitimate.

Tobacco and alcohol corporations tell us that their advertising leads only to purchases and non-problem use, and that it is some combination of other factors that transforms non-problem use into high-risk use, which may then manifest as problems. These other predisposing or triggering factors might include exposure to prolonged stress, trauma, disadvantaged environments, and poor role models. Personal attributes that contribute might include low coping skills or biological predisposition. The industries tell us that it is unfair to hold them accountable for the ills of society and the vulnerability of individuals that transform use of their products into misuse.

However, the evidence from research on reinforcement expectancies tells us that our beliefs about alcohol are directly related to high-risk use and harm. Those predisposing beliefs overlap very well with the messages of alcohol advertising. While stress, trauma, etc. certainly often do lead to high-risk use and harm, they are not required for problem drinking to occur. To be clear, my suggestion is not that drug promotion is the only cause of drug-related harm. But it should be included as a key component in a constellation of factors. It should also be regarded as one that has not received the attention it deserves. Drug product promotion is also a factor that, from a policy perspective, is relatively easy to address, given the regulatory will to do so.

I confess to being a bit of an ad nerd. I have an extensive collection. In this section, I will describe and discuss some specific examples of tobacco and alcohol advertising, from as early as the 1950s up to our current time. What becomes clear in this longitudinal treatment is that surface aspects of ads—language, hairstyles, dress, and activities—change with the dictates of ever-shifting fashions. However, the underlying communication strategies remain mostly constant—perhaps because they work so well.

We will see how alcohol and tobacco ads have associated their products with glamour and sophistication, machismo and athleticism, romance and sexuality, and acceptance and belonging—the tangible manifestations of the cultural mythology that I mentioned earlier. Alcohol and tobacco ads have been criticized for targeting vulnerable populations including youth, racial minorities, lower socioeconomic groups, and people with mental health problems. Beneath banners of philanthropy and diversity, tobacco and alcohol ad campaigns have also co-opted the arts, fashion, and sports, as well as the women's and pride movements. But at what cost, and with what disturbing ironies at play?

I will also look at the results of research studies that evaluated the impact of these ads and the public health policy dramas that ensued.

Tobacco Advertising and Market Segments

Women and Young Girls

Perhaps one of the most perverse market segmenting successes was the co-opting of the women's movement by the tobacco industry in its ads from the 1960s and 1970s. Women were encouraged to proclaim their independence by taking up smoking. Slogans such as "You've come a long way, baby" and "For women who can light their own cigarette" beckoned and congratulated the independent woman. More to the point, and more ironically, women were being encouraged to express their independence by becoming dependent upon a drug—a drug manufactured and advertised by male-dominated corporations.

People who know about my interest in ads sometimes send me interesting ones. One such gift was a cigarette ad that appeared in a German fashion magazine for a brand called West Lights. This ad gives us a revealing demonstration of how a market segment can be defined.

The ad features a young, overweight woman eating a large ice cream cone. A young, athletic man, wearing a Los Angeles Lakers basketball jersey and Houston Astros baseball cap, is offering her a cigarette.

This ad is the Magic Johnson and Jeff Bagwell of tobacco ads. It has an impressive four classic tobacco ad themes at play. The first is nicotine as an appetite suppressant. We see a woman who may wish to lose some weight, and the large confection she is holding suggests dieting may not be working so well. Inclusion of the word "Lights" in the cigarette brand name refers not only to lower tar levels in the cigarette but is also often used for lower calorie food products. The second theme is romance, as indicated by the man's attentive look and by addressing her as "sweetheart." The third theme is the athleticism of the young man. Finally, is the western United States theme captured in the brand name and in the swag of two teams from professional sports that are more popular in North America than they are in Europe.

If we deconstruct this image and infer the implied action, we see a crassly crafted depiction of the intended market segment: a young, European woman, who wishes to lose some weight (without making dietary sacrifices) and capture the affections of an attractive athletic guy sporting a western mystique.

If you wonder whether I might be reading too much into this ad, please stay with me. You may find the following example more convincing.

Thanks to a whistleblower at RJ Reynolds Tobacco Co., details of a planned ad campaign were leaked to, and published in, the *Washington Post*. The campaign plan was for a new cigarette brand called Dakota which targeted young, poorly educated, white women, referred to in the internal company documents as "virile females." The profile included eighteen- to twenty-year-old women with no education beyond high school, and whose favourite pastimes included mall cruising, tractor pulls, and watching television soap operas. RJ denied that Dakota was aimed solely at women. The Dakota exposure came just three weeks after R.J. Reynolds was forced, by strong opposition, to cancel plans to test market Uptown, a brand of cigarettes aimed at people of African descent. (Trueheart 1991).

The tobacco industry was also interested in attracting much younger girls and was quite successful in doing so as demonstrated by a 1994 report published in *The Journal of the American Medical Association* (Pierce, Lee, and Gilpin 1994).

The report showed that from 1944 to 1967, there was only a minor increase in the number of teenage girls who started smoking. Between 1967 and 1973, smoking initiation rates jumped:

- *35% among 17-year-old girls*

- *75% among 15-year-old girls*

- *110% among 12-year-old girls.*

Rates among teenage boys rose only negligibly during the same time span. During the same six years, aggressive marketing campaigns were mounted for cigarette brands Virginia Slims, Silva Thins, and Eve. All these brands targeted women.

Men

While women became a market segment of great interest to the to-bacco industry, the industry never gave up on the male segment and were hard at work slicing it into sub-segments to maximize sales. We can illustrate with two ads from the 1980s that depict two different cigarette brands targeting two different types of men—two market segments.

The ad for one brand, Magma, (with copy reading "MAGMATUDE") depicts a young man in denim and sunglasses, crouched beside his motorcycle. The image presents a very straight-forward manly celebration of the union between smoke and machine—roaring and billowing with machismo.

The other ad, for a brand called Montclair, is more ostentatious. It is also more complex. It depicts an older, stylish, and refined, wealthy yachtsman. It also employs some not-so-subtle stereotypes of him being effeminate or possibly gay. The man's upper-class stature is reinforced by the word "rich" to describe the flavour of Montclair.

But there is a clear contradiction in this ad. Below the word "rich" is a horizontal line and below the line the copy reads "about 1/2 price." The horizontal line juxtaposes the contradiction. A rich yachtsman does not need to smoke a half price discount cigarette. This ad is not targeted to wealthy yachtsmen, but rather to men who aspire to that lifestyle. If people are made up of two selves—who they are and who they want to be—this ad is aimed at the latter. Realistically, they probably will not ever reach their aspiration. But what they can do is smoke the same brand of cigarette as the wealthy yachtsmen of the world – and at a discounted price. The ever-hopeful are invited to share a small part of the lavish yachtsman lifestyle, however strictly voyeuristic that sharing may be.

This leads to a critical point. Ads do not simply try to sell us a product. The process is much more elegant than that. They offer us a surrogate fulfillment of an aspiration or fantasy. That *faux* fulfillment creates a positive association with the product and improves the likelihood of a purchase.

Children and Adolescents

Advertising of cigarettes with images that would appeal to children started at least as early as the 1950s. A notable example is a Lucky Strike ad depicting a typically jolly Santa Claus holding a cigarette. In later years, the practice of using images to appeal to children would intensify.

A few years after the Dakota and Uptown brand exposures, more company documents showed that Reynolds, undaunted by those earlier embarrassments, was also targeting youth. An industry document titled RJR Memo From Mr. C.A. Tucker January 23, 1975" (quoted in Campaign for Tobacco Free Kids 2001) read:

> To ensure increased and longer-term growth of Camel Filter, the brand must increase its share of penetration among

the 14-24 age group which have a new set of liberal values and which represent tomorrow's cigarette business. (Campaign for Tobacco Free Kids 2001)

That statement was quite different from the public one R.J. Reynolds made in 1994 which claimed "...that smoking is a choice for adults and that marketing programs are directed at those above the age to smoke" (Josefson 1998).

I have already mentioned Philip Hilts' book *Smokescreen* and its chapter called "For Starters." The chapter provides an in-depth treatment of tobacco companies targeting children in both the US and Canada during the 1990s (Hilts1996). So how effective were industry campaigns to capture youth as smokers?

A paper published in the journal *Tobacco Control* (Arnett and Terhanian 1998) reported that prior to the start of the Joe Camel campaign, Camel's share of the youth market (ages 12 to 17) was less than 1%. A year and a half later, it had risen to 8%, and five years later, it had risen to 13%. Market share increases of this size are very rare, and highly coveted in the marketing industry.

A 1998 US Center for Disease Control and Prevention report described a 73% increase in the number of American teens who became daily smokers over the nine years since the debut of the Joe Camel ad campaign in 1988 (Associated Press 1998).

The evidence for the effectiveness of tobacco promotion continued to mount. Drawing upon the 2012 US Surgeon General's Report, a review of the evidence on tobacco marketing and tobacco use by youth was published in a report *Cause and Effect: Tobacco Advertising Causes Youth Tobacco Use* (Tobacco Control Legal Consortium 2012).

First the Report summarized what had been learned from tobacco industry internal documents:

- *tobacco marketing is intended to recruit new users and increase use of tobacco products*

- *tobacco companies invest $ billions in marketing strategies that attract youth*

- *the tobacco industry is targeting youth at the point-of-sale*

From its examination of the peer-reviewed literature, the Report concluded that:

- *tobacco marketing causes youth tobacco use*

- *point-of-sale marketing increases youth tobacco use*

"Causes" is a strong word when used in a publication from a scientific organization. This says that the evidence is not just circumstantial or correlational but that they are declaring that an actual causal mechanism is at play.

Tobacco's Fall from Grace

The US Surgeon General's 1964 report (Surgeon General to the United States 1964) marked the beginning of a new era when the tobacco industry would increasingly feel the wrath of the public health movement, the courts, and government legislators and regulators. It was the first time that the SG's report warned of the health hazards of smoking tobacco. Its release on January 11 was, unusually, on a Saturday—reportedly to minimize or buffer the immediate impact on the stock market.

The release of the SG's Report was not a surprise for the tobacco industry. They knew it was coming and had been trying to prevent its release. When that failed, tobacco companies went into damage control mode. A major strategy was to counter the harms to health reported in the Surgeon General's report with highly suspect statistics behind claims such as "More doctors smoke Camels than any other cigarette."

The SG report also ignited a great deal of anti-smoking sentiment in the population, often setting smokers and non-smokers in conflict. Another cigarette brand, Tareyton, used the slogan "I'd rather fight than switch." The ads would always feature a man or a woman with bruising around one of their eyes. On the surface, the ad is about brand loyalty, but the more subtle message was for smokers to fight for their right to smoke. If you would rather fight than switch brands then presumably you would also rather fight than yield to pressure not to smoke when and where you chose to. This was perhaps the beginning of the "smokers have rights too" campaign that was launched by front groups for the tobacco industry.

From a public health perspective, there can be no right to expose others to a known health hazard. A person's right to swing a fist in the air ends where it contacts someone's nose.

Throughout the transitional decades from the twentieth to the twenty-first century the tobacco industry saw increasing exposures of its corporate malfeasance. This culminated in a high-profile court case, Philip Morris versus The United States Government. When the judicial dust settled, several US cigarette companies were convicted of engaging in racketeering to defraud the American people (United States District Court for the District of Columbia 2006). I will provide a more detailed account of these developments in Chapter 5.

As the reputation of tobacco corporations was increasingly tarnished, it became important for the industry to find ways to keep a favourable presence in the eyes of the public and, most importantly, with lawmakers. The industry was reasonably successful in doing so with its charitable donations in support of the arts and sports. However, the industry also earned a reputation for spending much more money on telling the world about its donations than it donated. I like to call this the strategic veneer of altruism. In the world of corporate sponsorship, nothing drives altruism like self-interest.

The tobacco industry's fall from grace coincided with a variety of policy, legal, and legislative reforms, including specific interventions to expose the threats of tobacco and of tobacco corporations. These included:

- *public education campaigns*

- *prohibitions on smoking in public places*

- *warning labels and graphic images on cigarette packages*

- *restrictions on advertising and promotion*

- *government and class-action lawsuits against the industry.*

I will also provide more coverage on some of these interventions in Chapters 5 and 10.

Implications for Cannabis Legalization: The commercial restraints currently imposed upon the cannabis industry were fashioned largely from those currently imposed upon the tobacco industry. Tobacco policy analysts and advocates did much of the heavy lifting to achieve this. However, the cannabis industry continues to lobby heavily to move the commercial environment for cannabis closer to that for alcohol. The next section of this chapter will provide some indication for why that is not a good idea.

Alcohol Advertising and Market Segments

The advertising of alcohol products is strikingly like the grand tradition of the tobacco industry—full of the promise of success, belonging, and the fulfillment of amorous desire.

Upwardly Mobile

A 1980s ad for Chivas Regal, a blended scotch, is a visually captivating image that just oozes with cultural mythology. It shows the scotch being poured from the ornate Chivas Regal bottle into a transparent glass slipper. If your childhood included exposure to western fairy tales, you know that it was through the magic of a glass slipper that Cinderella was delivered from a life of arduous work and drudgery to a life of happily-ever-after. The copy reads "Why settle for Champagne?" This ad beckons us to use Chivas Regal to move up to a higher lifestyle. I once showed this ad to a friend who is a bit of a scotch snob. With more than a small measure of indignation, she replied, "Not with a blended scotch you won't!" She explained that scotch aficionados insist upon a single malt scotch, rather than a blend. So, this ad, akin to the tobacco ad with the wealthy yachtsman, is not aimed at scotch snobs. It is aimed at people who see scotch as an icon for a higher lifestyle to which they aspire. Drinking Chivas Regal is positioned as a pathway towards achieving that lifestyle, or at minimum, an acceptable substitute for it. In another example, consider the Miller High Life beer ad slogan: "The champagne of beers."

A crucial point warrants repetition: ads offer us a surrogate fulfill-ment of an aspiration or fantasy. That creates a positive association with the product and leads to a purchase.

Children and Young Drinkers

Aass Winter is Norway's oldest brewery going back to 1834. Aass Winter boldly surpasses the Lucky Strike cigarettes ad that featured an im-age of Santa Claus holding a cigarette. Aass Winter put Santa's image on the bottle label, depicting a red-clad Santa-like figure pulling a keg on a sled across a snowy, alpine landscape. Party time for the little elves?

Closer to home, Crown Royal, makes a maple-flavoured whiskey. Imagine what an indignant whiskey snob might think about that! Why maple-flavoured? Why not creamy garlic cucumber or jalapeño-chipotle? Maple may represent a bit of Canadian nationalism. But the main reason is that maple has a sweet flavor. Similar to sweet fruity alcoholic coolers, fruit and candy-flavoured spirits are intended to usher young people from their soda pops years to the adult world of alcoholic beverages. These beverages are sometimes called cocktails with training wheels. In recent years the Canadian province of Ontario's alcohol retailer, The Liquor Con-trol Board of Ontario (LCBO), has been selling Pinnacle, a cotton candy fla-voured vodka imported from France. What sweet dreams are made of these?

Here is another interesting thing that happened in the alcohol in-dustry. In 2003, The Cool Beer Brewing Company released a product called Millenium Buzz. The beer is made from hemp, a plant of the same family as the cannabis plant. While the plants look similar, hemp does not contain more than a negligible amount of the most active ingredient, THC. But giv-en the family ties, the brewing company apparently thought it cool to make the connection to cannabis, and even display the leaf of the cannabis/hemp family on the label. And of course, the word buzz is drug use vernacular for being high. This is an interesting branding strategy, given that youth are a prominent demographic for cannabis use. Ads for the beer also became more commonly encountered during a time when discussions about can-nabis law reform were growing.

Women and the Singles Bar Scene

Hypnotiq is a beautiful blue coloured beverage made with fruit juices, vodka, and cognac. A girls' night out ad features four twenty-something women at a bar, dressed to kill. They all assume striking, animated, even provocative, poses. The copy reads "live louder" and "don't turn heads, break necks."

You may remember a series of television ads for the Keg Restaurant chain from the latter part of 2013. They depicted a table of women and a separate table of men at The Keg. The women take the initiative to make the connection in boldly flirtatious ways. Around the same time, a print ad for the Keg ran in magazines, featuring a seasonal cocktail named Forbidden Fruit made with lemon flavoured vodka. The ad copy read "tis the season to be sexy." It appears the Keg was also flirting with enhancing its traditional steakhouse brand with the allure of singles bar intrigue.

Not all ads with a singles bar theme are as blatantly aimed at women as the Hypnotiq or Keg ads. Some, more generically, emphasize romantic themes or the hunt culture of the singles bar scene. A 2013 ad for Crush Midnight Cab wine has the words "smooth enough to go home with you" splashed across the top of the ad. Beyond conveying a wine that is smooth to drink, the copy also hints at an impromptu sexual encounter initiated by a smooth talker, presumably at a club. An interesting feature of the ad is how the name of the wine in "Introducing Crush Midnight Cab" is revealed by peeling back the surface layer of the ad. Could this be symbolic for introducing oneself after deploying the superficial pick-up line ? There may be more play on the name of this wine. "Cab" is often used in the wine world as an abbreviation for cabernet sauvignon, the grape varietal from which Crush Midnight is made. But might Cab also be a reference to the mode of transport used at midnight to get to "your place or mine?" Just in case this all sounds too scurrilous for the more genteel denizens of the bar scene, the ad hedges its bets with more copy in smaller print at the bottom left that reads "you never know where a crush might lead"—perhaps an appeal to those interested in something more long-term.

I am deliberately reading a lot into this ad and perhaps more than was intended by its architects. I do so to make the point that there is always a challenge in knowing how much to read into the ads. It is true that many ads are meticulously designed, with multiple levels of intended meaning. But, like an irresistible Rorschach (ink blot) test, (or a cumulus cloud floating across a blue sky) it is also tempting for us to project our own affectations onto the ads. That alone is a powerful strategy for engaging consumers.

Ads with singles bar themes always remind me of a parody in which a man approaches a woman in a club and says "so, how do you like your eggs in the morning." The woman, unimpressed and deadpan, replies "Unfertilized."

The modern emphasis on women in ads depicting bar scenes is not accidental. It is strategic. Women have always been less likely to drink than men, to drink less often, and to drink less when they do. There was a time that this was much more a product of social structure than it is today. When I first became of age to drink I noticed that the older bars had two separate entrances. One was labelled something like Men Only and the other—Ladies and Escorts. The Men Only door led to the Men's Room where only men could enter and drink. The Ladies and Escorts sign over the other entrance was a not-so-subtle suggestion that women without a male companion were not welcome. That arrangement did not last for too many more years.

The alcohol industry was certainly happy to step up as a great champion for equality for women in this respect. The industry has encouraged more women to drink and to drink more—thus creating a more equitable, and for the industry, a more profitable, world. (Creating equity by encouraging men to drink less has not been part of the alcohol industry's strategy.) The plan may be working. Alcohol related harms are generally on the increase in Canada. However, a dramatic increase in harms among women and girls is especially notable as the increase is much greater than the increase among men (Spithoff 2019). This might be a suitable place to recall the half-century old tobacco ad slogan that beckoned women to smoke: "You've come a long way, baby."

Patrons of the Arts

An Absolut vodka ad is a good example of how advertising can reinforce a long-existing theme of cultural mythology for older, existing customers and introduce that mythology to the next generation of customers. The ad depicts a bottle of Absolut vodka with roses falling in mid-air around the bottle. The copy reads "Absolut Bravo." For many generations, roses, and shouts of "bravo" have been used in the performing arts to proclaim and reward a great performance. The calligraphy on the bottle has an Elizabethan look to it, perhaps suggesting a seventeenth century theatrical production. Roses are also a symbol for romance. (Check out the prices around Valentine's Day.) So maybe there is a celebration of another kind of performance intended as well. The roses are depicted out of focus which embellishes their movement of falling through the air. But there may be some perceptual psychology at play here as well. The out-of-focus roses, by contrast, direct one's attention to the very sharply focused product name on the bottle.

The Pride Movement

Alcohol manufacturers were early adopters in co-opting the pride movement. I recall an Absolut vodka ad, from almost two decades ago, with the rainbow motif running across the bottle. I photographed another ad, this one for Alexander Keith's beer, placed in a window of a Toronto downtown pub. The ad welcomed people to Toronto's Pride Parade with an image featuring the rainbow motif embedded as layers of beer within a frosted mug. The ad copy read: "welcoming you to Toronto with open taps."

Is there no better way to champion acceptance of diverse sexual orientations and preferences than with alcohol? Keep in mind that alcohol-related problems are generally considered to be higher among those of diverse sexual orientations and preferences than in the general population, perhaps because of the stigma and discrimination that must be endured (Hughes 2005).

Plant-based Diets. IT'S NEW!

The number of people with diets that are more plant-based is increasing, and it is not just students consuming beer and fries, as they always have. More vegetarian and vegan restaurants are popping up everywhere, and most restaurants are making vegetarian and vegan options available. The alcohol industry is paying attention. In 2020, the Liquor Control Board of Ontario's website featured a section: "These wines love veggies." The Spring 2021 issue of the LCBO's flagship marketing vehicle, *Food & Drink*, featured an article: "In honour of Earth Day, a plant-based menu featuring sustainable and organic wines alongside - naturally!"

As with the development of many new market segments, enthusiasm sometimes trumps execution. The March 19, 2022 issue of LCBO's *Vintages* magazine had an ad for Frogpond Farm organic wine that it trumpeted as "Vegan." The ad recommended pairing it with seafood. Someone did not think that one through. The appeal to a plant-based market segment is still in its infancy, but watch it grow!

Men, Sports, and Sex

For many years, sports and sex have been doing the heavy lifting for the corporate alcohol and marketing partnership to sell alcohol to men.

An Amstel beer ad from the 1970s referenced the United States football championship Super Bowl, with its ad copy reading "Hats off to a super beer." At the base of a single erect bottle of Amstel, on each side, are miniature helmets of the two teams competing that year. The sports theme is overt. Some people see other kinds of symbolism. I will let you decide how much you want to read into this one.

A more contemporary ad, circa 2010, came from Gnarly Head, a California winery. One of its wine ads depicted a well-dressed and well-groomed man, but with his nose bandaged and eyes bruised. The copy reads: "Bold, sophisticated, with a hint of gnarly." To me, he looks like a professional athlete in an endorsement-ready suit and tie. But maybe that is just my reading of it. A colleague once suggested that perhaps he had been in a bar fight. I rather doubt that was the winery's intent. The association of bar violence with alcohol is not something to which the industry would strategically want to draw attention. Bruising from a fight in a hockey game would be more consistent with western tolerances for violence.

Heineken was "the official beer" of the 2012 Summer Olympics in London, UK. I find it difficult to imagine how beer, like the McDonalds burgers and fries, might be of service to the athletic excellence needed to compete at an Olympic level.

One of the most sexually provocative ads I have seen for any product was one that could make even the most thick-skinned and grizzled curmudgeon blush. This Absolut vodka ad depicts a bottle of the product set in a red metallic looking pouch with a zipper running vertically on the front. It is unzipped about halfway, revealing the top half of the bottle. On either side of the bottle are the profile faces of a Caucasian woman and a woman of colour both with brightly coloured red lips. In front of the exposed part of the bottle float two red cherries each at the end of separate stems that join at the top. Each of the two cherries is firmly planted in the lips of one of the two women. And I do not think I need to say anything more.

I could not have a section on alcohol advertising without discussing the infamous matter of subliminal advertising. Perhaps the most notorious ad alleged to have used this form of influence is one from the 1970s for Gilbey's gin. The ad showed a bottle of Gilbey's beside a tall thin glass filled to the top with gin and three vertically set ice cubes. When the image of the glass is enlarged, it appears that the artist has, at least partly, penciled in the letters S E X, one letter in each ice cube, going from the top cube to the bottom one.

The Gilbey's ad was most likely an ad agency being playful. Obviously, the alcohol industry wants to move product. An effective way to do that is to advertise their products in a way that associates them with things near and dear to us. If Gilbey's ad were released today the agency might arrange for a social media influencer to expose it on the internet. The ad would go viral and the producer would enjoy millions of dollars of free advertising. And that would be the point.

The last time I looked at the literature on subliminal perception I did not think the evidence was compelling. However, one study stands out in a way that attracts our attention. A paper published in the journal *Nature* (North, Hargreaves, and McKendrick 1997) found that grocery store shoppers were more likely to buy German wine on days when traditional German music was played and more French wine on days when traditional French music was played. The data showed three-fold reversals in the number of wine purchases corresponding to the type of music played. And here is the punchline: the overwhelming majority of wine purchasers, when interviewed, denied that the music had any influence on their purchase. Perhaps we should keep an open mind on the matter of subliminal influence.

In 2021, US brewer, Coors, launched a promotion called "Big Game Dream" in conjunction with Super Bowl LV. Coors drew upon consultation from psychologist Dr. Deirdre Barrett at Harvard University's Department of Psychiatry, whose research had suggested that repeated exposure to specific content immediately before going to sleep could lead to increased likelihood of that content appearing in peoples' dreams. Under Barrett's supervision, Coors arranged for volunteers to watch a specific video clip a few times before going to sleep and report on whether the video inspired dreams that had images from the video and Coor's beer. The as-yet unpublished results showed that five of the eighteen volunteers (twelve of whom were paid actors) reported having dreams reflecting content from the video (Moutinho 2021).

The promotion generated a great deal of free media for the company and attention for Barrett and her work at Harvard. However, some of the attention was unwanted. A letter signed by forty scientists warned of the corporate incursion into people's dreams as a dangerous one. Barrett initially expressed some enthusiasm for the results of the initiative: "We saw the results come to life in the Dream Lab trial run when participants reported similar dream experiences including refreshing streams, mountains, waterfalls and even Coors itself" (McBreen 2021). However, once the topic became controversial among her peers, Barrett quickly distanced herself from the dream project that had become somewhat of a nightmare for her (Moutinho 2021).

I imagine that it is not necessary for me to make this next point, but just to be completely sure, I want to issue an important reality check: alcohol has nothing to do with either athletic or sexual prowess. This is not a new idea; nor is it one arising from an extensive meta-analysis of the peer-reviewed literature. It was plainly obvious to William Shakespeare over four centuries ago. In his famous tragedy, *Macbeth*, we read the following offering on the effects of alcohol on sexual appetite and performance:

> *What three things does drink especially provoke? Marry,*
> *sir, nose-painting, sleep and urine. Lechery, sir, it provokes,*
> *and unprovokes; it provokes the desire, but it takes away the*
> *performance; therefore, much drink may be said to be an*
> *equivocator with lechery: it makes him, and it mars him; it*
> *sets him on, and it takes him off; it persuades him, and dis-*
> *heartens him; makes him stand to, and not stand to; in con-*
> *clusion, equivocates him in a sleep, and, giving him the lie,*
> *leaves him.*

Shakespeare was a brilliant writer. Argue with me at your peril. Shakespeare was also reputed to be a passionate drinker and may have had a thing for cannabis as well. A recent excavation of one of his homes turned up several pipes from which forensic analysis showed traces of THC. Alleged references to cannabis in Shakespeare's plays are, in my opinion, too clouded in metaphor to be certain. I pray, let not your wish betray the truth. (I also pray there is at least one person reading this who appreciated the Elizabethan iambic pentameter of the previous sentence.)

Research on Alcohol Promotion

Shakespeare's firsthand experiences from the seventeenth century aside, let us continue our reality check on alcohol promotion and drinking by looking at what research from the twenty first century tells us. A report released by the Centre for Addiction and Mental Health (CAMH) in Canada reviewed twenty years of research on alcohol promotion and drinking (Giesbrecht et al. 2013.)

For young (underage) people, increased exposure to alcohol advertising is linked to earlier initiation of drinking and increased drinking among current drinkers. The research also shows that the increases are sustained.

For young adults of legal drinking age, greater exposure to alcohol portrayals in media is associated with increased drinking and positive attitudes about alcohol and associated drinking behaviors.

To consider the importance of positive attitudes, I ask you to reflect on the research on reinforcement expectancies as I discussed earlier in this chapter.

Research on event sponsorship by alcohol companies, as seen on TV, movies, online, buses, and bus shelters, billboards and other media showed that the sponsorships reinforce positive associations with alcohol, create unrealistic expectations of the effects of drinking, and increases consumption in high-risk contexts. Again, the research on reinforcement expectancies looms large.

It is not only CAMH that is talking about limiting exposure to alcohol advertising. There is a growing chorus in the global health policy community that includes:

- *World Health Organization (2010)*

- *Canadian Public Health Association (2011)*

Giesbrecht (2013) has listed the following organizations as well:

- *Canada's Alcohol Strategy (Canadian Centre on Substance Abuse)*

- *US Surgeon General*

- *American Academy of Pediatrics*

- *US Institute of Medicine*

- *(US) Center on Alcohol Marketing and Youth*

One might think that the gravitas of such an esteemed collection of organizations might give cause for pause to the alcohol industry. Apparently not.

In the spring of 2013, Old Milwaukee beer launched an ad campaign in Canada on billboards that I saw in two Ontario towns: Kingston and Hamilton. I would imagine that the billboards appeared elsewhere as well. The Kingston billboard depicted two revealingly dressed women leaning against a person-sized Old Milwaukee beer can, with a second equally large can resting on its side. The ad copy read: "Free girl with every can." The Hamilton billboard depicted a sparsely dressed woman sitting on a case of Old Milwaukee. The copy read: "Of course we're trying to seduce you" and offered a discount price. The billboard in Hamilton was located not far from McMaster University and even closer to a high school—probably not a coincidence. The ad disappeared around the time that the spring school term ended. The alcohol industry is living in a self-regulatory nirvana. It is no longer daunted nor restrained by a public health or feminist narrative. Everybody knows what is going on, and at least some companies are happy to openly proclaim it. If a scantily clad woman and a low price are what it takes to move product, then that is what they will do.

Implications for Cannabis Legalization: As mentioned earlier, the cannabis industry is lobbying hard for a more permissive regulatory structure for advertising. If it is granted such permission, we can expect all the themes discussed in this section to become prominently displayed in all the kinds of locations where alcohol ads are displayed. Even if you think cannabis businesses should be allowed to advertise, would you really want more billboards filling our community spaces? Could we not just plant trees instead? I'm confident that people who want to buy cannabis can figure out where to buy it.

ADVERTISING: WHAT DO WE DO ABOUT IT?

Most industries have their marketing boards, associations, and lobby groups to protect and advance their commercial and political interests. But as discussed earlier, alcohol and tobacco are not benign products. Their use is associated with an enormous amount of harm. So, for the regulation of product promotion, we need more discerning rules than those that apply to most consumer products. To some extent we have that, but this needs a closer look given the extent of harm involved. All too often the public's health gets trumped when public health goals collide with commercial interests. Meaningful change will take more than consensus in the health policy sector. Health policy authorities must make a consolidated and sustained effort, with wide-scale public engagement, to press the critical question to our legislators: what is the priority of their party—public health or corporate wealth?

The Internet and Social Media: A Minimally Regulated Environment

There is a great deal of drug promotion on the internet and specifically in social media that occurs through three avenues. Some of it is traditional corporate advertising, promoting specific brands. Some of this is legal. Some of it is not. Tobacco products are illegally promoted on social media platforms under the guise of promoting cultural and entertainment events. The promotions use code words also used in branding of tobacco products, or direct people to enter a contest by going to a website that includes tobacco ads (Chapman and Moeck 2021). This is sometimes referred to as stealth advertising.

Another type of stealth product promotion is also ambiguous in its legality. Company-compensated media influencers will promote specific brands through social media. Some of them have built up enormous followings. Finally, there is no shortage of spontaneous, unpaid, fan-based idolatry for specific products or product types. The internet is essentially an unregulated environment, and it renders national boundaries as fully permeable membranes. Even the great firewall of China has been vulnerable to the efforts of hacktivists with the required expertise and persistence. All this presents a formidable challenge for implementing restrictions on any kind of drug product promotion on the internet. Sometimes, when I consider the ubiquity with which drug product ads are sent careening our way from all directions, I marvel that drug problems are not more prevalent than they are.

Counter Advertising

An interesting strategic question is whether to ban drug product ads or to counter them with messages that try to subvert their impact. There is little political will on the part of government to ban product promotion or to implement meaningful penalties to motivate deterrence. Thus, there is increasing interest in counter-ad campaigns by health policy organizations. But campaigns can be launched by anyone having knowledge of how to post something on the internet or social media.

There was some controversy surrounding a widespread counter ad campaign in New Zealand in the 1980s. The campaign borrowed from the medical literature on alcohol-induced erectile dysfunction (and perhaps from Shakespeare). A billboard showed the customary male symbol of a circle and an arrow coming off the top right of the circle. However, rather than the arrow pointing upwards in the usual erect fashion, the arrow was hanging limply down. The ad copy read: "If you drink too much there's one part that every beer can reach." We can recognize that the same market-segmenting strategy that is used in product advertising can be repurposed to deliver counter ads. Identify what is important to a population segment of interest and configure your message accordingly.

Some people felt the ad was irreverent and in poor taste. The ad's defenders argued that it is difficult to change people's behaviour if you do not have their attention. The billboard certainly got people's attention. This debate raises interesting strategic and ethical questions. Should health advocates be confined to the high road of pious propriety and resist using the same persuasive techniques as drug industries? Or should it reject an unlevel playing field that gives advantage to the industry at the cost of the public's health? I expect that both views will continue to find expression in counter-ad campaigns which will, at minimum, keep the advertising landscape interesting.

Earlier, I mentioned a McDonalds Restaurant marketing campaign that aligned its products with the health and fitness brand of the Olympics. Sometimes when you are that presumptuous, you attract the wrong kind of attention. McDonalds has often been criticized by public health advocates and activists. Their mascot, Ronald McDonald, has been dubbed the Joe Camel of obesity. McDonalds was also lampooned by the anti-consumerism magazine, *Adbusters*, on one of its covers. The cover depicted a burger product of 10 patties with 10 cheese slices, stacked up with the usual condiments between the two parts of a bun. The caption read: "Are We Happy Yet?"—a reference to McDonalds' Happy Meal brand at the time. The image resonated with people. In Canada, it won the Gold Award for Best Magazine Cover at the 36th Annual National Magazine Awards.

You can also find many tobacco and alcohol ad parodies and counter-messaging on the web. Some of these images blatantly expose the dark side of alcohol and tobacco use and its promotion—sometimes in ways that radically challenge the traditional norms of polite and restrained public health messaging. The more extreme messages would probably not be allowed on a billboard in most or all municipalities. However, they find an unencumbered platform on the internet. One of the more provocative ones I have come across was a stinging indictment of alcohol impaired judgment with the world-famous Jack Daniels whiskey as the target. The image depicts a bottle of Jack Daniels with the copy reading: "I did WHAT with my sister?" You can find other parodies including ones from *Adbusters* for Joe Chemo (Joe Camel) and Absolute Mayhem (Absolut Vodka). For product advertising, the internet gives, and it takes away. But one of my favourite drug-themed parodies was on a package of napkins in the kitchen section of a home *décor* store. It read "What wine pairs best with living in a dystopian nightmare?" The meme wars will continue. Some of us will be amused, and others not. The critical question concerns the impact of all this activity on long-term alcohol-related attitudes and behaviour. The answer is not yet in sight.

Implications for Cannabis Legalization: We can also see the potential shape of things to come in US states that have commercialized cannabis. One billboard advertising a cannabis brand (reminiscent of tobacco billboards of earlier decades) depicted a young couple, with full pack, having just scaled a mountain peak. I have included the image of this ad in some of my presentations, prompting one young member of the audience to proclaim: "Climb a mountain? I have a tough time opening a bag of chips!"

The cannabis industry has already pushed the legal limits for advertising. In some cases, they blatantly violated the law. Will the cannabis industry continue to push for its perceived right to advertise in the same way as does the alcohol industry? Will it eventually prevail? Will there be a counter movement of parody ads—maybe a playful depiction of the opening of a bag of chips gone seriously awry?

This and the previous chapter have provided an indispensable foundation of understanding of the place in society of our long-established recreational drug products. The rest of the book will concentrate much more on cannabis legalization and its path forward. First, in the next chapter, I will provide a brief history of cannabis law reform, and how it brought us to the momentous events of October 17, 2018.

SUMMING UP

From an early age we receive an inconsistent, often contradictory, set of messages about drugs and drug use, often couched in a misleading framework of good drugs and bad drugs or safe drugs and harmful drugs. But any drug can be used safely, and any drug can be used in a manner that is harmful. It is not so much about the intrinsic properties of the drugs as it is about how we think about the drugs and the decisions we make in their use. It is also about how we are strategically socialized to think about them. Under commercialized legalization, we are not just allowed to use drugs, we are encouraged to use them. That encouragement martials high level knowledge on child development and social psychology combined with the ordnance of modern technology. Some manufacturing industries contaminate the physical environment—the air, water, and soil. This has led to illness, injury, and social disruption in communities. Drug manufacturing industries, through advertising, contaminate the perceptual environment with omnipresent visual and auditory messages that glamourize or valorize the use of their products. Those messages influence our behaviour and how we use the drug products. Advertising works. In the case of drug products, it may indirectly contribute to adverse consequences such as social disruption, injury, and illness. The current restrictions on cannabis advertising should not be reduced. They need to be maintained and enforced with meaningful penalties for infractions.

Section II

The Setup

Chapter 3

A Brief History
of Cannabis Policy

"What a long, strange trip it's been."
—**The Grateful Dead**

Et tu, Brute?

When I was in Grade 10 at Sarnia Central Collegiate Institute, we were studying William Shakespeare's play *Julius Caesar*. Our prim, proper, and kind-hearted teacher, Mrs. Barr, asked us to form groups of three, learn a segment of the play, and perform it in front of the class. A couple of classmates and I went to her with a slightly different proposal which was that we would write a parody of a segment of the play and perform that in front of the class. She agreed. We wrote the parody such that the rebellion against Caesar was prompted by his refusal to lighten up on the marijuana laws. And yes, we performed it in front of our amused classmates and with no small measure of consternation on the part of Mrs. Barr.

I suppose it is not a particularly interesting story, but what I find personally interesting about it is that a half century later, I was still standing in front of a room full of people talking about the need for cannabis law reform. While it had remained a prominent international social policy issue, it had still not been resolved in Canada. But it had not gone away either. The issue had staying power. And apparently its day was coming. But we'd heard that before.

The history of cannabis policy in Canada, within the broader context of drug policy, is not nearly as elevated as a Shakespearean history. But it certainly has tragic and comedic elements. It also, at times, seems like something conjured as part of an hallucinogenic episode in a B movie—a bad acid trip in the parlance of the 1960s and 1970s. And yet the story is a disturbingly real one.

This chapter does not provide a detailed history of drug prohibition or cannabis law reform. Others have already done a remarkable job of it (Boyd 2017; Carstairs 2022). I will describe only the major milestones of cannabis law reform in Canada with sufficient detail to help make one especially important point relevant to the rest of the book.

The long history of cannabis law reform in Canada, and elsewhere, has predominantly been about social justice and compassion. Advocates questioned the humanity and the wisdom of criminalizing the possession of a drug for which the legal consequences of conviction outweighed the likely harm from using the drug.

The prevailing discussions debated the merits and perils of cannabis decriminalization as a solution to the social justice problems arising from prohibition. Decriminalization meant that possession of cannabis would still be technically illegal. However, for small amounts, offenders would no longer receive criminal records. Rather, they would suffer confiscation of the cannabis in their possession and a fine. While that was the typical model, there have been a few variants proposed—but rarely implemented. I will provide more detailed descriptions of decriminalization and legalization as law reform approaches in the next chapter.

Cannabis law reform for strictly therapeutic (medical) use required an authorization from a licensed healthcare provider to possess cannabis. That path was very different from the path for non-therapeutic or recreational use for which decriminalization was still the prevailing policy discussion. A *Summary Report* from the Senate Special Committee on Illegal Drugs (2002, 34) supported "...regulation of the production, distribution, and consumption of cannabis...." But that recommendation was an outlier. Such an option did not join the mainstream of drug policy discussions for a decade. And it would be part of a vastly different kind of movement. The commercial legalization of cannabis for recreational use was a sudden major and unanticipated change in course from the prevailing narrative of decriminalization.

A major theme of this book is that this abrupt change from decriminalization to legalization, as the prominent policy reform choice for cannabis, was not rooted in the traditional concerns of social justice but in the monied interests of forging a new drug industry. This more avaricious ambition was entirely disconnected from the social justice reform movement.

CANNABIS POLICY: FROM ILLEGAL DEMONIZED STREET DRUG TO LEGAL MEDICINE TO GLAMOURIZED PASTIME

Prohibition

The prohibition of drugs for non-medical use became a major social force beginning in the early years of the 20th century. Cannabis was added to the Schedule of Restricted Drugs in Canada's Narcotics Drug Act in 1923.

I find it fascinating that the circumstances are obscured by a lack of detail in the legislative record. The specifics remain enshrouded in mystery and the subject of speculation. The legislative record shows that there was no debate on the matter, and there was no coverage in the media. There also appears to have been little arrest and seizure activity either before or immediately after the legislative changes. Nor was there any evidence that use of the drug was widely considered to be a serious social or health problem. There was a significant amount of demonization of the drug by one high profile populist advocate. However, the influence of such invective on both public thinking and government action has been discounted. A more likely line of speculation is that given Canada's active role in international drug policy reform at the time, it is possible that the *impetus* came largely from foreign, rather than domestic, influence (Schwartz 2014; Carstairs 2022).

Decriminalization

The absence of law enforcement activity related to cannabis in Canada would change as the twentieth century progressed with more people being charged under the new laws. Social justice advocates would come to increasingly question the utility and humanity of these laws. For more than a half century efforts to end the criminalization of cannabis in Canada and elsewhere were driven by a concern that criminalization was punishing a victimless crime. In doing so, it was having a harmful impact on peoples' lives. The twenty-first century brought increasing concern for the impact of criminalization on peoples' social determinants of health—particularly those from racialized and other vulnerable populations. All cannabis law reform campaigns, world-wide, selected decriminalization as the solution.

In Canada, the case for decriminalization was made in a series of reports from *The Commission of Inquiry into the Non-medical Use of Drugs*. The Commission is often credited with recommending that the Canadian government decriminalize cannabis. But this is not the case. The idea received support in a report from the Commission that was focused on the topic of cannabis (Commission of Inquiry into the Non-medical Use of Drugs 1972). The idea was also raised in a more general report the Commission submitted to the Minister of Health in 1970 which was later published as an *Interim Report of the Commission* (Commission of Inquiry into the Non-medical Use of Drugs 1973b).

The Commission's *Final Report* stated that it was supportive of the rationale for ending the criminalization of cannabis possession. However, the *Final Report's* formal recommendations did not support changing the law at that time. However, it did acknowledge a dissenting recommendation from one Commission member who asserted: "There should be no offence subject to criminal law sanctions for possession or use of any of the drugs" (Commission of Inquiry into the Non-medical Use of Drugs 1973a, 252). That is as close as the Commission's Final Report got—acknowledging a declaration by a single dissenting member.

A few years later, Patricia Erickson at The Addiction Research Foundation of Ontario and the University of Toronto published a book, *Cannabis Criminals* (Erickson 1980) which became an important milestone in cannabis policy reform. Erickson reported that for most cannabis users, the stigmatizing, marginalizing, and adverse economic impacts of a criminal record were more harmful than was use of the drug. Erickson also made a compelling case for the futility of cannabis prohibition as a deterrent to use.

It would not be until the 1990s that the Canadian Liberal Party formally declared its support for cannabis decriminalization and initiated legislative processes to achieve it. (Fischer 1997; Erickson and Hyshka 2010). The idea had the support of a wide range of stakeholders from The National Organization for the Reform of Marijuana Laws (NORML) to The Canadian Association of Chiefs of Police. Most revealingly, the Liberal Party of Canada maintained a majority government from 1993 until 2004—a full, continuous decade. Yet the Party did not assign a level of priority to the legislation that would make it happen. While legislative efforts continued to stall in Canada many other nations and state jurisdictions in the United States decriminalized cannabis possession. These bold campaigns abroad achieved a widely recognized international record of success (Erickson 1997; Room et al. 2010; Erickson, Van Der Maas, and Hathaway 2013; Room 2014; Caulkins et al. 2015). Accordingly, health policy organizations in Canada including The Canadian Drug Policy Coalition (Carter and Macpherson, 2013) and The Canadian Public Health Association (2014) continued to advocate for the liberalization of not only cannabis laws, but for laws pertaining to all illegal drugs. The last chapter of this book will return to the topic of decriminalization of all drugs during the current time.

Legalization for Therapeutic (Medical) Use: Catalyst for a Commercial Cannabis Industry

The approaching 21st century brought other unprecedented changes in both debate and legislation. Some nations including Canada and several US states legalized cannabis for therapeutic or "medical" use. Most of them licensed a commercial industry to produce and sell cannabis. Others allowed the establishment of not-for-profit co-operatives, or cannabis social clubs, or compassion clubs (Room, et al. 2010; Room 2014; Caulkins et al. 2015; Murkin 2015).

In the year 2000, The Supreme Court of Canada ruled that a government could not deny people their medicine and had a duty of care to provide a legal mechanism by which Canadians could access cannabis for therapeutic use. Access to medicine is a justifiable humanitarian principle. The question was to what extent, at that time, did cannabis legitimately qualify as medicine. The lack of clinical trial evidence would have prevented any new pharmaceutical product from coming to market. (This controversy, and its consequences, will receive more attention in Chapter 5.) In the following year, the Liberal government responded by passing the Marihuana Medical Access Regulations (MMAR) under the legislative umbrella of The Controlled Drugs and Substances Act. This prompted a series of unprecedented events in cannabis policy for Canada. The new set of regulations allowed a person, with authorization from a healthcare practitioner, to be in possession of cannabis and to apply for a licence to grow a limited amount of cannabis for their own therapeutic use. The person also had the choice of designating another person to grow cannabis on their behalf (Canada 2022).

It was this latter provision that would contribute significantly to the proliferation of "grey market dispensaries" that co-existed with other "dispensaries" that operated with no such licence and were thus blatantly illegal. As will be discussed in more detail in Chapter 7, it has been alleged by the RCMP that some of the personal cannabis cultivation licences fell into the hands of organized crime.

With the Progressive Conservative government achieving a majority in the 2011 election, the party moved to clean up the tainted production and retail landscape for therapeutic cannabis. The MMAR were replaced in 2013 with the Marihuana for Medical Purposes Regulations (MMPR), which curtailed the personal growing provisions of the MMAR and established a licensing system for commercial growers who could sell to authorized users by a mail order system (Canada 2013).

The MMPR was sometimes criticized as being unconstitutional since some patients, who claimed to be poorly served by the commercial licensing system, had been prohibited from growing their own medicine or arranging for someone to grow it for them. When the Liberal Party achieved a majority government in the 2015 election, it struck down the MMPR and in 2016 replaced it with the Access to Cannabis for Medical Purposes Regulations (ACMPR). The new regulations retained the licensing of commercial growers as well as the mail order system from licensed producers. The new regulations also reintroduced the provision that would allow medically authorized individuals to request permission to grow cannabis at home for their own therapeutic use or to appoint someone to grow it for them from the grower's home (Canada 2016).

Legalization for Recreational Use

Legalization for therapeutic use had been a pivotal moment in cannabis policy reform, setting the stage for legalization for recreational use. Beginning in 2012, the US state jurisdictions of Colorado, Washington, Alaska, and Oregon made up the first wave of legalized cannabis for recreational use through state-level ballot initiatives. The US District of Columbia (Washington DC) legalized possession of cannabis for recreational use but did not legalize sales. The significant difference of this approach from decriminalization is that there are no penalties for possession—not even a fine or confiscation of product. In 2013, Uruguay became the first nation to legalize sales for recreational use (Room 2014; Caulkins, et al. 2015).

These developments marked a significant shift in cannabis policy. The prevailing force for reform had also shifted from its traditional focus on social justice. The driving force had now become the creation of a commercial cannabis industry that would also supply a source of tax revenue for government, like our industries for alcohol, tobacco, and pharmaceutical products.

Legalization for Recreational Use in Canada

Proposals for legalization for recreational use were not unprecedented in the history of cannabis law reform. However, the rise of legalization from a fringe, less-politically viable policy option to one that was a successful contender was meteoric and caught many observers and policy analysts by surprise. In Canada, these discussions became publicly manifest during the Liberal Party of Canada's 2013-2015 federal election campaign when party leader and prime ministerial candidate Justin Trudeau announced that, if elected, the Party would legalize recreational cannabis use. In Chapter 6 I will chronicle, in more detail, the intriguing series of events leading to the Liberal Party of Canada abruptly changing its long-held official position of decriminalization to commercial legalization.

In 2014, The Centre for Addiction and Mental Health (CAMH) in Ontario released its *Cannabis Policy Framework* (Centre for Addiction and Mental Health 2014). The Framework's analysis favoured legalization—a significant departure from CAMH's own longstanding support for decriminalization since 2000. CAMH's *Framework* earned widespread attention for overtly recommending legalization—a potentially controversial move at the time that was later echoed by an article published in the *Canadian Medical Association Journal* (Spithoff, Emerson, and Spithoff 2015). However, the proposal in *CMAJ* differed in important aspects from the CAMH model—more on that in Chapters 5 and 6.

In 2015, The RAND Corporation in the US released a report (Caulkins et al. 2015) prepared for the State of Vermont. The report reviewed twelve policy models for cannabis law reform, describing the merits and perils of each. RAND did not recommend a specific model but issued an overarching warning that jurisdictions should not rush from prohibition to commercial legalization. It recommended that jurisdictions take the time to consider several options in their reform efforts.

After his successful 2015 election campaign, Prime Minister Trudeau, followed through on his promise in earnest, establishing a Task Force on Marijuana Legalization and Regulation, to consult with experts and other Canadians, and issue a report to the government. Canada took its intentions to the world when it announced at the United Nations General Assembly Special Session (UNGASS) in April 2016, that it would introduce legislation to legalize cannabis in the spring of 2017. This was a controversial move given that Canada was a signatory to at least two, arguably three, international treaties that included declarations against the legalization of cannabis, other than for therapeutic use or research.

On December 13, 2016, the Canadian government publicly released the Task Force's *Final Report* which included a change in the name of the Task Force—replacing Marijuana with Cannabis (Task Force on Cannabis Legalization and Regulation 2016). The Report supported the Canadian government's intent to expand the commercial therapeutic industry to include production and sales of cannabis for recreational use.

The Cannabis Act received royal assent on June 21, 2018, and came into effect on October 17 of that year. Other cannabis products including edibles, extracts and topicals were legalized a year later. It was a major milestone in the story of legalization, but not the end of the story. Consistent with the many troublesome experiences with the therapeutic cannabis industry and with the warnings from public health authorities, many problems arose with the newly expanded legal cannabis industry.

The case for caution was multi-faceted. As we saw in Chapter 1, the data showed us that most of our drug-related harm and economic costs were associated with legal drug industries, not the illegal drug trades. This harm was related to a long history of industry failure (alcohol, tobacco, pharmaceutical) to balance its relentless pursuit of revenue with protection of public health. (I cover that history in Chapter 5.) Government regulation had proven ineffective in enforcing measures to ensure that balance. As we saw in Chapter 2, there was a long history of mesmerizing market manipulation by tobacco and alcohol companies that contributed to the harm described in Chapter 1.

The Liberal Party was aware that it had options other than commercial legalization for cannabis but chose not to let expert advice guide its course. Decriminalization had a long history of international success. Commercial legalization had no such record. Decriminalization could have been enacted almost immediately. A second step could be to forge a not-for-profit legalization model that generated no private revenue and maintained a public health protection priority.

Chapters 5 through 8 will provide detailed accounts of a tainted process of legalization and the many problematic outcomes of Canada's chosen model of corporate legalization. Descriptions of not-for-profit models are provided in Chapter 9.

The next chapter provides a comparison of decriminalization and legalization as policy options. This serves the dual purpose of highlighting the mistake made in Canada as well as a warning to other jurisdictions currently involved in cannabis law reform.

SUMMING UP

The storyline for cannabis law reform in Canada in its incarnations of prohibition, attempted decriminalization, and legalization for therapeutic and then recreational use has been a strange one. The specific rationale for, and circumstances of, prohibition remain as mysteries. Despite a decade in power with a majority government, the Liberal Party of Canada never made good on its professed intentions to decriminalize possession of the drug, despite many states in the US and other nations having done so. Under unorthodox circumstances, the Supreme Court of Canada veered outside its lane to deem cannabis as medicine in the absence of the standard scientific requirements for doing so. The Liberal government promptly passed regulations to create a restricted home-grow supply system. Then alternating Liberal and Conservative governments introduced varying sets of regulations that had the unintended effect of creating a grey market in supply. Despite a history of supporting prohibition, it was the Conservative government that created the commercial cannabis trade for therapeutic use. This would prove to be the more politically palatable prerequisite and enabler for legalization for recreational use. Finally, with a level of commitment never seen in its attempts at decriminalization, the Liberal Party initiated a campaign to legalize cannabis for recreational use. The Cannabis Act came into effect on October 17, 2018.

A long, strange trip, indeed.

Chapter 4

Cannabis Decriminalization:
A Proven Success
Abandoned

*"We do not need to get good laws to restrain bad people. We
need to get good people to restrain us from bad laws."*
— **Gilbert K. Chesterton**

This chapter explores the decision by The Liberal Party of Canada to abandon an internationally successful cannabis law reform strategy in favour of creating a new revenue-driven drug industry—an approach that many drug policy analysts from around the world had cautioned against. The chapter is based upon a part of a manuscript that I hurriedly prepared and submitted to the Task Force on Marijuana Legalization and Regulation in August 2016, and later revised and included in a publicly available monograph called *Cannabis Law Reform in Canada: Pretense & Perils* (DeVillaer 2017). I have not updated the research in this chapter. I want it to be an authentic time-capsule of the information that was made available by myself and other analysts to the government in 2016 when it sought input for its new cannabis legislation.

In the last chapter of this book I will address developments in Canada and in the global decriminalization movement since 2016. These developments include and go beyond cannabis to address other, and even all, drugs.

Distinguishing Decriminalization and Legalization

In many of the conversations leading up to Canada's legalization of cannabis for recreational use (and even after it) I was surprised at how often decriminalization and legalization were used interchangeably and incorrectly by the public and in the media. So, I will make the distinction clear before going any further into this book.

The essence of decriminalization, as it literally suggests, is that people are no longer given criminal records for possession of personal amounts of cannabis. Stated more dramatically, they are no longer treated like criminals for using cannabis to alter their body chemistry—for healing, amusement, or both. Several variants of decriminalization have been proposed and implemented in jurisdictions around the world. Decriminalization can involve a formal legislative (*de jure*) process that removes possession of small amounts of cannabis from the criminal code. Criminal penalties are typically replaced with civil ones, such as a fine and confiscation of the cannabis. Decriminalization can also occur through a *de facto* approach, in which the laws are not changed. Technically speaking, possession is still illegal. However, apprehension practices of local enforcement and/or prosecution practices of local justice authorities are altered as a matter of chosen practice. Transgressions of the law are met with relatively minor consequences such as a fine or confiscation, or with an issuance of cautions. In other variations, fines are replaced with referrals to educational or therapeutic interventions—typically referred to as diversion. Another variation, sometimes referred to as depenalization, can involve removal of all kinds of penalties or requirements, but in a manner that is discretionary by law enforcement.

Legalization is something quite different. In a legalized commercial model, cannabis production and retail are typically provided by competitors in the private sector, colloquially, the beer store model, as this is how beverage alcohol is typically produced and sold, world-wide. Private sector, government licensed retail outlets, operate with legislated controls in place. The controls include restrictions on location, geographic or population-based density, storefront appearance, operating hours, and minimum age and sobriety requirements at the time of purchase. Provincial jurisdictions in countries such as Canada also have government-operated alcohol retailers or a mix of independent private operators and government operators. A key point is that government-controlled retail operations should not be equated with not-for-profit approaches. Government alcohol retail operations can be as market expansionist and revenue driven as any private sector system if they so choose. And they typically do—provincial government retailers in Canada being prime examples. I will have more to say about market expansion within government operations and about not-for-profit models in Chapters 5, 6 and 9.

THE UNLICENSED CANNABIS TRADE: BANEFUL OR BENIGN?

Common Depictions

There are dangerous criminal cartels involved in the international trade in illegal drugs such as heroin, fentanyl, cocaine, and methamphetamine. Product integrity and safety of these clandestine products is never assured. The trade in illegal drugs may also be aligned with other violent and exploitive forms of crime. This paradigm was reflected in the 2002 report of Canada's Senate Special Committee on Illegal Drugs which asked: "Who has not heard of drug traffickers, veritable anti-heroes, whom we find both repulsive and fascinating, all of whom we consider the worst kind of scum, who grow rich by selling adulterated and dangerous products to our children?" (Senate 2002b, 1). Such descriptions are consistent with the familiar paradigm of international drug cartels, led by a sinister drug lord sitting at the apex of a large distribution pyramid, the profits from which are used to fund other criminal enterprises. The question addressed here is whether this commonly accepted paradigm can be justifiably applied to the unlicensed trade in cannabis.

With regards to cannabis, the Senate Special Committee was more guarded, concluding that only an unspecified "portion of production is controlled by organized crime elements" (2002a,13).

The Centre for Addiction and Mental Health's (CAMH) *Cannabis Policy Framework* released in 2014 made a persuasive case for cannabis law reform and proposed specific changes to serve social justice and public health protection. The Framework also raised concerns about a dangerous criminal trade in cannabis at the time and the threat it posed to cannabis users. The Framework recommended legalization over decriminalization. It argued that the unlicensed trade in cannabis was a threat to the safety and propriety of Canadians and that decriminalization would do nothing to dislodge it. Thus, the profits would remain in the hands of criminals. It is true that decriminalization would do nothing to dislodge the unlicensed trade in cannabis. However, the body of research presented in this chapter disputes the premise that the unlicensed trade was a serious threat. With that premise discredited, there is little case for legalization as a singular solution. A stronger case can be made that both approaches, decriminalization and legalization, have their respective merits (and liabilities) and that a hybrid model involving components of each would be the best model. This chapter will draw upon some of the analysis put forward in CAMH's *Framework* as it relates to decriminalization. I will address the *Framework's* fuller analysis, including the case for legalization, in Chapter 6.

The Task Force on Marijuana Legalization and Regulation *Discussion Paper* (2016, 5) referred to 2015 data from the Criminal Intelligence Service Canada (CISC). It reported "657 organized crime groups are operating in Canada, of which over half are known or suspected to be involved in the illicit marijuana market." It is noteworthy that only a portion of this number is "known or suspected" to be involved in the unlicensed cannabis trade. Nor is it clear whether "organized crime groups" includes many small operations with no ties to crime other than the local small-scale sale of cannabis. As I will explore in the research literature shortly, this appears to be the norm.

The Task Force's reference to the CISC claim was consistent with other claims made against the unlicensed cannabis trade which found a home on the website of the Liberal Party of Canada during its legalization campaign. When accessed in late 2016, the Liberal Party's website declared: "Every day, our kids turn to dealers, gangs and criminals to buy marijuana, putting them in harm's way" (Liberal Party of Canada, n.d.).

Similarly pejorative statements prevailed throughout the Liberal Party's legalization campaign including allusions to the unlicensed cannabis trade as "...criminal organizations, street gangs and gun-runners" (Elliott 2015). Such content was also offered by many members of the Liberal and Progressive Conservative Parties in the June 2016 House of Commons debate on cannabis law reform (Canada 2016).

In contrast to such depictions of the unlicensed cannabis trade, research on illegal cannabis transactions by Coomber and Turnbull (2007) prompted them to offer a different perspective:

> Supply of this nature has been argued to be sufficiently
> different to 'dealing proper' to justify a different criminal
> justice approach in relation to it. This has been argued to be
> particularly true regarding social supply among young people
> who use substances such as cannabis.

In a University of Toronto newspaper article on the topic, Toronto attorney Steven Tress offered another less pejorative perspective.

> Almost all of the clients in that industry are not what the
> public would characterize as criminals. They are just guys
> who are in financial trouble, they heard of this thing, and they
> decided to take the risk. And then they get caught, and you
> have to deal with a potential criminal record. (Pasca 2016)

Despite a diversity of perspectives on the unlicensed cannabis trade, the commentary from the Liberal Party offered a more singular narrative that under prohibition and decriminalization, cannabis users are exposed to an unsafe supply of cannabis that is under the control of dangerous criminals who will introduce users to more harmful illegal drugs and to other types of criminal activity.

The Research Evidence

The research literature on the unlicensed cannabis trade tells a story that is vastly different from the frightful messages that most Canadians heard during the Liberal Party's legalization campaign.

First, the research showed that very few cannabis users buy from sellers who are part of a large criminal syndicate or who are dealers or criminals by vocation. Rather, they buy small amounts from friends, family members or other close acquaintances (Coomber and Turnbull 2007; Erickson, Van Der Maas, and Hathaway 2013; Hathaway 2004; Korf et al. 2008). Another study of regular cannabis users in four Canadian cities found that only 6% reported buying their cannabis from "street dealers." The rest bought from friends, acquaintances, or grew their own (Duff et al. 2011). It appears that most cannabis users would never have contact with violent, exploitive individuals or criminal organizations. CAMH's Framework (Centre for Addiction and Mental Health 2014) acknowledged research showing that most cannabis users do not use other illegal drugs and do not progress to use them. This suggests that there is little basis for believing that the illegal cannabis industry is acting as a gateway to the use of other drugs. Research by Korf et al. (2008) found that cannabis sellers tended to sell only small amounts of cannabis, did not traffic in other drugs, and that most cannabis sellers were not involved in any violent aspects of the drug trade.

While the great majority of cannabis users would have no direct contact with organized crime, a portion of cannabis users, including their typically small-volume suppliers, could form the broad base of a pyramid-shaped crime syndicate, and ultimately support its existence. This syndicate might also have tentacles that extended out to other criminal arenas. However, most unlicensed cannabis trade does not appear to occur within such structures. The already-cited work of Erickson, Korf, and Coomber and Turnbull compel us to recognize a very different paradigm resembling a disconnected cottage industry (colloquially, mom and pop ops) in which independent, and otherwise law-abiding people, sell cannabis to support themselves and their families. Boyd and Carter (2014) have similarly described most "grow-ops" as small-scale operations, managed by single site managers. These unlicensed businesses are servicing an existing demand in their community for a product for which most Canadians now believe should not be criminalized. Most people are unlikely to see egregious behavior in such a scenario. Furthermore, Bouchard, Alain, and Nguyen (2009) found that higher prevalence of cannabis cultivation in a community may be associated with a shortage of legal employment opportunities. They also reported that participants in the unlicensed cannabis trade are a demographically diverse group typically involved in small operations. Wilkins and Sweetsur (2007) found a relationship between unemployment in a community and the presence of cannabis purchases for resale. They also found that the net annual income from cannabis sales for these individuals was less than $3,000. We might be justified to regard a sizable portion of the participants in the illegal cannabis trade as people willing to take risks with their personal freedoms for typically small amounts of financial gain. More generously, we might think of them as resourceful victims of a society increasingly unable or unwilling to supply sufficiently gainful legal employment opportunities.

The government's own intel also disputed its frightful hyperbole against the unlicensed trade. An international review of the unlicensed cannabis trade published by the Canadian Drug Policy Coalition (Capler, Boyd, and MacPherson 2016) found that links between the cannabis trade and violent organized crime groups have been greatly exaggerated. Through an Access to Information request, the Coalition's report included data from the Canadian Department of Justice (Solecki, Burnett, and Li 2011) that showed that only 5% of unlicensed cannabis production was associated with organized crime or street gangs.

As of 2016, the most recent Annual Report of the Public Prosecution Service of Canada (PPSC) (2016) reported on prosecution files for 2015-16. It reported that "Drug prosecution files continue to represent the most significant portion of the PPSC's total caseload." For cases with organized crime involvement, PPSC's Report mentioned only cases with cocaine and none with cannabis. The findings in PPSC's report appear to be inconsistent with those from the Criminal Intelligence Service of Canada (CISC), as cited by the Task Force in its *Discussion Paper*. I tried to access that information from CISC. An emailed response from CISC indicated that the information for that time was classified.

The Canadian Drug Policy Coalition's Report also confirmed that the international picture of the unlicensed cannabis trade is similar to that seen in Canada. It described illegal cannabis operations as independent, small, local, non-violent, and modest in realized revenues. It also found that most people involved in the unlicensed trade are otherwise law-abiding citizens who are active in their communities and would welcome the opportunity to be part of a legal trade.

At the conclusion of its report, the Coalition recommended, among other things, that the Canadian government abandon its unsubstantiated descriptions of the unlicensed cannabis trade and base its policy on established research findings.

The research literature clearly describes a more diverse and less threatening unlicensed cannabis trade. This adds important nuance to the claim that decriminalization would keep profits in the hands of criminals.

There are other reasons why it is misleading to argue that users buy their cannabis from criminals in the sense that people typically think of the concept. Certainly, someone who sells a small amount of unlicensed cannabis to a friend is, technically speaking, engaging in a criminal act. The same would also be technically true of someone who sells a few bottles of beer or a pack of cigarettes to an adult acquaintance. In these cases, the criminality arises because the seller of these legal drugs does not possess the license needed to trade in a regulated drug product. Yet, few of us would regard such transactions as seriously criminal. Likewise, Canadians appear to be increasingly adopting more tolerant views about cannabis. It would be an uncharacteristically severe judgment to regard someone selling a couple joints of unlicensed cannabis to a friend as committing a condemnable act of criminality. The Liberal Party's discourse on dangerous drug dealers is based upon a narrow, unrepresentative, and ultimately self-serving view of the unlicensed trade. We might also see an ill-considered inconsistency in exonerating purchasers of a small amount of cannabis but to continue to demonize and harshly punish their typically small-volume suppliers.

The narrative of the Liberal Party was not a new one. At the dawn of the Party's legalization campaign, Boyd and Carter (2014) published a book titled Killer Weed. It detailed the long history of law enforcement and the media in spreading hyperbole and fabrication about the unlicensed cannabis trade as dangerous criminal activity. It also described the significant harm caused by anti-drug crackdowns and the potentially detrimental impact for civil society in Canada. The Liberal Party remained undaunted.

The existence of an unlicensed cannabis trade is not ideal. But neither is it the threat that it has been claimed to be. I am not trying to diminish or excuse serious criminal conduct. The point to be made is that enforcement/justice resources should be more judiciously deployed to those matters where they will do the most societal good. Organizations involved in a large-scale illegal drug trade, as well as in other violent or exploitive criminal activity, could still be subject to appropriately measured interventions from the enforcement/justice system. This should also apply to individuals who endanger the safety of others through conduct such as impaired driving or the adulteration of cannabis with harmful additives. My intent is simply to place cannabis use and the unlicensed cannabis trade within a more balanced context. This context refutes the anachronistic and overly dramatized rhetoric that has been used in the past to sustain prohibition and criminalization, and to sabotage justified reform.

We must exercise caution that a vestigial reefer madness-like depiction of the unlicensed cannabis trade is not repurposed to deny decriminalization its legitimate place on the menu of workable reforms. The politics of fear, played out with fabricated threats to our children's safety, may play well on an election campaign trail. But such jingoism falters upon scrutiny and has no place in evidence-based drug policy reform.

THE IMPACT OF DECRIMINALIZATION

The research literature on the impact of decriminalization, as studied in various parts of the world, is instructive on the likely impact of decriminalization in Canada. There has also been some revealing research conducted on the characteristics and practices of cannabis users during prohibition. This research has implications for their conduct in a decriminalization regime.

Impact on Consumer Demand, Ease of Access, Use, and Associated Problems

Studies of cannabis use patterns among regular users in four Canadian cities (Duff et al. 2011) demonstrated that under prohibition, cannabis users for the most part, even in times of easy access, moderate their cannabis use such that it does not interfere with their lives or lead to adverse health consequences. Such consumption patterns were also the norm in other countries where decriminalization was adopted. For decades, research on the impact of cannabis decriminalization showed that, in a variety of jurisdictions in Australia, Europe and the United States, decriminalization did not result in a sustained increase in ease of access or consumer demand. Nor did decriminalization lead to a sustained increase in prevalence of use or cannabis-related problems. However, decriminalization decreased the adverse social problems associated with criminal records from cannabis possession offences. Accordingly, it decreased enforcement and judicial costs. Detailed accounts of these findings can be found in Single (1989), Single, Christie, and Ali (2000), and Room et al. (2010). While these findings were acknowledged in CAMH's *Cannabis Policy Framework* (Centre for Addiction and Mental Health 2014), they appear to have carried no weight in shaping the Framework's conclusions and recommendations.

Impact on Cannabis Product Safety

CAMH's Framework juxtaposed decriminalization and legalization as mutually exclusive cannabis law reform options. It highlighted the lack of assurance of purity or known strength of unlicensed cannabis, thus raising concerns about decriminalization as a desirable reform model as it would do nothing to address these product safety issues. This is a legitimate concern which was supported by an analysis of cannabis samples from illegal dispensaries in Toronto.

Reporters from *The Globe and Mail* bought samples of leaf cannabis and cannabis edibles from unlicensed Toronto dispensaries and had them tested against the same criteria used by Health Canada for legal cannabis products. One report (Robertson and McArthur 2016a) found that leaf cannabis samples were contaminated with yeast, mould, and bacteria to the extent that one-third of them would not have passed Health Canada standards. Another report (Robertson and McArthur 2016b) found that almost all samples of tested cannabis edibles had much less THC (tetrahydrocannabinol, the principal psychoactive ingredient in cannabis) than was indicated on the label.

The *Final Report* of the government's Task Force on Cannabis Legalization and Regulation (2016, 10) drew more attention to the problem:

> *With decriminalization, the production, distribution*
> *and sale of cannabis remain criminal activities. Thus, indi-*
> *viduals remain subject to the potential dangers of untested*
> *cannabis. Criminal organizations continue to play the role of*
> *producer, distributor and seller, thereby increasing risk, par-*
> *ticularly to vulnerable populations.*

There is something the Task Force should have known but did not report. Licensed cannabis producers for therapeutic and recreational use in state jurisdictions in the United States, were also having frequent, and sometimes serious problems with product contamination. (I cover that problem in the next chapter.) The same problems were occurring in Canada with the therapeutic cannabis industry. As early as 2014, Health Canada required recalls of cannabis products for bacteria (Canada 2014b) and mould (Canada 2014c). In these and another recall because of unspecified "...issues with the company's production practices..." (Canada 2014a) the licensed producers' patients were advised "...to immediately discontinue use...." There have also been recalls for inaccurate labelling of the potency of products (Canada 2015). More seriously, by the end of 2016, recalls had also been issued because of the presence of unauthorized pesticides on flower product (Canada 2017). The latter case is an interesting one for several reasons—one of which was the very unusual delay between Health Canada's awareness of the problem in October 2016 and its posting in February 2017. I will revisit that story in the next chapter.

In its *Final Report*, the Task Force (2016, 4), apparently oblivious to the problem, praised "the good production practices of the current cannabis for medical purposes system."

Health Canada continued to issue cannabis product recalls for a variety of contamination and mislabelling infractions during the period leading up to legalization for recreational use in October 2018. I will return to the problem of product integrity failures among licensed producers in several later chapters.

The lesson for this chapter is that the claim that product integrity is sufficiently assured in a legalized regime has no basis in the evidence. Given that there was little reason to believe that the unlicensed trade would disappear any time soon, there is no assurance that legalization would improve the overall product integrity for consumers.

An improvement in product integrity in a legal trade provided perhaps the best opportunity to significantly diminish the unlicensed trade. We would expect that cannabis users would prefer a safer and more predictable product. By 2016, Canada's licensed producers had failed to grasp this opportunity. Canada's government and its Task Force had failed to grasp or acknowledge the problem as well.

Impact on Social Justice

Almost all known jurisdictions that had opted for decriminalization had implemented the traditional model. This is a testament to its demonstrated positive impact on reducing unwarranted criminal records, creating enforcement/justice savings and its neutral impact on public health and safety (Single, Christie, and Ali 2000; Room et al. 2010). However, the model as typically implemented remained punitive in nature, harboring social injustice and equity-related perils. Under such a punitive model, someone using cannabis was still seen as breaking the law. They were confronted by law enforcement officers and subjected to sometimes very public interrogation during the issuance of a ticket. This retained a lingering sense of wrong-doing and stigma which, as noted in CAMH's Framework, may also have prevented individuals from engaging with various health-related programs and services for fear of judgment and even legal reprisal. Room et al. (2010) cite evidence that these encounters were prejudicial against specific vulnerable or marginalized populations, and that the core element of punitive decriminalization, the imposition of fines, had more harmful economic, legal, and social impact on vulnerable populations. For some people, a $200 fine would be, to various degrees, a nuisance. But for others, that would mean the loss of their money for food for a month.

There is important context to the Framework's assertion that prejudice, inequity, and stigma exist within a decriminalization regime. These conditions did not emerge from the establishment of a decriminalization regime. They already existed under prohibition, and more importantly, they would also exist within a legalization regime. The societal problems of prejudice, inequity, and stigma have a life and trajectory of their own. Even in a legalization regime, there are cannabis offences that remain subject to law enforcement and penalties. Problems of prejudice and inequity will persist.

Cannabis-related stigma will also persist for quite some time in a legalization regime. The Canadian population carries several generations of prohibition-related stigma baggage. Such deeply ingrained societal judgments are unlikely to dissipate quickly and fully with the mere stroke of the legislative pen.

Fines are typically a default penalty under decriminalization. However, there appears to be little said about the actual utility of the fines. Clearly, they do not have a substantial general deterrent effect. So why have they remained a part of decriminalization initiatives?

At a time when there was less public support for decriminalization, the pejorative judgment associated with fines may have served as a political compromise to appease those who were more aligned with the traditional criminal justice approach. The fines may have also served as an incentive for policy change by maintaining a continuing source of revenue for government. However, it is important to recognize that the fines contributed nothing directly to either the public health or social justice goals that predominated in the justice-oriented narrative of the cannabis law reform movement. Single (2000) noted that decriminalization, as it had customarily been implemented, had more in common with prohibition than it did with reform driven by a non-punitive, public health and social justice priority.

IMPROVING THE TRADITIONAL MODEL OF DECRIMINALIZATION

The traditional approaches to decriminalization can be improved in two respects.

Non-punitive Decriminalization

First, for the reasons already cited, Canada could have adopted a non-punitive decriminalization model with no enforcement interventions or fines for personal use possession. Under such a regime, possession of a personal use quantity of cannabis would have no legal consequences.

Despite the relative simplicity and potential advantages of non-punitive cannabis decriminalization, there had been no evaluations of these early attempts. Even discussions of non-punitive approaches were rare in the literature at that time. Single, Christie, and Ali (2000) and Room et al. (2010, 82) referred to practices in several Australian states that provided "cautions" instead of penalties (although these approaches retained some punitive elements). The RAND Report (Caulkins et al. 2015, 52) made a reference to the merits of non-punitive elements in a decriminalized environment by suggesting "fully legalizing possession for personal use but not sales." The US District of Columbia (District of Columbia Office of the Attorney General 2015) adopted such a model. A non-punitive approach was achieved along a more evolutionary path in Alaska. After decriminalizing cannabis in 1975 and allowing for a $100 fine for possession of small amounts, Alaska dropped the fine altogether in 1982 (Edge and Andrews 2016). After two failed attempts to legalize cannabis for recreational use, a third attempt was finally successful, becoming effective in 2015.

There may have been evidence of early public support for a non-punitive approach in Canada. Fischer (1997) referenced a finding of a 1995 Health Canada survey:

...almost 70% of the Canadian population favoured a non-imprisonment penalty (fine only) for, or the complete decriminalization of simple cannabis possession as opposed to criminal punishment.

Given the continued liberalization of Canadian attitudes since the mid-1990s, it is reasonable to expect that support for non-punitive approaches had increased by the time of the 2013 cannabis law reform campaign in Canada.

A non-punitive decriminalization model could also have included a public health component, facilitated by a partnership of local education, public health, and drug treatment programs. The model could involve these sectors collaborating on the delivery of community-based programs of primary prevention, risk/harm reduction, and helping users' access to therapeutic intervention, if desired by the user. Such an approach might give cannabis users less cause to be intimidated from accessing prevention and treatment services.

Legislatively, decriminalization would have been considerably less onerous and time-consuming than would legalization with all its regulatory challenges and lengthy legislative process. In Canada, non-punitive decriminalization could be as simple as removing cannabis possession from The Controlled Drug and Substances Act. No new legislation and regulations would have been necessary. However, it is still possible that the approval process for making such a change could have taken some time to formalize and thereby continue to expose cannabis users to prosecution during that period. But an even more expedient solution was available.

De Facto Decriminalization

Another improvement to the traditional model of decriminalization might have been the prompt implementation of a *de facto* approach. This could be as simple as federal, provincial, and regional authorities diverting enforcement activities away from detection of cannabis possession. Laws did not have to change—only enforcement practices. This *de facto* model had already been used in several jurisdictions worldwide (Room et al. 2010), supplying a rich resource of lessons already learned that could have guided efforts elsewhere. Canadian law provides for such a *de facto* mechanism. In Chapter 6, I will describe how such an attempt was made through a motion introduced to the House of Commons in 2016 by the New Democrat Party (NDP), but was defeated.

THE IMPACT OF DELAYING DECRIMINALIZATION

When the Liberal Party formed a majority government in 2015, it had a premier opportunity to right the harms of cannabis criminalization as a first step in a comprehensive approach to cannabis law reform. It squandered this opportunity by maintaining a sole focus on expanding the existing commercial cannabis industry for therapeutic use to include recreational use.

In the summer of 2016, the Canadian government released a *Discussion Paper* (Task Force on Marijuana Legalization and Regulation 2016) that confirmed the government's commitment to a private sector commercial legalization approach. However, the government was not always entirely transparent in informing Canadians that the legalization would involve a complex process that would take years to achieve. Nor did the government clearly articulate that the introduction of legislation would mark only an early milestone in a lengthier process. The widespread availability of cannabis at legal retail outlets for recreational use would come years later.

There were several foreseeable possibilities that could produce a lengthy timeframe associated with legalization.

There was no evidentiary assurance of an aggregate net gain in public health protection, or even of an outcome that was near-neutral. Even enthusiastic supporters of legalization in the policy arena acknowledged that there were risks if this were not done with a public health priority (Centre for Addiction and Mental Health 2014). The risks and the uncertainty demanded a slow, thoughtful process to mitigate potential harm to the public's health.

There was not over-whelming public support for legalization across Canada. A Nanos poll from May-June 2016 was often cited as showing that "70%" (69% actually) of respondents supported legalization. However, only 43% showed unqualified support. The remaining 57% (including 26% who only partially supported legalization) were less enthusiastic (Tahirali 2016). This meant that more than half of respondents had at least some reservations, questions, or were unsure. If the lack of assurance among Canadians was communicated to their Members of Parliament, there could arise a more cautious demeanor in the pending House of Commons debates. The government had some work to do to convince most Canadians that commercial legalization for recreational use was a promising idea.

There was a daunting regulatory labyrinth to be navigated. How would various government department responsibilities and powers, and each department's relationships with industry, be decided? There was an extensive list of legal enforcement and justice issues to be resolved. What would be the interface of a recreational trade with the therapeutic trade? What were the implications for cannabis use in the workplace? What industry structural models would be considered? Regulations had to be developed to guide product development, retail, and product promotion practices. Would home cultivation be allowed? More daunting federal issues included taxation, importation, and exportation. The enormous complexities for each of these regulatory challenges had been described in detail by Caulkins et al. (2015). To make matters even more daunting, there was a paucity of research evidence and practical experience to guide the resolution of the multi-faceted, complex issues. This would need an enormous amount of cautious work from a variety of expertise domains. The complexity would demand a great deal of time.

The federal legislative approval process would be a complex and potentially protracted one. The bill would go through a first, second, and third reading in both the House of Commons and the Senate. Each could have its own public and expert consultation processes, internal negotiations, etc. followed by the preparation of reports and revisions. Only when both the House and Senate agreed upon the same wording of the bill, would it continue to the Governor General for royal assent. Then the bill would become law.

Additional pressures and delays would come from other levels of government. Thirteen provinces and territories, as well as Indigenous governments, would have their concerns and interests to pursue. Municipalities, through their associated local public health departments were also engaged on the issue and had been sending their expectations to the Prime Minister's Office. The *Final Report* of the Task Force on Cannabis Legalization and Regulation (2016) recommended that provinces, territories, Indigenous governments, and municipalities assume at least partial responsibility for several regulatory decisions and functions. These would include some of the potentially controversial ones: minimum age, distribution, retail, public use, and home cultivation. Assuming the federal government took the Task Force's advice, both provincial and local levels of governance would have their own legislative process to engage. Municipalities had specific and compelling reasons to be cautious. If anything went awry with cannabis legalization, the impacts might be most profoundly experienced at the local community level—in neighborhoods, workplaces, and in families.

The next arena of complexity would be introduced by a large and diverse number of interest groups. These groups, in some cases fueled by potent levels of passion, would pursue a variety of potentially competing interests including human rights, law and order, access to medicine, freedom of pursuit of pleasurable self-indulgence, protection of public health, responsible fiscal management, and the pursuit of entrepreneurial opportunities—by forceful competitors. The competition would extend beyond those companies operating in the cannabis industry. The alcohol, tobacco, and pharmaceutical industries would also have their interests to protect and op-portunities to cultivate. They possessed the means to bring powerful lobbying artillery to the legislative process. There were also potential benefactors with-in government and various government-funded services that would assert-ively pursue a share of a new tax revenue stream. All these interest groups would try in any way they could to influence the decision-making process. The diversity of the myriad interests and the intensity of their pursuit of those interests would not hasten legislative consensus or compromises.

There were also formidable business logistics to address in establish-ing the manufacturing, distribution, and retail capabilities for producing and delivering cannabis products to consumers. A process for granting licenses to manufacture and sell would be required. There would also be the acquisi-tion of financing and properties, acquisition, installation and testing of pro-duction equipment, establishment of supply chain logistics, and hiring and training of the workforce. Security would also be an issue in all aspects of the supply chain. The *Final Report* of the Task Force (2016, 7) acknowledged some of these challenging post-legislative challenges and a few others:

> *"Success requires federal leadership, coordination and in-vestment in research and surveillance, laboratory testing, li-censing and regulatory inspection, training for law enforcement and others, and the development of tools to in-crease capacity ahead of regulation."*

There were international treaties that restricted legalization of recre-ational cannabis among signatories of which Canada was one (Room 2012). The treaties may very well be archaic, not evidence-based, and possibly even counter-productive, at least in the case of cannabis. Nonetheless, they presented a challenge for a prime minister who, in 2015, was a novice among world leaders and was hopeful to secure a seat for Canada on the UN Security Council. Given this aspiration, the prime minister needed to be concerned about the optics of sidestepping treaties—particularly treaties that (with the lone exception of Uruguay) had not been challenged by his more seasoned peers. Canada had made a bold statement of intent to legal-ize cannabis at the 2016 United Nations General Assembly Special Session (UNGASS). However, the meeting ultimately gained no tangible progress in changing the prevailing international regime of prohibition that was main-tained by the treaties (Glenza 2016). This might have supplied another cause for caution and thoughtfulness.

All the above hurdles meant that recreational users would probably have to wait for quite some time for the opportunity to buy their cannabis legally. The rest of Canadians, regardless of their specific interests in the is-sue, would also have to be patient. The actual amount of time was difficult to estimate. In 2015, the Prime Minister acknowledged that it could take up to "a year or two" (CBC 2015). That same year, CAMH policy researcher, Jürgen Rehm, more realistically, estimated that the wait could be for as long as four years (Rehm and Nutt 2015). If correct, that would establish legal retail in 2019. A similar estimate had been provided by an unidentified senior federal government official in a *Globe and Mail* report (Leblanc 2016). So, why would an expected delivery date in 2019 pose a serious problem?

The campaign to reform cannabis law should have been guided by a principle borrowed from emergency medicine: first, stop the bleeding. The bleeding, in the case of cannabis law reform, was the large number of (mostly young) Canadians who were being charged for trivial cannabis offences each year and who would suffer the life-long consequences of a criminal record.

Data available from Statistics Canada at the time (Cotter, Greenland, and Karam 2015) suggested that in each of the years that legalization was delayed, approximately 59,000 criminal charges would be laid for simple possession of cannabis. The number of actual convictions that resulted in a criminal record would be at least 22,000 per year. The continuance of prohibition during the approximate four years from 2015 through 2019 would therefore result in the number of criminal records approaching 90,000 before there would be a legal alternative to buying cannabis. The adverse consequences for these individuals had been documented for decades since the publication of Patricia Erickson's *Cannabis Criminals* (Erickson 1980). A more recent update (Erickson and Hyshka 2010) reinforced the original findings of a disruptive interference with the victims' lives.

The potentially wide-ranging and devastating assault on basic social determinants of health could include restricted access to employment and housing, restricted entry into specific professions, international travel restrictions, financial hardship, and potentially exposing users to hurtful social judgments and stigmatization. Such hardship could have a profound impact on a person's overall well-being for many years. Some of these individuals would consist of those with mental health and drug-related problems who turned to the healthcare system for help. It is difficult to imagine how the acquisition of a criminal record could in any way help with a person's improved social stability or recovery. It would almost certainly present only another barrier. This danger placed an onus on health care and policy institutions to become active advocates for the shaping of policy configured primarily by humanitarian and health priorities.

Despite all these unsavoury possibilities, the government remained undeterred and went ahead with a cannabis law reform campaign focused primarily upon commercial opportunity. As I will discuss in later chapters, it would become increasingly clear that the government had no interest in decriminalization nor any concern for those harmed by continued criminalization. This was clear from the beginning. The government's *Discussion Paper*, issued by its Task Force on Marijuana Legalization and Regulation (2016, 19), appeared to portend the continuation of harsh and even increasing penalties in the new system: "...close consideration must be given to new or strengthened sanctions for those who act outside the boundaries of the new system." Those "who act outside the boundaries of the new system" would

"Who Knew Legalizing Marijuana Could Be So Complicated?"

Beginning in the spring of 2015, I began to give presentations to organizations interested in cannabis legalization. From my years of interest in drug policy, and the work of prominent academics and health policy authorities. I had acquired what I thought was a comprehensive understanding of the many issues that the government would need to address in the creation of a new legal drug industry. My audiences were usually astonished by just how complicated it would be. Here is my list from 2015:

- *centralized vs. decentralized authority: feds, provinces, municipalities*
- *can provinces or municipalities opt-out of legalization?*
- *government or private sector monopoly versus competitive*
- *can people grow their own? how much?*
- *security at production facilities, distribution, and retail*
- *inspection of facilities and product quality*
- *retail: cannabis only or combined with other (tobacco, alcohol, or pharma)*
- *how are retail licenses awarded?*
- *how many in a municipality? determined by population size or geographic density?*
- *what would they look like? restrictions on location and appearance*
- *days and hours of operation*
- *staff training and certification*
- *cannabis sold (legally) at bars and restaurants? cannabis lounges?*
- *-- should advertising be allowed? restrictions on content and location of ads?*
- *how to regulate advertising on the internet?*
- *product line: loose-leaf, pre-rolled, flavoured edibles, concentrates, topicals*
- *branding versus plain packaging*
- *health warning labels? what would they say?*
- *allowed potency levels*
- *driving and THC levels: testing and penalties*
- *minimum age; penalties for underage use*
- *penalties for adult buying for under-age user*
- *use in public allowed? where? maximum amount to possess?*
- *penalties: criminal record? fine?*
- *host liability for conduct of impaired guests*

- implications of impairment at work

- public education programs—how? content?

- how to deal with illegal growers and retailers? penalties?

- how much in taxes collected at federal and provincial levels

- excise taxes and sales taxes; tax by price, weight, or potency

- investment securities regulation? penalties for fraud?

- does medical marijuana become irrelevant? covered by health plans?

- edibles available at workplace social events? part of cash-bar?

- if there are more problems, increase funding for treatment programs?

- reduce or increase funding for local enforcement?

- eliminate criminal records of people with past convictions?

- allow imports, exports?

- cannabis tourism allowed? promoted?

On December 5, 2017, *The Globe and Mail* published an article by Gary Mason, titled: "Who Knew Legalizing Marijuana Could Be So Complicated?" A colleague, who was familiar with my presentations, sent Mason's piece to me, and kindly acknowledged that I had known how complicated it would be. The truth is, I barely knew the half of it.

potentially include those under the minimum legal age limit and those over the minimum limit who continue to use cannabis from an unlicensed source. Minor offences under legalization would remain the same victimless crime that they had always been.

And what of the hundreds of thousands of users who already had criminal records for simple possession? Neither the Task Force's *Discussion Paper* nor its *Final Report* showed concern for the plight of cannabis users who bore the legal and social scars of Canada's punitive history. Government should have explored a mechanism by which it could grant record expungement for those already convicted of simple possession only. It is difficult to imagine how record expungement would have brought substantial opposition from an increasingly enlightened and sympathetic public. It is also difficult to fathom how maintaining the status quo was consistent with a promised move from a criminal justice approach to one based on public health protection. Long-time advocates of reform, less mesmerized by the spectacle of a glamorous, lucrative, new cannabis industry, may have been left wondering what had happened to the compassion and sense of justice that had fueled the drive for reform for so much of the issue's history.

IMPLICATIONS OF LEGALIZATION WITHOUT DECRIMINALIZATION

Experience from state jurisdictions in the United States has made it clear that an unlicensed cannabis trade will survive legalization and thrive—as do contraband supplies for tobacco and pharmaceuticals, and to a lesser extent, alcohol. Given the long-standing existence of the unlicensed cannabis trade in Canada, was it realistic to expect many cannabis users to take seriously the distinction between legal and illegal cannabis? Was a young adult at a party, when passed a joint, likely to ask about the legal status of the offering, or to even care? And was it reasonable to expect law enforcement to be able to make the distinction between a joint rolled with legal or illegal product, and was it prudent to expect the justice system to spend time and resources on providing a ruling based upon making a distinction? If the new legislation intended to deal in a harsh manner on making a distinction that few key players recognized as critical, reasonable, or practical, did that not pose a risk of bringing discredit to the entire enterprise?

Beginning in 2016, the government should have been true to its word in taking "a public health approach" to cannabis law reform. Given the significant impact of criminalization upon people's social determinants of health, the government's approach should have avoided any continuance of punitive measures for the simple possession of cannabis. The continued existence of an unlicensed trade within either a decriminalization or a legalization regime was assured. Its continued monopoly under a decriminalization regime would not be ideal. However, the establishment of a decriminalization regime would have been a reasonable short-term compromise. It would have the immediate benefit of bringing an end to cannabis use criminalization and the attendant harms to Canadians. Our government would have done well to recognize these benefits and to have desisted with the exaggerated appeals to fear.

Outside of Canada, support for decriminalization continued to flourish as a preferred approach to reform. The American Academy of Pediatrics issued a strong statement of support for decriminalization while issuing an equally strong recommendation against legalization (Ammerman, Ryan, and Adelman 2015). By 2016, twenty-one US states had decriminalized cannabis (National Organization for the Reform of Marijuana Laws 2016). Canada's Task Force on Marijuana Legalization and Regulation's *Discussion Paper* (2016) provided an unreferenced statement that twenty-two countries had implemented some form of decriminalization of cannabis. As of November 2016, Wikipedia (2016), citing individual jurisdictional sources, provided a count of thirty-two. Why was Canada not one of them?

Historically, opposition to decriminalization had usually come from those who favoured continued prohibition. They expressed fears that decriminalization would send a counter-productive message that would increase cannabis use and related problems. They also asserted that decriminalization would sustain and possibly strengthen a criminally controlled illegal trade in cannabis and other illegal drugs. There were concerns that the proceeds would be used to fund other violent and exploitative activities of organized crime operations worldwide. However, this chapter has shown that, for cannabis, these fears were largely unfounded. A vast majority of the unlicensed trade is benign. So, many nations as well as state jurisdictions within the United States, had not been overly concerned about the continued existence of the unlicensed cannabis trade and proceeded to decriminalize possession of cannabis. In contrast, Canada's legalization of cannabis campaign embellished and exploited these unsubstantiated fears to increase public support for legalization. As we will see in later chapters, the rationale for doing so was apparently not out of a misguided intent to protect citizen propriety but out of a desire to protect market share of the new legal industry—which was about to experience an enormous expansion. It was the same old narrative of fear, but now repurposed for a more contemporary and lucrative objective.

The Canadian government maintained a harshly inflexible stance against the decriminalization option that had been its official position on cannabis for more than a decade. This was not an oversight. It was a strategic decision that was part of a larger plan that I will describe in Chapter 6. The decision was also inconsistent with the wave of discourse across Canada and much of the world, which was increasingly considering decriminalization, not just of cannabis, but of all drugs. I will return to that topic in the last chapter of the book. Finally, the path chosen by the Canadian government was one paved with warnings from the practices of other legal drug industries. I will dive into that topic in considerable detail in the next chapter.

SUMMING UP

The unlicensed cannabis trade has been unjustifiably characterized as a violent drug cartel affiliated with organized crime. This canard has been used to discredit decriminalization as a practical cannabis law reform alternative to prohibition. Both the research and the government's own intel showed the unlicensed trade to be much more benign than baleful. The research also shows that decriminalization has been an internationally successful approach to cannabis law reform. The consequences of not first doing so in Canada meant that cannabis users in possession of unlicensed cannabis were harshly punished for the same victimless crime it has always been. The Liberal Party of Canada once embraced decriminalization as its formal policy position for cannabis, but then abruptly abandoned it for a new objective that had little to do with social justice or an evidence-based approach to policy.

Chapter 5

A New Legal Drug Industry: What Could Possibly Go Wrong?

"...limbic capitalism is...global industries that basically encourage excessive consumption and even addiction...now they've reached the point where they're actually designing it."

— David T. Courtwright,

Presidential Professor Emeritus

I was not at the 8th Global Conference on Health Promotion held in Helsinki, Finland, in 2013. But I can imagine looks of astonishment when Margaret Chan, Director-General of the World Health Organization, had this to say in the conference's opening address:

> ... it is not just Big Tobacco anymore. Public health must also contend with Big Food, Big Soda, and Big Alcohol. All these industries fear regulation and protect themselves by using the same tactics. Research has documented these tactics well. They include front groups, lobbies, promises of self-regulation, lawsuits, and industry funded research that confuses the evidence and keeps the public in doubt. Tactics also include gifts, grants, and contributions to worthy causes that cast these industries as respectable corporate citizens in the eyes of politicians and the public. They include arguments that place the responsibility for harm to health on individuals and portray government actions as interference in personal liberties and free choice. This is formidable opposition. Market

power readily translates into political power. Few governments prioritize health over big business. As we learned from experience with the tobacco industry, a powerful corporation can sell the public just about anything. (Chan 2013)

This chapter reveals such unsavory dynamics within the tobacco and alcohol industries and the pharmaceutical industry as well. It also explores the early warnings that the upstart cannabis industry had begun its journey on the same path.

As with the previous chapter, this one began as part of a submission I sent to the Task Force on Marijuana Legalization and Regulation. Much of the content has since been rewritten, but the chapter includes only what was known during the Canadian government's cannabis law reform initiative. The purpose is to provide a time capsule of what could have played a significant role informing the legislation. In later chapters, I will address recent developments in the cannabis and other drug industries.

THE LEGACY OF DRUG CORPORATIONS

At the time of cannabis legalization, there was a long-established tradition of legal, government-regulated corporations supplying drug products to people. This included both recreational (alcohol and tobacco) and therapeutic (pharmaceutical) drug products. Governments were comfortable with the private corporate model and most people saw it as the only possibility. Within the traditional orthodoxy of drug policy, the private corporate model was presumed to be a superior and desirable panacea to the unlicensed trade in drugs. Licensed corporations were assumed to supply safe products and to operate within a legal framework that posed little threat to the propriety and safety of society. These beliefs prevailed, largely unchallenged, despite a substantial body of evidence on the perils of the corporate model. These perils gained increasing attention on the road to legalization of a new legal drug industry for cannabis.

In this chapter I will explore this body of evidence for each of our three long-standing types of drug corporations (tobacco, alcohol, and pharmaceutical) as well as the new one—cannabis. Well before Canada's campaign to legalize cannabis for recreational use, it had already established a private corporate model for therapeutic (medical) use, as had individual sub-national jurisdictions within The United States. A few sub-national jurisdictions had, more recently, also established a corporate model for recreational use.

Human rights and justice advocates welcomed the anticipated end of cannabis prohibition. Cannabis users, who had experienced, or lived in fear of, the legal and personal consequences of prohibition celebrated the liberation of their pastime. There were also those who saw an opportunity for financial benefit from the expansion of a therapeutic industry into one serving recreational use as well.

However, as discussed earlier, results from a Nanos poll (which were often only partially reported) showed that most Canadians were unsure or had at least some concerns. Some had major concerns. Many caregivers were troubled about the impact on the welfare of their patients, particularly those with drug-related problems and/or mental health challenges. Concerns also included the conduct of the cannabis industry itself. In an Environics Communications survey of Canadians' level of trust for twenty business sectors to "do what is right for Canada, Canadians, and our society." The cannabis industry was ranked dead last, behind even recently controversial sectors such as energy and resources, finance, and the pharmaceutical sector (Krashinsky Robertson 2017).

In the face of these concerns, the government insisted that Canadians should not worry because, in contrast to the illegal trade, cannabis corporations would be strictly regulated like our alcohol, tobacco, and pharmaceutical corporations.

In this chapter I will explore the question of whether Canadians, including the government, should have been concerned about the commercial legalization of cannabis. I will draw from several bodies of evidence available at the time of the legalization campaign in Canada that should have provoked more prudence. These include:

- *harms and costs associated with recreational drugs*

- *corporate misconduct and criminality*

- *quality control of legal drug products*

- *effectiveness of government regulation*

- *expected impact of legalization on cannabis use and problems.*

Discussions based upon these areas of evidence will weave their way through many of the topics covered in the chapter.

Harms and Costs from Recreational Drug Industries: Tobacco and Alcohol

I will once again address the levels of harms and costs of drug use in Canada as covered in Chapter 1, but much more succinctly. I will also restrict this summary to information that was available at the time of Canada's legalization campaign. I start with considering the combined impact of our legal drug industries that are most like the cannabis industry—tobacco and alcohol. The data provided a profound cautionary tale to the government for its ambition of creating a new legal recreational drug industry. The most recent aggregate data publicly available on harms and costs from drug use in Canada at that time was from 2002. Rehm et al. (2006) had shown that the combined annual health footprint of tobacco and alcohol use in Canada was 6.5 million days spent in hospital, and 41,467 premature deaths accounting for 663,178 potential years of life lost (PYLL). These numbers accounted for 66.8% of all drug-related days in hospital, and 96.1% of all drug-related premature deaths accounting for 91.4% of all drug-related potential years of life lost (PYLL). The remaining portions are attributable to all illegal drugs combined. Rehm's group also showed that this was more than a health crisis. The estimate for the cost of the combined alcohol and tobacco related harm to the Canadian economy was $31.6 billion annually, which made up 79.3% of drug-related economic costs. It is important to keep two points in mind. First, this data set did not include legally used pharmaceutical products, so the portion of harms and costs attributed to legal drug use is underestimated. Secondly, these figures correspond to the harms and costs encountered in just one year. An earlier study on the harms and costs of drug use in Canada in 1992 (Single et al. 1996, 1998) also reported high figures suggesting a long-term trend of health and economic harm concentrated on alcohol and tobacco.

These figures, by themselves, did not prove that the revenue-driven corporate model is the singular cause of the harm and costs observed. However, with such enormous levels of harm and cost, levels that significantly exceed those attributable to all illegal drugs combined, it would have been prudent for the government to consider the potentially perilous role of the commercial corporate model. It should also have been aware that the opioid crisis that began in the early-mid-1990s had its genesis in an aggressive, deceitful, and illegal promotional campaign of opioid products by legal pharmaceutical corporations. I will cover more on that story later in this chapter and provide an update in the last chapter. Based upon what we knew from these three legal drug industries, it should have been plain to the government that legalization and regulation of a drug trade was no assurance of public health protection as cannabis made its historic journey from an illegal drug to a legal one.

Corporate Misconduct, Harms, and Regulatory Oversight

This section will cover the misconduct of our three long-term drug industries—tobacco, alcohol and pharmaceutical and their permissive regulation by the government. We will also see how this perilous combination can have an impact on public health. As described earlier, the information presented in this section will focus on the point up to which cannabis legalization was unfolding in Canada. It will thus represent what was known, or should have been known, by the Canadian government at the time. I will provide updates in the last chapter.

Tobacco Corporations

The tobacco industry is made up of legal, government-regulated corporations.

The legal tobacco cigarette is designed and manufactured in accordance with industry-standardized, regulator-approved protocols. It is also our most toxic legal consumer product when used in its intended manner. As it is throughout much of the world, tobacco use is a public health crisis in Canada resulting in substantial morbidity, mortality, and economic loss. Using data available at the time of Canada's cannabis legalization campaign,

Rehm et al. (2006) demonstrated that the harm from tobacco included 2.2 million hospital days and 37,209 premature deaths resulting in 515,607 potential years of lost life (PYLL). The cost to the Canadian economy was $17 billion. I want to emphasize that these estimates of harm and cost were for one year only. There is no reason to believe that it was an atypical year.

A significant contributor to this perennial harm was more than a half century of nefarious conduct by the tobacco industry. The Canadian story was told in *Smoke & Mirrors: The Canadian Tobacco War* written by Rob Cunningham, Senior Policy Analyst with the Canadian Cancer Society (Cunningham 1996). A US account was provided in a Pulitzer Prize-winning history of the tobacco industry in America called *Ashes to Ashes*. It covers the rise of the public health movement, the policy clash between public health and commerce, and the political and legal machinations throughout (Kluger 1997). A third book, *Smoke Screen: The Truth Behind the Tobacco Industry Cover-up* (Hilts 1996) covered the industry's exploits in both countries. These books provided a comprehensive historical account of the epic battle involving the tobacco industry, public health authorities, government regulators and the courts. All were available at the time that the Liberal Party of Canada was crafting a new revenue-driven drug industry.

A high-profile exposure of tobacco industry malfeasance surfaced in the US landmark court case against Philip Morris USA presided over by Justice Gladys Kessler. After reviewing hundreds of depositions and thousands of exhibits, Kessler issued a stinging condemnation of the industry in her 1,742-page opinion (United States District Court for the District of Columbia 2006). Some highlights of Kessler's findings follow:

> *[This case] is about an industry, and in particular these Defendants, that survive, and profits, from selling a highly addictive product which causes diseases that lead to a staggering number of deaths per year, an immeasurable amount of human suffering and economic loss, and a profound burden on our national healthcare system. Defendants have known many of these facts for at least 50 years or more. Despite that knowledge, they have consistently, repeatedly and with enormous skill and sophistication, denied these facts to the public, the Government, and to the public health community (United States District Court for the District of Columbia 2006, 3).*

> *Defendants have marketed and sold their lethal products with zeal, with deception, with a single-minded focus on their financial success, and without regard for the human tragedy or social costs that success exacted (United States District Court for the District of Columbia 2006, 4).*

> *Over the course of more than 50 years, Defendants lied, misrepresented and deceived the American public, including smokers and the young people they avidly sought as 'replace-*

ment' smokers about the devastating health effects of smoking and environmental tobacco smoke (United States District Court for the District of Columbia 2006, 1500).

The evidence in this case clearly establishes that Defendants have not ceased engaging in unlawful activity.... For example, most Defendants continue to fraudulently deny the adverse health effects of second-hand smoke which they recognized internally; all Defendants continue to market "low tar" cigarettes to consumers seeking to reduce their health risks or quit; all Defendants continue to fraudulently deny that they manipulate the nicotine delivery of their cigarettes in order to create and sustain addiction; some Defendants continue to deny that they market to youth in publications with significant youth readership and with imagery that targets youth; and some Defendants continue to suppress and conceal information which might undermine their public or litigation position.... Their continuing conduct misleads consumers in order to maximize Defendants' revenues by recruiting new smokers (the majority of whom are under the age of 18), preventing current smokers from quitting, and thereby sustaining the industry (United States District Court for the District of Columbia 2006, 1603).

An important facet of Kessler's judgment was that it was not based only upon the harms of tobacco (which is a legal product), but upon what the industry knew and chose not to share and act upon. The judgment against the industry raised interesting questions about the culpability of other long-established industries whose products present public health perils. Considering Kessler's ruling and comments it would seem likely that industries such as alcohol and pharmaceutical (and perhaps gambling and fast food as well) would have been prompted to have conversations with their legal advisors. These conversations might address issues of transparency in how they conduct their business within the context of what they know about the harm of their products. While those conversations may very well have happened, it is not apparent that they had any affect on the conduct of these corporations.

The vast engagement in criminality and turpitude described by Justice Kessler was not restricted to the United States. Mahood (2013) alluded to the direct relationships between US and Canadian tobacco companies and noted that the crimes described by Kessler also occurred in Canada at the same time. Mahood's insightful accounts of this era supplement Cunningham's (1996) work, and described how in the early 1990's, Canada's three tobacco companies had been involved in tobacco smuggling operations which caused the government to lose billions of dollars in unpaid tobacco taxes. Charges were eventually laid against the companies and individual executives. Charges included fraud, conspiracy to commit fraud, possession of the proceeds of crime, deceit, fraudulent misrepresentation, spoliation [destruction of documents] and a "massive conspiracy." Mahood quoted presiding Justice E.F. Ormston: "The acts committed in furtherance of the conspiracy here represent the largest offense of its nature in Canadian history."

Mahood also described subsequent legal actions taken against Canada's tobacco companies by the Canadian government in 2008 and 2010. He noted that the eventual out-of-court settlements recovered only a small portion of the lost taxation revenue. Payment schedules of ten to fifteen years made it easy for the industry to pass the costs of the settlements on to their nicotine-dependant customers. Despite guilty pleas from the companies as part of these settlements, no individuals were convicted of any criminal wrongdoing.

The involvement of Canadian tobacco companies in so much deception, at least in part, prompted most Canadian provinces and territories to seek compensation for healthcare costs through individual lawsuits against Canadian cigarette manufacturers and their foreign parent companies (Ontario Tobacco Research Unit 2013). None of these lawsuits had gone to trial by the end of 2016. Tobacco control advocates (Mahood 2013) expressed concern that relatively small out-of-court settlements, as seen in the 2008 and 2010 actions, would provide an easy windfall of cash for governments but would comprise too modest of a financial sacrifice to reform industry perfidy.

It is interesting that the industry's initial reaction to the lawsuits in Canada was to demonstrate the partnership relationship it had maintained with the government for much of its activity. This argument was not accepted by the courts as a basis for dismissing the cost-recovery suits. However, given the descriptions provided by Mahood (2013), there was little doubt that the government, at best, had been negligent in its failure to effectively regulate the tobacco industry, and accordingly, was at least somewhat complicit as an enabler of some of the harm inflicted upon the public.

The absence of any grave consequences inflicted upon the industry from legal proceedings may have emboldened industry opposition to public health measures such as plain packaging (Hatchard et al. 2014), bans on flavourings (Brown et al. 2016), increased taxation (Zhang and Schwartz 2015), and improving the safety of e-cigarettes (Kusnetz 2016). All this suggested that the industry had little fear of serious repercussions from current legal actions brought against it in Canada. Brownson et al. (2016) also expressed concern about a lack of serious action on the part of regulators in addressing safety aspects of e-cigarettes. Delays of stricter regulation for e-cigarettes, allegedly based upon a desire for more convincing data, ultimately protected the interests of industry. This was eerily reminiscent of the history of traditional cigarettes. In the early days of research, industry influence, and policy development, the onus was placed upon health authorities to demonstrate the harm. Given what we knew from that experience, the protection of the public's health would be better served by placing the onus upon industry to provide evidence for safety.

It might be argued that more recent tobacco-related regulatory actions that had been taken by the Canadian federal and provincial governments provided assurance that government regulation of drug industries was alive and well and capable of protecting the public's health. For example, several provincial governments in Canada had recently passed legislation to ban flavouring in cigarettes, and the Canadian government had promised to introduce legislation for plain packaging. It may have been tempting to take some comfort in these recent developments in considering the implications for an improved regulatory regime for cannabis. However, there were also three reasons for caution.

1) Regulatory improvements had occurred in slow piecemeal fashion over a period of a half century since the US Surgeon General's landmark report prompted governments to regulate the tobacco industry more strictly. This is not a clock that health authorities would want to start running over again for an emboldened cannabis industry, hungering for the large market expansion that could accompany legalization for recreational sales.

2) For several years, public health authorities, academics, and advocates (including myself) had celebrated substantial reductions in cigarette smoking, particularly by younger age groups. However, more recent evidence at that time from The United States (Singh et al. 2016) suggested that there was a substantial replacement effect with many young people using other ways to ingest nicotine such as e-cigarettes, vaporisers, hookahs, and chew. Of considerable concern was a report on adolescent smoking by Leventhal et al. (2016) that found a positive relationship between higher frequency and heaviness of vaping at baseline and combustible tobacco smoking six months later. The future implications of continued nicotine ingestion through alternative means remained controversial. The tobacco industry was relentless, creative, and phenomenally successful in renewing its customer base with product innovations and thus protecting its commercial interests. No less should have been expected of its disciple—the cannabis industry.

3) As described by Mahood (2013), the tobacco regulatory changes implemented thus far had done little to seriously harm the industry. The industry had remained aggressive in its pursuit of new young smokers and enormously profitable. The architects of the industry's crimes remained largely unpunished. There had been no substantial deterrent effect on the tobacco industry by government regulation or by court judgments. This would be readily apparent to the emerging, watchful cannabis industry.

The tobacco industry's long-lived malfeasance had continued to persist on a global scale. In a report that detailed the industry's relentless attempts to sabotage international public health efforts, a World Health Organization report (2008, 22) concluded that "the tobacco industry is not and cannot be a partner in effective tobacco control." In the presence of this harsh, but deserved judgment, it is important to be reminded that the tobacco industry was made up of legal, government-regulated, corporations.

Alcohol Corporations

The alcohol industry is also made up of legal, government-regulated, corporations. Despite being produced and sold under standard, government-approved protocols, commercial beverage alcohol is associated with over 200 different diseases, conditions, and injury types (Rehm et al. 2009). Alcohol has been long recognized as a Group 1 carcinogen by the International Agency for Research on Cancer (1988). This is the same classification held by tobacco (when combusted), asbestos, and arsenic. Since the year 2000, alcohol has been verified as associated with six types of cancer by The World Health Organization, The International Agency for Research on Cancer, and The American Society of Clinical Oncologists. More recently, alcohol's carcinogenic potential has been extended to dosages that many would regard as quite low (Cao 2015).

As it is through much of the world, alcohol misuse is a public health crisis in Canada resulting in substantial morbidity, mortality, and economic loss. Using the most recent aggregate data available from 2002 at the time of Canada's cannabis legalization campaign, Rehm et al. (2006) provided estimates for several indicators of the country's annual harm from alcohol. This included 4.3 million days in hospital and 4,258 premature deaths resulting in 147,571 potential years of lost life (PYLL). The estimate for the costs of alcohol misuse to the Canadian economy was $14.6 billion annually. Again, I want to emphasize that those figures were for one year. As was the case for tobacco, there is no reason to believe that there was anything unusual about that year.

Alcohol's harmful footprint on public health is not necessarily an argument for prohibition. However, at minimum, it should compel us to consider the information about alcohol that is made available to consumers. The information disproportionately uses exciting, glamourous, and romantic depictions to promote the enjoyment of alcohol over disclosure of the risks associated with its use. In the policy arena, governments have appeared indifferent to the body of evidence on the harms and the expressed concerns of public health authorities. Thus, the legacy of revenue-centred corporate behaviour and of government regulatory permissiveness has continued—at enormous expense to the public's health and to the Canadian economy.

Some of the details of this legacy were made available in a book titled *Sober Reflections: Commerce, Public Health, and the Evolution of Alcohol Policy in Canada, 1980-2000* (Giesbrecht, Demers, and Stoduto 2006). The chapters by the authors in this compilation detailed the Canadian alcohol industry's disturbing heritage of malfeasance and disregard for public health. This included smuggling operations involving hundreds of on-premises drinking establishments, public disinformation campaigns to sway policy and public opinion, aggressive lobbying, threats to withdraw charitable donations, and corporate largess for elected officials including campaign contributions and free sports event tickets. Regulatory failure on the part of the government included a failure to implement compulsory labelling information on alcohol products. This occurred at a time when the exclusion of ingredient listings on alcohol products was unique among consumer products. And there were no health warning labels on this Group 1 carcinogen and cause of over two hundred kinds of morbidities. The authors also noted that regulation had allowed increased commercialization of alcohol as well as liberalization of restrictions on access at a time when increasing consumption was understood to lead to increased problems. The authors pointed to changes allowing lower-priced imported products, fewer restrictions on advertising of alcohol products, and the privatization (self-regulation) of the monitoring of advertisements.

Misdeeds in Canada's alcohol industry and failures in adequate regulation did not end at the turn of the century. Contraband alcohol product was commonly available in at least some parts of Canada, and the legal industry was involved. The *National Post* (Hamilton 2015) reported that in 2015, a Montréal, Québec, winery had been investigated for having imported and sold over two million bottles of "cheap Italian wine" outside of the Québec government's regulatory and distribution system over a four-year period. It was estimated that the fraudulent wine sales avoided approximately $14 million in provincial and federal tax payments. The police investigation culminated in the apprehension of a ring of twelve individuals including a former Ontario vineyard executive. The group was charged with fraud, conspiracy to commit fraud, trademark infringement and recycling the proceeds of crime. The Ontario winery, whose executive was involved, acknowledged having had a business arrangement with the Montréal winery, but said that it discontinued that arrangement upon hearing of the police investigation. These aspects of the case should have raised concerns about a blurring of the line between the legal and illegal alcohol trades, particularly given the prevailing narrative of the desirability of a legal, government-regulated industry over an unlicensed trade.

Two elements of the Montréal case, the Italian wine and a winery in Ontario, also arose in another case in which contraband wine appeared on the shelves of the Ontario Government's alcohol retailer, The Liquor Control Board of Ontario (LCBO). As reported by the *Toronto Star* (Rubin 2011), an investigation by York Region Police revealed that the LCBO was defrauded into selling sub-standard contraband wine in bottles bearing premium Italian brand labels. The fraud was detected not by government regulators or by its retailer, but by discerning customers. My email communications with York Region Police revealed that 221 bottles were returned to the LCBO in York Region, and that other LCBO outlets had also been defrauded in the same manner with the same contraband product. In York Region, several individuals were arrested, and charges laid for fraud, purchasing alcohol from other than a licensed establishment, and unlawfully receiving orders for the sale of alcohol. This case has clear implications for the ability and/or commitment of a government-regulated retail system to safeguard the integrity, and possibly the safety, of alcohol products.

There have also been product integrity issues in the manufacture of alcohol. In 2017, the LCBO recalled bottles of Bombay Sapphire London Dry Gin and Georgian Bay Vodka which, when returned by customers and tested, were found to contain 77% and 80% alcohol by volume, respectively, as opposed to the intended 40% as labelled (Canadian Press 2017a). Once again, it was not licensed producers, government regulators or staff of a government retailer, who detected these production failures. Detection occurred only at the point of consumption.

There was also a continued escalation in the aggressive and glamorous promotion of alcohol products by the industry and also by government-operated retail outlets such as the LCBO. There appeared to be little concern from regulatory bodies such as the Alcohol and Gaming Commission of Ontario. Apart from sporadic and vague platitudes related to responsible use of its product, the alcohol industry, government retailers, and regulatory bodies had remained mostly quiet on the significant harms associated with the product.

Much had been made of the social responsibility (SR) campaigns of the alcohol industry, in which the industry was, at least initially, embarrassed into participating. Nonetheless, the alcohol industry in Canada had become involved in a variety of initiatives intended to promote responsible drinking (Public Health Agency of Canada 2016). However, these efforts remained disproportionately small compared to the effort expended on promotion of the products. An obvious indicator of the relative importance of social responsibility to the industry is apparent in the amount of space in promotional materials or on product containers that is devoted to the SR message. It was minuscule, compared to the amount of space devoted to the glamorous depiction of the product. A casual inspection of alcohol ads in print media would have revealed that a social responsibility message, if there at all, would not typically amount to even one percent of the ad's total space. In contrast, by law, tobacco products sold in Canada were required to display a health warning making up no less than three quarters of the surface of the packaging (Canada 2011). Despite being associated with levels of harm like those for tobacco (Rehm et al. 2006), beverage alcohol containers sold in Canada are not required to carry health warnings.

The epidemic of alcohol harm in Canada is not occurring for lack of evidence on how to reduce it. International research has identified policies that can contain alcohol problems. These include:

- *increasing taxation*
- *decreasing maximum legal blood alcohol levels from 0.08 grams of alcohol in 100 millilitres of blood to .05*
- *setting the legal limit to zero grams for drivers under the age of twenty-one*
- *increasing the minimum drinking age to twenty-one*
- *Safer Bars training for staff in alcohol-serving premises*

> *- training in brief interventions for patients with alcohol problems*
> *for caregivers working in primary care settings.*

(Rehm et al. 2011)

Rehm, et.al. (2011) showed that the adoption of all these best practices in Canada would, on an annual basis, result in 800 fewer preventable deaths with a reduction of close to 26,000 years of lost life (PYLL) and more than 88,000 fewer acute care hospital days. The annual savings to the Canadian economy would amount to approximately $1 billion. The report emphasized that these were conservative estimates.

Stated another way, these annual harmful consequences were largely attributable to the perennial failure of the alcohol industry and government regulation to implement evidence-based policies for protecting the public's health. After the release of Rehm's report, there had been more warnings against increased liberalization of alcohol laws in Ontario (Giesbrecht 2015), and a call for a renewed comprehensive public health-based alcohol policy (Centre for Addiction and Mental Health 2015).

Despite such determined advocacy, the alcohol industry and the Ontario government did not heed the advice. And it implemented even higher risk practices and policies with the introduction of beer and expanded wine retail in grocery stores (Giesbrecht 2015). Even in those jurisdictions like Ontario where much of the alcohol was sold by a government retailer, the absence of a public health priority persisted in both alcohol industry practices and government regulation. The timing of the introduction of alcohol product to grocery stores in Ontario was particularly audacious. It followed on the heels of a *CBC* report (Griffith-Greene 2015) on how Loblaws, the premier grocery chain allowed to sell alcohol, had been found to be tampering with 'best before' dates of food products and selling unsafe food to customers to reduce monetary loss due to spoilage. Undaunted by this apparent callous disregard for the safety of consumers on the part of Loblaws, the Ontario Government proceeded to issue the grocery chain a license to sell alcohol, one of our most risk-laden consumer products.

There had been more concerns raised about how the LCBO, the Ontario government, and the alcohol industry conducted their business partnership. A variety of controversies had arisen with respect to:

> *- a lack of transparency on pricing amidst allegations of market manipulation (Cohn 2014)*
>
> *- the introduction of legislative changes to nullify a class action suit against the government for "price-fixing" (Gray 2015)*
>
> *- former government employees becoming lobbyists for the alcohol manufacturers (Morrow 2015)*
>
> *- a secretive practice of routine largess in the provision of alcohol products for foreign diplomats (Brennan 2015)*
>
> *- inadequate privacy protection for customers (Jones 2015)*

The Ontario government's approach to alcohol regulation has historically fallen significantly short of the integrity, diligence and transparency that comprise the gold standard in matters of public health protection.

The picture was no better in provinces outside of Ontario. In fact, it was worse. A Canada-wide study found that Ontario achieved the highest rating for regulatory practices among Canadian provinces. Giesbrecht et al. (2013) compared the provinces on a variety of alcohol policy domains and generated an overall score for each province as a percentage of the ideal score. The national average was below 50% and no province achieved a score as high as 60%.

The overall picture was that alcohol industry regulation in Canada was not simply less than perfect; it was substantially less than adequate, falling significantly short of evidence-informed regulatory practice. We would expect this shortfall to contribute towards the perennial high levels of personal and societal harm.

Canadian jurisdictions were not alone in alcohol industry regulatory shortcomings. Xuan et al. (2014) provided an account of how alcohol policies in the United States also fall short of best practices. An examination of the alcohol industry's conduct would not be complete without reference to its targeting developing countries to ensure market growth. Karnani (2013) reported on the role of alcohol in developing countries to precipitate and worsen poverty, and the role of the industry in exploiting poor and illiterate populations with its deceptive advertising. This work also exposed how the industry bribed corrupt governments for regulatory frameworks that were favourable to the industry's commercial interests at the expense of human welfare.

In summary, the alcohol industry had an established history of illegal and unethical activity. It misled governments and the public, and ignored, minimized, and concealed the known harms associated with its product. Government regulation of the industry had demonstrated several shortcomings. This included product quality assurance, a failure to implement evidence-based policy, and government-industry collusion. Sometimes the covert collusion furthered the industry's commercial interests at the expense of public health. Most notably, the alcohol industry had shown a chronic disregard for public health and human welfare, sometimes preying upon the most vulnerable populations. The industry and government continued to be rewarded with substantial revenues, while healthcare and social service systems struggled to keep pace with the enormous levels of alcohol-related harm.

American academic and alcohol policy researcher, Thomas Babor, had this to say of prospects for working with the industry to reform it: "...working in partnership with the alcohol industry is likely to lead to ineffective or compromised policy and is best avoided by governments, the scientific community and the NGOs" (Babor 2010).

In the wake of the harm, the reader is reminded that the alcohol industry, like the tobacco industry, is made up of legal, government-regulated corporations. The legacies of these recreational drug industries were unsavoury. We might expect better from an industry with a mandate to produce therapeutic drug products. And yet, the pharmaceutical industry may be the worst of the three. Surprised? Read on.

Pharmaceutical Corporations

The pharmaceutical industry is made up of legal, government-regulated, corporations.

By 2016, when Canada's cannabis legalization campaign was in full swing, the country, like much of the western world, was gripped in a crisis of opioid-related overdoses and deaths. While many of these deaths were caused by the illicit trade in opioids the catalyst lay with legal pharmaceutical corporations.

Except for a few hot-spots such as the Downtown East side of Vancouver, opioid dependence was not a widespread problem in Canada for almost all the twentieth century. This changed with the introduction of highly addictive oxycodone painkillers by legal pharmaceutical companies in the mid-1990s. Most notably, Purdue Pharmaceutical generated billions of dollars in annual revenues with its OxyContin product in both the US and Canada. This was achieved primarily through aggressive, misleading, and illegal marketing to prescribers, leading to large numbers of pain sufferers becoming dependent upon the medication (Van Zee 2009).

The problem was officially flagged in Canada as early as 2004 in The Government of Newfoundland and Labrador *Oxycontin Task Force Final Report* (2004, 22, 5). In recognition of the harmful marketing practices, it recommended "...that Health Canada ensure that pharmaceutical manufacturers use appropriate marketing strategies that includes information on the dangers of drug abuse and diversion." The Task Force also recommended strengthening "...the role of Health Canada in monitoring and auditing sales of controlled substances and investigating adverse drug events." And to implement "...legislative and regulatory amendments to facilitate investigation and intervention." Health Canada was not inspired to act.

Within a decade, an escalation of the opioid epidemic was clearly apparent. Ontario data on opioid-related mortality in 2013, showed the province recorded 638 opioid-related deaths (Martins et al. 2016), a substantial increase from the 165 deaths recorded in 1992 (Gomes et al. 2014). Gomes et al. also reported a three-fold increase in years of potential life lost (YLL) between 1991 and 2010. A later survey of provincial health authorities showed that the problem prevailed across Canada and suggested that the overall prevalence of opioid-related deaths had not diminished between 2014 and 2016 (The Canadian Press 2016). By 2016, yet another epidemic of harm, launched by a legal drug industry, was in plain evidence.

Canadian government regulators did not react before the extent of harm had reached epidemic levels bringing an intensification of criticism of the Canadian government's lack of pre-emptive action. Federal Health Minister at the time, Rona Ambrose, attempted to defend her department by noting that Health Canada's guidelines allowed it to consider only a medicine's effectiveness for its intended purpose (painkiller in this case) and not its potential for public health or safety implications (Ivison 2015). This is an astounding and unsettling statement. It seems to be an admission from the minister that Canada's regulatory regime for the pharmaceutical industry was inadequate for the public's protection.

Minister Ambrose would be the first of four consecutive Canadian federal health ministers, from two different political parties, to publicly acknowledge the rising opioid-related mortality. Ambrose declared that "Prescription drug abuse and addiction is a significant public health concern across Canada" (Canada 2015). Her successor, Dr. Jane Philpott, was reported by *The Globe and Mail* as referring to the current opioid epidemic in Canada as a national public health crisis (Kirkup 2016). Philpott's successor, Ginette Petitpas Taylor, likewise offered: "I would definitely say that it's a public health crisis right now" (Wells 2017). (As described in Chapter 1, the next Health Minister, Patti Hajdu, would also acknowledge the crisis in December 2019.)

In its coverage of the Purdue OxyContin story in Canada, *The Globe and Mail* (Robertson 2016b) reported that the President of Purdue Pharma Canada, Mr. John H. Stewart had sought to minimize Purdue's culpability. The story quotes Stewart saying: "The answer to abuse of prescription medications is greater education and substance-abuse treatment. The answer to diversion is tough law enforcement, not restrictions on patients and physicians who treat them."

While no governments in Canada brought criminal charges against any pharmaceutical companies or their executives, civil class actions against Purdue had been launched in almost all Canadian provinces, and the parties were negotiating a nation-wide settlement. The intent was to resolve all pending OxyContin-related class actions across the country (M. Branco, Siskinds LLP, email to author, December 5, 2016). There were no actions naming Health Canada as a defendant or co-defendant.

The opioid epidemic, and its wake of tragedy, continued to persist and mutate in Canada through the emergence of a contraband trade in other prescribed opioids, such as fentanyl (Fischer 2016). In most Canadian provinces, fentanyl appeared to be a major contributor to the continuing crisis (The Canadian Press 2016). A *Prescription Opioid Policy Framework* produced by the Centre for Addiction and Mental Health (2016a) reported that the fentanyl problem consisted of both legal diverted product and analogue product. The *Framework* also reported an increase in the use of street heroin. By early 2017, another opioid drug with high potential for overdose, carfentanil, was beginning to capture the attention of enforcement, public health authorities, and the media in Canada (CTV News 2017).

In November 2016, Health Canada released "Health Canada's Action on Opioid Misuse"—a plan, presented publicly in poster-style, that outlined the government's efforts to address the current epidemic of opioid-related harm. It listed five major areas for intervention. Conspicuous by its absence, was any onus placed upon the industry to promote its products in an accurate and responsible manner that would place the welfare of Canadians before the industry's revenue interests. Nor was there any indication of intent on the part of Health Canada to better regulate the industry to prevent such crises in the future (Health Canada 2016a). On November 18, 2016, a one-day Opioid Conference was hosted by Dr. Jane Philpott, Federal Minister of Health on behalf of Health Canada and by Dr. Eric Hoskins, Minister of Health on behalf of the Province of Ontario. The gathering was held in Ottawa and webcast live. The agenda provided an impressive list of pertinent issues. However, it too stopped short of including an item on the importance of improving regulation of the pharmaceutical industry or of using the justice system to introduce deterrents to industry malfeasance (Health Canada 2016b).

By 2017, Philpott and Hoskins were reportedly having some conversations about legal action against Purdue to recover healthcare costs (Howlett 2017). Both ministers eventually left their respective posts with no legal action in sight.

Health Canada continued to come under criticism for placing the fiscal interests of the pharmaceutical industry ahead of protecting public health. There were also calls for a revised regulatory framework (Lexchin and Kohler 2011; Centre for Addiction and Mental Health 2016a).

Despite the enormous amount of premeditated harm perpetrated by Purdue no one from the company had gone to prison. However, Walter James McCormick, a street dealer in British Columbia, did. In January of 2017, he was convicted of trafficking in fentanyl and sentenced to fourteen years in prison. Presiding Justice Bonnie Craig admonished McCormick for contributing to the suffering and potential death of others. But she may have shown some insight into the bigger picture when she added: "McCormick did not create the problem with opioid addiction in the community. He is just one of the players in a far more complicated problem" (McElroy 2017). McCormick is not alone in his treatment by the judicial system. Fentanyl street dealers in Alberta and Ontario have faced manslaughter charges (The Canadian Press 2017b).

As the epidemic grew in the United States, Purdue executives were found guilty of knowingly making false claims about the addiction potential of the drug and fraudulently marketing a drug for an unapproved use (CBC News 2007). The company paid a settlement of $634 million. No individuals were punished. Purdue US blamed the problems on lower-level employees who made "misstatements." It did, however, shortly thereafter announce the "retirement" of its CEO, a position that was filled, in 2007, by the previously mentioned Mr. John H. Stewart, who had been President of Purdue Canada. By 2012, the US Senate Committee on Finance was chastising Mr. Stewart. The Committee was concerned about the continued economic harm the company was doing to the health insurance industry and about Purdue's lack of cooperation in responding to the government's requests for information. Shortly thereafter, Mr. Stewart left Purdue (Robertson 2016b). But he would, intriguingly, resurface again in Canada's cannabis industry—an interesting story I will share later in this chapter.

While there were no criminal charges laid against industry executives related to opioids in Canada, federal and state authorities in the US had been more hawkish. US Federal authorities had charged six former Insys Therapeutics Inc. executives and managers with bribery of physicians to prescribe an opioid medication containing fentanyl for off-label purposes, and with misleading insurers to secure authorization of payment. Insys had already settled one case for similar claims in Oregon. Other similar legal actions against Insys were underway in at least five other states (Thomson Reuters 2016).

The substantial levels of human carnage from the opioid crisis continued to be heavily covered in the media. One would think that this extensive adverse coverage, or at the very least, the line-up of litigants, might give Purdue cause to proceed more responsibly with its opioid products in the future. This did not appear to be the case. Ryan et al. (2016) reported that, with the diminished North American market for OxyContin because of the controversy and of reduced prescribing of the drug, Purdue turned its attention elsewhere. The company was implementing a massive migration of its OxyContin campaign into Latin America, Asia, the Middle East, Africa, and other regions using the same marketing tactics that were employed in North America. The tactics included a notable addition to the arsenal of marketing memes—the company's intent to combat "opiophobia." Promotional videos prepared for the foreign markets featured people of diverse ethnicities and proclaimed: "We're only just getting started." Perhaps the most frightening aspect of such an expansion was that it would target less developed nations with much less capacity than that of Canada and the United States to effectively cope with the coming epidemics. The outcomes could be horrific. These countries also possessed less capacity to seek legal redress from Purdue for any harms incurred.

Harm from pharmaceutical products is not restricted to opioid medications. As early as 2013, Canada's National Advisory Committee on Prescription Drug Misuse noted that for prescribed opioids, sedative-hypnotics, and stimulants "the associated harms have become a leading public health and safety concern" (National Advisory Committee on Prescription Drug Misuse 2013, 1). In May of 2015, Canada's Minister of Health, Rona Ambrose, announced that "Prescription drug abuse and addiction is a significant public health concern across Canada" (Canada 2015).

The rarely discussed aspect of such epidemics was the role of the pharmaceutical industry in their genesis. An indispensable context is that the malfeasance of the pharmaceutical industry in the current opioid crisis was not an isolated case. There is a voluminous literature on the international, indiscriminate profiteering of the industry at the expense of both the public's health and of the credibility of government regulation.

The literature that detailed this bleak situation was effectively summarized by Dukes, Braithwaite, and Moloney in their book Pharmaceuticals, Corporate Crime and Public Health (2014). As a writing team, the authors brought impressive credentials to this work, not only as academics but also from experience in international regulation of the pharmaceutical industry with the World Health Organization and from employment within the pharmaceutical industry itself. Their findings arose from court cases, investigative journalism, a broad collection of government investigations and health/justice agency reports, and from papers published in highly-regarded peer-reviewed academic journals including, among others: The British Medical Journal, The Lancet, The Journal of the American Medical Association, California Law Review, The New England Journal of Medicine, The British Journal of Psychiatry, The American Bar Association Journal, The Journal of Law Medicine and Ethics, The International Journal of Epidemiology, and Nature.

Drawing from cases dating back to the 1950s, the authors provided an account of more than a half century of international industry misconduct in its relationships with customers, health care professions, researchers, research subjects, and government regulators and other bodies. The dizzying list of perfidy includes: withholding and ignoring evidence of harm in test trials; agreeing to testing protocols and then ignoring them; intimidation of researchers; manipulation of supply chains, research practices and findings; testing new drugs in countries with weak regulations thus exposing vulnerable populations to harm; deaths of infants and children resulting from the conduct of illegal trials in which parents were pressured into providing uninformed consent; non-payment of court-ordered settlements to parents whose children died in the trials; recruitment of unemployed vulnerable subjects onto research subject panels; use of prisoners as subjects; testing of experimental drugs without informing subjects of the availability, at no cost, of similar products already established as safe; fabricating research data from nonexistent patients; suppression of uncooperative investigators; ignoring consumer complaints; falsifying reports; forcing less senior executives to take the blame for CEO decisions; workplace safety infractions at manufacturing facilities; use of off-shore havens to avoid taxation; use of advertising content that is not evidence-based; overly-aggressive, misleading, and illegal advertising and marketing practices; imposing restrictions on the availability of drugs to countries that are not industry-friendly in their regulation; untruthful "public awareness" campaigns; tampering with court proceedings and legislative processes; abuses of international conventions; selling drugs to publicly-funded Medicare programs at inflated prices; failing to keep promises to increase research and development and create new employment in the sector; circumventing competition law, patent law, and safety laws; misleading patent offices to secure patents; bribery; collection of tax breaks from donations of expiring drugs that were useless or likely to do more harm than good to the recipients; use of patent protection to prevent promising research; creation of exploitive monopolies, engagement in anti-trust activity; price-fixing and insider-trading; environmental violations, and animal rights infractions.

Dukes and colleagues also detailed repeated failure of government regulation to prevent and effectively hold the industry accountable for its misconduct, including: allowance of high-risk, highly-profitable drugs on the market; insufficient fines to act as deterrents; lack of administrative or legal action on unpaid fines; not enforcing requirements for ethics review; industry whistle-blowers were not protected and sometimes prosecuted by the state; and complicity of regulators with the industry in the commission of crimes.

Early in the book, the authors recounted the infamous thalidomide case from the late 1950s-early 1960s. Any person with intact conscience might think that such an atrocity would have forever deterred industry carelessness or malfeasance in bringing a new product to market, but not so for the international pharmaceutical industry. One might also think that such a calamity would place government regulators on perpetual heightened alert to avert a repeat event. In contrast, the authors detailed a legacy of cases that were just as disturbing in their blatant disregard for human welfare. The authors also described how government regulation repeatedly failed to meaningfully deter misconduct and neglect by the industry. The norm for penalties appeared to be government-imposed fines and out-of-court civil settlements in amounts that may seem enormous to the average person but were clearly insufficient to deter continued malfeasance by the companies involved. The US-based organization, Public Citizen reported that between 1991 and 2012, US pharmaceutical companies settled at least 239 cases for a total of $30.2 billion (Almashat and Wolfe 2012). It is noteworthy that fines and settlements primarily punish company shareholders and are not targeted to the executives who make the decisions. Industry executives engaged in corrupt practices tended to go unpunished while continuing to receive extraordinarily high levels of remuneration.

Unfortunately, the bulk of misconduct cannot be dismissed as the actions of a few bad apples operating in a few outlier jurisdictions with weak regulation. By my count, Dukes and colleagues' accounting of the wrongdoing touched upon no less than sixty-four companies located in no less than thirty-one countries spread across all well-populated continents. This was not just a few bad apples. This was an orchard-wide blight. Companies with serial infractions were not uncommon. Some of the infractions were committed by companies operating in highly vulnerable developing countries or had victims in those countries.

Bogdanich and Kolimay (2003) described such a case. Cutter Biological, a division of the Bayer pharmaceutical company, knowingly produced and sold millions of dollars of HIV-infected blood-clotting product to Asia and Latin America. This happened after the Food and Drug Administration (FDA) in the US and European regulators had banned the product. The sales to Asia and Latin America contravened the company's promise to regulators that it would not continue to sell the old, infected product since it now had a new safe version which it was selling in the US. The result was that an un-

132

knowable number of overseas hemophiliacs would have been infected. In the face of concerns raised over such outcomes, a Bayer spokesperson insisted that the company had "behaved responsibly, ethically and humanely" in selling the older tainted product overseas. Bogdanich and Kolimay also reported that during the controversy, a senior FDA official had instructed FDA staff that the issue should be "...quietly solved without alerting the Congress, the medical community and the public."

Canada was not excluded from the global scourge of pharmaceutical industry turpitude and government regulatory failure. While the opioid epidemic provided the most recent well-known case of corporate wrong-doing and regulatory failure in Canada, there had been many other disturbing cases.

Dukes, Braithwaite, and Moloney (2014) recounted the 1993 abolition of compulsory licensing of medicines in Canada. This act was expected to raise the average price of medicines in Canada, but the industry had promised, in return for higher revenues, to increase its research and development activity and to create new employment. Dukes and colleagues cited a report by Lexchin (1997) that showed that the promises, four years later, had remained unfulfilled. Lexchin also provided a revealing overarching picture of pharmaceutical industry-government relations in Canada and the adverse impact upon users of medicines. Disregard for public health in the pursuit of revenue on the part of the Canadian pharmaceutical industry had persisted as had the failure of the Canadian government and of its regulatory body, Health Canada, to effectively regulate pharmaceutical corporations.

More examples had been revealed in a series of reports published by the *Toronto Star*. The first article in the series (Bruser and McLean 2014a) provided evidence that consumers had been exposed to defective and potentially unsafe prescription drugs that Canadian pharmaceutical companies knowingly sold. The investigation also revealed that some companies failed to divulge evidence of side-effects suffered by consumers. The companies attempted to hide the evidence by either destroying files or altering their contents. Between 2008 and 2014, over forty Canadian companies had been cited for "serious manufacturing violations" by Health Canada.

A second article in the series (Bruser and McLean 2014b), showed that an order by Health Canada to stop imports of suspect drugs from an Indian company to its Canadian subsidiary was simply ignored by the manufacturer. There was no follow-up from Health Canada. Once the story became public, Health Canada quickly took more formal and aggressive regulatory action to ban more than thirty drugs and approximately thirty drug ingredients from the manufacturer. This story provides a telling aspect of the current relationship between the pharmaceutical industry and government regulation. The Canadian subsidiary took legal action against Health Canada for its infringement of the manufacturer's commercial entitlements (McLean and Bruser 2015).

Such legal actions were facilitated by the North American Free Trade Agreement (NAFTA) -- still in effect at the time. Canada had been a frequent target for such actions (Sinclair 2015). In 2016, the Canada-European Union

Comprehensive Economic and Trade Agreement (CETA), another international trade agreement, threatened to extend such provisions across a much larger part of the globe (Nelson 2016). Such mechanisms provided an ongoing opportunity for emboldened corporate malfeasance within a context of regulatory weakness.

A third instalment of the *Toronto Star* series showed that in 2013 and 2014, twenty-four Canadian pharmaceutical companies had been found to be non-compliant with Health Canada regulations, and that nearly one-third had terms and conditions on their licenses. Such terms and conditions had been imposed by regulators in response to identified problems that could pose a threat to consumers (McLean and Bruser 2014).

A disturbing aspect of these stories was that the journalists did not acquire their information from Health Canada but rather from the website of the US Food and Drug Administration. The history of Health Canada's knowledge of the defective products remained as confidential information within Canada and was not available to the public. Other investigations had unearthed more examples of industry/Health Canada secrecy regarding acetaminophen overdoses (Yang and Cribb 2015) and medication for the treatment of nausea and vomiting during pregnancy (Crowe 2015). Such cases have led two Toronto-based health sciences academics to refer to "...the disgraceful culture of secrecy at Health Canada" (Persaud and Juurlink 2015).

Malfeasance in the Canadian pharmaceutical industry was not limited to the manufacturers. Criminality and fiscal irregularity had also been exposed in the retail arm of the industry. A Canadian pharmacist and seven others had been charged with trafficking narcotics through a community pharmacy (Wetselaar 2015). In a separate case tax auditors at Revenue Canada found $58 million in hidden income by Canadian pharmacies. Fines were levied but no charges were laid. The commission of tax avoidance was ill-timed by pharmacies. Some of them were applying to Health Canada to become retail outlets for therapeutic cannabis at the time. The Canadian Pharmacists Association supported the applications by noting that Canadians "trust pharmacists" (Beeby 2016).

The Canadian government's favourable and lenient orientation to the pharmaceutical industry had been demonstrated in an opinion piece (Ogilvie and Eggleton 2015) published in the *Toronto Star* by Kelvin Ogilvie and Art Eggleton. Ogilvie and Eggleton were, respectively, the Chair and Deputy Chair of the Standing Senate Committee on Social Affairs, Science and Technology. The Committee had just issued a report on Prescription Pharmaceuticals in Canada (Standing Committee on Social Affairs, Science and Technology 2015). The main thrust of the report, and particularly of the companion opinion piece in the *Star*, was to draw attention to Health Canada's wide-ranging regulatory ineffectiveness, even citing "...the department's failure to provide our Senate committee with reliable testimony." The opinion piece and the report provided little more than a timid insinuation of the culpability of the pharmaceutical industry in Canada. Unfortunately, the

Committee's approach probably sent a mixed message to Canada's regulator—that the government expects them to effectively regulate the industry, but that the regulator should not expect that government will have its back when Big Pharma pushes back. Health Canada apparently found itself in the unenviable position of having to work under constraints imposed by a government that is apparently loath to publicly call-out the pharmaceutical industry for its misdeeds.

The statements from the Standing Senate Committee on Health Canada's role in the country's pharmaceutical industry problems were consistent with commentary by Dukes, Braithwaite, and Moloney (2014) regarding a tendency for state issued punitive actions to focus on, or at least to include, its regulators. However, government sanctions against regulators in Canada have been less onerous than those invoked elsewhere. Dukes and colleagues (2014, 196, 193) cited a US example of a ring of Food and Drug Administration and industry employees who colluded in criminal acts. They were sentenced to prison as well as ordered to pay fines and provide community service. In another case, the Head of China's State Food and Drug Administration was found guilty of gross corruption. He had accepted 5.5 million yuan (approximately $3.3 million Cdn) in bribes to approve drugs that were, in some cases, known to be dangerous. The official was executed by the state.

This section of the report on the pharmaceutical industry has attempted to highlight Canadian cases set against the international backdrop described by Dukes and colleagues. It is important to keep in mind that the pharmaceutical industry is a global multi-national entity. This means that some of the harmful practices, while not occurring in Canada specifically, could have had a global impact and therefore still affected the well-being of Canadians. Examples would include tampering with research trials and published findings, misleading advertising in medical journals, as well as the manipulation of patent law, international supply chains, and international conventions. A deeper dive on the Health Canada and Canadian pharmaceutical industry axis of collusion is available in Lexchin's 2016 book *Private Profits versus Public Policy: The Pharmaceutical Industry and the Canadian State.*

Clearly, there is a disturbing culture of inhumanity that pervades the upper echelons of the pharmaceutical industry. We are challenged to imagine how such a culture could exist within a civil society and be tolerated by a government that held genuine concern for the welfare of its citizenry and humanity in general. The cases presented here show the enormity of the challenge before us in reforming these cultures of indifference within both the industry and government.

Before concluding this evaluation of the pharmaceutical industry's conduct, it must be acknowledged that, unlike the products of the tobacco and alcohol industries, many of the pharmaceutical industry's products have improved the health status of international populations. Some of its products have saved many lives. For this important and honourable role, the industry and its leaders are very handsomely compensated with an elevated standing in Canadian society that includes financial rewards and other entitlements that are far out of the reach of almost all Canadians. But what a civilized society should not do is to further entitle the captains of this industry by allowing them, at their convenience, to game and ignore legislation in a relentless attempt to gain even more wealth. All too often this pursuit had been at the expense of the public's health and safety. Neither should a civilized society abide government regulation that too often responded to industry turpitude with secrecy, silence, and distraction. The pharmaceutical industry, like the tobacco and alcohol industries, is made up of legal, government-regulated, corporations.

Three Legal, Government Regulated Drug Industries

For decades, disregard for public health protection, breaches of ethical business practices, and even blatant criminality, have been witnessed among tobacco, alcohol, and pharmaceutical companies. In many cases, these practices posed serious risks and adverse consequences for people. Quality control of legal recreational and therapeutic drug products has, at times, been substandard. Flawed, and even potentially dangerous products, have sometimes been the result of neglect by producers, retailers, and regulators. All this provided three important lessons:

- *legalization of a drug trade was no guarantee of product integrity and safety*

- *revenue-driven legal corporations could not be relied upon to temper their pursuit of profit with the protection of public health, business ethics, and respect for the rule of law*

- *government regulatory oversight had been typically accommodating of industry misconduct; accordingly, it had failed to deter and reform corporate malfeasance, which continued unabated, decade after decade, across all legal drug industries.*

These are painful lessons. And they are unacceptable. People should be able to expect that their government will protect them from the consequences of industry wrongdoing. Too often, government regulation failed to do so, and in the worst cases, was complicit with industry in the misconduct. There was little reason for optimism that corporate conduct and regulatory performance would be any better for a new cannabis industry.

With the legacies established by these three industries in Canada and abroad, and the failure of regulation to contain these juggernauts, one wonders why the Canadian government thought that the same industry model would be a good one to adopt for cannabis. The legalization of cannabis provided government with an opportunity to establish a regulatory approach that would get it right. The information was readily available in the government's own documentation, in the research that it had funded, and in the advice provided by health policy authorities during the consultation phase of legislative development. While the advice was occasionally ac-knowledged, and in a very few cases implemented, the disturbing evidence from our other drug industries ultimately would not play a significant role in guiding the development of cannabis legislation.

NEW KID IN TOWN: EARLY LESSONS FROM THE LEGAL CANNABIS INDUSTRY

The legacy of perilous conduct by legal drug corporations was a har-binger of what was possible with the establishment of a new revenue-driven drug industry. The studies, reports and data sets referenced in this chapter were all available at the time that the Canadian government was developing its plan to legalize cannabis for recreational use. Many of them were sent to the government through its Task Force. We made it easy for them. The warnings were in plain sight for all who were willing to heed them.

Undaunted by the evidence, Canada's legislators apparently had no appetite for considering alternatives to the traditional corporate commercial model. An extensive evidence-based report on cannabis law reform pub-lished by the RAND Corporation (Caulkins et al. 2015) in the United States stopped short of recommending a specific cannabis law reform model. However, one of its key recommendations was that jurisdictions should avoid moving, by default, from prohibition directly to commercial legaliza-tion, and described several alternative approaches. Many submissions from policy experts to the Canadian government also alluded to the perils of a commercial corporate model and described alternatives. As we will see later, these submissions were acknowledged by government, but the warnings and prescriptions ultimately went unheeded.

The legacy of our other legal commercial drug industries was not the only source of pertinent lessons to inform the legalization of cannabis for recreational use. There were also important lessons to be drawn from can-nabis legalization for therapeutic and recreational use at the state level in the United States, and from legalization for therapeutic use in Canada.

Legalization for Therapeutic (Medical) and Recreational Use in the United States

At the time of Canada's recreational legalization campaign, state-level cannabis legalization in the US had occurred widely for therapeutic use years earlier. More recently a few states had legalized for recreational use as well. Both developments south of the border provided transferable insights on what to expect from a commercial cannabis industry. The US corporate experience included an alarming indifference to public health protection and the law -- manifested as problems with product safety and unethical/illegal business practices. All the information cited in this section was available during Canada's legalization campaign for recreational use.

Product Quality and Safety Issues

A persuasive argument for legalization has been that illegal cannabis was of unknown potency and was often contaminated, thus posing a safety risk to users. However, there were clear and largely ignored warnings about the safety of legal product in the United States, particularly regarding pesticide contamination. As early as 2014, reports were appearing from both Maine and California of illegal pesticides being detected on cannabis products sold in legal medical cannabis dispensaries (Stone 2014).

Analysis of therapeutic cannabis samples had also revealed a problem with inconsistent product strength resulting in both insufficient and excessive dosing with particular concern expressed around edibles which have been found to be inconsistent in potency and inaccurately labelled (Thomas et al. 2015).

Colorado was the first state jurisdiction in the United States to legalize the sale of cannabis for recreational use. Retail carelessness and permissive regulation were apparent from the beginning. Similar problems arose in the ever-expanding legal recreational trade in other states. The problems of under-reported THC levels, along with the detection of dangerously elevated levels of pesticides drew added attention to the retail of cannabis edibles, often sold in a form (e.g., cookies) that would be attractive to children. The legalization of edibles was associated with increased hospitalization of children for treatment of toxic reactions from inadvertent ingestion (Rocky Mountain High Intensity Drug Trafficking Area 2014; Wang et al. 2016). According to a statement from Dr. Patricia Daly, the Chief Medical Health Officer for Coastal Health in British Columbia, THC ingestion in very young children can depress respiration and lead to coma (Brown and Corday 2016). The prevention of children ingesting potentially toxic pesticides as well as high levels of THC should have been a regulatory priority for the Canadian government. As we will see in the next chapter, that did not appear to be the case.

Industry Conduct and Government Regulation

Upon legalization for recreational use, it did not take long for the cannabis industry to demonstrate its indifference to public health protection. An interesting example (Gazette 2016) came from Colorado where the industry successfully manipulated the political system to sabotage the introduction of public health measures. States, including Colorado, legalized recreational cannabis through a mechanism known as ballot initiatives. This involves a sponsor collecting a minimum number of signatures from eligible voters for the initiative to continue to a ballot on which people can cast a vote. In Colorado, and eventually elsewhere, more people voted for legalization than against it. The state government was then obliged to create the necessary legislation within a prescribed period. Following successful legalization for recreational use in Colorado, Ballot Initiative 139 was a grass-roots-initiated attempt to introduce measures intended to protect the public's health. The proposed measures included child proof cannabis containers, lower product potency, and health warnings on container labels—all common public health protection measures for drug products. But the Colorado cannabis industry had other priorities. First, the industry tried to use the courts to prevent these changes, arguing among other things, that the provisions would substantially decrease the marketability of products—an infringement of their commercial freedom. That attempt was not successful.

The industry then tried a different approach. There are companies that have effective systems for collecting large numbers of signatures to support ballot initiatives. The cannabis industry paid all signature collection companies in the state of Colorado not to work on Ballot Initiative 139. When Initiative 139 sponsors attempted to hire a company from Arizona, the industry paid off that company as well. This effectively sabotaged the required documentation of public support to allow Initiative 139 to continue (Gazette 2016). This is a powerful demonstration of the industry's contempt not only for public health protection but also for the very democratic process that had allowed the industry to come into existence in the first place.

One might argue that Canada's political system is sufficiently different that such strategies would not be possible. However, this argument misses the key point. In pursuit of revenue maximization, the industry may be inclined to exploit whatever regulatory vulnerabilities or legislative mechanisms are available within any given jurisdiction. The Canadian cannabis industry would prove itself to be just as wily as its American counterpart.

Outright disregard for the rule of law in pursuit of revenue maximization was also demonstrated in the US through violations of tax law. Tax evasion by legal regulated medical cannabis retail outlets was documented in Washington State. Kleiman et al. (2015) estimated that reported sales of legal cannabis for tax purposes were barely one-fifth of actual sales. Other improprieties from the US experience included conflicts of interest among lawmakers and public officials with ties to the cannabis industry (Nirappil 2017). Based upon the US experience, the prospect of a strictly regulated, law-abiding cannabis industry in Canada should have been seen as a potentially risky bet.

Legalization for Therapeutic (Medical) Use in Canada

The Path to Establishing a Commercial Cannabis Industry

As described in the chapter on the history of cannabis law reform in Canada, the journey from prohibition to legalization for therapeutic, and then recreational use, was a tumultuous one. In 2013, the Marihuana for Medical Purposes Regulations (MMPR), established a licensing system for commercial growers who could sell directly to medically authorized patients by a mail order system. This marked the beginning of the corporatization of cannabis in Canada. The establishment of this infrastructure would serve as the proverbial foot in the door and provide a convenient foundation for the eventual commercial legalization of cannabis for recreational use.

From the beginning, cannabis as medicine was not provided to patients with the customary due diligence with which other medicines were prescribed and dispensed (Wilkinson and D'Souza 2014). Under the MMPR, the process of acquiring medicine fell short of what most people would assume to be in place. This included:

- *a diagnosis of a specific condition for which there is clinical trial evidence for cannabis as effective medicine*

- *the diagnosis is made, and the authorization issued, by a formally trained and licensed, knowledgeable health care professional working in a regulated health care facility*

- *the dispensing of the medicine is overseen by a formally trained and licensed, knowledgeable health care professional working in a regulated health care facility.*

A credible base of information to guide authorization of patients was very sparse at the time. There was no established body of clinical trial evidence demonstrating that cannabis was therapeutically effective for its alleged and practised applications of the time. Some portion of cannabis users may very well have benefited therapeutically from their use of cannabis. However, the point is that no medicine produced by a pharmaceutical company could be brought to market without the weight of convincing clinical trials. The status of cannabis, as medicine, was an anomaly. In the best of scenarios, authorization was granted by licensed health care providers with compassion and good intentions, but with a level of knowledge limited by the state of clinical trial evidence.

Largely unaffected by the MMPR was the chaotic system of retail that continued to prevail. The medicine was dispensed by the manufacturer by mail, not in person by a licensed professional outlet such as a pharmacy. These were the prevailing legal conditions at the time. All other commercial mechanisms for the acquisition of cannabis for therapeutic use, including the grey market dispensaries, were illegal. The qualifications of the dispensing staff ranged perilously from self-taught to non-existent. The confusing mosaic of options, dominated by these dispensaries, arose from the haphazard and incoherent way in which the therapeutic cannabis industry in Canada was designed and implemented.

A report filed by a journalist (CBC News 2015a) provides a typical account for the period. While in Vancouver on an assignment unrelated to cannabis, the journalist was approached on the street by a sales representative of a nearby cannabis dispensary. He was invited to apply for a card that would authorize the purchase of cannabis for therapeutic use. Recognizing the opportunity for an interesting story, the journalist obliged. Once at the dispensary, the journalist attended an interview with a naturopath via remote video connection. A few questions revealed that the reporter was under stress in his job, which was considered cause for the issuance of a card to purchase cannabis as a therapeutic intervention.

Increasingly, cannabis dispensaries dropped the pretense of an assessment altogether. The same *CBC* report told of another Vancouver operation dispensing cannabis product from a vending machine. Such a *laissez-faire* approach to supplying cannabis to patients prevailed across the country.

Despite repeated attempts by the federal government to rationalize the legislative oversight and mechanics of the cannabis trade, problems remained. The legally tenuous dispensaries continued to operate in a manner inconsistent with how medicine is customarily prescribed and dispensed, extracting private revenue from a clientele that was using cannabis for one or both of two purposes: questionably substantiated therapeutic use and illegal recreational use under the guise of therapeutic use. The line between therapeutic and recreational use could be a thin or blurred one.

The job of closing illegal dispensaries was left to local law enforcement where limited capacity, and perhaps limited interest in some jurisdictions, made intervention sporadic and seemingly haphazard with unsustainable impact. The wily dispensaries ventured on in full defiance of the law, often with the begrudged tolerance of municipal authorities. This would not substantially change until after legalization for recreational purposes occurred in October 2018.

Few Canadians would be inclined to challenge the foundational principle of legalization for the therapeutic use of cannabis -- that people have a right of access to their medicine. However, there is a valid question about whether, in the year 2000, cannabis could be considered as effective medicine. (I provide a review of more recent clinical trial evidence for cannabis as medicine in Chapter 10—which is more supportive.)

However, in 2000, cannabis advocates, paraded their compassion for supplying medicine—but without accepting the customary prerequisites for therapeutic legitimacy. These requirements are an important legal/social construct, having a long legacy of protecting us from nefarious mongers of fraudulent remedies.

There may very well have been benefits for some people who had been using cannabis. There were also increasing numbers of legitimate practitioners who authorized use with the appropriate caution, if not with compelling evidence. However, there is a simple principle which could have guided the use of cannabis for therapeutic use. If cannabis were to be legal medicine, then it should be treated as medicine in the same manner as any other controlled pharmaceutical product.

In the early years of legalization for therapeutic use, the clinical trial evidence for the use of cannabis as medicine was tenuous at best. Accordingly, one might expect the government to have made immediate arrangements for setting up a substantial funding stream for properly conducted clinical research. That did not happen.

Since 2000, two different Canadian political parties had formed three different federal governments and failed to effectively address the situation. The seemingly premature legislating of the drug's provision for therapeutic use was an anomaly in Canadian law and health policy. For those people who found therapeutic benefits from cannabis use, decriminalization, without penalization, would have done just fine.

As we will see in the next chapter, the journey to legalization for recreational use was no less tumultuous.

Product Quality and Safety Issues

A long-held justification for commercial legalization had been the lack of quality control in an illegal unregulated cannabis trade. Health Canada used such concerns when it trumpeted the government's establishment of licensed commercial cannabis production for therapeutic use. In announcing the new regulations, Health Canada proclaimed that the regulations "...will provide access to quality-controlled marihuana for medical purposes, produced under secure and sanitary conditions, to those Canadians who need it, while strengthening the safety of Canadian communities" (Canada 2013).

Quality control as a major talking point in the years leading up to legalization for recreational use prompted analyses of samples from illegal dispensaries in Toronto, which confirmed inaccurate labelling and contamination as problems (Robertson and McArthur 2016a; 2016b). A high level of quality control would provide a clear advantage of a legal, government-regulated industry over an unregulated system. This advantage was lauded in the cannabis legalization framework document produced by The Centre for Addiction and Mental Health (2014) and in two reports from the federal government's Task Force: The Task Force on Marijuana Legalization and Regulation (2016) and The Task Force on Cannabis Legalization and Regulation (2016). (Note the change in the name of the Task Force that replaced Marijuana with Cannabis.) Product integrity was also a major theme in many media discussions during the years leading up to recreational legalization.

As already discussed, legal cannabis product sold in the United States had failed to meet standards of accurate labelling and freedom from contaminants such as excessive or unapproved pesticides. Product contamination, including with illegal pesticides, had also arisen in Canada's legal supply for therapeutic use, and the problem was plainly apparent on the road to legalization for recreational use. As discussed in the previous chapter, Health Canada had reported recalls of medical cannabis from Canadian licensed producers as early as 2014.

A quite dramatic case involved a Toronto-based licensed producer, Mettrum Ltd. A *Globe and Mail* report (Robertson 2016a) revealed that Health Canada had detected two types of unauthorized pesticide in samples of product from Mettrum. The *Globe*'s investigation uncovered several other matters of interest, including:

- *reluctance on the part of the producer to disclose the full extent of contamination to its customers and to reporters*

- *conduct by the producer and Health Canada apparently intended to minimize public awareness of the problem*

- *a discrepancy between Health Canada's alleged "zero-tolerance" policy for use of banned pesticides and its lenient treatment of the producer.*

It is noteworthy that Health Canada became aware of the unauthorized pesticide use shortly before the release of the *Final Report* of the Task Force on Cannabis Legalization and Regulation. Consider the timeline of events:

October 2016: Health Canada detected unauthorized pesticides at Mettrum

November 2: Mettrum quietly initiated a "voluntary recall" of the contaminated product

December 13: The Task Force released its Final Report

December 29: the first Globe and Mail story was published

February 7 2017: the Mettrum recall is posted on Health Canada's Recalls and Alerts database

February 9: the second Globe and Mail story is published.

The length of time between the initial recall and the posting date of over three months is unusual. My inspection of all 9 other recall postings in 2016 and 2017 showed that 8 of them were posted on the same day that the recall began.

The Mettrum story took on added dimensions. A former Mettrum employee, interviewed and considered credible by a *Globe and Mail* journalist, made allegations that were published by the *Globe* (Robertson 2017). He alleged that Mettrum had been using the banned pesticide since 2014, fully aware that Health Canada was not testing for unauthorized pesticides. According to the employee, Mettrum hid the containers of the banned pesticide above the office ceiling tiles during Health Canada inspections of its production facility. Health Canada confirmed that it had not been testing for unauthorized pesticides and had assumed that the mere threat of a company losing its production licence would act as a deterrent. This would appear to be an ill-considered assumption given Health Canada's decades of experience regulating malfeasance in both the tobacco and pharmaceutical industries.

When Health Canada finally posted the recall in February 2017, it noted that "All tested lots contained low levels of myclobutanil or pyrethins that did not exceed any of the levels permitted in food production for these two pesticides."

This too, seems disingenuous. The reason that myclobutanil is approved for food and not cannabis is because myclobutanil becomes a more serious health risk when it is combusted, due to the release of hydrogen cyanide.

In a statement provided in March of 2017, Health Canada declared, without providing sources, that the combustion of myclobutanil produced much less hydrogen cyanide than did the combustion of cannabis. Accordingly, the regulator concluded that the additional amount was not judged to pose an added threat to cannabis users (Canada 2017).

However, Health Canada's statement may conflict with a perspective provided by an independent laboratory. A material safety data sheet issued by Santa Cruz Biotechnology, Inc. referred to myclobutanil as "a hazardous substance", rated as having moderate toxicity (Santa Cruz Biotechnology, Inc. 2011). Health Canada acknowledged in its March statement that it "received 10 adverse reaction reports related to Mettrum Ltd.'s products sold during the period covered by the recall."

Health Canada has also not addressed why myclobutanil was excluded as an approved pesticide for cannabis in the first place, and why it continues to be excluded from the list of approved pesticides. Other questions remain. With customary euphemism, the Health Canada "clarification" also asserted that "recently, two licensed producers undertook voluntary recalls after it was found that they had used unauthorized pesticides, including myclobutanil."

Can we really believe that this was a "voluntary recall" on the part of the producer? Had Mettrum not been caught after more than two years of committing the infraction, it likely would have continued using the banned pesticide.

Health Canada concluded its myclobutanil 'clarification' with the following statement:

> Health Canada would like to assure Canadians that had
> there been any evidence to show that a licensed producer had
> acted with indifference or recklessness and engaged in activit-
> ies that put the health or safety of Canadians in danger, the
> Department would have responded with appropriate enforce-
> ment actions, including licence suspension or revocation.
> (Canada 2017)

The harms of myclobutanil, potential or actual, are not the only important issue. Also relevant is the choice of Mettrum to use the banned pesticide and then allegedly attempt to conceal that use from the regulator. Health Canada has provided no indication that it investigated the alleged coverup. Health Canada seemed to ignore these aspects of the incident.

Given that the producers expected monthly inspections, there is a legitimate question concerning just how seriously the producers regarded their responsibility to respect regulations for the protection of their patients. Heightened concern was also called for given that the discovery of banned pesticides at Mettrum did not occur because of the customary testing protocol, but only through additional testing that was prompted by other independent contamination infractions. This raises the possibility that there may have been much more contaminated product in circulation, particularly since it was well known in the industry that Health Canada was not testing for unauthorized pesticides. It was also important to consider the importance of a company whistle-blower in making other aspects of Mettrum's conduct public. There is also a legitimate question about the levels of due diligence, transparency, and accountability demonstrated by Health Canada in addressing this incident.

Several elements of this story suggest a regulator in desperate damage control mode on the eve of the release of the Task Force's report. The story was certainly inconsistent with the Task Force's depiction of an industry operating for the safety of cannabis users.

We could certainly take some comfort in knowing that Health Canada ultimately detected the defective products. However, given that the inspections customarily occurred monthly, there should be concern about the welfare of patients who were ingesting, in some cases, a large amount of contaminated product daily for up to a month without warning. Some of these patients had compromised immune systems.

While the impact of cannabis tainted with pesticides on the health of patients remains uncertain, the politics of the matter are clearer. Health Canada publicly acknowledged that it had the authority to suspend and even revoke Mettrum's licence, but Mettrum received only the administrative sanction of more unannounced inspections. Again, one might ask where the deterrent effect lies.

I raised this issue in my testimony to The Senate Standing Committee on Social Affairs, Science and Technology. I noted that Mettrum had knowingly used a banned pesticide on a product sold to patients, some of whom are immuno-compromised. It did so for over two years, while allegedly covering up the evidence during Health Canada inspections. I asked the senators if deliberately poisoning medically vulnerable patients was not cause for license revocation or suspension, what would be?

The Canadian government now had indications from both the US and Canada that the promise of a safe supply of cannabis from a licensed and regulated trade was not assured. My own submission to the government's Task Force had provided an account of the recalls in Canada and of the pesticide problems in the US. The Chief Medical Officers of Health of Canada & Urban Public Health Network, in their report (2016), also anticipated the need for recalls of cannabis product in a legal regime.

In the next chapter, I will detail how the government's Task Force on Cannabis Legalization and Regulation (2016) praised the licensed producers for their high production standards, as the product recalls continued to mount.

Neither were the persistent problems with quality control apparent in the declarations of numerous cannabis trade associations which had sprung up to represent the interests of cannabis producers. In early 2017, there were no less than five such associations claiming to uphold the highest standards of product development. The associations included: Canadian Cannabis Industry Association, Canadian Medical Cannabis Council, Canadian National Medical Marijuana Association, Cannabis Canada Association, and Cannabis Trade Alliance of Canada. Only two of the trade associations listed their member organizations on their website and they listed only a few, thus openly accounting for a small portion of the licensed producers in Canada. However, those two associations still managed to include almost all the producers cited by Health Canada for product quality infractions. After four years of operation, the legal commercial cannabis trade in Canada appeared to be in a state of fragmented disarray while promising product integrity. At best, this promise was highly suspect.

It must be acknowledged that regulation provided a mechanism, however flawed, for detecting pesticides and irregularities in concentration. This provided a clear advantage for a legal, regulated regime over an unlicensed one. However, the finding that potentially harmful levels of contaminants were indeed found in legal product is disturbing and should have been a significant concern for government regulators, public health authorities, cannabis consumers, and the public who were being wooed by the promise of product safety in a legal, regulated regime. All considered, there seemed to be little assurance that a legal, government-regulated cannabis trade would ensure product integrity.

If the Canadian government were concerned about the quality and safety of illegal product and confident that a legal industry would produce safer product, it should have encouraged the legal industry to compete with the illegal supply on that aspect. It is reasonable to expect that most people would prefer to use a safer product. But consumer confidence could be achieved only if government transparently acknowledged the problem of contaminated legal product, and then dealt successfully with the problem.

The Canadian government had created a testing protocol for product integrity but had recklessly assumed full compliance by producers. It then provided negligible consequences for breaches of compliance, and of its trust. In doing so, the Canadian government had failed to earn the respect of the industry. Cannabis consumers would assume the risks arising from such a permissive regulatory milieu.

Finally, contamination or intentional adulteration of any drug product with a dangerous substance should be punishable with suitable consequences for such disregard for public safety. This should apply to licensed cannabis companies as well as to those operating in the unlicensed trade. Legislators would have done well to consider that a legal regulated cannabis producer who knowingly supplies contaminated product not only threatens the public's health (as does an unlicensed producer) but also violates the trust that the public has placed in the licensed provider. The setting of penalties for violations should consider the greater gravity of this dereliction of responsibility and trust. Administrative penalties appear to be insufficient to act as deterrents.

Product Promotion Violations

Product promotion is an inclusive term that includes advertising, marketing, event sponsorship, contests, and celebrity endorsements. Drug policy authorities in the US had raised concerns about product promotion given that a substantial research literature had shown that promotion of alcohol and tobacco was associated with increased use and harmful impacts of these drugs on adults (Babor 2010; Tobacco Control Legal Consortium 2012; Pacula et al. 2014.) However, product promotion was not a contentious regulatory issue in the US where an extension of the First Amendment to freedom of commercial speech gave the cannabis industry considerable freedom in promoting its products. Any restrictions that were introduced dealt with issues such as the proximity to schools of billboards with cannabis advertising.

In Canada, by virtue of the Controlled Drugs and Substances Act, the Marihuana for Medical Purposes Regulations (MMPR) that were introduced in 2013 prohibited advertising of cannabis products. In November 2014, Health Canada sent a warning letter to twenty producers about their illegal advertising practices. The warnings were sent after continued infractions following the issuance of an advertising standards bulletin to all producers five months earlier (Canada 2014). Health Canada did not release the names of the companies to whom it sent the warnings. One prominent producer, Aphria, was well-known for its very public (illegal) sponsorship of race car driving (BettingBruiser 2018).

Aphria was one of at least two licensed producers that resorted to unethical, if not illegal, promotional strategies to expand their markets, specifically targeting Canadian military veterans. The companies' strategies took advantage of the Canadian government's coverage, through Veteran's Affairs, of the cost of therapeutic cannabis for veterans who were experiencing trauma from their service in the military. Licensed medical cannabis producers, including Aphria and MedReleaf, set up separate websites specifically for veterans. The producers charged elevated prices for products on the veterans' sites and excluded some of their less expensive products that were offered on their public sites. In 2013, there were 112 Canadian veterans on the program at a total cost of $400,000. By 2016, there were 1,762 veterans on the program at a cost of $20,000,000 (Ling 2016). That represents more than a three-fold increase in cost per veteran—a windfall for the cannabis companies at the expense of the publicly-funded care system.

Unlike companies such as Aphria and MedReleaf who were working on expanding and exploiting the therapeutic cannabis market, other companies had their sights set on the much larger markets that would arise from the anticipated legalization of cannabis for recreational use.

In early 2016, licensed cannabis producer Tweed and American entertainer and self-described cannabis aficionado Snoop Dogg, announced a partnership to promote each other's commercial interests. In a *CBC* interview, Bruce Linton (CEO of Tweed at the time), spoke openly about Snoop

Dogg's role as a "key icon advisor" in Tweed's transition from the medical market to the recreational market (Foote 2016). The partnership was emblazoned on Tweed's web site as "Leafs by Snoop" when I accessed it on November 16, 2016.

The partnership between Tweed and Snoop Dogg was an interesting one. Bolstered by the notoriety of a minor criminal record, Snoop Dogg, as a rapper and cultural icon, consistently cultivated a reputation that glorifies gang culture, a fact reflected in his early artistic productions, replete with allusions to criminality and violence (Giovacchini 1999). Snoop was a high-profile celebrity with over seventeen million followers on his Twitter account which he used on a near daily basis to promote his own line of cannabis products and to share his provocative thoughts on gangsta lifestyle.

Tweed's choice of Snoop Dogg as a promotional partner gave cause to wonder about the branding strategy that Tweed had in mind for its entry into the recreational cannabis market. There is a stinging irony in this strategy given that the Canadian government's often-stated primary purpose for legalizing cannabis was to protect young people from being exposed to criminals, drug use, and their violent activities.

Tweed's clear violation of product promotion provisions was an act that appears to reflect a sense of entitlement and indifference to the rule of law, particularly after repeated warnings had been sent to licensed producers by Health Canada. Tweed's bold conduct occurred during a time of heightened political sensitivity over cannabis legalization, when good judgment might have advised a decorum of restraint.

I raised these concerns in my submission to the Task Force in late August 2016. The input provided a specific suggestion that the Task Force pursue a discussion with the government on this unsavoury and potentially embarrassing matter. When the report of the Task Force was released in December of 2016, the Snoop Dogg partnership had considerably less presence on Tweed's website with only low-profile references to its *Leafs by Snoop* product line. I do not know if my submission to the Task Force and/or possibly submissions from others had any influence on these changes.

The licensed cannabis producers that were entrusted to supply cannabis for therapeutic use to patients quickly established a reputation for indifference to both public health and the law. Mesmerized by the opportunities for market expansion, particularly by the potentially enormous nascent recreational market, licensed producers also showed a surprisingly cavalier attitude towards the sensitive political context of the time—an attitude that would only become emboldened as legalization for recreational use approached. We will explore that in considerable detail in the next chapter.

It might be offered that cannabis corporations were still in their infancy and that more time was needed to right the ship. That contention prompts consideration of the conduct of our more mature drug industries. This chapter has already provided that disturbing answer.

Licence Approvals: The Case of Mr. John H. Stewart
(From Pharma to Canna)

Imagine a scenario in which a principal figure in an epidemic of drug-related deaths could become a significant player in the emerging cannabis industry. Robertson (2016b) reported such a scenario in *The Globe and Mail*. As presented earlier, Mr. John H. Stewart, President of Purdue Pharma Canada, and later CEO of Purdue Pharmaceutical in the United States, was an ardent denier of Purdue's culpability in the genesis of the opioid epidemic. He also incurred the wrath of the US government for Purdue's continued chicanery and lack of cooperation with government information requests. After leaving Purdue in the US, Mr. Stewart returned to Canada to assume a leadership role in a company, Emblem Pharmaceutical, with an inconspicuous office in the charming community of Paris, Ontario. Emblem applied for and received a licence from Health Canada to produce and sell medical cannabis products. In a private investors meeting Mr. Stewart described Emblem's intent to innovate medical cannabis by producing pharmaceutical pills and capsules. With haunting irony, Mr. Stewart described how Emblem would promote cannabis as an alternative to opioid painkillers and their attendant harms. In granting Emblem's medical cannabis licence, Health Canada appears to have concluded that this was entirely acceptable. One might ponder the message that this might send to Canadians who lost a loved one in the still ascending opioid crisis. Mr. Stewart continued to build up the company's move into the cannabis industry in a private meeting with potential investors held at the Trump Hotel in Toronto (Robertson 2016b).

Shortly after legalization in October 2018, Emblem was acquired by Aleafia, another medicinal cannabis company, for a reported $173.2 million all-stock deal (Benic 2018). The trip from pharma to canna was a successful one for Mr. Stewart, largely aided by the munificence of the Canadian government.

Securities Violations

Entrepreneurs typically lack the financial resources or liquidity to enter an expensive enterprise such as cannabis production. They need investors and will try a variety of strategies to attract them, some of which may violate legal provisions. It is the job of government securities regulators to prevent delinquent companies and individuals from entering the industry in the first place. Failing that, the regulators attempt to detect improper or dishonest strategies and practices and to bring entrepreneurs in line with legal requirements. If that fails, the company's business license can be revoked. Investors who feel they have been wronged have also been inclined to hire legal representation to pursue remediation and compensation—typically in class action suits against the offending company. Many such undertakings are ultimately settled out of court.

There were early warnings that applications for cannabis production licences included some from players who would not provide the necessary protections or might try to mislead investors. Canadian securities regulators said it found serious investor protection concerns at twenty-five newly registered medical cannabis companies. The regulators did not disclose the identities of the non-compliant companies (Reuters 2015).

In an unusual case published in *The Globe and Mail*, US producer CEN Biotech had reached the final stage of Health Canada's seven-stage approval process. Health Canada had completed a site inspection and the company had been scrutinized by the RCMP. However, Health Canada staff had become aware that the company was issuing misleading statements and the company had been warned against such conduct by the regulator. However, there was no follow-up by Health Canada and the company continued with its misrepresentation. The problem became sufficiently serious that Health Minister Rona Ambrose eventually referred the matter to the RCMP again for further investigation.

Ultimately, CEN Biotech's plight reached a level of buffoonery that was absurd. The company continued to mislead investors by saying that it had already been approved by Health Canada. It falsely told investors that the CEO personally knew the Canadian health minister and had attended a barbeque at her home. The company also provided the name of a contact person -- who did not exist. When this was discovered, the company clarified that the name of the fictitious individual was a *nom de plume*, akin to McDonald Restaurants' use of its Ronald McDonald character. The company's CEO also took exception to the scrutiny of the Canadian government and publicly wondered whether Canada was "communist" (Robertson 2015). CEN Biotech's license application was not approved. The continuing problem of securities violations following legalization for recreational use will be addressed in Chapter 7.

Licensed Producers, Illegal Activities, and Organized Crime

One of the ambitions of the Liberal Party's legalization campaign was to significantly reduce and perhaps even eliminate the role of criminals, street gangs and organized crime in the cannabis trade. There were two problems with this aspiration.

The first problem is that there was no evidence of substantial involvement of organized crime or street gangs in the illegal cannabis trade. This was covered in considerable detail in the previous chapter. Interestingly, more recent information suggests that what little involvement of organized crime there was in the cannabis trade may have been enabled by legalization for therapeutic use. In 2013, *CBC-Radio Canada* had accessed an RCMP Report, through The Access to Information Act (ATIA), which had informed the Canadian Association of Chiefs of Police of an increase in organized crime involvement in the legal cannabis industry. *CBC News* (Pfeffer and Dumont 2017) reported that the alleged activity involved diversion of personal medical cannabis cultivation licences that had been issued by Health Canada. The licences were diverted to criminal organizations including at least one motorcycle gang. The criminal organizations would then produce and sell the product illicitly.

The significance of this story lies not only with organized crime's involvement but rather with cultivation licences being diverted from a legal framework to the illegal trade. This unintended consequence is exactly the opposite of what legalization was supposed to accomplish. At the time there was no reported evidence of diversion of Health Canada's production licences which allow producers to sell cannabis to patients through the mail. However, the RCMP Report did warn that "there is no shortage of organized criminal groups who have applied to produce medical marijuana" (Pfeffer and Dumont 2017). A statement provided to *CBC News* from Public Safety Minister Ralph Goodale's Office indicated: "The RCMP works with Health Canada to ensure that companies cultivating medical marijuana are not linked to organized crime. It conducts law enforcement record checks of all applicants referred by Health Canada under the Marijuana for Medical Purposes Regulations."

There was a second problem with the government's promise to eliminate the role of crime in the cannabis trade. In contrast to the government's proclamation of a licensed cannabis trade as a panacea, licensed cannabis companies were engaging in criminal conduct. Such conduct is more serious than the already discussed regulatory non-compliance related to the use of banned pesticides, product promotion, and securities infractions.

In the spring of 2014, licensed cannabis producers Tweed and Mettrum (later to become brands under Canopy Growth) illegally purchased and transported two shipments (a total of 705,000 grams) of ready-for-retail processed flower bud from illegal growing operations. This was done under the guise that the shipment was comprised of unprocessed plants only. (The latter, but not the former, was legally allowed if the transaction was pre-authorized by Health Canada.) Acting on notification from the Kelowna International Airport, the RCMP seized the illegal product on March 31, and was preparing a press release about the seizure. However, the RCMP was asked to stand down on the case and did not release its statement. The *National Post* filed an Access to Information request, and five years after the incident, The Post received the documents on what happened. Documents revealed that the government feared the news of the seizure would have a harmful impact on the stock values of the companies which had just recently become publicly traded. There was also concern about potential embarrassment for Health Canada which had authorized the shipment, albeit under false pretense. An RCMP spokesperson said that a press release from Tweed to its shareholders on the matter was "a long way from what transpired" and provided "brutally misleading" information about the seizure. The spokesperson also expressed frustration that the RCMP was not permitted to effectively respond to the details of the press release with its own account of events (Quan 2019). While the Canadian public would not hear the details of this case until 2019, the details were certainly very well known in the Ministry of Health, and we can safely assume at the office of the Attorney General.

The retreat by the RCMP, under government pressure, is unsettling. Investors in a company should be entitled to the benefit of accurate disclosure rather than the sanitized version of events provided by Tweed in its press release.

There is an interesting postscript to this story involving the RCMP and one of the companies, Mettrum. On June 18 2014, less than three months after the RCMP's seizure of the illegal cannabis, Mettrum announced that former RCMP Commissioner, Norman Inkster, had been appointed to its board of directors (Cinaport Acquisition Corp. 2014). Apparently neither the illegal actions of Mettrum, nor it and Tweed's conflict with the RCMP, dissuaded the celebrated law enforcement official from joining and staying involved with the company. As of September 2016, Inkster's salary from the company was reported as $99,500 along with $705,000 worth of company shares (Campbell 2017). Interestingly, the monetary value of those shares is exactly the number of grams of cannabis seized by the RCMP in Kelowna - possibly a coincidence. Or perhaps someone was having a bit of fun with this.

While reflecting on the varied improprieties of cannabis corporations discussed thus far, consider that the improprieties did not occur within illegal drug cartels or organized crime pyramids. They occurred within a licensed, government-regulated industry. That should have been a caution against significantly expanding the cannabis industry from a relatively small therapeutic one to a much larger industry for recreational use.

POTENTIAL IMPACT OF CANNABIS LEGALIZATION

Warnings from health policy experts went beyond the conduct of drug producing industries. They also included what we knew about how drug industry conduct and government regulation can combine to affect the patterns of use of the drug and the level of harms associated with use.

Known Harms from Cannabis Use

One of the prominent issues discussed during the legalization campaign was the potential for commercial legalization of cannabis to create a financial incentive for market expansion which would lead to increased consumption and increased problems. Cannabis represented nowhere near the extent of harm as seen with alcohol and tobacco. But there was evidence that it's use was not entirely benign either.

Cannabis use disorder (CUD), like alcohol use disorder, is characterized mainly by the experience of problems directly related to use of cannabis and difficulty in transitioning to non-problem use or abstinence.

The Canadian Tobacco, Alcohol and Drugs Survey (Canada 2021) reported that in 2015, 3.6 million Canadians of age fifteen and over reported having used cannabis in the previous year. Fischer et al. (2016) had estimated that each year, 380,000 Canadians (10.5% of users) show signs of cannabis use disorder. Annual individual participation in specialized addiction treatment for cannabis problems in Canada was estimated at: 76,000 - 95,000. The authors also provided estimated annual ranges of 89–267 for cannabis-related motor vehicle accident (MVA) fatalities, and 6,825–20,475 MVA injuries. The acknowledged imprecision of these estimates was an unavoidable result of the limited capacity for collecting data on cannabis-related harm at the time of cannabis legalization. The absence of better data on potentially harmful consequences should have been another reason for more caution on the part of the Canadian government.

The Province of Ontario's addiction treatment system has a client monitoring system called the Drug Addiction Treatment Information System (DATIS), which provided a more complete picture of admissions to addiction treatment programs, albeit for only one province. DATIS (Centre for Addiction and Mental Health. Drug and Alcohol Treatment Information System (DATIS) 2015) provided a report on assessments of 62,951 individuals at 173 reporting agencies from calendar year 2014. The report showed that 24,408 individuals identified cannabis as one of their problem substances. This was higher than the number for each of tobacco, opioids/opiates, and crack/cocaine. Only alcohol, at 42,131, was higher than cannabis. A subsequent report from DATIS (Centre for Addiction and Mental Health. Drug and Alcohol Treatment Information System (DATIS) 2017) was based on assessments of 64,476 individuals at 170 reporting agencies from calendar year 2016. It showed that 23,945 individuals identified cannabis as one of their problem substances. This was also higher than the number for each of tobacco, opioids/opiates, and crack/cocaine. Again, only alcohol, at 42,270, was higher than cannabis.

The impact of a legal cannabis supply on use of cannabis and associated harm was uncertain. However, there are several points to be made arising from the above data sets.

The number of individuals in treatment self-identifying cannabis as a problem in Ontario, as well as even the low end of the ranges provided by Fischer and colleagues made it clear that popular notions of cannabis use as harmless were unsupported by the data available.

These estimates and counts of people with cannabis problems occurred during prohibition of recreational use. Thus, they did not reflect the potential for commercial legalization to increase both use and associated problems—an issue which will be addressed in the subsequent sections of this chapter. Thus, the right question was not whether legalization would create a public health problem with cannabis, but whether the existing problem would get worse and by how much? Might levels of harm eventually approach the much higher levels now associated with alcohol?

The numbers of individuals experiencing harm from their cannabis use did not comprise an argument for continued harmful criminalization of its use; however, the data were sufficient to warrant caution in any legislative change that could potentially exert an impact for the worse.

Finally, the period for how long it would take to see a potential increase in use and problems, was uncertain. Drug problems in individuals rarely develop quickly. They have an incubation period, sometimes of years, before becoming obvious. The same could be true for assessing the public health impact of legalization at the population level. The last chapter will include a section on what is known into the fourth year of legalization. But even that is unlikely to capture the more pertinent, longer-term trajectory. My guess is that it will be at least a decade, and maybe two or three, before we have a sufficiently complete understanding of the impact on the public's health.

Impact on the Unlicensed Cannabis Trade

The impact of a legal cannabis supply on the unlicensed trade was uncertain. There were optimistic aspirations here in Canada that criminal activity "...should shrink significantly and potentially disappear" (Centre for Addiction and Mental Health 2014, 11). In the *Final Report* of the Canadian Government's Task Force on Cannabis Legalization and Regulation (2016, 38), the less ambitious intent to simply "curb the illicit market" appeared.

Early impact from legalization in state jurisdictions in the United States was more consistent with the latter of the two predictions. The unlicensed cannabis trade still flourished in Colorado (Stuart 2014) and Washington (Kleiman et al. 2015). The Washington data showed that more than a year after legalization, illegal sources still accounted for an estimated 28% of cannabis sold in the state.

The Task Force's more modest goal was advisable given that anything more ambitious was also inconsistent with actual experience related to other long-established legal drug industries and their unlicensed counterparts. Despite having had legal and regulated regimes for tobacco and alcohol for over a century in Canada, contraband product remains widely available for both drugs. Knockoff pharmaceuticals can be ordered over the internet -- with unintentional home delivery by the Canadian government's postal service. The magnitude of contraband sales is sufficiently significant that tobacco, alcohol, and pharmaceutical producers and retailers, government regulators, and enforcement agencies have all expressed concern. Some have lobbied government for tougher controls on the trade of counterfeit drug products (Task Force on Illicit Tobacco Products 2009; National Coalition Against Contraband Tobacco 2016; Lockington 2015; Hamilton 2015; Rubin 2011; Smithers 2012; RCMP 2014; Canada 2010; Elash 2006; Standing Senate Committee on Social Affairs, Science and Technology 2015).

It would be difficult to fathom how a newly established legal, regulated cannabis industry would somehow cause a large, deeply entrenched, diversely manifested unlicensed industry to disappear. A new legal cannabis industry in Canada would be realistically expected to capture only a piece of the action. Many of-age cannabis users would be expected to buy from the new legal industry, simply because they can. But others would continue to buy from their established and trusted unlicensed sources. Underage users would access the legal supply through their older peers and continue to access a thriving, if somewhat smaller, unlicensed supply. Canada's unlicensed cannabis trade would almost certainly persist and thrive as does the unlicensed trade in alcohol, tobacco, and pharmaceuticals.

The continued existence of an unlicensed cannabis trade is not ideal. But it is less of a threat to the safety and propriety of cannabis users than it is to the revenue of the new legal industry. It was irresponsible of the Canadian government to engage in hyperbole and fabrication primarily in service of the monetary interests of its emerging corporate cannabis trade.

Impact on Public Health

At the time of Canada's cannabis legalization campaign, there was no certainty about commercial legalization's impact on public health. But there was no reason to believe that it would play out any differently than had commercial legalization for other recreational drugs—alcohol and tobacco. We could expect that the impact would be mediated, in large part, by four relationships. The first relationship is the impact of the newly granted permission that comes with legalization of a previously illegal drug. That alone will provide an exciting attraction to a portion of current, former, and non-users, and an increase in demand. The second relationship is the added impact of product promotion (advertising, marketing, sponsorships, and endorsements) upon consumer demand. The third is the impact of increased ease of access to cannabis on its consumption. The fourth relationship is the impact of changes in consumption upon changes in associated problems. These mediating relationships are closely tied to how the industry is allowed to conduct its business by government.

It is to be expected that any company (and therefore any drug company) will have a primary purpose of maximizing financial return for owners/shareholders. A company attempts to do so largely by overall market expansion and by capturing as much of that market as possible. Prominent strategies for market expansion include product promotion to increase demand, and industry lobbying of government for facilitation of policy. These two strategies will weave their way through some of the discussion that follows.

Legal Permission

It is obvious that many Canadians decided that they did not require a legal industry nor permission from their government to use cannabis. However, survey data collected at the time of the legalization campaign in Canada told us that many people would feel sufficiently more comfortable to try cannabis for the first time if it were provided by a legal industry with government support. A poll of Canadians conducted by Forum Research (CBC News 2015b), suggested that the number of Canadians using cannabis could increase by over 50% after legalization.

Market Expansion and Consumer Demand

As introduced in Chapters 1 and 2, legal drug products with their potential for harm, are no ordinary commodity. Drug companies, primarily through their attempts at market expansion, thus pose a greater potential threat to public health than do ones supplying more benign consumer products. The heightened liability of drug products requires additional constraints on how they are promoted to the public. It is reasonable to expect that, at minimum, the sum of information provided to consumers for any legal recreational drug product would achieve a balance between promotion of the use of the product and information that encourages and facilitates its safe use.

Reports from The Chief Public Health Officer for Canada (Public Health Agency of Canada (2016) and The Canadian Public Health Association (2011) cited the research demonstrating an association of increased consumption with promotion of alcohol. Research also demonstrated an impact on children and youth (Heung, Rempel, and Krank 2012). Babor (2010) referenced the body of research showing that the largely self-regulation of alcohol advertising practices world-wide does not appear to prevent marketing that would appeal to younger people. Accordingly, Babor has recommended a complete ban on the advertising of alcohol products, as has been achieved for the publicly visible promotion of tobacco in Canada. The Tobacco Control Legal Consortium (2012) cited a decade of evidence on the relationship between increased promotion and increased tobacco use. Further evidence for alcohol and tobacco has been cited by Babor (2010) and Pacula et al. (2014).

It is important to consider that the projected increased demand for cannabis, as reflected in the survey data, did not include the potential added impact of an industry's market expansion tactics that could have followed legalization. The report from the Office of the Parliamentary Budget Officer (2016, 43) acknowledged the complexity of factors at work that would determine levels of use of cannabis after legalization. The report acknowledged that the literature is not conclusive on the expected level of impact, but states that "...on balance, legalization appears more likely to increase aggregate consumption." The report made an estimate of approximately 600,000 new cannabis smokers after legalization and identified advertising and marketing as a factor that would increase use.

We might also consider that almost all commercial enterprises, from street corner mom and pop shops to the largest international corporations, advertise their products and services—an assured expenditure of billions of dollars each year. Should we believe that the global commercial enterprise is run by people who would carelessly assign such expenditures to a practice that did not produce substantial results? The power of product promotion is widely recognized and could be reasonably expected to have a profound impact upon the consumption of cannabis.

Ease of Access

Another way to expand a market for a product is to increase the ease of access to the product. The Canadian Public Health Association (2011) and Pacula et al. (2014), have cited the research demonstrating a relationship between increased accessibility to alcohol with increased use. The Ontario Tobacco Research Unit (2011) has done so for tobacco. These findings had significant implications for how cannabis should be made available to the Canadian public for recreational use. It is reasonable to expect that the establishment of local retail outlets for legal recreational cannabis would increase comfort and access for those adults who may have been uncomfortable with accessing, or unable to access, illegal sources. Under legalization, a legally protected, assured supply of product at fixed, known locations with predictable hours of operation would arise. This would provide a much more reliable and convenient source for product than could most unlicensed supply mechanisms, including the grey-market and illegal dispensaries of the time. Consumers would no longer have to worry about a police incursion while making a purchase.

The Report of The Office of the Parliamentary Budget Officer (2016) and the previously mentioned polling results (CBC News 2015b), both suggested that market expansion would be expected because of some current non-users trying the product, and some of them continuing to use it. Current users might also be expected to buy cannabis more often from a legal retail option.

From another perspective, we might question the assumption that an increased legal supply would subtract from the illegal supply. It is also possible that a new legal supply would add to the illegal supply, thus substantially increasing availability and purchase.

A major aspiration of legalization was that it would reduce access to cannabis by underage youth. Pre-legalization data from The Centre for Addiction and Mental Health's Ontario Student Drug Use and Health Survey (Boak et al. 2015) showed that, among grade 7 to 12 students, 46% reported that it would be 'fairly easy' or 'very easy' for them to obtain cannabis. The corresponding figures were 65% for alcohol and 53% for cigarettes. Alcohol and cigarettes are regulated drug products that would not be legally accessible to almost all students in these grades. Yet, based upon their daily experience, more students perceive them to be more accessible than illegal cannabis. This suggests that legalization may increase access for underage users. At minimum, it suggests there is little reason to accept the notion that ease of access to cannabis for underage users will substantially diminish under legalization. Underage youth are likely to access legal cannabis in the same way they access legal tobacco and alcohol—through their peers of legal age. A literature review by the United States Institute of Medicine had already established this finding for tobacco (Bonnie, Stratton, and Kwan 2015, 5-6). I will return to that fascinating and important study in greater detail in Chapter 6.

A prediction of increased use of cannabis due to increased access is based upon traditional retail models for alcohol and tobacco. This was at a time when regulations allowed at least some product promotion for tobacco. The implications of this for cannabis led to consideration of alternative retail mechanisms such as ordering by mail/phone/internet and delivery by postal service or courier. Such a model had been adopted for Canada's therapeutic cannabis supply and was listed as an option for recreational use in the government's *Discussion Paper* (Task Force on Marijuana Legalization and Regulation 2016). It was also supported as one option in the Canadian Public Health Association's (2016) submission to the Task Force. The option was recommended in the Task Force's *Final Report* (2016) but only for those consumers who were mobility-disadvantaged or living in remote, sparsely populated areas where a free-standing retail facility might not be sustainable. No toker left behind.

Increased Use and Associated Problems

As the prevalence of use of a drug product increases in a population it will also presumably increase among the more vulnerable portion of the population. Thus, the prevalence of problems associated with the drug's use will also increase.

The relationship between higher smoking rates and higher rates of smoking-related disease had been known for quite some time (National Institutes of Health 2012). The data demonstrating the same relationship for alcohol use and associated harms has been reported by Babor (2010), Canadian Public Health Association (2011) and Giesbrecht et al. (2013).

CAMH's *Cannabis Policy Framework* (The Centre for Addiction and Mental Health 2014), the Canadian government's Discussion Paper (Task Force on Marijuana Legalization and Regulation 2016), and the United Kingdom Expert Panel Report (Rolles 2016) all expressed the potential for the relationship to hold for cannabis. The Chief Medical Officers of Health of Canada & Urban Public Health Network (2016) recommended that government be prepared for an increased demand for mental health and addiction treatment services following legalization.

The Cascade of Increased Demand, Use, and Problems

The evidence cited in this section is consistent with a perspective I propose for any legal, commercial drug industry, including a newly created cannabis industry. The perspective predicts the potential cascade of a new drug product's impact on a population:

- *legal permission leads to more demand for the product*
- *more product promotion leads to more demand for the product*
- *more demand plus easier access leads to more use of the product*
- *more use leads to more associated harms.*

This section has referenced reports citing evidence from tobacco and alcohol research supporting the individual components of this perspective. The epidemic of opioid overdoses and deaths in North America illustrates that the perspective can apply to legal therapeutic drug products as well.

Legal permission, in the form of regulatory approval of opioid medications, created demand from people with pain-management issues. Aggressive promotion of opioid products by pharmaceutical companies to prescribers further increased the demand. This increased demand, along with ease of access from prescribers and dispensers at pharmacies, led to substantially increased levels of use. Unprecedented levels of opioid-related harm ensued.

It should be acknowledged that other social forces (for example, a pandemic) might also have an impact on use and problems.

Implications for Policy

The relationships between legalization and product promotion and the cascade of demand, use, and harm, had clear implications for health authorities' recommendations to the Canadian government. They did not recommend mere restrictions on product promotion for recreational cannabis use. They recommended a full ban. Calls for such a ban came from The Chief Medical Officers of Health of Canada & Urban Public Health Network (2016), The Canadian Public Health Association (2016), *The Canadian Medical Association Journal* (Spithoff, Emerson, and Spithoff 2015), The Canadian Paediatric Society (Grant and Bélanger 2016), The Centre for Addiction and Mental Health (2016b) and the United Kingdom Expert Panel (Rolles et al. 2016). It is also noteworthy that Uruguay, the only nation that legalized cannabis for recreational purposes before Canada, banned all forms of product promotion for recreational use.

The recommended bans are justified given that cannabis has considerable potential for market growth as a recreational drug in Canada. The most recent data from The Canadian Tobacco Alcohol and Drugs Survey (CTADS) (Canada 2021) at the time of the legalization campaign was from 2015 and showed that 77% of Canadians fifteen years of age and older used alcohol in the past year. The comparative figure for cannabis at that time was 12%. Cannabis companies would covet the alcohol industry's high level of market penetration and be expected to set that as their target. As was the case for alcohol (and once was for tobacco), and in the absence of a ban, a full battery of proven approaches including marketing, advertising, sponsorships, and celebrity endorsements could be expected. Throughout the legalization campaign in Canada, the cannabis industry continued to aggressively lobby for license to promote cannabis use. In a meeting I attended in Ottawa in February 2017, with The Federal Tobacco Control Program and The Cannabis Secretariat, a representative from The Cannabis Secretariat confirmed that a desire to advertise was the major issue raised by cannabis industry lobbyists. From the tone of the meeting, it appeared to be a very sensitive matter in the federal bureaucracy.

Undaunted by the advice from health policy experts, The Task Force on Cannabis Legalization and Regulation's *Final Report* (2016) recommended restrictions on promotional practices, rather than the complete ban that was put forward by health authorities. The inevitable risks of that compromise will be addressed in the next two chapters.

As discussed earlier, industry lobbying of government can also be a powerful supplement to product promotion to expand a market. Lobbying strives for less-restrictive regulations of many kinds, including reduced surveillance and enforcement of the regulations, and reduced penalties for infractions. The goal is a regulatory regime that facilitates, or does not obstruct, market expansion and the revenues that ensue.

Given that market expansion increases risk to the public's health, several health policy organizations in Canada and abroad warned against the perils of industry lobbying in cannabis law reform. These organizations included: *The Canadian Medical Association Journal* (Spithoff, Emerson, and Spithoff 2015), The Centre for Addiction and Mental Health (2014), The RAND Corporation (Caulkins et al. 2015), and The United Kingdom Expert Panel (Rolles et al. 2016). As we will see in the next chapter, cannabis industry lobbying of the federal government was intense on the road to legalization. Government was receptive.

It was obvious that commercial recreational legalization would bring substantially increased revenues for the cannabis industry and increased tax revenues for government. But there was more to consider. From a public health perspective, there was a sufficiently compelling case that commercial legalization would also bring increased cannabis use, associated problems, and presumably economic costs. The government should therefore have moved cautiously along this policy terrain. It would have been prudent to legislate with public health as a priority over industry and taxation revenue. I will explore this as a major topic in the next chapter.

This chapter has drawn upon what was known at the time of Canada's legalization campaign and should have been known by government and more seriously considered in its campaign. The last chapter of the book will examine the extent to which the concerns were verified during the fourth year of legalization.

As we will see in the following chapters, this new drug industry, and its partnership with the Canadian government, had not yet hit the zenith of its systemic perfidy. In the next chapter, I will describe how the foundation of the government's ambitious plan for cannabis legalization, however perilous, appears to have been set early on, and impervious to suggestions for a more cautious and prudent approach. In my admittedly challengeable opinion, the government's approach was not an implementation failure. It was a premeditated, strategic plan. I believe the broad strokes of The Cannabis Act may have been set before the Task Force held a single consultation.

SUMMING UP

This chapter presented the evidence that our long-established legal drug industries engage in activities that are illegal or otherwise inconsistent with business ethics and the protection of public health. This appears to be a contributing factor to their products being associated with international public health crises. We knew how drug industry conduct, drug use patterns, and government regulation could shape the creation of a new legal commercial drug industry. The most worrisome interpretation is that we may have more to fear from the legal industries that produce drugs than we do from the drugs themselves. In its early years, the cannabis industry appeared to be following the same path as its elder drug industry siblings. We saw this in therapeutic and recreational legalization in the United States, and in therapeutic legalization in Canada. The various incidents and flags should have prompted more caution. Government remained undaunted.

Section III

The Main Event

Chapter 6

Legalization for Recreational Use in Canada: How It Really Happened and Why

"Drug reformers get seduced by politicians who co-opt our language but who make no meaningful change. And when we don't hold politicians accountable, we contribute to harm."

— Dr. Carl Hart

"Politics is the entertainment branch of industry."

— Frank Zappa

The legislative and regulatory quagmire that had prevailed for therapeutic cannabis in Canada did not bode well for the development of sound public policy for recreational use of the drug. Despite the Liberal Party's promise to take a public health approach for recreational use, there were yellow flags that raised concern:

- *the legal therapeutic market for cannabis was minuscule compared to the potential size of the legal recreational market*

- *the threat that market expansion posed for public health protection*

- *the licensed cannabis industry's demonstrated disregard for public health protection and the law during therapeutic use legalization*

- *the permissive regulation of the cannabis industry by government.*

As seen in the previous chapter, these flags were even more prescient given the legacy of harm from more seasoned drug industries. And yet, these threats received scant acknowledgement by the government on the road to recreational use legalization. Casual observers, and even some policy analysts, appeared to be unaware that a licensed cannabis industry crime spree had only put its boots on. I will cover that in Chapter 7. This chapter tells how we got there.

WHAT IS A PUBLIC HEALTH APPROACH?

As an alternative to the continued criminalization of drug use, health policy organizations in Canada had, for several years, articulated and encouraged a "public health approach" for legal and illegal drugs, including cannabis.

The Liberal Party of Canada was apparently enamoured by the politically auspicious appeal of a public health approach that conveyed safety for Canadians. The Party took up the banner for its legalization campaign. This would include a strictly regulated, law-abiding system, that would provide safe product. My evaluation of the Party's success in delivering on this promise is addressed through five criteria which I will draw upon in this and subsequent chapters:

- *the selection of an industry model and overarching policy approach*

- *the process of informing federal legislation*

- *the intent and content of the legislation (with a focus on a juxtaposition of market expansion versus public health protection)*

- *industry regard for public health protection, regulatory compliance, and the rule of law*

- *regulatory performance by government.*

THE LIBERAL PARTY OF CANADA AND CANNABIS LEGALIZATION

An Inside Job?

The process of developing federal legislation for recreational cannabis use is best understood with a brief reminder of some pertinent historical context. Decriminalization of cannabis had a well-established international record of success, and the Liberal Party of Canada had declared its formal position of support for decriminalization. It had even made attempts to introduce legislation (Erickson and Hyshka 2010). However, despite the Party having maintained a majority government from 1993 through half of 2004, it never assigned a sufficient level of priority to the initiative to get the job done. Canada remained an outlier among nations with its continued criminalization of cannabis.

A renewed momentum for reform within the party arose in 2011. Entrepreneur Chuck Rifici was approached by Ian McKay, then National Director of the Liberal Party of Canada, to join the party's board as a volunteer Chief Financial Officer (Kirkup 2015; Rinaldi 2019; Wikipedia 2019). Mr. Rifici's and Mr. McKay's shared backstory is an interesting one. They were well-acquainted as classmates at Queen's University in the early 2000s. In 2011, Rifici reportedly sustained a painful injury and after a perilous trial of prescribed hydromorphone, came to regard cannabis as a safer alternative with commercial possibilities. Rifici invested a substantial amount of time exploring the opportunities and began to meet with potential investors. In 2013, Rifici, along with Bruce Linton, became co-founders of Tweed, Canada's largest licensed cannabis producer at the time. Ian McKay was one of the founding investors (Rinaldi 2019).

Leading into the Liberal Party's Ottawa convention in January 2012, cannabis law reform had quietly acquired an elevated profile within the party that was unprecedented. It became a prominent topic at the convention. However, it is interesting that when interviewed at the outset of the convention, Justin Trudeau, The Honorable Member of Parliament for Papineau, Québec, showed appropriate deference to the Party's legacy of support for de-criminalization. He was less enthusiastic about legalization: "I don't know that it's entirely consistent with the kind of society we're trying to build" (Di Fiore 2016). Mr. Trudeau's caution was understandable. At that time, the official position of the Liberal Party of Canada, like the federal New Democrat Party (NDP), was to support decriminalization. The then-ruling Progressive Conservatives were unflinchingly committed to continued criminalization of the drug's recreational use. Only the Green Party had gone on public record supporting cannabis legalization (Cannabis Digest 2010).

But it appears that leanings among the Liberal Party's executives had quietly shifted, and The Honourable Member from Papineau was not on the inside. Neither were Canadian drug policy analysts. Almost all of us were still focused on making a case for decriminalization. In the United States, legalization for recreational use was nothing more than an uncertain ballot initiative in Colorado, which was still a year away from becoming the first state jurisdiction to legalize. Uruguay, the first nation to legalize, was also still a year away from doing so. In Canada, legalization was, at best, a fringe discussion at the time of Mr. Rifici's appointment in 2011.

But the winds were shifting. They caught more sail at the Liberal Party's convention where the Party would forge a platform for the 2015 federal election. It was later revealed that, in 2011, the same year that Rifici joined the Liberal Party executive, a filmmaking/communications company was hired to create video content for the convention. The company was also asked to promote the idea of cannabis legalization among the delegates. In two articles, and in a conversation with me in the autumn of 2021, the firm's principal, Mr. James Di Fiore told the story. During our conversation, Fiore, disclosed that it was the National Director of the Party, Mr. Ian McKay, and the outgoing President of the Liberal Party of Canada Board of Directors, Mr. Alfred Apps, who had met with him and ultimately hired his team to work on the convention.

As for the part of the job concerning the promotion of cannabis legalization, Di Fiore tells the story:

> In 2011 I was hired by the Liberal Party of Canada's upper brass to pressure their delegates to vote yes on a policy initiative that would push for legalization. For three months, my team approached marijuana advocacy groups and rallied their

members to bombard LPC delegates via email, tweets, and Facebook messages. The plan was to put enough pressure on delegates until they voted for a Canada who would shed its draconian views on weed. When we started, just 30 per cent of delegates were in our camp. After the votes were tallied at the Liberals' 2012 convention, more than 75 per cent of delegates voted yes. (Di Fiore 2017)

In his articles, and during our discussion, Mr. Di Fiore named other members of the Liberal Party upper brass and their respective positions on cannabis legalization. As already discussed, party leader heir apparent, Justin Trudeau was not in support of it. Interim leader, Bob Rae and former leader Stephane Dion appeared to share Trudeau's reticence (Di Fiore 2016). Former Prime Minister, Paul Martin, appeared oblivious to the issue at the time. Only former leader, Michael Ignatieff, embraced the idea. Overall, this was not exactly a hearty endorsement from the Party's elected silver-backs. Rather, the enthusiasm seemed to exist within the Party's board of directors—the same board on which future cannabis magnate Chuck Rifici sat as Chief Financial Officer, and his long-time friend and cannabis investor, Ian McKay, sat as National Director.

The Campaign Trail: Not the High Road

In 2013, Justin Trudeau became Party Leader and was now sporting a more ardent perspective on legalization. He made the announcement midway through the year and campaigned enthusiastically for legalization throughout his 2013-2015 run for Prime Minister. Upon winning the 2015 election with a majority, the Liberals promptly reaffirmed their commitment to cannabis legalization. In early 2016, the Government announced the striking of a Task Force to study and make recommendations on legalizing and regulating cannabis for recreational use. The government expected to introduce legislation in the spring of 2017. The expedited level of commitment to achieving legalization stood in stark contrast to the less enthusiastic inclination towards decriminalization that had languished within the Party for more than a decade.

In September 2014, amidst some internal turmoil at licensed cannabis producer Tweed, Chuck Rifici left the company he had founded—presumably to spend more time with his lawyers. He left The Liberal Party Board of Directors in June 2016. Mr. Rifici would go on to pursue a variety of other cannabis ventures which continue into 2022.

It is important to recognize the correlated period of Mr. Rifici's generous, and unprecedented, contributions of his time to a political party and that party's dramatic change in cannabis policy. The change was unprecedented for the Liberal Party, as it was for any major political party in the world, except for in Uruguay.

There is no doubt that legalization, in contrast to decriminalization, would bring substantial monetary benefit to the business ambitions of Mr.

Rifici and many other big players who were the risk-tolerant early adopters in a legal cannabis industry. This group included some elite members of the Liberal Party—more on that later. Both Mr. Rifici and the Liberal Party have publicly denied that there was any causative connection between Mr. Rifici's short-lived and timely role with the Party executive, the legalization campaign, and Rifici's cannabis business interests (Cannabis Life Network 2015).

Beginning in the early days of the government's legalization campaign, the federal New Democrat Party repeatedly called on the Liberals to decriminalize cannabis possession at once while it was forging the new blueprint for legalization. Canada could have joined dozens of US state jurisdictions and nations world-wide by promptly implementing decriminalization of minor cannabis offences—a policy choice with an established record of long-term international success. In contrast, legalization had no such record.

But the Liberal Party now unapologetically dismissed decriminalization as a policy option. It began developing a communication strategy in support of legalization which it anticipated to be a tough sell in some quarters of the country. The strategy was loudly trumpeted on multiple platforms including the Party's website, formal press releases, and Mr. Trudeau's frequent statements to the media for which the press showed an unquenchable thirst. The Party's communication strategy consisted of two components: demonizing the unlicensed trade in cannabis and extolling the virtues of a legal, regulated trade as a panacea.

Demonizing the Unlicensed Cannabis Trade

The illegal trade in street drugs like cocaine, methamphetamine, heroin, and fentanyl has, at least in part, been conducted by unscrupulous individuals and organizations. Some of these players trade in carnage as well as drugs. Some policy analysts, stuck in traditional orthodoxy, indiscriminately generalized that scenario to the unlicensed cannabis trade. Some journalists piled on with the same misinformation. So did the Liberal Party of Canada—with substantial enthusiasm. One of the Party's favourite depictions of the unlicensed cannabis trade was "...criminal organizations, street gangs and gun-runners" (Elliott 2015).

With relentless derisive hyperbole directed against the unlicensed cannabis trade, the Liberal Party hoped to invoke concern for the safety and propriety of cannabis users, including children. Most notably, the vitriol was designed to invoke parents' protectiveness of their children. The unlicensed cannabis trade was thus viewed as the stereotypical organized crime pyramid with an imagined evil drug lord at the top. The cartel would allegedly direct proceeds to hidden violent and exploitative criminal enterprises in Canada and abroad. As described in the earlier chapter on decriminalization, the research evidence told a different story. To summarize, most cannabis users buy from friends, family, or other acquaintances, not from sketchy strangers in poorly lit parking lots. The evidence also revealed that the unlicensed cannabis trade, in Canada and elsewhere, is not the stereotypical drug cartel pyramid. Rather, it is mostly benign, consisting largely of a disconnected cottage industry of small operations earning modest revenues that supported local legal economies. The research also showed that most people in the unlicensed cannabis trade did not sell other drugs and were not associated with street gangs or organized crime. Nor were they involved in violent or exploitative crime, or any form of crime other than selling cannabis.

Nor was it likely that typical unlicensed sellers were sheltering large caches of revenue in offshore accounts and using it to fund international criminal activities. We can expect that, like many Canadians, they were buying Registered Retirement Saving Plans and Tax-Free Savings Accounts to support their retirement. Nor were they realizing a level of revenue that would allow them to buy opulent vacation properties, yachts, and a fleet of luxury automobiles. But they might rent a cottage for a week and buy a kayak and a roof rack for their mid-size sedan.

This is not to say that there were no bad actors or problematic practices in the unlicensed cannabis trade. Far from it. In Chapter 4, I wrote about its problems with product contamination and package labelling errors. Recently there have been reports of reckless practices such as using packaging that is similar in appearance to popular children's candy products (Marchitelli 2021). Is the unlicensed cannabis trade illegal? By definition—yes. Is it irresponsible? Sometimes. Is it using cannabis to recruit our children as gun runners? Not so much.

The evidence discredited the hyperbole and outright fiction that became a mainstay of the Liberal Party's narrative in the period leading up to and following legalization. The evidence was made available to the government during the consultation phase of its legalization campaign but with no discernible impact on its narrative.

The final critical point made in the chapter on decriminalization was that the government's own documentation from its Department of Justice and the Public Prosecution Service of Canada indicated that there was little basis for concern about a major role for organized crime in the unlicensed cannabis trade.

Undaunted by the research and its own intelligence, the Liberal government persisted with its dishonest mission to associate the unlicensed cannabis trade with violent organized crime. The campaign was essentially a contemporary remake of the alarmist, prohibition era film, *Reefer Madness*. The fact-famished exhortations were now repurposed to terrify Canadians into supporting a new ambitious objective in a modern era—the creation of a new lucrative drug industry.

A Legal Regulated Cannabis Trade as Panacea

The second part of the government's communication strategy was to cultivate support for its legalization campaign by praising the merits of a legal, government-regulated, safe cannabis trade over an illegal, unregulated, dangerous one. The premise possesses a surface-level appeal that has been buoyed by decades of drug policy orthodoxy.

As we saw in the previous chapter, there is a legacy of misconduct by licensed drug companies that challenges the veracity of this orthodoxy. Licensed drug industries, such as alcohol, tobacco, and pharmaceutical have shown frequent indifference to public health in their pursuit of revenue, and sometimes engaged in unethical and criminal conduct in this pursuit. Government regulation of such conduct has been generously tolerant and, in the worst cases, intentionally facilitative, even collaborative. That chapter also showed that a healthy skepticism of the propriety of a legal, regulated cannabis industry is warranted by observations of recreational use in US state-jurisdictions and of therapeutic use in both the US and Canada.

On the road to cannabis legalization, The Liberal Party's pitches became an ever-shifting mosaic of jingoistic seductions that bore little resemblance to the real world of cannabis and other drug trades, licensed and unlicensed. Over time, the Party evolved a comforting rubric of taking a public health approach, protecting children, fighting organized crime, and strengthening the economy. By the time legalization arrived, the Liberal Party's spin-masters had crafted the marquee slogan to seduce a wary segment of the public into acceptance. But that is getting ahead of the story; more on that later.

The Centre for Addiction and Mental Health's
Cannabis Policy Framework

The government's case for legalization was reinforced by a highly supportive *Cannabis Policy Framework* produced by The Centre for Addiction and Mental Health (CAMH) (2014). The Framework had its merits, including a convincing case in support of policy change:

- *the popularity of cannabis as a recreational drug*

- *increased public support for liberalization of cannabis laws for both therapeutic and recreational use*

- *cannabis-related harm is potentially serious, but the most serious harm is experienced by a relatively small proportion of users*

- *failure of the criminal justice approach to curtail cannabis use and related harm*

- *the added social harms that arise from our criminal justice approach*

- *the importance of implementing a reform model that places priority on public health considerations.*

Arising from that analysis, the *Framework* made a strong statement on the importance of ending prohibition in service of social justice. It also provided a warning about threats to public health policy from industry lobbying and recommended a full ban on all promotion of cannabis products. This is laudable, evidence-based, public health advocacy.

However, the Framework's analysis also engaged in hyperbole about the harms of the unlicensed trade and gave insufficient attention to research on the merits of decriminalization. It also fell short in its attention to the legacy of harm, malfeasance, and economic costs associated with established legal drug industries. The Framework also juxtaposed decriminalization and legalization as incompatible alternatives to policy reform and concluded that legalization alone was the only defensible evidence-based policy option for cannabis law reform.

CAMH's *Framework* drew upon two familiar groups of assertions to make its recommendation for legalization over decriminalization.

The first was that the unlicensed cannabis trade was characterized by dangerous criminality, cannabis product of uncertain integrity, risk to the safety and propriety of users, and the retention of all revenue in the hands of criminals; decriminalization does nothing to dislodge the unlicensed trade.

The second assertion was that legal, government-regulated cannabis industry would supply safe product, protect public health, safety, and propriety, and provide revenue for a new industry, government, and worthy causes.

The *Framework* further asserted that the unlicensed trade "...should shrink significantly and potentially disappear" (CAMH, 2014, 11).

As with the Liberal Party, the recommendation for legalization was an unexpected and momentous change for CAMH. CAMH and one of its precursor organizations—The Addiction Research Foundation of Ontario (ARF)—had maintained a formal position favouring decriminalization since 1990.

In a conversation I had in June 2015 with a prominently placed individual at CAMH with intimate knowledge of the *Framework*'s development, I was told that a request to CAMH for a report on cannabis legalization had been initiated by a CAMH board member connected to the Liberal Party of Canada. Based upon the credibility of the source and my near four decades of experience at ARF and CAMH, some as a Director, I regard that information as highly credible. And while it could be entirely coincidental, it is noteworthy that, according to his Wikipedia page (Wikipedia 2022), Alfred Apps, the Liberal Party executive who hired a communications firm to champion legalization within the Party, had also served as Chair of the CAMH Foundation Board of Directors from 2006-2007. This was confirmed in an email to me (Centre for Addiction and Mental Health Foundation 2021) which also indicated that Mr. Apps served as a member of the Foundation Board from 2003 to 2009 and that Mr. Apps had also served on CAMH's Transforming Lives Campaign Cabinet from 2007 to 2011 which helped raise $108 million. An impressive and prominent contribution indeed!

On the same day that CAMH publicly released its *Framework* (October 9, 2014), no less than the Leader of the Liberal Party and Prime Minister heir apparent, Justin Trudeau, expressed the gratitude of the Party in a press release issued not from Ottawa, but from Toronto—the location of CAMH's headquarters. The release read: "Liberals welcome the call for the legalization and regulation of marijuana by the CAMH..." (Liberal Party of Canada 2014).

Clearly, Liberal Party leadership was prepared for the release of the report that it may very well have catalyzed. Along the path to legalization, the government and media outlets would often refer to CAMH's *Framework* as providing support for the legalization campaign. CAMH's continued support for the campaign was further realized with the appointment of Dr. Catherine Zahn, CAMH CEO at the time, to the government's Task Force on Marijuana Legalization and Regulation.

Decriminalization is Out; Criminalization is In

In 2016, The Honourable Murray Rankin was a Member of Parliament (NDP) for Victoria, British Columbia. He was also Vice-Chair of the federal government's Standing Committee on Justice and Human Rights and a former law professor at the University of Victoria. Mr. Rankin introduced a motion to the Canadian House of Commons on June 13, 2016. The motion recommended invoking the Director of Public Prosecutions Act to allow the federal Attorney General to direct enforcement and prosecution authorities to stop arresting and prosecuting people for minor cannabis offences. Attorney General Jody Wilson-Raybould spoke against the motion, and it was defeated in the House by a large block of Liberal and Progressive Conservative votes. The arguments against the motion were replete with the traditional Progressive Conservative party-line vitriol about the enrichment of dangerous criminals who threaten children's safety and propriety—arguments parroted that day by members of the Liberal Party as well (Canada 2016a). Once again, the Liberal Party of Canada had perpetuated its long legacy of the criminalization of mostly young, cannabis users.

Privileged Access to Influence Policy

An important role of government in health policy development is to ensure a balance of an industry's pursuit of revenue with the protection of public health. Policy development can be seen as an arena where these two interests compete for influence in policy direction. The neutrality of the political process to enable equitable opportunity to influence the policy outcomes is an important and expected safeguard.

One of the principal ways by which an industry can influence government policy is through a system of privileged access, most notably, industry lobbying. The potential of lobbying to serve market expansion and profitability while potentially increasing the risk of harm to public health has already been discussed. This is the reason health policy organizations warn against the practice of industry lobbying. Cannabis would be no exception.

In 2016, a report from *CTV News* had documented eighty-five entries in the federal government's Lobbyist Registry as of March of that year (Woodward 2016). These were private meetings between cannabis industry representatives and senior government officials. On February 10, 2017, I did a subsequent search of the Registry on "Canopy Growth" and found that between April and December 2016, Canopy Growth alone had ten such meetings. Canopy was represented by a consultant from Ensight Canada, a public relations firm with a self-declared specialty in government relations. The consultants are typically people who have worked at senior levels in the government bureaucracy. They possess seasoned expertise on which levers to pull, how, when, and with whom. Representatives of the government in these meetings included Directors of Policy Affairs, Policy Advisors, Members of Parliament, and Senators (Office of the Commissioner of Lobbying of Canada 2017). Two years later, I conducted another check of the Registry and discovered that, as of April 17, 2019, lobbying activity by "Canopy Growth" and "Aurora Cannabis Inc", two major players in the cannabis industry, had continued throughout the pre-legalization period (Office of the Commissioner of Lobbying of Canada, 2019).

The arena of influence is not restricted to Parliament Hill. Liberal Party cash-for-access fund-raising events also provided cannabis industry executives with the opportunity to ply their elevator pitches to key government decision-makers. One such event, held in Toronto in the spring of 2016, included a substantial presence of cannabis industry people, most noticeably representing interests of the licensed producers. This premium-priced event provided an opportunity to speak privately with Bill Blair who, at the time, was the government's point-person on cannabis legalization (Fife and Chase 2017).

The intended outcome of industry-government meetings, typically employing the lobbying wisdom of professional consulting firms, is industry-friendly policy. This privileged type of influence stands in stark contrast to that accessed by most non-industry players, including public health authorities. For the most part, they provided their input in large gatherings, made written submissions, or completed an online questionnaire—their voices potentially lost amidst a faceless bleating herd.

Along the road to legalization, The Liberal Party frequently warned us that dangerous criminals were selling cannabis to our children. It may have been more prudent for us to worry about the greater danger of legislators selling influence to corporate lobbyists.

Establishing The Task Force on Marijuana Legalization and Regulation

An inequitable level of influence can also come into play as part of the study phase of introducing new legislation. This phase began promptly after the Liberal Party formed the new government, beginning with the appointment of The Task Force on Marijuana Legalization and Regulation. The Task Force would consult with experts and other Canadians and issue a report with recommendations to government. To orient Canadians to the issue, the Task Force released a *Discussion Paper* in June of 2016 (Task Force on Marijuana Legalization and Regulation 2016). The *Discussion Paper* acknowledged that it was a work in progress and was written, in part, to ask for and guide advice on the many daunting legislative and regulatory challenges. The paper also reinforced aspects of the government's core messages of demonizing the unlicensed trade and exalting the benefits of a licensed one. The *Discussion Paper* invited Canadians to send their thoughts and advice through an online template which was available during July and August 2016. This is a time of year when most Canadians are preoccupied with more pleasurable pursuits than informing government policy. However, the Task Force would later announce that it had received approximately thirty thousand submissions! Canadians were interested.

The appointed leadership for the study phase of new legislation can have a profound impact on the process. The professions of law and health care are traditionally considered as highly relevant to health policy development. Accordingly, The Task Force leadership consisted of a lawyer as chair and a physician as co-chair. The Task Force membership included additional representatives from the health and legal professions, as well as from municipal politics, law enforcement, public health, social policy, and academia.

There were no representatives from the cannabis industry thus precluding any direct conflicts of interest. The government has a procedure for declaring "indirect interests" to identify the potential for undue influence of any financial or personal interests among members of a study group in the development of legislation. These are declared in the "Summary of Responses from Task Force Members Regarding Their Interests and Affiliations."

The Chair of the Task Force, Ms. Anne McLellan, had a very impressive past political record in service of Liberal Party of Canada governments. These included:

- *Minister of Natural Resources and Federal Interlocutor for Métis and Non-Status Indians.*

- *Minister of Justice and Attorney General of Canada.*

- *Minister of Health.*

- *Deputy Prime Minister of Canada.*

- *Minister of Public Safety and Emergency Preparedness.*

Ms. McLellan quite properly declared "indirect financial interests" arising from her role as "Senior advisor with Bennett Jones, a law firm in Edmonton since 2006. The firm represents some clients with interests in the legal marijuana business" (Canada 2016b). Upon scrutiny, this was an understatement of Ms. McLellan's interests.

Among the business associates of Bennett Jones was the previously discussed cannabis producer, Tweed, the same producer whose co-founder, Mr. Chuck Rifici, had been an executive member of the Liberal Party of Canada's National Board of Directors. It was apparent that Bennett Jones LLP had been cultivating a particularly close relationship with Tweed. An item displayed on the law firm's website on June 18, 2014 described two partners from Bennett Jones' Toronto office having been invited to, and attending, Tweed's official launch of their Smith Falls, Ontario, production facility (Bennett Jones 2014). The article acknowledged Tweed as a "...front-runner in the hotly anticipated "Green Rush"...." It was also clear that the law firm's interests in the green rush went much further than Tweed. In a *Toronto Star* article, one of the same Toronto partners at Bennett Jones, Hugo Alves, spoke of the changing and growing cannabis industry and of Bennett Jones' ambitions for that industry: "We want to be the go-to advisors" (Flavelle 2015). "Bennett Jones LLP" was also listed under "General Membership" on the website of the cannabis trade association, Cannabis Canada.

Bennett Jones clearly had an interest in seeing the cannabis industry prosper financially, and it is reasonable to expect that Ms. McLellan would be predisposed to supporting her employer's ambitions. There was nothing improper with any of that. It was all appropriate, and smart, networking among like-business interests. But matters went awry when Ms. McLellan accepted the appointment as Chair of the government's Task Force on Marijuana Legalization and Regulation. With its *Final Report* submitted directly to Cabinet members, the Task Force was positioned to have substantial and unparalleled influence on the key decisions that would shape Canada's legal cannabis regime. This included decisions on how this industry would be allowed to conduct its business, and how government would regulate it. Many of those decisions would resolve potential trade-offs between industry revenue and public health protection. For example, a higher minimum age of twenty-one for cannabis use would better protect public health and safety while a lower age of eighteen would generate more sales and revenue for the industry. Restricting product innovation such as a ban on cannabis confections would likely limit increases in cannabis use and associated problems, while allowing edibles would increase sales and revenues. An online-only system for buying cannabis would prevent increased normalization and glamourization of cannabis while allowing highly visible retail outlets (as exist for alcohol) would increase visibility, purchases, and revenue. A ban on advertising, versus allowing advertising, would carry the same potential impacts on market expansion. Clearly, any interest of a Task Force member that leans towards industry interests had the potential to compromise protection of the public's health. The financial interest may be indirect, but that does not eliminate its potential impact. The fact that the Task Force member concerned was the Chair is particularly noteworthy.

Following the work of the Task Force, Ms. McLellan was speaking at cannabis industry meetings. When a journalist asked her about these appearances as a potential conflict, she responded: "When I do these speaking engagements, I do so in my role as the former chair of the task force. I'm not there as senior adviser at the law firm of Bennett Jones LLP." An article in *The Globe and Mail* reported that Ms. McLellan was handing out her Bennett Jones business cards at industry meetings (Hager and Robertson 2017).

The conflicts did not end with the Chair of the Task Force. The Co-chair, Dr. Mark Ware, is a physician and renowned cannabis researcher and academic at McGill University in Montréal, Québec. Dr. Ware's declaration in the "Summary of Responses from Task Force Members Regarding Their

Interests and Affiliations" included an impressive list of contributions to various academic/health-related organizations. He also declared indirect "financial" and "intellectual" interests (Canada 2016b).

Before the work of the Task Force began, it appears that Dr. Ware maintained a consulting business with at least one licensed cannabis producer as a client. Michael Haines, CEO of Mettrum, had this to say about Dr. Ware's assistance to his company: "Mark Ware is a leading pain researcher. With Ware's help, and a few more strains, the company is expecting double-digit growth" (Shaw 2016).

In customary circumstances, there is nothing wrong with academics consulting with industry. There are potential benefits for all involved. However, as in the case with Ms. McLellan, the conflict arose when Dr. Ware accepted the post of Co-chair of the Task Force.

That conflict intensified when, two months after the release of the Task Force Report, licensed cannabis producer Canopy Health Innovations (owned by Canopy Growth Corporation) announced that it was entering "...into a 3-year consulting agreement with EPIC Consulting Inc., the Québec-based consulting firm of Dr. Mark Ware" (Canopy Growth Corporation 2017).

Barely a year into that consulting agreement, Dr. Ware was appointed Canopy's Chief Medical Officer and took a leave from his academic post at McGill University (Canopy Growth Corporation 2018).

In another case, one month after the Task Force released its Report, Task Force member Raf Souccar, a former RCMP Deputy Commissioner, became the President and CEO of Aleafia. This medical cannabis company became incorporated in the month following the release of the Task Force Report (Platt 2017). It is unknown whether Mr. Souccar was considering this interest before or during his tenure with the Task Force. He had not declared an interest with the government.

It Sure Looks Like an Inside Job: The Fully Permeable Membrane Between Government and Industry

In the previous chapter, I presented the legacy of industry-government alliances and industry-friendly regulatory practices seen in our longer-established drug industries. It is reasonable to expect that similar dynamics might come into play in the emerging cannabis industry as well. Commercial interests of Task Force members may understandably compromise the confidence that public health advocates and the public would have in the integrity of a process meant to ensure the "public health approach" the government had promised.

When selecting its Task Force leaders, The Liberal Party would have done well not to supply fuel for these reasonable concerns. It seems clear that commercial interests were in play for both the Chair and Co-chair. The financial and intellectual property interests were properly declared, but that makes them no less of interests. The purpose of declaring the interest is to expose it to public consideration for whether it is a conflict of interest. I believe that these interests of the Task Force's Chair and Co-chair represented unacceptable conflicts of interest. I also believe that the conflicts were incompatible with an equitable process to ensure a balance of industry revenue opportunity and the protection of the public's health.

An important cascade of events began with the therapeutic legalization of cannabis and the later creation of a legal commercial production capacity. The cascade continued with the Liberal Party's announcement of its intent to legalize recreational use, it's majority victory in the 2015 election, and its prompt establishment of an industry-friendly task force. As this cascade further progressed, there was a large-scale transport of political players through the fully permeable membrane between government and industry. Chuck Rifici and Ian McKay, apparent principal catalysts of the Liberal Party's legalization campaign, and the leadership of the Task Force, comprised only a few of the many Liberal Party elites with aspirations in the cannabis industry. With visions of wealth dancing in their heads, they became officers, board members, advisors, and investors, positioning themselves for substantial financial gain from recreational legalization.

Liberal Party Elites Join the Green Shine List

Liberal Party elites becoming involved in the cannabis industry included individuals at both federal and provincial levels. Some of the federal level players included the following:

- *John Turner, a former prime minister, became a board member of Muileboom Organics Inc. (Sheikh 2016).*

- *Martin Cauchon, a former justice minister, became chair of the board for 48North (Press 2018).*

- *Herb Dahliwal, a former minister of finance became chair of NG BioMed (DiMatteo 2018).*

- *Larry Campbell, called to the senate by former Liberal Prime Minister Paul Martin, became an advisor to Vodis Pharmaceutical Inc. (Campbell 2017).*

- *Ian McKay, as discussed earlier, had served as a national director of the Liberal Party, and played a key role as a catalyst for recreational legalization. He had also served as a senior policy adviser to a minister of industry under former Prime Ministers Jean Chretien and Paul Martin. Apart from being an initial investor in Tweed Inc., McKay eventually became the director of Knightswood Financial Corp., a company with concentrated investments in the cannabis industry (Levesque 2017).*

178

Provincial level players included the following:

- *Kash Heed, a former British Columbia solicitor general, became a consultant with National Green BioMed (DiMatteo 2018).*

- *Adam Miron had been a national director of Young Liberals of Canada and a provincial coordinator for the British Columbia Liberals. He started a cannabis producer, Hydropothecary (Fayerman 2017). The company would eventually change its name to HEXO and become a prominent and (as we will see later) controversial player in the industry.*

- *Terry Lake was a former British Columbia health minister. A longtime associate of Miron's, he became vice-president of corporate and social responsibility at Hydropothecary (Fayerman 2017).*

- *Dr. John Gillis, a Halifax physician specializing in pain management, and a former president of the Liberal Party of Nova Scotia, became the vice president of medical development at the Truro Herbal Company (Atlantic Business Magazine 2017).*

- *George Smitherman was a former Ontario deputy premier and health minister who became affiliated with two cannabis producers. He was a shareholder (Campbell 2017) and board member for Alta Vista Ventures Ltd. and was a director and investor at THC BioMed International (Sheikh 2016). In 2020, Mr. Smitherman became President and CEO of the Cannabis Council of Canada, one of the country's foremost cannabis industry lobbyist groups (Cannabis Council of Canada, n.d.).*

- *Charles Sousa was a former Ontario Liberal finance minister with responsibility for the government's cannabis retail plan. He joined the board of Lobo Genetics (Subramaniam 2018).*

Senior Bureaucrats Serving Under Liberal Governments

Apart from elected officials, senior government bureaucrats were also keen to join the green rush:

- *Mark Zekulin was a former senior advisor to former Ontario finance minister Dwight Duncan. He became president of Tweed Inc. (Sheikh 2016).*

- *Cam Battley was a former legislative assistant to a Canadian minister of Consumer and Corporate Affairs. He became the chief corporate officer for Aurora Cannabis (DiMatteo 2018).*

- *Shane Morris was a former director of policy leadership in the federal government. He took a leave of absence to become a vice-president at Hydropothecary (HEXO) and held shares in the company (Campbell 2017).*

- *Courtney Betty, a former crown attorney with the federal justice department, became the CEO of Timeless Herbal Care, which included therapeutic cannabis in its product line (Sheikh 2016).*

- *Joshua Tepper was a president of Health Quality Ontario. He became a director and shareholder at Mettrum Ltd. (Campbell 2017).*

Players from Other Political Parties

Most political party players moving to the industry were affiliated with the Liberal Party. However, a few from other parties were also eager to make the move:

- *James Moore was a former federal Progressive Conservative minister of industry and minister of Canadian Heritage. He joined the board of directors of Benchmark Botanics (Stockhouse 2019).*

- *Ernie Eves, a former Ontario Progressive Conservative premier, became chair of Timeless Herbal Care (Sheikh 2016).*

- *Mike Harcourt was the former New Democrat Party premier of British Columbia. He became chair and a shareholder in True Leaf Medicine (Campbell 2017).*

- *Darrell Dexter, a former New Democrat Party premier of Nova Scotia, became vice chair of global affairs at the Cannabis Beverage Producers Alliance (GrowthOp 2019).*

Law Enforcement: From Arresting to Cashing In

With justified indignation, seasoned, internationally known Canadian cannabis activist, Jodie Emery, had much to say about the movement of law enforcement figures into the cannabis industry. Ms. Emery has bewailed tirelessly on social media about the hypocrisy of former law enforcement officials who built careers, at least in part, by arresting and charging cannabis users (including she and her former partner, Marc Emery). Ms. Emery took great offence to former law enforcement officials now profiting from their recent vesting in the licensed cannabis industry. She reasonably sees the industry as being built on a foundation of social acceptance that she and Marc had played a leading role in forging at significant cost to their and many others' social freedoms. Emery curated and posted links to media stories providing examples of enforcement figures having moved into the industry (Emery 2017).

A few notable examples follow. Emery's coverage is more extensive:

- *Norman Inkster, a former head of the Royal Canadian Mounted Police, became a director at Mettrum.*

- *Raf Souccar was a former undercover drug officer and RCMP deputy commissioner. He was a member of the Task Force on Cannabis Legalization and Regulation. He became president and CEO of Aleafia Inc.*

- *Julian Fantino was a former Conservative member of parliament, Ontario provincial police commissioner, and Toronto police chief. He had once infamously equated the legalization of cannabis to the legalization of murder. Mr. Fantino became the executive chair of licensed cannabis producer Aleafia Inc.*

- *Kim Derry was a former Toronto deputy police chief. He became senior advisor of safety and security at Alta Vista Ventures. Along with George Smitherman, he lobbied his former boss, Bill Blair, former chief of police for Toronto. Blair was then the Liberal Party's point person on cannabis legalization. The pair were asking Blair for a tougher response to unlicensed cannabis operators (Di-Matteo 2018).*

When I first encountered the lists of prominent government and enforcement people moving into the industry, I was reminded of a discussion at the University of Waterloo's student pub circa 1977. One of the discussants offered that his greatest concern about the future of cannabis would be the day that he would have to buy his weed from "the man." The rest of us around the table smiled and rolled our eyes. In retrospect, it appears this young man was somewhat of a prophet.

Wither Impartiality and Integrity

There lingers a tempting conclusion from the formative years of the Liberal Party's cannabis legalization campaign, including the Party's un-ceremonial abandonment of decriminalization as its preferred policy choice. The new direction appears to have been inspired, in large part, by the envisioned enrichment of a lucrative commercial drug industry. Many of the Party's prominent members had invested in the therapeutic forerunner of an industry poised to undergo significant growth with the arrival of recreational legalization. Such an expanded market was also expected to generate a substantial amount of tax revenue—play money for the party in power. Subsequent events (as discussed later) would prove to be largely consistent with these early indications.

In the best possible scenario, all the declared and undeclared interests may ultimately have been inconsequential to the deliberations and recommendations of the Task Force. A definitive conclusion on this question is not possible. A significant barrier is that the minutes of Task Force meetings were sealed from public access.

When one considers the broader entanglement of events, it would not be unreasonable to declare a serious credibility risk to the impartiality and integrity of the overall legalization process. To summarize, these events include:

- *prompt and assertive action taken by Liberal Party Board Executives to change party policy from decriminalization to legalization*

- *at least two of those executives were invested in a prominent cannabis company*

- *membership of an executive of that prominent licensed cannabis producer on the executive of the Party's Board of directors*

- *the Liberal government's tolerance of that cannabis producer's illegal business relationship with a violent serial criminal in the United States, and of that producer's other illegal activities*

- *extensive industry lobbying of decision makers*

- *many Liberal Party elite members and senior bureaucrats being vested in the cannabis industry*

- *the Party's selection of Task Force leadership with cannabis industry connections and ambitions*

- *the lack of transparency in the deliberations of the Task Force.*

Overall, the process was incompatible with the maintenance of public confidence in the impartiality and integrity of the Canadian government in its campaign to legalize cannabis for recreational use.

DID WE GET A PUBLIC HEALTH APPROACH?

The Government Proclaims a "Public Health Approach"

For several years, prominent health policy organizations in Canada had issued reports encouraging a public health approach for drug policy reform. These included The Canadian Drug Policy Coalition (Carter and Macpherson 2013), The Canadian Public Health Association (2014), The Centre for Addiction and Mental Health (2014) and The Canadian Medical Association (2016).

The Liberal Party appeared to recognize the pacifying appeal of a public health approach and adopted it as its cannabis legalization banner for the 2015 federal election campaign. A public health approach was recommended in both documents released by the government's Task Force: its *Discussion Paper* (Task Force on Marijuana Legalization and Regulation 2016) and its *Final Report* (Task Force on Cannabis Legalization and Regulation 2016). The "Summary" of Bill C-45, The Cannabis Act included the intention "to protect public health and public safety" in both its first and final versions (Canada 2018a, 2018b). Specific mention of a public health approach also appeared in Minister of Health Ginette Petitpas Taylor's public announcement at the time of the Act's coming into force on October 17 2018 (Canada 2018c).

Tension Between Market Expansion and a Public Health Approach

The Task Force's *Discussion Paper* was released in June of 2016 to support its solicitation of advice on the many legislative and regulatory challenges of legalization (Task Force on Marijuana Legalization and Regulation 2016). The *Discussion Paper* acknowledged the importance of a public health approach, but also suggested that the Canadian government was interested in only one path for cannabis law reform—a private sector, commercial cannabis industry:

> *Experience with both home cultivation and government-controlled production in the context of relatively small numbers of medical users suggests neither approach would be in the public interest in the context of the larger numbers of users expected in a legalized market. Therefore, some form of private sector production with appropriate government licensing and oversight could allow for safe and secure production of legal marijuana with adequate choice (both price and strain) for consumers. (Task Force on Marijuana Legalization and Regulation 2016, 16)*

Later that year, The Task Force's *Final Report* (Task Force on Cannabis Legalization and Regulation 2016) was submitted directly to the Ministers of the three lead Ministries responsible for cannabis legislation: Health, Justice, and Public Safety and Emergency Preparedness. The Report would be highly predictive in determining the course of the legislation, and accordingly receives considerable attention in this chapter.

The government's apparent enthusiasm for a public health approach never acknowledged the unavoidable tension between public health protection and a profit-driven corporation's priority for market expansion. This is especially important when the product is a potentially harmful drug.

It is expected that any revenue-driven company, including a drug company, would have a principal interest in expanding its market. Such is the essence of the entrepreneurial spirit. However, drug products, by their nature and associated harm, are no ordinary commodity. A drug industry's attempts at market expansion thus pose a greater potential threat to public health than does an industry expanding its market for less risk-laden products. The potential for significant individual and societal harm from drug products is the source of the tension that exists between market expansion and public health protection. This tension will likely be pervasive in any attempt to marry a public health priority with a commercial enterprise.

First, Chapter 1 demonstrated perennial high levels of harm to people and costs to the Canadian economy from the use of products from our long-established drug industries for alcohol and tobacco. Chapter 5 demonstrated several key points that are pertinent to the tension that exists between public health protection and an industry's desire for market expansion. Here are the key points.

- *An association of alcohol and tobacco industry market expansion activities (advertising, marketing, lobbying) with increased harm.*

- *An association between market expansion and harm was also demonstrated by the opioid overdose pandemic that began with illegal marketing practices by legal pharmaceutical companies.*

- *Despite the evidence of harm, drug industries remained relentless in their pursuit of market expansion, even to the point of breaking the law.*

- *Government regulation has not succeeded in containing the problems associated with legal drug trades.*

The cannabis industry in Canada, since legalization for therapeutic use, had also engaged in illegal market expansion tactics, not only to support the growth of the therapeutic market but also in anticipation of a much larger and more lucrative recreational market.

Given the group of perils above, it was no surprise that public health authorities approached cannabis legalization for recreational use with caution. These concerns were buoyed when The Canadian Centre on Substance Abuse (2015) dispatched a team to interview key stakeholders in the states of Colorado and Washington which had just recently legalized recreational use. The team produced a report, detailing a variety of challenges with ensuring public health protection in those commercial legalization environments.

The importance of addressing this challenge would not be lost on many health policy organizations in Canada and abroad. They are familiar with the well-documented, decades-long, malfeasance in pursuit of market expansion as witnessed in our existing legal, revenue-driven, corporate drug industries. It seems unavoidable that the tension between market expansion and public health prevention will be pervasive in attempts to marry a public health approach with a commercial enterprise in the legalization of a recreational drug.

The Task Force found itself the arbiter of this tension between two approaches with an apparent unresolvable underlying incompatibility. One approach prioritized health protection, while the other prioritized revenue maximization. I will now try to evaluate how, and how successfully, the Task Force addressed this conflict. First, I will attempt an operational definition of a public health approach.

Key Elements of a Public Health Approach

Despite the clearly stated preference for a conventional private industry model in The Task Force's *Discussion Paper*, health policy organizations were apparently not inclined towards immediate acquiescence. In their submissions to the Task Force, there was a consensus on the importance of using a public health approach to avoid market expansion. These organizations provided advice for doing so in three ways:

1. *considering not-for-profit approaches as a supply model*

2. *resisting industry lobbying*

3. *banning all forms of product promotion (advertising, marketing, celebrity endorsement, event sponsorship).*

To these three, I add four key issues that emerged as controversial ones and required the Task Force to make choices between public health protection and revenue maximization:

4. *a minimum age for purchase and possession*

5. *edible products*

6. *treatment of the unlicensed cannabis trade*

7. *product quality control.*

This provides seven issues which juxtapose market expansion and public health protection. For each of the seven issues, I will review evidence that supports a public health priority, the recommendations of the Task Force in its *Final Report*, and the legislation ultimately created by the government in The Cannabis Act.

Written legislation is intended to provide comprehensive and clear provisions to serve its stated objectives. In the case of the development of Bill C-45, The Cannabis Act, Canadians were told that the Act would reflect a public health approach for supplying cannabis to Canadians within a law-abiding commercial framework. The Task Force declared its adoption of a public health approach as a guiding principle for its work. I have accordingly used it as the guiding principle for my analysis of the work of the Task Force and the provisions of the Act. In most cases, the recommendations in The Task Force's Report were assigned a great deal of weight in determining the provisions of The Cannabis Act.

The Task Force Releases Its *Final Report*

The Task Force publicly released its *Final Report* in December 2016, with a change to the Task Force's name, replacing "Marijuana" with "Cannabis" (Task Force on Cannabis Legalization and Regulation 2016).

The release of the report occurred amidst two controversies arising from the already established legal trade in cannabis for therapeutic use. I already covered one controversy in the previous chapter. Cannabis producer, Mettrum, had been exposed by a whistle-blower for using illegal pesticides and hiding the evidence during Health Canada inspections. Health Canada was (uncharacteristically) less than enthusiastic in promptly making the case details public—possibly because of the imminent release of the Task Force Report.

The other controversy revolved around a sudden near doubling in the value of Canopy Growth's stock of which former Liberal Party CFO, Chuck Rifici, held a considerable amount. Rifici had left the Liberal Party Board of Directors in June 2016. By October, there was no mention on the Liberal Party's website of Rifici's involvement with the Board. In November, the Canopy Growth stock surge occurred just a few weeks before the public release of the Task Force's Report. The Report was highly favourable towards the interests of licensed producers such as Canopy. Members of the Conservative Party accused Mr. Rifici of having access to inside information that benefited him financially—an allegation which Rifici denied (Bagnall 2018). More than three years later, under threat of legal action, the allegations against Rifici made by two members of the Conservative Party were withdrawn (Stratcann 2020). The conservative members claimed they wanted only to hold the Liberal Party to account for placing someone in a senior position who held a significant interest in the cannabis industry as the party was launching a major cannabis policy initiative (Bagnall 2018).

Crafting Legislation: Market Expansion Versus Public Health Protection

Controversies aside, The Task Force Report was released among great fanfare with extensive media coverage. The Report acknowledged some of the perils inherent in commercial legalization as had been raised by many health policy organizations during the consultation phase: "As with other industries, this new cannabis industry will seek to increase its profits and expand its market, including through the use of advertising and promotion" (Task Force on Cannabis Legalization and Regulation 2016, 18).

However, the Report provided no specific explanation for why market expansion could be detrimental to public health. There was no mention of drug industries perpetually gaming regulations or of their involvement in criminal activity to increase revenues. The Report acknowledged the extraordinary complexity of cannabis law reform and the challenge of striking a balance that fairly represents the myriad interests including those of an emerging industry and the protection of public health. The enormity of this challenge should not be underestimated.

It is to be expected that a commercial cannabis company will have a primary mandate to maximize financial return for owners/shareholders. It tries to do so by expanding the overall market for cannabis and capturing as much of that market as possible. (Other factors, such as minimizing costs and taxes are also relevant, but are less germane to this discussion.)

To its credit, The Task Force made some recommendations that were consistent with a public health approach. Some examples include:

- *allow no promotion that would be appealing to children*

- *prohibit products with high THC potency*

- *avoid criminalizing youth*

- *provide public education and prevention programs*

- *improve access to treatment*

- *prevent impaired driving.*

(Task Force on Cannabis Legalization and Regulation 2016, 2-7)

These were commendable recommendations. They were also recommendations that would have no or minimal impact on the industry's ambitions for market expansion.

But when market expansion was at stake, the Task Force's recommendations tended to be more favourable to the fiscal interests of the industry than to protection of public health. This will become clear in my analysis of the seven juxtapositions of market expansion and public health protection.

1. A Not-For-Profit Model

My submission to the Task Force provided an account of the decades-long legacy of public health harm arising from the conduct of revenue-driven alcohol, tobacco, and pharmaceutical industries, and their permissive regulation by government. The submission also drew attention to early warnings of problems in the commercial legalization campaigns in the United States as well as in the legal therapeutic cannabis regime in Canada. My submission included this recommendation:

> The Task Force should request that government allow it the time to explore the logistics of establishing a government-controlled, not-for-profit cannabis authority that will place protection of public health over market expansion and revenue maximization.

The submission also included a general outline of what such an approach would look like with citations to more detailed descriptions of specific aspects. I later prepared a more detailed manuscript available for public access (DeVillaer 2017). A further revised and updated description of a not-for-profit model is included in this book's "Chapter 9: Let's Try Something Different."

I was not alone with my concerns about a commercial model of legalization and my recommended solution. Prominent health policy authorities in Canada and elsewhere expressed similar concerns about a private industry model and proposed alternatives compatible with my own suggestions.

An article on cannabis law reform published in *The Canadian Medical Association Journal* (Spithoff, Emerson, and Spithoff 2015) noted the legacy of "permissive alcohol and tobacco regulation" and made the following recommendation:

> The government should form a central commission with a monopoly over sales and control over production, packaging, distribution, retailing, promotion and revenue allocation. The primary goal should be public health promotion and protection (to reduce demand, minimize harms and maximize benefits). The commission should be at arm's length from the government to resist interference with this goal, such as industry influence and the government's desire to increase revenues from promoting sales, fees and taxation.

A report by Institut national de santé publique du Québec had this to say:

> The commercialization of cannabis products, even within the context of a strict regulatory framework, sets up an opposition between the profit motive of businesses and the public health goal of reducing cannabis use within the population as a whole. In contrast, a not-for-profit approach makes it possible to focus squarely on prevention, health and safety. (Chapados et al.,1)

The Report of the Chief Medical Officers of Health of Canada & Urban Public Health Network (2016, 12) recommended that cannabis supply be controlled through "a government monopoly and supply management systems" that would oversee production, distribution, and retail and would ensure that retail outlets do not promote use of the product.

The RAND Corporation in the United States had produced a report for The State of Vermont to advise the state on its deliberations on cannabis law reform (Caulkins et al. 2015, 49). The report described a dozen different approaches. RAND did not recommend any one approach over the others, but it made one strong recommendation—that governments do not move, by default, directly from prohibition to commercial legalization. RAND described commercial legalization as "...a for-profit commercial marijuana industry that is licensed and regulated somewhat like the alcohol industry..." and distinguished it from a not-for-profit approach that would entail "...barring for-profit corporations but allowing co-ops or nonprofits whose boards include public-health and child-welfare advocates."

RAND also addressed the retail component of the supply chain. RAND cited research showing that a regulated government retail monopoly is a better model for protecting public health than are less-regulated options (Pacula, et al. 2014). The report articulated four advantages of a government retail monopoly specific to cannabis:

- reduced diversion, which would reduce enforcement costs
- easier reversibility—easier to go from a government monopoly to a commercial competitive model than the reverse

- reduced or eliminated advertising and product innovation

- can prevent a price drop prompted by increased production efficiency by countering with a tax increase.

The United Kingdom's advocate for drug policy reform, Transform Drugs, has a long history of addressing the liabilities of corporate drug industries. Chaired by Transform Drugs' Steve Rolles, The UK's Expert Panel expressed support for not-for-profit approaches such as cannabis social clubs "...so long as they are subject to a formal regulation framework..." (Rolles 2016, 13).

So, how did the Task Force react to these recommendations from within Canada and abroad?

The Task Force's *Final Report* (2016, 31, 33) acknowledged that it had received from stakeholders "...strong calls for a diverse marketplace in which barriers to the participation of smaller producers (sometimes referred to as "craft" or "artisanal") and not-for-profit entities are kept to a minimum" and proposals for a "...centralized, government monopoly...", and that there be opportunity for "...those for whom profit is not their principal motive (e.g., compassion clubs)."

None of these proposals were included in the Task Force's recommendations to the government.

Among public health authorities, drug policy analysts, and various other stakeholders in Canada and elsewhere, there was an interest, even an urgency, to try something different. In the end, the Task Force and the federal government remained undaunted by the data and recommendations for a not-for-profit approach. In both its early *Discussion Paper* and its *Final Report*, The Task Force supported a private sector cannabis industry. This single-minded perspective was built upon the legacy of the Canadian producers that had been licensed for therapeutic use. The perspective may also have been reinforced by continued successful ballot reforms in state jurisdictions in the US. Private sector cannabis producers in Canada were poised to see enormous growth of their industry upon legalization of cannabis for recreational use. The Task Force enabled their ambition and the federal government made it so in The Cannabis Act.

2. Industry Lobbying

The capacity of industry lobbying of government to serve market expansion and profitability at the expense of public health protection was discussed earlier. More specific cautions about the threat it posed for cannabis legalization had been issued by health policy organizations in three countries. In Canada, the warnings appeared in a paper published in *The Journal of the Canadian Medical Association* (Spithoff, Emerson, and Spithoff 2015) and a *Framework* produced by The Centre for Addiction and Mental Health (2014). More warnings appeared in a report from the RAND Corporation in the United States (Caulkins et al. 2015), and a report from the Expert Panel in the United Kingdom (Rolles et al. 2016).

Undeterred by domestic and international alerts, the Task Force's report contained no discussion on industry lobbying, nor did it recommend any discouragement of lobbying activity. The Cannabis Act followed suit. The government opened its doors to the cannabis lobbyists. Private meetings between cannabis industry lobbyists and senior government officials continued throughout the legalization process (Office of the Commissioner of Lobbying of Canada 2019).

3. Product Promotion Practices

Another critical juxtaposition of public health protection and cannabis industry ambitions for market expansion can be seen in the Task Force statements and recommendations on product promotion. More than anything else, the cannabis industry wanted to expand its market for recreational use. The most recent data available to the Task Force from CTADS was from 2015 (Canada 2021). It showed that alcohol was consumed by 77% of the Canadian population age fifteen and over. The corresponding figure for cannabis was 12%. The 77% figure for alcohol was likely to become the benchmark for success for the cannabis industry's long-term market expansion ambitions. One of the best ways to get there is with product promotion—finding ways to get more people to try and keep using cannabis. Of course, the industry also wants current users to continue to use it, and that both groups of customers use more cannabis, more often.

While product promotion is an important market expansion tool for the cannabis industry, it represents a significant concern for public health authorities. Accordingly, several of Canada's health policy organizations called for a full ban on all forms of product promotion for cannabis, including advertising, marketing, celebrity endorsements, and event sponsorships. These calls can be viewed in reports issued by the Chief Medical Officers of Health of Canada and Urban Public Health Network (2016), The Canadian Paediatric Association (Grant and Bélanger 2016), The Canadian Public Health Association (2016), The Centre for Addiction and Mental Health (2016) and a paper published in *The Canadian Medical Association Journal* (Spithoff, Emerson, and Spithoff 2015).

Product promotion was a critical issue for the Task Force in providing its advice to government. Its *Final Report* (Task Force on Cannabis Legalization and Regulation 2016, 19) issued the following statement: "The Task Force agrees with the public health perspective that, in order to reduce youth access to cannabis, strict limits should be placed on its promotion".

On first read, this statement may seem reasonable, even laudable. But there are two problems with it. The first problem runs through much of the Task Force's analysis and recommendations on product promotion. There is an apparent attitude that drug advertising is a threat only to youth. Youth may very well be the most vulnerable target for drug product promotion. Much has been said about the effects of cannabis, the drug, on the developing brain. However, we need to be equally concerned about the effects of advertising on these developing brains in terms of the pervasive and sustained attitudes that can be formed in young fertile minds.

However, youth are not the only vulnerable target. Much of the research on recreational drug advertising involved the perils to adults. I was quite clear on this point in my submission to the Task Force's consultation process, as were other health authorities. The impact of drug advertising on adults was not addressed in the Task Force's report.

The second problem with the statement is that it misrepresents the "public health perspective" as it was provided to the Task Force by public health authorities. These organizations did not, in fact, call for "strict limits", but rather a full ban on all forms of product promotion. The difference between strict limits and a full ban is an important one. Public health authorities are familiar with the wile and creativity of drug companies in gaming regulations. Limits, however strict, are much more open to interpretation than is a full ban. Limits present more opportunity for industry to game the restrictions by exploiting unintended omissions or ambiguities in the written provisions. They also invite industry lobbying of government for flexibility in their interpretation. Surveillance and enforcement of vaguely defined limits, however strictly intended, can be a resource and morale-exhausting undertaking for a regulator's staff.

The concerns of public health agencies were justified given Health Canada's repeated communications with cannabis producers on the issue of product promotion. The notices threatened disciplinary action, including license suspension, for repeated advertising-related violations. When confronted with violations, some companies plead ignorance, declaring difficulty understanding which forms of communication are illegal advertising and which are not. Taken at face value, this defence demonstrates how the understanding and enforcement of product promotion limits can be a nuanced and difficult task for industry and regulators. The public health recommendation of a less ambiguous full ban on product promotion, was justified based on years of experience in the trenches of regulatory surveillance.

On a related matter, The Task Force (2016, 18) wrote: "The industry representatives from whom we heard, while generally supportive of some promotion restrictions—particularly marketing to children and youth, and restrictions on false or misleading advertising—made the case for allowing branding of products." The report also offered: "It was suggested that brand differentiation would help consumers distinguish between licit and illicit sources of cannabis, helping to drive them to the legal market".

The sincerity and credibility of the first statement should be appraised within the context of Health Canada's repeated admonitions of many licensed producers for advertising violations (Canada 2014). Clearly, this industry had not established a track record of being "generally supportive" of restrictions on advertising. The industry's track record of violations of such restrictions, received no mention in the Task Force's report. Taken at face value, industry concessions of not trying to sell cannabis to children or of not lying in its advertising are hardly worthy of accolades from the Task Force.

The second claim—regarding branding—seems disconnected from the dynamics of retail. The distinction of legal from illegal cannabis by consumers will not be primarily made upon the basis of brand differentiation, but by the point of purchase. The illegal retail stores or grey-market dispensaries would soon be closed. The legal product is the one that can be bought from the remaining retail stores. This is unlikely to be a point of confusion among consumers. Any differentiation of licensed and unlicensed product could also be made, not by branding elements, but based upon several federally imposed packaging requirements, including health warnings and excise stickers. Few unlicensed sellers would adopt these added and costly packaging measures.

Furthermore, an unlicensed online site can be just as creative in branding as can a licensed one. While cannabis branding may shift preferences among all types of brands, licensed and unlicensed, there is no reason to believe branding will shift brand preference from unlicensed products to licensed ones.

What the cannabis industry really wanted was to use a brand aesthetic in packaging as advertising for market expansion. The skilful use of brand packaging as a form of advertising has been documented for tobacco in a World Health Organization report that cites supportive research from Australia, Brazil, Canada, France, New Zealand, the United Kingdom, and the United States (World Health Organization 2016).

There is a classic piece of advice in the advertising business: "Don't sell the steak, sell the sizzle." The metaphoric "sizzle" is a powerful force of product promotion that, when applied to cannabis, or any other drug product, is unlikely to contribute to consumer education or protection. Its sole purpose is to seduce a consumer into making a purchase. Cannabis users are best served by accurate information pertinent to the product, such as thc:cbd ratio and dosage—not the sizzle of stylized, focus-group tested logos and slogans, which serve solely to expand overall market size and a company's share of it. Sizzle begets revenue.

The industry's pitch for branding to the Task Force was a preemptive attempt to derail public health efforts to limit the extent and risks of product promotion and to serve the industry's aspiration for market expansion.

In the end, The Task Force recommended "plain packaging" for cannabis product, and "restrictions" if branding were allowed. Apart from information related to the product's composition and strength, and warning labels, the restrictions would allow only the company's name.

But the cannabis industry had far greater ambitions for market expansion and increased revenue. Unhappy with the Task Force's recommendations on product promotion and branding, several cannabis companies and the industry's lobby organizations made their own formal submission on the matter to the government. The submission described a self-regulated industry approach to cannabis product promotion (Aphria et al. 2017). The proposal is candid in its attempt to adopt the promotional playbook of the alcohol industry. It identified the intent to advertise cannabis "...in all types of media, including print, television, radio, out-of-home, digital, and social media platforms." It also expressed an interest in advertising "...on television, radio, or on any websites or social media platforms where at least 70% of the audience is over eighteen years of age or over a province's or territory's legal age for purchase..." (Aphria et al. 2017, 3).

Adoption, by government, of these proposals would mean that much of the publicly visible ad media landscape would be populated with cannabis ads—as much of it is now with alcohol ads. It also means that websites with as much as 30% of underage visitors could promote cannabis. In sum, that could mean potentially millions of underage Canadians exposed to the siren song of cannabis sizzle.

Ultimately, The Cannabis Act did not grant the industry its full wish list with regards to product promotion. Nor did it enact the full ban that was recommended by public health authorities. Following the advice of the Task Force, The Act defined advertising as including marketing, event sponsorship, contests, and celebrity endorsements. It restricted advertising to venues that would not be accessible to those under the legal age. It also prohibited content that would associate company brand elements with "a way of life such as one that includes glamour, recreation, excitement, vitality, risk or daring" or would otherwise evoke "positive emotions" or appeal to youth.

The problem with these limits is that they provide an opportunity for the industry to employ its infinite creativity in gaming them. The Act also allowed limited package branding—either a logo or a slogan and only a few restrictions on the use of colour. These are all features that public health experts recognize as intended not to educate the consumer but to induce purchases and establish brand loyalty. This was the "sizzle" on packaging that is such a powerful tool for product promotion and market expansion.

Some may consider that, on the issue of product promotion, The Cannabis Act arrived at a reasonable compromise of the tension between industry market expansion and public health protection. However, a compromise is not necessarily equitable if only one of the parties begins with a reasonable proposal while the other party begins with a less defensible one. While the public health position is based upon research intended to protect the public, the industry proposal to market cannabis like alcohol is one rooted in market expansion and most likely a detriment to public health. Recall the elevated levels of morbidity, mortality, and economic costs associated with alcohol misuse. Recall the research showing an association between alcohol advertising, alcohol use, and related problems as presented in the previous chapter. Given that context, the alcohol playbook on product promotion was not a reasonable and responsible starting proposal for cannabis product promotion.

The avoidance of a full ban on product promotion was the best the cannabis industry could have realistically hoped for. In this respect, the Task Force and Cannabis Act were sufficiently obliging for the cannabis industry's prosperity.

With limited resources for surveillance and enforcement, and no commitment from government to support sufficiently punitive responses to violations, it would be difficult for even a keen regulator to adequately perform its function. That struggle became clear in the period leading up to and following legalization—a story I will tell shortly.

In the worse case scenario, cannabis promotion might ride a slippery slope of increasing regulatory permissiveness, and eventually reach a visual ubiquity in our communities and media as is currently the case with alcohol.

A final point is a reminder that Uruguay, the only other nation to have legalized cannabis sales for recreational purposes, banned product promotion (Cerdá and Kilmer 2017).

4. Minimum Age

The setting of a legal minimum age for cannabis purchase and possession was one of the most divisive issues in cannabis law reform in Canada. The Task Force received recommendations ranging from a low of eighteen years to a high of twenty-five. Recommendations of nineteen and twenty-one were most common. Ultimately, the Task Force recommended eighteen—the lowest point in the range of recommendations.

The Task Force argued that a higher minimum age creates an opportunity for the unlicensed trade to sell cannabis to underage users. This is a legitimate point, but it should be considered within the context of two other legitimate points.

First, it can be acknowledged that some underage people would acquire cannabis through the unlicensed trade, as they already do. But this does not necessarily mean that, post-legalization, they would only buy it from the unlicensed trade. Many of them would get it from older siblings or friends who bought it legally. When they did buy from the unlicensed trade, it was unlikely to be from dangerous drug dealers. As demonstrated in Chapter 4, buying cannabis from most unlicensed sources is unlikely to place anyone in the kind of serious peril as alleged in the Liberal Party's alarmist campaign. Such invective was also echoed in some of the Task Force's comments on the matter.

Second, as discussed in Chapter 5, data from The Centre for Addiction and Mental Health's *Ontario Student Drug Use and Health Survey* (Boak et al. 2015) challenged a common urban myth that illegal drugs are easier for youth to obtain than are legal ones. In contrast, the CAMH data showed that underage youth tend to report that legally available alcohol and tobacco were easier for them to obtain than was illegal cannabis. So, keeping youth aged eighteen to twenty out of the legal cannabis market should reduce overall access by those in that age range. By virtue of social networks being the principal supply mechanism for underage youth, it should also reduce access by those of immediately younger ages—that is, fifteen to seventeen.

This contention finds support in a literature review of social networks and tobacco use by the United States Institute of Medicine (Bonnie, Stratton, and Kwan 2015, 5-6) which concluded that underage tobacco smokers typically acquire their tobacco from legal-aged peers in their social networks. Youth aged fifteen to seventeen were shown to have peers aged eighteen and nineteen in their social networks, but not peers aged twenty-one and older. Accordingly, the authors argue that a minimum age for tobacco use of twenty-one would be much more effective at keeping tobacco out of the hands of, not only those of eighteen to twenty years, but also those of fifteen to seventeen years. The authors recommended a change of the minimum age for tobacco use from eighteen (as existed in most US state-level jurisdictions) to twenty-one. Many states were doing just that at the time of the Task Force deliberations (Campaign for Tobacco-Free Kids 2020).

In Canada, the importance of a minimum age of twenty-one for tobacco use has been recognized in a report from the Ontario Tobacco Research Unit (Pope, Chaiton, and Schwartz 2015). For alcohol, Babor (2010) has summarized a well-established literature in support of the currently recommended best practice to raise the minimum drinking age to twenty-one.

The US Institute of Medicine rationale for setting a minimum age for tobacco extends perfectly well to cannabis in Canada and would suggest that a minimum age of twenty-one would be optimal for reducing access and use for those between fifteen and twenty—potentially an important public health measure.

The Task Force was not inclined to recognize the increasing legislative precedents or the public health research and recommendations that would support a minimum age of twenty-one for cannabis, as well as other recreational drugs. Rather, it seemed to regard the current minimum age set for tobacco and alcohol in Canada as a gold standard to be emulated for cannabis. The Task Force's rationale for the lower age seemed tenuous: "Many [stakeholders] suggested that 18 was a well-established milestone in Canadian society marking adulthood" (Task Force on Cannabis Legalization and Regulation 2016, 17). The age of eighteen is just one such milestone. Both nineteen and twenty-one have also traditionally served as milestones of adulthood in Canada.

The Task Force acknowledged that all US states that had legalized cannabis for recreational use had set twenty-one as the minimum age. But the Task Force expressed concern that a higher minimum age would expose young users to the legal consequences of illegal use. This was insincere. The cause of these consequences is not a higher legal age. It was the determination of the Liberal Party to resist, and now discredit, a half century of research-based advocacy supporting the decriminalization of the drug. As previously discussed, decriminalization was for many years the official position of the Liberal Party until the Party became mesmerized with the financial rewards of commercial legalization. Recommending decriminalization as a first step towards legalization was apparently not an option within the Task Force's mandate.

The Task Force acknowledged that "Health-care professionals and public health experts tend to favour a minimum age of 21" (Task Force on Cannabis Legalization and Regulation 2016, 17). Those healthcare professionals included the Canadian Medical Association and the Canadian Psychiatric Association both of whom emphasized the scientific literature on the impact of cannabis use on brain development in their recommendation of a minimum age of twenty-one and a restriction on higher potency products until age twenty-five (Dehaas 2017).

With the Task Force's recommendation of eighteen as the minimum age, it was clearly, and seemingly knowingly, paddling against the current of the public health research and thinking as well as the legislative trends of the time. It was also contrary to a proposal to the House of Commons by the NDP Justice Critic of the time. A minimum age of eighteen was also contrary to my own advice on the matter to the Task Force and to my testimony to the House of Commons Standing Committee on Health.

There may be an unacknowledged pressure that guided the Task Force's choice of eighteen. In contrast to the Task Force's overt disclosure of the preference of public health authorities for a minimum age of twenty-one, there was no disclosure of the minimum age proposed by cannabis industry stakeholders. This information is perhaps conspicuous by its absence in the Task Force's Report. However, on behalf of its industry members, the Cannabis Trade Alliance of Canada (2016, 3) posted its submission to the Task Force online. The Alliance recommended that "A minimum age of 18 or 19 is suitable...." Imagine the industry's surprise, and glee, to be granted the lower-end of its recommended range! One might imagine a big party and celebration that night. Let's explore the likely cause for their merriment.

Data collected in 2015 by the Canadian Tobacco Alcohol and Drugs Survey (CTADS) estimated 426,000 cannabis users aged fifteen to nineteen and 715,000 aged twenty to twenty-four. We can accordingly envision a substantial legal cannabis market boost with a minimum age of eighteen compared to twenty-one (Canada 2021). Also recall the US Institute of Medicine study that suggested that fifteen to seventeen year olds will have more access to legal recreational drugs with a minimum age of eighteen than they would with a minimum age of twenty-one. A minimum age of eighteen would not protect young cannabis users from a dangerous illegal trade. But it would expand overall market size for the licensed cannabis industry. It might also expand market share from its competition from the unlicensed trade.

On the matter of minimum age, the Task Force received vastly different advice from public health authorities and from the cannabis industry. In the end, it did not side with the evidence-based public health approach. Nor did it find a midpoint as a compromise.

The Task Force gave the cannabis industry the expanded market it coveted as did the Cannabis Act. The Task Force's recommendation of 18 was adopted into law with the proviso that provinces could raise it. All provinces except Alberta and Québec did—but only to nineteen. In 2020, after a change in government, Québec raised its minimum age from eighteen to twenty-one (CBC News 2020).) The Prime Minister publicly expressed his displeasure with that development.

5. Edible Products as Confections

In the lead-up to legalization, the discussion of cannabis edible products was not always explicit that cannabis edibles would typically involve cannabis-infused confections. These would include sweet, fruit-flavoured beverages, candy, and baked goods. Any product innovation that pairs a drug with a pleasantly tasting experience is a potentially powerful tool for market expansion and increased revenue. Public health analysts working on alcohol and tobacco policy performed all the heavy lifting in documenting the role of fruit and sweet flavours as training wheels for alcohol and tobacco use by young people. Products such as "Cotton Candy" vodka, sold by The Liquor Control Board of Ontario, serve to seamlessly usher young drinkers from their soda pop years to the adult world of alcohol consumption. Cannabis candy would have the same appeal to young people and to novice cannabis users, particularly those who did not already smoke or vape cannabis or tobacco.

The Task Force cited input from observers in Colorado, the first state in the US to legalize cannabis for recreational use: "Expect edibles to have a broad appeal. Cannabis products such as brownies, cookies and high-end chocolates are attractive to novice users" (Task Force on Cannabis Legalization and Regulation 2016, 20).

The pairing of a drug with sweet, or otherwise pleasant-tasting, confections is particularly powerful when combined with the exciting and seductive allure of lifestyle advertising. Recall the lesson from Chapter 2 that many ads do not try to sell only a product. They also sell a surrogate fulfillment of an aspiration or fantasy. Many ads these days also invoke environmental sustainability themes. Imagine this ad copy for a fictional THC-infused *crème brulée*: "...using only certified organic ingredients, locally sourced from artisans, supporting sustainable agricultural practices within a fair-trade framework." With all the boxes checked for the contemporary *zeitgeist* of sustainability, equity, and social justice, how could a THC-infused *crème brulée* possibly be a bad thing?

A potential advantage of cannabis edible products is that they could reduce combustion of cannabis plant material, which would provide a reduced risk to public health. However, this assumes that large numbers of existing cannabis smokers would completely replace smoking with edibles. The more certain impact of edibles would be their appeal to people not currently using cannabis.

Observers in Colorado also warned that confection edibles were attractive to young children who were being taken to hospital in increasing numbers from unintended ingestion at their homes (Rocky Mountain High Intensity Drug Trafficking Area 2014; Wang et al. 2016).

The Task Force could have avoided the risks of cannabis edibles for both adults and unsuspecting children by recommending more thoughtful provisions on the types of edible products allowed. For example, edibles could have been restricted to thc/cbd oils sold in small vials. Users would simply place drops on their tongue. This type of ingestion avoids the perils of smoking and vaping. The vials would have less glamourous appeal for market expansion with underage and adult users and would not provide as much of a visual attraction to young children in the home as would confections.

This approach would have alleviated another expressed concern of the Task Force related to the legalization of edibles: "The net result is that any discussion about regulating a new cannabis industry quickly leads to an understanding of the complexity of regulating not one but potentially thousands of new cannabis-based products" (Task Force on Cannabis Legalization and Regulation 2016, 20). This was a valid observation. However, the challenge that it presents for edibles could have been substantially reduced by simply not allowing cannabis confections to be sold and therefore require regulation. The Task Force could have made a case for restricting edibles to oil drops, at least initially, simply as a cautious approach. Again, the Task Force appeared loath to recommend anything that might diminish the opportunity for market expansion that would be presented by "...thousands of new cannabis-based products."

The Task Force also acknowledged that public health stakeholders in Canada had advised against the legalization of edibles. However, The Task Force stopped short of recommending against the legalization of edible confections.

The Cannabis Act delayed but did not prevent the market expansion opportunity presented by drug infused confections. Edibles were legalized one year later. That was another monumental victory for the cannabis industry with potential peril for public health and safety.

6. Treatment of the Unlicensed Cannabis Trade

Claims of an alleged danger posed by the unlicensed cannabis trade to the propriety and safety of cannabis users, including children, were common throughout The Liberal Party's legalization campaign. As discussed earlier, the research literature found such threats to be highly exaggerated, even fabricated. The immediate intent of these claims was to provoke parental fear and protectiveness of their children to create public support for the establishment of legal cannabis corporations and for harsh measures aimed at competition from the unlicensed trade.

Licensed producers, including one promoted by George Smitherman, a former Ontario Liberal Deputy Premier (Leblanc 2016a), were lobbying hard with a campaign targeting "...top Liberal officials" to eliminate the unlicensed trade (Leblanc 2016b).

Thus, the ultimate intent of the Liberal Party's claims was to steer purchases away from the unlicensed trade and concentrate revenues in the licensed industry. There is nothing necessarily wrong with that aspiration. However, the methods used in its pursuit were unjustified and likely as harmful as they were beneficial.

Policy wise, decriminalization and legalization did not have to be mutually exclusive options. Since my 2016 submission to the Task Force, I have made the case that decriminalization and non-commercial legalization could be first and second stages in a stepped hybrid approach to cannabis law reform. That has been the standard template in sub-national jurisdictions in the United States—although it was not always necessarily planned that way.

Consideration of decriminalization as a policy option was not included in the Task Force's terms of reference. Accordingly, the Task Force's report made little mention of it. Rather, the Task Force's report repeatedly decried the unlicensed cannabis trade as a serious threat to public safety and propriety. The substantial body of research to the contrary was not introduced. Nor was the impact of the continued criminalization of Canadians during the long legalization process and beyond.

The press conference that announced the striking of the Task Force provided an unexpected glimpse into the government's attitude, potentially reflecting its direction to the Task Force. In response to a journalist's question, the reply was surprisingly candid and stark. It escaped like a razor edge ray of light from the opaque box of Party intent:

> "...decriminalization does not meet any of our objectives"
> (CBC News 2016).

There was apparently no appetite for evidence-based policy, social justice, or compassion. This was business.

Accordingly, the Cannabis Act carried some severe provisions. Penalties included criminal records and prison terms of up to five years for possession of unauthorized cannabis. An adult who sold cannabis to a person under the legal age was also subject to a criminal record as well as a maximum penalty of fourteen years in prison. In the latter case, a social justice perspective might question the wisdom of creating the potential for such a harsh penalty applying to a scenario in which a nineteen-year-old sells a small quantity to a seventeen-year-old. While we might discourage such transactions, any length of prison term and a lifelong criminal record would seem to constitute a counter-productive overreach.

Such harsh provisions came as a disappointing and even shocking surprise to long term advocates of cannabis law reform who were less mesmerized by the spectacle of a glamourous new cannabis industry. These advocates were left wondering what had happened to the compassion and sense of justice that had fuelled the half-century drive for reform. The unsavoury reality is that under a corporate cannabis legalization regime, the motivation for criminalizing the unlicensed trade in cannabis is very different. It is no longer about imposing an arbitrary, anomalous form of morality on society. It is now about market domination—which may be a much more formidable motivator for oppression than a perverse proxy for morality ever was.

In the months leading up to The Cannabis Act coming into force, Prime Minister Trudeau continued to beat the demonization drum in the media: "...anyone who is currently purchasing marijuana is participating in illegal activity that is funding criminal organizations and street gangs..." (Harris 2018).

I wonder if the Prime Minister ever considered such a harsh view of cannabis use being applied to himself and the several members of his immediate family who had been well-known cannabis users during prohibition. The profound disconnect between Justin Trudeau's familial penchants and his hyperbolic political talking points is sadly embarrassing. In June 2022, The Liberal Party of Canada's website still carried the discredited pronouncement: "Every day, our kids turn to dealers, gangs and criminals to buy marijuana, putting them in harm's way" (Liberal Party of Canada, n.d).

The continued existence of an unlicensed cannabis trade is not ideal, and we should work towards minimizing its appeal to cannabis users. We could also explore ways to allow participation in the licensed trade for those who are willing to respect regulatory requirements and the law. Government should not attempt to eliminate the unlicensed trade with fear mongering and the imposition of laws that would continue to criminalize cannabis users for the same victimless crime that it had always been. The unlicensed cannabis trade posed far more of a threat to the revenues of the Liberal Party elites in the emerging legal trade than it did to the safety and propriety of Canadians and their children. With its harsh provisions, The Cannabis Act was legislating the creation of more cannabis criminals for the gain of profit. Another loss for social justice and public health protection. Another victory for industry profits.

7. Product Quality Control

Product quality control includes product integrity (including safety) and the accuracy of labelling on the product package.

One of the most promising strategies for reducing the unlicensed trade in cannabis is one that may be readily achievable. However, it remains mostly untapped by large licensed producers. Government has done little to motivate industry to take advantage. While price is very important to consumers, we would expect that they would also be inclined to buy product that is consistently of decent quality, accurately labelled, and free from contamination. Product of unknown strength or compromised quality, or perhaps even contaminated, was often identified as a problem with cannabis from unlicensed sources. Mislabelling of the product for amounts of tetrahydrocannabinol (THC) and cannabidiol (CBD) was also an ongoing concern. The absence of quality control was widely cited as part of the rationale for legalization and regulation. Yet, in the previous chapter, we saw that from the early days of commercial legalization for therapeutic use, production failures were common. This resulted in product recalls related to product integrity and labelling accuracy. This had been an opportunity for licensed producers to increase and stabilize market share through uncompromised attention to quality control. However, much of the licensed industry appeared to choose the easier road of mass production with insufficient attention to production rigour and checks on quality. This easier road is one that, in the short-term, may lead to lower production costs and a desirable impact on profitability. However, it may ultimately be a short-sighted and counterproductive strategy for the industry if it diminishes consumer confidence in the licensed trade. Without the assurance of improved quality, there could be a continued consumer allegiance to the unlicensed trade.

I included multiple reports of contaminated and mislabelled product from licensed cannabis producers in both Canada and the United States as part of my submission to the Task Force near the end of August 2016. Many incidents of contamination had been reported in Health Canada's Recalls and Alerts database before the work of the Task Force was completed. And yet, this problem received no attention by the Task Force. Its *Final Report* noted that "Task Force members had the opportunity to visit some of these producers and were impressed by the sophistication and quality of their work" (Task Force on Cannabis Legalization and Regulation 2016, 9). The Report also recommended: "Regulate the production of cannabis and its derivatives (e.g., edibles, concentrates) at the federal level, drawing on the good production practices of the current cannabis for medical purposes system" (Task Force on Cannabis Legalization and Regulation 2016, 33). The Task Force appeared to have little interest in exploring the issue of quality control—perhaps because the status quo effectively served the industry's immediate profitability.

Opportunities for improving quality control could have arisen within Task Force discussions on packaging of cannabis products. A claim made to the Task Force by industry stakeholders was that to achieve "brand loyalty", producers would be motivated to produce high quality products and be more accountable to their customers. On the surface, this may sound like a reasonable strategy for achieving product integrity and consumer protection through trusted brand loyalty. However, as described in the previous chapter, there was a disappointing legacy of product quality control in the early days of the cannabis industry in both the United States and Canada.

Product integrity, consumer protection, and fair market competition could be more reliably served in two ways. The first would be by unannounced inspections of all production facilities. Samples for testing would be selected not by staff of the producer, but by regulatory staff. There would be independent product testing. There would also need to be meaningful penalties, including license suspension and revocation, for repeated serious failures to meet safe product standards.

The second mechanism would be a requirement that the dates of past recalls for a given producer's product be included on its respective product packaging. This requirement would motivate more care in production practices and improve consumer protection. The requirement to print recall dates on labels would provide a clear market advantage for those producers who take more care to avoid product contamination and labelling errors. I provided some suggested wording for this consumer protection provision in my testimony before The Standing Senate Committee on Social Affairs, Science and Technology in April 2018. The recommended provision was not included in the Cannabis Act. Another victory for the industry; another continued threat to public health and safety; and another lost opportunity to diminish the prominence of the illegal cannabis trade. As discussed earlier, numerous product recalls continued throughout therapeutic legalization. In the next chapter, we will see that this problem has persisted well past legalization for recreational use as well.

That completes my analysis of the seven policy juxtapositions of public health protection and market expansion. The general conclusion is that the Task Force was willing to recommend measures put forward by public health authorities only when those measures would not compromise the aspirations of the industry to expand the market for cannabis and to serve profits. For the most part, the Cannabis Act followed suite.

IT'S NOT ABOUT THE MONEY. OR IS IT?

At a Canadian Press round-table in December 2015, Mr. Trudeau was quoted as saying: "The Liberal plan to legalize pot has always been about public health and safety, not making money." The PM further asserted that "any cash that flows to public coffers through marijuana taxation should go towards addiction treatment, mental health support and education programs—not general revenues" (Bronskill 2015). Well into the fourth year of legalization, that has not happened.

The Task Force identified several principles that would guide its work towards recommendations. One such principle read: "...it is also our view that revenue generation should be a secondary consideration for all governments, with the protection and promotion of public health and safety as the primary goals" (Task Force on Cannabis Legalization and Regulation 2016, 12).

This is a worthy principle. However, its restriction to government revenues is disappointing. There was no suggestion that revenue generation would be secondary to public health and safety, where the industry was concerned. My examination of seven critical issues—all examples of juxtaposition of market expansion and public health protection—would suggest that these two considerations were reversed in importance by the Task Force. Public health and safety were strategically compromised for the increased revenues that would come for both industry and government with increased market expansion. The proof is plainly apparent in the recommendations of the Task Force and their codification in The Cannabis Act. The priority of cannabis legalization in Canada seems indisputable—industry revenue. This also became clear in the time leading up to the day of legalization. This period was one of excessive gaming of regulations by the industry and permissive responses from Health Canada as the regulator. The unfathomable story of non-compliance and forgiveness follows.

Product Promotion Violations

The path to recreational use legalization was paved with promises of strict regulation, including for advertising and marketing. However, the permissive regulation of product promotion for therapeutic use should have prompted a healthy skepticism for the level of regulatory rigour to be applied to recreational use.

In the months leading up to The Cannabis Act coming into force, some licensed cannabis producers entertained a presumptuous entitlement. They contended that the restrictions on product promotion would not come into effect until the date of legalization on October 17, 2018. Therefore, they would engage in as much promotion as possible before that date (Fabian 2018; Miller 2018a). That period witnessed an intensification of blatantly illegal product promotion by some of the larger licensed producers.

Advertising before October 17 was illegal by virtue of the Controlled Drugs and Substances Act. The Act provided the legislative umbrella for the Access to Cannabis for Medical Purposes Regulations (ACMPR), as well as for ACMPR's predecessors—the Marihuana Medical Access Regulations (MMAR) and the Marihuana for Medical Purposes Regulations (MMPR). As previously discussed, licensed producers have a history of repeatedly violating these restrictions despite repeated warnings from Health Canada (Canada 2014). Violations continued after the warnings, as did more warnings. The licensed producers were very much aware that they were breaking the law. Health Canada indicated that, in 2018, it again issued warnings—this time to seven companies (Canada 2018d). Consistent with past practice, Health Canada did not divulge the identity of the companies that were in violation.

Two articles in the *Ottawa Citizen* (Miller 2018a; Miller 2018b) demonstrated how the industry's gamesmanship of product promotion regulations took on many guises in the months leading up to legalization—despite the additional warning from Health Canada. Health Canada's admonitions of the producers were timely given newly published research on the impact of therapeutic cannabis advertising on youth in the United States. The study found that between 2010 and 2017, the percentage of youth reporting exposure to ads increased from 25% to 70%. Advertising for therapeutic use was allowed in the US, but the ads were not specifically directed at youth. Nonetheless, the study demonstrated that among seventh and eighth grade students (average age thirteen), a higher frequency of exposure to medical cannabis ads was associated with more use of cannabis, more positive beliefs about cannabis use, higher rates of intention to use cannabis in the future, and more adverse consequences from cannabis use (D'Amico et al. 2018). (If these associations seem familiar, you might be remembering the alcohol research on reinforcement expectancies that I covered in Chapter 2.) A more recent Canadian study also documented exposure of youth to cannabis advertising—despite the practice being illegal in Canada (Noël et al. 2021).

The results of both studies raised concerns about the potential impact of cannabis company sponsorship of events. In Canada, such sponsorships are a violation of The Cannabis Act. There were additional concerns about events where children would see cannabis branding—another violation of the Act. In the spring of 2018, I gave a community presentation in rural eastern Ontario where I was told stories of mayors of small towns being approached by representatives from Canopy Growth's nearby Smith Falls production facility to discuss holding summer festivals in their communities. These stories were given credence in the summer of 2018, when Health Canada took exception to the sponsorship of festivals by licensed producers (Canada 2018d). The *Ottawa Citizen* investigations (Miller 2018a; Miller 2018b) reported that in one instance, cannabis producer, Aurora Cannabis Inc., argued that its sponsorship of a music festival under the name of simply "Aurora" did not violate the law. Aurora branded the festival as a celebration of art, legalization, and culture.

The *Ottawa Citizen* investigations also reported that during the 2018 Toronto International Film Festival (TIFF) which took place September 6 to 16, many cannabis companies established a prominent, even brazen, visual presence. Aurora was a major sponsor of the festival. Both Aurora and Tweed installed large signs in the public square at the Yonge and Dundas intersection. This is possibly the most pedestrian-heavy intersection in the city, and particularly so given nearby venues for the film festival and pleasant summer temperatures. The Aurora and Tweed signs contained corporate logos, playful, enigmatic narrative, and the company website addresses. The signs were a violation of the federal laws in place at the time. They also ran afoul of the impending restriction against advertising in places where it could be seen by those under the legal age, for which there would be an abundance in the vicinity.

The companies defended the signs by saying that since the signs provided only information and did not promote any products, they were not in violation of product promotion restrictions. However, the signs were clearly providing direction to the companies' websites where very aesthetically appealing depictions of the products could be found. Aurora and Tweed were not the only cannabis brands to display a notable presence at the festival. Licensed producers Aphria, HEXO, and Up Cannabis were also prominent.

The *Ottawa Citizen* articles also described how several licensed producers had already forged business partnerships with pop culture celebrities in anticipation of recreational legalization. Apart from the previously discussed ground-breaking partnership between Canopy's Tweed brand and Snoop Dogg, The *Citizen* also described how celebrities such as Canadian rock band The Tragically Hip, and the actors of the television series *Trailer*

Park Boys, were working with cannabis producers to position themselves as cannabis brand icons. Several cannabis strains from licensed producer Up Canada were named after some of The Tragically Hip's song titles. Organigram, the cannabis producer associated with the *Trailer Park Boys*, issued a statement that it was the television show that was associated with the cannabis products, and not the individual actors. Thus, the company's view was that the association was not a violation of the restrictions on celebrity endorsement. The *Trailer Park Boys* partnership is an interesting one. Presented in a comedic genre, the television series painted a somewhat endearing portrait of an adventurous lifestyle of cannabis use and crime, including illegal large volume cultivation and selling of cannabis and various other forms of comically-presented crime, including theft and weapons violations. I thought that, at times, the slapstick antics of the three main characters borrowed a great deal from *The Three Stooges* television series of the 1950s and 1960s. A major difference was the *Trailer Park Boys'* liberally applied f-bombs and sundry vulgarities that would make a stand-up comedian blush. The most notable examples included name-calling related to other characters' alleged participation in male genital-oral congress.

The Organigram Cannabis and *Trailer Park Boys* partnership was also somewhat reminiscent of the Tweed and Snoop Dogg relationship. In both cases, there was a romanticized association of cannabis with criminal activity. This association stood in stark symbolic contrast to the Liberal Party's sustained justification for legalization—to protect cannabis users, including children, from the perils of a criminal cannabis trade.

The *Citizen*'s coverage of promotional violations also included how major media companies (including its owner, Postmedia) were receiving revenue for media placements from cannabis companies. The legality of these ads, and of the revenues received, was dubious at best. Writing that part of the story was courageous of the journalist, as was its inclusion by the paper's editor-in-chief.

As mentioned earlier, the various promotional strategies of licensed producers in 2018 were all illegal by virtue of preexisting federal legislation. The companies' attempts to justify their infractions were frivolous. The arrival of legalization in October would do little to discourage many other forms of non-compliant and illegal conduct by the industry. I will get into that in the next chapter.

The Big Day: Cannabis Is Legalized for Recreational Use

The Cannabis Act was introduced on April 13, 2017. It was passed by the House of Commons on November 27, 2017, and by the Senate on June 20, 2018. I had been invited to testify before the House of Commons Standing Committee on Health and the Standing Senate Committee on Social Affairs, Science and Technology. My experience with both bodies left me feeling pessimistic about the potential for a public health advocate to have a major impact on this piece of legislation.

Once passed by the Senate, The Cannabis Act was set for the final stage of Royal Assent at which Governor General Julie Payette would sign the bill into law. However, according to a report from the *National Post* (Smith and Platt 2018) Payette was resisting her responsibility. She was asked to preside over the ceremony on short notice and already had plans for the designated day. It apparently required the insistence of no less than the Clerk of the Privy Council, Michael Wernick, to persuade the Governor General to change her plans. Payette signed Bill C-45 into law on the morning of June 21—the very next day after passage in the Senate. We are left wondering what motivated such haste on the part of the government.

I smiled upon reading the story about the Governor General's reluctance. Julie and I played on the same recreational baseball team when she was an undergraduate student many years earlier at McMaster University. I've had no contact with her since then, but she remained in my memory because of her days of celebrity as an astronaut. As for her baseball days, I recall her as a quiet, but skilled and intense competitor.

On October 17, 2018, The Cannabis Act, came into force—seven years after cannabis magnate Chuck Rifici was appointed to The Liberal Party's Board of Directors and six years after the Party's adoption of a motion at its convention to legalize cannabis for recreational use. Viewed in retrospect, despite the controversies and embarrassments, many aspects of the campaign had met the objectives of the Party. The Task Force performed its function as assigned, operating beneath a veneer of impartiality and academic, legal, and public health gravitas. The Liberal Party's ever-shifting rhetorical seduction had kept the media and much of the public mesmerized by the spectacle of the creation of a new legal drug industry. The campaign was forged from the scrap heap of a widely discredited, anachronistic, and stigma-laden mythology from the era of the drug's criminalization. October 17 marked the zenith of the spectacle of legalization and generated a sustained, unbridled media frenzy. A *CBC Radio 1* producer offered me the opportunity to be interviewed five separate times for coast-to-coast coverage. I declined due to a day long previous engagement. There was no call from the Clerk of the Privy Council.

The Liberal Party was neither timid nor humble in its celebration of the delivery of this election promise. By the time the big day had arrived, Party spin-masters had settled on the marquee slogan to cement public comfort with the legislation:

> *"Keep cannabis out of the hands of youth and profits out of the pockets of criminals."*

The government's October 17 press release (Canada 2018c) began with the statement:

> *"The old approach to cannabis did not work. It let criminals and organized crime profit, while failing to keep cannabis out of the hands of Canadian youth."*

And then asserted:

*"The Cannabis Act will keep profits from going into the
pockets of criminal organizations and street gangs."*

The same news release provided reinforcement with redundant, on-message statements from each of the government's meticulously prepped, short-leashed spokespersons:

*"The Government of Canada is committed to keeping can-
nabis out of the hands of youth and keeping profits from
criminals and organized crime."*
*— The Honourable Bill Blair, Minister of Border Security and
Organized Crime Reduction*

*"With a strictly regulated market for adults, we will help
keep cannabis out of the hands of youth and profits out of the
pockets of criminals."*
*— The Honourable Jody Wilson-Raybould, Minister of Justice
and Attorney General of Canada*

*"We have prioritized public health and safety to keep can-
nabis out of the hands of Canadian youth. We have taken a
public health approach..."*
— The Honourable Ginette Petitpas Taylor, Minister of Health

Just in case Canadians still did not get the message, the very first bullet in a section at the bottom of the press release titled "Quick facts" read:

*The Cannabis Act will better protect the health and safety
of Canadians by keeping cannabis out of the hands of youth
and profits out of the hands of criminals and organized crime.*

What was going on here? It would seem likely that a staff writer was given the marquee slogan and asked to write several variants on that message, which would create the slightest impression of individuality among cabinet ministers while ensuring that everyone's statement was unwaveringly on-message. This was apparently an administration careful to control every bit of minutia related to communicating the spectre of legalization to the Canadian public, apparently with little concern that Canadians might see through the charade.

Nonetheless it was a powerful and compelling slogan with embedded promises assured to hold high favour with Canadians—protecting their children and combating dangerous crime. As one would expect, there was no shortage of media mimicry in the ensuing days. Amidst all the drama, Canadians got the message.

In an isolated piece of comedic relief, social media had a field day with a day one blooper courtesy of the Ontario Cannabis Store, the Ontario Government's online retailer. Eager customers were either indignant or gleeful to discover that a THC and CBD-infused genital spray from HEXO had been mislabelled as a sub-lingual (oral) product. Oops. How much fun could a *Trailer Park Boys* episode have with that?

The days ahead would be a tumultuous time with a new industry mired in regulatory non-compliance and corporate crime—all within a permissive and forgiving regulatory environment. And that is where the next chapter picks up the story.

SUMMING UP

The Liberal Party's cannabis legalization campaign had its genesis in a principal purpose of enriching elite members of the Party who were already deeply vested in the therapeutic industry. That market was very small relative to the much larger recreational one, with its enormous financial rewards. The strategy to secure the support of the Canadian public was two-fold: to demonize the unlicensed trade and offer a law-abiding legal substitute as a panacea. The legitimacy of both parts of the strategy were challengeable. A compromised investigation process ensued, involving a Task Force with leadership that was tainted with conflict of interest. In many instances, the Task Force's recommendations discounted the advice of health policy authorities in support of the industry's market expansion agenda. Many of the Task Force's recommendations were adopted in the Cannabis Act. On the road to legalization for recreational use, we saw sustained regulatory non-compliance in the licensed therapeutic cannabis industry, foreshadowing what was to come in a legal recreational use industry.

Chapter 7

Post-Legalization: More Regulatory Non-Compliance and Corporate Crime

"If justice perishes, human life on earth has lost its meaning."
— **Immanuel Kant**

"I have worked in the legal side of cannabis for many years & in the unlicensed market of cannabis many years. In my experience there are more shady people in the legal market than the unlicensed market. It's amazing what you can get away with legally nowadays."
— **Jon Grow** (@Grow_Supplies), Twitter Feb. 3, 2019

As provocative as the previous chapter was, this one may be even more so. The promise of legalization for recreational use was to take a public health approach that would replace a dangerous criminal supply system with a safer licensed one. The licensed system would supply accurately labelled, uncontaminated product within a strictly regulated, law-abiding industry. It didn't quite happen like that.

The Cannabis Act has some meaningful provisions for holding industry accountable for the protection of public health. These include, for serious offences, suspension and revocation of production licenses and administrative penalties of up to $1million. However, a critical determinant of the ultimate effectiveness of legislation is the fidelity of enforcement efforts with the intent and provisions of the legislation. The impact of even the best-crafted provisions can be significantly compromised if surveillance is lacking or if non-compliance is met with consequences that do not motivate future compliance. As described in Chapter 5, we have seen decades of this problem with the regulation of alcohol, tobacco, and pharmaceutical corporations.

This chapter addresses the post-legalization conduct of licensed producers and regulatory responses by government using information available as of the first half of 2022. I will begin with a broad sweep of non-compliance recorded by the regulator and will then focus on two notable areas of infractions: product integrity and product promotion. Later sections will describe incidents of corporate crime and address issues of overall enforcement consistency and accountability. The cannabis business news platform, *Marijuana Business Daily*, was an important source of information on developments in the industry. More so than any other, MBD provides a balanced account of successes and failures. This chapter drew extensively upon MBD, especially the work of Matt Lamers—a seemingly tireless curator of noteworthy developments.

REGULATORY NON-COMPLIANCE

Health Canada Surveillance

I will draw upon Health Canada's annual Compliance and Enforcement Reports to examine the results of surveillance of cannabis producers. The reports arise from Health Canada's inspections of licensed producers' growing facilities which can occur in less than a day or over a few days.

Health Canada has developed a standard nomenclature for recording regulatory non-compliance during its inspections. All individual instances of non-compliance noted during an inspection visit are recorded as "observations" which can include infractions ranging from minor ones to serious criminal conduct. Each site visit also receives an overall rating of "compliant" or "non-compliant." Non-compliance is defined as: "...at the time of the inspection, the licensed producer has not met the applicable legislative and regulatory requirements, and is not in control of the regulated activities" (Canada 2019a).

In 2015-16, Health Canada rated its observations of production infractions as either "critical" or "non-critical."

Critical observations included instances of non-compliance that may pose a risk:

- *of diversion to the illegal trade*

- *to the health and safety of medical users*

- *to security of the site*

- *to the confidence of Canadians in the marijuana product or the MMPR program.*

Non-critical observations included instances of non-compliance that were less likely to have a serious impact on the integrity of marijuana production.

I counted 311 inspections conducted in 2015-16 by Health Canada (Canada 2019b). It logged 239 critical and 174 non-critical observations. All inspections noting critical observations received an overall site visit rating of non-compliant. However, it appears that only 4 resulted in "significant compliance actions." Of those, 3 occurred at Aphria, Aurora Cannabis Enterprises Inc., and Emerald Health Botanicals Inc. which all resulted in "seizure of products due to Good Production Practices non-compliance." A fourth action at CannTrust Inc. suffered a "seizure of products due to contravention of Physical Security Directive" and the issuance of a warning letter. The details of the infractions remain enshrouded by brevity and non-specificity.

Beginning in 2016-17, Health Canada introduced new nomenclature for rating the seriousness of observations:

"Minor observations" will likely not increase the risk of diversion, prevent the detection of diversion, and/or health risk.

"Major observations" may increase the risk of diversion, prevent the detection of diversion, and/or health risk.

"Critical observations" are the most serious deviation or deficiency of the act or regulations and include those that are likely to:

- increase the immediate risk of diversion

- prevent the detection of diversion

- present an imminent health risk

- involve the possibility of deliberate fraud, misinterpretation, or falsification of information.

The changes to the nomenclature are important. They represent a shift towards the recognition of infractions that could not be explained by, and excused as, errors from inexperience. The nomenclature was clearly revised to capture infractions that were more wilful. This shift is captured by the addition of terminology such as "prevent the detection", "deliberate fraud", and "falsification." It was plain that Health Canada was encountering and acknowledging the types of conduct of a revenue-driven industry that had been predicted by health policy authorities during the consultation phase of legalization.

As in 2015-16, Health Canada did not report the actual number of inspections conducted for 2016-17 and 2017-18. From the reports, I made approximate counts of 230 and 260, respectively. For 2018-19, Health Canada reported that it conducted 293 inspections. This would produce an approximate total of 783 inspections conducted between April 1, 2016, and March 31, 2019, from which the regulator logged 500 minor, 216 major, and 10 critical infractions (Canada 2019a, 2020). Many of these infractions involved product seizures due to potential compromises of product quality and safety. I will address that issue shortly.

Examples of unspecified critical and major infractions, and the actions taken by the regulator, are reported below. Most are reported *verbatim* as recorded by Health Canada.

- *RedeCan Pharm: warning letter for contravention of Physical Security Directive*
- *CannTrust: warning letter for contravention of Physical Security Directive*
- *Aurora: warning letter issued and seizure of products due to a contravention of Physical Security Directive*
- *Agrima Botanicals: warning letter issued due to activities taking place at the site that were not authorized by the licence*
- *Green Quality Inc.: corrective actions monitoring due to inventory, security, record keeping and Good Production Practices non-compliance*
- *Agrima Botanicals: seizure of products and licence suspended due to the conduct of unauthorized activities with cannabis*
- *Green Quality Inc.: warning letter issued due to destruction, security measures and record keeping non-compliance and to a false or misleading statement made to an inspector*
- *Aphria: warning letter issued due to Good Production Practices non-compliance and to a false or misleading statement made to an inspector*
- *BC Tweed Joint Venture Inc.: warning letter issued due to plant inventory non-compliance*
- *BC Tweed Joint Venture Inc. (second site): warning letter issued due to plant inventory and record keeping non-compliance*
- *Bonify Medical Cannabis: warning letter, seizure of products and licence suspended due to possession, distribution and selling of product that was purchased from an unlicensed source and was not compliant with Good Production Practices.*

As in 2015-16, licensed producers can also receive an overall non-compliant inspection rating which means that at the time of the inspection, the licensed producer has not met the applicable legislative and regulatory requirements and is not in control of the regulated activities.

Between April 1, 2016 and March 31, 2019, there were 13 instances of producers receiving non-compliant ratings from Health Canada. They included: Agrima (twice), Aphria, Aurora, BC Tweed Joint Venture Inc. (two sites), Bonify, Hydropothicaire/ Hydropothecary (HEXO), Mettrum, Mettrum (Bennett North), Natural Med Company, and Quality Green Inc. (two sites).

POST-LEGALIZATION

As of May 2022, the most recent Compliance and Enforcement Report from Health Canada provided data available from April 1, 2019 through March 31, 2020 (Canada 2022). The regulator reported that it conducted 417 inspections and made 283 minor and 153 major observations. There were 7 critical observations.

With only two exceptions, all entries for major observations provided no information on the nature of the infractions or on the course of action taken by Health Canada. The entry indicated only "Corrective actions required." The two exceptions were:

- *Aurora Cannabis Enterprises Inc.: Warning letter issued due to unauthorised sale of cannabis products and to not providing notice to Health Canada before selling a new cannabis product.*

- *We Grow BC: Warning letter due to recurring good production practices and record keeping non-compliances and to lack of knowledge of the responsible person.*

For all instances of receiving a critical observation, the company received a non-compliant rating. These are new entries and do not include instances of a non-compliant rating that was still in effect from the previous year (as was the case for Bonify). The little detail provided by Health Canada on the 7 instances of non-compliance is provided below. It is noteworthy that in 3 instances the company had its license suspended, and in 2 instances, permanently revoked. I will explore those stories in more detail later in the chapter.

- *Toronto Research Chemical Inc.: Warning letter issued due to false and misleading information provided to an inspector and to obstructing an inspector*

- *Bloomera Inc.: Warning letter, detention of products and licence revoked due to non-compliance to security requirements*

- *Alberta Green Biotech Inc.: Seizure of products conducted on follow-up targeted inspection(s), and licence suspended and subsequently revoked due to lack of overall control at the site and other non-compliances*

- *CannMart Inc: Warning letter issued due to Good Production Practices non-compliance*

- *CannTrust Inc.: (two sites) Seizure of products conducted on follow-up targeted inspection(s) and licence suspended due to unauthorized activities with cannabis and additional non-compliances*

- *Evergreen Medicinal Supply Inc.: Seizure of products conducted on follow-up targeted inspection(s) and licence suspended due to unauthorized activities with cannabis and additional non-compliances.*

Compromised or Uncertain Product Quality and Safety

Between April 1, 2015 and March 31, 2019, Health Canada's Compliance and Enforcement Reports described the following 15 instances of noncompliance by licensed producers related to product quality and safety. The types of responses include warning letters, seizure of product, and licence suspension. There were 11 seizures of product.

- *Agrima Botanicals Corp.: seizure of products and licence suspended due to the conduct of unauthorized activities with cannabis*

- *Aphria: seizure of products due to Good Production Practices noncompliance*

- *Aphria: warning letter issued due to Good Production Practices non-compliance and to a false or misleading statement made to an inspector*

- *Aurora: seizure of products due to Good Production Practices noncompliance*

- *Aurora: seizure of products due to Good Production Practices noncompliance*

- *Aurora: seizure of products due to Good Production Practices noncompliance*

- *Aurora: warning letter issued and seizure of products due to a contravention of Physical Security Directive*

- *Bonify Medical Cannabis: warning letter, seizure of products and licence suspended due to possession, distribution and selling of product that was purchased from an unlicensed source and was not compliant with Good Production Practices*

- *CannTrust: seizure of products due to contravention of Physical Security Directive and issuance of a warning letter for non-compliance*

- *Emerald Health Botanicals: seizure of products due to Good Production Practices non-compliance*

- *Hydropothicaire/Hydropothecary (HEXO): warning letter and seizure of products due to Good Production Practices non-compliance*

- *Mettrum: seizure of unauthorized material*

- *Mettrum: warning letter issued due to Good Production Practices non-compliance*

- *Mettrum (Bennett North): warning letter issued due to Good Production Practices non-compliance*

- Natural Med Company: warning letter issued due to non-compliance with Good Production Practices (two instances) (Canada 2019a, 2020).

Health Canada's Compliance and Enforcement Report for April 1, 2019, through March 31, 2020, listed 21 product seizures. CannTrust's two sites were responsible for 16 of them. There were 3 seizures from Evergreen Medicinal Supply Inc. and 2 from Alberta Green Biotech Inc. (Canada 2022). Health Canada disclosed to *Marijuana Business Daily* that all the seizures totalled more than 35 million grams of cannabis products and 7,800 plants (Lamers 2022b).

Another source of data on problems with product integrity is Health Canada's Recalls and Alerts database. This includes recall of products that are now in the marketplace. I conducted a search on "cannabis OR marijuana" in the database (Canada, n.d.) on June 16, 2021. The search yielded 68 records occurring between January 1, 2014 and May 19, 2021. Of the 68 records, 9 were advisories (providing public education messages only). The remaining 59 posts involved (sometimes large) product recalls involving multiple product types from many licensed producers. Of the 59 recalls, 37 were for labelling and packaging errors. The most frequent problem was mislabelling of products, typically involving incorrect concentrations or thc:cbd ratios. Many of these were not serious errors, but some were sufficiently so to evoke complaints from customers. In one such incident, Aurora sent out product with the box labelled as "CBD caps" (capsules) but containing a bottle labelled as "THC Sativa caps." Big difference.

Of the remaining 22 recalls, 3 involved marijuana drug test kits and there was 1 recall of a faulty cannabis vape pen from HEXO that would heat up to the point that its plastic parts would melt. The remaining 18 incidents all involved recalls for cannabis products due to contamination. In all cases, the contamination was of a sufficiently serious nature that Health Canada was prompted to advise customers to "immediately stop using the product."

There were three types of product contamination encountered.

- *mould was the cause of 7 recalls from Natural MedCo Ltd., Agro-Greens Natural Products Ltd., Up Cannabis Inc., Redecan, THC BioMed Ltd., and TerrAscend Canada (2 products).*

- *use of unauthorized pesticides led to 6 recalls from Broken Coast Cannabis Ltd., Peace Naturals Project Inc., Hydropothecary (HEXO), Mettrum, and Organigram. Product provided by Organigram to Aurora led to a recall from there as well.*

- *microbial or chemical contaminants led to 4 recalls from Bonify, Natural Advancement Canna Master Blend, Tilray, and Peace Naturals Project Inc.*

The remaining case was a recall by Greenleaf Medicinals for unspecified "issues with the company's production practices."

215

I searched the Recalls and Alerts database ("cannabis OR marijuana") again on May 28, 2022 (Canada, n.d.). During the near one-year period since the previous search, an additional 5 recalls were posted. There was one recall for mislabelling in which the actual amount of THC was approximately 3.5 times higher than indicated on the package (Peace Naturals project Inc.). The other 4 recalls involved the actual or potential presence of contaminants including yeast (Atlas Growers), mold/mildew (Atlas Growers; Joint Ventures Craft Cannabis), bacteria (Atlas Growers, Trichrome JWC), and apparently small pieces of metal wire (WPCP). There were no recalls posted in Health Canada's database after October 28, 2021. While customer complaints for some of the products were received, there were no reports of adverse reactions.

I should also point out that product failures are not restricted to cannabis plant products. I already mentioned a faulty vape pen and three instances of cannabis test kits being recalled. Another incident involved a cannabis producer, Tree of Knowledge, which supplied faulty masks to hospitals during the height of the COVID-19 epidemic in Canada. In response, the courts froze the company's assets (McArthur 2020).

The amount of information provided on recalls in Health Canada's database is customarily scant. In some cases, journalists uncovered more details. The more newsworthy stories included tales of the reckless, the comedic, and the criminal.

A licensed producer, Redecan, had customers complaining that its product, bought through the Ontario Government's online Ontario Cannabis Store, contained "bugs". Redecan responded that it used a specific strain of mites to control spider mites. Spider mites pose a serious threat to a cannabis crop. The type of mite introduced did not eat cannabis—only spider mites. The company described its approach as an organic one since it avoids the use of pesticides. Neither Redecan nor the Ontario Cannabis Store acknowledged that there was a problem with mites in the product at the point of retail (Little 2018; Windowswear 2018).

In another incident, Sundial Growers was required to recall a shipment because it was contaminated with mould and pieces of rubber gloves (Underwood 2019).

Health Canada's Recalls and Alerts database described another interesting case as follows: "The recalled product may not meet some of the microbial and chemical contaminant limits as specified by the Good Production Practices requirements of the Cannabis Regulations. Documentation confirming test results could not be matched to the lot specific numbers" (Canada, n.d.). The wording of this passage is euphemistic to the point of obfuscation. At the end of 2018, the offending producer, Bonify, in Winnipeg, Manitoba, admitted to having purchased two hundred kilograms of illegal cannabis which it sold to legal retail outlets in Saskatchewan. None of these details were promptly disclosed in Health Canada's Recalls and Alerts database. I will revisit the remarkable Bonify story in more detail later in the chapter.

The less than forthright description of the Bonify infraction in Health Canada's database is an altogether separate source of concern as it prompts us to wonder what unreported circumstances may have lain behind other seemingly unremarkable entries in the database. Health Canada's database was equally sparse in the most disturbing details of the story behind the previously discussed Mettrum recall as well. In both cases, it took a whistle-blower in the company and the tenacity of investigative journalists to expose the disturbing nature and magnitude of events.

It must be acknowledged that regulation allows for detection of some of the production failures, providing a clear advantage of the licensed trade over the unlicensed trade in this respect. However, the finding of numerous production failures—some among repeat offenders, and none in others, prompts two conclusions:

- *it is possible to produce non-tainted cannabis and*

- *there is an irregular standard of production in this industry that is not being effectively addressed by regulation.*

Given that Health Canada's inspections generally occur monthly, this is obviously a significant concern for regular cannabis users who might be using a defective product for up to a month before a defect is detected and a recall is issued. This might be particularly worrisome for users for therapeutic purposes, some of whom are immuno-compromised.

A New Brunswick licensed producer, Organigram, became caught up in a pesticide scandal. Some of the company's patients, who claimed to have been made very ill from products bought from Organigram, were successful in having a class action suit against the company approved (CBC News 2019a). However, in the subsequent hearing, Justice Peter Bryson ruled: "There is no evidence that there is a workable methodology to determine that the proposed adverse health-effects claims have a common cause," and reduced the scope of the action such that there could be no compensation for illness experienced by the plaintiffs (Magee 2020a). The Supreme Court of Nova Scotia refused to hear an appeal of that ruling (Magee 2020b). However, in June 2022, Organigram issued a proposal to refund customers the cost of the products purchased (less any refunds already received) and to compensate them for legal and administrative costs. The proposed settlement, worth $2.3 million, requires the approval of the Supreme Court of Nova Scotia. The case is scheduled to be heard in August 2022 (Business Wire 2022).

Potentially harmful contamination should also be a concern for government regulators and public health authorities as well as for industry investors, customers, and the public who are being placated and misled by the promise of product safety in a legal regime. If government is concerned about the quality and safety of unlicensed product and confident that a legal industry is a safer alternative, it should do more to compel the legal industry to compete with the unlicensed supply on that aspect. Consumer confidence can be achieved only if industry and government transparently acknowledge the full extent and nature of production failures and take corrective measures beyond the euphemistic "voluntary recalls."

Inconsistent product integrity, especially when involving contamination, also poses a threat to research on both the therapeutic and harmful effects of cannabis. Any harm observed in research studies can be confounded. Is the observed harm due to cannabis or to the contaminants? Also, potential therapeutic benefits of cannabis might be masked, or compromised, by the harmful effects of contaminants. Research programs are wise to be concerned.

A deeper dive on the types of contamination and possible consequences is described in a review published by the Michael G. Degroote Centre for Medicinal Cannabis Research at McMaster University (2021, 5). The report noted:

> Contamination of cannabis takes numerous forms and can be a significant health concern, especially for individuals with health problems or compromised immune systems. Deliberate contamination of cannabis product should occur only in the black market, as legal operators are under the obligation to conform to state or national safety standards utilized for food and drugs. Nonetheless, there are gaps in safety standards and the standards are only as strong as the level of enforcement. In Canada, there is a national testing and reporting system, which should ensure limited contamination and consistency between provinces/territories, although violations are documented. Thus, vigilance is nonetheless required to ensure cannabis producers meet the mandated standards and minimize contamination.

Many licensed producers will attempt to keep their product failures as quiet as possible. A social media post by Saskatchewan micro producer, North 40 Cannabis, offered a refreshing change. North 40 showed that there are conscientious people in the business who have more respect for the well-being and intelligence of their customers when things go awry. The company's social media post explained: "Well, it happened. More powdery mildew. Time to shut the facility down and deal with it. I refuse to sell product that is contaminated with mildew or fungicides. Thanks to everyone who has supported us and I promise we'll be back even stronger. Chin up, shoulders back, carry on" (North 40 Cannabis 2020).

Just as impressive are the replies to the post from other micro growers and customers who show the solidarity among those in the business with more conscientious business models. Health Canada has appeared to be indifferent on this issue, but Big Cannabis needs to take notice of this counter-veiling force in the business. Customers certainly are. Shifts in market share are happening. I will cover that in the next chapter.

And no, using social media to distract customers from a company's failures by loudly trumpeting the hiring of a Vice-President of Equity will not cut it.

Product Promotion

Health Canada's Compliance and Enforcement Reports also covered investigations of product promotion violations, including inspections at promotional events. Advertising and Promotions inspections are not assigned ratings, as are other regulatory violations since observations are not made. The (Canada 2020) report states: "The purpose is to support the assessment of compliance for promotion and advertisement activities and the associated requirements by gathering information."

I think this might mean that Health Canada investigates product promotion activities to help them learn how to investigate product promotion activities. But it is difficult to tell.

It is also noteworthy that product promotion violations are the only type of infraction for which the non-compliant company is not named, thus providing leniency and anonymity.

Between October 17, 2018, and March 31, 2019, Health Canada conducted 85 promotions-related compliance verification activities which resulted in 48 actions taken by the regulator. These actions included:

- *9 compliance promotion phone calls*

- *3 compliance promotion letters*

- *4 warning letters*

- *32 referrals to the RCMP.*

(Canada 2020)

It should be noted that these responses do not include action taken by Health Canada in response to the flurry of illegal advertising activities that occurred in the months leading up to legalization (as described in the previous chapter).

Between April 1, 2019, and March 31, 2020, Health Canada conducted 234 promotions related compliance verification activities which resulted in 130 actions taken. These actions included:

- *18 compliance emails*

- *108 compliance promotion emails or calls*

- *4 warning letters*

(Canada 2022).

Polite phone calls and emails, and even "warning letters" are consistent with the overall lenient approach of Canada's regulator with cannabis producers. The referrals to the RCMP in 2018-19 certainly have some potential for getting the industry's attention. But thus far, there have been no reports of action taken by the RCMP on those referrals. On January 27, 2022, I filed an Access to Information Request with the RCMP and received an auto-response acknowledging my request. On March 2, I also asked Health

Canada for information on the status of the referrals. As of June 2022, I had not received a response to either request.

There appears to have been some curtailment of the most brazen product promotion violations of the Act following legalization. But promotional activities on the legal borderline, as well as some seemingly clear violations, continue to occur.

Celebrity Affiliations

Organigram eventually dropped its references to Trailer Park Buds. At Up Canada, there remained only one vague brand reference to a Tragically Hip song, with Hundredth Meridian being changed to Meridian. The latter surrender prompted howls of protest of a double standard from cannabis advocates who noted that Niagara Peninsula Stoney Ridge vineyard had named a wine after the T-Hip's album "Fully Completely." The wine even used the album cover artwork on the bottle label. The wine was featured by The Liquor Control Board of Ontario's marketing vessel "Vintages" (Liquor Control Board of Ontario, n.d.). I was able to view the T-Hip product online without even the flimsy (but annoying) age-gate requiring the entry of my date of birth or age.

The protests of a double standard are reasonable. The question is how the double standard should be resolved. Should cannabis producers be allowed the same promotional liberties reserved for the alcohol industry? Or should the alcohol industry be required to follow the less permissive rules set for cannabis brands? If you have come this far in the book, you know that alcohol problems are an international public health crisis and might consider why we would want to emulate the libertarian approach towards alcohol for another recreational drug product.

By the time of legalization in October 2018, the presence of Snoop Dogg on Tweed's website was almost entirely abated. Cryptic references to the acronym "*LBS*" (Leafs by Snoop) were the last vestige of an attempt by Canopy Growth (now Tweed's Corporate umbrella) to retain at least some element of the partnership. Shortly thereafter, even the acronym, had almost disappeared into obscurity. By mid-2021 Canopy Growth's website had kept the "LBS" brand acronym, but had effectively laundered it of any reference to Snoop Dogg:

"The LBS brand slogan—"Worth Its Weight In Gold"—is a reference to the care and quality put into the brand's products and to its roots in California, the Golden State. The company name is also a nod to the abbreviation for pounds. In addition to positioning itself as the gold standard in the cannabis industry, LBS is focused on embracing diversity and inclusiveness throughout its brand messaging and company initiatives."

Undaunted, Snoop sold his semblance for a wine product – 19 Crimes Snoop Dogg Cali Red – with California-based, Treasury Wine Estates. In early 2022, the product was selling in retail outlets of the Liquor Control Board of Ontario. The promotion on LCBO's website described the wine as:

POST-LEGALIZATION

"19 Crimes wines are defiant by nature, bold and always uncompromising, just like the D-O-double-G!" Cannabis advocates will be certain to point to this as another example of how alcohol products are not tethered by the same commercial constraints as are cannabis products.

However, a few concessions aside, major cannabis industry players were not in full retreat from product promotions.

Another visit to the site of the Office of the Commissioner of Lobbying of Canada on September 30, 2021, showed that lobbying activity by the industry with key players in the federal bureaucracy persisted well past legalization. Aurora and Canopy maintained a prominent presence into July 2021 (Office of the Commissioner of Lobbying of Canada 2021). I wonder about the association between these industry efforts and the lack of meaningful penalties for their promotional infractions.

Illegal industry-celebrity partnerships continued. Canopy Growth had now emerged as one of the country's largest cannabis producers. It appeared to be immune from meaningful consequences for its regulatory breeches. Undaunted by its loss of the Snoop Dogg partnership, Canopy persisted in establishing other celebrity partnerships. A November 2019 press release provides an example of what seems to be a tolerated violation of the ban on celebrity endorsements. Canopy announced its "partnership" with Canadian entertainer Drake in a relaunch of a Canopy subsidiary More Life Growth Company. The press release described how Canopy would retain 40% of the shares and would control production and distribution of cannabis product. Drake would contribute his "vision", "perspective as a culture leader and entrepreneur", and "innovative eye." In exchange for his 60% of shares, Drake would allow More Life to "exploit certain intellectual property and brands in association with the growth, manufacture, production, marketing and sale of cannabis and cannabis-related products, accessories, merchandise and paraphernalia in Canada and internationally" (Canopy Growth Corporation 2019).

Canopy also announced its investment in a company called Houseplant, headed by Canadian entertainer and self-acknowledged cannabis enthusiast, Seth Rogan (Ligaya 2019b).

Another seeming departure from the rules was reminiscent of the Canopy and Snoop Dogg collaboration. In 2021, Canopy announced its partnership with internationally recognized *bon vivant* and convicted felon, Martha Stewart. In Canopy's press release, Martha was quoted as saying: "Working with the top researchers and scientists at Canopy Growth, I saw first-hand how dedicated the company is in producing high quality, safe and consistent products."

The partnership announcement came on the heels of another of Martha's ventures into the cannabis business – "Martha Stewart CBD for Pet" which Canopy's press release described as "oil drops and soft-baked chews in three gourmet flavour combinations and formulas designed to support pet mental and physical well-being" (Canopy Growth Corporation 2021).

221

Another perspective to keep in mind is that just the announcement of a celebrity partnership, with assured media coverage, carries a great deal of the promotional benefit associated with a celebrity partnership. Such is the fine art of product promotion as news. The illegal, alluring, celebrity buzz in the cannabis marketplace appears not to have been fully extinguished by Health Canada.

Event Sponsorship

In March of 2019, *CTV News* reported that Health Canada was investigating a sponsorship of a Toronto children's charity event by Canopy Growth and Halo Labs (Ligaya 2019a). The specific violation involved the logos of the companies appearing in a list of sponsors on the website for the event and at the event itself, contrary to the Act which prohibits cannabis "brand elements" to be used in a promotion of an event or activity.

Responses from spokespeople for the event, and for Canopy Growth, pleaded a lack of knowledge of the Act. Such pleas serve to reinforce the importance of calls for a full ban on product promotion to avoid the ambiguity inherent in mere restrictions. However, at that stage, the reaction, particularly from Canopy, seems disingenuous. Large cannabis companies lobbied quite aggressively on these issues and should be very aware of the outcome of those efforts. The law is quite clear in this regard. There is also no shortage of law firms declaring a specialty in cannabis law that are available to provide guidance above and beyond whatever in-house counsel might be retained by a well-resourced, licensed cannabis producer. There is no credible excuse for not understanding the law in the matter.

Sponsorship of events can also go awry with unintended consequences. In Dawson Creek, British Columbia, an 8-year-old boy won $200 worth of cannabis products in a raffle at a minor league hockey tournament (Jones 2020). The boy's father picked up the boy's prize, and his grandfather, a retired police officer, filed a complaint with the hockey league. The league promised to review its policies on the matter.

Licensed Producer Websites

With most publicly visible product promotion now contained, the industry held onto one last venue for the glamourous presentation of its products to expand the market—the producers' own websites.

The Cannabis Act placed a variety of restrictions on promotional content for cannabis products. It prohibited content that would associate company brand elements with "a way of life such as one that includes glamour, recreation, excitement, vitality, risk or daring" or would otherwise evoke "positive emotions." These restrictions do not apply only to ads that might be seen by youth. All advertising that might be seen by youth is illegal. These restrictions apply to advertising that is intended to be seen by adults.

These restrictions do not allow much room for seductive enticement and, if followed, would equate cannabis promotion to that of a banal consumer product where the only information needed is what is necessary to help a customer choose a suitable product. That being the case, the type of information available to consumers buying cannabis online would not be any different than purchasing something as pedestrian as the following hypothetical plumbing part:

> *Product #: NJ315-2*
> *Length: 10 cm*
> *Inside diameter: 10 mm*
> *Price: $4.20*

Accordingly, under such a model, and consistent with the regulations, one would expect to visit a licensed cannabis producer's or retailer's website and encounter something with no more glam than a plain font listing such as this:

> *Product   Acme Oral Cannabis Spray (15 ml bottle)*
>
> *Concentration: THC 10 mg/ml*
> *CBD 13 mg/ml*
> *thc:cbd   10:13*
> *Price $30.00.*

However, upon visiting several licensed producer's websites in the early months of 2019, I encountered a very different world. There is perhaps no other aspect of non-compliance with the Act that has employed so much creative wile on the part of the licensed producers.

Their websites employed powerful colour and design aesthetics, imagery, product nomenclature, and narrative that shamelessly flirted with the restrictions in the Act. Canopy's products were depicted with minimal restraint with the focus on its product containers, presented in a sleek uniform format, but differentiated by striking colours associated with respective products. More boldly, Aurora used a captivating combination of colour and design that invoked the awe and grandeur of nature and outdoor spectacles. Product names and imagery at the Organigram site depicted a rugged, athletic, outdoor lifestyle.

Product presentation at these sites employed top shelf graphic design at its most alluring. The imagery would "evoke positive emotions" in anyone—whether a passionate user or the most indifferent policy analyst.

The connection of product names with cultural lifestyles was equally flirtatious. Product names encountered at a variety of producers' websites included allusions to famous classic and contemporary pop culture icons such as "Skywalker", "Rockstar", "Treasure Island", "Flower Power", and "Warlock'. Some allusions were more nature-based: "Purple Pines", "Sugar Bush", and "Sunburst." Others were more romantic: "Fleur de Lune", "Midnight." The Ontario Cannabis Store website offered a product wryly called "Plain Packaging."

My revisit to the websites of these companies in mid 2020 found little had changed overall. Canopy's Tweed site still focused on high end graphic design highlighting its product packaging with product descriptions that emulate wine reviews: "earthy, woody, and spicy flavours."

A visit to the websites of Aphria and HEXO also found a focus on the product containers. Aphria explained how its products were named after Canadian Lakes. HEXO featured high-definition images of cannabis buds with names steeped in the natural world: Terra, Tsunami, Lagoon, and Nebula.

Aurora had stayed with its formula of aesthetically appealing nature scenes of mountains, forests, lakes, waterfalls, starry skies, and of course, auroral displays. On its website's home page, Aurora proclaimed: "Our garden is home to thousands of happy plants growing in the foothills of the Canadian Rocky Mountains, sipping fresh mountain water in gentle breezes and basking in ideal lighting conditions." Aurora had also added the enticement of creating anticipation for a new product. Some product images were supplemented with a tag – "now growing."

Interestingly, Organigram had toned down the aesthetics of its product depictions somewhat, with less imagery and hyperbole, and limiting the content more to the specifications of the products.

My mid 2021 visit to the websites of some of the more prominent brands found results like previous years, but perhaps with a bit more restraint in some cases. Tweed continued to display colour-coded packaging for infused chocolate and drinks, and an enticing pitch for choosing edible "soft gels" over smoking and vaping.

Aurora featured "medical" brands and "consumer" brands using lifestyle icons such as Whistler and Woodstock. Overall, Aurora toned down the picturesque views of nature, but did include these themes on the Whistler pages that depicted sheer faces of rock, trees, and cascading waterfalls. The images of cannabis bud are not up to usual Aurora graphic design standards. They fell below the technical skill and aesthetic appeal of images posted on Twitter by craft grower, cultivation consultant, and cannabis philanthropist Grow Supplies. Aurora's Woodstock brand is presented in the recognizable font of the famous and infamous music festivals and as "a line of cannabis products for the thriving music and festival lover." But there is no imagery. The section of "Branded Products" (clothing) also featured nature scenes – some of which were presented out of focus to direct attention to the lithe models wearing the branded clothing.

Aphria continued to feature its branding as "Proudly Canadian, Aphria's medical cannabis products are named after lakes from across our country." Its medical products featured oils, soft gels, and dried cannabis that also sport campy retro names such as Headstash, Royal Highness, Alien Dawg, and the enigmatic Great Bear (Exodus Cheese).

HEXO's main page prominently declared "New Vapes. Lower Prices." HEXO has continued to focus on the images of the product line with at least one provocative brand name – a high-THC vape cartridge called "Trainwreck". HEXO also proudly displayed its several industry awards.

Organigram also continued to sport a more restrained depiction on its site, with a major focus on its production processes and facilities, including a video tour of the production facility. I thought the video had a bit of an Orwellian dystopian feel to it, but maybe that's just me. In its product section, Adult Recreational, the product line included playful names such as Shred and Big Bag O' Buds.

Almost all the producer's sites examined also used the indica/sativa nomenclature to describe their products, sometimes with subtle, or not so subtle, indications of associated effects. Given that there has never been a scientifically established basis for these differences in effect, one might question whether this invokes the Act's provision against false claims in advertising.

It is also noteworthy that access to the prohibited lifestyle elements on licensed producer websites are protected only by a self-report age gate, which serves as more of a nuisance to adults than as a barrier to the underaged. The ease with which an underage user can enter the company websites where, in some cases, enticing product promotion prevails, raises another potential violation of the Act.

The Cannabis Act provides authority for Health Canada to inspect producers' websites for promotion compliance. There has been no mention of the regulator having done so in its Compliance and Enforcement Reports.

One might think that a provincial government run retailer would be more attentive to the finer or even most rudimentary aspects of federal law on advertising, but, at least in Ontario, this is apparently not the case. The Ontario Government's online cannabis retailer, the Ontario Cannabis Store also appears not to be above a blatant departure from following the federal regulations on product promotion. On Twitter, the retailer posted: "Originally from California, Blue Dream has made its mark here in Ontario. Read more about this unique strain here" (@ONCannabisStore, October 13, 2020). A link provided in the Twitter post, led to a blog page on the OCS website on a "featured flower." The article contained enticing accolades and descriptions such as: "exceptional aroma", "a crowd favourite", "The aroma profile includes pine, pepper and lemon", and "If you like high-THC strains, strong scents and blueberry cobbler, Blue Dream is worth a try" (Ontario Cannabis Store, n.d.).

Access to the OCS website is only protected by an age gate. On October 14, 2020, I replied to the post asking how the OCS post was not illegal given that it promotes a product in a place where children could see it. I did not receive a reply.

Regulatory Response

In the early days of recreational legalization, the imagery and product names of cannabis products were consistent with the glamourous depiction of alcohol products and reminiscent of the tobacco ads of a bygone era. If one of The Cannabis Act's intentions was to eliminate the seductiveness of cannabis promotion, compared to the current alcohol standard, and that of tobacco at the pinnacle of its popularity, the Act initially failed to do so.

While the bolder incarnations of product glamourization have been toned down at some producers' websites, the transformation is not complete. Some analysts may still see some of the current industry conduct in product promotion as blatant violations of the law. Others may be more inclined to see the conduct more as transgressions of the spirit of the Act. And yet, others of a more libertarian persuasion will think the current legislated restrictions on ads to be an unnecessary and even harmful obstacle to the freedom of commercial speech.

But all these arguments may be beside the essential point. Public Health authorities are concerned about the effects of advertising for alcohol, tobacco, and cannabis. There was enough concern expressed during the legalization of cannabis campaign that the government was moved to pass legislation that was restrictive. Any reversal on that legislation is a betrayal of the promise that was made to get the country on board with legislation. The other disturbing aspect of the numerous product promotion offences is that the companies typically receive only warnings from the regulator. While some cases of product promotion violations have been referred to the RCMP, there has been no indication that any of them have been acted upon.

As discussed earlier, the research evidence shows that advertising drug products to adults is not a benign practice. And yet, much has been made of the legislation's requirement that advertising be restricted to places where children are prohibited to enter. Even in cases of industry compliance with this requirement, there would remain many legal places where adult purchasers could come under the influence. These potentially include alcohol retail outlets, tobacco and vaping retail outlets, bars, gambling casinos, some massage parlours and spas, euphemistically named adult stores, adult movie venues, and perhaps even on-screen ads when regular movie theatres are showing an adult-rated film.

It is to be expected that the industry will continue to seek out even more venues and strategies for its market expansion agenda. At the April 25-27, 2019, O'Cannabiz Expo in Toronto, the schedule included a moderated panel discussion titled: "Subtle Sales: How to Brand and Market Within the Regs." The panel description in the schedule included the statement: "How do you portray your product in a positive light without glamourizing it? Believe it or not, there is a way to stick-handle the "regs" and get the word out. Our industry strategists have advice on judicious packaging, branding, copy writing and logo differentiation that will attract attention..." (O'Cannabiz Conference & Expo 2019).

It appears that at least part of the cannabis industry has no intention to embrace the letter or even the intent or spirit of the regulations, but rather to find creative solutions in their gaming. This is the challenging landscape of product promotion and other strategies of market expansion that lay before the already-beleaguered government regulators. How have they responded thus far?

POST-LEGALIZATION

The *Ottawa Citizen* coverage of industry advertising included the following statement from a Health Canada spokesperson: "The purpose of any message by a licensed (cannabis) producer, its content, its context and its intended audience are all factors to consider when determining whether that message falls within the definition of advertising..." (Miller 2018). A *CTV* report (Ligaya 2019a) quoted a Health Canada spokesperson saying that each potential violation is addressed on "a case-by-case basis."

As a regulatory response, this raises the kind of concerns anticipated by Canada's health policy organizations in their recommendations to the government at the time of legalization. They recommended not just restrictions on product promotion, but a less ambiguous, less easily gamed, full ban on product promotion. Cannabis companies are likely to perpetually game the Act with boundless enthusiasm and creativity, and presumed entitlement. They do so always for market expansion, and perhaps sometimes just for sport. They can always plead ignorance when challenged. This relentless tendency, in concert with the inherent ambiguity of restrictions, will generate enormous costs in Health Canada's "case-by-case" surveillance, analysis, and responses to product promotion activities by the industry. The problem is much bigger than just product promotion. I will have more to say shortly on the high level of regulatory maintenance required by this industry.

A year later, in mid-2020, Health Canada was still displaying a timid posture in its admonitions of the industry. Health Canada spokesperson Tammy Jarbeau explained to *Marijuana Business Daily*: "Health Canada discourages any federal cannabis licence holder, cannabis retailer, or any other regulated party from undertaking any celebrity-affiliated promotions or packaging and labelling" (Israel 2020a). "Discourages" is not regulatory language that is likely to evoke serious apprehension about breaking the law. It falls far short of the strict enforcement of regulations Canadians were promised in the government's pitch for legalization.

Health Canada's permissive reactions to product promotion violations have, in effect, given the cannabis industry much of what it wanted—only partially-encumbered promotional access to the public, including youth. This access has a clear, ambitious purpose—the expansion of overall market size and increased revenues. The available evidence from our experience with alcohol and tobacco tells us this is likely to occur at the expense of public health.

The above-mentioned O'Cannabiz Expo panel was moderated by Trina Fraser, a prominent Canadian lawyer specializing in cannabis law. Ms. Fraser has been a persistent advocate for regulatory adherence in the industry and was not shy about calling out the questionable practices that have prevailed. When interviewed for a *Marijuana Business Daily* article she said: "generally speaking, even if the primary intention is to encourage compliance, and not to penalize, at some point there has to be some real consequences imposed to keep everybody in line, in terms of all aspects of enforcement, whether it's license suspensions or monetary penalties." Fraser continued:

"I feel like sooner or later someone will be made an example out of, because there is blatant, flagrant noncompliance out there. We know that. Eventually it becomes de facto permitted" (Lamers 2021a).

Fraser was speaking more broadly than product promotion violations, but her comments are certainly pertinent to the advertising infractions, and the shortage of meaningful consequences issued thus far from Canada's regulator.

It is not the case that Health Canada has no legislative teeth available to it for dealing with product promotion violations. The Controlled Drugs and Substances Act provides for suspension or revocation of a licence or prosecution. The Cannabis Act provides for up to a $5 million fine, up to 3 years prison, or both.

But no punitive consequences have occurred over eight years of legal cannabis company violations – for first therapeutic, and then recreational, use. Health Canada has provided transgressors with full immunity for their disregard for the restrictions on product promotion. It is puzzling that legislators thought that product promotion was a sufficiently serious infraction to create substantial penalties, but the regulator appears to have no intention to use them. The fear factor associated with a regulatory scarecrow is likely to have a limited life span.

Neither has the regulator ever named a company that committed a product promotion violation. It is indeed a strange set of circumstances that Health Canada has named companies committing other serious infractions, but still provides those with product promotion violations with the favour of anonymity as well.

Interestingly, in the latter part of 2020 and extending into the autumn of 2021, the publicly visible promotion of cannabis became considerably less brazen. This may have been in part because the COVID-19 pandemic had put a damper on festivals and events that provided attractive promotional venues for the industry. But one might also wonder if Health Canada had quietly issued an ultimatum to the industry on its non-compliant product promotion practices. In the summer and autumn of 2022, with diminished COVID-19 restrictions on entertainment events, there was little if any event sponsorship activity.

One thing is clear. The industry is not done with its interest in advertising to expand the market for its products. Mr. Irwin Simon is Chairman and Chief Executive Officer of recently merged cannabis industry leader, Tilray. As we will see in the next chapter, Mr. Simon is not just one of the highest paid cannabis executives in Canada and the United States, but also one of highest paid executives in any industry in Canada. Perhaps buoyed by his recent meteoric rise in stature and compensation, Mr. Simon appears ready to take on government, public health authorities, and perhaps the courts as well given his thoughts and intentions on market expansion as expressed in an October 2021 address to Tilray shareholders:

*It's coming up on three years, October 18 with the Cana-
dian government on legalization. There has to be some
changes to the regs out there. And we will be out there lobbying the politicians with the liberal government now how to
make some of these changes, how to get out there and advertise safely, how we can sell more products. Because I'll tell you
what, we pay a lot of tax dollars toward this, and there's a lot
of benefits, and there's a lot of data that we've collected to
show why legalization made sense and what happened in the
last three years. (Tilray Inc. 2021)*

CORPORATE CRIME AND "UNAUTHORIZED ACTIVITIES"

Securities Violations

As discussed in Chapter 5, securities violations have been a problem in the Canadian cannabis industry since the early days of the corporatization of cannabis for therapeutic use in 2013. As Canada enacted legalization for recreational use in October 2018, the Canadian Securities Administrators (CSA), an umbrella organization for provincial securities regulators, issued a warning of a higher incidence of "problematic promotional activities." As with product promotion violations in Canada, the regulator's warning stopped short of naming specific companies (Lamers 2018). However, two high profile cases at the time attracted considerable attention in the business media.

Just to clarify, the "problematic promotional activities" in this case does not refer to promotion of cannabis products. It refers to companies promoting themselves to would-be investors. A Toronto-based e-commerce cannabis company called Namaste Technologies was accused by investors of several counts of securities fraud. A report from Citron Research alleged that "Namaste has lied to its shareholders, Canadian Regulators, US Regulators; and most of all has attempted to hide US assets from the Justice Department in an attempt to obtain a US listing" (Swaby 2018). The CEO was consequently fired for "breaches of fiduciary duty" and "evidence of self-dealing" (Subramaniam 2019). While the company denied the allegations, a class action lawsuit was pursued by investors (Law Offices of Howard G. Smith, n.d.).

Aphria is another Ontario medical cannabis producer discussed earlier for its advertising violations and exploitation of Canada's publicly funded system for covering the cost of therapeutic cannabis for veterans. A couple years later, Aphria ran afoul of investors and securities fraud investigators. A December 2018 report from Quintessential Capital Management and Hindenburg Research alleged that Aphria had acquired foreign assets, at vastly inflated prices, which were essentially worthless. The report also alleged that this was done as part of a scheme to divert funds away from shareholders to company insiders (Ligaya 2018).

While the company has denied the allegations, the law firm of Kessler Topaz Meltzer and Check, LLP sought Aphria investors as plaintiffs for a securities fraud class action lawsuit (Kessler Topaz Meltzer and Check, LLP. 2018). At least four other law firms had announced that they were investigating the Aphria case.

While embroiled in securities fraud investigations, Aphria applied to Health Canada for a licence amendment to expand its cannabis growing operations. Seemingly unconcerned about Aphria's past and current business indiscretions, Health Canada approved the amendment allowing Aphria to become an even more prominent player in the industry (Aphria 2019).

A previously discussed case involved Sundial Growers, in which a cannabis shipment was recalled because it was contaminated with mould and pieces of rubber gloves. Sundial ran afoul of its investors who alleged that the company did not report the recall prior to going public and launched a class action lawsuit (Underwood 2019).

The British Columbia Securities Exchange Commission has named several cannabis companies in fraud investigations. Ontario-based producer Beleave has acknowledged its violations while five other cannabis companies remained under investigation by the Commission. These included: Affinor Growers Inc., Liht Cannabis Corp. (formerly Marapharm Ventures Inc.), PreveCeutical Medical Inc., Speakeasy Cannabis Club Ltd., and Abattis Bioceuticals Corp. (Rendell 2019a).

Another class action alleging securities violations against prominent Ontario licensed producer CannTrust was approved in early 2020, along with an investigation of CannTrust's activities by the Ontario Securities Commission. I will tell the CannTrust story shortly.

I conducted a follow-up of the securities fraud allegations made in this chapter in June 2021. Almost all cases were still in process. The case against Beleave had been settled. The cases against Sundial Growers and Abattis Bioceuticals had been fully dismissed.

Collaboration with the Illegal Cannabis Trade: Bonify Medical Marijuana

The promise of replacing a criminal cannabis trade in Canada with a law-abiding one has been further betrayed by outright collusion of the legal trade with the illegal one. This would not be a surprise for anyone who has followed the history of our other legal drug trades (DeVillaer 2019). Chapter 5 showed that licensed alcohol and tobacco companies have a history of collaboration with their respective illegal counterparts, largely for the purpose of tax avoidance.

Winnipeg, Manitoba, licensed cannabis producer, Bonify Medical Marijuana, had maintained a reasonably good inspection history with Health Canada, with only 4 minor observations of infractions, and no noncompliant ratings. However, on December 7, 2018, Bonify issued what Health Canada prefers to call a "voluntary recall' of product that had been sold to several legal Saskatchewan retailers. The official reason for the recall was Bonify's inability to prove that the product had passed laboratory testing. However, in a disclosure to the *Winnipeg Free Press* publication *The Leaf* a month earlier, a Bonify employee reported that the company had purchased two hundred kilograms of cannabis from an unlicensed supplier, and that the recalled cannabis was part of the illegal purchase. The whistleblower also said that on December 13, Health Canada seized a supply of cannabis from Bonify. At the time, Health Canada would only confirm that its inspectors had visited the Bonify site. A statement from Bonify's Board of Directors acknowledged only that "irregularities pertaining to the recalled product" had been uncovered, that it was investigating, and would have more to say on the matter later (Israel 2018c).

By December 21, Health Canada would say only that it had been "...unable to verify that the required laboratory testing had occurred", and that it had not determined whether Bonify or anyone else broke the law. At the same time, it was revealed that Bonify's Board of Directors had "removed company executives" and that Bonify had secured the services of a third-party consultant, RavenQuest Technologies, to manage the company's operations (Israel 2018a).

On December 24, Health Canada announced another recall of Bonify product for inadequate record-keeping and mislabelling (Froese 2018). Given Health Canada's penchant for euphemism in such matters, it remains uncertain whether the inadequate record-keeping and mislabelling is related to the purchase and sale of the illegal product.

On December 27, RavenQuest CEO George Robinson, who had conducted an investigation, announced that in addition to the dismissal of Bonify executives, a Board Member had also been suspended. Other details included that unrealistic production targets may have led to "poor choices" in trying to fulfill supply obligations. Robinson also acknowledged: "What they did was not at all remotely close to following the regulations" (Malone 2018).

Robinson also acknowledged that Bonify employees had been "bullied" by managers into inappropriate practices and had felt compelled to take the issues to Bonify's Board of Directors. He also suggested that his investigation led him to believe that other licensed producers were engaged with illegal suppliers. Exaggerated production targets can be used to attract investors—a practice that can run afoul of securities regulators. When those in-house production targets cannot be achieved, there is a temptation to quickly acquire cannabis product from a source that leaves no paper trail.

Robinson provided assurance that, in Bonify's case, the company was working closely with Health Canada "to right the ship" and he was confident that the company would eventually return to full production capacity with the blessing of the regulator (BNN Bloomberg 2019).

Two weeks later, Health Canada announced that it had suspended Bonify's licence. Robinson explained to the *Winnipeg Free Press* that this happened because of Health Canada's concern that "...the company wouldn't have proper management after March 31, when his management contract with Bonify is due to expire." However, Health Canada told the *Free Press* that the suspension was because Bonify had been found to be "...possessing, distributing and selling product that was purchased from an illegal source." It was also announced that the RCMP had begun an investigation of the company's supply chain. Consistent with customary practice, Bonify was given ten days to explain why the suspension should not occur (Israel 2019). It is not known whether Bonify submitted such an explanation.

Another disturbing aspect of this story was the lack of transparency on the part of Health Canada. Upon being notified of the situation, not by Health Canada but by Bonify, Manitoba Premier Brian Pallister expressed concern over the lack of communication with his government by Health Canada. This is at odds with a statement on the matter from Health Canada which asserted: "The department remains fully committed to sharing information with partners, including provincial and territorial officials and law enforcement, as appropriate." However, the lack of transparency did not end with Health Canada. When Mr. Pallister's Office contacted the RCMP, a spokesperson would neither confirm nor deny whether Bonify was being investigated (Israel 2018a). The office of Bill Blair, Minister of Border Security and Organized Crime Reduction, who was responsible for cannabis legalization, was equally evasive when contacted by *The Free Press* (Israel 2018a).

Apart from the ongoing lack of transparency during the investigation stage, many details of the case remain privileged information. Mr. Robinson admitted that the illegal cannabis purchase had occurred through "a broker" but that his investigation did not determine the source of the unauthorized cannabis. However, Mr. Robinson also disclosed that the findings had been provided to Manitoba and federal regulators, but with the names of individuals redacted (Malone 2018). Health Canada's and Manitoba's reaction to the redaction remains unknown.

By early February 2019, the Bonify matter was being investigated, not just by the RCMP, but also by Canada Revenue Agency (CBC News 2019b). The interest of CRA evokes consideration of instances of collusion by Canadian licensed alcohol and tobacco companies with the illegal trade in those products (DeVillaer 2019).

Health Canada indicated that it referred the Bonify case to the RCMP in December 2018. The RCMP initially denied that the case was referred to them, but later indicated that it had reviewed the case and decided not to investigate. The RCMP indicated that it would be a matter for the jurisdictional police, which would be the Winnipeg Police Service. However, WPS indicated that it had not been asked to investigate and would not be investigating (Lamers 2021d). A *CBC* report (Froese 2019) indicated that the RCMP said it had referred the case to the provincial Justice Department which indicated that the matter required further review before it could comment.

At the same time, Mr. Robinson, now in charge of Bonify, announced that Bonify was still producing cannabis and was hoping to regain its licence from Health Canada so it could sell the product again (Froese 2019).

Bonify's licence was reinstated by Health Canada in October 2019, less than a year after its suspension (Gowriluk 2019).

In stark contrast to the charitable disposition of crimes committed by large, licensed producers was a case occurring at the same time as the Bonify case, involving a Winnipeg Aboriginal man. He was charged with possession of 85 grams of cannabis (above the federal legal limit of 30 grams) and of paraphernalia that could be used for further distribution of the cannabis. The judge referred to the man not as "a broker" but as a "drug dealer" and sentenced him to ten months in prison – a reduction from the fifteen months sought by the prosecutor in the case (Geary 2019). No charges were ever laid against Bonify by any level of law enforcement.

However, in August 2021, Bonify announced that it was "winding down" its production facility (Stratcann 2021). A Bonify employee, who wished to remain anonymous, told me that the company had employed mostly very conscientious people who were now out of work because of the reckless conduct of the company's handsomely compensated executives.

Multiple Instances of "Unauthorized Activity": CannTrust

CannTrust Inc., an Ontario licensed cannabis producer, has been heralded as a leader in the cannabis industry. In early 2019, CannTrust's website home page proclaimed that in 2018 the company had received seven Canadian Cannabis Awards, including the top award, Licensed Producer of the Year (2018). However, in mid-2019 CannTrust found itself under joint investigation by the Ontario Securities Commission, the RCMP Financial Crime Program and the Ontario Provincial Police Anti-Rackets Branch (Canadian Press 2019c).

In an unscheduled inspection of CannTrust's Niagara (Pelham), Ontario, facility in early July 2019, Health Canada discovered the company had allegedly been growing cannabis in unauthorized rooms and had provided false information to Health Canada. CannTrust quickly accepted Health Canada's findings and indicated its intention to become compliant with all regulations (Nair and Roy 2019). On July 9, Board of Directors Chair Eric Paul told BNN Bloomberg: "It was quite a shock when I found out about it." Paul also said that he remained confident in the company's leadership including CEO Peter Aceto and suggested that the problem was due to "pretty flawed logic" by the company's employees (George-Cosh 2019c).

More details emerged from a former CannTrust employee. Nick Lalonde, told a reporter at the *Globe and Mail* that he and others were asked to stay after work by their manager to erect walls of vinyl sheets to obscure illegal plants from photos submitted to Health Canada (Rendell 2019b). The decision by Lalonde to alert Health Canada appeared to anticipate the decision by CannTrust executives to blame employees: "To me it was any day Health Canada is going to come in here and see these rooms and we're all going to get arrested and I'm going to go to jail and I'm going to be screwed for the rest of my life and I'm making $15 an hour doing it" (Ferreira 2019).

Shortly after the surprise inspection at the Niagara facility, Health Canada found problems at a second CannTrust facility in Vaughan, Ontario – citing inadequate security, quality assurance, operating proced-ures, and record keeping. Health Canada put a hold on over 12,000 kg of cannabis product. These developments prompted the company's auditor to withdraw its endorsement of CannTrust's 2018 financial statements (Sarkar and Jain 2019).

CannTrust's internal investigation found that both Chairman Paul and CEO Aceto knew about, and encouraged, the illegal activities well be-fore they were brought to the attention of Health Canada. It was also dis-covered that some of the unauthorized product had been sold to legal government retailers in Canada and to a Danish partner. Aceto was "ter-minated with cause" by CannTrust's Board of Directors which also asked for and received Chairman Paul's resignation (Canadian Press 2019a).

Records from the Canadian System for Electronic Disclosure for In-siders (SEDI) showed that Paul and another director had sold, through a holding company, over $6 million worth of CannTrust stock. The transac-tions occurred almost immediately after the irregularities came to the atten-tion of CannTrust's Board, and before the results of Health Canada's investigations had become public (Milstead and Rendell 2019). As would be expected, the value of CannTrust stock plummeted dramatically following the public announcement.

A few months later, company documents surfaced that showed that CannTrust had, without applying for authorization from Health Canada, purchased cannabis seed from the illegal trade. CannTrust also misrepres-ented the strain of some of those seeds as strains that it was authorized to cultivate. At least a thousand plants were grown from the illegal seed, con-verted to product, and sold on the legal market (George-Cosh 2019b).

Health Canada should not have been too surprised by these revela-tions. It was not as if CannTrust had an unblemished record before the July 2019 incident. Unlike the reasonably compliant history at Bonify, Health Canada's Compliance and Enforcement Reports showed that between April 1, 2015, and March 31, 2019, CannTrust had 10 minor and 11 major observa-tions recorded during the regulator's inspections. This included 8 non-com-pliance inspection ratings in 2015-16. Consequences imposed by the regulator included seizure of product for contravention of the Physical Se-curity Directive and warning letters (Canada 2019a, 2020).

Recall CannTrust's outstanding recognition at the 2018 Canadian Cannabis Awards. It invites wonder about what the criteria might be for achieving such accolades.

On September 17, 2019, CannTrust announced that Health Canada had imposed a partial suspension of its licences. This meant that the com-pany could continue to grow, process, and sell currently held legal product, but could not begin any new cultivation, pending further investigation by the regulator (CannTrust Holdings Inc. 2019). A month later, CannTrust also announced that to regain full regulatory compliance, it would destroy $77 million worth of plants and inventory (Reuters 2019).

By early 2020, a class-action lawsuit against CannTrust had been approved by an Ontario court. The lawsuit named all those who had served on the Board of directors including the executives between October 2018 and July 2019, along with the new CEO Robert Marcovitch, given his role on the audit committee at CannTrust. The lawsuit also identified the illegal selling of company stock by Chairman Paul, and another director, Mark Litwin. It also named the company's auditors KPMG LLP and its underwriters for having supported those trades (Subramaniam 2020).

In March, CannTrust was granted creditor protection so it could avoid falling into bankruptcy (Financial Post Staff 2020), thus joining several other licensed producers including AgMedica Bioscience, Ascent Industries, Beleave, Invictus Group, James E. Wagner Cultivation Corp., and Wayland Group (Israel 2020b). For at least the short-term such protection prevents plaintiffs from collecting on any civil actions—a very generous arrangement under Canadian law when pertaining to wayward corporate conduct.

Following a disastrous plunge in its stock value, CannTrust lost its listing on both the Toronto Stock Exchange and the New York Stock Exchange (NYSE). Both Aurora and HEXO have narrowly escaped a similar fate with the NYSE (Israel 2020b).

In an act of almost unfathomable regulatory generosity, the licences for CannTrust's Niagara facility and for its Vaughan facility were reinstated by Health Canada in May (CannTrust Holdings Inc. 2020) and in August 2020, respectively. Health Canada said it was "satisfied with the actions the company has taken in response to the suspension" and added: "CannTrust Inc. will be subject to additional oversight measures, which may include increased frequency of inspections" (Lamers 2020). The Cannabis Act carries a provision of administrative fines of up to $1 million. Despite CannTrust having committed several serious infractions under the Act, Health Canada chose not to fine the company. Once again, Canada's health regulator had failed to impose actions that would send a message to other licensed producers that there would be meaningful consequences for industry executives who were indifferent to regulatory requirements.

The embattled company appeared to be on the road to recovery with its licenses restored and making amends with its shareholders. In early 2021, the company announced that it was setting up a trust fund of $50 million for the compensation of securities claimants (Marijuana Business Daily 2021). Ultimately, a primary settlement was reached for $126 million (A. Dimitri Lascaris Law Professional Corporation et al. 2022) which included a US settlement for $83 million (Top Class Actions 2021).

In mid 2021, the CannTrust case took a surprising and unprecedented turn.

Following the completion of a joint investigation by the Ontario Securities Commission and the RCMP Integrated Market Enforcement Team, three former CannTrust directors and officers were charged with quasi-criminal offences under the Securities Act of Ontario. The quasi-criminal designation means that the offences are not prosecuted under the Criminal Code by the Ministry of the Attorney General. However, a provincial court trial means that potential sanctions include fines, jail time, or both (Ontario Securities Commission 2021).

Charged were Eric Paul, Peter Aceto, and Mark Litwin with a variety of offences including fraud, insider trading, making a false prospectus and false preliminary prospectus, making false or misleading statements to the OSC and to the market, and authorizing, permitting, or acquiescing in the commission of an offence (Ontario Securities Commission 2021). Health Canada has claimed that it was unaware that Litwin was under investigation when it restored CannTrust's production licenses (Lamers 2021e). This was despite media coverage of Litwin having been named as a defendant in the ongoing class action (Subramaniam 2020). The three individuals retained legal representation. In all three cases, counsel has made public statements assuring the complete innocence of their respective clients (Lamers 2021a).

At a pretrial hearing in May 2022, the charges related to making false or misleading statements to the Ontario Securities Commission were withdrawn. A spokesperson for the OSC indicated that this would reduce the scope and time required for what is expected to be a complex case (Canadian Press 2022). In December 2022, the three CannTrust executives were acquitted of all charges (Shecter 2022).

In yet another stunning development in 2022, CannTrust announced that it had insufficient liquidity to survive beyond the short term and may have to "wind-down" in the absence of a significant infusion of investment (CannTrust Holdings Inc 2022a). That infusion appeared to have come in an investment from a Netherlands private equity firm (CannTrust Holdings Inc 2022b). On May 3, the company announced a name change from CannTrust to Phoena. The press release explained: "The name Phoena is derived from the word 'phenotype' which describes the traits taken from a plant's genetic code that we use to merge nature, purpose, and science to produce the best cannabis products on the market" (Phoena 2022).

License Revocations

RavenQuest (Bloomera Inc., Alberta Green Biotech Inc)

Mr. George Robinson's company, RavenQuest, which had been brought in to temporarily manage Bonify through its troubles, ultimately had its own problems. The locks on the doors to Bloomera, Inc., a RavenQuest grow facility in Markham, Ontario, had been changed by the property owner. Health Canada had been unable to gain entry to conduct an inspection and suspended the company's licence in early 2020. Another RavenQuest subsidiary, Alberta Green Biotech Inc., also had its license suspended around the same time. Following the resignation of Robinson and all board members, save one, the remaining director alleged that Mr. Robinson had

"...fled, taking with him the company financials and subsidiary paperwork." Robinson denied the allegation (Parry 2020). Ultimately, Health Canada revoked the licenses of both Bloomera and Alberta Green Biotech.

Agrima Botanicals Corporation

Agrima Botanicals Corporation, a British Columbia licensed cannabis producer and subsidiary of Ascent Industries Corporation, had only a moderately spotted inspection record with 3 minor observations and 1 critical one resulting in a non-compliance rating. Health Canada issued a warning letter due to activities taking place at the site that were not authorized by Agrima's licence. Compliance with the regulations was achieved following the warning letter. However, beginning in August 2018, matters turned more serious for Agrima. A Health Canada inspection found that the company "did not meet all of its record keeping and other compliance requirements" and partially suspended Agrima's licences (Ascent 2018b). A later release from Ascent (2018a), disclosed that Health Canada was also concerned about "unauthorized activities with cannabis" on the part of Agrima and that the company had failed to defend the activities to Health Canada's satisfaction. Health Canada was consequently considering the full revocation of Agrima's licence. Ascent announced that its chief executive, chief operating officer and head of business development had all resigned, and that it would continue to try to protect its licences from revocation. Neither the company nor Health Canada has been more specific about the nature of the violations. There was some speculation that the revocation was due to Agrima's selling of cannabis vape pens, which are sold legally in the United States by another of Ascent's subsidiaries, TOKO, but are not legal in Canada (Israel 2018b). There has been no confirmation that this was the case.

In February 2019, Sweet Cannabis (another subsidiary of Ascent), located in Nevada, received a notice from state authorities of the potential suspension or revocation of its licences arising from its having held a cannabis consumption event in Las Vegas and for the now familiar "record keeping and inventory errors." The notice also referred to the Health Canada licence suspension for the Canadian subsidiary (Ascent 2019).

In March, embattled Ascent was granted creditor protection for its Canadian subsidiary by The Supreme Court of British Columbia (Canadian Press 2019d). In July, Health Canada revoked its licence. A Health Canada spokesperson said: "These findings of non-compliance were based on evidence obtained during inspections by Health Canada that indicated that the company was conducting unauthorized activities with cannabis both before and after the company was issued licences..." (Canadian Press 2019b).

The acknowledgement from Health Canada that Ascent was involved in "unauthorized activities" before the company was issued licenses is an important one. It speaks to the vulnerability of what Canada's regulators have referred to as their "robust" and "exhaustive" screening procedures for issuing licenses (Harris 2018). Whether Agrima was guilty of criminal, or the less stigmatized, unauthorized conduct also remains unknown.

Evergreen Medicinal Supply Inc.

In 2019, Evergreen had some of its products seized and its licence suspended. In an interview with BNN Bloomberg, Health Canada spokesperson, Tammy Jarbeau, was uncharacteristically slightly more forthcoming with detail on the suspension, noting that on August 9, 2019: "Health Canada suspended Evergreen Medicinal Supply's licences to protect public health and safety, including preventing cannabis from being diverted to the illegal market, as a result of non-compliance with certain provisions of the Cannabis Act and Cannabis Regulations." Evergreen was also sued by its property owner for unpaid rent of $425,061 and for the continued occupation of the land by its production facility after the lease had expired (George-Cosh 2019a). As of February 25, 2022, the company was no longer included on Health Canada's list of licensed producers (Canada 2022).

Wither Accountability?

Health Canada's Cannabis Compliance and Enforcement system is an important accountability measure. However, without the contributions of company whistle-blowers, it is uncertain how successful it may have been in uncovering some serious violations. Two recent developments raise concerns that the effectiveness of the system may be further compromised.

Near the end of 2021, a Health Canada communication with *Stratcann*, an online cannabis communications platform, noted that between the beginning of 2020 and almost the end of 2021, the number of license holders to be inspected grew from about 250 to nearly 800. While there was a time that license holders would be visited several times a year, this growth in their numbers means that some facilities are now inspected only once per year or not at all during the year (Brown 2021).

The additional concern is that the single inspection might be a virtual one. The Canadian government funded a Health Canada proposal to reduce its "carbon footprint" by conducting virtual inspections of licensed cannabis producers. The project summary states: "This project is a pilot to replace certain physical inspections that are a significant source of carbon emissions, with virtual inspections. If successful, the program's carbon footprint will be reduced while still maintaining (and perhaps augmenting or enhancing) regulatory oversight. There is also significant potential for broader application within Health Canada and beyond" (Canada 2021).

The COVID-19 pandemic also provided a justification for a move to virtual inspections. The same Health Canada communication with *Stratcann* cited the challenges of the pandemic. The regulator divulged that it had conducted most of its 2020 and 2021 inspections virtually (Brown 2021).

Environmental concerns and COVID-19 protections are obviously important. However, the downside of virtual inspections is that they limit opportunity to improve oversight of an industry that so persistently attempts to circumvent the regulations. Rather, a virtual approach could make surveillance even more susceptible to the industry's wily gaming of the regulations and less effective at detection of non-compliance. The outcome of having conducted mostly virtual inspections between April 1, 2020, and March 31, 2021, will would not be publicly available until the release of the 2020-21 Cannabis Compliance and Enforcement Report.

The potential withering of Health Canada's regulation of the industry may also be predicated upon financial concerns. The industry's pursuit of a more lucrative commercial landscape, at seemingly any cost, is one that creates a heavy workload for regulators—an industry buffer borne partly by taxpayers.

To offset regulatory costs, Health Canada charges fees to cannabis businesses. However, the fees only partially cover the total costs of regulation. In March of 2021, Health Canada told *Marijuana Business Daily* that in fiscal 2018-19, Health Canada's regulatory fees recovered $4.2 million of $92.4 million in total regulatory costs. In 2019-20, the recovery was $50.5 million of the $110.2 million in costs. However, even with a system of only partial recovery of the total costs, many companies have fallen behind in their remittance to Health Canada. As of December 31, 2021, the total amount in arrears since September 2020 was $914,000—a more than ten-fold increase from the previous year. Industry spokespeople speculated that the shortfall might be due to some companies facing daunting financial hardships such that they may have to choose between paying regulatory fees to Health Canada or excise taxes to Canada Revenue Agency (Lamers 2022c).

However, a subsequent report from *Marijuana Business Daily* showed that some cannabis companies were not paying their excise taxes either. As of March 2021, there was $16 million in unpaid excise tax by cannabis companies. That figure ballooned to $52.4 million by March 2022. During the same period, the number of companies in arrears had increased from 68 to 141. Industry spokespeople cited falling marijuana prices and fierce competition, as creating a business landscape in which companies must choose between paying taxes and paying employees and keeping the lights on (Lamers 2022a).

None of the spokespeople mentioned the excessive amounts of money spent by some companies on the excesses of shuttered greenhouses and executive salaries—a topic I will cover in the next chapter. Given the reluctance of Health Canada and Canada Revenue Agency to disclose the identities of cannabis companies in arrears, it is not possible to know if the companies in arrears on their regulatory fees are the same ones that have spent excessively on some operational costs.

The great majority of Canada's 856 licensees had apparently made their excise payments in full. A point that can be made in favour of some of the companies' plights is that excise tax provisions do not differentiate between large companies and medium-small ones. Rather than drop the excise tax, perhaps it can be sensitized to company size.

Organized Crime in the Licensed Cannabis Industry

The euphemistic "unauthorized activities" in Canada's cannabis industry do not end with the non-compliance and criminal conduct described thus far. Earlier in this book I referred to a *CBC News* report (Pfeffer and Dumont 2017) on a 2013 RCMP disclosure of an increase in organized crime involvement in the licensed (then therapeutic-only) cannabis trade. It may seem counter-intuitive that legalization would enable organized crime's involvement in the licensed cannabis trade. And yet, this became apparent upon the results of an investigation by the *Québec Radio-Canada* investigative program *Enquête*. A November 2018 *CBC News* account of the investigation (Denis 2018) reported evidence of ties between licensed cannabis growers and organized crime. *Enquête* examined hundreds of documents available to the RCMP, Canadian securities regulators and Health Canada. *Enquête* discovered ties between known "Mafia members", "drug traffickers", the well-known Montréal crime family – the Rizzutos, and "a major Canadian cannabis company" as well as an individual identified as "one of the big players in the industry." Enquête chose to not name the companies or individuals involved.

Enquête claimed that the major vulnerability in the screening process of the Canadian government is that the identities of investors and applicants for cannabis production licences are sometimes protected by trusts, whose beneficiaries are not disclosed in the applications. Expert testimony recommending a default rejection of production applications that are financed through trusts was made to the Canadian Senate during its deliberations on cannabis legalization. Recognizing the opportunity for organized crime to establish a stronger presence in the licensed cannabis regime, Senator Carignan and other senators tried, unsuccessfully, to amend The Cannabis Act in this respect.

A *CBC News* follow-up to the story (Harris 2018) provided reactions from government officials, including Border Security and Organized Crime Reduction Minister Bill Blair:

"We have robust physical and personnel security screening processes in place for the existing industry designed to guard against infiltration by organized crime."

Health Minister Ginette Petitpas Taylor claimed that the current verification system was "exhaustive" and had uncovered no such connections between licensed producers and organized crime. Prime Minister Trudeau was reported as acknowledging that there is still work to do, but that he was happy with progress thus far.

These platitudes are not compelling and are inconsistent with statements from the RCMP. When asked how it had failed to identify the ties discovered by the journalists, an RCMP spokesperson cited a need for sophisticated technological tools which the RCMP could not afford (Denis 2018).

None of the government spokespersons specifically addressed the critical issue of trusts concealing the identities of persons with connections to organized crime. The expert testimony on the perils of trusts during the Senate hearings was not heeded by the government. This left the application process open to exactly the type of risk that finance experts had predicted, and exactly what eventually appears to have happened.

In a May 2019 statement on improvements in Health Canada's licence application process for cultivation, processing, and retailing cannabis, the regulator announced: "There are no changes to the regulatory requirements, including the rigorous security clearance process for key personnel and corporate directors" (Canada 2019b). There was no mention of the issue of trusts.

A more recent investigation into connections between licensed cannabis producers and organized crime was more forthcoming with the names of individuals involved in familial, social, and business relationships among producers, Redecan and HEXO, and motorcycle club and crime organization, Hells Angels (Blais et al. 2021).

The report notes that businessperson, Josh Hill, was a major shareholder in Redecan when it was purchased by HEXO in May 2021. Mr. Hill also maintained an office at Redecan. When a journalist contacted the HEXO office in November of 2021, it was confirmed that Hill was an employee, but was not there at the time. Separate social media posts that have since been removed showed Hill posing with two HEXO directors and with members of Hells Angels. Both Health Canada and Québec's Permanent Anti-Corruption Unit (UPAC) were investigating the matter. HEXO claimed that Hill is not part of the company and that Health Canada's investigation is complete. As of January 2022, Health Canada had not publicly issued any conclusions from its investigations (Cloutier 2022). That was still the case in June 2022.

CONSEQUENCES AND CRONYISM

Commonality and Inconsistency

Regulatory responses to non-compliance and criminal conduct by cannabis corporations holds some interesting and disturbing commonalities. There are also puzzling inconsistencies.

The first commonality occurred among at least four major cases that we know of. These include Mettrum and Tweed (for purchase and transportation of unauthorized product), Mettrum (for use of unapproved pesticides), Bonify (for purchase and sale of unlicensed cannabis), and CannTrust (for unauthorized cultivation). All these violations came to the attention of Health Canada, not because of its scheduled or even its unscheduled inspections, but because third parties alerted them. In the Mettrum/Tweed case, employees in airport security notified the RCMP. In the other cases, an employee of the respective cannabis producer notified Health Canada of the improprieties. These cases raise questions about the rigour and ultimate effectiveness of Health Canada's regulatory surveillance. Certainly, Health Canada identifies many infractions, but what might be the size of the denominator—the larger number of infractions that include the undetected? Of greater concern is that in all cases, it is possible that the violations could have continued perhaps even to the present time if not for the conscientiousness of the employees. In the case of CannTrust, the whistle-blower specifically mentioned to the *National Post*, that he expected Health Canada may not have become aware of the infractions if he had not come forward (Ferreira 2019). That is despite CannTrust having a history of major infractions.

The second commonality in regulatory response is the lenient treatment, in most cases, of cannabis producers who are non-compliant and/or break the law. It is also here where some puzzling inconsistencies appear.

Marijuana Business Daily reported that Canada Revenue Agency (CRA), in 2019 and 2020, issued 22 cannabis-related fines totalling $1.3 million dollars for violations of the Excise Act by licensed cannabis companies. The most common reasons included:

- *production without an excise license*

- *unaccounted for excise stamps*

- *inadequate records*

- *purchase of cannabis by an excise licensee from an unlicensed person.*

All but two fines were small. Excluding these outliers of $434,611 and $507,660, the average annual fine amounts were approximately $14,000 in 2019 and $19,000 in 2020 (Lamers 2021c).

As we saw with Health Canada's treatment of licensed cannabis producers for product promotion violations, CRA did not reveal the names of the offending companies. This is a peculiar accommodation on the part of the regulators for companies that have broken the law. The granting of anonymity is also a departure from any regulatory due diligence to protect other companies, customers, and shareholders who might be inclined to avoid doing business with a non-compliant company.

The initial involvement of the RCMP in the charges against Ontario's CannTrust is also a departure from past action. The RCMP's inaction with Manitoba's Bonify was reminiscent of the 2014 incident in British Columbia in which the RCMP followed a directive to stand down on a seizure of illegal cannabis shipments by licensed producers Tweed and Mettrum. Health Canada's justification for the issuing of this astonishing directive stressed the importance of protecting the stock values of the offending companies which had just become publicly traded. This is another betrayal of shareholders' rights to accurate information about the companies to whom they have entrusted their investments. Securities regulators also failed to weigh in.

It is noteworthy that in the cases of companies committing offences involving unauthorized cannabis, the Cannabis Act provides a maximum sentence of fourteen years imprisonment. However, no criminal charges were brought for this case or for similarly serious offences committed by Bonify or Agrima. Yet, quasi-criminal charges have been brought in the CannTrust case—a lone instance. Suspended production licences at Bonify and CannTrust were reinstated after a few months. The licenses were permanently revoked at Agrima, Bloomera, Alberta Green Biotech, and Evergreen. We know nothing of the reasons for the profoundly different fates.

Health Canada's approach to violations has remained generally permissive, having thus far chosen not to fine any licensed producers despite their commission of major offences. CRA's pursuit of fines, and the provincial court action of the Ontario Securities Commission against CannTrust, invites questions about why different government regulators take such different approaches. One apparent difference is that OSC and CRA have taken more punitive actions to protect the financial interests of investors and of the government itself. Health Canada appears less punitive in the exercise of its core mandate—the protection of the health interests of Canadians.

There has been another profound inconsistency in the Canadian government's enforcement of the Cannabis Act. This inconsistency involves the permissive treatment of cannabis companies for unauthorized production of cannabis versus the harsh treatment of cannabis users and unlicensed sellers for the use/sale of unauthorized product.

Cannabis company executives who engaged in serious crimes under the Act lost their jobs but remain at large with the entitlement of being able to roam free to negotiate an executive position elsewhere with typically seven figures in annual compensation and bonuses.

The generous treatment of felonious executives from licensed cannabis producers prompts an important question. Might a lone unlicensed cannabis "dealer", found to be in possession of copious amounts of illegal product, be treated so generously? What about a person caught in simple possession of unauthorized cannabis? Would these individuals be more likely to face the punitive provisions of the Act—certainly a fine, probably a criminal record, and possibly a prison sentence?

For its part, the RCMP continues to charge unlicensed growers and retailers more so than legal producers who violate the conditions of their licenses (Royal Canadian Mounted Police 2021). Controversy also continues regarding diversion of cannabis grown by individuals for supposed therapeutic use, and potentially through organized crime networks. This allegation has been contested by advocates for therapeutic use but remains a concern that the RCMP has been raising since 2013. There appears to have been little progress in addressing the matter (Lamers 2021b; M. Robertson 2020).

Data from The Public Prosecution Service of Canada (PPSC), as introduced in Chapter 4, indicates that other branches of law enforcement also remain active exclusively with unlicensed cannabis operators. As for cannabis users, Canada's crime statistics showed reductions in arrest rates for some cannabis use related offences since legalization. But overall, they still show high levels of criminalization of cannabis users for a variety of cannabis related offences, including mostly minor ones. I will present the detailed statistics on charges for cannabis users in Chapter 10 as part of a larger discussion of the impact of cannabis legalization in Canada.

For now, I will say that the differential regulatory responses between cannabis corporations and individual Canadians raises fundamental questions about the consistency with which the Liberal government responds to corporate transgressions versus much less significant transgressions committed by individual Canadians. This also raises questions from legal and human rights perspectives on justice and equity in the application of the Cannabis Act.

When challenged on these seemingly inequitable responses to violations of the Act, a Health Canada spokesperson noted that the regulator's practices for cannabis are consistent with its practices in other regulatory arenas (K. Robertson 2020). The statement seems not so much a defence of inequitable responses for cannabis enforcement as it is an admission of inequitable treatment in other arenas of regulation in Canada. Chapter 5 provided a detailed account of permissive approaches to the regulation of Canada's other legal drug industries—tobacco, alcohol, and pharmaceutical.

It Sure Looks Like Cronyism

Chapter 6 referred to a "green shine" list of connections between political party elites and licensed cannabis producers in the then-nascent cannabis industry. Connections were most notable among affiliates of the Liberal Party of Canada—the party that engineered legalization for recreational use. Liberal Party figures and their high-ranking bureaucrats played particularly important roles in the establishment of some of the industry leaders at that time. Tweed and Mettrum (now both subsidiaries of Canopy Growth) were prominent on the green shine list, as was Hydropothecary (now HEXO). In the cases of corporate malfeasance and impropriety discussed thus far, Canopy, or one of its subsidiaries (Tweed, Mettrum), has come up repeatedly. It was also prominent in the rash of illegal product promotion that occurred in the months before legalization. As far as has been disclosed, there have been no meaningful consequences for this company for any of its infractions. I sometimes wonder if parochial monetary interests are, at least in part, driving the decisions and the inconsistencies in regulatory consequences for infractions.

An additional instance involving Canopy occurred in 2019, when it found itself in the middle of a Newfoundland Auditor General Office's probe. The Auditor General was investigating concerns from opposition members in the legislature related to the province's process of awarding a $40 million supply contract to Canopy. There were also concerns with Canopy's payment of exorbitant levels of rent for production facilities to a numbered company owned by associates of Provincial Liberal Party members. The company had also received millions of dollars in tax-free loans from the provincial Liberal government. Newfoundland Auditor General, Julia Mullaley, stated: "All I can tell you is that it is something that I think is a really important area of work, so we will be looking at that, as resources become available."

The Auditor General noted that a first report was expected to be released within a month and that others would follow (Breen 2019). Julia Mullaley left her position as AG in March of 2020 (VOCM Local News 2020). Searches of the website for the Office of the Auditor General Newfoundland and Labrador in July 2020 and October 2021 found no reports of progress or on the status of the case.

In the next chapter I will describe Canopy's receipt of millions of dollars in federal COVID-19 wage subsidies from the Liberal federal government—while it laid off hundreds of employees.

Hydropothecary (HEXO) is another company that was prominent on the green shine list. Its licence has also survived a lengthy list of infractions detailed earlier in this chapter from Health Canada's compliance inspections. Like Canopy, it was among the most brazen of companies engaged in illegal product promotion just before legalization came into effect. As described earlier in this chapter, it also appears to have survived indications of possible ties to organized crime.

Ultimate accountability for such government/industry relationships does not lie with regulators like Health Canada. In some ways, regulators are among the victims of it—having to carefully carry out regulatory responsibilities while remaining attentive to whose personal financial interests might be at stake.

Cabinet is ultimately where the accountability must lie. For much of the tumultuous history of cannabis legalization, it would be too easy, and unreasonable, to throw Health Canada (or any regulator) under the bus—to use the vernacular of political culture. A regulator can only be as effective as the Cabinet that directs it. It is also relevant to recall the apparent importance of The Liberal Party of Canada Board of Directors as a catalyst in the establishment of the cannabis industry, and of the vested interests of key people in the Party. One wonders how far up the chain lies the origin of the tolerance for so much non-compliance and criminal conduct among the many companies identified in this chapter. Regardless of the level of its hierarchical origin, the ongoing protection and enabling of corporate wrongdoing by the Liberal Government continues to make a mockery of Canada's law enforcement and justice systems. Canada is not alone in the blatant and unapologetic displays of cronyism in the licensed cannabis industry. The problem has also been endemic in state jurisdictions in the United States (Government Accountability Institute 2021). Perhaps the time has arrived for an RCMP investigation into the same problem here in Canada—and this time, with no stand-down provision.

Another solution—a much more unorthodox one—might be for concerned provincial governments to offer financial incentives for whistle-blowers to come forward with allegations of serious company malfeasance that regulators are able to verify. Whistle-blowers have been instrumental in bringing industry malfeasance to the attention of regulators and the public eye through the media. They are a resource to be leveraged. The valour and the vulnerability of the whistle-blower—a misfit within a corrupt corporate culture—was effectively captured in a *Financial Times* column: "Hidden corporate misbehaviour comes to seem normal to those engaged in it. Everyone else is doing it, management seems to encourage it and it takes a brave, or foolhardy, soul to ask: what would happen if the outside world knew what we were getting up to?" (Skapinker 2012).

The big players in the cannabis industry have never been inclined to acknowledge their positions of privilege that have afforded them so much leniency in bearing any meaningful consequences for their various violations. Astonishingly, they have often attempted to camouflage their persistent regulatory non-compliance, illegal conduct, and financial failures with indignant cries of "nanny state" regulation. They claim it is unrealistic and unfair rules that impede the industry's propriety and success. These claims are a profound departure from the truth. As we will see in the next chapter, the big players have, to a significant extent, been the architects of their companies' misery. They have demonstrated an embarrassing lack of business acumen within an orgy of self-indulgent executive excess. This is exactly what we should expect when political party cronyism dominates the formative years of an industry.

SUMMING UP

The legalization of cannabis promised to replace a criminal cannabis trade with a law-abiding one that would supply safe product for consumers. That did not happen. Health Canada has an Enforcement and Compliance system that has detected numerous acts of non-compliance, including for product integrity, among licensed producers. It has also detected illegal activity on the part of licensed producers. Other serious instances of criminal activity were not detected by the regulator but reported by company whistle-blowers. The sum of illegal activity included securities fraud, illegal transport of cannabis, unlicensed cultivation and attempted cover-ups, financial crimes, collusion with the illegal trade, and connections with organized crime. In almost all cases, the regulator responded with consequences that are unlikely to motivate future compliance. Permissive and inconsistent regulatory actions are an expected outcome of an apparent dynamic of cronyism between political party and industry.

Chapter 8

Green Rush in The Red

> *"Anyone who wanders into Major League Baseball can't help but notice the stark contrast between the field of play and the uneasy space just off it, where the executives and the scouts make their livings. The game itself is a ruthless competition. Unless you're very good, you don't survive in it. But in the space just off the field of play there really is no level of incompetence that won't be tolerated."*
>
> — **Michael Lewis,** *Moneyball*

Halfway through 2022, well into the fourth year of recreational legalization, the licensed cannabis industry in Canada was in fiscal chaos. This chapter tells the story. Even while quarterly sales for some companies were increasing, most companies were still reporting enormous deficits. The biggest, long-established companies have yet to have a profitable year. The industry has been hurt by what appears to be a serious lack of basic business competence.

Poorly performing, inappropriately incentivized, and crime-bent executives have left their posts with six or seven-figure payouts—following a record of significant monetary loss and reputation damage for the company, insolvencies, plunging stock values that devastated investors, closure of production facilities, and massive staff layoffs. Retail is now oversubscribed and will result in financial calamity for many hopeful entrepreneurs with modest to high ambitions.

This chapter examines five areas related to strategic and fiscal performance in the licensed cannabis industry:

- *over supply of cannabis*

- *financial losses by companies*

- *investor loss, job loss, executive excess*

- *multiple retail problems*

- *surviving fiscal calamity*

As in the previous chapter, this one drew extensively upon the diligent work of Matt Lamers at *Marijuana Business Daily*.

OVER SUPPLY OF CANNABIS

First, an overview. Legalization for recreational use offered enormous potential for market expansion and the realization of large revenues and profits. However, an initial shortage of supply was a problem. But the big, licensed cannabis producers did not set the creation of more supply as their immediate priority. Rather, with bold aspirations for a future global market, and flush with cash from unprecedented levels of investor enthusiasm, the producers set increased capacity for future production growth as their priority. Executives were effectively incentivized to build greenhouses. They built some of the largest greenhouses this world has ever seen. But the international market did not develop as anticipated. Many of those greenhouses sat empty, for months. Some were sold at large losses. One abandoned and empty greenhouse suddenly burst into flames in the dark of night. Executives still received substantial bonuses for financing them with investors' money.

The domestic market for cannabis was also not proving to be profitable. The slow development of retail capacity was one, probably exaggerated, reason. Inadequate production processes yielding enormous amounts of unsaleable product were another. However, the major reason was an inexcusable over-estimation of demand—both domestic and international. Even when production was finally ramped up, the product sat—its limited shelf-life hovering menacingly.

This was an important lesson already understood by anyone familiar with the applicable epidemiological survey results. As we saw in the data presented in Chapter 1, at the time of legalization, about three quarters of Canadian adults used the recreational drug alcohol, while about one-sixth used the recreational drug cannabis. Since legalization, imprecise survey estimates show that the number of people using cannabis has been increasing but is still only about one-quarter that of alcohol. (I will cover recent prevalence estimates in the last chapter.)

The comparative prevalence figures for use of these recreational drugs are not new information. Nor are they obscure information that was hidden away in arcane academic journals. They were, and remain, easily accessible online from the Canadian government. I, and others, mentioned the data in presentations and media interviews in the years preceding legalization. I also mentioned it as an invited panelist at a 'Cannabis Summit' organized by The Economist in Toronto during the summer of 2019. An investment-eager crowd of several hundred hopefuls blanketed the large banquet-style room. They looked at me like I was a skunk at their picnic. I guess I was.

In terms of consumer demand, cannabis was not the new alcohol. If cannabis executives understood this critical point, they were apparently incentivized to ignore it. Let's explore some of the details of the many profound failures.

The good news for the industry was that sales volume of legal recreational cannabis was increasing. According to data from Health Canada (Canada 2022), dried cannabis sales (which represent about two-thirds of all cannabis sales) rose from 4,405 kilos in October 2018 to 11,707 kilos in September 2019. Beginning in October of 2019, Health Canada began to report sales in 'packaged units' rather then kilos. October sales of recreational dried cannabis were at 5.2 million packaged units and rose to 8.7 million units in September 2021. Edibles and extracts also showed gains in sales.

The bad news was that sales were no where near the unrealistic, bordering on fraudulent, forecasts that so seductively lured investors. *Marijuana Business Daily* reported the astonishing finding that, as of the end of December 2020, the total size of unsold inventory was over a billion grams (Lamers 2021c). In September 2021, sales of all cannabis products, for both medical and non-medical use, reached 14.2 million packaged units. However, that represented only 22% of the 65.1 million packaged units held in inventory. There were also 6.3 million unpackaged plants held by licensed producers. As of September 2021, packaged inventory of dried cannabis was 3.7 times higher than sales. Packaged inventory of edibles and extracts were 6.5 and 5.5 times higher than sales, respectively (Canada 2022).

Part of the plan for serving a priority of expanding market opportunities, both domestic and international, had included the acquisition and development of massive greenhouse space—at massive costs—and ultimately, at massive loses. Some of the country's largest producers purchased greenhouses at which they eventually had to reduce or shut down operations. In the worst cases, operations were abandoned before even starting.

Medicine Hat, Alberta, was a town probably too dependent or hopeful upon oil and gas for sustainable prosperity. So it was with high hopes, in 2019, that Medicine Hat welcomed Aurora's intention to construct what it called the largest greenhouse in the world by square footage (Subramaniam 2019). In anticipation of the 650 jobs promised by Aurora, the financially struggling municipality used $6 million in reserve funds to waive development levies. Aurora's facility, named Sun, opened amidst great fanfare. However, it began cannabis production activities on only a small scale, and the building remained uncompleted. It was listed for sale in early 2021 (Gallant 2021). In mid 2022, Aurora announced that it had a tentative offer of $47 million—representing a sizable loss from the $250 million it had invested. The pending sale follows the closure of Aurora's Polaris facility in Edmonton (Lamers 2021a), its flagship Sky facility, also in Edmonton, and a British Columbia outdoor operation. Aurora had also bought a greenhouse manufacturing company which it eventually sold back to the original owner for far less than what it had paid (Lamers 2022a).

Canopy announced that, in total, it was closing five growing facilities including one of the largest in the world in Delta, British Columbia (Deschamps 2020). The facility had been abandoned and unused for months when it erupted into flames in the early hours of November 1, 2020. The

Delta Fire Department and Emergency Services said the cause of the fire was under investigation (Carrigg 2020). I submitted a request for Access to Records under the Freedom of Information and Protection of Privacy Act and received the report which included a variety of peculiar elements. The onsite security detail at the greenhouse was not available upon arrival of the fire department. That is difficult to fathom given the prominent flames reportedly visible from kilometers away. There was also the assured wailing of sirens audible for at least several minutes before arrival. Once located, security personnel were unsuccessful in finding keys to allow the fire department to enter the compound—while the fire continued to rage on. The firefighters had to cut chains and locks to gain entry.

The report concluded that the exact origin and cause of the fire was inconclusive and that while the evidence pointed to an accidental cause "...arson could not be completely ruled out due to the destruction of evidence in the fire." One of the firefighting detachments on the scene submitted its report which included a note that the natural gas service to the abandoned greenhouse had been turned on for a single hour—within the time range of when the fire was believed to have started. This observation was not included in the chief investigator's summary report.

The report also stated that investigators were unable to rule out rodents as a cause of the fire. The evidence may be inconclusive, but I think I smell a rat!

Between 2019 and 2021, prominent licensed producer HEXO purchased, and then closed, facilities in Kirkland Lake, and Brantford, Ontario, as well as in Stellerton, Nova Scotia (Lamers 2021m). In 2022, it closed its "centre of excellence" facility in Belleville, Ontario (HEXO 2022).

In September 2021, Tilray announced the closing of its flagship facility in Nanaimo, British Columbia, choosing to concentrate its production at its facilities in Vancouver, Germany, and Portugal (Marijuana Business Daily 2021c).

According to the most recent aggregate data available, greenhouse space in Canada appears to be on the decline. Data from Health Canada on indoor growing area show the peak was reached in May 2020 at 2.2 million square meters. That fell by 22% to 1.7 by September 2021 (Lundy and Galea 2022).

Even without fully capitalizing on its massive greenhouse space, the industry was still producing far more cannabis than it could sell. Apart from low demand, this was for two reasons. One was inadequate quality product that could not be sent to market. The other was that the acceptable product could not be sold within the product's shelf life. This meant that a lot of product had to be destroyed. A revelation published by *Marijuana Business Daily* was nothing short of devastating news for the industry. MBD's analysis came to the astounding conclusion that between 2018 and 2020, Canadian cannabis companies destroyed more cannabis than they sold (Lamers 2021f).

During that time, annual sales were in the tens of thousands of kilograms. Health Canada's data show that between 2018 and 2020, licensed producers destroyed 447,118 kilograms of unpackaged cannabis. *Marijuana Business Daily* (Lamers 2021h) quotes industry analysts who suggest that this is an underestimate of the total amount destroyed because it does not include any packaged cannabis that was destroyed. It is also considered an underestimate of the total liability given that some producers are reportedly holding large volumes of product "in the vault" to avoid additional bad publicity. Deloitte partner Karina Lahnakoski remarked: "I've seen one company that has built-in their own incinerator because they anticipated having more waste."

In 2020, Health Canada reported that 19% of unpackaged cannabis had been destroyed. Industry consultant, Mary Durocher, commented that 20-30% wastage is not uncommon at some licensed cannabis producers, while that for other agricultural products is typically about 5%. Ryan Douglas, former expert grower for Tweed (now Canopy) noted "Massive waste and repeated crop failures in commercial horticulture are the exceptions, not the norm, and it's no way to run a profitable business" (Lamers 2021h).

Surplus inventory is expected to diminish. Nonetheless, it appears that the most likely fate of almost all the excess inventory will involve an encounter of the incinerating kind. And I don't mean in a bong. The valuable lesson has been learned—albeit the painful, expensive way. That too is progress, however hard-earned. So how did all this happen? Was erroneous industry market forecasting the sole harbinger of so much calamity?

Industry analysts have proposed various explanations for the excess inventory and mass wastage. One explanation is a lack of expertise in producing large yields which led to poor quality product. Another is questionable priorities among executives. *Marijuana Business Daily* cited Av Singh, cultivation expert at Nova Scotia-based Flemming and Singh Cannabis: "The mentality of money over quality is flawed, but unfortunately for most of those who entered the cannabis space, it was not their own money" (Lamers 2021f).

Another report suggests an additional factor. *Marijuana Business Daily* cited a regulatory filing by Aurora that showed that executive bonuses encouraged unbridled expansion through mergers and acquisitions, increasing growing capacity domestically, and opening new foreign facilities (for, initially, the therapeutic market). The MBD report concludes that "They were effectively incentivized to build greenhouses, fuelling investor—not consumer—demand." The same report quoted Daniel Sax, a cannabis industry investor and adviser: "This became not a business-building industry for a bit. It was a press-release industry. Everything was a press release. The bigger the number, the better. The more grandiose the vision, the better." Sax added "there was a component of it that was a gamesmanship of the stock market" (Lamers 2020e). Beleaguered investors might ask "where were the securities regulators?"

The excess inventory, along with intense competition for market share—not only among producers, but also in an over-subscribed retail environment, created a perfect storm for a drop in price for consumers. An analysis by economy reporters at *The Globe and Mail* reported that excess inventory and intense competition were causing a plunge in cannabis retail prices while the consumer price index was showing dramatic price increases for all other products during the mid 2022 period of the COVID-19 pandemic (Lundy and Galea 2022). While frequent cannabis users may appreciate the price drop, the risk is that increased price-based accessibility is likely to increase consumption and the risk of related health and social problems. As described in Chapter 5, such a relationship has been demonstrated for both alcohol and tobacco products. The customary regulatory solution is to raise taxes on the product to prevent a price-fuelled increase in consumption and problems. In 2022, the cannabis lobbyists are aggressively arguing for tax reductions. It is interesting that the placement of a premium on executive compensation over fiduciary duty could have such a domino effect with unintended circumstances. It will be interesting to observe if, and how, government will respond to the sizable retail price decline.

An ill-considered premium placed on executive compensation was also suggested by an interesting lawsuit. *Marijuana Business Daily* (Lamers 2021j) reported on a lawsuit filed in The Ontario Superior Court of Justice by a numbered Ontario company against Canopy Growth and subsidiaries. The suit alleged that the Canopy collective of companies engaged in fraud, civil conspiracy, breach of fiduciary duty, and bad faith when it agreed to purchase large amounts of cannabis from the plaintiffs—a purchase which it never intended to make. The suit further alleged that the promise to purchase was intended solely to artificially increase stock prices and earn returns for company executives including Canopy co-founders Bruce Linton and Mark Zekulin. When the product was produced, Canopy refused delivery citing its own substantial surplus and prevailing low market price for cannabis. The plaintiffs also claimed that Canopy refused their product because of imposed production standards that were unrealistic and not achieved at Canopy's own growth facilities. The plaintiffs claimed to have suffered huge financial losses and damage to their reputation with employees, the community, the greenhouse industry, and lenders. The lawsuit seeks $500 million in compensation. The Canopy collective of companies denied all allegations contained in the suit.

I will have more to say shortly about the excesses of executive compensation within the context of tragic losses for companies, investors, and employees. I will also explore similar examples of industry in-fighting as attempts to survive in a difficult fiscal environment.

FINANCIAL LOSSES BY COMPANIES

First, the good news for the industry. The market for licensed cannabis experienced significant sales growth in the first three years of legalization. An (unadjusted) $42 million market for recreational use in October

2018 reached $355.4 million in October 2021. Then, sales gradually declined to $324.1 million in February 2022, but increased in March to $358.8 million, and again in April to $372.4 million (Statistics Canada 2022). The trajectory for the remainder of 2022 remains uncertain, but there appears to be reason for cautious optimism in the industry.

While the market has seen substantial sales growth since legalization, the demand has not grown at a rate that is close to what was forecast by many large producers in the early speculative days of the nascent industry. Israel (2020a) reckoned the problem to over-estimation of the growth rate of the market both domestically and internationally and to slow domestic retail development.

The enormous surplus provided verification of the over-estimation of the growth rate as a significant factor. Anticipation that increased retail capacity would help to move the surplus was less certain. By mid 2022, retail capacity has ballooned, probably beyond sustainability, and the surpluses remain. A substantial increase in sales would depend upon one or both of two developments: increased demand for product (market expansion) and a significant shift in purchases from the unlicensed to the licensed trade.

Weighing heavily against quick market expansion is the already discussed reality that demand for cannabis is not even close to that for alcohol. Restrictions on marketing, intended to protect public health, will pose a hurdle for expedited market expansion. There is neither the demand nor the opportunity to quickly expand sales.

As we saw in Chapter 7, the licensed trade has failed to convincingly demonstrate the integrity of its product. This remains as a potentially significant hurdle for an expedited change in market loyalty away from the unlicensed trade.

On October 17, 2018, when Canada legalized recreational cannabis, the market capitalization (total value of all shares) of the country's ten largest publicly traded cannabis businesses was slightly below $60 billion. By October 2019, the same ten companies were down to about $25 billion—a drop of more than 57% (Konyukhova and Avis 2020).

A report compiled by ATB Capital Markets showed large losses in 2020 for the major players. Aurora was reported to have led the pack in net losses at $3.3 billion, followed by Canopy at $2.3 billion. Both companies also lost market share in the recreational use sector, as did other producer juggernauts Tilray, Organigram, and Cronos. Some companies, including some smaller ones gained market share—including HEXO Corp., Redecan, Auxly, and Cannabis Village Farms International (Lamers 2020b). In March 2021, the market share held by Canada's largest licensed producers (Tlray, HEXO, Canopy, and Aurora) was at 54%. But a year later, it had declined to 28% (Lundy and Galea 2022).

Of course, market share and revenues do not tell the whole story. Chuck Rifici's company, Auxly, for example, increased its market share and reported its highest revenues ever in the 2021 quarter ending September 30.

However, it still netted a sobering loss of $15.4 million (Marijuana Business Daily 2021b).

Isolated, modest successes of the industry are overshadowed when its largest, long-established players perform so poorly. *Marijuana Business Daily* starkly captured the status in 2021: "Canopy has lost CA$3.8 billion since its inception; Aurora has run a CA$4.1 billion deficit. Neither company has ever reported a profit" (Lamers 2021i). Despite high hopes, there was no major turnaround in the early part of 2022. Aurora's net loss for the quarter ending March 31 2022, was $1.1 billion. That brought its net losses since 2015 to approximately $5.3 billion (Marijuana Business Daily 2022d).

Another Canadian producer, WeedMD, reported a net loss of $9 million for the quarter ending March 31, 2020. Undaunted by the company's lacklustre performance, the LiUNA Pension Fund of Central and Eastern Canada, a retirement plan associated with the Laborers' International Union of North America, invested $30 million in the cannabis company (Marijuana Business Daily 2020b).

INVESTOR LOSS, JOB LOSS, EXECUTIVE EXCESS

The ultimate tragedy of many fiscal failures at companies is the loss of investors' savings and loss of jobs by company employees. Companies that had the financial reserves or backing to avoid bankruptcy still had to endure massive declines in stock value and implemented substantial downsizing measures. Much of this fiscal carnage occurred within a context of almost unimaginable executive excess in the industry. I will return to that shortly.

Like other kinds of publicly traded companies, public cannabis companies are listed in stock exchanges which allow investors to buy and sell their stock. Examples include the Toronto Stock Exchange, the New York Stock Exchange, the NASDAQ (National Association of Securities Dealers Automated Quotations) and The Standard and Poor Dow Jones.

Given the prominent levels of hype around the creation of a recreational cannabis industry, stocks were initially doing very well. But by the first anniversary of legalization, a Forbes market analyst observed that most stocks had crashed by 50% or more. Following conventional stock market wisdom of 'buy low', many investors continued to buy, expecting a recovery and enormous returns (McBride 2019). Market orthodoxy tells us that the market always bounces back. Well, until it doesn't.

On the second anniversary of cannabis legalization, most cannabis stocks were "in the pits" as one *Globe and Mail* analyst put it. Even the major industry players such as Canopy Growth, Cronos Group, Aphria, Tilray, Aurora, and HEXO had all lost stock value, and some of these big players were among the biggest losers (Milstead 2020).

The stock market picture has not improved since then. A company can be deemed "non-compliant" by a stock exchange if its stock value falls below a specified dollar amount for a specified number of days. In that circumstance, the company can lose its listing, and that is a serious blow to the reputation and viability of the company.

On February 16, 2022 (well into the fourth year of legalization), there were four Canadian cannabis companies on the NASDAQ list of non-compliant companies: Cronos, HEXO, Neptune, and Sundial (NASDAQ Listing Center 2022). This occurs at NASDAQ if a company's stock value remains below $US 1.00 for thirty consecutive business days. The company is given 180 calendar days to get its stock value back to at least $1.00 for ten consecutive business days. Failure to do so results in the company losing its NASDAQ listing. While this would not affect the company's listing on other stock exchanges, the loss of the NASDAQ listing would be a serious consequence for the companies. On March 3, it was reported that NASQAQ had granted extensions to Sundial and Neptune to allow the companies to remain compliant (Marijuana Business Daily 2022a). HEXO hoped for salvation from its woes through a merger with Tilray (Tilray Inc 2022). Aurora had narrowly avoided such a fate with the NYSE (Israel 2020b).

Canopy Growth was not so fortunate. In March 2022, Canopy was dropped from The Standard and Poor Dow Jones (S&P Dow Jones Indices LLC. 2022). This was a dramatic fall from grace. The company had risen from a modest start-up (Tweed, Inc.) operating out of an abandoned chocolate factory in the rural town of Smith Falls, Ontario, to become Canada's premier cannabis producer and brand. As we saw in Chapter 6, it was also one with intimate ties to the ruling Liberal Party of Canada in the early days of the industry. Even with so much entitlement, the company continues to struggle in its sustainability.

Lesser-known players were also not immune from increasing fiscal peril. They included GW Pharma ADR, Innovative Industrial Properties, Charlotte's Web Holdings, Village Farms International, and Scotts Miracle-Gro Company (Milstead 2020).

The crucial point made earlier was that the market demand just was not there to support the high levels of production, surpluses, and ultimately the investor-funded fodder for the incinerators. The truth is plain and simple, such that it bears repeating. Cannabis is not the new alcohol. There was insufficient demand and little opportunity for market expansion through legal product promotion.

The cannabis industry has also been criticized for the use of deceptive accounting practices. Industry and forensic analysts have criticized the use of inappropriate practices that are intended for well-established industries with years of sales data to justify projections for future sales. In the case of the nascent cannabis industry, projections are typically arbitrary and overly optimistic guesses that can mislead investors (Castaldo 2018). Sadly, investors lost not only their savings and loans, but also their dreams and trust in what has, so far, remained a losing venture. This is in stark contrast to the rewards realized by the early entry entrepreneurs. Cannabis legalization in Canada might be viewed as a Ponzi scheme. Again, I propose the question "Where were the securities regulators?"

As so much financial hardship beset the industry, a reduction in its workforce was sure to follow. One might think it unfortunate but unavoidable. However, another dark side of this industry is revealed when the loss of jobs, savings, and dreams is considered within the context of sometimes unfathomable excess in the compensation of industry executives—including companies that had performed poorly.

Canopy Growth's closing of five growing facilities led to hundreds of layoffs (Deschamps 2020). After the company lost $1.7 billion, Canopy executives were rewarded with salary raises and bonuses. As cannabis companies laid off employees, some collected emergency wage subsidies during the COVID-19 pandemic (Subramaniam 2021). Canopy Growth collected payroll subsidies worth $11 million while eliminating 220 full-time positions (Lamers 2021i).

An analysis by *Marijuana Business Daily* found that licensed cannabis producers pulled in $140 million in federal subsidies which were intended to prevent layoffs, or to help rehire those who had been, during the pandemic. However, since early 2020, 5,997 employees at licensed cannabis producers lost or left their jobs. The most layoffs and highest subsidies occurred at industry giants—Canopy Growth, Aurora Cannabis, Sundial Growers, and Tilray (Lamers 2021g). At Canopy Growth, the layoffs continued into April 2022, when it announced another workforce reduction of 245 jobs. This brought its total workforce down to 2,839 from a 2020 high of 4,434 (Lamers 2022b).

While reporting a loss of over $3 billion in 2020, Aurora executives were compensated at almost $15 million—an increase of 58% from the previous year. A spokesperson for the company offered that the compensation was based upon good corporate governance practices and that "executive bonuses are administered in line with company performance" (Lamers 2020a).

Aurora also reported massive layoffs. The closing of its Polaris facility in Edmonton alone was expected to result in job loss for 8% of Aurora's workforce (Lamers 2021a). Several other large Aurora closures would follow—each with an attendant significant loss of jobs.

In 2020, HEXO laid off 200 people, about 20% of its workforce. While reporting a loss of $546.5 million, its executive compensation increased by almost 20% to $14.4 million (Lamers 2021k). Things did not improve for HEXO in 2021. Early that year, HEXO acquired cannabis producer Zenabis (for $245 million), which operated a facility in Stellarton, Nova Scotia. HEXO also acquired cannabis producer 48 North for $50 million—with facilities in Kirkland Lake and Brantford, Ontario. However, HEXO quickly found itself overextended and announced it would be closing the facilities early in 2022, with a loss of 155 jobs (Lamers 2021m).

The happenings at HEXO seem nothing less than chaotic. Amidst all the uncertainty described above, HEXO unveiled a new "Centre of Excellence" production facility in Belleville, Ontario, in December, 2020. The facility also housed the Truss Beverage Co., a bottling company, as a joint venture with Molson Coors Canada (HEXO 2020). But just 16 months later, HEXO announced that it was closing its Centre of Excellence, which would mean the termination of 230 employees. The announcement indicated that the bottling operation would remain active (HEXO 2022).

I posted a link to this story on Twitter. It was liked by both Kevin Sabet and Jodie Emery, two high profile individuals at opposite ends of the spectrum in their level of enthusiasm for cannabis as a consumer product. I then tweeted: "You know you have hit upon a universal truth with your tweet when both Kevin Sabet and Jodie Emery like it..."(@MikeDeVillaer, April 22, 2022). Both Jodie and Kevin liked that post as well. Maybe there is some cause for hope for unity against corporate cannabis.

In 2020, cannabis producers Aphria and Tilray merged into a new company adopting the name Tilray. Just before the merger, Aphria gave its CEO, Irwin Simon, an annual compensation package totalling $8.1 million. Simon has now become the CEO of Tilray (Lamers 2021d). In Leamington, Ontario, 120 people lost their jobs when Tilray closed its cannabis production facility (Schmidt 2020). Another 170 Tilray employees lost their jobs when the company closed its flagship Nanaimo, British Columbia, production facility that was established in 2014. The closing of the facility occurred while Tilray made a US$211 million investment in HEXO (Ball 2022).

Amidst an 88% revenue plunge and the resignation of its Chief Financial Officer, Medipharm reduced its workforce, saving approximately $3 million annually. At the same time, the company reported 2019 executive compensation at $7 million, up from $1.3 million in 2018 (Lamers 2020f).

A licensed British Columbia company, Pasha Brands Ltd, once described itself as a "vertically integrated prohibition-era brand house firmly rooted in BC's craft cannabis industry...." Pasha later changed its name to B.C. Craft Supply Company Ltd. In the first quarter of 2020, Pasha earned $15,052 in net revenues (not a typo), while posting a loss of $4.65 million which included some debt payment. Stock values in the company plummeted to near zero. Despite the company's disastrous performance, former CEO Jason Longden, was paid more than $1 million in compensation for half a year's work while Patrick Brauckmann, who had held a variety of executive positions with the company, collected $737,656 (St Anthony 2020). There were unconfirmed claims that wage payments of some employees at the company were months in arrears. On January 25, 2022, the company filed for bankruptcy (Global Newswire 2022).

CannTrust, because of fiscal pressures created by its executive level charges that I covered in Chapter 7, decided to cut 140 jobs, about a quarter of its workforce (Gaviola 2019).

In mid 2022, *Canadian Business* reported that one third of the industry's approximate 20,000 jobs had vanished between 2019 and the end of 2021 (Mouallem 2022).

The greatest demonstration of excess in executive compensation in Canada, and perhaps in the world, may have occurred at Neptune Wellness

Solutions, a Québec-based company that has entered the cannabis industry. Michael Cammarata, CEO and President, received over $58 million in various forms of compensation in 2020 (Neptune Wellness Solutions 2020). Once again, I want to be clear—that is not a typo.

One might wonder if the executive compensation levels in the cannabis industry are in line with other Canadian industries, and with cannabis producers elsewhere.

A report by the Canadian Centre for Policy Alternatives revealed that cannabis executives in Canada are among the top paid executives in the country across many large industries (Macdonald 2021). In another analysis conducted and reported by *Marijuana Business Daily*, Canadian cannabis executives' compensation was found to compare very favourably, and in some cases greatly exceed, the compensation of their counterparts in the cannabis industry in the United States (Smith 2021a).

The extraordinary compensation levels of Canada's cannabis executives must be regarded within the context of an industry that has performed at a subpar level fiscally, is frequently non-compliant with regulations, and sometimes engages in criminal conduct.

An interesting aspect of executive life in the licensed cannabis trade is the high level of turnover in the positions. The closure of production facilities coincided with an upheaval of executive turnover at some of Canada's largest licensed producers such as Aphria, Canopy, and Aurora (Israel 2020b). Smaller players were also affected. The Green Organic Dutchman replaced its CEO, Brian Athaide, after reporting a $76 million loss in 2020. However, Althaide was entitled to a severance package that could approach $700,000 (Lamers 2020d).

In 2020, Zenabis appointed its fourth CEO in two years. The company was also served by three different chief financial officers over an 18 month period (Marijuana Business Daily 2020a). In the same year, HEXO appointed its fourth chief financial officer in two years (Marijuana Business Daily 2020c). In mid 2022, *Canadian Business* reported that there had been an 80% turnover in CEO leadership since October 17, 2018 (Mouallem 2022).

To be fair to the private sector, executive instability also prevailed at the Ontario government's cannabis wholesaler and online retail store. In 2021, the Ontario Cannabis Store (OCS) appointed its sixth president in three years. None of the six had remained in the position for longer than a year (Lamers 2021o).

RETAIL

One of the prevailing narratives in the nascent days of the recreational cannabis industry was that the success of the industry would be assured once full retail capacity had been achieved. Several years later, retail is over-subscribed, but the industry's financial woes remain as serious as ever. Retail is struggling as much as the production sector. This is true for even Canada's largest retail chains. For example, Fire & Flower Holdings Corporation, for its quarter ending August 31 2020, reported revenues of $23.4 million but a net loss of $29.1 million. Another leading cannabis retailer, Meta Growth Corporation, for its quarter ending May 31 2020, reported revenues of $13.7 million, but a net loss of $23.7 million. Meta attributed its loss to "...corporate expenses and start-up costs." Meta has since been bought out by a competitor, High Tide, forming Canada's largest retail chain (Marijuana Business Daily 2020d).

In response to industry assertions that its surplus was primarily due to a laggard retail capacity (increase local supply and demand will follow), Canadian provinces complied. Most dramatically, The Ontario Cannabis Store, the Ontario Government's monopoly cannabis wholesaler and online retailer, announced in August 2021, the licensing of the province's 1000th store (Ontario Cannabis Store 2021.)

This seems unlikely to be the solution, even for the big chains. Fire & Flower, while opening 32 new stores in 2021, continued to have bottom line problems. It realized annual revenues of $175.5 million, but still recorded a net annual loss of $63.6 million (Marijuana Business Daily 2022e). Another major retail chain, Choom, with 17 operating stores and an additional 6 licenses, was granted creditor protection in April 2022 (Marijuana Business Daily 2022c).

Independent retail businesses also have their challenges. *Marijuana Business Daily* has repeatedly quoted industry insiders who expect that the recent proliferation of retail outlets means that many independent licensed retail outlets will not survive, and some may not even open (Israel 2021b, 2021a).

Retailers have additional challenges. A *CBC* investigation found that banks are reluctant to provide even the most basic services to cannabis retailers (Ballard 2021). While the investigation showed that retailers are inclined to blame stigma for the reticence on the part of banks, it is likely that financial prudence is more at the heart of it. Statements from the banks were typically vague with public relations corpo-speak as seen in this statement from CIBC: "We support emerging Canadian industries and seek to offer clients the best products and services to suit their needs. For the cannabis sector, we review opportunities on a case-by-case basis." A spokesperson from a British Columbia credit union that offers financial services to cannabis retailers was more candid in his assessment of the banks' perspective: "I think the banks have made an economic decision that there is no big profit in this."

It is also possible that given the regulatory non-compliance and illegal conduct, as well as the fiscal carelessness, of some of Canada's largest producers, lending institutions may not be willing to extend their level of risk tolerance with any part of this industry.

At least in the Province of Ontario, the conduct and oversight of cannabis retail outlets has not been helpful in establishing their credibility. The Office of the Auditor General of Ontario has conducted audits of the Ontario Cannabis Retail Corporation (OCRC), and its regulator—The Alcohol and

Gaming Commission of Ontario (AGCO). OCRC resides within the province's Ministry of Finance. It includes the province's online Ontario Cannabis Store (OCS) and is the wholesaler for all private retail outlets in the province.

The Auditor General audit of AGCO identified some major problems. Between September 2019 and July 2020, retail cannabis stores reported the destruction of 5,477 units of cannabis products. They also reported 84,228 fewer units of cannabis in the stores than recorded in their inventory. The AGCO could provide no assurance that these units were not lost, stolen, or diverted elsewhere. The AG report also noted that the AGCO had never conducted store inventory counts to ensure reliability of reports. Nor had it requested surveillance videos from store operators to review the destruction of cannabis products. The report also expressed specific concerns about sales to minors, diversion to or from the illicit market, and selling to intoxicated individuals (Office of the Auditor General of Ontario 2020).

Among the problems identified the following year in the audit of the OCRC were:

- *no standard approach to monitoring the performance of retail outlets*

- *significant over payment for leased equipment*

- *inadequate customer service*

- *no consistent criteria for measuring progress on non-financial objectives*

- *inadequate sales forecasting and revenue management*

- *lack of formal procedures for product selection, with an attendant lack of transparency and accountability for selection decisions*

- *lack of documentation to support non-competitive procurement*

- *inadequate reporting on performance to the board of directors*

- *inadequate attention to OCRC's social responsibility mandate*

- *inadequate verification of age for purchases made through the online store and at home delivery*

- *inadequate safeguards on stored customer information*

(Office of the Auditor General of Ontario 2021).

The item on " inadequate safeguards on stored customer information" is noteworthy. In May 2022, just five months after the publication of the AG's report, the Ontario Cannabis Store reported a misappropriation of confidential sales data. A spokesperson for OCS indicated that this was not an IT failure, but a misappropriation of data that was being unlawfully distributed within the cannabis industry (Deschamps 2022). OCS was conducting an internal investigation and referred the matter to the Ontario Provincial Police (Deschamps 2022).

In March 2022, the Ontario Government announced that home delivery of cannabis product from retail stores, as introduced as a temporary COVID-19 measure, would now become a permanent service. It also announced the establishment of new rules for the service. The new rules introduced conditions pertaining to product leaving the retail outlet but did not address the issue of age verification at the point of delivery as identified in the audit (Marijuana Business Daily 2022f).

Another important aspiration of the licensed cannabis trade is a shift of consumer purchases from the unlicensed to the licensed trade. Here there has been only modest progress—a problem identified in both Auditor General reports cited above. In the third quarter of 2020, two years after legalization, sales in the licensed cannabis trade finally overtook Health Canada's estimates of unlicensed sales. This resulted from both an increase in licensed sales and a decrease in unlicensed sales. That dual trend continued into the fourth quarter (Lamers 2021b).

Statistics Canada's 2018 and 2019 National Cannabis Survey provides data on approximately 6,000 Canadians aged fifteen years and older. An analysis by Hathaway, Cullen, and Walters (2021) found that after legalization, 12% of survey respondents purchased primarily from dealers, compared to the 19% doing so before legalization—a decrease of 37%. Controlling for the effect of potentially confounding variables reduced the decrease to 28%.

While this is encouraging, we should consider that the crossover reported by Health Canada could have occurred sooner and the decrease in use of dealers could have been more significant if licensed producers assigned a greater priority to satisfying consumers than to attracting investors with grandiose, sometimes fraudulent, promises. Finally, we might also worry about the social justice cost of using highly punitive law enforcement as a means of intimidating buyers away from the unlicensed trade.

SINK OR SWIM: SURVIVING FISCAL CALAMITY

The Industry Turns on Itself

It has been widely reported, but (despite my efforts) neither confirmed nor repudiated, that Ray Kroc, architect of the McDonald's restaurant empire, once said: "If any of my competitors were drowning, I'd stick a hose in their mouth and turn on the water."

The profound financial downturn for the cannabis industry has ignited intense competition for the over-estimated market. This has led to companies turning against each other with increasing complaints filed with Health Canada. *Marijuana Business Daily* (Lamers 2021n) reported that, in 2020, the regulator received 182 complaints from cannabis companies about the conduct of other cannabis companies. That is almost double the 97 complaints received in 2019. Apart from intense, even desperate, competition, industry analysts also blame vague, ever-shifting rules at Health Canada.

Inconsistency and non-transparency in enforcement have also been cited as contributory factors. A permissive regulatory environment, with minimal or no consequences for violations can also be expected to lead to increased risk-taking with regulatory non-compliance.

Canopy Growth is a company that often appears to be balancing precariously on the perimeter of the regulations, and sometimes clearly beyond the spirit if not the rule of the limits. A complaint filed against Canopy by Pure Sunfarms, a subsidiary of Cannabis Village Farms International, involved "static labelling" of product potency. This practice uses an historic test result for potency for the labelling of all future lots of the same product (George-Cosh 2021). The complaint, filed with Health Canada, prompted another one of the regulator's euphemistic "updates" to, once again, explain the law to producers. The bulletin titled "Cannabis License Holders Update: Displaying THC and CBD Content on Dried Cannabis Product Labels and Kief", was apparently sent only to licensed producers, but was made available publicly by Fox D Consulting (2021) on its Twitter account. Specifically, the bulletin noted that the potency labels on all lots of products must correspond to testing results for that specific lot.

As described earlier in this chapter, a lawsuit filed in The Ontario Superior Court of Justice by a cannabis producer against Canopy Growth suggests that the launching of legal action against competitors is another strategy that may be increasingly employed by cannabis companies to sink or swim in the currently competitive and turbulent environment.

Insolvency

On the sinking side of the available options is the declaration of insolvency (bankruptcy). A company is declared insolvent when it has more debt than can be paid even if its total assets are mortgaged or sold.

By November 2020, at least twenty-one cannabis businesses were undergoing or had undergone insolvency proceedings in Canada. Legal analysts were predicting that the number would grow. A detailed account of cannabis company insolvencies was published by the Canadian Legal Information Institute (Konyukhova and Avis 2020).

One interesting case demonstrates the priorities of the insolvency process. Eve & Co. is Canada's first female-founded cannabis company. It's subsidiary, Natural Medco Ltd (NML) was licensed by Health Canada in 2016 and operated in Stratford, Ontario. In March 2022, Eve & Co. was granted creditor protection, and was arranging the sale of assets. The company announced that it intended to fulfill its agreement with its senior secured creditor (Royal Bank of Canada) and that the bank would be repaid, in full, from the proceeds of the sale (Marijuana Business Daily 2022b). There appears to be no such priority for the near $2 million the company owes to Canada Revenue Agency. Seemingly, under any circumstances, the interests of banks trump the requirements of the tax revenue system, and the interests of the public .

Corporate Edibles: Mergers and Acquisitions

As either a growth or coping strategy, licensed cannabis producers also entered a period of voracious consumption of other cannabis companies through mergers and acquisitions.

Consolidation of cannabis producers became a major force in a changing business environment. Canopy Growth acquired another Canadian producer, The Supreme Cannabis Co. for $435 million. HEXO acquired Zenabis Global for $235 million (Marijuana Business Daily 2021d) and 48 North for $50 million (Lamers 2021m).

The most significant merger yet, referred to by industry analysts as a blockbuster, occurred between Aphria and Tilray. This merger was really a takeover of Tilray by Aphria. The consolidated company took on the name of Tilray. The acquisition made Tilray the largest cannabis producer in Canada and one of the largest globally with combined market capitalization reported at $10.07 billion (Marijuana Business Daily 2021f).

Not all mergers and acquisitions appeared to go just swimmingly. Ontario-based WeedMD acquired Starseed Medicinal for more then $50 million and sold it to Final Bell Canada less than two years later for $2.5 million (Lamers 2021p). Weed MD defended the loss by noting that it retained possession of all intellectual property and the right to future revenue arising from the patient roster.

Despite the wave of mergers and acquisitions, Canada's largest cannabis companies have been losing market share to smaller players. Analytics firm Hifyre has provided data that show that between the first quarters of 2020 and 2021, the market share of the top five licensed producers fell from slightly more than half to less than 40%, and the market share of the top nine fell from almost 80% to 62%. These plunges occurred at a time that month to month sales across Canada were at an all time high (Lamers 2021e).

In April of 2021, HEXO CEO, Sebastien St. Louis, expressed surprise at the performance of craft growers in some markets, but also indicated that he thought it was a short-term, not a long-term, victory for craft (Lamers 2021l). Tilray CEO, Irwin Simon, was more provocative in his delivery of a similar message about craft growers. In early October of 2021, Mr. Simon caused a social media storm when he referred to his competition as "ankle biters" (Tilray Inc. 2021).

Future shifts in market share will determine the fate of these ankle biters—as a rising force with which to be reckoned—or as corporate edibles within a continued trend of mergers and acquisitions. Nonetheless, the big players might be wise to display some humility. It has been said that anyone who thinks the little guy cannot make a difference has never spent an evening in a tent with a mosquito.

In an interesting turn of events in which HEXO found itself in serious financial trouble and in peril of losing its NASDAQ listing, the fates of HEXO and Tilray came together. In an agreement reached in March 2022, the two LPs formed a partnership from which Tilray would "acquire a significant equity ownership position in HEXO." Tilray would also appoint one of its officers to the HEXO Board of Directors as well as a board "observer" (Tilray Inc. 2022).

Mergers and acquisitions are also becoming a major force in retail and are expected to proliferate (Israel 2020a).

Investment by Alcohol, Tobacco, and Pharmaceutical Companies

A central theme of this book has been that a very real threat of a commercialized cannabis industry is that it will adopt the playbook of its elder sibling drug industries: alcohol, tobacco, and pharmaceutical. This playbook brandishes an unfathomable indifference to public health protection in a relentless pursuit of revenue through breaking and gaming regulations and violating the law. A considerable amount of evidence has already been provided in support of that theme in Chapters 5 and 7. The second stage of that story line may very well lie within the increasing investment in cannabis from those industries.

The first major play began as early as 2017 by Constellation Brands—an American Fortune 500 company and producer of alcohol products Corona beer and Svedka vodka. Constellation made an initial modest investment in Canopy Growth and then followed up with a 2018 purchase of a 38% stake for $4 billion. There are provisions for Constellation to acquire a majority financial interest if it chooses (Krane 2018). As of April 2022, five of seven board directors at Canopy were current or former executives and/or board members at Constellation (Canopy Growth Corporation, n.d.).

Canadian beer icon, Molson (now a part of the US-based Molson Coors Beverage Company) partnered with cannabis producer Hydropothecary (HEXO) to create a non-alcohol, cannabis infused beer product (Krane 2018).

These developments fortify something I referenced earlier in the book about marketing and advertising—that beer companies are not just in the beer business; they are in the party business.

Altria, the parent of tobacco company, Philip Morris, became another early adopter when it invested $1.8 billion in Canadian cannabis producer Cronos for 45% of the company, with an option for investing an additional $1.05 billion to increase the share to 55% (Krane 2018).

The often-controversial Canadian cannabis pioneer, Chuck Rifici, who has emerged in several places in this book, is now the CEO of the Auxly Cannabis Group. Auxly was another of the first cannabis companies in Canada to welcome investment from another drug industry. It struck a deal in 2019 with the United Kingdom-based Imperial Brands tobacco company. Imperial took possession of a 19.9% stake in Auxly with an investment of $123 million. Imperial also designates one of the five voting director positions on Auxly's board of directors (Canadian Press 2019). In 2021, Auxly appointed Murray McGowan, Imperial's chief strategy and development officer, to its board of directors (Marijuana Business Daily 2021b).

British American Tobacco (BAT), the UK's largest tobacco firm, has publicly declared cannabis a part of its future (BBC News 2021). BAT made good on the declaration when it acquired a 20% stake in Canadian cannabis producer Organigram for about £126 million ($210 million CAD). BAT has become Organigram's largest shareholder and has appointed two directors to Organigram's board of eight directors. David O'Reilly, Director of Scientific Research at BAT, noted: "This move takes us into a new space and we are not ruling out any product innovation" (Khan and Cavale 2021). That sounds somewhat ominous considering that tobacco companies such as BAT innovated the cigarette into an optimum nicotine delivery device, effectively maximizing the potential to quickly create and maintain dependence on the drug.

Cannabis producer, Tilray, made the pioneering move of partnering with pharmaceutical company, Novartis, to provide therapeutic cannabis products (Krane 2018). Aurora Cannabis added Theresa Firestone, a former executive with Pfizer and Shoppers Drug Mart, to its board of directors (Marijuana Business Daily 2021a). Shoppers Drug Mart continues to press for a role in the retail of cannabis for therapeutic use that would extend beyond its online retail service to include its many community-based retail stores (Lamers 2020g).

With accelerating talks in the United States about federal legalization, some Canadian cannabis producers are acquiring US cannabis producers (Smith 2021b). The acquisitions are not limited to cannabis. Canadian licensed cannabis producer, Aphria, now under the Tilray brand, purchased US brewer, Sweetwater (NASDAQ 2020).

There are companies in other industries that are also natural partners with the cannabis industry. A growing number of confirmed or potential players have included Scotts Miracle Gro and Coca Cola (Krane 2018).

Controlling the Narrative

For the most part, the Liberal Party of Canada handed the legal cannabis trade to corporate juggernauts, too many of whom clearly possessed an inclination towards public health indifference, regulatory non-compliance and in the worst cases, premeditated criminality. The predominate orientation of entitled, expansionist, corporate commercialism is unlikely to change. (Maybe some hope for a better future lies with the craft growers.) What we can expect from Big Cannabis is a communication strategy that will attempt to distract us all—including law makers—from the prevailing corporate self-indulgence. The industry will attempt to change and control the narrative in its own interests.

First, the industry is in dire need of success stories. Upon the second anniversary of cannabis legalization in the autumn of 2020, two-year reviews of cannabis legalization, like one by cannabis community advocate,

Leafly, (Porter 2020) were mostly laudatory. Leafly's review raised worthy issues for improvement such as the importance of amnesty for those with past convictions and the lack of diversity in the industry. However, it missed acknowledging the importance of ending the possession-related criminal charges that are very much a part of The Cannabis Act. There was also no mention of continued quality and safety issues like product contamination and package labelling errors. There was nothing about product promotion violations, or securities fraud leading to significant losses for investors while industry executives enjoyed lifestyles of the rich and famous. There was not a word about collusion of the legal industry with the unlicensed one and with organized crime.

Marijuana Business Daily, has an established legacy of balanced coverage of the industry—warts and all. In its two-year review, MBD proclaimed: "Legalization in Canada has been a major success, and the market is growing exactly as fast as rational analysts predicted" (Lamers 2020c).

There are two aspects of this proclamation that warrant comment. First, the appraisal delicately implies the valid and key point that many of the early growth projections were irrational, and when those are eliminated from consideration, the actual growth is in line with what a rational analyst would predict. However, this is as much an indictment of the industry for early securities irregularities, as it is an exoneration of rational industry analysts.

The second aspect is that, like the Leafly review, the MBD statement evaluates the success of cannabis legalization from mostly a market growth perspective. Of course, that is a central part of MBD's mandated orientation. But legalization is much more complex than purely bottom-line considerations.

There was a similar orientation in a report from Deloitte on the third anniversary of legalization. The report, titled "An industry Makes its Mark: The Economic and Social Impact of Canada's Cannabis Sector", carried the logo of the Ontario Cannabis Store on its cover (Deloitte 2021). This report also had a preponderance of information on economic contributions. Using a timeline from October 2018 through 2021, the report declared a contribution to the nation's economy of $43.5 billion. It also reported direct and indirect tax revenues at $15 billion. Finally, Deloitte celebrated the $11 billion worth of cannabis purchased in Canada during that period.

This achievement, along with this chapter's previous mentions of increasing annual cannabis sales, needs to be considered within the context of how much of those purchases are concentrated among heavy cannabis users. An Ontario Auditor General report noted that heavy consumers comprise 40% of cannabis users and are responsible for 90% of total provincial spending on cannabis products (Office of the Auditor General of Ontario 2021, 1). This prompts consideration of the public health implications of heavy consumption. These include the development of dependence and of cannabis use disorder, as well as the impact on families, and the burden placed on publicly funded care systems. As we saw in

Chapter 1, Ontario alone has a perennial 20,000 individuals in drug treatment programs for problems related to their cannabis use. An increase in cannabis sales is not all up-side.

The Deloitte report also notes that the cannabis industry has directly and indirectly sustained 151,000 jobs across Canada. As is often the case with economic reports, there is no mention of the security of this employment, including whether the jobs pay a living wage or provide benefits and safe working conditions.

On the social equity side of matters, Deloitte referred to a 2020 study that found that 72% of cannabis executives and directors were Caucasian males. The report recommended movement towards "...a more diverse, equitable, and inclusive industry."

Like the Leafly review, Deloitte also notes the failure of legislation to provide easily accessible and effective removal of criminal records for cannabis convictions prior to legalization. However (also like Leafly), Deloitte makes no acknowledgement of the continued criminalization of cannabis users for minor cannabis offences. Continued criminalization under the Cannabis Act serves industry commercial interests in its intent to intimidate people away from the unlicensed trade. Forgiveness of past transgressions provides no such threat to the industry's interests in market expansion. Neither do the laudable aspirations of improved diversity, equity, and inclusiveness. This is the same dynamic I described in Chapter 6 in the work of the Task Force. Social good is pursued only in ways that do not threaten the fiscal interests of the industry.

To be fair, Deloitte raised some issues that, if remedied, might increase industry production costs. Its report decried the 5,184 kilograms of carbon emissions for every kilogram of dried flower produced, as well as the estimated 5.8 to 6.4 million kilograms of cannabis packaging that went to landfills during 2018 and 2019. Deloitte also raises production issues related to excessive water use and impact on local air quality and safety. The report also suggests that environmental degradation may be even worse among unlicensed production facilities.

Environmental issues, social justice, and social equity are matters that should receive increased attention in the industry and cannabis law reform efforts. However, the many problems with this industry and its regulation as described in this and the previous chapter were excluded from Deloitte's report. One is unavoidably struck with the inequity of Deloitte's coverage of economic impact and social impact.

Nearing the third anniversary of legalization, the narrative appeared to be getting more desperate. *Marijuana Business Daily* was almost exultant in its August 9, 2021 lead story "Pure Sunfarms posts quarterly profit on surging marijuana revenue." Imagine that—a medium-large cannabis company turning a quarterly profit! (Marijuana Business Daily 2021e). As mentioned earlier, I have a high level of respect for MBD's overall balanced coverage of the industry. Perhaps it was just a slow week for news.

But that was nowhere near the worst of it. The Cannabis Council of Canada (CCC), an industry lobby group, emblazoned a "Not Done Yet Report Card" on cannabis legalization across the home page of its website (Cannabis Council of Canada 2021), and promoted the report on social media. The report denounced the "nanny state over-regulation of cannabis" and provided a treatise for regulatory liberalization in service of market expansion. The Council's report was also fashioned with a veneer of social justice colloquialisms. But the report was not primarily a plea for social justice. It was about bigger profits for big players in the cannabis industry. It was a brazen march under a banner of US-style commercial freedom of speech and self-regulation. There was no hint of the public health implications.

While the Council's report listed Cannabis Amnesty, Medical Cannabis Canada, and NORML Canada as collaborators, neither the report, nor any mention of it, appeared on any of these other organizations' websites in early January of 2022. This social distancing from The Council's Report Card is understandable, given the more ardent and sincere commitment of these organizations to social justice issues. I hope they do not place too much hope in the ambitions of The Council as a path for improved social justice. I fear they will be deeply disappointed.

As discussed earlier in this book, market growth and protection of public health seem to be unavoidably adversarial forces in a revenue driven enterprise. The tobacco industry remains one of the most financially successful industries on the planet. The public health impact of that industry's success is not so laudable. It was not my primary intent to criticize *Marijuana Business Daily*, Leafly, or Deloitte. Their coverage is necessarily in line with their organizations' missions. My intent is simply to introduce the bigger picture to which we will return with considerable detail in the next two chapters.

WHAT DOES THE FUTURE LOOK LIKE?

I do not know. This and previous chapters have told a story of an industry that quickly spiralled out of control, and thus far has struggled to right the ship. The lack of strict regulation to hold industry accountable has not provided the required buoyancy for that righting. Rather, permissive regulation from a ruling party with connections to the industry has only encouraged and enabled non-compliance.

After discussing the industry's multiple filings for creditor protection, plummeting stock values, delisting from stock exchanges, forced downsizing, and enormous unsold product surpluses, MBD writer Solomon Israel (2020a) arrived at the admirably restrained conclusion that "investors just aren't as excited about cannabis as they used to be." Solomon has a gift for gentle understatement. I've talked to a few investors who are livid, even vengeful.

From my perspective the take-home lesson is that the first wave of legalization was driven by immaturity, emotion and entitlement-fuelled avarice rather than sound and prudent strategic and financial stewardship. It remains to be seen if the second wave will fashion a less recklessly ambitious demeanour with a more mature business acumen. However, the achievement of a financial turnaround for the industry is unlikely in the short term. Longer term fiscal viability remains a matter for longer term observation.

While cannabis trade publications acknowledge the problems in the early years of legalization, they also hasten to add causes for optimism of a turnaround, mostly around fiscal gains. But within the realm of public health protection and legal adherence—not so much. When I read these statements, I consider the century long performance of our elder drug industries—all remarkably successful fiscally. But none have managed, over an extensive time frame spanning a century and longer, to marry fiscal performance with due diligence in public health protection and adherence to the laws of the land. With the alcohol, tobacco, and pharmaceutical conglomerates now investing in the cannabis industry, with their well-honed, proven playbook in hand, there can be little doubt about some aspects of the future trajectory of the cannabis industry. It is slowly and quietly becoming part of a formidable multi-headed hydra of drug industries. I am inclined to call it Big PACT (Pharma, Alcohol, Cannabis, Tobacco).

Resistance is futile. Cannabis will be assimilated. There remains a lingering absence of effective oversight from a government that has repeatedly demonstrated a permissive protectionism for the cannabis industry and a stubborn indifference to preventative and corrective guidance offered from many fields of expertise. This places substantial strain on one's optimism for us achieving a true public health approach in the short term.

On several occasions on social media, I have quipped that only capitalism could cause cannabis law reform to fail. Maybe that is just my personal skepticism. Or maybe not. Canada's cannabis legalization has been a story of just about everything that can go wrong in a capitalist economy.

One of the world's foremost drug policy authorities is Jonathon Caulkins, now Professor of Operations Research and Public Policy at Carnegie Mellon University. Dr. Caulkins is a former Co-director of the RAND Corporation's Drug Policy Research Center, and lead author of RANDs 2015 ground-breaking and widely celebrated report *Considering Marijuana Legalization: Insights for Vermont and Other Jurisdictions.* Seven years later, I still regard that report as one of the most important and useful treatments of cannabis legalization.

Caulkins brought stinging clarity to the likely future of cannabis legalization, when he told delegates at the 2016 National Cannabis Science and Policy Summit: "We are going, in the United States, to legalize marijuana nationally, and roughly along the alcohol model, and there's a good chance that people in 25 to 40 years will look back and shake their heads and ask, what were you thinking? Why did you think it was a good idea to create an industry of titans to market this drug?" (Fernholz 2016).

I share his dystopian view. It fits well with an observation from the World Health Organization that I presented in an earlier chapter. I raise it again because it so effectively addresses the inequitable juxtaposition of market power and health protection within the battleground of government regulation: "Market power readily translates into political power. Few governments prioritize health over big business" (Chan 2013). If this is the future of the cannabis industry, it will strengthen the arguments of the industry's harshest critics.

Despite my pessimism, I remain interested in, and receptive of, any evidence that provides cause for hopefulness that the cannabis industry might depart from the well established, century old ways of its elder drug industry siblings. Perhaps there is hope in an emerging legal craft trade in cannabis that aspires to assign a greater priority to social responsibility than to unbridled expansion. However, with enormous start-up costs, including daunting licensing fees, the deck was stacked against the craft growers, making their plight difficult to say the least. But some of the craft growers appear to be getting a foothold, and the big players are beginning to take notice.

I have encountered a few craft growers and retailers who appear to have a genuine intent to marry business with social responsibility. I sincerely invite everyone in the craft and retail sectors to make me a believer.

The next chapter of this book will not look to industry for solutions to the failure of cannabis legalization in Canada. Rather, it will explore, with all due humility and candor, some potential public health-based remedies for the current dilemmas. It will also propose a much bolder policy alternative. Some analysts will be inclined to see it as somewhat subversive of traditional drug policy orthodoxy. I would not be inclined to dismiss that interpretation.

SUMMING UP

The legalization of cannabis for recreational use held promise for revenues and profits that would dwarf those from the therapeutic market. And yet, some of Canada's largest cannabis companies have experienced only perennial losses. The cannabis industry complains of being restrained by nanny-state over-regulation. But it has clearly been the architect of its own despair. It has failed financially in many respects owing largely to weak business acumen, especially in its strategic planning, and in a counter-productive system of incentivizing executives. An over-supply of cannabis led to massive amounts of product destruction, the purchase and construction of some of the world's largest greenhouses that sat empty, investor losses, job losses, insolvency, in-fighting, and risk-laden mergers and acquisitions—all telling signs of a struggling industry. At the same time, executives enjoyed extraordinary levels of compensation. The industry's current rescue by alcohol, tobacco, and pharmaceutical corporations will bring financial backing and expertise, but at what cost? These are industries that have a long track record for sacrificing public health and the rule of law at the alter of profit. The early days of the cannabis industry were characterized by greed, immaturity, and incompetence. The future incarnation may be one of greed, maturity, and competence—potentially a much more dangerous combination. The future may not be so friendly.

Section IV

Preparing for the Future

Chapter 9

Let's Try
Something Different

*"They are ill discoverers who think there is no land when
they can see nothing but sea."*
— **Francis Bacon**

"Failure should be our teacher, not our undertaker."
—**Denis Waitley**

SUMMARY OF THE FAILURE OF
COMMERCIAL LEGALIZATION

Canada

The failure of cannabis legalization in Canada has been a multi-faceted story. A summary of the key points made in the book thus far may be helpful before moving on to alternative approaches that could have been taken. They still could happen, but probably not in Canada. That opportunity has been squandered.

The creation of a revenue-driven drug industry that is neglectful of regulatory compliance and inclined towards criminal activity was never a part of the Liberal Party's pitch to Canadians for cannabis legalization. But that is what we have.

Promises of a public health approach and strict regulation were apparently no more than the bait on the hook of corporate capture of the unlicensed cannabis trade—a trade that was mostly benign. Many of the early-day beneficiaries of legalization were intricately connected to the Liberal Party of Canada. The additional gift to the cannabis industry has been the milquetoast posture of government regulation. With only a few exceptions, it has neglected to meaningfully enforce its own laws pertaining to the industry. Unfathomably, despite all these advantages bestowed upon corporate cannabis, many of the largest companies are in a fiscal shambles, brought down by their own avarice and lack of business acumen. Many seasoned cannabis users complain of a legal supply of low-quality, mass-produced product. Many industry investors lost their savings or went into debt when stock prices plunged following reckless business practices. But there was no loss for the Big Cannabis executives. They walked away with millions. None have been held accountable. In contrast, without decriminalization, there are still cannabis users receiving criminal records for trivial cannabis-related offences. And the industry lobbyists encourage this. The industry has betrayed many of the most ardent supporters of legalization.

We can recall the government's marquee slogan that it trumpeted on the day of legalization: "Keep cannabis out of the hands of youth and profits out of the pockets of criminals." Well into the fourth year of legalization, the key elements of this promise have not been realized.

As we will see in Chapter 10, there is no evidence that cannabis is less in the hands of youth. Only half of the profits have been transferred from the illegal trade to the legal one. Some analysts may think that is laudable, but there are counterpoints to consider. Chapter 7 demonstrated that a portion of legal cannabis revenues was earned illegally. On paper, those sales are legal. In reality—not so much. Thus, some of the revenues went from the pockets of unlicensed criminals to the pockets of licensed criminals—therefore, not legalized so much as laundered. Most ironic is that legalization has apparently led to cannabis production licenses landing in the pockets of organized crime—exactly the opposite of what it was supposed to accomplish.

The United States

As discussed in earlier chapters of this report, state-level commercial legalization in the United States has also not gone just swimmingly. It has major trials before it. A report published by the Ohio State Drug Enforcement and Policy Center (Title 2022) described the state-level legalization of cannabis in the United States as facing serious challenges and harms from the increasing monopolization of the industry by a few large and powerful players.

The Center's report mentioned many of the same problems that have arisen with the corporatization of the cannabis trade in Canada. It described a legalization landscape dominated by big business, mega mergers, vertical integration, and manipulative public relations campaigns. The report cited compelling examples of the agile gaming by cannabis corporations of anti-monopoly provisions, including predatory pricing and collusion to fix prices. Legislators becoming increasingly vested in the industry has given rise to political motivation for the creation of daunting barriers that exclude new and smaller entrants to the industry. The banking industry has piled on with predatory loaning and unethical business practices. The US cannabis industry has also seen tobacco and alcohol companies making significant investments. Corporate influence through aggressive lobbying has overtly and covertly shaped regulations, and the industry has launched lawsuits against regulators. The report has lamented the cumulative threat of all this conduct to equity, diversity, and public health protection.

While acknowledging the potential of federal legalization and regulation in the US to improve some aspects of the trade, the report also had this to say:

> "Unfortunately, in their current form, the major comprehensive reform bills being considered (MORE Act, States Reform Act, and CAO Act) would likely eviscerate a key component of state social equity programs, trigger a race to the bottom to roll back valuable public health protections, and potentially create dangerous gaps in regulation until new federal rules are promulgated" (Title 2022, 3).

CANADA HAS A DRUG POLICY PROBLEM —HELP IS AVAILABLE

A Hybrid Approach:
Social Justice and Public Health Protection

When a person has a drug problem, the first step towards recovery is to recognize and acknowledge the problem. Canada has a serious drug problem—a drug policy problem. The evidence is in the magnitude of harms and costs related to our long-term drug industries and the legacy of industry indifference to public health and the rule of law. The warning signs from the newborn cannabis industry were aplenty.

In its ongoing reluctance to acknowledge the serious shortcomings of its cannabis legalization campaign, our government remains in a state of denial. It did not have to be this way. Many of us, including some of the foremost health policy organizations and academic policy analysts in the world, intervened. We tried to help the Liberal Party of Canada recognize the perils of commercial legalization of cannabis. The intervention was not successful.

The Canadian Government has, in most cases, exonerated the corporate criminals in the cannabis industry who chose to operate outside the law. However, the government has been less forgiving of Canadians who chose to access their cannabis outside the law. The Cannabis Act retains harsh criminal penalties for minor offences involving unauthorized cannabis—the same victimless crime it has always been.

When I submitted my report and recommendations to the Task Force on Marijuana Legalization and Regulation in 2016, I suggested a two-step hybrid approach to cannabis law reform. The first step was immediate decriminalization. (I covered some of the options for decriminalization in Chapter 4.) The second step was the development of an alternative to commercial legalization—a not-for-profit approach with a priority of public health protection over market expansion. This hybrid approach prioritized not only public health but also social justice. It borrowed a directive from emergency medicine: "first, stop the bleeding!" In the case of cannabis law reform, the bleeding was the thousands of mostly young Canadians perennially receiving criminal records for possessing cannabis of the wrong kind or in the wrong place. That needed to change. With the destructive criminalization of Canadians out of the way, efforts could focus on developing a genuine public health approach as an alternative to commercial legalization and the inevitable devotion to market expansion. I was not alone in my thinking about a new way of doing things.

Health Policy Organizations Support a Not-For-Profit/Public Health Approach

Canada's campaign to legalize recreational use of cannabis prompted input from health policy authorities from across Canada and abroad. In Chapter 6, I described various proposals for a not-for-profit approach that were made at the time of Canada's legalization campaign. The organizations included:

- *The Canadian Medical Association Journal (Spithoff, Emerson, and Spithoff 2015)*

- *The Chief Medical Officers of Health of Canada & Urban Public Health Network (2016)*

- *Institut national de santé publique du Québec (Chapados et al. 2016)*

- *The United States' RAND Corporation (Caulkins et al. 2015)*

- *The United Kingdom's Expert Panel (Rolles et al. 2016)*

Since that time, additional organizations have come on board. From the US, The Stanford Network for Addiction Policy (SNAP) works to foster interaction and mutual learning between addiction researchers and policy makers. SNAP expressed concerns about commercialization of cannabis and suggested a not-for-profit approach (Stanford Network for Addiction Policy 2020). More recently, a similar recommendation came from the field of criminology. A paper published in The British Journal of Criminology noted:

"The lesson for the cannabis industry may be that, instead of taking the large step of moving from prohibition straight to a fully commercial market, a more measured approach might be to begin with a state-controlled supply system—coupled with home cultivation and local growing co-operatives—as a strategic 'circuit-breaker' in order to establish some social norms for legal cannabis" (Seddon 2020).

France's Conseil analyse économique joined the chorus with its proposal for a national public monopoly for the production and distribution of recreational cannabis (Auriol and Geoffard 2019).

Among national governments, only Uruguay has a well-established regime with some common ground with a non-commercialized approach. Other countries, many in Europe, are in various stages of implementing co-

Proposal for a Not-For-Profit Approach for the Tobacco Industry

The idea of a not-for-profit approach for a drug industry did not originate with campaigns to legalize cannabis. In Canada, much of the innovation of thought began with early models of provincial government-operated alcohol retail outlets (more on this later). There were similar proposals at the federal level from tobacco policy advocates. In 2005, Physicians for a Smoke-Free Canada (PSC) (Callard, Thompson, and Collishaw 2005a) recommended transitioning Canada's for-profit tobacco industry to a not-for-profit model. The authors offered a rationale and strategies for doing so, as well as three models for what the not-for-profit approach might look like, including examples of not-for-profits currently operating for various purposes in Canada. The descriptions are impressively detailed and compelling. PSC asserted that the essence of the problem was that tobacco companies are legally required to make profits for their shareholders. They can only do that by selling tobacco products and will never willingly temper that pursuit with public health considerations.

PSC accordingly recommended that responsibility for tobacco production and sale be moved to a not-for-profit organization with a public health mandate to decrease demand for smoking. Callard, Thompson, and Collishaw (2005b) offered some encouragement with their observations regarding reform of the tobacco industry: "The decision to put tobacco in the hands of business corporations was made through government, and can be changed through government. The choice between keeping corporations in tobacco manufacture or replacing them with something else is ours to make."

Unfortunately, the proposed solution did not exactly sprout wings and soar triumphantly about the corridors of power in government. Nor did it become a prominent idea in the tobacco policy community of the day. Perhaps, just too far ahead of its time, the idea languished. But given the current trend for tobacco control efforts to achieve diminishing returns on impact, public health academics and advocates are increasingly considering less traditional approaches as part of an "endgame strategy" for the tobacco industry (Tobacco Endgame Cabinet 2019). The Cabinet's Report acknowledged PSC's work with its reference to a "...nonprofit enterprise with a public health mandate" as an option for regulatory reform. They also recommended several other options to remove a considerable amount of control from tobacco corporations.

Physicians for a Smoke-Free Canada persists in its advocacy for an endgame to the commercialized tobacco trade. In 2021, it submitted a report to Canada's newly appointed Minister and Associate Minister of Health declaring:

"Endgame approaches recognize the need to change the structural, political and social dynamics that sustain the tobacco epidemic. Measures in this category include more powerful interventions such as decommercializing the supply of tobacco products..."(Physicians for a Smoke-free Canada 2021).

I'm on board.

operatives or cannabis social clubs (CSCs) as not-for-profit entities. I will
have more to say on these developments shortly.

How Does a Public Health Approach Differ from a Commercialized One?

The recommendations from health policy authorities introduced a
variety of descriptors: "public health approach", "government monopoly",
"central commission", "not-for-profit approach", "for-profit", "state-controlled supply system", "national public monopoly" "commercial legalization", and "public" versus "private." For many readers, these descriptors may
raise more questions than they provide understanding. I will try to provide
some context of supply systems that may make these descriptors more
meaningful. The overarching question is how a public health approach dif-
fers from a commercialized one.

When talking about what we want in the establishment of a new drug
trade, whether it is cannabis, psychedelics, or whatever other types of reform
campaigns are yet to come, it is tempting to get caught up in juxtapositions
such as private versus public, and for-profit versus not-for-profit approaches.
These constructs obviously have implications for creating a public health approach, but we must be more specific. So, what do we want?

Generally, we want a genuine public health approach, not the fraudulent one that the Liberal Party of Canada promised while apparently concealing its true intent of establishing a commercialized, market expansionist
regime with a priority of generating massive amounts of private profit and
taxation revenue for government.

It is important to describe specifically what we mean by a genuine
public health approach. In this chapter, I will try to make a substantial contribution towards that goal. I hope others might be inspired to explore and
to build on it.

As a starting point, I suggest that there are five fundamental features
that distinguish a genuine public health approach from a commercialized one:

- *the priority goal is protecting public health, not the generation of profit*
- *the salient process is to provide a public service to meet existing demand, not to increase demand (market expansion) to sell more product*
- *the source of revenue should be one that expects reimbursement of only startup and initial operating costs, not profit, or return on investment*
- *the disposition of revenue beyond operating costs should support only the public health mission of the organization, and not become private assets, or fully discretionary funds for government*

- governance should be by individuals with public health expertise and commitment, not with expertise in, and commitment to, market expansion and profit maximization.

I will add much more detail to these features later in the chapter when I recommend a specific approach for cannabis.

To better define a genuine public health approach, it helps to consider the organizational types in play—some of which are far more compatible with the approach than others. Let's consider a few types.

For-Profit Corporations

This is, by far, the most common model for providing drug products (and all products) to consumers in western democracies. Whether privately owned (like Purdue Pharmaceutical L.P. by the Sackler family) or publicly traded like most of the large cannabis companies in Canada, for-profit corporations have often proven themselves to be perilous entities when it comes to protection of public health as defined by the five features listed above. The priority goal is the generation of profit, not the protection of public health. The salient process is to sell a product through commercialized market expansion, not to provide a public service as needed. The source of revenue is the assets of the owners or investors all of whom expect to realize a profit or return on investment, which also determines the disposition of revenue primarily towards privately held profits. Finally, governance rests with owners or a board of directors with expertise in, and commitment to, market expansion and profit maximization, not with expertise in and commitment to, public health protection.

For-profit corporations are prone to mergers and acquisitions, and ultimately monopolization which concentrates enormous amounts of market power in the hands of a few players. A variation on the for-profit corporation that intends to avoid monopolization is receiving some spirited advocacy in the United States. The previously mentioned report published by the Ohio State Drug Enforcement and Policy Center (Title 2022) described a near calamitous march towards heightened monopolization in the current campaign for federal cannabis legalization in the US. To avert that, the report lays out several policy proposals that would attempt to promote a diverse and competitive market with a priority on consumers and public health protection. The proposals include:

- allowance for limited home grow

- prohibition of vertical integration

- limit how much of a market any one person or entity may control

- enforce ownership limits

- create incentives for states to license small or disadvantaged businesses

- review mergers for existing evidence of predatory or anti-competitive tactics in state jurisdictions

- *disqualify corporations for criminal conduct, defrauding the public, or causing significant public health damage*
- *create a task force to enforce anti-monopoly limits*
- *allow states to challenge interstate commerce to preserve state-level advantages to local businesses.*

Many of these proposals are applicable to other jurisdictions considering cannabis legalization. Those jurisdictions would be wise to heed the advice. The proposals could also be considered in Canada with its significant levels of regulatory non-compliance, corporate crime and disregard for consumers and health protection. Canada's perilous experience with national legalization could serve as a pertinent case study in support of many of the report's key messages.

The Center's report is clearly in support of a commercial cannabis industry—just one that prevents large monopolies. This support appears to rest upon the assumption that smaller, more equitable, and diverse businesses will be more compliant with regulations and the law, more attentive to consumer needs and public health protection, and easier to regulate. We would all like this to be the case. However, in Ontario, Canada, audits of mostly small cannabis retailers documented large-scale misconduct (Office of the Auditor General of Ontario 2020, 2021). Accordingly, we would be wise to retain a healthy level of skepticism towards this aspiration. Nonetheless, a smaller scale, less monopolized industry has its merits and is worth a try. At the very least, an industry of smaller players would possess a smaller stick with which to assail the rule of law and public health protection. It should not be as harmful as large cannabis monopolies. But it is not likely to be a panacea either.

Private, Not-For-Profit Organizations

Given the bleak prospects for public health protection by for-profit organizations (especially large ones), many drug policy experts have expressed support for not-for-profit approaches. These too can be both private and public. Private, not-for-profit organizations are widely recognized as foundations serving a variety of charitable causes. These foundations are typically funded by a single donor with a substantial contribution. The donation is invested in the stock market and the foundation's activities are funded from the return on investment. The foundation exists only to support its chosen charitable causes. It has no need to sell products to generate revenue. The foundations have a board of directors. But there are no requirements for the directors to be selected from, or otherwise represent, the beneficiaries of the foundation's activities or from any other constituencies. Ultimately, governance may rest with the donor.

A variation on the model of private not-for-profit organizations includes the small cooperatives or cannabis social clubs (CSCs) established in some European jurisdictions (Room et al. 2010; Murkin 2015; Pardal et al.

2020). This model supplies cannabis to people who support the organization with their membership fees. The cooperatives are viable entities for supporting a public health approach to the legalization of any drug, including cannabis. They have no mandate for generating revenue beyond operating costs. There is no need to satisfy owners or shareholders with profits. Nor do they have an imperative to expand their membership numbers. Governance is by elected members of the co-op. Nations continue to explore variants of this model for making cannabis available.

There is now an international organization (Encod.org) that provides advocacy and support for the development of cannabis social clubs. The results of a mapping exercise showed that cannabis social clubs have been established in 13 European countries. However, not all of them are legal. So, many clubs continue to engage in cannabis law reform activism as well (Pardal et al. 2020).

Public Not-For-Profit Organizations

There are also many public not-for-profit entities serving a wide variety of social causes. Some of them are very large—including hospitals, universities, colleges, and research institutes. Annual funding comes from various branches of government. They also receive time limited grants from government and private doners. They may occasionally sell their services to private industry. Individual employees may earn personal revenue from intellectual property rights on inventions, and a portion of those revenues usually defaults to the organization. But the organization's salient process is to provide a public service in return for public funding. There is also a diverse collection of smaller and medium sized charitable organizations. They too may engage in limited commercial activities. For any size of these public not-for-profit organizations, the realization of assets beyond what is required for ongoing operational costs remains public capital. It will be reinvested exclusively towards the organization's mission. Governance must include a board of directors that is representative of the organization's community of interest.

Government Enterprises as Public Not-For-Profit Organizations

Another very different incarnation of a public not-for-profit approach is when governments become involved in the retail and wholesale of consumer products. In Canada, this includes alcohol, gaming, and cannabis products. These government initiatives can provide a public service with no need to perpetually increase market size and sales to realize a profit for owners or shareholders. Governments provide their own revenue for start-up and initial operating costs, which are eventually covered by revenues earned. The excess revenues remain public assets that can be reinvested in similar or other public services. The enterprise provides its own governance, usually resting with an appointed board of directors, and ultimately with a minister of the government. Thus, these not-for-profit enterprises provide an opportunity to establish a public health priority in the delivery of these consumer products. However, these government enterprises are no panacea. There are several aspects that can, and typically do, fall short of a public health protection gold standard—sometimes, significantly short.

These government enterprises are commonly referred to as government monopolies. In almost all cases, this is a misnomer. For alcohol, gaming, and cannabis in Canada, these government enterprises play their role alongside private for-profit players. The retail sector for alcohol, cannabis, and gambling services in Canadian provinces is typically a mix of private for-profit and government not-for-profit providers. In these circumstances, government is not completely replacing a commercialized approach. It is just attempting to get a piece of the action.

As described in Chapter 5, public not-for-profit retail enterprises tend to perform better than do private for-profit ones on public health and safety indicators. However, these government enterprises did not adopt all or even most public health's best practices. The Ontario Government's mixed public and private alcohol retail system was found to have the highest level of fidelity with public health best practices—higher than other Canadian provinces with a strictly private for-profit system.

Given that stature, let's take a closer look at the leader of the pack—Ontario's public not-for-profit enterprise—The Liquor Control Board of Ontario (LCBO).

Given its public funding, the priority goal of the LCBO could be to simply deliver a public service of providing alcohol in a manner to maximize public health protection. Yet, the salient process is one of omnipresent product promotion to facilitate market expansion. The LCBO is nearly as market expansionist as any private sector retail system. This is in full compliance with the province's regulator—the Alcohol and Gaming Commission of Ontario. With no private owners or shareholders providing investments and expecting returns on those investments, the LCBO has no legal obligation to expand the market, sales, and revenues. Yet, across three different political parties having formed governments in Ontario during my adult lifetime, the appetite for revenue from alcohol sales has remained rapacious. It is true that the revenue remains as public funds. But the revenues are not directed exclusively to public health or public welfare initiatives. The revenues can find their way into general accounts that can be used for any desired purpose by the Ontario government—potentially including subsidization of private for-profit enterprises.

Governance of the LCBO is by an appointed board of directors that reports to the Minister of Finance (not Health). A key predictor of fidelity with a public health approach is the membership of the enterprise's board of directors which will reflect the intentions and ambitions of the government. A membership comprised mainly of directors with business and finance expertise and market expansion inclination will conduct the organization very differently than will one comprised mainly of public health professionals. In the case of the LCBO, the board maintains only token membership of directors with public health expertise.

Implications for Government Cannabis Enterprises

A report from The Canadian Centre on Substance Use and Addiction (2019) noted that legislation for cannabis legalization in Canada promised to have a focus on public health and safety. However, the legislation has no requirements for public health appointees to boards of directors of cannabis producers or retailers. Accordingly, the Centre's analysis of the composition of boards overseeing retail sales and distribution of cannabis in Canadian provinces and territories, found that board membership did not reflect a public health and safety priority. Rather, there is a preponderance of members whose expertise lies within business and finance. Directors with an academic or vocational background in public health and safety were very few.

While the report did not cover the boards of licensed cannabis producers, I have also noted the same preponderance of expertise there. There appears to be little genuine interest in the industry, or in government, in assigning priority to public health.

The Ontario government's online Ontario Cannabis Store (OCS), like private for-profit cannabis businesses in Canada, is prohibited from advertising in places where the ads can be seen by those under the legal age. However, OCS takes full advantage of its easily gamed, age-gated website to showcase cannabis product monographs. Some of the descriptors have adopted the metaphoric sizzle of commercial advertising:

- *"infused high-THC pre-rolls are beyond basic"*

- *"get the latest buzz about infused foods and beverages."*

As of March 2022, public health expertise on the OCS board of directors was questionable at best. If government retail enterprises for cannabis and other consumer drug products continue to be directed primarily by individuals with no experience in, or inclination towards, the protection of public health, we will likely continue to see its subjugation to market expansion and revenue generation. That systemic determinant must change. It is therefore important not to, by default, conflate government enterprises (even if a true monopoly) with a public health approach. While government enterprises present an opportunity, the devil, or saviour, will always reside in the details.

Three Steps Forward in Québec

The Canadian Province du Québec has taken three important steps forward in its approach to retail for cannabis. The Institut national de santé publique du Québec (INSPQ) was successful in its advocacy for provincial legislation to establish a not-for-profit government retail monopoly for cannabis—the Société Québécoise du cannabis (SQDC). This first step has gone

one step further than the province's Société des alcools du Québec (SAQ) which maintains only a near monopoly for alcohol retail.

In its 2021 Annual Report, SQDC described its mission to: "Sell cannabis in compliance with the Cannabis Regulation Act and with a focus on health protection to attract and retain users from the illegal cannabis market without encouraging use" (Société Québécoise du cannabis 2021, 8).

The opening statement of SQDC's report declares: "In its 2020-2021 fiscal year, the Société Québécoise du cannabis (SQDC) generated comprehensive income of $66.5 million, nearly double the figure for the preceding fiscal year. Remitted in full to the Gouvernement du Québec, the monies will be used primarily to fund cannabis-related research, education and harm prevention efforts. At this point, more than 50% of illegal market sales have been converted to the SQDC, fulfilling a key part of the company's mission. The Québec model, which focuses the SQDC on health protection, can thus be seen as having clear public health and safety benefits in addition to being profitable for Québec society."

The second step forward for the province is the legislated designation that all cannabis sales revenue (beyond covering SQDC operational costs) goes to a cannabis revenue fund. That fund is then split between cannabis prevention and research activities (at least 51%) with the balance going towards more general programs for psychoactive substances in general.

Thus, revenues above operating costs cannot become discretionary funds within general government accounts. This significantly reduces the incentive for government to increase cannabis sales for revenue-generation.

The third step is that the Québec provincial legislation also established a "vigilance committee" with public health leadership to advise government (l'Assemblée nationale du Québec 2018).

The Québec model has taken on some key characteristics of a public health approach to cannabis retail. This comprises a significant milestone in the evolution of drug policy, world-wide. A more detailed description of the Québec system is available in a 2021 report from the Institut national de santé publique du Québec. It describes the early achievements of the not-for-profit system and, ominously, the ongoing threats from market expansionists in the private for-profit sector (Gagnon 2021).

The Québec model also suggests that a not-for-profit, public health approach may be feasible at a national level as well. The nation of Uruguay holds some promise.

Uruguay's Public Health Approach

Uruguay, the first nation to legalize the sale of cannabis for recreational use, adopted a model with many features of a national, public health, not-for-profit approach. The Institut national de santé publique du Québec (INSPQ) reviewed available literature on the Uruguayan approach and provided a summary of its key features, which include:

- *the Instituto de Regulación y Control del Cannabis (IRCCA) acts as a government purchasing monopoly and regulator*

- *the Board of directors of the IRCCA is chaired by the chair of Uruguay's national drug council—a government agency overseeing drug prevention, treatment, and drug law enforcement*

- *other members equally represent public health, social development, and agriculture*

- *sales of cannabis to the public occur through community pharmacies and not-for-profit growers' clubs which are accessed by members only*

- *unlike most jurisdictions which intend to limit use only by youth, Uruguay has the explicit objective of containing, and not expanding, the market for cannabis*

(Gagnon 2021).

Uruguay's approach is a dramatic departure from the profit-driven corporate model adopted by Canada and U.S sub-national jurisdictions. More detail of the Uruguayan regime can be found at the Uruguayan institute's website (https://www.ircca.gub.uy/).

What Happened in Canada at the Federal Level?

Canada was the second nation to legalize the recreational use of cannabis. It had access to the same thinking from health policy authorities as did Uruguay. Yet, Canada took a vastly different path. So, what became of the expertise offered to the Canadian government on how to implement a public health approach for cannabis, specifically, within a not-for-profit model? What did the *Final Report* of the Canadian Government's Task Force on Cannabis Legalization and Regulation say, and what did the Cannabis Act put into force? As already described in Chapter 6, The Task Force's report acknowledged having received proposals for not-for-profit entities, but stopped short of recommending the approach, instead favouring a for-profit private sector model. Expert advice was not heeded by the government on most of the fundamental aspects of creating a new recreational drug industry. A commercial, market expansionist approach was apparently exactly what the Liberal Party of Canada wanted, and that is exactly what Canada got in the Cannabis Act—a perilous policy model predicated upon near surrender to corporate dominance.

In Canada, we have often heard that cannabis legalization was not an event but will be a process. We are accordingly invited to see cannabis law reform as a long-term, dynamic undertaking that will be subject to many forces in its ongoing evolution. Reform efforts, favouring a public health approach, can only hope to adopt individual components (à la carte) from a comprehensive model. In the most optimistic scenario, reform in Canada will evolve slowly towards a more genuine public health approach.

However, other nations considering cannabis law reform options could establish a national not-for-profit cannabis commission with all it's holistic merits for supporting a health protection priority. The next section of this chapter provides the case and begins to lay out the key features of such an approach.

A NATIONAL NOT-FOR-PROFIT CANNABIS COMMISSION

The Case for a National Not-For-Profit Cannabis Commission

I readily acknowledge the subversive potential of recommending a national not-for-profit cannabis commission. Such a proposal will provoke no shortage of critics who will prefer the more familiar and comfortable ground of the traditional private sector model—despite its ruinous track-record for protecting the public's health.

There will be those who protest the loss of an opportunity for creating yet another lucrative drug industry and the potential for many spin-off industries. Fiscally oriented leaders in government will lament the loss of a new unrestricted revenue stream. Even worse, I often worry that high ranking individuals within political parties that come to power have personal financial interests and are inclined to prioritize those interests. There will be no sympathy for not-for-profit approaches among such legislators.

Some cannabis users may be concerned about how pursuing a not-for-profit model will affect the supply of cannabis. There will also be some drug policy analysts who will be uncomfortable with adopting an approach that moves beyond the prevailing orthodoxy of mere tinkering with the broken model around which their careers have developed. I sometimes worry that some are constrained by their reliance on government funding, which may be predicated upon support for the status quo. I worry that this fiscal muzzling of some analysts may effectively exclude unorthodox ideas from their policy work.

There will also be those who will argue that a large government bureaucracy will not operate with purity of intent, and that noble aspirations will be sometimes compromised by political machinations and bureaucratic careerism. After decades of working in a large, government-funded bureaucracy, I too might be tempted to join that chorus. It's been said that the road to hell is paved with good intentions.

However, the advantages of a not-for-profit cannabis commission are potentially considerable—effectively eliminating the many harmful activities and influence of revenue-driven corporations, including:

- *compromised quality control in the interest of cost containment*

- *product innovation for market expansion, potentially at the expense of public health protection*

- *aggressive, misleading, and exploitative product promotion for market expansion*

- *disinformation campaigns aimed at the public to generate support for industry-friendly policy development*

- *lobbying government legislators and bureaucrats for regulatory favour*

- *securities fraud that cheats investors out of their savings*

- *regulatory violations and gaming of regulations*

- *corporate crime*

- *the necessity of extensive resource-consuming regulatory surveillance and adjudication—funded largely from taxes.*

Part of the case for a national not-for-profit cannabis commission is also the advantage of coherence. As is the case with alcohol, cannabis distribution in sub-national jurisdictions also varies considerably with various models adopted. Regulatory uniformity and fidelity with public health best practices would be difficult to achieve under such a decentralized system—alcohol distribution in Canada as a case in point. A more manageable approach might be to have all components of the supply chain, from production to retail, come under the control of a single national cannabis commission under public health direction. It might be worthwhile for the sub-national jurisdictions to have logistical control over distribution and retail, but authority for policy would remain with the national commission. A single coordinating commission could also help to bring order to the early chaotic days of legalizing a new recreational drug supply.

A nation-wide commission may also provide a level of political heft that may not exist in not-for-profit operations that operate on a smaller stage. For example, the small local cannabis social clubs and cooperatives discussed earlier are under persistent threat from players with commercial ambitions (Decorte 2015). This will be a threat for other approaches to cannabis law reform as well such as those established in Spain, Mexico, Georgia, South Africa, and Washington, D.C, which have legalized possession of cannabis, but not commercialization. Events in Washington, D.C provide a telling case. In May 2019, D.C Mayor Muriel Bowser introduced The Safe Cannabis Sales Act which would have overturned the ban on commercialization and allowed the sale of cannabis in licensed facilities (Washington, D.C 2019). However, the Act was blocked in March 2022 by virtue of federal legislation (Marijuana Business Daily 2022).

Nonetheless, the threat of these commercial turns needs to be taken seriously, as they can occur in ways that are more subtle than by a change in legislation. They can occur through a gradual erosion of public health practices. This has also been observed in provincial government alcohol retail in Canada. They were once less privatized and more aligned with public health best practices than they are today. These commercial turns for alcohol retail have been described for both Québec (Quesnel 2003) and Ontario (Giesbrecht et al. 2021). The association of such turns with increased harm has also been described (Myran et al. 2019). The existence of a national cannabis commission might mean fewer active fronts at which these for-profit incursions must be repelled.

If the idea of a national not-for-profit cannabis commission seems desirable, but too unconventional, consider that not-for-profit organizations are numerous in Canada and most other places in the world. Callard, Thompson, and Collishaw (2005a) noted that some of our largest organizations: hospitals, universities, colleges, and research institutes are not-for-profit organizations. National not-for-profits in Canada include federal crown corporations such as Canada Post, the Canadian Broadcasting Corporation, VIA Rail, and many others. Not-for-profits also include many medium-sized and smaller grass-roots organizations serving a variety of social, human rights, environmental, and charitable causes. Similar organizations exist in many countries world-wide.

A willingness, and even an urgency, to try something different is emerging in Canada and elsewhere. Canada's legalization of recreational cannabis use provided an opportunity to do so. Tobacco control advocates who proposed switching the tobacco industry to a not-for-profit model faced a daunting challenge given how well-entrenched tobacco corporations were at the time. This was not the case for the emerging cannabis industry. There was an opportunity to shape the budding industry while it was still in a relatively pliable infancy. The cannabis industry has now become firmly established in law and in practice as a legion of mostly large, well-resourced, sometimes politically connected and powerful, partly foreign-owned, corporate entities. The force of its escalating momentum makes its reversibility increasingly difficult and unlikely. There was a warning of this development within a recommendation from the Chief Medical Officers of Health of Canada & Urban Public Health Network (2016): "Proceed with much caution, and err on the side of more restrictive regulations, since it is easier to loosen regulations than to tighten them afterwards."

The RAND Corporation discussed a similar dynamic of reversibility. They argued that it would be much easier to move from a monopoly model to a competitive commercial one later than to transition from a competitive commercial model to a monopoly model (Caulkins et al. 2015, 61).

290

What Would a National Not-For-Profit
Cannabis Commission Look Like?

The following description should be viewed as representing only an initial offering of ideas. The ideas arise, as much as possible, upon the evidence-based public health principles presented throughout this book. Many of the ideas came from an earlier proposal from Physicians for a Smoke-free Canada (PSC) for converting the legal tobacco trade in Canada to a not-for-profit model. This description will not provide the level of detail that is offered in the PSC's proposal. I recommend that the passionate or skeptical reader consult their original work for more detail (Callard, Thompson, and Collishaw 2005a).

The ideas proposed here are not intended to be specifically definitive, restrictive, or comprehensive. Rather, they are intended to be sufficiently tangible to stimulate a process towards developing a more detailed model. I would expect (and insist!) that a complete model would benefit from the input of many specialties of knowledge and experience that I do not possess.

Mission and Goals

The mission of a national not-for-profit cannabis commission would be to produce and distribute cannabis in a manner that would minimize the harm to public health and safety.

The goals would be to:

- *contain or lower the prevalence of cannabis use and aggregate cannabis use*

- *substantially reduce higher risk use and its harmful consequences.*

The Commission would achieve these goals by:

- *drawing upon public health evidence, best advice, principles*

- *serving only the existing level of demand, with no attempt at market expansion*

- *making no attempt to induce non-users to try cannabis*

- *providing uncontaminated, accurately labelled, lowest-risk format product*

- *providing only evidence-based information on low-risk use with no metaphoric hyperbole intended to stimulate purchases.*

Much of the structure and daily operations of a not-for-profit cannabis commission would not necessarily be that different from a for-profit model. The commission would be responsible for cultivating cannabis, processing it into consumer products, and distributing it to affiliated retail outlets. It would also maintain oversight of the retail function. There would be some important differences—most notably, the over-arching priority of protecting public health over market expansion. The long-term goal could be to decrease cannabis consumption and therefore the revenue of the Commission. From a traditional business perspective, this will seem like an entirely counter-intuitive idea. Some entrepreneurs will have other, less kind, adjectives for it. Yet, the goal of containing and reducing the use of any drug for recreational purposes is entirely consistent with a true public health approach. The specific objectives of the commission would be set at a more programmatic level. Ideally, they would be identified in consultation with key partners including representatives from government, public health, researchers, addiction/health/social services, educators, and representatives from marginalized communities.

Governance and Staffing

The commission would be nationally legislated but independent of government. It would be led by a commissioner and a board of trustees principally comprised of individuals with public health and related expertise. The trustees would possess a proven track record of experience and commitment to health, social justice, and not-for-profit organizations. They might bring specific experience from addictions, public health, social policy, research, law, education, and working with marginalized communities. Individuals affiliated in any way with specific drug companies or drug industries would not be eligible.

In Canada, this has already become the norm in many public health initiatives, for example in the development of dietary and opioid guidelines. Direct cannabis industry involvement was also excluded from the membership of Canada's Task Force for Cannabis Legalization and Regulation. However, as described in Chapter 6, the cannabis industry still found indirect ways to be influential. The establishment of governance would have to be very diligent in its protection of a public health priority to eliminate all risk of encroachment by expansionist business interests.

Staff would report to a management structure which would be ultimately accountable to the commissioner. The management team and operations staff would possess experience related to their respective operational responsibilities (e.g. agriculture, computer technology, finance, human resources, supply chain, security, maintenance). They would also have an appreciation for, and experience working in, not-for-profit organizations.

Source of Funding and Disbursement of Revenue

The start-up capital for the commission would come as an investment from the national government. If sub-national governments were to take on roles in distribution and retail, they could also make initial investments to support the establishment and initial operation of these components. All investments would be repaid from revenues over a suitable period. Once in full operation, the commission would be self-funded through its cannabis sales. Private investment would not be allowed or pursued to avoid any potential pressures for market expansion or other potential conflicts with the public health priority.

A major difference between a for-profit drug company and a not-for-profit commission is with regards to the disbursement of revenue after covering operating costs. Excess revenue would remain as public, not private, assets. Generation of a new unrestricted revenue stream for government should be avoided given that it could create an appetite for increasing sales as a means for increasing that revenue stream. An unrestricted stream might serve any number of government initiatives either irrelevant to, or a threat to, a public health imperative. Funding from the commission for public health services would not replace existing government funding for the programs. That would be equivalent to creating a new unrestricted revenue stream for government with the former funding envelopes. Revenue that accumulated above repayment of start-up and ongoing operating costs would be directed only to initiatives relevant to the organization's public health mission. The intent to avoid the creation of a new unrestricted revenue stream for government would also mean that taxation would not come into play. Taxation would also not be necessary given that the commission alone could control pricing to contain consumption. This departure from the traditional approach would arise directly from, and be protected by, the organization's mission which would be enshrined in legislation.

Transition from Private to Not-For-Profit

It is unlikely that Canada or another jurisdiction that had already adopted a private sector model would transition to a not-for-profit approach. (Have you ever tried to get toothpaste back into the tube?) If this were to occur, existing private cannabis producers, distributors, and retailers would be subject to the expiry of their licences within a reasonable time frame and eventually bought out at fair market value.

Scope of Operations

The scope of operations would include the basic components of a complete cannabis supply chain, including cultivation, processing, distribution, and retail. There could be a role for sub-national monopolies in the logistics of distribution and retail, and these public monopolies would also be accountable to applicable sub-national legislation. Retail outlets would also be subject to municipal bylaws. All components would remain accountable to the policies of the national commission.

Cannabis Product Production

The daily operational aspects of the commission's cannabis production would be very much like the current legal private sector operations. The commission would employ experienced people to run and supervise the production line for cultivation and conversion of cannabis plants to packaged consumer product—quite possibly the same people who are already performing these functions in the private companies. In the case of conversion from a private to a not-for-profit approach, there would need to be very little job loss, if any. Without multi-million-dollar salaries and ill-earned bonuses going to executives, pay levels could be substantially improved to more equitable levels—certainly well above the minimum wage that prevails for many employees in the industry.

There would be other differences that reflected a public health priority. Strict quality control would supersede the low standard of mass production that currently prevails in many large cannabis factories. As seen in earlier chapters, this model, too often, resulted in low quality product contaminated with bacteria, mould, mildew, unauthorized pesticides, and apparently even bugs and pieces of plastic gloves!

Something that would be worth exploring is a transition away from large scale production factories to smaller craft growers that would still be part of the commission. Without a priority for generating revenue, these smaller production units would not have to worry so much about economies of scale. They could concentrate on product quality. There would also be a priority placed on accurate labelling of thc:cbd ratios and potency which has been another problem in mass production cannabis factories. Quality would rise above a mere marketing slogan. Verified product integrity and labelling accuracy would become measured, tangible requirements as a basis for bonuses for production teams.

Product Line

There would be no product innovation that would increase the risk of harm for cannabis consumers. For example, synthetic products, products with elevated levels of tetrahydrocannabinol (THC), and cannabis products combined with other drugs would not be produced. Pre-rolled joints that can only be consumed with combustion inhalation would also not be manufactured. Any flower product sold in containers would bear evidence-based cautions concerning harms associated with combustion and vaping. Ideally, flower product might eventually be phased out, but this will be a challenge as flower product remains, by far, the most popular cannabis product with consumers. Perhaps a sustained, evidence-based, public education program on the health risks associated with combustion and vaping might help with that.

Product innovations that could serve market expansion, or otherwise the glamourization of the product, would also not be allowed. An example would be cannabis edibles in the form of confections (candy, baked goods, soft drinks). Such confections also represent a risk for young children in the home when the children and cannabis confections are not being attended to by the adults. However, low dose edible products such as capsules, or oils which can be applied to the tongue, could be produced. The significant advantage of these products is the risk reduction value in replacing combustion and vaping. There would also be less glamourous appeal of this product to attract new users for market expansion. There would also be little visual attraction for a young child in the home.

Packaging

All cannabis products would be available only in plain, child-proof containers that displayed only clear and accurate potency indication and risk reduction information. Company logos, colours, slogans, or other labelling design features that have been employed to stimulate purchases would be replaced with a standard symbol verifying that the product was genuine commission issue.

Distribution

To ensure surveillance of movement of product from cultivation to retail, a seed to sale system would monitor inventory movement at all stages of the supply chain. The responsibility for distribution logistics could be retained by sub-national government monopolies.

Retail

All retail outlets would be held accountable to the policies of the commission. Legal online sales of cannabis products could continue. Physical retail outlets would be licensed as stand-alone operations, that would not sell any other types of consumer products, including drug products such as alcohol and tobacco. Swag (clothing and/or trinkets featuring cannabis related images or references) would not be sold through any of the Commission's retail outlets—physical or online. Nor would devices for combustion be available for purchase. The sale of vaping devices would be subject to policies based upon the continuing unfolding of the pertinent research literature on their safety as a consumption method and effectiveness as a harm reduction approach.

There would be reasonable containment of retail outlets in terms of their numbers, location, density, and hours of operation. It would also be worthwhile to have discussions about the appearance of the store fronts. It may be that the current approach to allowing stylized appearances provides effective advertising for cannabis use. If so, that would undermine approaches to limit the role of advertising in market expansion. As an alternative, storefronts could be made consistent with a 'plain-packaging' look. Finally, all staff working in retail would be trained in the knowledgeable and responsible service of the product.

There would be no licensing of cannabis consumption lounges, given the potential health threats to staff from daily exposure to second-hand smoke or vapour.

As discussed in Chapter 6, the public health literature and legislative trends for legal recreational drugs alcohol, tobacco, and cannabis are strongly supportive of changing the law for the minimum age for the purchase of these drugs to twenty-one. The minimum age for cannabis purchase should be set, nationally, to twenty-one.

Avoid Market Expansion:
No Product Promotion; Demand Reduction Strategies

Under the authority of a national commission, there would be no promotion of cannabis products of any kind across the supply chain. This would mean no advertising, marketing, product giveaways, event sponsorships, or celebrity endorsements, in any medium—print, electronic, or involving actors—human or otherwise. (I was once regaled with a story of a California cannabis retail outlet that paid people to adorn their dogs with t-shirts that promoted the retail outlet. The agreement specified that the doggie t-shirts were to be worn during a minimal number of walks per day in areas with pedestrian traffic. This gives an entirely new meaning to "dog-walker"—a high thc cannabis strain.)

Without sustained attempts at market expansion, there would be reduced need to worry about increases in problematic use as has been associated with market expansion for alcohol, tobacco, and opioid products.

In contrast to attempts at market expansion, the Commission could be responsible for implementing demand reduction strategies as articulated for tobacco by Callard, Thompson, and Collishaw (2005b). Barry and Glantz (2016) have also advocated for applying evidence from tobacco control to develop a similar demand reduction strategy for cannabis.

The circumstances may be somewhat different for cannabis than for tobacco, but the general principle would be to not reward increased sales, but rather practices that supported, rather than acted to sabotage, public health efforts. So, ultimately this could mean achieving a reduction in aggregate sales. In the case of cannabis, demand reduction strategies might include plain packaging and the elimination of flavouring—other than the natural flavours of cannabis. This could also involve providing information at the point of retail on potential health risks, low-risk cannabis use practices including low-risk methods of ingesting THC and accessing help for cannabis-related problems. The successful implementation of some of these demand reduction strategies could also be subject to performance-based incentives for employees of the Commission.

Other Responsibilities of the Commission and the Big Payoff!

Apart from maintaining responsibility for the production, distribution, and retail of cannabis products, the Commission could also have a responsibility for working with relevant partners to sponsor and fund an ambitious research and development program for the development, dissemination, and evaluation of projects that served the Commission's public health mandate. The Commission could work with academics to identify research priorities and to maintain a research program with dedicated research staff and hard funding. It could also contract out research projects to investigators working in existing research institutions. These arrangements would be a welcome replacement for the perilous practice of funding research with money provided by a commercial cannabis company.

Projects could address prevention, harm reduction, and therapeutic initiatives related primarily to the use of cannabis and other drugs, and possibly also to more general health, social, and social justice issues. More specifically, the projects might include:

- *educating the public on the lower risk use of cannabis and other drugs*

- *supporting the implementation of evidence-based prevention, risk and harm reduction, and treatment programs in communities and evaluating their impact*

- *making cannabis products, or methods of ingestion, less hazardous*

- *designing cannabis products in ways that reduced their potential attractiveness, particularly to underage or specific at-risk populations*

- *development of technology for road-side impairment testing and determination of optimal legal per se limits of impairment*

- *product testing for quality control could maintain an ongoing evaluation program for perpetual product integrity improvement*

- *conducting research on the health impact of the use of cannabis and other drugs*

- *expanding capacity for evidence-informed treatment for those with cannabis and other drug or mental health-related problems*

- *conducting research towards the development of more successful treatment interventions for those with cannabis and other drug-related problems*

- *conducting research on the effectiveness of cannabis for therapeutic applications*

- *monitoring the progress of the commission in meeting its goals*

- *surveillance of the unlicensed trade in cannabis; development of non-punitive strategies to minimize its capacity*

- *pilot projects to bring unlicensed operations under the umbrella of the commission; or to improve the safety of its products (think of these provocative ideas within a harm reduction framework)*

- *assessing the longer-term impact of cannabis legalization upon public health and safety*

- *monitoring cannabis law reform in other jurisdictions for further insights*

- funding think-tanks for innovative drug and health policy development

- sponsoring local, national, and international consultations and meet-ings for sharing new knowledge.

The Commission would consult with legislators, regulators, national, sub-national, and local health authorities, international drug policy organiz-ations, academics and community-based, grassroots organizations. The in-put would be used to identify needed changes in cannabis and other drug policy, and to ensure that change was informed by research evidence and otherwise compelling experiences and perspectives from marginalized and diverse communities.

I find the above possibilities to be enormously exciting. This is what could be done if the revenues beyond cost coverage remained public rather than private where they enrich only an elite few. In contrast, the deploy-ment of the revenues to such activities would have a positive impact on the quality of life for many individuals, communities, and nations. And that is a big payoff for a not-for-profit organization!

A NATIONAL NOT-FOR-PROFIT CANNABIS COMMISSION: MISSION IMPOSSIBLE?

Well, maybe. For certain, it is an unorthodox and ambitious idea. Gov-ernments, entrepreneurs, regulators, policy analysts all have their respective reasons to be comfortable with, and supportive of, the traditional private in-dustry model, and wary of such a dramatic change in course.

But we must all be mindful that drugs are no ordinary commodity. For the sake of the public interest there should be no accommodation of a perspective that sees a licence to commodify cannabis as a licence to gener-ate extravagant revenue at any cost to public health and purse.

Regulators like Health Canada bear the responsibility for the surveil-lance of drug industry conduct and enforcement of regulatory provisions in a meaningful manner that motivates compliance. An important question for our regulators is: What would it be like to have a cannabis commission that genu-inely believed in, and wanted to follow, the regulations? I expect this would be a welcome change to trying to regulate corporations that possessed little but contempt for regulation and perpetually tried to game the regulations.

The championing of a not-for-profit approach to any drug trade will be a difficult and likely long-term proposition. But what are the implications of not attempting a radically new approach to drug policy? It means the status quo is maintained. We will continue to endure more decades of elev-ated levels of drug-related mortality, morbidity, and economic costs.

But what is important to appreciate is that Canada's cannabis legaliz-ation campaign prompted statements of support for a not-for-profit ap-proach from health policy organizations, both here in Canada and in several other major countries. Hopefully, this will inspire similar efforts elsewhere, and strengthen the momentum.

The good news is there is already more than momentum. As discussed earlier in this chapter, Institut national de santé publique du Québec was the first in Canada, and perhaps worldwide, to develop logistics and formally advocate with its provincial government for a not-for-profit approach for cannabis (Chapados et al. 2016). More importantly, along with Uruguay, it was also one of the first jurisdictions worldwide to be successful in convincing a government to implement and operate a not-for-profit system for cannabis—albeit at the provincial level. Hopefully, this too will inspire similar efforts elsewhere.

A point to be emphasized in the case for a not-for-profit approach to the legalization of cannabis involves a remarkably simple concept. Cannabis sales anywhere in the world are likely to generate substantial amounts of revenue beyond operating costs. That will continue for many years. How do we want to spend that excess revenue? Should we use it to reward principally a small group of business elites? Do we pay executives millions of dollars annually to fail at running their companies—while the companies' employees work precariously at low wages, and investors lose their savings and go into debt? Do we want to use it to allow these executives to purchase multiple luxury cars, yachts, and vacation homes? Should we spend it building some of the largest greenhouses in the world that are ultimately abandoned (and maybe mysteriously burn down in the middle of the night)? Most dangerously, do we want to gift these cannabis lords with the financial resources to purchase the influence over government and the leniency from our justice system that massive wealth sometimes allows?

Or do we want to spend those revenues on programs and activities that will help to prevent and alleviate the substantial levels of harm and suffering that is the legacy of our drug trades—both licensed and unlicensed? Would we not prefer to spend the revenues on health initiatives that make a safer, healthier world for all to enjoy?

Cannabis law reform is happening in many nations across much of the world. In the next and concluding chapter, I will look at the impacts of cannabis legalization in Canada thus far. I will also explore developments in cannabis law reform elsewhere.

However, cannabis law reform is no longer the only or the lead story in drug policy. Legalization of psychedelics for therapeutic and recreational use also has a place in the international spotlight—as does the decriminalization of all drugs. Canada's cannabis legalization experience has provided important lessons to bring to those policy initiatives—in how we define drug policy problems, and how we attempt to solve them.

How might it all come together? Read on.

SUMMING UP

The legalization of cannabis in Canada stimulated worldwide attention on the legacy of harm from our current legal drug industries—alcohol, tobacco and pharmaceutical. It also prompted health policy organizations from Canada and abroad to propose alternative not-for-profit approaches to cannabis legalization. These approaches aspire to reduce the importance of revenue generation and to make public health protection the priority to reduce the perennial burden of harm. Various jurisdictions are making bold attempts at implementing a variety of such not-for-profit approaches. This chapter presented a brief overview of these approaches and describes one model in more detail—a national not-for-profit cannabis commission.

Chapter 10

What's Next in Drug Policy Reform?

"Civilization had made them men of learning, but in order to save it they must leave their studies and become men of action."
— **Iain Pears,** *The Dream of Scipio*

THREE WAVES OF DRUG POLICY REFORM

I begin by reminding readers that drug reform is currently a highly dynamic issue in Canada and globally. Given the passage of time between the last major edit of this book and its public availability, there will be some significant developments that are not captured here.

Some people appear to believe that cannabis legalization is "done" in Canada, and it is time to move on. Entertaining such a notion is understandable, but it is not a prudent conclusion.

The cannabis industry in Canada is very active; it continues to take on new ambitions and directions. In the latter part of 2021 and first half of 2022, the industry was lobbying more heavily and more publicly for tax reductions and more freedom to innovate its products and advertise them.

A review of the federal lobbying registry for 2021 was published in BNN Bloomberg. It reported entries for seven companies and two associations. Canopy and Aurora led the pack with a combined sixty-five meetings with federal representatives of cabinet and ministries. George Smitherman, Chief Executive Officer of the Cannabis Council of Canada, when interviewed, disclosed that he had lobbied the government ten times and planned to escalate his meetings with government over the coming year. Mr. Smitherman's principal issues included the reduction of excise taxes and restrictions on cannabis edible products (George-Cosh 2022).

Finally, the increasing investment in, and control of, some of Canada's largest cannabis producers by pharmaceutical, alcohol and tobacco companies may pose the greatest threat yet to a public health priority. And it is not just about cannabis, anymore. A campaign to legalize psilocybin for both therapeutic and recreational purposes is becoming increasingly prominent in Canada and elsewhere. The similarity to cannabis in the trajectory of this new initiative is striking. There are important lessons from how a legal cannabis trade took shape that can be applied to psychedelics. And psychedelics will not be the last category of drugs to be targeted with entrepreneurial ambition. We are also seeing increased interest in Canada and elsewhere in the decriminalization of all drugs. The social justice lessons from the cannabis law reform experience are indispensable for these bold initiatives. The cannabis story is as pertinent as ever.

In mid 2022, there were three major waves of drug policy reform at play in Canada and much of the western world:

- *legalization of cannabis*

- *legalization of psychedelic drugs (e.g. psilocybin, MDMA, LSD)*

- *decriminalization of all drugs and creation of a safe supply*

I will discuss these waves within a global context—considering opportunities for social justice, the implications of further commercialization of drug trades, and the current inadequate regulatory approaches of governments. I will attempt to pull together some of the key data and ideas from earlier in the book and apply them to the current events and emerging trends in drug policy reform

Finally, I will make the case for why it is important that jurisdictions, including Canada, pursue a revolutionary reformulation of their approach to drug policy. I will describe what should concern us and to what long-term ambitions we might realistically aspire. And what we should do as soon as possible.

CANNABIS: THE IMPACT OF LEGALIZATION IN CANADA

Legalization of cannabis for recreational use in Canada will continue to morph in ways expected and unexpected. This book has already chronicled the impact of legalization in creating an industry motivated far more by market expansion than by consideration of public health protection.

But there are other impacts to address. I will provide a brief treatment of some of these questions based upon what we know in the fourth year of legalization. As I indicated earlier, my caution is that four years is still early.

Prevalence of Use of Cannabis

Given the liberal access to cannabis for therapeutic use since 2001, and the steady upwards trend in prevalence of cannabis use across the country following 2001, one might expect a ceiling of demand may have been met by the time recreational legalization occurred. That is, any potential for a large additional increase in market size arising from legalization for recreational use may have already been tapped out. However, prevalence of use has continued to climb. Data from The National Cannabis Survey (NCS) (Rotermann 2021) indicated that reported use of cannabis in the past three months among those age fifteen and higher increased from 14% in 2018 Q1 to 20% in 2020 Q4. The great majority of the increase was accounted for by those aged 18-44. A survey of the Canadian experience, conducted by the US organization, Public First (Gibbs, Reed, and Wride 2021, 29) in May 2021, estimated use in the past three months at 31%. Data from the Canadian Cannabis Survey (CCS) also showed increases for use in the past twelve months among those age sixteen and higher:

- *2018: 22%*

- *2019: 25%*

- *2020: 27%.*

However, use decreased in 2021 to 25% (Canada 2021b). Future estimates may clarify the significance, if any, of that decrease.

While there is considerable variability among the more recent population estimates from these surveys, the general picture appears to be that cannabis use is on the rise, given the newfound legal permission to use it, and the more accessible means to acquire it. One additional consideration in interpreting this data is the potential impact of the COVID-19 pandemic which may also have contributed towards increased consumption.

During Canada's legalization campaign, there was a great deal said about already high, and climbing, rates of use by underage youth, and the potential impact of legalization. There were hopes that youth use would be reduced as legal access was denied and the illegal trade diminished. There were also dire warnings of use increasing with a toxic effect on still-developing brains. After reviewing several datasets pertaining to the impact of legalization on youth use, the Public First evaluation offered: "In summary, therefore, it is difficult to make any conclusion about the degree to which the prevalence of youth cannabis use has been impacted by legalization. If anything, the data suggest that the policy goal of reducing youth access through legalization has been unsuccessful" (Gibbs, Reed, and Wride 2021, 39).

Daily or Almost Daily (DAD) Use

Daily or almost daily (dad) use is a likely indicator of dependence and a risk factor for problem use. Both the CCS and the NCS provided an estimate for dad use in the Canadian population of near 6% for 2018 and 2019. The NCS estimate rose from 6.1% in Q3 of 2019 to 7.9% in Q4 of 2020. This increase appears to be primarily the result of an increase in dad use among females which had become as high as that for males—a rare, perhaps unprecedented, event in surveys of cannabis use. Dad use was highest for the 18-44 age range (Rotermann 2021). There is some reasonable speculation and suggestive data that the COVID pandemic played a role in the increases of dad use of cannabis (Gibbs, Reed, and Wride 2021).

Cannabis Related Harms

After addressing several sources pertaining to the impact of legaliza-tion on the harms arising from cannabis use, the Public First evaluation re-ported "in these areas, crucial data in Canada is missing" (Gibbs, Reed, and Wride 2021, 35). The lack of data on such a critical question is not so much a failure of legalization as it is a failure of due prudence on the part of the Ca-nadian government. A genuine commitment to taking a public health ap-proach to cannabis would have included establishing an immediate priority for data gathering and analysis on cannabis-related harms. It's minimal presence four years into legalization is consistent with a central theme of this book: that the Liberal Party of Canada—before and after it formed a government —had other priorities. While studies funded by The Canadian Centre for Substance Use and Addiction (CCSA) are now underway, the outcomes are not imminent.

Such research should have been fast-tracked. Cannabis-related ad-missions remain high at addiction treatment programs in Ontario. Data from The Centre for Addiction and Mental Health's Drug and Alcohol Treatment Information System (DATIS) (2022) indicate that, in 2021, there were 18,532 distinct individuals who entered an addiction treatment pro-gram in the province and identified cannabis as one of their problem sub-stances. That was higher than cocaine and higher than opioids and opiates. Only alcohol was higher with 26,886 distinct individuals. As noted earlier, the number of people entering treatment programs during the pandemic years is lower than the pre-pandemic years. This also appears to have impacted the counts of individuals with specific problem sub-stances—which are also lower than usual.

One study suggests a specific threat that should continue to be mon-itored. An analysis by Myran et al. (2022) showed significant increases in cannabis-related emergency department visits following the proliferation of cannabis retail stores in Ontario.

Cannabis Poisoning in Children

There were warnings about increased hospital admissions for child poisonings from cannabis confections in the United States, as well as advice from health policy organizations in Canada to not allow cannabis edibles as confections. Some of us recommended allowing only non-confection edibles which would not be attractive to children. Neither the warnings nor advice were given sufficient priority in the Task Force's recommendations or in the provisions of the Cannabis Act. It was no surprise to health authorities when a study at Sick Kids Hospital in Toronto reported a higher severity of cases for cannabis-related child poisonings following legalization. The study noted: "The recreational cannabis legalization in Canada is associated with increased rates of severe intoxication in children. Edible ingestion is a strong predictor of ICU admission in the pediatric population" (Cohen et al. 2022).

This represents yet another disturbing testament to the Liberal Party's prioritization of market expansion over the safety of our most cherished. The harm was mostly preventable.

Source of Cannabis

Survey data suggest that there has been a shift in source of cannabis acquisition from the illegal trade to the legal trade. The National Cannabis Survey (NCS) found that the percentage of cannabis users who reported having acquired cannabis from a legal source increased as follows:

- *just before legalization in 2018 22.9%*

- *2019 47.4%*

- *2020 68.4%.*

Over the same period, users acquiring cannabis from illegal sources decreased from 51.3% to 35.4% (Rotermann 2021).

Data from the Canadian Cannabis Survey (CCS) is not directly comparable to the NCS, but nonetheless sheds some light on the transfer from illegal to legal sources. The CCS showed that, in 2021, unambiguously legal sources such as legal stores or legal online sites were identified as sources by 53% and 11% of respondents, respectively. This represents an overall increase from the 2020 figures of 41% and 13%, respectively. Unambiguously illegal sources ("illegal storefront", "illegal online", or "dealer"), were identified, in 2021, by 2% of respondents for each of the three categories Those figures were lower than the 2020 figures of 3% for each of the three categories (Canada 2021a). Well into the third year of legalization, the transfer had not been as complete as hoped by some legalization advocates. But the trend is encouraging.

Arrest Rates

Canada's crime statistics have shown reductions in cannabis arrest rates, especially for youth. However, the statistics continued to show high levels of criminalization of individuals for a variety of cannabis related offences. These included mostly minor offences but with harmful legal consequences for the individuals involved.

The good news is that a significant improvement became apparent in an analysis of police arrest rates of Canadian youth (ages 12-17) between 2015 and 2018 (Callaghan et al. 2021). The investigators reported decreases in arrest rates of 55% and 65% in males and females, respectively. This is an important accomplishment as the criminalization of Canadians at such an early age is potentially a serious disadvantage going forward with one's life. However, it is also important to recognize that this could have been achieved even more so with decriminalization. Furthermore, while the decrease in youth arrest rates is an important part of the story, it is only one part of a larger story.

A report from Statistics Canada showed that while 2019 saw less than half of the reported offences for all ages in 2018 (most of which occurred before the Cannabis Act came into force), there were still 16,868 police-reported cannabis offences in 2019. There was also a major change in the type of offences reported since the Cannabis Act came into force. Before legalization, possession accounted for 75% of cannabis related offences. In 2019, possession accounted for 10.8% and importation or exportation accounted for 67.6%. The authors of the report indicated that many of the importation or exportation charges appeared to arise from people not considering the law regarding carrying personal amounts of cannabis across a border (Moreau, Jaffray, and Armstrong 2020). Yes, that is reckless behaviour, especially given the prominent warning signage at airports. But charging these individuals with importation and exportation seems excessive. The appearance of such charges in someone's criminal record may conjure up interpretations of serious criminality that is misleading, unjust and harmful for the individuals involved. The Canadian government remains oblivious to these social justice issues.

Diversity in the Cannabis Industry

Another social justice issue has continued to provide unfavourable press for the industry. A study from the University of Toronto (Centre on Drug Policy Evaluation 2020) surveyed 700 executives and board members at 222 Canadian cannabis producers and parent companies. Only 14% of the executives and board members were women. Only 16% were non-white.

Post-legalization Attitudes on Contentious Issues: Legal Age and Product Promotion

The Public First Survey included several opinion/attitude questions addressing respondent views on key issues. The minimum legal age for purchase and possession of cannabis was one of the most contentious issues to arise during the legalization campaign in Canada. Of a variety of ages offered for a minimum legal age in the survey, more respondents favoured twenty-one than any other age (Gibbs, Reed, and Wride 2021, 76). As discussed in Chapter 6, the health policy research and general trends in drug policy tend to support twenty-one as a minimum age. It appears that the public is more onboard with the science than was the government's expert Task Force that recommended eighteen; as well as the Canadian government that adopted it. Again, other priorities appear to have been at play.

Product promotion remains a controversial issue. The cannabis industry lobbied tirelessly and aggressively to be able to market cannabis as aggressively as alcohol is currently marketed (Aphria et al. 2017). The Cannabis Council of Canada continued to do so at the end of 2021. In it's *Not Done Yet Report Card* (2021), The Council laid out an intoxicating buffet of evidence-deficient assertions flavoured with a sprinkling of social justice platitudes.

The Council's libertarian mindset was reminiscent of the industry's 2017 pitch for near complete freedom in advertising (Aphria et al. 2017). In it's 2021 *Report Card*, The Council included a section titled "Financial Viability." The section made no mention of the industry's legacy of regulatory non-compliance, criminal activity, financial mismanagement, and the excesses of its executive compensation. Rather, it attributed the industry's financial hardships to "nanny-state over-regulation of cannabis", with specific mention of "prohibitions on promotion."

We can juxtapose the Council's report with the United Nations' 2021 call for a full ban on cannabis advertising: "A comprehensive ban on advertising, promoting and sponsoring cannabis would ensure that public health interests prevail over business interests. Such a ban would need to apply across all jurisdictions. The measures could work in a way similar to the provisions of the WHO Framework Convention on Tobacco Control" (United Nations 2021,10).

As of mid 2022, the Canadian government has not yielded to the industry on this issue. Nor has it taken the advice of health policy experts from Canada and abroad to put a full ban on advertising in place. Rather, it has chosen to place restrictions on product promotion that continue to be creatively gamed and ignored by the industry. The Public First Report noted: "Overall, the Canadian public are strongly in favour of the current restrictions around cannabis advertising." About two in five Canadians supported an outright ban (Gibbs, Reed, and Wride 2021, 76-77).

Another perspective is that although cannabis advertising is legally restricted from public visibility (e.g. no billboards), it is omnipresent in most populated areas in the form of cannabis retail storefronts. The storefronts are a form of advertising with a potentially significant impact on market expansion. Have you ever seen a billboard with a door you can walk through to make a purchase? It is also noteworthy that any underage person who is willing to misrepresent their age on a cannabis company's age-gated website, has full access to appealing cannabis branding. There should be no misunderstanding on this point. Cannabis advertising is already ubiquitous in Canada. The Cannabis Council wants more. Canadians do not.

Cannabis Legalization in Canada: The Whole World is Watching

I have a presentation titled: "Cannabis Legalization in Canada: The Whole World is Watching." Other nations that are observing Canada will need to carefully consider the disparate goals of public health protection and industry market expansion. The people of those nations should be vigilant as to how attentive are their governments to the science and to the desires of their people, versus the desires of the industry, in the legislation being forged.

There is another suggestion I make to people from other nations who tell me they are watching Canada's legalization. I advise: "Don't watch Canada, watch Québec." It is too early to know if Québec will have lower rates of cannabis related harm. However, its policies on government revenues, public health oversight, product promotion, and minimum age are certainly more aligned with public health practices known or reasonably believed to lower drug-related harms.

International observers would also do well to study the Uruguay model and to watch developments in Malta, which appear to be avoiding the establishment of a market expansionist approach. I will return to these developments shortly.

A 2022 report from the Social Market Foundation, a U.K think tank, looked at cannabis policies in Portugal, Spain, the Netherlands, Uruguay, Canada, and the U.S states of Colorado and Oregon (Shepherd 2022). The report references the Public First report cited here earlier. The two organizations are similar in their findings for Canada's legalization regime in terms of impact.

However, the Social Market Foundation was more candid in its assessment of the adverse corporate influences in commercialized cannabis regimes. The report warned: "...market-regulated models, such as in Canada, Colorado, and Oregon, raise concerns about the corporate capture of cannabis markets and the undermining of public health efforts, potentially increasing harm" (Shepherd 2022, 27). With regards to Canada, the report noted criticisms related to monopolization, corporate exploitation abroad, and investments in the cannabis trade by alcohol and tobacco companies. The report concludes: "...there are signs that Canada's legal cannabis industry may have become more commercialized than intended in the public health-first framing of the Cannabis Act, potentially hindering its policy objectives, with social justice and equity elements of the Cannabis Act now considered to have been an afterthought in the legalization process" (Shepherd 2022, 27).

In the final analysis, the Social Market Foundation report noted that of the regimes it had researched, "Uruguay's state-controlled model of regulation appears to be the most effective in reducing cannabis-related harm and demonstrating drug control" (Shepherd 2022, 6).

In June 2022, The Canadian Centre on Substance Use and Addiction issued a report providing its observations and recommendations on cannabis legalization (Canadian Centre on Substance Use and Addiction 2022). The report emphasized the growth of the legal cannabis market and the decrease in cannabis-related charges since legalization. It also raised concerns about a variety of issues such as accidental cannabis intoxication in children, increased association between cannabis use and mental health problems, advertising and promotion claims of health benefits from CBD use, and an association between outlet density and low-income residential areas. There was no mention of problems in the legal trade with product integrity, other regulatory violations, corporate crime, and the industry's disastrous fiscal performance.

Pending: Health Canada Evaluation of Legalization

The Cannabis Act holds the Canadian Government responsible for evaluating its legalization campaign at the third anniversary of legalization (October 2021). That responsibility has been assigned to Health Canada. As of June 2022, the process has not been formally announced. However, in February, Health Canada spokesperson, Tammy Jarbeau, told *Marijuana Business Daily* that preparations had begun, but declined to provide a more specific time frame (Israel 2022).

The report can make observations and perhaps even recommendations. However, government is under no obligation to make any changes. Nonetheless, as already discussed, the industry is lobbying hard for regulatory changes in its favour (Israel 2022). These are not proposals that are in the best interests of public health protection.

Industry advocates have no interest in talking about the industry's widespread misconduct, nor of the attendant high cost to taxpayers of the surveillance and adjudication of their conduct. They are also unlikely to acknowledge the highly permissive and forgiving regulatory approaches taken by Health Canada and the Attorney General.

My concern is that the government's evaluation will not address the self-imposed failures of this industry. The worse scenario would be if the government gives in to the industry's lobbying. I am also concerned that this evaluation will be little more than performative and will provide media camouflage for a more serious play simmering quietly in the background. A section of the Canadian Government's 2022 Budget was titled "Engaging the Cannabis Sector." It reads: "As a relatively new sector of the Canada economy, it is important that the federal government and all stakeholders have a clear understanding of the challenges and opportunities that are facing Canada's legal cannabis sector. Budget 2022 proposes launching a new cannabis strategy table that will support an ongoing dialogue with businesses and stakeholders in the cannabis sector. The Department of Innovation, Science and Economic Development will lead this, and will provide an opportunity for the government to hear from industry leaders and identify ways to work together to grow the legal cannabis sector in Canada" (Canada 2022, 80).

I think it unlikely that stakeholders other than industry leaders will include individuals who will ensure that The Department of Innovation, Science and Economic Development strategy table will understand the importance of public health protection in the face of such a strong commitment to "grow the legal cannabis sector" (market expansion). The strategy table also needs to be fully apprised of how the cannabis industry has, so profoundly, been the architect of its own fiscal calamity.

Earlier in this book, I described how Liberal Party elites had invested heavily in the cannabis industry. If they are still invested, their stocks are now seriously diminished in value, and that can only be rectified by ushering in a successful resurrection for the industry. We should expect that this aspiration will determine much of what comes out of the strategy table.

The Centre for Addiction and Mental Health's Continued Support for Commercial Legalization

When the Liberal Party of Canada was rolling out its cannabis legalization campaign, The Centre for Addiction and Mental Health (CAMH) was keen to help with its *Cannabis Policy Framework* (Centre for Addiction and Mental Health 2014). (See Chapter 6.) Now, as the Liberal government will attempt to account for itself, it appears that CAMH has once again stepped up. In April 2022, CAMH released a commentary, *Regulating the Legal Cannabis Market: How is Canada Doing?* (Crépault and Jesseman 2022). The report asserts that the Canadian government has chosen a public health approach over a commercial one and finds that: "Canada's regulations are optimal in the area of advertising, marketing and promotion, adequate with respect to minimum age as well as tax and price, while some provinces and territories—especially those with private retail systems—have work to do around controlling availability" (Crépault and Jesseman 2022).

I have not sufficiently investigated the matter of tax and price and so I will not comment on that topic. I agree with the suggestion that retail systems (which are the responsibility of provincial governments, not the federal Liberal government) remain a liability. However, to suggest that product promotion is "optimal", and that minimum age is "adequate" appears to be at odds with the much more comprehensive picture that I presented in Chapter 6. How could this be? The answer appears to reside in the criteria used in the CAMH report to define success. It used fidelity between what the Task Force recommended and what the Cannabis Act enacted. In other words, the conclusions are based upon an assumption that the Task Force recommendations were based upon a public health approach. In Chapter 6, I explored the details of how the Task Force *Final Report* fell short of that standard.

I have already acknowledged the fidelity between Task Force recommendations and Cannabis Act provisions. But a demonstration of that fidelity does not establish that Canada has adopted a public health approach. This book, most notably Chapters 6 and 7, makes a comprehensive case that a public health approach was compromised for industry market expansion, and remains so. One of the major lessons, even with good regulations and surveillance in place, is that failure has arisen from frequent non-compliance and even criminal conduct on the part of cannabis companies. Except for the most extreme cases, the misconduct has occurred without meaningful consequences that prompt a deterrence effect. CAMH's report makes no acknowledgement of this major failing. This is particularly surprising given that this problem resides, not just within cannabis policy, but within drug policy in general—whether related to cannabis, alcohol, tobacco, or pharmaceutical. It is a difficult problem to miss. This book has provided numerous examples.

Apart from agreement on the unsatisfactory retail environments across Canada, I would agree with another assertion of the CAMH report.

The cannabis industry is attempting to reduce the public health protections that are currently in place, and this must be resisted.

Given the broader scope of information available, CAMH's 2022 report has fallen short of a compelling exoneration of private sector legalization in Canada —as did its 2014 Framework as a justification for private sector legalization.

THE INTERNATIONAL WAVE OF CANNABIS LEGALIZATION

A wave of interest in cannabis law reform is sweeping across much of the world. With various forms of decriminalization in place in many jurisdictions, there has been an increasing shift towards interest in legalization for both therapeutic and recreational use. Global status is provided on a regularly updated page on Wikipedia (2022) which cites jurisdictional sources for reference. Given the dynamic nature and definitional variation of cannabis law reform initiatives, these counts should be regarded as approximate, and certain to change. As of March 2022, there were forty-five countries that had legalized cannabis for therapeutic use. A few more had legalized only the use of cannabis-derived pharmaceuticals.

The Canadian cannabis industry has not just been passively sitting back waiting for foreign governments to pass legislation. They have become increasingly active internationally with established footholds in Europe, Asia, Africa, and Latin America. As early as 2019, Canopy was already in fourteen countries, Aphria in ten, and Aurora in twenty-five. Canadian cannabis companies have been criticized for their practices in some of these jurisdictions which include:

- *lobbying for supportive national legislation*

- *encouraging criminalization of traditional growers*

- *acquiring remote locations for establishing large plantation-style operations*

- *appropriating water supplies without local consultation*

- *exploitation of raw materials and cheap labour without a fair-trade framework for proportional sharing of profits*
        (Paley 2019).

Paley points out that such exploitative and unfettered colonialism is strikingly familiar to those who have monitored the exploitative conduct of the Canadian mining industry abroad—another perilous playbook adopted by the cannabis industry.

A countervailing force against the ambitions of Canada's cannabis companies is that many countries have been more cautious when it comes to legalization for recreational use, and even more so for commercial legalization. Uruguay and Canada remain the outliers —being the only countries (as of June 2022) that have formally and fully legalized sales for recreational use. Yet, the two remain vastly different, with Uruguay's commercialization being much more restrained than Canada's.

Reforms in Spain, Mexico, South Africa, and Georgia also differ from Uruguay and Canada. These jurisdictions have "legalized" possession in a variety of ways which do not fit the strict commercial model. It would be more accurate to say that these nations tolerate the possession of cannabis —emulating the approach taken in Washington, D.C. What they all have in common is that they have not legalized commercial sales of cannabis for recreational use.

Switzerland appears to be getting closer to commercial legalization. In September 2020, the country amended its laws to allow pilot trials for "the dispensing of Cannabis for non-medicinal purposes" with an intent to use experience from the trials to move into full legalization in the future. The new laws came into effect in May 2021 (Federal Office of Public Health 2021).

Major legislative efforts at recreational legalization have also been occurring in several other nations. As of the end of 2021, France (Pascual 2021), Israel (Times of Israel 2020), Luxembourg (Arellano 2021), and Malta (Berger 2021) were in various stages of legislative process that intend to legalize cannabis for recreational use—using a variety of models. The model chosen by Malta is particularly interesting. It allows personal possession of cannabis leaf/flower of up to seven grams, and up to fifty grams in one's home. Possession of larger amounts are subject to confiscation and fines. Small scale personal cultivation is also allowed. For-profit production and retail businesses are not allowed. However not-for-profit cannabis social clubs can be licensed to sell to adult members only (BBC News 2021).

New Zealand held a non-binding referendum on cannabis legalization for recreational use for September 2020. A frequent commentator on the topic was Benedikt Fischer at Auckland University's Faculty of Medical and Health Sciences. While with The Centre for Addiction and Mental Health in Canada, Dr. Fischer was a principal architect of CAMH's *Cannabis Policy Framework*. Fischer continues to warn about the potential for over-commercialization, but also remains on message with an otherwise generous anointing of a licensed, regulated commercial trade, and a harsh, hyperbolic critique of the unlicensed cannabis trade. The proposed legislation for New Zealand had some interesting features including the full ban on product promotion that CAMH and other health authorities had advocated for Canada. New Zealand's proposal would have production and retail residing with private sector licensees, but no single licensee could hold more than 20% of a total cap imposed upon production. It is noteworthy that the 20% limit does not restrict market expansion, only monopolization. While the proposed New Zealand bill appeared to have a somewhat less harsh demeanour towards the unlicensed cannabis trade, it still retained convictions and prison sentences for some offences. Ultimately, New Zealand's referendum in support of commercial recreational legalization was narrowly defeated, having received 48.4% support (Roy 2020). The reform movement for legal recreational cannabis use has since stalled in the country.

In late October 2020, the Green Party in Germany tabled a motion for legalization of cannabis for recreational use. Despite optimism from Canadian cannabis executives in search of another large foreign market, the motion was firmly defeated (Pascual 2020). However, by mid 2022, the German government announced that it was moving forward with legalization of cannabis sales and would be holding consultations to shape the legislation (AP News 2022). Legalized cannabis for therapeutic use remains in place in both New Zealand and Germany.

In an unfortunate irony, the United Kingdom, which has no significant legislative process underway to reform its cannabis laws, possesses one of the world's most prolific drug policy advocacy organizations. The UK's Transform Drug Policy Foundation continues to advocate tirelessly for cannabis law reform. In April 2022, Transform released the third edition of its *How to Regulate Cannabis: A Practical Guide*. It is an important resource for jurisdictions considering cannabis law reform.

There also remains the legendary case of the Netherlands where discretionary enforcement allows the sale and possession of cannabis for recreational use when purchased in designated coffee shops. What has always struck me as quaint about these cafes is that the cannabis comes in the back door as blatantly illegal product and goes out the front door as legally tolerated product. The cafes have effectively served as contraband laundering operations. However, legislative maneuvers are now afoot via a Closed Coffeeshop Circuit Act, that would provide for select (currently illegal) commercial cannabis growers to be "strictly regulated" to legally supply the coffee shops (Transform Drug Policy Foundation 2021).

The status of legalization becomes more complex when we consider the United States. While there continues to be increased activity at the federal level to legalize cannabis for recreational use, it remains illegal federally. Cannabis law reforms in the US have been accordingly confined to subnational jurisdictions which have legalized possession and (except for the District of Columbia) adopted legalized sales as in Uruguay and Canada. As of March 2022, the count for recreational legalization had risen to eighteen states, two territories and The District of Columbia (Wikipedia 2022). Some states have only decriminalized possession, while others still fully prohibit possession of cannabis in any amount for any reason. Within each of those scenarios there are nuanced differences to consider. The US process also remains very dynamic with the prospects of federal legalization waxing and waning unpredictably in a climate of political intrigue. At the federal level, the United States passed legislation for legalization in the House of Representatives for a second time in April 2022 (Smith 2022). The federal legislation also follows the commercial legalization template. As covered in Chapter 9, there is concern that federal legalization could increase the monopolization of the trade. However, widespread anti-legalization sentiment in the Senate makes its passage there a formidable challenge.

Several other nations pursuing cannabis legalization appear to be leaning towards adopting the commercial model that has become the favourite in North America. This may be a strategic error. The failure of legalization campaigns, as seen in New Zealand and Germany, are often attributed by activists to cannabis related stigma among the population of these nations. This may very well be part of the resistance, but there appears to be more to it. During a failed 2015 ballot initiative in Ohio, polls showed strong support for ending prohibition, but opposition to control of the trade resting with a few wealthy landowners (Lopez 2015).

Adams, Rychert, and Wilkins (2021) found that strategies used by the nascent cannabis industry to influence government policy and public opinion were strikingly like those used by the alcohol, tobacco, and gambling industries. Earlier chapters of this book demonstrated that the business practices of the cannabis industry are likely to follow suit. It is not just about stigma. People are wise to be concerned about the creation of a Big Cannabis.

Non-commercial models may be much more appealing to citizens of nations that are uncomfortable with creating large profit driven cannabis industries. Policy analysts, activists, and legislators of these nations would do well to consider approaches that may have more appeal to the citizenry and be less likely to spark resistance.

IAQ (Infrequently Asked Questions) about Cannabis Legalization

Before moving away from a concentration on cannabis policy to a broader terrain of drug policy, I would like to add a few more perspectives on key cannabis issues. These are issues that should be considered in any country addressing cannabis law reform.

Is Commercial Legalization the Answer to Criminalization?

As detailed in Chapter 5, the problems with legalization seen in Canada also have a long-established history among the early adopters of legalization at the state level in the United States. The problems continue both sides of the border. Relatively little of that story is heard in the current discussions on legalization.

Given near world-wide attention to its legalization sojourn, it is important that Canada gets it right. If Canada did not get it right, we must be entirely candid and clear in describing the details as provided in Chapters 5 through 8. These include:

- *the misleading campaign of the Liberal Party to generate support for legalization*

- *conflicts of interest in the consultation and study phase*
- *cronyism within government-industry relations*
- *prioritization of industry revenue over public health protection*
- *poor product quality from mass production factories*
- *use of illegal pesticides and other forms of contamination*
- *incorrectly labelled product*
- *industry misleading government inspectors*
- *securities fraud*
- *product promotion violations*
- *illegal cultivation (by licensed companies)*
- *collaboration with the unlicensed trade and with organized crime*
- *lack of meaningful consequences for regulatory non-compliance and criminal activity*
- *lack of business acumen among some of the largest cannabis companies*
- *increasing monopolization through mergers and acquisitions*
- *increasing control of Canadian cannabis businesses by foreign alcohol, tobacco, and pharmaceutical companies*
- *insolvencies, plant closings, layoffs*
- *excessive compensation packages for company executives*
- *questionably justified access of funds intended for victims of the COVID-19 pandemic*
- *prohibitive barriers to small craft growers*
- *lack of diversity and equity in the industry*
- *continued criminalization of cannabis users for petty offences*
- *no program for expungement of past convictions*
- *exploitation of the people and natural resources of foreign markets.*

And of course, all this occurred within a permissive regulatory environment maintained by the Canadian Government. With the whole world watching, and potentially a lot at stake, Canadian analysts and foreign observers share a critical responsibility. Countries considering commercial legalization should not go into it even partially naïve. Their citizens deserve the full story, unequivocally told. Commercial legalization should not be adopted in a short-sighted, impassioned attempt to end criminalization.

Will the Unlicensed Cannabis Trade Disappear?

The trajectory of cannabis law reform in Canada, from prohibition through full legalization had five roughly sequential, partially overlapping stages:

- *prohibition and criminalization*

- *legal self-supply for therapeutic use*

- *commercial legalization for therapeutic use with a mail order supply system*

- *emergence of "dispensaries" - some properly licensed with medical supervision, some of uncertain legality (but tolerated), and some clearly illegal (less tolerated).*

- *commercial legalization for recreational use; legal retail stores open.*

The unlicensed trade in cannabis maintained a persistent co-existence through all these stages and continues to thrive globally. In Canada, after 21 years of legalization for therapeutic use, and four years for recreational use, the unlicensed trade is declining, but slowly. Its demise is not imminent.

Can Social Equity Programs Be Expanded?

An interesting aspect of the cannabis legalization narrative is the emergence of advocacy for social equity programs. While the topic has received a fair bit of attention in Canada, it has been a particularly salient topic of discussions and a component of legislation in subnational jurisdictions in the United States.

The concept of social equity, and its foundation, is a laudable one. It is widely recognized that some communities have been, and continue to be, victimized more than others in the ongoing war on drugs. People of colour and other marginalized populations in America have had to navigate negative stereotypes as well as systemic racism and intolerance. These forces constrain choices in life and possibilities for career development (Bourgeois 1995; Lagalisse 2018).

Social equity initiatives intend to compensate for these wrongs by providing victims in these communities with business opportunities subsidized with the actual or anticipated cannabis-related tax revenues received by government. Some jurisdictions, such as Oakland, California, have provided priority licensing for cannabis businesses to individuals with cannabis-related charges.

But why shouldn't all social equity initiatives provide a wider range of opportunities that extend beyond entering the cannabis industry? There is simply no reason to assume that someone who had a conviction involving cannabis, or any drug, would necessarily be interested in starting a cannabis-related business. Why not help the person start any type of legal viable business? The programs could also cover costs related to other enablers of achieving a better livelihood—such as tuition support for career training, housing or legal assistance, debt payment, childcare, or recreational programs for children and adults. With so many dire social/economic needs in communities ravaged by limited opportunity and exacerbated by the war on drugs, why would any community choose to focus only on providing help with starting a cannabis business? The narrow scope of many social equity programs tied to cannabis business opportunities leads me to wonder if this is as much about cannabis fetishism as it is about social equity. And that may not be the worst of it.

There is a potential peril that could arise from a social equity program that focused only on starting cannabis businesses. The benefits may be fleeting with unintended consequences. Imagine a scenario in which a small, successful cannabis company was launched with help from social equity subsidization. Then consider the wave of acquisitions of small cannabis companies by large ones that is already rampant in North America. Imagine that small business owner being offered more money for her company than she had ever imagined possessing. Is she likely to resist? Is it reasonable to expect her to? Of course, allowing her company to become an acquisition-edible for Big Cannabis is her choice to make. And the acquisition will generously compensate her for the harm endured from any drug criminalization she previously experienced. But what is the ultimate community justice impact of the social equity program in this highly likely scenario? Essentially, the publicly funded program subsidized the start-up costs for an eventual corporate takeover. There is a real danger that cannabis-focused social equity programs will ultimately be the alluring bait on the hook of corporate capture.

Might it be better to implement a broad menu of social equity opportunities that does not include subsidization for starting a cannabis business? Such questions tend not to surface in social equity discussions arising from cannabis legalization campaigns. Social equity, as a movement for justice, should be expanded in its conceptual scope.

How Effective is Cannabis as Medicine?

Before moving from cannabis to law reform for other psychedelic drugs, I want to make some comments about legalization of cannabis for therapeutic use. The case for law reform related to psychedelics is beginning with a case for therapeutic use, but with clear plans emerging for a transition to recreational use. This is very much like the trajectory of the legalization of cannabis.

For decades, there has been no shortage of personal testimonials from Canadians claiming therapeutic benefits from the use of cannabis and its derivatives. The benefits in some cases border on the miraculous. There are licensed health care practitioners who provide aggregate data on patients who report benefits from cannabis. Such testimonials played the key role in convincing the Supreme Court of Canada that cannabis is medicine, and people should have access to it. It is difficult to imagine someone disagreeing with the principle that people should have access to medicine. But the critical question is: was cannabis well-established as effective medicine in the year 2000?

Personal testimonials played a key role because there was little clinical trial evidence to consider at the time. Clinical trials are the long-established gold standard for evaluating the effectiveness of a medicine. A pharmaceutical company would not have been allowed to bring a new medicine to market with the dearth of clinical trial data available at the time for cannabis.

Two decades after the Supreme Court made its ruling, we now have some moderately strong clinical trial evidence that demonstrates that some trial participants report some therapeutic benefits for some conditions, some of the time. However, the power of clinical trials is revealed as these same studies also show that some subjects report therapeutic benefits when they unknowingly receive a placebo. There are also participants who report no or negligible benefits. And some report that their conditions get worse. Some report unpleasant side effects. Results for a single condition vary, sometimes dramatically, from patient to patient and study to study. The results of many studies can be combined into a meta-analysis to create a forest for the trees perspective. In these cases, the authors of several meta-analyses have been consistent in their conclusions that practitioners should exercise caution in their recommendations of cannabis as medicine (Whiting et al. 2015; Goldenberg et al. 2017; Stockings et al. 2018; Hill et al. 2019; Wang et al. 2019). A team of researchers at the University of Alberta, Canada, investigated cannabis as medicine by conducting a systematic review of systematic reviews. (Yes, there is such a thing). It came to the same conclusion —that caution is warranted (Allan et al. 2018).

Health Canada remains cautious in its formal actions and declarations concerning cannabis as medicine. While a synthetic THC product and a cannabis extract product have been assigned Drug Identification Numbers (DINs), cannabis flower (the most popular, and most frequently authorized product for therapeutic use) has not. As of June 2022, Health Canada's website still carried the following disclaimer:

> *Cannabis is not an approved therapeutic product and the*
> *provision of this information should not be interpreted as an*
> *endorsement of the use of cannabis for therapeutic purposes,*
> *or of marijuana generally, by Health Canada. (Canada 2016)*

Given the tenuous evidence base when cannabis was approved in Canada in 2000, one might expect the government to have made immediate arrangements for establishing a substantial funding stream for research to support this bold move. Two decades later, substantial research funding was only beginning to become available. Researchers and professional practitioners were still lamenting a lack of evidence to guide therapeutic use by their patients (Hill 2019; Boseley 2019). Patients should have a right to their medicine. They should also have the right to confidence that their practitioner is acting with the best possible evidence. In 2021, a petition to Health Canada launched by cannabis investigators argued that the process of obtaining a license to conduct cannabis research was stifling much needed clinical knowledge (Webster 2021). I was happy to sign on to that petition.

Part of the policy challenge arising from the approval of cannabis as medicine, and apparently for conducting research as well, may lie with the motivation for policy reform. As of March 2022 in the United States, cannabis had been approved as medicine in thirty-seven states, four territories, and the District of Columbia (Wikipedia 2022). This wave of reform may have been motivated at least as much by government accommodation of the pursuit of private revenue as by the provision of therapeutic benefit. A US website, Marijuana Doctors, claims to be "The #1 Medical Marijuana Platform." In August of 2021, the site listed 391 conditions that had been approved for treatment with cannabis across US states (Marijuana Doctors 2019). The last condition on the list was "writer's cramp."

Anyone who has ever toiled in a laboratory to accumulate convincing evidence for an effective treatment of even a single health condition will appreciate how unlikely it is that a single drug would be effective for treating so many conditions. Something seems awry.

I want to complete this discussion with a few important points. The first is that the therapeutic cannabis enterprise has gone awry with hyperpromotion that attracts business with fantastic therapeutic claims and often requires patients to pay high prices for cannabis therapy. Not everyone has sufficient disposable income or health insurance subsidization to cover the costs, so there is a built-in inequality in affordable access. Just as people who are suffering should not be disadvantaged by oppressive laws in seeking relief, neither should their suffering be exploited by over-zealous businesses charging high prices for their products.

Secondly, high quality clinical trials on the potential benefits of cannabis therapy should be funded with a reasonable licensing process. Studies should not be funded directly by cannabis companies, but by government. Government may wish to collect increased levies from the industry to support this research, but it must always position itself in an intermediary role, drawing upon independent scientific review for what research proposals should be funded. Government should also ensure that all trial results are made available to the scientific community. The information should also be easily accessible, and comprehensible, to anyone else who is interested.

Finally, any person who finds therapeutic relief from cannabis, should not be disadvantaged in their access to it. For that person, whether the benefit is wholly or partially due to a placebo effect may not be the most important consideration. One of my health care providers once told me that there is nothing wrong with a placebo effect. I replied that there would be as soon as my insurance coverage reached the maximum.

Cannabis appears to have therapeutic value for some people. But it is not a panacea. The commercial hype far exceeds the science. We need to reduce the hype and increase the science.

Some People Are Harmed by their Use of Cannabis;
Will Legalization Make It Worse?

The indispensable context is that most cannabis users engage with the drug in a responsible manner with no serious harm to their lives. That is also the case for alcohol. However, cannabis use can be extremely disruptive to the lives of a portion of those who use it. That is also the case for alcohol.

Folklore has it that cannabis does not pose the same level of risk for personal harm as does alcohol or tobacco, and therefore presents no threat to pose the levels of societal harm we see with those recreational drugs. Yes, and no. Before the legalization of cannabis for recreational use, cannabis had nowhere near the impact of alcohol and tobacco on the number of hospitalizations and deaths, as seen in the CSUCH data sets presented in Chapter 1 (Canadian Substance Use Costs and Harms Scientific Working Group, n.d). However, we also see that in any given year, before and after legalization, Ontario alone has approximately 20,000 people in addiction treatment programs for cannabis problems (Centre for Addiction and Mental Health 2015; 2017; 2021a). A less certain estimate from Fischer et al. (2016) placed the figure between 76,000 and 95,000 for all of Canada.

While most cannabis use is not associated with serious harm, frequent users of cannabis are more likely to have negative impacts on their lives. In a 2016 publication in National Affairs, Caulkins (2016) summarized the evidence that demonstrates that among frequent users, cannabis has at least as high a potential as alcohol for producing dependence and for disruption of one's life. Caulkins does not argue against cannabis legalization. He sees it as inevitable and asserts that the role of academics is to ensure that emerging policy is based on evidence and not folklore and industry expansionism.

Another important point is that we must be careful of comparisons that cherry pick indicators of harm that serve a foregone conclusion. Too many arguments in support of cannabis consumption focus on low death counts relative to alcohol and tobacco. While the claim is justified, deaths are only one measure of a drug's negative impact on society.

Even arguments based upon data sets portraying dependence have their limits. While some drugs may have a greater potential for creating dependence, dependence is also only one type of drug problem. Much harmful drug use is not so much the result of compulsive use, but rather of occasional reckless use. To illustrate, one study found that among 327 alcohol-impaired drivers, only 48% of the drivers fulfilled the criteria for alcohol dependence (Brinkman et al. 2002). Apparently, the remaining 52% did not have an alcohol dependence problem; they had a decision-making problem.

Ultimately, whether one drug is more harmful than another is not the most critical issue. The important thing to appreciate is that the evidence shows that indiscriminate use of both alcohol and cannabis has significant potential for harm. To take this further, any drug can be used safely, and any drug can be used in a manner that is harmful.

Drug problems are not just about the intrinsic properties of drugs. Their misuse has at least as much to do with how we think about drugs. Anyone who understands a placebo effect can also understand this important point. In Chapter 2, we learned that there is a well-established body of evidence that demonstrates how we think about a drug can have a dramatic effect on how we use and misuse it.

Public health academics warn about the promotion of drug products under a legal regime. Adults are not just allowed to use legal drug products like alcohol and tobacco; we have also been encouraged to use them, and since well before we became adults.

In this line of thinking, the world may have more to fear from an expansionist cannabis industry than it does from cannabis itself. The data are clear that heavy alcohol users consume most of the alcohol sold by the alcohol industry. In Canada, about 20% of the drinkers account for about 70% of the alcohol consumption (Thomas 2012). The same phenomenon appears to be happening with cannabis. Caulkins (2017) has reported that in the United States, 80% of marijuana is consumed by daily and near-daily users. The Canadian Tobacco, Alcohol and Drugs Survey (CTADS) showed that of those who had used cannabis in the past 3 months, 32% reported daily or almost daily use (Canada 2021c). Callaghan et al. (2019) have shown that the upper 10% of users in Canada accounted for approximately two-thirds of all cannabis consumed. As presented in Chapter 8, an Ontario Auditor General report also noted that heavy consumers comprise 40% of cannabis users and are responsible for 90% of total provincial spending on cannabis products (Office of the Auditor General of Ontario 2021, 1).

Drug industries have a fiscal interest in encouraging frequent and/or heavy use of their products. And that is where the harm lies. And that is where public health authorities must assume a role—not in prohibition, but in prevention and in risk and harm reduction.

People often ask if cannabis use will become a major drug problem following legalization. Given excessive amounts of consumption among the most frequent users and the number of people seeking help for problems related to their use of cannabis, it obviously already is a major problem. The infrequently asked and more relevant question is whether it will become a worse problem following legalization.

The short answer is that it is too early to tell. Any clinician with experience in helping people with drug problems knows that the problems do not typically develop quickly. Drug problems in most people follow a trajectory that has a gestation period—typically years. We should expect a parallel process to happen at a societal level. Even once problems begin to develop among a larger segment of the population, there may be a delay in detection. Prevailing levels of stigma delay open discussion and help-seeking. Accessing addiction treatment services remains difficult. For this reason, anonymously conducted general population surveys that ask about harms associated with cannabis use are important for earlier detection of an increasing societal cannabis problem.

321

Worldwide cannabis law reform has marked one of the most significant and controversial drug policy developments of the 21st century. It has potential to end the criminalization of the use of cannabis. But it may also represent the thin edge of the wedge for a different kind of threat to public health and safety. These two possibilities are not mutually exclusive. Much suffering could be averted with an end to criminalization of drug use. But new drug-related pandemics may emerge from commercial enterprises that assign priority to market expansion and maximizing revenue. We need government to play a strong role to enable the former and prevent the latter.

I assign the final word on this matter to Jonathon Caulkins, professor of public policy at Carnegie Mellon University in the US and one of the world's foremost drug policy academics. I already used this quote in Chapter 8, but its pertinence warrants repetition: "We are going, in the United States, to legalize marijuana nationally, and roughly along the alcohol model, and there's a good chance that people in 25 to 40 years will look back and shake their heads and ask, what were you thinking? Why did you think it was a good idea to create an industry of titans to market this drug?" (Fernholz 2016)

Dr. Caulkins makes two important points. First, it may be decades before we really understand the impact of these natural experiments in drug policy. Secondly, we have good reason to believe that commercial legalization may not turn out so well.

Closing: Broad Policy Recommendations for Cannabis Law Reform

In my 2017 report, *Cannabis Law Reform in Canada: Pretense & Perils* (DeVillaer 2017), I included recommendations which I had already passed on to the Canadian Government's Task Force. The essence of those recommendations remains unchanged five years later. But time has allowed some improved nuance. In 2022, my recommendations for any government considering cannabis law reform are as follows.

All approaches to cannabis law reform should take a hybrid approach. It should begin promptly with full decriminalization for possession of cannabis, regardless of its source. It should then patiently and thoughtfully implement a not-for-profit model for a licensed supply.

All individuals with pre-legalization criminal charges for simple possession should have their cannabis-related records fully expunged as part of a reconciliation initiative. They have already suffered too much from the foolishness of criminalization.

Enforcement efforts aimed at the unlicensed cannabis trade should focus only on players that are engaged in violent or exploitative activities or are selling contaminated or misrepresented product. Penalties issued should be proportional to the seriousness of the offence. For unlicensed cannabis trade activity that is outside the above circumstances, penalties beyond product confiscation should be considered only when warranted by appropriate circumstances. Another approach to consider is to find ways to bring unlicensed traders within a licensed regime. At the time of legalization in Canada, many in the unlicensed trade said they would prefer to be part of the legal trade but were systemically denied access. Of course, these players would have to realize that, in the legal system, they would be subject to laws and regulations. Violations could result in the loss of their licenses.

In the case of a commercial legalization regime already in place, enforcement should be mostly concerned with ensuring compliance of the legal supply with regulations and the law. Penalties for repeated regulatory non-compliance must be meted out with near-zero tolerance and include fines large enough to encourage compliance. License suspension and revocation should be considered as warranted. The identities of chronically non-compliant companies should be public information. License suspensions should become more common for more serious cases of repeated non-compliance. Criminal activity within the licensed industry should be met with mandatory revocation of licenses. To provide effective deterrence for executives engaged in criminal activity there should be mandatory confiscation of salary, bonuses, and severances earned at the time of illegal activity. Prison terms of reasonable length should also be considered, as appropriate. I make these harsher recommendations not out of a desire for inhumane punishment, but as a hopeful means of preventative deterrence. The guaranteed get-out-of-jail-free card must disappear from the cannabis industry, as it should from the larger corporate world.

LEGALIZATION OF PSYCHEDELIC DRUGS: DÉJÀ VU ALL OVER AGAIN, AGAIN?

The second wave of drug policy reform is the increasing groundswell of calls in many jurisdictions for legislative reform pertaining to psychedelic drugs, most notably psilocybin (magic mushrooms), but also including drugs such as LSD (acid) and MDMA (ecstasy).

In Chapter 2, I referred to the practice of toad licking in the 1990s to get hallucinogenic effects from a substance, bufotenin (5-HO-DMT), secreted by the Bufo, or Cane, toad. A quarter century later, the bufotenin/DMT (dimethyltryptamine) story lives on. An academic psychiatrist has authored a book called "DMT The Spirit Molecule: A Doctor's Revolutionary Research into the Biology of Near-Death and Mystical Experience" (Strassman 2001). His research used pharmaceutical grade DMT. More recently, a lab has produced a synthetic version of the drug, 5-MeO-DMT. The article speculated on benefits for both human and toad populations (Bauer 2021).

Toad-licking, near-death, and mystical experience aside, the continued interest in psychedelics should be taken seriously. These substances are not only the subject of increasing calls for decriminalization, but also of increasing research on their therapeutic applications. We are also seeing increasing development of legal enterprises with both therapeutic and recreational ambitions. The policy reform trajectory for the broader group of psychedelics most notably psilocybin, appears to be unfolding in a manner that is reminiscent of the one for cannabis. Calls for the commercial legalization of psychedelics (or for any currently illegal drug) add significant import to the story about cannabis commercialization within the context of our long-established commercial drug industries.

Research Evidence

The case for a therapeutic benefit from psychedelics, as in the early days of advocacy for therapeutic use of cannabis, has been based mostly upon personal testimonials and studies without a control group. Thus, the potential for reported benefits being accounted for by placebo effect looms large. A few clinical trials with modestly promising results have begun to emerge, but most were compromised by small numbers of participants (Griffiths 2016).

However, by the autumn of 2021, the case of therapeutic value of psychedelics was beginning to look more promising. A meta-analysis that combined the results from nine randomized, placebo-controlled trials found that psychedelics worked better than placebo across four mental health conditions—post-traumatic stress disorder, anxiety/depression associated with a life-threatening illness, unipolar depression, and social anxiety among autistic adults. The size of the effect was found to be larger than that typically reported for interventions with psychotherapy or other drugs (Luoma et al. 2020).

However, a subsequent study claiming to be the largest placebo-controlled trial on psychedelic micro-dosing involved 191 participants who completed measures on cognitive function, affect, mental well-being, anxiety, and life satisfaction, among others. The micro-dosing group did not show greater improvement than the placebo group. The authors concluded that "anecdotal benefits of micro dosing can be explained by the placebo effect" (Szigeti et al. 2021).

At this point, advocates for the use of psychedelics in clinical practice should be cautious regarding their recommendations to policy makers, as should practitioners in their recommendations to patients. But hopefully, research with clinical trials will continue.

Therapeutic Use: Emerging Policy and Research Capacity

In the United States, psilocybin is still a restricted substance under federal law. However, given sustained enthusiasm for discovering therapeutic benefits from psilocybin (Farah 2019), MDMA and LSD (Rosner 2020), the US Food and Drug Administration has granted "breakthrough therapy" designation for psychedelics to facilitate prompt approvals for research (Peesker 2019). More clinical trials are in progress, testing the therapeutic value of LSD for a diverse group of conditions including Alzheimer's disease, alcohol dependence, and adult ADHD (Haridy 2020).

Johns Hopkins University's Center for Psychedelic and Consciousness Research became the US's first such research center. The Center plans to study the effectiveness of psilocybin for opioid addiction, Alzheimer's disease, post-traumatic stress disorder (PTSD), Lyme disease, anorexia nervosa, and alcohol use in people with major depression. The intent is to "create precision medicine treatments tailored to the specific needs of individual patients" (The Johns Hopkins Center for Psychedelic and Consciousness Research 2021). Johns Hopkins obviously brings considerable academic credibility to the emerging psychedelics campaign. In October 2021, Johns Hopkins announced that it had received funding from the National Institutes of Health (NIH) to study the effectiveness of psilocybin as a nicotine dependence treatment. This is the first NIH grant awarded in more than a half century to investigate therapeutic benefits of an established psychedelic (Johns Hopkins Medicine Newsroom 2021).

In the political world, Andrew Yang, Democratic Party hopeful for the 2020 nomination for President of the United States, expressed his support on social media for the exploration of therapeutic uses for psilocybin (Yang 2019).

Change is also occurring in the policy world. Cities in the US decriminalizing possession of psychedelics include Denver, Washington, D.C, Ann Arbour, Seattle, Oakland, Santa Cruz, and four municipalities in the state of Massachusetts: Easthampton, Northampton, Somerville, and Cambridge (Jaeger 2021). Oregon became the first state to legalize psilocybin for medical use. Personal use cultivation has been legalized in the State of New Mexico (Bogot, Horn, and Kwan 2021; Prieb 2021).

In Canada, psilocybin is still a restricted substance under the Controlled Drugs and Substances Act. Thus far, formal campaigns are restricted to securing exemptions from the Act to use psilocybin for therapeutic purposes where there are no viable or currently allowed alternatives. On August 4, 2020, four Canadians were granted exemptions by Canadian Minister of Health, Patti Hajdu. This allowed the inclusion of psilocybin as part of psychotherapy for the treatment of psychological distress associated with a cancer diagnosis and anxiety in an end-of-life situation (TheraPsil 2020). By late 2020, sixteen health care practitioners had been granted exemptions by Health Canada for the experimental use of psilocybin for patient care (Dubinski 2020). The granting of such exemptions continued in 2021. This well-intentioned, humane gesture on the part of the Minister served as a starting pistol for additional players to engage with an expanded set of ambitions.

A company called Numinus Wellness Inc. describes itself as a wellness company that aspires to use psychedelic therapies as treatments to enhance mental health. It has received permission from Health Canada to test MDMA for its effectiveness in the treatment of Post Traumatic Stress Disorder (PTSD). Numinus will collaborate on the study with MAPS Public Benefit Corporation which is a subsidiary of the Multidisciplinary Association for Psychedelic Studies (McIntyre 2021). Numinus was also the first Canadian company to complete a legal harvest of psilocybe mushrooms (Numinus Wellness Inc 2021).

ATMA Journey Centers, has been approved by Health Canada to conduct legal psychedelic-assisted therapy for patients in palliative care.

PsiloTec Health Solutions is a psychedelic drug development company that wants to provide an alternative for those struggling with a variety of mental health issues who do not find relief with currently available therapies. The company is acquiring a 23,000 square-foot facility to produce psilocybin (Kindleman 2021).

Canadian academia has also joined in with the establishment of a research chair of a program to study psychedelics at the University of Calgary (Graveland 2021). University Health Network in Toronto has received private funding to establish a Psychedelic Psychotherapy Research Centre (UHN 2021).

In May 2022, a conference was held titled "From Research to Reality: Global Summit on Psychedelic-Assisted Therapies and Medicine." Sponsors and planners included the Centre for Addiction and Mental Health (CAMH) the Canadian Centre on Substance Use and Addiction (CCSA) and the Mental Health Commission of Canada (MHCC).

Reminiscent of the early days of cannabis for therapeutic use, illegal storefront dispensaries for psilocybin are now popping up like mushrooms in major population centres in Canada and have also established an online presence. For the time being, most enforcement agencies are standing down.

Expansion to Recreational Use: Many Shades of Many Colours

Anticipation of broader liberalization for several psychedelics is clearly apparent. Alex Blumenstein, CEO of Leaf Forward, a Canadian cannabis investment and consulting business, tells of "some [therapeutically oriented] companies building 'psychedelics-adjacent' brands that appear poised to move into a recreational market if it became legal..." (Peesker 2019).

The increasing liberalization of attitudes regarding psychedelics can also be seen in social movements and popular culture. World Psychedelics Day is a non-profit organization that seeks to "increase global awareness of the therapeutic and life-enhancing potential of psychedelics when used responsibly" (https://worldpsychedelicsday.org/). The annual celebration is set at June 20 (6/20)— a tribute to the long-established April 20 (4/20) annual day of cannabis liberalization celebrations.

The recreational use of psychedelics is also appearing in mainstream popular culture. The drama series, *Riverdale*, one of the most popular series on streaming service Netflix, is aimed at an older adolescent and young adult viewing audience. Season 5, Episode 11 featured a first experience with "shrooms" by two young women—depicting the experience as a mostly benign and enjoyable one. Conversations elsewhere in the episode also referenced psilocybin use by two other characters and suggested that use might be problematic for one of them.

Thrill Kill: The Corporatization of Psychedelics?

The many parallels between the early stages of psilocybin and cannabis law reform are striking, and perhaps ominous given the meteoric rise of the cannabis trade from humble, illicit beginnings, to a revenue-driven, too-big-to-regulate, corporate juggernaut, with increasing ties to tobacco, alcohol, and pharmaceutical corporations.

There are already hints of the beginning of such a transformation for psilocybin. In the United Kingdom, Compass Pathways started out as a non-profit start-up but recently adopted a for-profit model. Biopharmaceutical company, ATAI Life Sciences, is a major shareholder. This change has prompted allegations from the psychedelic community that the company was attempting to monopolize the drug's production (Farah 2019).

Christian Angermayer, founder of ATAI Life Sciences, has declared his ambitious vision for psychedelic treatments being integrated into healthcare systems with coverage by insurers (Rosner 2020).

In the US, a California-based company has successfully trademarked the word psilocybin, to be used as the name for a chocolate product (that does not contain psilocybin). The company claims it wants to protect the word for purely educational purposes to prevent psilocybin from becoming a corporate commodity like cannabis. Grass roots advocates have expressed skepticism (Jaeger 2020).

Others are more cautious about the potential for psilocybin as a commercial success. Millar (2020) makes an argument that would likely extend to other psychedelic substances as well. He asserts that psilocybin's low capacity for producing dependence and the potentially intense effects might mitigate against the frequent use by individuals that typically leads to a lucrative drug business. A company, MindMed, also has this concern and is working on pharmaceutical solutions that would make a therapeutic LSD experience less lengthy and intense (Reader 2020).

Similarly, Millar accepts that there are already players in an unlicensed trade promoting micro-dosing of psilocybin for therapeutic purposes. He speculates that mass appeal could be realized with micro-dosing of psilocybin. Such an operation already exists in Canada as www.mushroom-dispensary.com, an unlicensed service providing "Access to micro-doses of psilocybin mushrooms for therapeutic purposes." It's founder, Dana Larsen, also founded and operated an online, unlicensed cannabis dispensary for several years.

Millar also acknowledges that some corporations may be able to "systematize and franchise" a therapeutic enterprise. MindMed certainly has such ambitions. Its co-founder and co-CEO, J.R. Rahn, described the company's ambition to be "...one of the first publicly listed neuro-pharmaceutical companies developing psychedelic medicines" and is targeting a valuation of approximately $50 million (Owram 2020).

CYBIN is a Canadian life sciences company that aspires to provide psychedelic pharmaceuticals for psychiatric and neurological conditions.

CYBIN's 2020 offering for investors worth $45 million was oversubscribed and sold out (Psychedelic Finance 2020).

Mark Haden, founder of Multidisciplinary Associations for Psychedelic Studies (MAPS) Canada, acknowledged that the legalization of cannabis has helped to clear the way for psychedelics (Kindleman 2021). Accordingly, players from the cannabis industry are stepping into the psychedelics corporate space. Tweed co-founder and former Canopy Growth CEO, Bruce Linton, has become a senior advisor on the Board of Trustees for Red Light Holland, an Ontario company poised to grow and sell psilocybin (Lim 2020). Linton has also joined MindMed as a director (Owram 2020).

Former politicians are also getting interested. Tony Clement is a former federal health minister with the Progressive Conservative Party of Canada who strongly opposed many drug liberalization initiatives during his tenure in politics. Following an apparent epiphany since leaving politics, the once-honourable member has joined Red Light Holland as a senior advisor (Lim 2020). Canadian television personality, and once-candidate for the leadership of the Progressive Conservative Party of Canada, Kevin O'Leary, is an investor in MindMed (Owram 2020).

The now humbled cannabis green rush may seek salvation in a shroom boom. *Marijuana Business Daily* has published a case for why those in the cannabis industry might be interested in the emerging psychedelics industry, which has potential to grow well beyond a strictly therapeutic market. MBD cites industry analysts predicting that market size will reach $10.75 billion by 2027 and create investment opportunities worth close to $100 billion. Analysts also predict that the companies that emerge as the most successful in the psychedelic market are those "that have deep pockets, patentable products and a well-thought-out reimbursement strategy" (Bogot, Horn, and Kwan 2021). (If you know people who are so inclined, be a good friend and introduce them to Chapter 8 of this book.)

The path of corporatization of psychedelics is not without its problems. Just as significant momentum was accumulating, a counter-force of failure and disillusion also materialized. Inexperience and naivete on the part of companies and investors appears to be at the heart of it. In the spring of 2022, stocks in psychedelic companies were dropping. Some plummeted significantly (Bryant 2022).

To help those with ambitions in the emerging psychedelics landscape in Canada, a group of cannabis industry professionals formed a specialized public relations agency for "cannabis, psychedelics and other emerging regulated markets" (Alan Aldous Inc. 2020). This suggests that ambitions extend beyond a trade in cannabis and psychedelics alone. Early indications are that the familiar trajectory of cannabis legalization will be repurposed for psilocybin, and perhaps with other currently illegal drugs. A potentially unlimited list of currently illegal designer drugs, both current and future, lies in waiting, not just for decriminalization, but for commercial exploitation. At the end of 2020, the European Monitoring Centre for Drugs and Drug Addiction was monitoring approximately 830 new psychoactive substances (European Monitoring Centre for Drugs and Drug Addiction 2021). Given the legacy of our current legal drug corporations, it is prudent to consider the impact of multiple emerging, permissively regulated, drug industries on public health and safety.

Major movements in psychedelics law reform do not reside exclusively in North America but are gaining momentum in Europe and Australia as well (Farah 2019).

Closing: Some Suggestions

Psychedelics have a fascinating history as a catalyst for spiritual experience in many Indigenous cultures. They also stand as a romanticized icon of twentieth century counterculture. Even in the absence of a compelling evidence base, they now appear to be ushering in a new age of tenuous chemical interventions for the prevalent mental health challenges of modern society. As with cannabis, the greater perils may not reside so much with the intrinsic properties of the drugs themselves, but with the social structures and narratives we construct about them. Are we looking at another revenue driven, evidence anemic, campaign for therapeutic benefit? Is this campaign the foot in the door for an ensuing *zeitgeist* of legalized, corporatized, commodified, McPsychedelics? It may not be just about therapy, but also about playing with our body chemistry. It will also be about making a lot of money. And we can expect public health implications.

I will end this section with similar points I made at the end of the section on the therapeutic use of cannabis. Effective as soon as possible, there should be no further criminalization of those who use psychedelics for either therapeutic or recreational use. A safe supply should be made available to people through not-for-profit health-mandated organizations. More clinical trials should be funded immediately to eventually provide guidance to legislators, clinical practitioners, and potential patients. The creation of another hyper-commercialized drug industry will be counter productive. Research funding from commercial interests in the psychedelics industry should be avoided. We must be vigilant that the laudable goals of decriminalization and access to medicine do not become yet more alluring bait on the hook of corporate capture.

DECRIMINALIZATION OF ALL DRUGS AND CREATION OF A SAFE SUPPLY

A defensible case can be made for the decriminalization of all types of drugs and creation of a safe supply. This is the third major wave of drug policy reform around the world. Moving away from a century of oppressive and ineffective criminalization of drug users is welcomed by many drug policy analysts and activists alike. A new paradigm for drug policy based upon social justice, harm reduction and public health protection continues to gather momentum.

An important part of improved drug policy is the de-stigmatization of drug users. A secondary, and much less popular, proposal is ending the indiscriminate demonization of unlicensed drug sellers. Yes, there are some bad actors in the unlicensed drug trade, responsible, at least in part, for many of the deaths linked to the current crisis of drug-related overdoses. However, as we have seen, there are bad actors in licensed drug trades as well, also responsible for many deaths—and who are typically entitled to operate without violent incursion by the state and even exonerated for their criminal and unethical conduct. Not so for the unlicensed trade. They have faced prison sentences of a decade or longer. For drug trade cases that do not involve violence, exploitation, or other serious crimes, we might consider a different approach. Instead of providing convicted drug traders with tax funded accommodation in prison, what if we provided them with tax funded counselling, skills development, job placement, and affordable housing? Maybe then, they could pay for their own accommodation—without the imprisonment part.

Academic studies are emerging that demonstrate the importance of nuance in our discussions of the unlicensed drug trade. A study conducted in Vancouver, Canada, showed that some unlicensed traders have genuine compassion for their clientele and go to lengths to ensure their safety (Betsos et al. 2021). A United States Federal Bureau of Investigation (FBI) document that was intercepted from a law enforcement website and made publicly available demonstrated that the Bureau had documented similar kinds of benevolent behaviour among illegal traders in some of its investigations (Blanchard 2020). The world possesses more complexity than drug policy orthodoxy has tolerated. Revelations on the diverse nature of the typically demonized players in the unlicensed drug trade will be slow to find their way into policy reform initiatives, or even discussions. Almost all efforts and discussions thus far are limited to reform of the treatment of drug users only.

International/Other Countries

A considerable amount of academic credibility was brought to the international decriminalization movement by The Johns Hopkins-Lancet Commission on Public Health and International Drug Policy (Csete et al. 2016). It conducted a review of decriminalization in Portugal and the Czech Republic. The review found: "...significant financial savings, less incarceration, significant public health benefits, and no significant increase in drug use." The Commission recommended international decriminalization of all minor drug use. The Commission's recommendation received further support in 2017, when the United Nations (UN) and World Health Organization (WHO) issued a joint statement encouraging countries to review and repeal laws that criminalize drug use and possession for personal use (Rajagopalan 2017).

The recommendations are consistent with, and may have prompted, a proliferation of international change. As of August 2021, countries that had decriminalized possession of all drugs at the national level included Argentina, Armenia, Chile, Costa Rica, Croatia, Czech Republic, Estonia, Italy, Kyrgyzstan, Lithuania, Peru, Poland, Portugal, Russian Federation, Slovenia, Spain, Switzerland, and Uruguay (Talking Drugs, n.d.). You will notice the list does not include many of the world's largest economies such as Australia, Brazil, Canada, China, France, Germany, Israel, Japan, Mexico, New Zealand, Saudi Arabia, the United Arab Emirates, the United Kingdom, or the United States. A wide variety of political regime types appear among those that have supported reform. A wide variety also appear in the group that remains prohibitive. Drug law reform appears to have little to do with self-righteous declarations of "freedom."

A federal bill has been introduced to the United States House of Representatives that would decriminalize all drugs that are currently illegal (Sutton 2021). Such a bill would reduce prosecution in states which had no decriminalization provisions as well as introduce some harmonization of disparate models of drug decriminalization across US states.

At the state level, Oregon has taken on the role of early adopter. In the autumn of 2020, Oregon voters approved a ballot measure to decriminalize possession of small amounts of street drugs such as heroin, methamphetamines, and cocaine. Possession would be punishable by no more than a $100 fine which can be waived by completing a health assessment for drug dependence. Tax revenue from legal marijuana sales in the state will be used to establish free drug treatment centers (Castronuovo 2020).

One of the contentious issues that arises in all attempts at decriminalizing drugs is the maximum amount of drug allowed to be in a person's possession—typically referred to as the "threshold." Drug use activists claim that thresholds that are typically set do not allow drug users to possess the amount required to prevent withdrawal. Thus, their required carries can still result in criminal charges if they exceed the legal threshold. This is a legitimate concern. On the other hand, we should probably not tolerate possession of a knapsack full of illegal, untested, possibly dangerously contaminated drugs. That is obviously an extreme scenario, but where do we draw the line? This issue is also central to discussions and controversy in current attempts to decriminalize drug use in Canada.

Canada Federal

Canada allocates a substantial portion of its nation-wide prosecutorial expenditure to drug charges. The Public Prosecution Service of Canada (PPSC) 2015-16 annual report declared that drug prosecution files represent, by far, the most significant portion of the PPSC's total caseload (Public Prosecution Service of Canada 2016). Subsequent Annual Reports from PPSC reaffirm this through the first quarter of 2021, showing that drug-related files perennially account for approximately three quarters of its total caseload. The reports show modest decreases from 78.2% in 2015-16 to 73.6% in 2019-20. There was then a slight increase to 75.0% in 2020-21 (Public Prosecution Service of Canada 2016, 2017, 2018, 2019, 2020, 2021).

It has been clear for quite some time that we cannot prosecute our way out of our drug problems. Canada's concurrent epidemics of COVID-19 and drug-related deaths are exacerbating the problem. COVID has shone a spotlight on our drug problems to emphasize, to anyone who had not already noticed, just how serious the problem is.

In Canada, the decriminalization of drugs at the federal level has been suggested by several prominent organizations with a mandate in health policy advocacy. These include The Canadian Public Health Association (2016), The Centre for Addiction and Mental Health (2018; 2021) and The Canadian Society of Addiction Medicine (2020).

In July of 2020, the Canadian Chiefs of Police recommended the decriminalization of possession offences for all drugs (Zimonjic 2020). In August, Theresa Tam, Canada's Chief Public Health Officer, was more cautiously encouraging discussions about decriminalizing hard drugs (T. Wright 2020).

That same month, the Director of Public Prosecutions, Kathleen Roussel, issued a directive that revised the approach of the Public Prosecution Service of Canada to drug possession offences under the Controlled Drugs and Substances Act. PPSC prosecutors were instructed to consider whether a prosecution for simple possession serves the public interest and were further instructed to divert cases away from the criminal justice system. However, charges could still be pursued if major public safety concerns involving weapons or violence, or other criminal activities were also at play (Tunney 2020).

While the directive did not specifically mention the Cannabis Act, The PPSC clarified in an email exchange with me between August 22 and 26, 2020 that "...the directive would also apply to simple possession charges under the Cannabis Act."

This is the same mechanism that was proposed to the House of Commons by Murray Rankin in 2016 for minor cannabis offences (as described in Chapter 6). The difference is that the 2020 directive would apply to all drugs, not just cannabis. On the downside, it came four years later—too late for the tens of thousands of Canadians who received criminal records for cannabis possession during that time.

So, did the order from the Director of the PPSC make a difference in the number of drug files it handled during the seven months it was in effect for 2020-21? The year of the new order saw a relatively small decrease in files involving drug-related offences. This occurred within a pre-existing declining trend in the number of drug-related files since at least 2015. The difficulty for the PPSC is that it is police who lay the charges that land with the PPSC. PPSC can only act in how it chooses to address those charges. The impact of the new order can be demonstrated by the percentage of simple drug possession charges that are withdrawn and/or granted a stay of proceedings by the Crown. As seen below, compared to the two previous years, that percentage increased considerably in 2020-21 when the new order was in effect for seven months.

- 2018-19 53.3%

- 2019-20 47.4%

- 2020-21 81.0%

There are two qualifiers. A stay in proceedings can be permanent or temporary. It is therefore possible that a stay in proceedings for a drug charge could resume in the future. The other qualifier is that 75% of files for all crimes are withdrawn and/or granted a stay of proceedings by the Crown. So, because of the new directive, the stay or withdrawal of drug charges is a modest 6% higher than that granted for the other crimes dealt with by PPSC. Hopefully a more substantial improvement will be seen in the next annual report from the PPSC. The 2021 Report also disclosed that there were 4,646 charges laid under the Cannabis Act in 2020-21 but provided no information on the disposition of those charges. (Public Prosecution Service of Canada 2021)

There is more cause for optimism from data released by the Province of Ontario. Between July 2020 and June 2021 Ontario courts withdrew 85% of drug possession charges before they came to trial. That compares to 45% in the previous one-year period (McMillan 2021).

The federal and Ontario data on the high number of drug-related charges being withdrawn prompt a question. Why are we paying for the police to lay so many drug-related charges when 4 out of 5 of them are being withdrawn by prosecutors? Something seems awry. Perhaps our local police forces should adjust their priorities with greater attention applied to more serious crimes.

In February 2021, the Canadian government introduced Bill C-22 which would alter sections of the Controlled Drugs and Substances Act to repeal mandatory minimum sentences for drug possession. The changes would also require enforcement, prosecution, and the courts to exercise more favour towards conditional sentencing or diverting cases of simple possession to treatment programs. The repeal of mandatory minimums is an important step. However, conditional sentencing and diversion are already part of Canada's justice system. While Bill C-22 would place a greater expectation on the players in the criminal justice system to consider other options, the bill stops short of the full decriminalization of simple drug possession (Tunney and Noel 2021).

In May and June of 2021, the Health Canada Expert Task Force on Substance Use released two reports (2021a, 2021b). The reports supported decriminalization of all drugs and proposed related measures such as free expungement of past records for drug charges for simple possession.

Bill C-22 died on the Order Paper when the Liberals called an election in September. It was re-introduced near the end of 2021 as Bill C-5. If all goes well, we might expect passage sometime in 2023.

On June 1, 2022, the federal New Democrat Party (NDP) introduced a private members bill (C-216) to the House of Commons that proposed to:

- *decriminalize drugs across the country*

- *expunge criminal records for past offences*

- *develop a national strategy for a safe supply.*

I was asked to provide some commentary on these proposals and did so with my full support for the bill. Unfortunately, the bill was defeated by block voting of the Liberal and PC Parties (T. Wright 2022). Such is the life of a drug policy analyst.

The Canadian Government's approach-avoidance performance has not satisfied policy advocates. Almost seventy organizations from across the country have written a letter to PM Justin Trudeau asking that drug possession be immediately decriminalized. Such a resolution to that effect was approved by Liberal delegates at the Party's 2018 convention (Bryden 2021). Four years later, the Party's leadership has failed to follow through on the resolution. This lack of action stands in stark contrast to the high priority that was given to the resolution passed by the Party at its 2012 convention in support of the much more lucrative ambition of cannabis legalization.

Therein lay a lesson pertaining to priorities in politics. After coming to power with a majority government in 2015, the Liberal Party took only three years to enact the extraordinarily complex Bill C-45, The Cannabis Act. The needs of Party elites vested in the cannabis trade were well served. But cannabis users are still receiving criminal records for minor cannabis offences. The Party's less enthusiastic effort to lessen the penalties for drug possession in general is reminiscent of when the Party proclaimed an intent to decriminalize cannabis possession in the early 1990s. Despite holding a majority government for a continuous decade, the Party failed to make it happen.

The Liberal Party's trepidation on the decriminalization issue may also land them in court. In September 2021, The Canadian Association of People Who Use Drugs filed a lawsuit against the federal government arguing that drug criminalization is a charter violation (Owen 2021).

Canada Municipalities

In Canada, much of the most recent high-profile advocacy for the decriminalization of drugs has occurred at the municipal level. This is no surprise given that when federal or provincial policy goes seriously awry, it is in our communities, neighbourhoods, and homes where the fallout can be most profoundly experienced. This has most certainly been the case for drug policy in Canada.

To support the active involvement of municipalities and provinces, the HIV Legal Network, a Canada based organization with an international mission, has developed a *Primer* for provincial and municipal governments. The guide provides a logistical road map to petitioning the federal government in Canada to grant exemptions from the Controlled Drugs and Substances Act (HIV Legal Network, 2020).

Efforts in Vancouver have been particularly strong and tumultuous. Mayor Kennedy Stewart proposed that Vancouver City Council send an application to Health Canada that, if granted, would allow residents of the city to be exempt from some provisions of the Controlled Drugs and Substances Act. This could effectively decriminalize all drug use. In making his case to City Council, the mayor cited support from British Columbia Premier John Horgan, provincial health officer Dr. Bonnie Henry, and Vancouver Coastal Health chief medical officer Dr. Patricia Daly. Other key organizations supporting decriminalization are the Vancouver Police Department, PIVOT Legal Society, Canadian Drug Policy Coalition, Canadian HIV/AIDS Legal Network, and the Overdose Prevention Society (Mooney 2020). The proposal received the unanimous approval of City Council.

The Vancouver Area Network of Drug Users (VANDU) was invited to work with Council on the proposal to the feds. However, early in the process, the mood at VANDU went from wary to frustrated. VANDU felt it was being marginalized in the decision-making process, which it claimed resulted in serious shortcomings in the details of the proposal. Specific complaints included the small amounts that people were legally allowed to have (threshold limits) and provisions that would give the police greater powers in arresting drug users. Ultimately, VANDU announced that it would no longer work with the city (Steacy 2021). The city carried on and announced on June 1, 2021 that it had submitted the proposal to Health Canada (Canadian Press 2021). Shortly afterwards, the mayors of several other British Columbia cities signed a letter in support of Vancouver's approach. However, advocacy groups have continued to express their concerns (CBC News 2021).

Activists have resorted to more provocative measures. The Drug User Liberation Front has partnered with VANDU to give away tested substances purchased from the dark web "so they won't be arrested for saving lives" (Grochowski 2021). The Drug User Liberation Front also held an event in front of the Vancouver Police Department on August 24, 2021, at which they gave away free heroin, cocaine, and crystal methamphetamine (Shepert 2021). Apparently the VPD elected to stand down and resist making any arrests—probably a good call.

In October 2021, The City Council of Vancouver gave unanimous support to a proposal to provide a safe supply of drugs to individuals at high risk of overdose. The program, if approved by the federal government, would be coordinated by Vancouver's Drug User Liberation Front. According to a statement from City Counsellor Jean Swanson, the program would be the first compassion club in North America that provided its members with prescription-grade heroin, methamphetamine, and cocaine (Grochowski 2021).

In late 2020, Toronto's Medical Officer of Health, Dr. Eileen de Villa, issued a report calling for decriminalization of small amounts of drugs along with other harm reduction measures. Ontario Premier Doug Ford and his Minister of Health, Christine Elliott, both publicly expressed their opposition to aspects of the report, including decriminalization (Passifiume 2020). A more recent report from the Toronto Public Health Department takes the same approach as Vancouver in asking for an exemption from the federal health minister. The report also noted that the Canadian Association of Chiefs of Police had backed decriminalization of personal possession as had the Ontario Association of Chiefs of Police. Toronto Mayor John Tory was more cautious, saying he supported exploring decriminalization (Pagliaro 2021).

Similar petitions to Health Canada are also in process in Montréal (Crockett 2021), Ottawa (Egan 2021), and Victoria (City of Victoria 2021). Calls for decriminalization are not just occurring in large urban centres. In Ontario, calls have also come from small town/rural areas such as Chatham-Kent (P. Wright 2021) and the Kingston, Frontenac, and Lennox & Addington Region (Goulem 2022).

Canada Provinces

Some provincial authorities have offered support to the municipal efforts. British Columbia's Minister of Mental Health and Addictions, Sheila Malcolmson, sent a letter to the federal Ministry of Health formally asking for an exemption (Zussman 2021).

On May 31, 2022, the federal government granted an exemption for British Columbia to decriminalize opioids, cocaine, and amphetamines. The exemption comes into effect on January 31, 2023 (Woo and Gee 2022). However, thresholds remain controversial (Harper 2022). The federal government was also criticized for granting this exemption for British Columbia but voting to defeat a proposal from the NDP to extend the same provisions to the rest of the country (P. Wright 2022.)

Ontario's chief medical officer of health, Dr. Kieran Moore, has publicly stated his support for federal decriminalization as part of a larger basket of reforms to drug policy (DeLaire 2021).

Closing: Some Daunting Challenges

The prospects for domestic and international decriminalization of drug use face several challenges.

Decriminalization of all drugs is still a highly stigmatized idea among significant portions of populations. To compound the challenge, some governments choose oppressive drug laws as a proxy for a law-and-order approach to create a semblance of propriety among the citizenry. The populations of most of these jurisdictions could benefit from government using the resources they allocate to drug criminalization to resolve far more pressing social/economic issues. But in many cases, political gaming will prevail. Decriminalization of all drugs is likely to remain a long-term objective in most jurisdictions.

Decriminalization is complex with many possible configurations. As with other ambitious drug policy reforms such as legalization and providing safe supplies of drugs, the devil is always in the details. Stevens et al. (2019) published a thorough description of alternate configurations of decriminalization in the European Journal of Criminology. Another paper published in the International Journal of Drug Policy also explored the complex facets of decriminalization with some commentary on what can go wrong with insufficient attention to the complexities (Greer et al. 2021).

Any drug reform movement based on social justice can be undermined and exploited. It's broad appeal to progressive and humane thinkers can become the alluring bait on the hook of corporate capture of a legalized drug trade. In the case of cannabis in Canada, a long-term social justice movement for decriminalization was suddenly subverted into a revenue-driven legalization campaign that ultimately transferred much of the cannabis trade from unlicensed, mostly benign mom and pop operations to licensed, avaricious corporations with little regard for regulatory restraint. Clearly, it is desirable to steer cannabis users towards a legal market to minimize the influence of an unlicensed, completely unregulated one. However, meting out criminal records comprises the same unjustified overreach of law enforcement that it always has been. For many years, the criminalization of cannabis use was fuelled by a perverse sense of morality. There is a very real danger that profit protection of licensed cannabis industries will provide a far more fierce and more destructive motivation for continued criminalization of those who, perhaps justifiably, choose to take their business elsewhere. These are more lessons from cannabis policy reform for the broader landscape of drug policy reform.

The voices of those most dramatically impacted by oppressive drug laws might be under-represented in reform campaigns. The Canadian Association of People Who Use Drugs (CAPUD) is one chapter of The International Network of People Who Use Drugs. INPUD's report, *Drug Decriminalisation: Progress or Political Red Herring?* indicates that it is not wholly impressed with the progress of decriminalization efforts, worldwide. INPUD's own words state their case better than I could:

> *Over the past decade there have been increasing claims that the world is moving towards a critical turning point in international drug policy, based on a growing recognition that governments must consider alternative approaches to drug policy which include decriminalization. While this shift has been hailed as a sign of progress by many, INPUD believes there are still important and overlooked questions regarding the extent to which the needs and rights of people who use drugs are being prioritized in countries that have decriminalized drug use.*

The report also offers:

> *Decriminalization is often discussed as if there is only one model, leading to a view that decriminalization anywhere equals progress. However, there are many different models of*

decriminalization in operation, all with different impacts. This report was published because we believe current reforms have not gone far enough. This situation means that in the overwhelming majority of countries, people who use drugs continue to be criminalized, punished, and stigmatized despite decriminalization. Furthermore, no existing reviews of decriminalization models have specifically included the perspective of people who use drugs in their analysis, a glaring oversight which reflects the historical exclusion of the voices of people who use drugs within policy discussions.

(International Network of People Who Use Drugs 2021)

INPUD's report also includes a call for "...full decriminalization without sanctions as the new baseline for measuring progress on decriminalization in the future."

INPUDS case is not inconsistent with what some academics are recommending. But governments, at all levels, apparently have a long way to go to address the problems of drug criminalization as drug users experience them. That is not the only, or the worst, aspect of sub-par government performance in the drug policy arena. As we will see in the next section, this story does not get any prettier.

Activists have also argued that decriminalization may prevent unjust criminalization, but it will not stem the tide of drug-related deaths. That requires the establishment of a safe supply of currently illegal opiates/opioids and stimulants. The challenge would be how to scale up from giving away free drugs in front of the Vancouver Police Department to meeting a much larger demand.

The concept of providing a safe supply is a defensible one, but it is another example of the devil residing in the details of how a safe supply would be implemented and regulated. The opioid crisis was born with all the customary boxes for safe supply checked off. Legal opioid medications were:

- *discovered and developed by qualified scientists working for government-regulated pharmaceutical companies*

- *manufactured by qualified technicians working for government-regulated pharmaceutical companies*

- *evaluated for effectiveness and safety in clinical trials conducted by qualified scientists employed by reputable research organizations, and published in reputable, peer-reviewed journals*

- *approved for use by a government regulatory body*

- *marketed by educated employees working for government-regulated pharmaceutical companies*

- *prescribed and dispensed by licensed health care providers accredited by their respective professional colleges*

- monitored for ongoing safety by qualified health care providers, expert academics, and government regulators.

Within the rubric of widely accepted drug policy orthodoxy, that sounds like a very safe supply. What could possibly go wrong? Well, lots. And it did.

We must ensure that the provision of a safe supply cannot be exploited by avaricious and deceitful manufacturers, subverted by reckless, single-minded prescribers, and compromised by impotent government regulation. If the political parties we elect continue to deploy slogans over thoughtful, humane, evidence-based policy reform, Canada's drug crises will continue and quite possibly worsen. Saying "we are taking a public health approach" must be more than a slogan that camouflages a campaign guided primarily by the pursuit of revenue and steeped in cronyism. Saying "establish a safe supply" could be equally susceptible to the same dynamics.

DRUG PROBLEMS: THE INDUSTRIAL-REGULATORY COMPLEX

It is often pointed out that corporations are required by law to make profits for shareholders. That is true. But the law does not require corporations to break the law to make those profits. But they do so anyway because sometimes it becomes easier through non-compliance with regulations and committing crimes.

Drug problems are not simply a result of someone's personal failing. Regulatory violations and criminal conduct can have profound consequences for public health and safety. We rely upon government to protect us from drug-related harms, especially when the harms are at least partially attributable to the misconduct of drug trades—including legal ones. When government fails to do so, the harms can be far-reaching. They are visited not only upon individual drug product consumers, but also upon their family, friends, neighbours, and co-workers. Even total strangers who had the misfortune of being in the wrong place at the wrong time can be affected. These extensions of harm beyond drug users make the misuse of drugs not just an individual problem. It is, profoundly, a community and a societal problem. Given the impacts on the Canadian economy that we explored earlier in the book, nefarious industry conduct and sub-par regulation is also an economic problem that translates into an enormous industry externality borne by the taxpayers.

Industry Conduct as a Cause of Drug Problems

With our alcohol, tobacco, and pharmaceutical industries, we already have three long-lived, legal, revenue-driven, corporatized drug industries. We also have three major international public health crises. The cannabis industry is becoming increasingly infiltrated by financial investments and board memberships from these same industries. It is thus perilously on track to become a part of Big PACT (Pharmaceutical, Alcohol, Cannabis, Tobacco)—a treacherous epicenter for what Professor Emeritus David Courtwright at the University of North Florida has described as "limbic capitalism." Most disturbingly, the commodification of our vulnerabilities occurs within a government-enabled, corporate free-for-all with mostly performative regard for public health and safety.

The traditional model of legal, commercial drug industries and regulatory regimes has had more than a century to adequately arrive at an acceptable balance of revenue generation and public health protection. The corporate model has repeatedly failed—at enormous individual and societal cost. In contrast, industries continue to reap massive revenues from the scourges they perpetrate. Industries then externalize the fiscal harms to health and social support systems that struggle to keep pace with it all. Long waiting lists for treatment and care add to the suffering of people with drug problems and their families. Canada's cannabis legalization venture has increased access to cannabis, and we have seen increases in cannabis use. There is likely to be an increase in problems and demand for services from these already chronically underfunded, stressed programs. Cannabis legalization in Canada has made overt an important principle for drug policy. The establishment of a new recreational drug industry should not provide opportunities for entrepreneurs to become multi-millionaires at the expense of the rule of law and public safety.

Regulatory Conduct as an Enabler

The Canadian government, and other governments, possess the knowledge and authority to prevent a future with an ever-growing pandemic of drug-related harm. But with continued, inexplicable, shortsightedness, governments choose not to. To borrow from child poverty advocate Sir Michael Marmot—countries will continue to have exactly the amount of drug-related harm that their governments want them to have.

Public health policy efforts to address drug-related harm meet with perpetual opposition and sabotage from the drug industries, and often with indifference from government. There has been progress with tobacco, but it has been slow and costly. The progress has also been compromised with the emergence of the tobacco-vaping industry—which I now call the nicotine addiction industry.

An equally worrisome scenario has arisen with the drug overdose crisis. In Canada, regulatory progress seems limited to initiatives that are directed towards dealing with perils after they happen. This has been likened to parking an ambulance at the bottom of the hill. By comparison, there is relatively little that addresses industry actions that cause the problems. Prescription monitoring programs may detect emerging problems early. However, early detection was not the principal problem for our opioid overdose crisis. Nor was it the problem for the arrival of vaping technologies. In both cases, the problem was a slow, reluctant response by Health

Canada to warnings issued years earlier by public health authorities. There is little in the way of policy initiatives to improve industry regulation to prevent the next drug product crisis, and the one after that, *ad finitum*. The next drug-related pandemic could be looming on a very short horizon.

In perhaps the worst scenario, the regulatory environment is degrading with increased liberalization of access to alcohol—a move that is contraindicated by the research and strongly discouraged by the very public health authorities that government funds to advise it on such matters.

Governments are also prone to gaming their own role in regulating industry. The Cannabis Act is a good example. As described earlier, The Act contains some impressive provisions based upon recommendations from health policy authorities. But the problem lies, most notably, with consequences for non-compliance that are insufficient to foster deterrence. Without meaningful consequences for infractions, the best-written regulations will be rendered impotent in their potential for deterrence. We should be concerned that the impressive provisions were apparently written only to appease health policy authorities, with no intention to be used. This is only one aspect of a legacy of regulatory permissiveness. The legacy has been forged over decades of industry lobbying acumen, government-industry social networking, and industry largess for political parties.

Drug problems are accordingly also a political problem. Canada's federal and provincial governments, spanning many decades and several political parties holding power, have allowed this dire situation to continue and worsen. Neither the current Canadian federal government nor any of the current provincial or territorial governments have a promising plan for improving matters.

It would be too convenient, and unfair, to lay the blame only upon regulatory bodies for the culture of corporate entitlement that prevails in government. I have no doubt that regulators such as Health Canada employ many conscientious and diligent people. But a regulator can only be as good as the Cabinet that directs it. Ultimately, it is Cabinet that must be held to account when regulation falters.

In contrast to the observed permissiveness for drug corporations, is the much harsher policy response for individual drug users. For the last century, governments have taken a judgmental and punitive, rather than a compassionate, public health approach. This may have been a well-intentioned, if ultimately ill-conceived, effort to prevent widespread societal harm from drug use. However, in some cases, questionable political objectives have given fuel to the harsh judgments and punitive laws. In Canada (and elsewhere) countless people have been imprisoned and/or had to bear the burden of a lifelong criminal record—for playing with their body chemistry. Regulators such as Health Canada cannot be blamed for this cruel and tragic incursion against our nation's people. That too falls upon Cabinet.

The criminalization of drug use is inhumane and ineffective. But commercial legalization is not the solution. The data from CSUCH told us that the major drug-related social/health threats with which Canadians are confronted is not from illegal drug cartels but from government licensed and protected corporations. Many of these corporations are willing to violate any laws in an unbridled pursuit of revenue—a kind of organized crime that is quite different from the customary definition. But these crimes must stop. We must somehow marshal the humanity and courage to explore and demand evidence-based alternatives.

Canada's approach to drug policy has been an example of governance at its worst. It was time for a change. Cannabis law reform in Canada provided an opportunity. The Liberal Party of Canada, with full intention, squandered that opportunity. In retrospect, it seems that there was never cause for optimism that Canada would make a significant change, or that the traditional corporate approach would fare any better with cannabis.

Drug Policy Orthodoxy as an Enabler

The continued practice in Western democracies to hand responsibility for drug trades to corporations is deeply embedded in long-lived drug policy orthodoxy.

Increasingly, the conduct of the industrial-regulatory complex exposes major flaws in this orthodoxy. The first flaw is the customary indiscriminate valorization of licensed drug trades and the unqualified demonization of unlicensed trades. Both unlicensed and licensed trades violate the law, giving us two types of drug crime. Unlicensed trades commit drug crimes by selling drugs that are illegal. Licensed trades commit drug crimes by selling legal drugs in a manner that is illegal. Licensed companies therefore not only violate the law but also the trust that society places in them to trade in a potentially harmful product in a manner that is respectful of the law and protective of society. So, which trade perpetrates the greater offence against society—the illegal or legal one? In contrast to our prevailing drug policy orthodoxy, I would argue that it is the latter.

Another flaw in drug policy orthodoxy arises from its assertion that regulation is not perfect. But we are nonetheless encouraged to accept the imperfections as unavoidable. We are encouraged to be grateful that imperfect regulation is better than no regulation. In other words, our regulatory regimes are better than nothing. On that, I can agree. But that seems to be setting the bar rather low. Canadians, like the people of any nation, deserve better than "better than nothing." The assertion is also disingenuous. The problem is not that regulation is tolerably less than perfect. The problem is that it is intolerably less than adequate—as evidenced by the enormous, perennial levels of harm associated with legal drug use. Furthermore, a large portion of the failures are both preventable and solvable. There is an abundance of research to show us the way forward, and it has all been brought to the attention of industry and government, repeatedly. All we lack is the political will to improve regulatory compliance by industry and enforcement by government. That is doable. Corporations and governments simply choose not to.

Finally, there are limits to what policy analysts can do. While many analysts have publicly recommended major paradigm shifts, there are hurdles to their optimal effectiveness in the advocacy arena. Analysts working on tobacco, alcohol, pharmaceutical, or cannabis policy are often in competition for government funding. This tends to discourage cross silo collaboration to form a united front for cohesive drug policy pertaining to the conduct of all drug industries and their sub-par regulation by government. The other problem is that criticism of government regulation that is too candid can pose a threat to the future funding of an organization and to even an individual's career trajectory. You are labelled a troublemaker.

Then there are policy analysts who accept funding from drug corporations. This is most prominent with pharmaceutical companies, but there have also been cases of analysts receiving support from the alcohol and tobacco industries. In Canada, I have heard of two researchers funded by the cannabis industry. That introduces even more limiting constraints on any possible advocacy role that addresses the harmful conduct of the industry. Another problem is the customary acceptance that declaring a conflict of interest somehow neutralizes it. Some policy analysts, who possess the knowledge to improve the propriety of the industrial-regulatory complex are, to some degree, muzzled by their reliance upon funding from government and industry. All these dynamics tend to contribute towards perpetuating a less-than-adequate regulatory environment.

There are serious liabilities with our traditional drug policy orthodoxy. It seems context-blind, tone-deaf, and implication-mute. It is context-blind to blatant conflicts of interest and cronyism within the industrial-regulatory complex, and the resulting regulatory forgiveness of widespread non-compliance and bold corporate crime. It is tone-deaf to increasing public concern about the inhumanity of corporate conduct and its tolerance by governments with questionable priorities. Finally, traditional drug policy orthodoxy is implication-mute on the perilous perennial harm to public health.

Canada requires a major reformation for how drug products are provided to its people. There are those in industry and government and other defenders of drug policy orthodoxy who are inclined to resist the idea. My response to them is a straight-forward one. The data on the alarming levels of drug harms presented in this book make it clear that the current corporate system and the industrial-regulatory complex is not working. In fact, they comprise a major public health and economic liability.

The question of the day is whether cannabis, and potentially other drugs that make the transition from illegal to legal trades, will take on the same level of harm as currently seen with alcohol and tobacco. There can be no certainty in predicting that future, but the yellow and red flags are waving for our attention. We ignore them at the potential peril of the next generation and beyond.

WHAT IF CANADA DOES NOT MAKE A MAJOR PARADIGM SHIFT IN DRUG POLICY?

The best response to this provocative question is one based upon the most telling evidence available. Without a major shift, the pandemics of harm associated with the products of legal recreational drug industries will continue unabated. The annual numbers for alcohol and tobacco, as I presented them in Chapter 1, are alarming. I am re-posting the key figures here for convenience and emphasis. Inpatient hospitalizations numbered over 105,000 for alcohol and over 141,000 for tobacco. Premature deaths totalled over 18,000 for alcohol and over 61,000 for tobacco. The costs to the Canadian economy were over $17 billion for alcohol and over $12 billion for tobacco (Canadian Substance Use Costs and Harms Scientific Working Group 2020). Again, I emphasize that these figures represent the harms and costs for just one year.

It is also important to recall from Chapter 1 that high levels of harm and cost have been occurring for at least three decades and appear to be on the increase. The data also demonstrated that alcohol and tobacco, our two long-term legal recreational drugs, account for almost all the drug related harm—another unsavoury reality that has prevailed for decades.

Under the current drug policy paradigm, Canadians can expect similar counts year after year with no cause to expect significant improvement. In mid 2022, an epidemic of opioid dependence and overdoses, many fatal, continued across the country—another pandemic—this one initiated by a revenue-obsessed, ineffectively-regulated pharmaceutical industry. By the end of December 2021, more than 29,000 opioid-related deaths had been officially recorded—an assured under-count. There is no credible reason to believe that any of these drug trends will reverse, or their curves flatten, in the near future.

SOLUTIONS: IS THERE CAUSE FOR OPTIMISM?

It is customary, and expected, to follow such a bleak account as provided in this book with a discussion of potential causes for optimism. This is not easy. And I am not spontaneously inclined to do so. Speculation on the future of drug harms and the trajectory of drug policy in Canada is too well-informed by more than a half-century of experience with governments failing to adequately regulate our long-established drug industries.

But I will surrender to custom and see what I can do. As Leonard Cohen once sang:

There is a crack, a crack in everything

That's how the light gets in.

But I can also hear the ice cracking beneath my feet.

In the absence of something quite unexpected, advances in drug policy will continue to occur primarily through the efforts of health policy authorities waiting for opportunities to convince governments to make small incremental improvements on micro policy issues. This opportunistic, incremental approach is the same one that has prevailed for more than the last half century and coincides with escalating pandemics of harm in all of Canada's long-established legal drug industries. Cause for optimism for significant improvement within this incremental approach remains scant. Ultimately, such efforts yield, at best, hard earned, modest success, over a long period of time. And the approach comes with risks. One potential risk is that a long campaign of evidence-based, methodically planned, cumulative progress can be undone by sudden and major reversals arising from an ideological shift associated with a change in government. More typically, a lengthy process of gains can gradually erode over successive government regimes, bending to industry influence.

There is, however, an increasing societal awareness of the role played by drug industries in our drug problems. There is also an increasing recognition that the metaphorical pandemic of drug industry addiction to profits is a gateway to our pandemics of literal drug addiction. The courts are also becoming aware of this dynamic. Thus, one possible cause for cautious optimism involves the launching of class action lawsuits against drug corporations.

As of September 2021, over 3,000 class actions had been listed against Purdue Pharmaceutical for its role in the opioid epidemic. That same month, a US federal bankruptcy judge gave conditional approval to a primary settlement between Purdue and various plaintiffs that included states, local governments, Native American tribes, hospitals, unions, and other plaintiffs across the United States. Purdue is owned by members of the Sackler family. As part of the settlement, members of the family involved with Purdue can no longer own the company or be able to own a company anywhere in the world that sells opioid medications. The drug maker will be reorganized into a new company with a board appointed by public officials and will funnel its profits into government-led efforts to prevent and treat opioid dependence.

Reminiscent of the big tobacco settlement in the US, a public repository of documents from the company will be created. Purdue would pay out at least $4.5 billion in damages. None of the Sackler family have admitted responsibility for the opioid crisis and none have offered an apology. They agreed to the settlement on the condition that none of them would be personally sued. When the dust settles, the Sackler owners of Purdue will still be worth billions.

There has been substantial criticism of the settlement amount given that the company, by its own admission, made $10 billion in sales from the drug. Several states, as well as Washington, D.C, Seattle, and the US bankruptcy trustee expressed dissatisfaction with the settlement's protections of the Sacklers and were considering an appeal of the decision (Mulvihill 2021). The United States Department of Justice has filed for a stay of the settlement claiming that the owners of the company, the Sackler family and associates, were abusing the bankruptcy system to avoid meaningful liability (Mann, 2021).

In December 2021, a federal judge overturned the $4.5 billion settlement which led the way for the Sackler family to increase its offer to $6 billion. That led to several dissenting state attorneys general to withdraw their objection as well. As of April 2022, the new deal still required approval from a bankruptcy judge to be finalized. None of the Sackler family have been granted immunity from criminal charges (Mann and Bebinger 2022).

Another major opioid settlement has been reached with drug maker Johnson & Johnson and three major distributors (AmerisourceBergen, Cardinal Health, and McKesson) who have agreed to pay $26 billion US. The amount would be distributed to nearly every state and local government in the US (Associated Press 2022). One of the states that did not participate in the class action in favour of pursuing its own action was West Virginia which was particularly hard-hit by the opioid crises. Ultimately, West Virginia received $99 million from Johnson & Johnson—almost double the estimated $50 million it would have gained by joining the class action (Knauth 2022).

As part of the class action deal, Johnson & Johnson admitted no wrongdoing but has agreed not to sell prescription opioids in the future. None of the $26 billion will go directly to victims of opioid addiction or their survivors. Advocates have suggested a variety of unmet community needs such as housing, education, and expanded clinical services. John F. Kelly, a professor of psychiatry in addiction medicine at Harvard Medical School, advocated for a more systemic and preventative response: "Some kind of national board or organization could be set up ... to prevent this kind of lack of oversight from happening again — where industry is allowed to create a public health hazard" (Associated Press 2022).

In early 2022, it was discovered that the four firms were seeking tax breaks to offset the settlement. In March, members of Congress asked for a federal review of the process (MacMillan 2022). Another settlement on the horizon addresses the role that pharmacies played in the opioid epidemic (Mulvihill 2021).

In Chapter 5, I mentioned that in Canada, civil class actions against pharmaceutical companies had been launched in almost all Canadian provinces, and the parties were negotiating a nation-wide settlement. In June 2022, British Columbia Attorney General David Eby announced a proposed $150 million settlement with Purdue Pharma Canada for the recovery of health-care costs arising from Purdue's illegal marketing of its opioid medications. The settlement would apply to all provinces and territories. Purdue is just one of forty companies named in the class-action suit. On the upside, the settlement prevented Purdue from selling off its Canadian holdings to meet obligations from American claims. That would have left Canada with nothing. However, continued action against the other thirty-nine companies is crucial given that the Purdue settlement does not come close to covering the billions in health-related costs. The certification of the class action against the remaining companies is scheduled for a hearing in the autumn of 2023 (Charlebois 2022).

In Chapter 5, I also described court cases against the tobacco industry in Canada for smuggling. Gilmore and Rowell (2018) would later demonstrate that the tobacco industry had continued to engage in global smuggling operations. At the same time, Canadian tobacco manufacturers were in court again. In 2019, a Québec court of appeals unanimously upheld a judgment for close to $15 billion against Canada's three tobacco companies—Imperial Tobacco Canada, JTI-Macdonald, and Rothmans Benson & Hedges. However, the cases remain unsettled with the companies seeking creditor protection which also effectively shields them from making payments to successful plaintiffs. On March 22, 2022, The Ontario Superior Court granted an extension to the stay until September 30, 2022—the eighth such extension which increased the extension period to forty-two months (Physicians for a Smoke-free Canada 2022). The extension also prevents Canada's provinces from collecting from the tobacco companies on their judgment for health care recovery costs with claims in the hundreds of billions of dollars.

Lawsuits have also been brought against e-cigarette company Juul in the United States. In 2015-16, Juul rejected a proposed ad campaign that was aimed strictly at adult smokers in favour of another campaign featuring attractive young models in provocative poses. It then placed the ads on websites catering to young people. These included Nickelodeon, the Cartoon Network, Seventeen magazine and educational sites for middle and high school students. A lawsuit was filed against Juul by the Massachusetts Attorney General in 2020 and has not been settled as of April, 2022 (Kaplan 2020). Other state actions have proceeded more expeditiously. Juul has been ordered to make payments in the states of Washington, Arizona, and North Carolina for amounts of $22.5, $14.5, and $40 million, respectively. The company disclosed that it has also reached an unspecified settlement with Louisiana. The funds from the Washington case will be used to fund programs to protect youth and vulnerable populations from deceptive practices. This will include a secret shopper program to detect sales of vaping products to youth. The company has agreed to making the payments without admitting to any wrongdoing. At least nine other states have cases pending against the manufacturer (Gutman 2022).

Canadian political parties are entertaining a different approach for the tobacco epidemic. The Liberal, Progressive Conservative, and New Democrat parties included measures in their respective platforms for the 2021 federal election that would impose significant financial taxes or penalties on the tobacco industry. The victorious Liberal Party committed to requiring tobacco manufacturers to pay for the cost of federal public health investments in tobacco control at $66 million per year (Liberal Party of Canada 2021, 73, 75). This is a concept that could be applied to supplement the recovery of healthcare costs as well. In addition to using the overly-patient courts to recover past costs, government could tax drug industries to recover future healthcare liabilities. It requires only the political will to do so.

Near the end of 2021, New Zealand announced its intent to implement a quite different and certainly controversial strategy—a complete ban on tobacco smoking. However, the ban will not apply to vaping, and it will not be implemented all at once. The legislation will be crafted such that the legal age for smoking will increase each year. In effect, the legislation prevents anyone born after 2008 from being able to legally smoke (Fickling 2021).

This is a bold move that will invoke the time-worn references to the failure of alcohol prohibition. There will be concerns about the impact of the law on the contraband trade, and there will be questions about infringement of personal liberties. On the latter point, a writer for Bloomberg News provided an interesting counterpoint: "Liberal societies will rightly seek to enhance individuals' sovereignty over their bodies, and tread carefully when they take those freedoms away. Addictive drugs already violate that sovereignty, though, by making it physically or psychologically painful to give them up. Tobacco prohibition in New Zealand will certainly infringe on people's freedoms. Tobacco addiction, however, has been doing that for centuries" (Fickling 2021).

Other countries will watch the New Zealand experience with interest. For those who are inclined to be critical of prohibition efforts, it may be helpful to consider that prohibition does not necessarily have to involve criminalization. Enforcement efforts could be restricted to confiscation of product in the case of those not legally allowed to be in possession.

A problem with many court awards against drug companies is that, even in amounts of hundreds of millions of dollars against a single company, the awards are insufficient to motivate change in a large, abundantly lucrative drug corporation. Such judgments also punish mostly the shareholders, not the company executives who are typically the decision makers. However, when the settlements are in the billions of dollars, they become potentially ruinous of individual companies. Cannabis companies (and certainly their shareholders) would be wise to watch the legal developments in the pharmaceutical and tobacco industries closely. As described earlier in this report, class actions have already appeared against cannabis companies from plaintiffs seeking redress for alleged securities violations and illness arising from contaminated product.

Recent developments in the US have even more portents for the cannabis industry. Lawsuits against the cannabis industry have tripled in the past two years in that country. Cannabis company board members and officers are scrambling to find affordable insurance coverage that will adequately protect them. Many insurers are reluctant to take the risk (Rahn 2022). Another yellow flag for Canadian cannabis companies.

A harbinger of changing awareness is that the media are increasingly covering stories related to drug problems. This includes the court actions—thus spreading the perspective that our legal drug corporations are, at least in part, culpable for drug-related harms. By extension, they may also be seen as culpable for the attendant costs of drug-related harms to the Canadian economy which were estimated at $46 billion for 2017 alone (Canadian Substance Use Costs and Harms Working Group 2020). There is no reason to believe that the annual costs may have decreased since then. As discussed earlier, data on past trends suggests that the costs are more likely to have increased.

There is another cause for mild optimism. If I may be granted the privilege of a casual observation from over the course of my career, I would say that the public is now better informed about drugs and drug problems than at any other time. I would also suggest that stigma towards drug users has decreased over that time. There is still a lot of progress required on that front, but the change, as modest as it is, is in the right direction.

Windows of opportunity for establishing more evidence-based and humanitarian drug policy will continue to occasionally open within the architecture of the status quo. On solitary policy issues, it is possible that larger unprecedented successes can be built upon initial improvements. Some possibilities follow.

Despite push back from the federal Liberals, Québec raised the minimum age for cannabis possession from 18 to 21 (CBC News 2020b), as was recommended by several health policy authorities during the consultation phase of legalization. There have also been overtures that a change in ruling party at the federal level could result in a similar change nationally (Gilmore 2018).

Health Canada may continue to bring licensed cannabis producers more in line with the laws on product promotion, following up on its modest success with curtailing illegal practices such as public advertising and sponsorship of events.

The Ministry of Health continues to log individual instances of failures of integrity in product from licensed producers. Yet, government has not explicitly acknowledged the ongoing systemic quality control problem in the mass production model of Canada's larger cannabis producers. If the industry were to make a shift away from large factories to smaller craft growers, there may be more product of elevated integrity available. A major hurdle is the substantial licensing fees for a small craft operator to enter the cultivation business. Perhaps market forces, both legal and illegal, will ultimately have some impact on government policy in this regard. Ryan Stoa, in his book *Craft Weed*, makes a case for an increased emphasis on craft growers in the cannabis industry (Stoa 2018).

While it will be met with controversy, I would also argue that there should be a different orientation of government towards the unlicensed trade. It should be less concerned with demonizing and punishing it, and more interested in bringing unlicensed growers within the fold of licensed operations. Perhaps the licenses of companies who have repeatedly misbehaved could be transferred to non-licensed operators who demonstrate a willingness to behave. Of course, the requirements of product integrity and regulatory adherence would apply to the new licence holder.

The Liberal Party's false claims tying the unlicensed cannabis trade to organized crime, have continued to be discredited by its own intel. Annual reports from The Public Prosecution Service of Canada (PPSC) have little to say of a connection between the unlicensed cannabis trade and organized crime. Out of hundreds of thousands of drug-related cases from a six-year period spanning April 1, 2015 to March 31, 2021, only two cases of organized crime involvement with cannabis were reported. Organized crime activity was focused on drugs such as cocaine, crack cocaine, carfentanil, fentanyl, heroin, ketamine, MDMA and methamphetamine (Public Prosecution Service of Canada 2016, 2017, 2018, 2019, 2020, 2021).

Criminal Intelligence Service Canada (CISC) curates intelligence and provides reports for law enforcement agencies on organized and serious crime in Canada. I was able to access annual report summaries from CISC for 2019, 2020 and 2021. (I wrote to CISC in January 2022 asking for reports from 2015 through 2018. I received a response indicating that there was no unclassified information available before 2019.) The 2019, 2020, and 2021 CISC reports identified organized crime involvement with cocaine, synthetic drugs, fentanyl, and methamphetamine. There was no mention of organized crime involvement with cannabis (Criminal Intelligence Service Canada 2019, 2021, 2022). These reports coincide with the time after recreational use was legalized. It is unfortunate that the same information is not available for the years immediately preceding legalization. An important side note to this issue is that while organized crime has not, historically, had a prominent presence in the unlicensed cannabis trade, it is also true that some licensed companies have been shown to have connections to organized crime.

The campaign of associating the unlicensed cannabis trade to dangerous organized crime has also had a stigmatizing impact upon those who buy cannabis from the unlicensed trade. It has also acted to justify harsh measures against them. Given the legacy of falsehood on which the legislative provisions are based, this must stop.

Potential solutions to the continued criminalization of Canadians for minor cannabis offences include:

- *de jure provisions that would remove criminal penalties for possession of unlicensed cannabis from The Cannabis Act or introduce new separate legislation that would decriminalize possession of cannabis*

- *de facto agreements between enforcement and prosecutorial authorities that would reduce cannabis-related charges*

- *de jure or de facto provisions pertaining to the decriminalization of all drugs that would include cannabis*

There has been little recent discussion of *de jure* or *de facto* changes that are specific to penalties for cannabis possession. Most of the discussion has been around the decriminalization of all drugs.

The Public Prosecution Service of Canada directive for a change in prosecutorial approach is a *de facto* intervention and a positive development. The increase of drug possession charges being dropped before trial in Ontario is particularly promising.

WHAT'S NEXT IN DRUG POLICY REFORM?

Despite sustained public pressure, *de jure* decriminalization of all drugs in Canada seems unlikely soon. In September of 2020, Prime Minister Trudeau rejected the idea saying: "I think in any crisis like this, there is not one silver bullet" (CBC News 2020a). This same metaphor had apparently been test-marketed for the PM days earlier by his Health Minister, Patti Hajdu (T. Wright 2020). The Prime Minister went on to say that his government was considering other options such as greater access to a safe supply of opioids.

There are no silver bullets in drug policy. As this book has demonstrated, commercial legalization of a drug, cannabis in this case, was not a silver bullet.

But decriminalization would stop the criminalization of drug users that only makes their plight more difficult. It would also yield a significant reduction in inhumane and ineffective expenditures of Canadians' taxes. The Public Prosecution Service of Canada alone has an annual budget of just over $200 million. Imagine what it might accomplish by redeploying the approximate three quarters of that annual budget that it spends on drug prosecutions each year. Then imagine a broader redeployment of funds from enforcement, judicial, and incarceration services.

As described earlier, the provision of a safe supply of currently illegal drugs would save lives but also present challenges and perils. A genuine public health priority must be our uncompromising guide to all regulatory design decisions. That is a tall order but the status quo is not immutable. Political will, fuelled by large scale public demand for a genuine public health and social justice imperative could lead to a new era of much improved drug policy. Such a transformation could reduce the extensive harm and costs associated with the misuse of drug products. It could probably do so substantially and sustainably.

Canada should continue its legal, regulated cannabis regime as an alternative to an unregulated illegal one. However, a vastly different kind of supply and regulatory paradigm is required. Large, monied licensed producers continue to resist reform. They attempt to sabotage what they see as regulatory infringement on their entitlement to maximize market expansion and profit. Even under a generously forgiving regime, these producers complain of being chaffed under the yoke of regulation. If the current regulatory model remains unpalatable for the industry and infeasible for government to adequately enforce, then the alternative is to remove the profit motive altogether and replace it with something else. In the previous chapter, I introduced such a not-for-profit model for the licensed cannabis industry that was inspired by one proposed for the licensed tobacco trade. That chapter also introduced proposals of support for such a revolutionary model from Canada, the United States, The United Kingdom, and France. The chapter also noted that other countries, including Uruguay, Spain, and Malta, are pursuing other kinds of not-for-profit approaches. Clearly, international momentum for an approach that removes the profit motive is building, however slowly.

In Canada, la Province de Québec continues to be a leader with its bold legislative initiatives. One such initiative followed the evidence-based advice of public health authorities across Canada to raise the minimum age for cannabis possession to twenty-one years. The move was criticized by those who feared that this would open cannabis users under the increased legal age to criminal prosecution. But this is disingenuous or ill-considered. Simple decriminalization provides a safeguard.

Another progressive Québec initiative directs all revenues from the provincial government's cannabis retail monopoly to cover operational costs first and to then be directed exclusively to addiction prevention and treatment programs. These reforms have risen far above the shallow sloganeering of the Canadian Government. They possess genuine potential to help keep cannabis out of the hands of children and profits out of the pockets of (corporate) criminals.

The widespread realization of not-for-profit approaches within cannabis law reform initiatives is probably not imminent. However, the discussion is happening internationally, and the appearance of such models on the menu of options, both in Canada and abroad, appears to be increasing.

Psychedelics are following the same path as cannabis, which means the lessons from cannabis failures can be applied if the political will exists to do so.

Finally, the decriminalization of all drugs continues to maintain a high profile globally and at multiple levels of government within nations.

While meaningful change usually happens slowly, if at all, we can sometimes be surprised. Let's consider the recent history of cannabis legalization for recreational use in Canada. Attempts at cannabis law reform, through decriminalization, remained fruitless for decades, despite the Liberal and NDP parties having formal positions in favour of decriminalization. Many drug policy authorities and advocates also supported decriminalization. As of 2010, only the national Green Party supported the less politically palatable legalization for recreational use (Cannabis Digest 2010). The then-ruling Progressive Conservative Party favoured continued prohibition. But just 2 years later, the Liberal Party adopted a motion to support legalization and made it a premier issue in the 2015 federal election. It happened 3 years after that. Within 8 years, a fringe idea became functioning Canadian law.

So, it may be premature to conclude that other dramatic shifts could not occur within a surprisingly short period under the right circumstances. Opportunities may arise from changes in a government or from the occurrence of a dramatic, high-profile event that creates political leverage for change.

Canada's national, provincial, and community health organizations are equipped to advise government and inform the public, to mobilize interest and public action, and to shepherd movement towards significant innovations in health policy. I acknowledge this is a daunting ambition. But, if those legislatively mandated to protect public health will not assume this responsibility, then who will? Perhaps our health organizations need some encouragement and publicly visible support from the people whose taxes provide their funding.

As daunting as such an undertaking may be, we must consider the consequences if we do not do this. We will most likely see continued, and perhaps increasingly, elevated levels of harms and costs. And for how much longer—years, decades, generations? Most of the harms and costs will continue to arise from our legal drug trades—under the cover of duplicitous rhetoric about the threats of drug dealers and organized crime. As cannabis and perhaps other psychedelic drug trades make their way from illegal to legal ones, will their respective industries add to the predominance of our legal trades in the harms and costs? This is difficult to predict. But if we had to guess, based upon what we know, I believe the wisest guess would be 'yes'.

I may not witness global revolutionary reforms in drug policy during my career or even my lifetime. But I am cautiously hopeful for the future. There is simply no strategic advantage to pessimism. My aspiration for this book is that it will provide one rung in a ladder. Other advocates for reform will add their own rungs. It will remain for a future advocate to climb the ladder.

We now have myriad opportunities for the exchange of ideas through print and digital audio and video technologies. The internet provides an instantaneous world-wide communication capacity. In the history of civilization, there has never been a better time nor greater capacity to spread an idea. What miraculous innovations might be available to our future ladder climber?

Now is the time for curating and communicating what we know about the potential harmful impact of creating new, monolithic, revenue-driven, drug product corporations. It is also the time for guiding evidence-based policy reform with a public health and social justice priority. The lessons learned from Canada's experience with cannabis law reform are indispensable. As drug law reform continues to proliferate in Canada, and abroad, those lessons will be ignored at our peril. The content of this book has never been more relevant or timely.

The onus for producing change should not reside solely with the drug policy professionals. Now is the time for all of us to speak to our government about cannabis and other drug law reform. What if we all replaced just a small portion of our leisure activities with participation in the democratic process? There are many options available. We can write to, and attempt to meet with, political leaders and try to educate them. Most importantly, we can let the politicians know that we are prepared to vote based on the answers to our questions and the party's policies on drugs. We can look for opportunities when governments are holding public consultations. We can write letters to the editor of the daily and weekly newspapers or articles for the many monthly journals or to the many burgeoning independent online news platforms. Or any one of us could really go down the rabbit hole and write a book! Educators, at all levels, can raise exciting new ideas in the classrooms, as can religious leaders in their weekly address to congregations. We can take advantage of the enormous reach of blogging platforms and social media. But, for the latter, a thick skin is helpful. Social media can be a nasty environment. Unfollow/mute/block are indispensable and easily deployed tools. But social media is also a platform with many well-informed and respectful contributors. For those who prefer in-the-flesh community participation, join in on a day of community action. Handing out free crystal meth in front of the police station may not be your thing. Such bold actions are probably best left to the activists who are well-seasoned in the nuance and strategy of civil disobedience. But there are other types of less provocative and less perilous options. Apart from demonstrations, people can organize strikes, boycotts, and petitions. Democracy gives us these gifts. Let's use them and encourage others to do the same.

Ultimately, the most toxic and damaging addiction in our society may be the corporate addiction to ever-increasing revenues—an addiction that appears insatiable. It is also an addiction that is enabled by governments, by the parties that form those governments, the economic interests represented by those parties, and ultimately the people who vote for the parties. This is a systemic problem in Canada that goes far beyond drug industries and drug problems. An increasingly prominent literature on "regulatory capture" and "corporate bias theory", has described governments' endangerment of public welfare in service of corporate welfare and expansion for many industries including fossil fuels, nuclear power, pharmaceuticals, construction, transportation, mining, and finance (Campbell 2022). This provides a much broader base of injured parties for counteraction. Elections are another gift of democracy. Attend candidate fora. Inform yourself, ask tough questions, and ask again if you do not like the first answer you get. Regard your vote as a precious tool for change. And when a party breaks a promise once it forms a government, hold a grudge. And do not forget. Holding our politicians accountable for what they promise us at election time is both a strategic and a moral/ethical necessity. But more so the latter. We always have been, and still are, good at figuring stuff out. Except for the occasional misfit, the world's contemporary leaders are intelligent people with advanced educational accomplishments. They are advised by people who are equally well-educated, intelligent, and politically savvy, as are the less-conspicuous people of monied interests who quietly instruct our leaders. Most of our leaders are also magically articulate and charismatic. Or at least they are regarded as such by enough people that they get installed as party leaders and elected. But beneath the veneer of all those prized personal assets lies a core of conflicted loyalties - juxtaposing elitism against opportunity for the many—the proverbial 1 versus 99%. When the priority tips towards the needs of elites, our leaders' laudable assets make them more dangerous.

The world is not in an intellectual crisis. It is in a moral/ethical crisis. Within the context of broader political/economic reforms, Canada and most other nations need a revolutionary change in drug policy. The change may be ushered in partly by a new generation of drug policy researchers and analysts. They may be the undergraduate and graduate students of today, reading this book and imagining a better way. Or the task may fall to a subsequent generation. Whoever feels the passion and grasps the opportunity, will hopefully and necessarily join with a much broader group of justice-minded advocates and activists. They will work towards a world of more equitable opportunity, safety, and perhaps even prosperity, for all. And they will not tolerate governments that willingly sacrifice their people at the alter of corporate dominion. And that is as optimistic as I can be while trafficking in the truth.

References

1. Playing with Our Body Chemistry: Drugs and Society

Brinkmann, Bernd, Justus Beike, Helga Köhler, A. Heinecke, and Thomas Bajanowski. 2002. "Incidence of Alcohol Dependence Among Drunken Drivers." *Drug and Alcohol Dependence* 66 (1): 7-10. https://www.sciencedirect.com/science/article/abs/pii/S0376871601001776#!.

Canada. 2015. "Government of Canada Invests in Research to Tackle Prescription Drug Abuse and Addiction." Modified May 1, 2015. https://www.canada.ca/en/news/archive/2015/05/government-canada-invests-research-tackle-prescription-drug-abuse-addiction.html.

Statistics Canada. 2019. "Causes of Death, 2017." Modified May 30, 2019. https://www150.statcan.gc.ca/n1/daily-quotidien/190530/dq190530c-eng.htm.

———. 2021 "Canadian Tobacco, Alcohol and Drugs (CTADS) Survey: 2017 Detailed Tables." Modified August 12, 2021. https://www.canada.ca/en/health-canada/services/canadian-alcohol-drugs-survey/2017-summary/2017-detailed-tables.html.

Canadian Centre on Substance Use and Addiction. 2013. "Canada's Low-Risk Alcohol Drinking Guidelines Frequently Asked Questions." https://ccsa.ca/sites/default/files/2019-04/2012-FAQs-Canada-Low-Risk-Alcohol-Drinking-Guidelines-en.pdf.

Canadian Substance Use Costs and Harms Scientific Working Group. 2018. "Canadian Substance Use Costs and Harms (2007–2014)." Canadian Centre on Substance Use and Addiction. November 2018. https://ccsa.ca/sites/default/files/2019-04/CSUCH-Canadian-Substance-Use-Costs-Harms-Report-2018-en.pdf.

———. 2020. "Canadian Substance Use Costs and Harms 2015–2017." Canadian Centre on Substance Use and Addiction. June 2020. https://csuch.ca/publications/CSUCH-Canadian-Substance-Use-Costs-Harms-Report-2020-en.pdf.

———. .n.d. "Canadian Substance Use Costs and Harms." Database Version 2.0.0. Canadian Centre on Substance Use and Addiction. Accessed April 12, 2022. https://csuch.ca/explore-the-data/.

Canales, Rodrigo. 2013. "The Deadly Genius of Drug Cartels." Filmed September 2013 at TEDSalon NY2013. Video, 17:43. http://www.ted.com/talks/rodrigo_canales_the_deadly_genius_of_drug_cartels/transcript?language=en.

Centre for Addiction and Mental Health. Drug and Alcohol Treatment Information System (DATIS). 2022. "Characteristics of Substance Abuse, Open, Individuals, Calendar Year 2021." Data file sent to author, June 14, 2022.

DeVillaer, Michael. 1996. "Establishing and Using a Community Inter-Agency Client Monitoring System to Develop Addictions Treatment Programs." *Addiction* 91 (5): 701-09. https://onlinelibrary.wiley.com/doi/abs/10.1046/j.1360-0443.1996.9157016.x.

DeVillaer, Michael and Vicki Smye. 1994. "Understanding Injection Drug Users: The First Step in Planning Needle Exchange Programs." Addiction Research Foundation (Hamilton) and The Department of Public Health Services, Regional Municipality of Hamilton-Wentworth. https://ia801607.us.archive.org/32/items/understandinginj00devi/understandinginj00devi.pdf.

Hajdu, Patti. 2019. "Minister Hajdu Answers Question on the Opioid Crisis." Hon. Patti Hajdu Website. December 10, 2019. Accessed online April 8, 2020; no longer available on January 27, 2021.

REFERENCES

Hilts, Philip J. 1996. *Smoke Screen: The Truth Behind the Tobacco Industry Cover-up.* Reading: Addison-Wesley Publishing Company, Inc.

Kirkham, Chris. 2019. "Juul Disregarded Early Evidence It Was Hooking Teens." *Reuters*, November 5, 2019. https://www.reuters.com/investigates/special-report/juul-eci-garette/.

Konefal, Sarah, Bridget Maloney-Hall, Karen Urbanoski, and the National Treatment Indicators Working Group. 2021. "National Treatment Indicators Report: 2016–2018 Data." Canadian Centre on Substance Use and Addiction. https://ccsa.ca/sites/default/files/2021-01/CCSA-National-Treatment-Indicators-2016-2018-Data-Report-2021-en.pdf.

Kornik, Slav and Caley Ramsay. 2017. "Alberta MLA Says Marijuana Legalization Could Lead to Communist Revolution." *Global News*, November 30, 2017. https://globalnews.ca/news/3889241/alberta-mla-says-marijuana-legalization-could-lead-to-communist-revolution/.

Mavrellis, Channing. 2017. "Transnational Crime and the Developing World." Global Financial Integrity. March 27, 2017. https://secureserver-cdn.net/50.62.198.97/34n.8bd.myftpupload.com/wp-content/uploads/2017/03/Transnational_Crime-final.pdf?time=1657208668.

National Advisory Committee on Prescription Drug Misuse. 2013. "First Do No Harm: Responding to Canada's Prescription Drug Crisis." Canadian Centre on Substance Abuse. March 2013. https://ccsa.ca/sites/default/files/2019-04/Canada-Strategy-Prescription-Drug-Misuse-Report-en.pdf.

National Institute on Drug Abuse. 2020. "Misuse of Prescription Drugs Research Report: What Is the Scope of Prescription Drug Misuse?". June 2020. https://www.drugabuse.gov/download/37630/misuse-prescription-drugs-research-report.pdf?v=add4ee202a1d1f88f8e1fdd2bb83a5ef.

Nigatu, Yeshambel T., Tara Elton-Marshall, Edward M. Adlaf, Anca R. Ialomiteanu, Robert E. Mann, and Hayley A. Hamilton. 2020. "CAMH Monitor e-Report: Substance Use, Mental Health and Well-Being Among Ontario Adults, 1977–2019." Centre for Addiction and Mental Health. https://www.camh.ca/-/media/files/pdfs---camh-monitor/camh-monitor-2019-ereport-pdf.pdf.

Nigatu, Yeshambel T., Tara Elton-Marshall, Jürgen Rehm, and Hayley A. Hamilton. 2021. "CAMH Monitor e-Report: Substance Use, Mental Health and Well-Being Among Ontario Adults, 2020." Centre for Addiction and Mental Health. https://www.camh.ca/-/media/files/pdfs---camh-monitor/2020-cm-full-report-pdf.pdf.

Oxford Martin School. n.d. "Number of Deaths by Risk Factor, World, 2019." Accessed June 1, 2022. https://ourworldindata.org/grapher/number-of-deaths-by-risk-factor?time=latest.

Rehm, J., D. Baliunas, S. Brochu, B. Fischer, W. Gnam, J. Patra, S. Popova, A. Sarnocinska-Hart, and B. Taylor. 2006. "The Cost of Substance Abuse in Canada 2002. Highlights." Canadian Centre on Substance Abuse. March 2006. https://www.ccsa.ca/sites/default/files/2019-05/ccsa-011332-2006.pdf.

Seddon, Toby. 2020. "Immoral in Principle, Unworkable in Practice: Cannabis Law Reform, The Beatles and the Wootton Report." *British Journal of Criminology* 60 (6): 1567–84. https://doi.org/10.1093/bjc/azaa042.

Sherk, Adam. 2020. "The Alcohol Deficit: Canadian Government Revenue and Societal Costs from Alcohol." *Health Promotion and Chronic Disease Prevention in Canada Research, Policy and Practice* 40 (5-6): 139-42. https://www.ncbi.nlm.nih.gov/pmc/articles/PMC7367422/pdf/40_5-6_2.pdf.

Single, Eric, Lynda Robson, Xiaodi Xie, and Jürgen Rehm. 1996. "The Costs of Substance Abuse in Canada 1992." Ottawa: Canadian Centre on Substance Abuse.

___. 1998. "The Economic Costs of Alcohol, Tobacco and Illicit Drugs in Canada, 1992." *Addiction* 93 (7): 991-1006. https://doi.org/10.1046/j.1360-0443.1998.9379914.x.

Special Advisory Committee on the Epidemic of Opioid Overdoses. 2022. "Opioid- and Stimulant-Related Harms in Canada." Public Health Agency of Canada. June 23, 2022. https://health-infobase.canada.ca/substance-related-harms/opioids-stimulants.

Wilt, James. 2018. "Alcohol Industry Officials Lobbied Yukon to Halt Warning Label Study, Emails Show." *The Globe and Mail*, May 22, 2018. https://www.theglobeandmail.com/canada/article-alcohol-industry-officials-lobbied-yukon-to-halt-warning-label-study/.

2. Persuasion and Influence

Alfayad, Khaldoon, Rachael L. Murray, John Britton, and Alexander B. Barker. 2021. "Content Analysis of Netflix and Amazon Prime Instant Video Original Films in the UK for Alcohol, Tobacco and Junk Food Imagery." *Journal of Public Health* 44 (2): 302-9. https://academic.oup.com/jpubhealth/advance-article/doi/10.1093/pubmed/fdab022/6155840.

Arnett, Jeffrey Jensen and George Terhanian. 1998. "Adolescents' Responses to Cigarette Advertisements: Links Between Exposure, Liking, and the Appeal of Smoking." *Tobacco Control* 7 (2): 129-33. http://www.jstor.org/stable/20207485.

Associated Press. 1998. "Youth Smoking Rises 73% in 9 Years." *The New York Times*, October 9, 1998. https://www.nytimes.com/1998/10/09/us/youth-smoking-rises-73-in-9-years.html.

Banks, Emily, Amelia Yazidjoglou, Sinan Brown, Mai Nguyen, Melonie Martin, Katie Beckwith, Amanda Daluwatta, Sai Campbell, and Grace Joshy. 2022. "Electronic Cigarettes and Health Outcomes: Systematic Review of Global Evidence". Australian Department of Health. National Centre for Epidemiology and Population Health. https://openresearch-repository.anu.edu.au/bitstream/1885/262914/1/Electronic%20cigarettes%20health%20outcomes%20review_2022_WCAG.pdf.

Bauer, Barbara E. 2021. "Hamilton Morris Synthesizes 5-MeO-DMT in 'Pharmacopeia.'" *PSR*, January 5, 2021. https://psychedelicreview.com/hamilton-morris-synthesizes-5-meo-dmt/.

Campaign for Tobacco Free Kids. "Tobacco Company Quotes on Marketing to Kids." May 14, 2001. https://www.tobaccofreekids.org/assets/factsheets/0114.pdf.

Canada. 2021. "Canadian Tobacco, Alcohol and Drugs (CTADS) Survey: 2017 Detailed Tables." Modified August 12, 2021. https://www.canada.ca/en/health-canada/services/canadian-tobacco-alcohol-drugs-survey/2017-summary/2017-detailed-tables.html#t2.

Canadian Public Health Association. 2011. "Too High a Cost: A Public Health Approach to Alcohol Policy in Canada." December 2011. https://www.cpha.ca/sites/default/files/assets/positions/position-paper-alcohol_e.pdf.

Carstairs, Catherine. 2022. "From Prohibition to Legalization: Cannabis Use and the Law." In *The High North: Cannabis in Canada*, edited by Andrew D. Hathaway and Clayton James Smith McCann, 29-51. Vancouver: University of British Columbia Press.

Centre for Addiction and Mental Health. Drug and Alcohol Treatment Information System (DATIS). 2013. "Characteristics of Substance Abuse, Open, Admissions, Calendar Year 2012." Data file sent to author, September 25, 2013.

REFERENCES

Chapman, Matthew and Ferdinand Moeck. 2021. "Tobacco Giant JTI Placing Stealth Adverts for its Brands on Facebook and Instagram." The Bureau of Investigative Journalism. April 25, 2021. https://www.thebureauinvestigates.com/stories/2021-04-25/tobacco-giant-jti-placing-stealth-adverts-for-its-brands-on-facebook-and-instagram.

Giesbrecht, Norman, Ashley Wettlaufer, Nicole April, Mark Asbridge, Samantha Cukier, Robert Mann, Janet McAllister, et al. 2013. "Strategies to Reduce Alcohol-Related Harms and Costs in Canada: A Comparison of Provincial Policies." Centre for Addiction and Mental Health. https://www.uvic.ca/research/centres/cisur/assets/docs/report-strategies-to-reduce-alcohol.pdf.

Hilts, Philip J. 1996. *Smoke Screen: The Truth Behind the Tobacco Industry Cover-up.* Reading: Addison-Wesley Publishing Company, Inc.

Hughes, Tonda. 2005. "Alcohol Use and Alcohol-Related Problems Among Lesbians and Gay Men." *Annual Review of Nursing Research* 23: 283-325. https://pubmed.ncbi.nlm.nih.gov/16353369/ .

Hurt, R.D., K.P. Offord, I.T. Croghan, L. Gomez-Dahl, T.E. Kottke, R.M. Morse, R.J. Melton.1996. "Mortality Following Inpatient Addictions Treatment. Role of Tobacco Use in a Community-Based Cohort." *Journal of the American Medical Association 275* (14): 1097-103. https://pubmed.ncbi.nlm.nih.gov/8601929/.

Josefson, Deborah. 1998. "Tobacco Company Targeted Marketing Campaign at Teenagers." *British Medical Journal* 316:327. doi: https://doi.org/10.1136/bmj.316.7128.327f .

Lexchin, Joel, Sharon Batt, Devorah Goldberg, and Adrienne Shnier. 2022. "National Patient Groups in Canada and Their Disclosure of Relationships with Pharmaceutical Companies: A Cross-Sectional Study." *British Medical Journal Open* 12 (3). https://bmjopen.bmj.com/content/12/3/e055287.

Lopez, German. 2018. "Imagine If the Media Covered Alcohol Like Other Drugs." *Vox*, September 20, 2018. https://www.vox.com/2015/6/15/8774233/alcohol-dangerous.

McBreen, Kelen. 2021. "Coors Light Promo Runs in Your Dreams by Unlocking the Subconscious." *Newswars*, February 8, 2021. https://www.newswars.com/coors-light-promo-runs-in-your-dreams-by-unlocking-the-subconscious/.

Moutinho, Sofia. 2021. "Are Advertisers Coming for Your Dreams?" *Science* June 11. https://www.science.org/news/2021/06/are-advertisers-coming-your-dreams.

North, Adrian C., David J. Hargreaves, and Jennifer McKendrick. 1997. "In-Store Music Affects Product Choice." *Nature* 390 (132). https://www.nature.com/articles/36484.

Pierce, John P., Lora Lee, and Elizabeth A. Gilpin. 1994. "Smoking Initiation by Adolescent Girls, 1944 Through 1988. An Association with Targeted Advertising." *Journal of the American Medical Association* 271 (8): 608-11. https://jamanetwork.com/journals/jama/article-abstract/365740.

Spithoff, Sheryl. 2019. "Addressing Rising Alcohol-Related Harms in Canada." *Canadian Medical Association Journal* 191 (29): E802-E803. https://www.cmaj.ca/content/191/29/E802.

Surgeon General to the United States. 1964. "Smoking and Health: Report of the Advisory Committee to the Surgeon General of the United States." https://www.pbs.org/newshour/health/first-surgeon-general-report-on-smokings-health-effects-marks-50-year-anniversary.

Tobacco Control Legal Consortium. 2012. "Cause and Effect: Tobacco Marketing Increases Youth Tobacco Use, Findings from the 2012 Surgeon General's Report." June 2012. https://www.publichealthlawcenter.org/sites/default/files/resources/tclc-guide-SGReport-Findings-Youth-Marketing-2012.pdf.

Trueheart, Charles. "Marketers Test Dakota Cigarettes." *The Washington Post*, August 14,

1991. https://www.washingtonpost.com/archive/lifestyle/1991/08/14/marketers-test-dakota-cigarettes/61904df8-3375-46dc-8145-acbe67da63b7/.

United States District Court for the District of Columbia. "United States of America vs. Philip Morris USA, Inc., Amended Final Opinion (Civil Action No. 99-2496 GK)." 2006. http://www.publichealthlawcenter.org/sites/default/files/resources/doj-final-opinion.pdf.

World Health Organization. 2010. "Global Strategy to Reduce Harmful Use of Alcohol." May 31, 2010. https://www.who.int/publications/i/item/9789241599931.

3. A Brief History of Cannabis Policy

Boyd, Susan C. 2017. *Busted: An Illustrated History of Drug Prohibition in Canada*. Halifax: Fernwood Publishing.

Canada. "Marihuana for Medical Purposes Regulations." Modified June 10, 2013. https://www.canada.ca/en/news/archive/2013/06/marihuana-medical-purposes-regulations.html.

___. Health Canada. 2016. "Understanding the New Access to Cannabis for Medical Purposes Regulations." Modified September 30, 2016. https://www.canada.ca/en/health-canada/services/publications/drugs-health-products/understanding-new-access-to-cannabis-for-medical-purposes-regulations.html.

___. Justice Laws Website. 2022. "Marihuana Medical Access Regulations." Modified June 29, 2022. https://laws-lois.justice.gc.ca/eng/regulations/SOR-2001-227/index.html.

Canadian Public Health Association. 2014. "A New Approach to Managing Illegal Psychoactive Substances in Canada. CPHA Position Paper." May 2014. https://www.cpha.ca/sites/default/files/assets/policy/ips_2014-05-15_e.pdf.

Carstairs, Catherine. 2022. "From Prohibition to Legalization: Cannabis Use and the Law." in *The High North: Cannabis in Canada*, edited by Andrew D. Hathaway and Clayton James Smith McCann. Vancouver: University of British Columbia Press.

Carter, Connie I. and Donald Macpherson. 2013. "Getting to Tomorrow: a Report on Canadian Drug Policy." Canadian Drug Policy Coalition. May 2013. https://www.drugpolicy.ca/wp-content/uploads/2013/01/CDPC2013_en.pdf.

Caulkins, Jonathan P., Beau Kilmer, Mark A. R. Kleiman, Robert J. MacCoun, Gregory Midgette, Pat Oglesby, Rosalie Liccardo Pacula, and Peter H. Reuter. 2015. "Considering Marijuana Legalization: Insights for Vermont and Other Jurisdictions." The RAND Corporation. January 2015. https://www.rand.org/content/dam/rand/pubs/research_reports/RR800/RR864/RAND_RR864.pdf.

Centre for Addiction and Mental Health. 2014. "Cannabis Policy Framework." October 2014. https://www.camh.ca/-/media/files/pdfs---public-policy-submissions/camh-cannabispolicyframework-pdf.pdf.

Commission of Inquiry into the Non-medical Use of Drugs. 1972. "Cannabis: A Report of the Commission of Inquiry into the Non-Medical Use of Drugs." Information Canada. https://archive.org/details/cannabis0000unse.

___. 1973a. "Final Report." Information Canada. http://publications.gc.ca/site/eng/9.699765/publication.html.

___. 1973b "Interim Report." Information Canada. https://openlibrary.org/books/OL20999867M/Interim_report_of_the_Commission_of_Inquiry_into_the_non-medical_use_of_drugs.

Erickson, Patricia G. 1980. *Cannabis Criminals: The Social Effects of Punishment on Drug Users.* Toronto: The Addiction Research Foundation of Ontario.

Erickson, Patricia G., Diane M. Riley, Yuet W. Cheung, and Patrick A. O'Hare. eds., 1997.

Harm Reduction: A New Direction for Drug Policies and Programs. Toronto: University of Toronto Press.

Erickson, Patricia G. and Elaine Hyshka. 2010. "Four Decades of Cannabis Criminals in Canada: 1970-2010." *Amsterdam Law Forum* 2 (4): 1-14. http://doi.org/10.37974/ALF.144.

Erickson, Patricia G., Mark Van Der Maas, and Andrew D. Hathaway. 2013. "Revisiting Deterrence: Legal Knowledge, Use Context and Arrest Perception for Cannabis." *Czech Sociological Review* 49 (3): 427-48. https://www.jstor.org/stable/23535185.

Fischer, Benedikt. 1997. "The Battle for a New Canadian Drug Law: A Legal Basis for Harm Reduction or a New Rhetoric for Prohibition? A Chronology." In *Harm Reduction: A New Direction for Drug Policies and Programs*, edited by Patricia G. Erickson, Diane M. Riley, Yuet W. Cheung, and Patrick A. O'Hare, 47-68. Toronto: University of Toronto Press.

Murkin, George. 2015. "Cannabis Social Clubs in Spain: Legalisation Without Commercialisation." Transform Drugs. January 2015. https://transformdrugs.org/assets/files/PDFs/cannabis-in-spain-briefing-2018.pdf.

Room, Robin, Benedikt Fischer, Wayne Hall, Simon Lenton, and Peter Reuter. 2010. *Cannabis Policy: Moving Beyond Stalemate*. Oxford: Oxford University Press.

Room, Robin. 2014. "Legalizing a Market for Cannabis for Pleasure: Colorado, Washington, Uruguay and Beyond." *Addiction* 109 (3): 45–51. https://www.ncbi.nlm.nih.gov/pubmed/24180513.

Schwartz, Daniel. 2014. "Marijuana Was Criminalized in 1923, but Why?" *CBC News*, May 6, 2014. https://www.cbc.ca/news/health/marijuana-was-criminalized-in-1923-but-why-1.2630436.

Senate Special Committee on Illegal Drugs. 2002. "Cannabis: Our Position for a Canadian Public Policy. Summary Report." September 2002. http://www.parl.gc.ca/Content/SEN/Committee/371/ille/rep/summary-e.pdf.

Spithoff, Sheryl, Brian Emerson, and Andrea Spithoff. 2015. "Cannabis Legalization: Adhering to Public Health Best Practice." *Canadian Medical Association Journal* 187 (16): 1211-16. http://www.cmaj.ca/content/187/16/1211.figures-only.

Task Force on Cannabis Legalization and Regulation. 2016. "A Framework for the Legalization and Regulation of Cannabis in Canada: Final Report." Health Canada, December 2016. http://healthycanadians.gc.ca/task-force-marijuana-groupe-etude/framework-cadre/alt/framework-cadre-eng.pdf.

4. Cannabis Decriminalization: A Proven Success Abandoned

Ammerman, Seth, Sheryl Ryan, and William P. Adelman. 2015. "The Impact of Marijuana Policies on Youth: Clinical, Research, and Legal Update. AAP Policy Statement." *Pediatrics* 135 (3): e769-85. https://pubmed.ncbi.nlm.nih.gov/25624385/.

Bouchard, Martin, Marc Alain, and Holly Nguyen. 2009. "Convenient Labour: The Prevalence and Nature of Youth Involvement in the Cannabis Cultivation Industry." *International Journal of Drug Policy* 20 (6): 467-74. https://pubmed.ncbi.nlm.nih.gov/19345079/.

Boyd, Susan C. and Connie Carter. 2014. *Killer Weed: Grow Ops, Media, and Justice*. Toronto: University of Toronto Press.

Canada. 2014a. "Recall of Marijuana for Medical Purposes - Greenleaf Medicinals." April 18, 2014. https://www.healthycanadians.gc.ca/recall-alert-rappel-avis/hc-sc/2014/39183a-eng.php.

___. 2014b. "Recall of Marijuana for Medical Purposes - Peace Naturals Project Inc." May 9, 2014. https://www.healthycanadians.gc.ca/recall-alert-rappel-avis/hc-sc/2014/39457a-eng.php.

___. 2014c. "Recall of Marijuana for Medical Purposes - Whistler Medical Marijuana Corp." August 15, 2014. https://www.healthycanadians.gc.ca/recall-alert-rappel-avis/hc-sc/2014/41115a-eng.php.

___. 2015. "Recall of Marijuana for Medical Purposes - Peace Naturals Project Inc." February 10, 2015. https://www.healthycanadians.gc.ca/recall-alert-rappel-avis/hc-sc/2015/43677a-eng.php.

___. 2017. "Recall of Cannabis for Medical Purposes—Mettrum Ltd." February 7, 2017. http://www.healthycanadians.gc.ca/recall-alert-rappel-avis/hc-sc/2016/62102r-eng.php.

___. House of Commons. 2016. "Opposition Motion: Decriminalization of Marijuana Possession." *House of Commons Debates*, 42nd Parl, 1st Sess, No 071 (June 13) 4368 (1200-1400) (Hon Geoff Regan). https://www.ourcommons.ca/DocumentViewer/en/42-1/house/sitting-71/hansard.

Capler, Rielle, Neil Boyd, and Donald MacPherson. 2016. "Organized Crime in the Cannabis Market: Evidence and Implications." Canadian Drug Policy Coalition. August 9, 2016. https://www.drugpolicy.ca/wp-content/uploads/2016/11/CDPC_Submission_Cannabis-and-Organized-Crime_Aug9-2016_Full-Final-1.pdf.

Caulkins, Jonathan P., Beau Kilmer, Mark A. R. Kleiman, Robert J. MacCoun, Gregory Midgette, Pat Oglesby, Rosalie Liccardo Pacula, and Peter H. Reuter. 2015. "Considering Marijuana Legalization: Insights for Vermont and Other Jurisdictions." The RAND Corporation. January 2015. https://www.rand.org/content/dam/rand/pubs/research_reports/RR800/RR864/RAND_RR864.pdf.

CBC News. 2015. "Trudeau Pledges to Work on Pot Legalization Policy 'Right Away' if Elected." October 1, 2015. http://www.cbc.ca/news/politics/trudeau-pot-marijuana-legalization-timeline-1.3252088.

Centre for Addiction and Mental Health. 2014. "Cannabis Policy Framework." October 2014. https://www.camh.ca/-/media/files/pdfs---public-policy-submissions/camh-cannabispolicyframework-pdf.pdf.

Coomber, Ross and Paul Turnbull. 2007. "Arenas of Drug Transactions: Adolescent Cannabis Transactions in England - Social Supply." *Journal of Drug Issues* 37: 845–65. https://journals.sagepub.com/doi/10.1177/002204260703700406.

Cotter, Adam, Jacob Greenland, and Maisie Karam. 2015. "Drug-Related Offences in Canada, 2013." Statistics Canada, Modified November 30, 2015. http://www.statcan.gc.ca/pub/85-002-x/2015001/article/14201-eng.htm.

DeVillaer, Michael. 2017. "Cannabis Law Reform in Canada: Pretense & Perils." McMaster University, The Peter Boris Centre for Addictions Research. February 2017. https://fhs.mcmaster.ca/pbcar/documents/Pretense%20&%20Perils%20FINAL.PDF.

District of Columbia Office of the Attorney General. 2015. "Office of the Attorney General Releases Frequently Asked Questions Document on District's Marijuana Laws." February 26, 2015. https://oag.dc.gov/release/office-attorney-general-releases-frequently-asked.

Duff, Cameron, Mark Asbridge, Serge Brochu, Marie-Marthe Cousineau, Andrew. D. Hathaway, David Marsh, and Patricia G. Erickson. 2011. "A Canadian Perspective on Cannabis Normalization Among Adults." *Addiction Research & Theory* 20 (4): 271-83. https://doi.org/10.3109/16066359.2011.618957.

Edge, Megan and Lauren Andrews. 2016. "Timeline: Notable Moments in 40 Years of Alaska's History with Marijuana." *Alaska Dispatch News*, September 28, 2016. https://www.adn.com/cannabis-north/article/alaska-weed-history/2014/04/14/.

REFERENCES

Elliott, Josh. 2015. "Liberals 'Committed' to Legalizing Marijuana: Trudeau." *CTV News*, September 30, 2015. http://www.ctvnews.ca/politics/election/liberals-committed-to-legalizing-marijuana-trudeau-1.2588260.

Erickson, Patricia G. 1980. *Cannabis Criminals: The Social Effects of Punishment on Drug Users*. Toronto: The Addiction Research Foundation of Ontario.

Erickson, Patricia G. and Elaine Hyshka. 2010. "Four Decades of Cannabis Criminals in Canada: 1970-2010." *Amsterdam Law Forum* 2 (4): 1-14. http://doi.org/10.37974/ALF.144.

Erickson, Patricia G., Mark Van Der Maas, and Andrew D. Hathaway. 2013. "Revisiting Deterrence: Legal Knowledge, Use Context and Arrest Perception for Cannabis." *Czech Sociological Review* 49 (3): 427-48. https://esreview.soc.cas.cz/pdfs/csr/2013/03/04.pdf.

Fischer, Benedikt. 1997. "The Battle for a New Canadian Drug Law: A Legal Basis for Harm Reduction or a New Rhetoric for Prohibition? A Chronology." In *Harm Reduction: A New Direction for Drug Policies and Programs*, edited by Patricia G. Erickson, Diane M. Riley, Yuet W. Cheung, and Patrick A. O'Hare, 47-68. Toronto: University of Toronto Press.

Glenza, J. 2016. "UN Backs Prohibitionist Drug Policies Despite Call for More 'Humane Solution'." *The Guardian,* April 20, 2016 . https://www.theguardian.com/world/2016/apr/19/un-summit-global-war-drugs-agreement-approved.

Hathaway, Andrew D. 2004. "Cannabis Users' Informal Rules for Managing Stigma and Risk." *Deviant Behavior* 25 (6): 559–77. https://doi.org/10.1080/01639620490484095.

Korf, Dirk J. Serge Brochu, Annemieke Benschop, Lana D. Harrison, Patricia G. Erickson. 2008. "Teen Drug Sellers: An International Study of Segregated Drug Markets and Related Violence." *Contemporary Drug Problems* 35 (1): 153-76. https://doi.org/10.1177/009145090803500107.

Leblanc, D. 2016. "Ottawa Plans to Open Up Legal Market for Cannabis by 2019." *The Globe and Mail*, December 13, 2016. http://www.theglobeandmail.com/news/politics/federal-task-force-advises-wide-ranging-legalization-of-recreational-marijuana/article33307322/.

Liberal Party of Canada. n.d. "Keep Marijuana Out of Our Kids' Hands." Accessed April 25, 2022. https://liberal.ca/keep-marijuana-out-of-our-kids-hands/.

National Organization for the Reform of Marijuana Laws. 2016. "States That Have Decriminalized." November 7, 2016. http://norml.org/aboutmarijuana/item/states-that-have-decriminalized.

Pasca, Teodora. 2016. "A Perfect Storm: Marijuana Regulation Is on the Horizon." *Varsity Magazine*, University of Toronto, April 1, 2016. http://magazine.thevarsity.ca/2016/04/01/a-perfect-storm/.

Public Prosecution Service of Canada. 2016. "Annual Report 2015–2016." June 30, 2016. https://www.ppsc-sppc.gc.ca/eng/pub/ar-ra/2015_2016/ar16-ra16.pdf.

Rehm, Jürgen and David Nutt. 2015. "Cannabis Without the Hot Air." Filmed November 2015 at University of Toronto, Munk School of Global Affairs, Toronto ON. Video. Accessed online January 24, 2017; no longer available April 5, 2022.

Robertson, Grant and Greg McArthur. 2016a. "What's in Your Weed?" *The Globe and Mail*, July 29, 2016. http://www.theglobeandmail.com/news/investigations/globe-investigation-whats-in-your-weed-we-tested-dispensary-marijuana-to-findout/article31144496/.

____. 2016b. "What's Not in Your Weed?" *The Globe and Mail*, July 29, 2016. Accessed online January 24, 2017; no longer available April 6, 2022.

Room, Robin, Benedikt Fischer, Wayne Hall, Simon Lenton, and Peter Reuter. 2010. *Cannabis Policy: Moving Beyond Stalemate*. Oxford: Oxford University Press.

Room, Robin. 2012. "Reform by Subtraction: The Path of Denunciation of International Drug Treaties and Reaccession with Reservations." *International Journal of Drug Policy* 23 (5): 401-6. https://www.ncbi.nlm.nih.gov/pubmed/22613198.

Senate Special Committee on Illegal Drugs. 2002a. "Cannabis: Our Position for a Canadian Public Policy. Summary Report." September 2002. http://www.parl.gc.ca/Content/SEN/Committee/371/ille/rep/summary-e.pdf.

Senate Special Committee on Illegal Drugs. 2002b. "Cannabis: Our Position for a Canadian Public Policy, Volume I: Parts I and II." September 2002. https://sencanada.ca/Content/SEN/Committee/371/ille/rep/repfinalvol1-e.pdf.

Single, Eric W. 1989. "The Impact of Marijuana Decriminalization: An Update." *Journal of Public Health Policy* 10 (4): 456–66. http://www.michelepolak.com/200spring11/Weekly_Schedule_files/Single.pdf.

Single, Eric, Paul Christie, and Robert Ali. 2000. "The Impact of Cannabis Decriminalisation in Australia and The United States." *Journal of Public Health Policy* 21 (2): 157-86. http://www.parl.gc.ca/content/sen/committee/371/ille/presentation/single-e.htm.

Solecki, A., K. Burnett, and K. Li. 2011. "Drug Production Cases in Selected Canadian Jurisdictions: A Study of Case File Characteristics 1997–2005." Canada, Department of Justice (Access to Information Request). Cited in Rielle Capler, Neil Boyd, and Donald MacPherson 2016. "Organized Crime in the Cannabis Market: Evidence and Implications." Canadian Drug Policy Coalition.

Tahirali, Jesse. 2016. "7 in 10 Canadians Support Marijuana Legalization: Nanos Poll." *CTV News*, June 30, 2016. http://www.ctvnews.ca/canada/7-in-10-canadians-support-marijuana-legalization-nanos-poll-1.2968953.

Task Force on Cannabis Legalization and Regulation. 2016. "A Framework for the Legalization and Regulation of Cannabis in Canada: Final Report." Health Canada, December 2016. http://healthycanadians.gc.ca/task-force-marijuana-groupe-etude/framework-cadre/alt/framework-cadre-eng.pdf.

Task Force on Marijuana Legalization and Regulation. 2016. "Toward the Legalization, Regulation and Restriction of Access to Marijuana: Discussion Paper." June 2016. http://healthycanadians.gc.ca/health-system-systeme-sante/consultations/legalization-marijuana-legalisation/alt/legalization-marijuana-legalisation-eng.pdf.

Wikipedia. 2016. "Legality of Cannabis." November 21, 2016. https://en.wikipedia.org/wiki/Legality_of_cannabis_by_country.

Wilkins, Chris and Paul Sweetsur. 2007. "Individual Dollar Expenditure and Earnings from Cannabis in the New Zealand Population." *International Journal of Drug Policy* 18 (3):187-93. https://www.ncbi.nlm.nih.gov/pubmed/17689365.

5. A New Legal Drug Industry: What Could Possibly Go Wrong?

Almashat, Sammy and Sidney Wolfe. 2012. "Pharmaceutical Industry Criminal and Civil Penalties: An Update." September 27, 2012. Public Citizen. http://www.citizen.org/documents/2073.pdf.

Babor, Thomas F. 2010. "Alcohol: No Ordinary Commodity—A Summary of the Second Edition." *Addiction* 105 (5): 769–79. https://onlinelibrary.wiley.com/doi/10.1111/j.1360-0443.2010.02945.x.

Beeby, Dean. 2016. "Revenue Canada Probe of Pharmacies Finds $58M in Hidden Income." *CBC News*, July 7, 2016. http://www.cbc.ca/news/politics/generic-drugs-pharmacies-canada-revenue-agency-tax-penalties-1.3667050.

REFERENCES

Benic, Geoffrey. 2018. "Aleafia to Acquire Emblem for $173M in All-Stock Transaction." *BNN Bloomberg*, December 19, 2018. https://www.bnnbloomberg.ca/video/aleafia-to-acquire-emblem-for-173m-in-all-stock-transaction~1568754.

BettingBruiser (@bettingbruiser). 2016. Twitter photo, December 4, 2018. https://twitter.com/BettingBruiser/status/1070002859452915712.

Boak, A., H.A. Hamilton, E.M. Adlaf, and R.E. Mann. 2015. "Drug Use Among Ontario Students, 1977-2015: Detailed OSDUHS Findings." (CAMH Research Document Series No. 41). Toronto: Centre for Addiction and Mental Health. (Accessed online January 23, 2017; no longer available April 5, 2022).

Bogdanich Walt and Eric Kolimay. 2003. "2 Paths of Bayer Drug in 80's: Riskier One Steered Overseas." *The New York Times*, May 22, 2003. http://www.nytimes.com/2003/05/22/business/2-paths-of-bayer-drug-in-80-s-riskier-one-steered-overseas.html.

Bonnie, Richard J., Kathleen Stratton, and Leslie Y. Kwan, eds., 2015. "Public Health Implications of Raising the Minimum Age for Purchasing Tobacco Products." U.S. Institute of Medicine. https://nap.nationalacademies.org/catalog/18997/public-health-implications-of-raising-the-minimum-age-of-legal-access-to-tobacco-products.

Brennan, Richard J. 2015. "LCBO Keeps Its Discount Booze Sales Secret." *Toronto Star*, May 8, 2015. https://www.thestar.com/news/canada/2015/05/08/lcbo-keeps-its-discount-booze-sales-secret.html.

Brown Chris and Chris Corday. 2016. "Pesto with a Punch: Edible Marijuana in Canada's Future." *CBC News*, April 9, 2016. http://www.cbc.ca/news/canada/british-columbia/edible-marijuana-legalization-canada-1.3522292.

Brown, Jennifer, Theresa DeAtley, Kevin Welding, Robert Schwartz, Michael Chaiton, Deidre Lawrence Kittner, and Joanna E. Cohen. 2016. "Tobacco Industry Response to Menthol Cigarette Bans in Alberta and Nova Scotia, Canada." *Tobacco Control* July 19, 2016. https://tobaccocontrol.bmj.com/content/26/e1/e71.

Brownson, Elisha G., Callie M. Thompson, Sarah Goldsberry, H. Jonathon Chong, Jeffrey B. Friedrich, Tam N. Pham, Saman Arbabi, Gretchen J. Carrougher, and Nicole S. Gibran. 2016. "Explosion Injuries from E-Cigarettes." *New England Journal of Medicine* 375:1400-02. https://www.nejm.org/doi/10.1056/NEJMc1608478.

Bruser, David and Jesse McLean. 2014a. "Canadians Kept in Dark About Defective Drugs." *Toronto Star*, September 11, 2014. http://www.thestar.com/news/canada/2014/09/11/canadians_kept_in_dark_about_defective_drugs.html.

-. 2014b. "Health Canada Bans Drugs from Two Apotex Factories in India." *Toronto Star*, September 30, 2014. http://www.thestar.com/news/canada/2014/09/30/health_canada_bans_drugs_from_two_indian_factories.html.

Campbell, Meagan. 2017. "How Public Officials Got into the Weed Game." *Maclean's*, April 13, 2017. https://www.macleans.ca/politics/how-public-officials-got-into-the-weed-game/.

Canada. Health Canada. "Policy on Counterfeit Health Products." May 14, 2010. http://www.hc-sc.gc.ca/dhp-mps/compli-conform/activit/pol_0048_counterfeit-contrefacon-eng.php.

___. "Health Labels for Cigarettes and Little Cigars." Modified December 12, 2011. https://www.canada.ca/en/health-canada/services/publications/healthy-living/health-labels-cigarettes-little-cigars.html.

___. "Marihuana for Medical Purposes Regulations." Modified June 10, 2013. https://www.canada.ca/en/news/archive/2013/06/marihuana-medical-purposes-regulations.html.

___. "Information Update - Marijuana for Medical Purposes - Advertising and Licensed Producers." Modified November 25, 2014. http://www.healthycanadians.gc.ca/recall-alert-rappel-avis/hc-sc/2014/42677a-eng.php .

___. "Government of Canada Invests in Research to Tackle Prescription Drug Abuse and Addiction." Modified May 1, 2015. https://www.canada.ca/en/news/archive/2015/05/government-canada-invests-research-tackle-prescription-drug-abuse-addiction.html

___. "Clarification from Health Canada on Myclobutanil and Cannabis." Modified March 9, 2017. https://www.canada.ca/en/health-canada/news/2017/03/clarification_-fromhealthcanadaonmyclobutanilandcannabis.html.

___. 2021. "Canadian Tobacco Alcohol and Drugs Survey (CTADS): 2015 Summary." Modified August 12, 2021. https://www.canada.ca/en/health-canada/services/canadian-alcohol-drugs-survey/2015-summary.html.

Canadian Press. 2016. "A Province-by-Province Look at Opioid-Overdose Stats, Including Fentanyl." *Global News*, November 17, 2016. http://globalnews.ca/news/3072316/a-province-by-province-look-at-opioid-overdose-stats-including-fentanyl/.

___. 2017a. "LCBO Recalled Bottles of Bombay Sapphire London Dry Gin and Georgian Bay Vodka," *CBC News*, May 3, 2017. https://www.cbc.ca/news/canada/toronto/lcbo-gin-recall-bombay-gin-1.4096746.

___. 2017b. "Manslaughter Charges Against Alleged Fentanyl Dealers Mount Across Canada," *CBC News*, October 9, 2017. https://www.cbc.ca/news/canada/toronto/fentanyl-manslaughter-dealers-overdose-death-1.4346539.

Canadian Public Health Association. 2011. "Too High a Cost: A Public Health Approach to Alcohol Policy in Canada." December 2011. https://www.cpha.ca/sites/default/files/assets/positions/position-paper-alcohol_e.pdf.

___. 2016. "A Public Health Approach to the Legalization, Regulation and Restriction of Access to Cannabis. Submission from the Canadian Public Health Association to the Task Force on Marijuana Legalization and Regulation." August 29, 2016. https://www.cpha.ca/sites/default/files/assets/policy/cannabis_submission_e.pdf.

Cao, Yin, Walter C. Willett, Eric B. Rimm, Meir J. Stampfer, and Edward Giovannucci. 2015. "Light to Moderate Intake of Alcohol, Drinking Patterns, and Risk of Cancer: Results from Two Prospective US Cohort Studies." *British Medical JournA al* 351:h4238. http://www.bmj.com/content/351/bmj.h4238.

Caulkins, Jonathan P., Beau Kilmer, Mark A. R. Kleiman, Robert J. MacCoun, Gregory Midgette, Pat Oglesby, Rosalie Liccardo Pacula, and Peter H. Reuter. 2015. "Considering Marijuana Legalization: Insights for Vermont and Other Jurisdictions." The RAND Corporation. January 2015. https://www.rand.org/content/dam/rand/pubs/research_reports/RR800/RR864/RAND_RR864.pdf.

CBC News. 2007. "Court Fines OxyContin Maker $634M US." May 10, 2007. http://www.cbc.ca/news/technology/court-fines-oxycontin-maker-634m-us-1.636582.

___. 2015a. "Medical Marijuana Easily 'Dispensed' in Vancouver." February 2, 2015. http://www.cbc.ca/news/canada/medical-marijuana-easily-dispensed-in-vancouver-1.2938574.

REFERENCES

___. 2015b. "20% of Canadians Smoked Pot Last Year, But More Than 30% Would If Legal, Poll Suggests." November 10, 2015. http://www.cbc.ca/news/business/marijuana-pot-poll-survey-1.3312151.

Centre for Addiction and Mental Health. 2014. "Cannabis Policy Framework." October 2014. https://www.camh.ca/-/media/files/pdfs---public-policy-submissions/camh-cannabispolicyframework-pdf.pdf.

___. 2015. "Why Ontario Needs a Provincial Alcohol Strategy." September 2015. https://www.camh.ca/-/media/files/pdfs---public-policy-submissions/why_ontario_needs_an_alcohol_strategy-pdf.pdf.

___. 2016a. "Prescription Opioid Policy Framework." October 2016. https://www.camh.ca/-/media/files/pdfs---public-policy-submissions/camhopioid-policyframework-pdf.pdf.

___. 2016b. "Submission to the Cannabis Legalization and Regulation Secretariat Re.: Consultation on the Legalization, Regulation and Restriction of Access to Marijuana in Canada." August 29, 2016. https://www.camh.ca/-/media/files/pdfs---public-policy-submissions/camhsubmission_cannabistaskforce_20160829-pdf.pdf.

___. Drug and Alcohol Treatment Information System (DATIS). 2015. "Characteristics of Substance Abuse, Open, Individuals, Calendar Year 2014." Data file sent to author, August 12, 2015.

___. "Characteristics of Substance Abuse, Open, Individuals, Calendar Year 2016." Data file sent to author, October 25, 2017.

Chan, Margaret. 2013. "Opening Address at the 8th Global Conference on Health Promotion, Helsinki Finland." World Health Organization, June 10, 2013. https://www.foodpolitics.com/wp-content/uploads/DG-WHO-speech-to-Health-Promotion-Conference.pdf.

Chief Medical Officers of Health of Canada & Urban Public Health Network. 2016. "Public Health Perspectives on Cannabis Policy and Regulation." September 26, 2016. http://uphn.ca/wp-content/uploads/2016/10/Chief-MOH-UPHN-Cannabis-Perspectives-Final-Sept-26-2016.pdf.

Cinaport Acquisition Corp. 2014. "Cinaport Acquisition Corp. Enters into Letter of Intent with Mettrum Ltd. in Respect of a Proposed Qualifying Transaction." June 18, 2014. https://www.sedar.com/GetFile.do?lang=EN&docClass=8&issuerNo=00031711&issuerType=03&projectNo=02224737&docId=3563646.

Cohn, Martin Regg. 2014. "The Beer Store's Secret Sweetheart Deal with LCBO Revealed." *Toronto Star*, December 9, 2014. https://www.thestar.com/news/queens-park/2014/12/09/the_beer_stores_secret_sweetheart_deal_with_lcbo_revealed_cohn.html.

Crowe, Kelly. 2015. "Health Canada Requires Doctor to Sign Confidentiality Agreement to See Drug Data." *CBC News*, October 15, 2015. http://www.cbc.ca/news/health/health-canada-drug-confidentiality-data-1.3269107.

CTV News. 2017. "RCMP Seize Lethal Opioid Carfentanil in Nanaimo." February 8, 2017. http://vancouverisland.ctvnews.ca/rcmp-seize-lethal-opioid-carfentanil-in-nanaimo-1.3277111.

Cunningham, Rob. 1996. *Smoke & Mirrors: The Canadian Tobacco War.* International Development Research Centre. November 2007. https://www.idrc.ca/en/book/smoke-mirrors-canadian-tobacco-war.

Dukes, Graham, John Braithwaite, and J.P. Moloney. 2014. *Pharmaceuticals, Corporate Crime and Public Health*. Cheltenham: Edward Elgar Publishing.

Elash, Anita. 2006. "WHO Launches Taskforce to Fight Counterfeit Drugs." *Bulletin of the World Health Organization* 84 (9). https://www.ncbi.nlm.nih.gov/pmc/articles/PMC2627462/pdf/17128332.pdf.

Fischer, Benedikt, Sameer Imtiaz, Katherine Rudzinski, and Jürgen Rehm. 2016. "Crude Estimates of Cannabis-Attributable Mortality and Morbidity in Canada—Implications for Public Health Focused Intervention Priorities." *Journal of Public Health* 38 (1): 183-8. http://jpubhealth.oxfordjournals.org/content/early/2015/01/28/pubmed.fdv005.full.pdf+html.

Fischer, Benedikt. 2016. "Fentanyl: Canada's Homemade Drug Crisis." *The Globe and Mail*, April 14, 2016. http://www.theglobeandmail.com/opinion/fentanyl-canadas-homemade-drug-crisis/article29626211/.

Foote, Andrew. 2016. "Snoop Dogg Deal Represents Changing Marijuana Industry: Tweed CEO." *CBC News*, February 13, 2016. http://www.cbc.ca/news/canada/ottawa/snoop-dogg-tweed-smiths-falls-1.3445854?cmp=rss.

Gazette. 2016. "Editorial: Big Marijuana Trashes Democratic Process." July 8, 2016. https://gazette.com/opinion/editorial-big-marijuana-trashes-democratic-process/article_ffcb8b46-a4e1-5c82-97ec-8b52a26267cc.html.

Giesbrecht, Norman, Andree Demers, and Gina Stoduto. 2006. "Alcohol Smuggling in the 1990s: Policy Opportunism and Interventions." In: *Sober Reflections: Commerce, Public Health, and the Evolution of Alcohol Policy in Canada, 1980-2000*, edited by Norman Giesbrecht, Andree Demers, Alan Ogborne, Robin Room, Gina Stoduto, and Evert Anthony Lindquist. Montréal: McGill-Queens University Press, 2006.

Giesbrecht, Norman, Ashley Wettlaufer, Nicole April, Mark Asbridge, Samantha Cukier, Robert Mann, Janet McAllister, et al. 2013. "Strategies to Reduce Alcohol-Related Harms and Costs in Canada: A Comparison of Provincial Policies." Centre for Addiction and Mental Health. https://www.uvic.ca/research/centres/cisur/assets/docs/report-strategies-to-reduce-alcohol.pdf.

Giesbrecht, Norman. 2015. "Selling Alcohol in Grocery Stores: Hidden Risks and Alternative Options." Centre for Addiction and Mental Health. March 17, 2015. https://onlineacademiccommunity.uvic.ca/carbc/2015/03/17/selling-alcohol-in-grocery-stores-hidden-risks-and-alternative-options/.

Giovacchini, Anthony M. 1999. "The Negative Influence of Gangster Rap and What Can Be Done about It." Savannah State University, June 4, 1999. https://www.coursehero.com/file/29727933/The-Negative-Influence-of-Gangster-Rap-And-What-Can-Be-Done-About-Itpdf/.

Gomes, Tara, Muhammad M. Mamdani, Irfan A. Dhalla, Stephen Cornish, J. Michael Paterson, and David N. Juurlink. 2014. "The Burden of Premature Opioid-Related Mortality." *Addiction* 109 (9): 1482-8. https://onlinelibrary.wiley.com/doi/10.1111/add.12598.

Grant, Christina N. and Richard E. Bélanger 2016. "Position Statement: Cannabis and Canada's Children and Youth." Canadian Paediatric Society. November 24, 2016. https://www.researchgate.net/publication/310818915_Cannabis_and_Canada's_children_and_youth.

Gray, Jeff. 2015. "Ontario Accused of Changing Law to 'Protect' Beer Store, LCBO." *The Globe and Mail*, October 26, 2015. http://www.theglobeandmail.com/report-on-business/industry-news/the-law-page/ontario-accused-of-changing-law-to-protect-beer-store-lcbo/article26995551/.

Griffith-Greene, Megan. 2015. Grocery Store Secrets: Best-Before Dates Tampered With, Workers Claim. *CBC News*, November 6. http://www.cbc.ca/news/health/loblaws-best-before-tampering-1.3306395.

Hamilton, Graeme. 2015. Illegal Tipple. *National Post*, December 12, 2015. http://www.pressreader.com/canada/national-post-latest-edition/20151212/281569469671180.

REFERENCES

Hatchard, Jenny L., Gary J. Fooks, Karen A. Evans-Reeves, Selda Ulucanlar, Anne B. Gilmore 2014. "A Critical Evaluation of the Volume, Relevance and Quality of Evidence Submitted by the Tobacco Industry to Oppose Standardised Packaging of Tobacco Products." *British Medical Journal Open* 4 (2): e003757. https://bmjopen.bmj.com/content/4/2/e003757.

Health Canada. 2016a. "Health Canada's Action on Opioid Misuse." July 5, 2016. https://www.infoway-inforoute.ca/en/component/edocman/3180-health-canada-s-action-on-opioid-misuse/view-document?Itemid=0.

Health Canada. 2016b. "Opioid Conference." November 18, 2016. http://video.isilive.ca/hcsc/2016-11-18/english.html.

Heung, Carly M., Benjamin Rempel, and Marvin Krank. 2012. "Strengthening the Canadian Alcohol Advertising Regulatory System." *Canadian Journal of Public Health* 103 (4): e263-e266. https://link.springer.com/article/10.1007/BF03404232.

Hilts, Philip J. 1996. *Smoke Screen: The Truth Behind the Tobacco Industry Cover-up.* Reading: Addison-Wesley Publishing Company, Inc.

Howlett, Karen. 2017. "Ottawa Urged to Prosecute Purdue Pharma over Marketing of OxyContin," *The Globe and Mail*, July 19, 2017. https://www.theglobeandmail.com/news/national/ottawa-urged-to-prosecute-purdue-pharma-over-marketing-of-oxycontin/article35729663/ .

International Agency for Research on Cancer. 1988. "Alcohol Drinking." *Monographs on the Evaluation of Carcinogenic Risks to Humans* 44: 416. https://publications.iarc.fr/62.

Ivison, John. 2015. "Ottawa Moves to Rein in Oxycontin," *National Post*, May 15, 2015. http://www.pressreader.com/canada/national-post-latest-edition/20150515/281492159894340.

Jones, Allison. 2015. "LCBO Runs Afoul of Privacy Commissioner." *CBC News*, November 1, 2015. http://www.cbc.ca/news/canada/toronto/lcbo-wine-club-1.3299030.

Karnani, Aneel. 2013. "Impact of Alcohol on Poverty and the Need for Appropriate Policy." In *Alcohol: Science, Policy, and Public Health*, edited by Boyle Peter, Paolo Boffetta, Albert B. Lowenfels, Harry Burns, Otis Brawley, Witold Zatonsky, and Jürgen Rehm, 354-60. Oxford: Oxford University Press..

Kirkup, Kristy. 2016. "Canada Must Examine Why It Tops Opioid-Consuming Countries: Health Minister Jane Philpott." *CBC News*, July 26, 2016. http://www.cbc.ca/news/politics/opioid-canada-us-philpott-1.3695805.

Kleiman, Mark A.R., Steven Davenport, Brad Rowe, Jeremy Ziskind, Nate Mladenovic, Clarissa Manning and Tyler Jones. 2015. "Estimating the Size of the Medical Cannabis Market in Washington State." BOTEC Analysis Corporation. December 15, 2015. https://static1.squarespace.com/static/5e5fc3d054a9e32eaf6411e0/t/5ea1173fcf24b67402f5b936/1587615552578/BOTEC-MMJ-Report+-+2015.pdf.

Kluger, Richard. 1997. *Ashes to Ashes.* New York: Vintage Books.

Krashinsky Robertson, Susan. 2017. "Marijuana Industry Faces Challenge in Gaining Canadians' Trust, Survey Finds," *The Globe and Mail*, June 15, 2017. https://www.theglobeandmail.com/report-on-business/industry-news/marketing/marijuana-industry-faces-challenge-in-gaining-canadians-trust-survey-finds/article34466751/.

Kusnetz, Nicholas. 2016. "How Big Tobacco Lobbies to Safeguard E-Cigarettes." The Center for Public Integrity. March 25, 2016. https://www.publicintegrity.org/2016/03/25/19468/how-big-tobacco-lobbies-safeguard-e-cigarettes.

Leventhal, Adam M., Matthew D. Stone, Nafeesa Andrabi, Jessica Barrington-Trimis, David R. Strong, Steve Sussman, and Janet Audrain-McGovern. 2016. "Association of E-Cigarette Vaping and Progression to Heavier Patterns of Cigarette Smoking." *Journal of the American Medical Association* 316 (18): 1918-20. http://jamanet-work.com/journals/jama/article-abstract/2579858.

Lexchin, Joel. 1997. "After Compulsory Licensing; Coming Issues in Canadian Pharmaceutical Policy and Politics." *Health Policy* 40 (1): 69-80. https://www.sciencedir-ect.com/science/article/abs/pii/S016885109600886X.

Lexchin Joel, and Jillian Clare Kohler. 2011. "The Danger of Imperfect Regulation: Oxycontin Use in the United States and Canada." *International Journal of Risk and Safety* 23: 233-40. https://pubmed.ncbi.nlm.nih.gov/22156088/.

Ling, Justin. 2016. "High Prices." *Vice News*, November 16, 2016. https://news.vice.com/en_ca/article/9kn95y/veteran-medical-marijuana-benefits-are-costing-canada-a-fortune.

Lockington, Nikki. 2015. "OCSA Butt Study 2015 Results Are In." The Ontario Convenience Stores Association. December 8, 2015. http://ccentral.ca/ocsa-butt-study-2015-results-are-in/.

Mahood, Garfield. 2013. What Were They Smoking? The Smuggling Settlements with Big Tobacco. Toronto: The Non-Smokers Rights Association. September 25, 2014.

Martins, Diana, Simon Greaves, Mina Tadrous, Michael Paterson, Dana Bandola, Samantha Singh, David Juurlink, Muhammad Mamdani, and Tara Gomes. 2016. "Opioid Use and Related Adverse Events in Ontario." The Ontario Drug Policy Research Network. November 2016. https://odprn.ca/wp-content/uploads/2016/11/ODPRN-Opioid-Use-and-Related-Adverse-Events-Nov-2016.pdf.

McElroy, Justin. 2017. "B.C. Fentanyl Dealer Sentenced to 14 Years in Prison," *CBC News*, January 30, 2017. https://www.cbc.ca/news/canada/british-columbia/fentanyl-dealer-mccormick-1.3959167.

McLean, Jesse and David Bruser. 2014. "Canadian Drug Companies Violating the Law." *Toronto Star*, November 5, 2014. https://www.the-star.com/news/canada/2014/11/04/canadian_drug_companies_violat-ing_the_law.html.

___. 2015. Inside Look into Health Canada Battle with Apotex. *Toronto Star*, June 1, 2015. https://www.thestar.com/news/canada/2015/06/01/inside-look-into-health-canada-battle-with-apotex.html.

Morrow, Adrian. 2015. "Former Ontario Liberal Staffers Among Beer Store Lobbying Ranks. *The Globe and Mail*, April 15, 2015. http://www.theglobeand-mail.com/news/politics/former-ontario-liberal-staffers-among-beer-store-lobbying-ranks/article23964098/.

National Advisory Committee on Prescription Drug Misuse. 2013. "First Do No Harm: Responding to Canada's Prescription Drug Crisis." Canadian Centre on Substance Abuse. March 2013. https://ccsa.ca/sites/default/files/2019-04/Canada-Strategy-Prescription-Drug-Misuse-Report-en.pdf.

National Coalition Against Contraband Tobacco. 2016. "National Coalition Against Contraband Tobacco 2016 Pre-Budget Recommendations." http://www.parl.gc.ca/Con-tent/HOC/Committee/421/FINA/Brief/BR8126162/br-external/NationalCoalitionAgai nstContrabandTobacco-e.pdf.

National Institutes of Health. 2012. "Nearly 800,000 Deaths Prevented Due to Declines in Smoking. March 14, 2012. https://www.nih.gov/news-events/news-releases/nearly-800000-deaths-prevented-due-declines-smoking.

REFERENCES

Nelson, Joyce. 2016. "Canadians Launch Constitutional Challenge Against CETA." *Counterpunch*, October 28, 2016. http://www.counterpunch.org/2016/10/28/canadians-launch-constitutional-challenge-against-ceta/.

Nirappil, Fenit. 2017. "Maryland Lawmaker Reprimanded by Ethics Panel Over Marijuana Business Ties." *The Washington Post*, March 2, 2017. https://www.washingtonpost.com/local/md-politics/maryland-lawmaker-reprimanded-by-ethics-panel-over-marijuana-business-ties/2017/03/02/811cb468-ff94-11e6-8ebe-6e0dbe4f2bca_story.html.

Office of the Parliamentary Budget Officer. 2016. "Legalized Cannabis: Fiscal Considerations." November 1, 2016. http://www.pbo-dpb.gc.ca/web/default/files/Documents/Reports/2016/Legalized%20Cannabis/Legalized%20Canabis%20Fiscal%20Considerations_EN.pdf.

Ogilvie, Kelvin and Art Eggleton. 2015. "Prescription Drug Regulation Needs Transparency and Openness." *Toronto Star*, March 11, 2015. https://www.thestar.com/opinion/commentary/2015/03/11/prescription-drug-regulation-needs-transparency-and-openness.html.

Ontario Tobacco Research Unit. 2011. "Prohibition of Tobacco Sales in Specific Places: Monitoring Update." Modified February 19, 2011. http://otru.org/wp-content/uploads/2012/06/tobacco_sales2011.pdf.

____. 2013. "Litigation Against the Tobacco Industry: Monitoring Update." Modified September 2013. http://otru.org/wp-content/uploads/2013/10/litigation2013.pdf.

Oxycontin Task Force. 2004. "Oxycontin Task Force Final Report." Government of Newfoundland and Labrador. June 30, 2004. http://www.he alth.gov.nl.ca/health/publications/oxycontin_final_report.pdf.

Pacula, Rosalie L., Beau Kilmer, Alexander C. Wagenaar, Frank J. Chaloupka, and Jonathon P. Caulkins. 2014. "Developing Public Health Regulations for Marijuana: Lessons Learned from Alcohol and Tobacco." *American Journal of Public Health* 104 (6): 1021-28. https://www.ncbi.nlm.nih.gov/pmc/articles/PMC4062005/.

Persaud, Nav and David Juurlink. 2015. "The Importance of Investigative Reporting on Drug Safety." *Toronto Star*, February 22, 2015. https://www.thestar.com/opinion/commentary/2015/02/22/the-importance-of-investigative-reporting-on-drug-safety.html.

Pfeffer, Amanda and Guillaume Dumont. 2017. "Police Warn Organized Crime, Including the Hells Angels, Has Infiltrated the Medical Marijuana Market." *CBC News,* April 13, 2017. https://www.cbc.ca/news/canada/ottawa/police-warn-organized-crime-including-the-hells-angels-has-infiltrated-the-medical-marijuana-market-1.4067112.

Public Health Agency of Canada. 2016. "The Chief Public Health Officer's Report on the State of Public Health in Canada 2015: Alcohol Consumption in Canada." January 2016. http://healthycanadians.gc.ca/publications/department-ministere/state-public-health-alcohol-2015-etat-sante-publique-alcool/alt/state-phac-alcohol-2015-etat-aspc-alcool-eng.pdf.

Quan, Douglas. 2019. "RCMP Went Silent About Massive Pot Bust Over Concern for Marijuana Producer's Stock Price, Documents Reveal." *National Post*, May 31, 2019. https://nationalpost.com/news/canada/rcmp-went-silent-about-massive-pot-bust-over-concern-for-marijuana-producers-stock-price-documents-reveal.

RCMP. 2014. "Customs and Excise. Quick Facts." December 2, 2014. http://www.rcmp-grc.gc.ca/ce-da/index-eng.htm.

Rehm, J., D. Baliunas, S. Brochu, B. Fischer, W. Gnam, J. Patra, S. Popova, A. Sarnocinska-Hart, and B. Taylor. 2006. "The Costs of Substance Abuse in Canada 2002 Highlights." Canadian Centre on Substance Abuse, 2006. https://www.ccsa.ca/sites/default/files/2019-05/ccsa-011332-2006.pdf.

Rehm, Jürgen, Colin Mathers, Svetlana Popova, Montarat Thavorncharoensap, Yot Teer-awattananon, and Jayadeep Patra. 2009. "Global Burden of Disease and Injury and Economic Cost Attributable to Alcohol Use and Alcohol-Use Disorders." *The Lancet Alcohol and Global Health Series* 373 (9682): 2223-33. http://www.thelancet.com/pdfs/journals/lancet/PIIS0140-6736(09)60746-7.pdf.

Rehm, Jürgen, Jayadeep Patra, William H. Gnam, Anna Sarnocinska-Hart, and Svetlana Popova. 2011. "Avoidable Cost of Alcohol Abuse in Canada". *European Addiction Research* 17 (2): 72-9. https://www.ncbi.nlm.nih.gov/pubmed/21150206.

Reuters. 2015. "Canadian Regulators Warn on Medical Marijuana Disclosures." February 23, 2015. https://www.reuters.com/article/canada-regulator-marijuana-id-CAL1N0VXI4220150223.

Robertson, Grant. 2015. "Health Canada Puts Medical Marijuana Firm under Further RCMP Review." *The Globe and Mail*, January 30, 2015. http://www.theglobeandmail.com/report-on-business/health-canada-puts-medical-marijuana-firm-under-further-rcmp-review/article22716002/.

Robertson, Grant and Greg McArthur. 2016a. "What's in Your Weed?" *The Globe and Mail*, July 29, 2016. http://www.theglobeandmail.com/news/investigations/globe-investigation-whats-in-your-weed-we-tested-dispensary-marijuana-to-findout/article31144496/.

___. 2016b. "What's Not in Your Weed?" *The Globe and Mail,* July 29, 2016. Accessed online January 24, 2017; not available April 6, 2022.

Robertson, Grant. 2016b. "OxyContin Creator Expands into Canadian Pot Industry." *The Globe and Mail*, December 2, 2016. http://www.theglobeandmail.com/news/national/leadership-behind-canadian-medical-marijuana-company-has-an-oxycontin-past/article33200287/.

___. 2016a. "Canadians Not Told About Banned Pesticide Found in Medical Pot Supply." *The Globe and* Mail, December 29, 2016. http://www.theglobeandmail.com/news/national/canadians-not-told-about-banned-pesticide-found-in-medical-marijuana-supply/article33443887/.

___. 2017. "Two Medical Marijuana Companies Face New Rules After Banned Pesticide Use." *The Globe and Mail*, February 9, 2017. http://www.theglobeandmail.com//news/national/health-canada-adds-new-rules-to-licences-of-two-medical-marijuana-companies/article33976056/?cmpid=rss1&click=sf_globe.

Rocky Mountain High Intensity Drug Trafficking Area. 2014. "The Legalization of Marijuana in Colorado: The Impact." Volume 2. August 2014. https://wp-cpr.s3.amazonaws.com/uploads/2019/06/august_2014_legalization_of_mj_in_colorado_the_impact.pdf.

Rolles, Steve, Mike Barton, Niamh Eastwood, Tom Lloyd, Fiona Measham, David Nutt, and Harry Sumnall. 2016. "A Framework for a Regulated Market for Cannabis in the UK: Recommendations from an Expert Panel." UK Liberal Democrat Party. March 2016. https://d3n8a8pro7vhmx.cloudfront.net/libdems/pages/10794/attachments/original/1457398164/A_framework_for_a_regulated_market_for_cannabis_in_the_UK.pdf?1457398164.

Rubin, Josh. 2011. "Fake Wine Discovered at LCBO Prompts Police Probe." *Toronto Star,* March 18, 2011. http://www.thestar.com/business/2011/03/18/fake_wine_discovered_at_lcbo_prompts_police_probe.html.

Ryan, Harriet, Lisa Girion, and Scott Glover. 2016. "OxyContin Goes Global - 'We're Only Just Getting Started.'" *Los Angeles Times*, December 18, 2016. http://www.latimes.com/projects/la-me-oxycontin-part3/.

REFERENCES

Santa Cruz Biotechnology, Inc. 2011. "Myclobutanil. Material Safety Data Sheet." May 13, 2011. https://datasheets.scbt.com/sc-205759.pdf.

Sinclair, Scott. 2015. "NAFTA Chapter 11 Investor-State Disputes to January 1, 2015. Canadian Centre for Policy Alternatives." January 12, 2015. https://policyalternatives.ca/sites/default/files/uploads/publications/National%20Office/2015/01/NAFTA_Chapter11_Investor_State_Disputes_2015.pdf

Singh, Tushar, René A. Arrazola, Catherine G. Corey, Corinne G. Husten, Linda J. Neff, David M. Homa, and Brian A. King. 2016. "Tobacco Use Among Middle and High School Students - United States, 2011-2015." *Centers for Disease Control and Prevention, Morbidity and Mortality Weekly Report*, 65 (14): 361–67. http://dx.doi.org/10.15585/mmwr.mm6514a1.

Single, Eric, Lynda Robson, Xiaodi Xie, and Jürgen Rehm. 1996. "The Costs of Substance Abuse in Canada 1992." Ottawa: Canadian Centre on Substance Abuse.

___. 1998. "The Economic Costs of Alcohol, Tobacco and Illicit Drugs in Canada, 1992." *Addiction*, 93 (7): 991-1006. https://doi.org/10.1046/j.1360-0443.1998.9379914.x.

Smithers, Rebecca. 2012. "Seizures of Fake Alcohol Increase Fivefold in Two Years." *The Guardian*, February 3, 2012. http://www.theguardian.com/society/2012/feb/03/huge-rise-alcohol-seizures.

Spithoff Sheryl, Emerson Brian, and Spithoff Andrea. 2015. "Cannabis Legalization: Adhering to Public Health Best Practice." *Canadian Medical Association Journal* 187 (16): 1211-16. http://www.cmaj.ca/content/187/16/1211.figures-only.

Standing Senate Committee on Social Affairs, Science and Technology. 2015. "Prescription Pharmaceuticals in Canada: Final Report." Government of Canada. March 2015. http://www.parl.gc.ca/Content/SEN/Committee/412/soci/rep/rep18mar15-e.pdf.

Stone, Dave. 2014. "Cannabis, Pesticides and Conflicting Laws: the Dilemma for Legalized States and Implications for Public Health." *Regulatory Toxicology and Pharmacology* 69 (3): 284-8. https://www.sciencedirect.com/science/article/abs/pii/S027323001400097X.

Stuart, Hunter. 2014. "Black Market for Weed Still Thriving in Colorado." *The Huffington Post*, January 6, 2014. http://www.huffingtonpost.com/2014/01/06/weed-colorado-black-market_n_4548338.html.

Task Force on Cannabis Legalization and Regulation. 2016. "A Framework for the Legalization and Regulation of Cannabis in Canada: Final Report." Health Canada. December 2016. http://healthycanadians.gc.ca/task-force-marijuana-groupe-etude/framework-cadre/alt/framework-cadre-eng.pdf.

Task Force on Illicit Tobacco Products. 2015. "Report on the Status of the Contraband Tobacco Situation in Canada." Ministry of Public Safety. Modified December 2, 2015. http://www.publicsafety.gc.ca/cnt/rsrcs/pblctns/archive-stts-cntrbnd-tbcc/index-eng.aspx.

Task Force on Marijuana Legalization and Regulation. 2016. "Toward the Legalization, Regulation and Restriction of Access to Marijuana: Discussion Paper." June 2016. http://healthycanadians.gc.ca/health-system-systeme-sante/consultations/legalization-marijuana-legalisation/alt/legalization-marijuana-legalisation-eng.pdf.

Thomas, Brian F. and Malmoud ElSohly. 2015. *The Analytical Chemistry of Cannabis: Quality Assessment, Assurance, and Regulation of Medicinal Marijuana and Cannabinoid Preparations (1st Edition): Emerging Issues in Analytical Chemistry, Volume 1*. Cambridge, MA: Elsevier & RTI Press.

Thomson Reuters. 2016. "6 Ex-Pharma Executives Arrested in U.S. in Fentanyl Bribe Case." *CBC News*, December 9, 2016. http://www.cbc.ca/news/health/fentanyl-bribery-1.3887631.

Tobacco Control Legal Consortium. 2012. "Cause and Effect: Tobacco Marketing Increases Youth Tobacco Use: Findings from the 2012 Surgeon General's Report." June 2012. http://publichealthlawcenter.org/sites/default/files/resources/tclc-guide-SGReport-Findings-Youth-Marketing-2012.pdf.

United States District Court for the District of Columbia. "United States of America vs. Philip Morris USA, Inc., Amended Final Opinion (Civil Action No. 99-2496 GK)." US Department of Justice. September 2006. http://www.publichealthlawcenter.org/sites/default/files/resources/doj-final-opinion.pdf.

Van Zee, Art. 2009. "The Promotion and Marketing of Oxycontin: Commercial Triumph, Public Health Tragedy." *American Journal of Public Health* 99 (2): 221-27. https://www.ncbi.nlm.nih.gov/pmc/articles/PMC2622774/.

Wang, George Sam, Marie-Claire Le Lait, Sara J. Deakyne, Alvin C. Bronstein, Lalit Bajaj, and Genie Roosevelt. 2016. "Unintentional Pediatric Exposures to Marijuana in Colorado, 2009-2015." *Journal of the American Medical Association Pediatrics* 170 (9): e160971. https://www.ncbi.nlm.nih.gov/pubmed/27454910.

Wells, Paul. 2017. "Canada's New Health Minister Faces the Opioid Crisis." *Maclean's*, September 12, 2017. https://www.macleans.ca/politics/ottawa/canadas-new-health-minister-faces-the-opioid-crisis/.

Wetselaar, Sean. 2015. "Keswick Pharmacist, Seven Others Charged in Drug Trafficking Case." *Toronto Star*, January 12, 2015. https://www.thestar.com/news/crime/2015/01/12/keswick_pharmacist_seven_others_charged_in_drug_trafficking_case.html.

Wilkinson, Samuel T. and Deepak Cyril D'Souza. 2014. "Problems with the Medicalization of Marijuana." *Journal of the American Medical Association* 311 (23): 2377-78. http://jamanetwork.com/journals/jama/article-abstract/1874073.

World Health Organization. 2008. "Tobacco Industry Interference with Tobacco Control." May 22, 2008. https://www.who.int/publications/i/item/9789241597340.

Xuan, Ziming, Jason Blanchette, Toben F. Nelson, Timothy Heeren, Nadia Oussayef, and Timothy S. Naimi. 2014. "The Alcohol Policy Environment and Policy Subgroups as Predictors of Binge Drinking Measures Among US Adults." *American Journal of Public Health* 105 (4): 816-22. https://www.ncbi.nlm.nih.gov/pubmed/25122017.

Yang, Jennifer and Robert Cribb. 2015. "Painkiller Reform is Painfully Slow: Experts." *Toronto Star*, September 17, 2015. https://www.pressreader.com/canada/toronto-star/20150917/281500750041632.

Zhang, Bo and Robert Schwartz. 2015. "What Effect Does Tobacco Taxation Have on Contraband? Debunking the Taxation-Contraband Tobacco Myth." Ontario Tobacco Research Unit. February 2015. http://otru.org/wp-content/uploads/2015/02/special_tax_contraband_final.pdf.

6. Legalization for Recreational Use in Canada: How It Really Happened and Why

Aphria, Aurora Cannabis, Canadian Medical Cannabis Council, Cannabis Canada, CannTrust Inc., Canopy Growth, Cresco Pharma, et al. 2017. "Adult Use Cannabis Advertising and Marketing Self-Regulatory Guidelines for Licensed Producers." November 2017. https://cannabislaw.report/wp-content/uploads/2017/11/GuidelinesforCannabis-EN-Nov6.pdf.

Atlantic Business Magazine. 2017. "Growth Op." July 4, 2017. https://atlanticbusinessmagazine.ca/article/growth-op/.

REFERENCES

Babor, Thomas F. 2010. "Alcohol: No Ordinary Commodity—A Summary of the Second Edition." *Addiction* 105: 769–79. https://onlinelibrary.wiley.com/doi/10.1111/j.1360-0443.2010.02945.x.

Bagnall, James. 2018. "Growing Pains: Tale of a Smiths Falls Marijuana Start-Up." *Ottawa Citizen*, October 9, 2018. https://ottawacitizen.com/business/local-business/growing-pains-co-founders-of-smiths-falls-marijuana-start-up-in-legal-battle/.

Bennett Jones. 2014. "Bennett Jones Attends the Official Launch of Tweed Inc.'s Medicinal Marijuana Facility." June 18, 2014. https://www.bennettjones.com/en/Publications-Section/Announcements/Bennett-Jones-Attends-the-Official-Launch-of-Tweed-Inc,-d-,s-Medicinal-Marijuana-Facility.

Boak, A., H.A. Hamilton, E.M. Adlaf, and R.E. Mann. 2015. "Drug Use Among Ontario Students, 1977-2015: Detailed OSDUHS Findings." (CAMH Research Document Series No. 41). Toronto: Centre for Addiction and Mental Health, 2015. Accessed online January 23, 2017; no longer available April 5, 2022.

Bonnie, Richard J., Kathleen Stratton, and Leslie Y. Kwan, eds. 2015. "Public Health Implications of Raising the Minimum Age for Purchasing Tobacco Products. Institute of Medicine." https://nap.nationalacademies.org/catalog/18997/public-health-implications-of-raising-the-minimum-age-of-legal-access-to-tobacco-products.

Bronskill, Jim. 2015. "Justin Trudeau Not Banking on Financial Windfall from Legalized Pot." *CBC News*, December 17, 2015. www.cbc.ca/news/politics/legal-marijuana-taxes-1.3370358 .

Campaign for Tobacco-Free Kids. 2020. States and Localities That Have Raised the Minimum Legal Sale Age for Tobacco Products to 21. August 2020. https://www.tobaccofreekids.org/assets/content/what_we_do/state_local_issues/sales_21/states_localities_MLSA_21.pdf.

Campbell, Meagan. 2017. "How Public Officials Got into the Weed Game." *Maclean's* April 13, 2017. https://www.macleans.ca/politics/how-public-officials-got-into-the-weed-game/.

Canada. 2014. "Information Update - Marijuana for Medical Purposes - Advertising and Licensed Producers." November 25, 2014. http://www.healthycanadians.gc.ca/recall-alert-rappel-avis/hc-sc/2014/42677a-eng.php.

___. 2016a. "Opposition Motion: Decriminalization of Marijuana Possession." *House of Commons Debates,* 42nd Parl, 1st Sess, No 071 (June 13) 4368 (1200-1400) (Hon. Geoff Regan). https://www.ourcommons.ca/DocumentViewer/en/42-1/house/sitting-71/hansard.

Canada. 2016b. "Task Force on Marijuana Legalization and Regulation - Summary of Expertise, Experience, and Affiliations and Interests." Modified June 30, 2016. http://healthycanadians.gc.ca/health-system-systeme-sante/consultations/legalization-marijuana-legalisation/affiliations-eng.php.

Canada. 2018a. "Bill C-45: An Act Respecting Cannabis and to Amend the Controlled Drugs and Substances Act, The Criminal Code and Other Acts—Summary." Parliament of Canada. June 21, 2018. http://www.parl.ca/DocumentViewer/en/42-1/bill/C-45/royal-assent.

Canada. 2018b. "News Release: Bill C-45, The Cannabis Act, Passed in Senate." Health Canada. Modified June 20, 2018. https://www.canada.ca/en/health-canada/news/2018/06/bill-c-45-the-cannabis-act-passed-in-senate.html.

Canada. 2018c. "News Release: Canada Legalizes and Strictly Regulates Cannabis." Health Canada. Modified October 17, 2018. https://www.canada.ca/en/health-canada/news/2018/10/canada-legalizes-and-strictly-regulates-cannabis.html.

Canada. 2018d. "Statement on Event Sponsorship and Other Promotional Activities by Federally Licensed Producers of Cannabis." Health Canada. Modified July 13, 2018. https://www.canada.ca/en/health-canada/news/2018/07/statement-on-event-sponsorship-and-other-promotional-activities-by-federally-licensed-producers-of-cannabis.html.

Canada. 2021. "Canadian Tobacco Alcohol and Drugs Survey (CTADS): 2015 Summary." Modified August 12, 2021. https://www.canada.ca/en/health-canada/services/canadian-alcohol-drugs-survey/2015-summary.html.

Canadian Centre on Substance Abuse. 2015. "Cannabis Regulation: Lessons Learned in Colorado and Washington State." November 2015. https://ccsa.ca/sites/default/files/2019-04/CCSA-Cannabis-Regulation-Lessons-Learned-Report-2015-en.pdf.

Canadian Medical Association. 2016. "Legalization, Regulation and Restriction of Access to Marijuana. Submission Government of Canada—Task Force on Marijuana Legalization and Regulation." August 29, 2016. https://policybase.cma.ca/documents/Briefpdf/BR2017-01.pdf.

Canadian Public Health Association. 2014. "A New Approach to Managing Illegal Psychoactive Substances in Canada. CPHA Position Paper." May 2014. https://www.cpha.ca/sites/default/files/assets/policy/ips_2014-05-15_e.pdf.

___. 2016. "A Public Health Approach to the Legalization, Regulation and Restriction of Access to Cannabis. Submission from the Canadian Public Health Association to the Task Force on Marijuana Legalization and Regulation." August 29, 2016. https://www.cpha.ca/sites/default/files/assets/policy/cannabis_submission_e.pdf.

Cannabis Council of Canada. n.d. "George Smitherman Named President and CEO of the Cannabis Council of Canada." Accessed April 25, 2022. https://cannabis-council.ca/media/george-smitherman-named-president-and-ceo-of-the-cannabis-council-of-canada.

Cannabis Digest. 2010. "An Interview with Elizabeth May. The Greens on Mandatory Minimums and Legalization." November 1, 2010. https://cannabisdigest.ca/an-interview-with-elizabeth-may/.

Cannabis Life Network. 2015. "Liberal CFO Rifici Sees Green from Tweed." October 29, 2015. https://cannabislifenetwork.com/liberal-cfo-rifici-sees-green-from-tweed/.

Cannabis Trade Alliance of Canada. 2016. "Public Consultation: Toward the Legalization, Regulation and Restriction of Access to Marijuana." August 29, 2016. https://issuu.com/sustainablecannabis.ca/docs/consultation_submission__final_.

Canopy Growth Corporation. 2017. "*Canopy Health Innovations Enters into Agreement with Dr. Mark Ware.*" *Cision*, February 10, 2017. https://www.newswire.ca/news-releases/canopy-health-innovations-enters-into-agreement-with-dr-mark-ware-613388233.html.

___. 2018. "Dr. Mark Ware Joins Canopy Growth Corporation as Chief Medical Officer." *Cision,* May 28, 2018. https://www.newswire.ca/news-releases/dr-mark-ware-joins-canopy-growth-corporation-as-chief-medical-officer-683849601.html.

Carter, Connie I. and Donald Macpherson. 2013. "Getting to Tomorrow: A Report on Canadian Drug Policy." Canadian Drug Policy Coalition. May 2013. https://www.drugpolicy.ca/wp-content/uploads/2013/01/CDPC2013_en.pdf.

Caulkins, Jonathan P., Beau Kilmer, Mark A. R. Kleiman, Robert J. MacCoun, Gregory Midgette, Pat Oglesby, Rosalie Liccardo Pacula, and Peter H. Reuter. 2015. "Considering Marijuana Legalization: Insights for Vermont and Other Jurisdictions." The RAND Corporation. January 2015. https://www.rand.org/content/dam/rand/pubs/research_reports/RR800/RR864/RAND_RR864.pdf.

REFERENCES

CBC News. 2016. "Marijuana Task Force to be Led by Former Deputy PM Anne McLellan." June 30, 2016. https://www.cbc.ca/news/politics/liberals-marijuana-task-force-1.3659509.

___. 2020. "Legal Age to Buy Cannabis in Quebec is Now 21, the Highest in Canada." January 1, 2020. https://www.cbc.ca/news/canada/Montréal/legal-age-cannabis-edibles-1.5399211.

Centre for Addiction and Mental Health. 2014. "Cannabis Policy Framework." October 2014. https://www.camh.ca/-/media/files/pdfs---public-policy-submissions/camh-cannabispolicyframework-pdf.pdf.

___. 2016. "Submission to the Cannabis Legalization and Regulation Secretariat Re.: Consultation on the Legalization, Regulation and Restriction of Access to Marijuana in Canada." August 29, 2016. https://www.camh.ca/-/media/files/pdfs---public-policy-submissions/camhsubmission_cannabistaskforce_20160829-pdf.pdf.

Centre for Addiction and Mental Health Foundation. 2021. Personal Communication, October 19, 2021.

Cerdá, Magdalena and Beau Kilmer. 2017. "Uruguay's Middle-Ground Approach to Cannabis Legalization." *International Journal of Drug Policy* 42: 118–120. https://www.sciencedirect.com/science/article/abs/pii/S0955395917300555.

Chapados, Maude, François Gagnon, Geneviève Lapointe, Sébastien Tessier, Nicole April, Richard Coovi Fachehoun, and Onil Samuel. 2016. "Legalization of Non-Medical Cannabis: A Public Health Approach to Regulation." Institut national de santé publique du Québec. October 2016. https://www.inspq.qc.ca/sites/default/files/publications/2233_legalization_non_medical_cannabis_0.pdf.

Chief Medical Officers of Health of Canada and Urban Public Health Network. 2016. "Public Health Perspectives on Cannabis Policy and Regulation." September 26, 2016. http://uphn.ca/wp-content/uploads/2016/10/Chief-MOH-UPHN-Cannabis-Perspectives-Final-Sept-26-2016.pdf.

D'Amico, Elizabeth J., Anthony Rodriguez, Joan S. Tucker, Eric R. Pedersen, Regina A. Shihb. 2018. "Planting the Seed for Marijuana Use: Changes in Exposure to Medical Marijuana Advertising and Subsequent Adolescent Marijuana Use, Cognitions, and Consequences Over Seven Years." *Drug and Alcohol Dependence* 188 (1): 385-91. https://doi.org/10.1016/j.drugalcdep.2018.03.031.

Dehaas, Josh. 2017. "Psychiatrists Ask Liberals to Keep Cannabis Illegal up to Age 21." *CTVNews*, April 13, 2017. http://www.ctvnews.ca/health/psychiatrists-ask-liberals-to-keep-cannabis-illegal-up-to-age-21-1.3366167.

DeVillaer, Michael. 2017. "Cannabis Law Reform in Canada: Pretense & Perils." McMaster University, The Peter Boris Centre for Addictions Research. February 2017. https://fhs.mcmaster.ca/pbcar/documents/Pretense%20&%20Perils%20FINAL.PDF.

Di Fiore, James. 2016. "Justin Trudeau and the Great Pot Hypocrisy." *Huffington Post*, May 14, 2017. https://www.huffpost.com/archive/ca/entry/justin-trudeau-marijuana-hypocrisy_b_9944286?utm_hp_ref=ca-liberal-party-of. Accessed April 6 2022.

___. 2017. "I Would Never Have Pushed for Legal Pot if I Knew It'd End This Way." *Huffington Post*, September 14, 2017. https://www.huffpost.com/archive/ca/entry/i-would-never-have-pushed-for-legal-pot-if-i-knew-itd-end-this-way_a_23202887.

DiMatteo, Enzo. 2018. "The Ex Cops, Politicians and Friends of Bill Blair Cashing in on Legal Weed. *NowToronto*, January 29, 2018. https://nowtoronto.com/news/cops-politicians-cashing-in-on-cannabis/.

Elliott, Josh. 2015. "Liberals 'Committed' to Legalizing Marijuana: Trudeau." *CTV News*, September 30, 2015. http://www.ctvnews.ca/politics/election/liberals-committed-to-legalizing-marijuana-trudeau-1.2588260.

Emery, Jodie (@JodieEmery). 2017. "Unfairness. Thousands of peaceful people continue to suffer." Twitter, December 17, 2017. https://twitter.com/JodieEmery/status/942434747946373121.

Erickson, Patricia G. and Elaine Hyshka 2010. "Four Decades of Cannabis Criminals in Canada: 1970-2010." *Amsterdam Law Forum* 2 (4): 1-14. http://doi.org/10.37974/ALF.144.

Fabian, Sabrina. 2018. "Pot Producers Seek Ways to Promote Brands in Light of Federal Restrictions." *CBC News,* July 17, 2018. https://www.cbc.ca/news/canada/nova-scotia/cannabis-producer-government-marketing-rules-1.4749109 .

Fayerman, Pamela. 2017. "Former B.C. Health Minister Terry Lake to Join Growing Marijuana Company." *Vancouver Sun*, August 31, 2017. https://vancouversun.com/news/national/former-b-c-health-minister-terry-lake-to-join-growing-marijuana-company/.

Fife, Robert and Steven Chase. 2017. "Trudeau's Lead on Legalizing Marijuana Lobbied During Cash-for-Access Fundraiser." *The Globe and Mail*, April 10, 2017. http://www.theglobeandmail.com/news/politics/trudeaus-marijuana-czar-lobbied-during-cash-for-access-fundraiser/article33084843/.

Flavelle, Dana. 2015. "Bay St. Law Firms Cash in on Pot Industry." *Toronto Star*, January 8, 2015. https://www.thestar.com/business/2015/01/08/bay_st_law_firms_cash_in_on_pot_industry.html.

Grant, Christina N. and Richard E. Bélanger 2016. "Position Statement: Cannabis and Canada's Children and Youth." Canadian Paediatric Society. November 24, 2016. https://www.researchgate.net/publication/310818915_Cannabis_and_Canada's_children_and_youth.

GrowthOp. 2019. "Cannabis Beverage Alliance Calls for Rules on Par with Alcohol Industry." April 24, 2019. https://www.thegrowthop.com/cannabis-business/cannabis-beverage-alliance-calls-for-rules-on-par-with-alcohol-industry.

Hager, Mike and Grant Robertson. 2017. "Questions Raised Over Marijuana Task Force Chair's Ties to Industry." *The Globe and Mail*, April 13, 2017. https://www.theglobeandmail.com/news/national/questions-raised-over-marijuana-task-force-chairs-ties-to-industry/article34694710/.

Harris, Kathleen. 2018. "Trudeau Says Pot Purchasers Are Funding Gangs, Organized Crime and Must Be Charged." *CBC News*, January 1, 2018. https://www.cbc.ca/news/politics/liberal-marijuana-pardon-legal-1.4484496.

Kirkup, Kristy. 2015. "Justin Trudeau Prepares to Tackle Pot Politics with Conservative Framework." *The Globe and Mail*, October 28, 2015. http://www.theglobeandmail.com/news/british-columbia/justin-trudeau-prepares-to-tackle-pot-politics-with-conservative-framework/article27024564/.

Leblanc, Daniel. 2016a. "Ex-Colleague Will Lobby MP Bill Blair to Restrict Field of Pot Growers." *The Globe and Mail*, January 10, 2016. https://www.theglobeandmail.com/news/politics/ex-colleague-will-lobby-mp-bill-blair-to-restrict-field-of-pot-growers/article28102506/.

___. 2016b. "Medical Pot Growers Lobby Ottawa to Shut Down Pot Dispensaries." *The Globe and Mail*, January 21, 2016. https://www.theglobeandmail.com/news/politics/medical-pot-growers-lobby-ottawa-to-shut-down-pot-dispensaries/article28331133/.

Levesque, Maurice. 2017. "Knightswood Enters Pot Deal with PanCann for $1M." *Stockwatch*, April 26, 2017. https://www.stockwatch.com/News/Item.aspx?bid=Z-C:KWF-2463886&symbol=KWF&region=C.

Liberal Party of Canada. 2014. "Liberals Welcome CAMH Call for Marijuana Legalization." October 9, 2014. https://www.liberal.ca/liberals-camh-call-marijuana-legalization/.

REFERENCES

Liberal Party of Canada. n.d. "Keep Marijuana Out of Our Kids' Hands." Accessed April 25, 2022. https://www.liberal.ca/keep-marijuana-out-of-our-kids-hands/.

Marchitelli, Rosa. 2021. "Copycat Pot Edibles That Look Like Candy Are Poisoning Kids, Doctors Say." *CBC News*, January 25, 2021. https://www.cbc.ca/news/canada/british-columbia/cannabis-gummies-poisonings-kids-illegal-sites-1.5879232.

Miller, Jacquie. 2018a. "Cannabis Companies Ramp Up Marketing as Health Canada Warns Them Not to Advertise Pot." *Ottawa Citizen*, October 11, 2018. https://ottawacitizen.com/news/local-news/warning-on-ads.

___. 2018b. "Trailer Park Buds? Cannabis Companies Devise Catchy Brand Names Amid Strict Health Canada Rules." *Ottawa Citizen*, October 15, 2018. https://ottawacitizen.com/cannabis/cannabis-business/pot-names#click=https://t.co/0KeKObrzms.

Noël, Chelsea, Christopher Armiento, Anna Koné Péfoyo, Rupert Klein, Michel Bédard, and Deborah Scharf. 2021. "Adolescent Exposure to Cannabis Marketing Following Recreational Cannabis Legalization in Canada: a Pilot Study Using Ecological Momentary Assessment." *Addictive Behaviors Reports* 14 Article 100383. https://doi.org/10.1016/j.abrep.2021.100383.

Office of the Commissioner of Lobbying of Canada. 2017. "Registry of Lobbyists." February 10, 2017. https://lobbycanada.gc.ca/app/secure/ocl/lrs/do/advSrch.

___. 2019. "Registry of Lobbyists." April 17, 2019. https://lobbycanada.gc.ca/app/secure/ocl/lrs/do/advSrch.

Pacula, Rosalie L., Beau Kilmer, Alexander C. Wagenaar, Frank J. Chaloupka, and Jonathon P. Caulkins 2014. "Developing Public Health Regulations for Marijuana: Lessons Learned from Alcohol and Tobacco." *American Journal of Public Health* 104 (6): 1021-28. https://www.ncbi.nlm.nih.gov/pmc/articles/PMC4062005/.

Platt, Brian. 2017. "Marijuana Task-Force Member's Move to Legal Weed Company Raises Conflict-Of-Interest Concerns." *National Post*, September 25, 2017. https://nationalpost.com/news/politics/marijuana-task-force-members-move-to-legal-weed-company-raises-conflict-of-interest-concerns.

Pope, Marilyn, Michael Chaiton, and Robert Schwartz. 2015. "Raising the Minimum Age for Access to Tobacco to 21". Ontario Tobacco Research Unit. August 2015. http://otru.org/wp-content/uploads/2015/08/update_august2015.pdf.

Press, Jordan. 2018. "From Politics to Pot: Legislators Now in the Cannabis Business." *National Post*, October 18, 2018. https://nationalpost.com/pmn/news-pmn/canada-news-pmn/from-politics-to-pot-legislators-now-in-the-cannabis-business.

Rinaldi, Luc. 2019. The CPA Who Helped Build Canada's Cannabis Industry. *Pivot Magazine*, December 20, 2019. https://www.cpacanada.ca/en/news/pivot-magazine/2019-12-20-chuck-rifici-interview.

Rocky Mountain High Intensity Drug Trafficking Area. 2014. "The Legalization of Marijuana in Colorado: The Impact." Volume 2. August 2014. https://wp-cpr.s3.amazonaws.com/uploads/2019/06/august_2014_legalization_of_mj_in_colorado_the_impact.pdf.

Rolles, Steve, Mike Barton, Niamh Eastwood, Tom Lloyd, Fiona Measham, David Nutt, and Harry Sumnall. 2016. "A Framework for a Regulated Market for Cannabis in the UK: Recommendations from an Expert Panel." UK Liberal Democrat Party. March 2016. https://d3n8a8pro7vhmx.cloudfront.net/libdems/pages/10794/attachments/original/1457398164/A_framework_for_a_regulated_market_for_cannabis_in_the_UK.pdf?1457398164.

Shaw, Barbara. 2016. "Marijuana, Inc: The Buzz Behind the Canadian Bud Biz." *Now-Toronto*, April 13, 2016. https://nowtoronto.com/news/marijuana-inc-the-buzz-behind-the-bud-biz-canada/.

Sheikh, Iman. 2016. "These Prominent Canadians Want You to Buy Their Weed." *TVO*, February 25, 2016. https://tvo.org/article/current-affairs/the-next-ontario/these-prominent-canadians-want-you-to-buy-their-weed.

Smith, Marie-Danielle and Brian Platt. 2018. "Failure to Launch: Inside Julie Payette's Turbulent First Year as Governor General." National Post, September 22, 2018. https://nationalpost.com/news/politics/failure-to-launch-inside-julie-payettes-turbulent-first-year-as-governor-general.

Spithoff, Sheryl, Brian Emerson, and Andrea Spithoff. 2015. "Cannabis Legalization: Adhering to Public Health Best Practice." *Canadian Medical Association Journal* 187 (16): 1211-16. http://www.cmaj.ca/content/187/16/1211.figures-only.

Stockhouse. 2019. "Benchmark Botanics Appoints Hon. James Moore to Board of Directors." January 9, 2019. https://stockhouse.com/news/press-releases/2019/01/09/benchmark-botanics-appoints-hon-james-moore-to-board-of-directors.

Stratcann. 2020. "Two Conservatives Apologize Over Cannabis Conspiracy Theory." April 11, 2020. https://stratcann.com/2020/04/11/two-conservatives-apologize-over-cannabis-conspiracy-theory/.

Subramaniam, Vanmala. 2018. Former Ontario Finance Minister Is Latest Politician to Join the Cannabis Industry. *Financial Post*, November 27, 2018. https://financialpost.com/cannabis/former-ontario-finance-minister-is-latest-politician-to-join-the-cannabis-industry.

Task Force on Cannabis Legalization and Regulation. 2016. "A Framework for the Legalization and Regulation of Cannabis in Canada: Final Report." Health Canada. December 2016. http://healthycanadians.gc.ca/task-force-marijuana-groupe-etude/framework-cadre/alt/framework-cadre-eng.pdf.

Task Force on Marijuana Legalization and Regulation. 2016. "Toward the Legalization, Regulation and Restriction of Access to Marijuana: Discussion Paper." June 2016. http://healthycanadians.gc.ca/health-system-systeme-sante/consultations/legalization-marijuana-legalisation/alt/legalization-marijuana-legalisation-eng.pdf.

Wang, George Sam, Marie-Claire Le Lait, Sara J. Deakyne, Alvin C. Bronstein, Lalit Bajaj, and Genie Roosevelt. 2016. "Unintentional Pediatric Exposures to Marijuana in Colorado, 2009-2015." *Journal of the American Medical Association Pediatrics* 170 (9): e160971. https://www.ncbi.nlm.nih.gov/pubmed/27454910.

Wikipedia. 2019. "Chuck Rifici." March 20, 2019. https://en.wikipedia.org/wiki/Chuck_Rifici.

Wikipedia. 2022. "Alfred Apps." June 10, 2022. https://en.wikipedia.org/wiki/Alfred_Apps.

Woodward, Jon. 2016. "Political Pot Donations Sign of 'Normalized' Industry: Advocate." *CTV News*, March 22, 2016. http://bc.ctvnews.ca/political-pot-donations-sign-of-normalized-industry-advocate-1.2826836.

World Health Organization. 2016. "Plain Packaging of Tobacco Products: Evidence, Design and Implementation." March 2017. https://apps.who.int/iris/bitstream/handle/10665/207478/9789241565226_eng.pdf;jsessionid=67031CE9989365E04069D2D157642407?sequence=1.

7. Post-Legalization: More Regulatory Non-Compliance and Corporate Crime

A. Dimitri Lascaris Law Professional Corporation, Henein Hutchison LLP, Kalloghlian Myers LLP, Strosberg Sasso Sutts LLP, Labaton Sucharow LLP, and Weisz Fell Kour LLP. 2022. "Settlement of CannTrust Holdings Inc. Securities Litigation: Current and Former Shareholders May be Entitled to Compensation." Cision, January 19, 2022. https://www.newswire.ca/news-releases/settlement-of-canntrust-holdings-inc-securities-litigation-current-and-former-shareholders-may-be-entitled-to-compensation-829031607.html.

Aphria. 2019. "Aphria Receives Health Canada License Amendment, Approving Fully Expanded Production at Aphria One." *Market Insider,* March 4, 2019. https://markets.businessinsider.com/news/stocks/aphria-receives-health-canada-license-amendment-approving-fully-expanded-production-at-aphria-one-1028000364.

Ascent. 2018a. "Ascent Industries Corp. Provides Health Canada Update and Announces Appointment of Interim CEO." *Cision,* November 21, 2018. https://www.newswire.ca/news-releases/ascent-industries-corp-provides-health-canada-update-and-announces-appointment-of-interim-ceo-701007181.html.

____. 2018b. "Health Canada Partially Suspends Cannabis Cultivation and Production Licenses of Ascent Industries Unit Agrima Botanicals." *New Cannabis Ventures* September 27, 2018. https://www.newcannabisventures.com/health-canada-partially-suspends-cannabis-cultivation-and-production-licenses-of-ascent-industries-unit-agrima-botanicals/.

____. 2019. "Ascent Industries Faces License Suspension or Revocation in Nevada." *New Cannabis Ventures,* February 15, 2019. https://www.newcannabisventures.com/ascent-industries-faces-license-suspension-or-revocation-in-nevada/.

Blais, Annabelle, Jean-François Cloutier, Jean-Michel Genois Gagnon, Marc Sandreschi, and Marie Christine Trottier. 2021. "A Relative of The Hells at a Big Seller of Legal Pot." *Le Journal de Montréal,* November 18, 2021. https://www.journaldeMontréal.com/2021/11/18/un-proche-des-hells-chez-un-gros-vendeur-de-pot-legal#cxrecs_s.

BNN Bloomberg. 2019. "Other Firms May Have Cheated on Cannabis Supply: Industry Consultant." January 22, 2019. https://www.bnnbloomberg.ca/video/other-firms-may-have-cheated-on-cannabis-supply-industry-consultant~1592631.

Breen, Katie. 2019. "AG to Investigate N.L. Marijuana Industry - Including Canopy Growth Deal." *CBC News,* June 5, 2019. https://www.cbc.ca/news/canada/newfoundland-labrador/auditor-general-investigating-weed-1.5164277.

Brown, David. 2021. "Health Canada's Cannabis Compliance and Enforcement Report." *Stratcann,* December 20, 2021. https://stratcann.com/2021/12/20/cannabis-compliance-and-enforcement-report-coming-in-january/.

Business Wire. 2022. "Proposed Settlement Reached in 2016 Class Action." June 23, 2022. https://www.businesswire.com/news/home/20220623005993/en/Proposed-Settlement-Reached-in-2016-Class-Action.

Canada. 2019a. "Quarterly Compliance and Enforcement Report - Inspection Data Summary - Access to Cannabis for Medical Purposes Regulations. Background." Modified May 31, 2019. https://web.archive.org/web/20190813135237/https:/www.canada.ca/en/health-canada/services/drugs-medication/cannabis/compliance-enforcement/medical-cannabis-quarterly-compliance-enforcement-report-inspection-data-summary.html#a2.

___. 2019b. "Statement from Health Canada on Changes to Cannabis Licensing." May 8, 2019. https://www.canada.ca/en/health-canada/news/2019/05/statement-from-health-canada-on-changes-to-cannabis-licensing.html.

___. 2020. "Compliance and Enforcement of the Cannabis Act Report: Inspection Data Summary 2018-2019." Modified December 18, 2020. https://www.canada.ca/en/health-canada/services/drugs-medication/cannabis/research-data/compliance-enforcement-report-cannabis-inspection-data-summary/2018-2019.html.

___. 2021. "Greening Government Fund." Modified April 1, 2021. https://www.canada.ca/en/treasury-board-secretariat/services/innovation/greening-government/greening-gov-fund.html.

___. 2022. "Compliance and Enforcement of the Cannabis Act Report: Inspection Data Summary 2019-2020." Modified February 2, 2022. https://www.canada.ca/en/health-canada/services/drugs-medication/cannabis/research-data/compliance-enforcement-report-cannabis-inspection-data-summary/2019-2020.html .

___. n.d. "Recalls and Alerts." Accessed June 16 and May 28 2022. https://www.healthycanadians.gc.ca/recall-alert-rappel-avis/search-recherche/result-resultat/en?search_text_1=cannabis+OR+marijuana.

Canadian Press. 2019a. "CannTrust CEO Fired, Chairman Resigns Amid Health Canada Investigation." *Global News*, July 31, 2019. https://globalnews.ca/news/5684890/canntrust-ceo-fired-chairman-resigns/.

___. 2019b. "Health Canada Revokes Licences of Pot Producer Agrima Botanicals." *Toronto Star*, July 15, 2019. https://www.thestar.com/business/2019/07/15/health-canada-revokes-licences-of-pot-producer-agrima-botanicals.html.

___. 2019c. "OSC Launches Investigation into Unlicensed Pot Growing at CannTrust." *Toronto Star*, August 1, 2019. https://www.thestar.com/business/2019/08/01/canntrust-says-osc-launches-investigation-into-unlicensed-pot-growing.html.

___. 2019d. "Pot Producer Ascent Granted Creditor Protection After Licenses Suspended." *CTV News*, March 4, 2019. https://www.ctvnews.ca/business/pot-producer-ascent-granted-creditor-protection-after-licenses-suspended-1.4321430.

___. 2022. "OSC Withdraws Some Charges Against Former CannTrust Leaders at Pretrial Hearing." BNN Bloomberg, May 25, 2022. https://www.bnnbloomberg.ca/osc-withdraws-some-charges-against-former-canntrust-leaders-at-pretrial-hearing-1.1770650.

CannTrust Holdings Inc. 2019. "CannTrust Discloses Notice of Licence Suspension." *Cision*, September 17, 2019. https://www.prnewswire.com/news-releases/canntrust-discloses-notice-of-licence-suspension-300920121.html.

___. 2020. "CannTrust Receives Notice from Health Canada of License Reinstatement for its Fenwick Facility." *Cision*, May 29, 2020. https://www.prnewswire.com/news-releases/canntrust-receives-notice-from-health-canada-of-license-reinstatement-for-its-fenwick-facility-301067527.html.

___. 2022a. "CannTrust Announces Implementation of CCAA Plan, Settlement of Class Action Lawsuits and Board Changes." *Cision*, January 6, 2022. https://www.newswire.ca/news-releases/canntrust-announces-implementation-of-ccaa-plan-settlement-of-class-action-lawsuits-and-board-changes-892098468.html.

___. 2022b. "CannTrust Announces New Investment Partners, Provides Timeline for CCAA Exit." *Cision*, February 25, 2022. https://canntrust.com/canntrust-announces-new-investment-partners-provides-timeline-for-ccaa-exit/.

REFERENCES

Canopy Growth Corporation. 2019. "Canadian Icons Come Together: Canopy Growth and Drake Launch New Cannabis Wellness Company. *Cision*, November 7, 2019. https://www.prnewswire.com/news-releases/canadian-icons-come-together-canopy-growth-and-drake-launch-new-cannabis-wellness-company-300953763.html.

___. 2021. "Canopy Growth Welcomes Martha Stewart as Official Strategic Advisor." May 20, 2021. https://www.canopygrowth.com/investors/news-releases/canopy-growth-welcomes-martha-stewart-as-official-strategic-advisor/.

CBC News. 2019a. "Class-Action Lawsuit Against Organigram Gets Green Light." January 21, 2019. https://www.cbc.ca/news/canada/new-brunswick/class-action-lawsuit-medical-cannabis-organigram-1.4986632.

___. 2019b. "Health Canada Suspends Licence of Winnipeg Cannabis Producer Bonify." February 6, 2019. https://www.cbc.ca/amp/1.5007446.

Cloutier, Jean-Francois. 2022. "Health Canada Investigation into HEXO Competed, Conclusions to Come." *Le journal de Québec*, January 6, 2022. https://www.journaldequebec.com/2022/01/06/enquete-de-sante-canada-sur-HEXO-terminee-les-conclusions-a-venir.

Denis, Marie-Maude. 2018. "Licensed Cannabis Growers Have Ties to Organized Crime, Enquête Investigation Finds." *CBC News*, November 2, 2018. https://www.cbc.ca/amp/1.4887997.

DeVillaer, Michael. 2019. "Cannabis Legalization: Lessons from Alcohol, Tobacco, and Pharmaceutical Industries." In *High Time: The Legalization and Regulation of Cannabis in Canada,* edited by Andrew Potter and Daniel Weinstock, 182-201. Montréal: McGill-Queens University Press.

Ferreira, Victor. 2019. "CannTrust Whistleblower Says Health Canada Would Never Have Found Unlicensed Rooms Without Him." *National Post*, July 12, 2019. https://financialpost.com/cannabis/cannabis-business/canntrust-whistleblower-believes-health-canada-would-never-have-found-unlicensed-rooms-without-him.

Financial Post Staff. 2020. "Cannabis Company CannTrust Granted Creditor Protection." March 31, 2020. https://financialpost.com/cannabis/cannabis-business/cannabis-company-canntrust-granted-creditor-protection.

Froese, Ian. 2018. "Health Canada Recalls More Strains from Troubled Cannabis Producer." *CBC News,* December 24, 2018. https://www.cbc.ca/amp/1.4958715#click=https://t.co/lKOiBdGjkO.

___. 2019. "RCMP Not Investigating Winnipeg Cannabis Producer that Sold Unauthorized Weed." *CBC News,* March 25, 2019. https://www.cbc.ca/amp/1.5070578#click=https://t.co/JIgM1IYSt9.

Geary, Aidan. 2019. "Winnipegger Sentenced for Possession of 85 Grams of Cannabis a Month After Legalization." *CBC News,* April 2, 2019. https://www.cbc.ca/news/canada/manitoba/winnipeg-cannabis-act-trafficking-1.5082152.

George-Cosh, David. 2019a. "B.C. Pot Firm Evergreen Medicinal's Licence Suspended by Health Canada." *BNN Bloomberg*, September 16, 2019. https://www.bnnbloomberg.ca/b-c-pot-firm-evergreen-medicinal-s-licence-suspended-by-health-canada-1.1316783.

___. 2019b. "Black Market Pot Entered Canntrust Facility, Flowed into Legal Market Last Year: Sources." *BNN Bloomberg*, September 6, 2019. https://www.bnnbloomberg.ca/black-market-pot-entered-canntrust-facility-flowed-into-legal-market-last-year-sources-1.1312150.

___. 2019c. "'Quite a shock': CannTrust Chair Stands by CEO Amid Penalty Threat." *BNN Bloomberg*, July 9, 2019. https://www.bnnbloomberg.ca/quite-a-shock-canntrust-chair-stands-by-ceo-as-threat-of-penalties-linger-1.1284353.

Government Accountability Institute. 2021. "Cannabis Cronyism." February 2021. https://cannabislaw.report/wp-content/uploads/2021/02/Cannabis-MC2Changes-2-1-2021-PDF-FINAL.pdf.

Gowriluk, Caitlyn. 2019. "Winnipeg-Based Cannabis Producer Bonify Has Licence Reinstated by Health Canada." *CBC News*, October 23, 2019. https://www.cbc.ca/news/canada/manitoba/bonify-licence-reinstated-after-health-canada-suspension-1.5332637.

Harris, Colin. 2018. "Federal Ministers Defend Cannabis Rollout After Enquête Uncovers Ties to Organized Crime." *CBC News,* November 2, 2018. https://www.cbc.ca/news/canada/Montréal/federal-ministers-defend-cannabis-rollout-after-enqu-te-uncovers-ties-to-organized-crime-1.4890238.

Israel, Solomon. 2018a. "Bonify Sold 'Unapproved Cannabis Products' Health Canada Confirms." *Winnipeg Free Press, The Leaf,* December 21, 2018. https://www.theleafnews.com/news/bonify-sold-unapproved-cannabis-products-health-canada-confirms-503358182.html.

___. 2018b. "Regulatory Action for Alleged Cannabis Infraction." *Winnipeg Free Press, The Leaf,* November 23, 2018. https://www.theleafnews.com/news/leaflet-Regulatory-action-for-alleged-cannabis-infraction-501144772.html.

___. 2018c. "Winnipeg Cannabis Company Sold Illegal Weed in Saskatchewan: Source." *Winnipeg Free Press, The Leaf,* December 20, 2018. https://www.theleafnews.com/news/winnipeg-cannabis-company-sold-illegal-weed-in-saskatchewan-source-tells-free-press-503246402.html.

___. 2019. "Health Canada Pulls Bonify's Licences for Selling Illegal Weed." *Winnipeg Free Press, The Leaf,* February 5, 2019. https://www.winnipegfreepress.com/local/health-canada-pulls-bonifys-licences-for-selling-illegal-weed-505382112.html.

___. 2020a. "Health Canada: 'Any Celebrity Affiliation with Cannabis Has Potential to be Noncompliant'." *Marijuana Business Daily*, July 2, 2020. https://mjbizdaily.com/health-canada-any-celebrity-affiliation-with-cannabis-has-potential-to-be-noncompliant/.

___. 2020b. "The Lay of the Land." *Marijuana Business Magazine*, 7 (8): 50-56. https://mjbizmagazine.com/digital-issues/september-2020/40/.

Jones, Alexandra Mae. 2020. "Eight-Year-Old Wins $200 Worth of Cannabis Products at Youth Hockey Tournament. *CTV News*, March 2, 2020. https://beta.ctvnews.ca/national/canada/2020/3/2/1_4836083.html.

Kessler, Topaz, Meltzer, and Check, LLP. 2018. "Securities Fraud Class Action Filed Against Aphria Inc.—APHA." *Cision,* December 10, 2018. https://www.prnewswire.com/news-releases/kessler-topaz-meltzer--check-llp--securities-fraud-class-action-filed-against-aphria-inc--apha-300762608.html.

Lamers, Matt. 2018. "Regulator Warns Canadian Marijuana Firms Against 'Problematic Practices'." *Marijuana Business Daily*, December 6, 2018. https://mjbizdaily.com/canadian-cannabis-firm-regulatory-warning/.

___. 2020. "With All Licenses Reinstated, Canntrust Aims for Cannabis Product Relaunch." *Marijuana Business Daily*, August 6, 2020. https://mjbizdaily.com/with-all-licenses-reinstated-canntrust-aims-for-cannabis-product-relaunch/.

___. 2021a. "3 Former Executives of Cannabis Producer Canntrust Charged with Fraud." *Marijuana Business Daily*, June 22, 2021. https://mjbizdaily.com/cannabis-producer-canntrusts-former-directors-face-fraud-insider-trading-charges/.

___. 2021b. "British Columbia Urges 'Rethink' of Canada's Medical Cannabis Program, Citing Diversion to Illicit Market." *Marijuana Business Daily*, March 30, 2021. https://mjbizdaily.com/british-columbia-urges-rethink-of-canadas-medical-cannabis-program/.

REFERENCES

____. 2021c. "Canada Revenue Agency Has Fined Cannabis Firms CA$1.3 Million Since Adult-Use Market Launch." *Marijuana Business Daily*, March 2, 2021. https://mjb-izdaily.com/canada-revenue-agency-has-fined-cannabis-firms-ca1-3-million-since-adult-use-market-launch/.

____. 2021d. "Health Canada Declines to Fine Cannabis Companies for Violations, Opting for Other Penalties." *Marijuana Business Daily*, February 8, 2021. https://mjb-izdaily.com/health-canada-declines-to-fine-cannabis-companies-for-violations/.

____. 2021e. "Health Canada Unaware Canntrust Exec Was Under Investigation When Cannabis Licenses Reinstated." *Marijuana Business Daily*, July 7, 2021. https://mjb-izdaily.com/health-canada-unaware-canntrust-cannabis-executive-was-under-in-vestigation/.

____. 2022a. "Canadian Cannabis Producers' Overdue Excise Taxes More Than Triple to CA$52M." *Marijuana Business Daily*, May 25, 2022. https://mjbizdaily.com/canadian-cannabis-producers-overdue-excise-taxes-more-than-triple-to-ca52-million/.

____. 2022b. "Health Canada Seized More Than 35M Grams of Marijuana, 7,800 Plants After Inspections." *Marijuana Business Daily*, February 23, 2022. https://mjb-izdaily.com/health-canada-seized-more-than-35-million-grams-of-cannabis-7800-plants/.

____. 2022c. "Unpaid Canadian Marijuana Regulatory Fees Jump Tenfold to Almost CA$1 Million." *Marijuana Business Daily*, March 28, 2022. https://mjbizdaily.com/unpaid-canadian-cannabis-regulatory-fees-jump-tenfold-to-almost-ca1-million/.

Law Offices of Howard G. Smith. n.d. "Namaste Technologies, Inc. (OTC: NXTTF)." Accessed April 5 2022. http://www.howardsmithlaw.com/SecuritiesFraudCases/NamasteTechnologies.html.

Ligaya, Armina. 2018. "Aphria Shares Plunge 28 Per Cent After Short Seller Report." *CTV News*, December 3, 2018. https://www.ctvnews.ca/business/aphria-shares-plunge-28-per-cent-after-short-seller-report-1.4202897.

____. 2019a. "Health Canada Looking into Cannabis Company's Sponsorship of Charity Event." *CTV News*, March 6, 2019. https://toronto.ctvnews.ca/health-canada-look-ing-into-cannabis-company-s-sponsorship-of-charity-event-1.4323661.

____. 2019b. "Seth Rogen Teams Up with Canopy Growth to Launch Cannabis Brand Houseplant." *CTV News*, March 27, 2019. https://beta.ctvnews.ca/national/busi-ness/2019/3/27/1_4353608.html#click=https://t.co/V6aBm8raF0.

Little, Simon. 2018. "Mouldy Ontario Pot Recall Extended to B.C." *Global News*, November 29, 2018. https://globalnews.ca/news/4713509/pot-recall-bc-cannabis-stores/.

Liquor Control Board of Ontario. n.d. "The Tragically Hip Fully Completely Reserve Red." Accessed June 1, 2022. https://www.lcbo.com/webapp/wcs/stores/ser-vlet/en/lcbo/the-tragically-hip-fully-completely-reserve-red-2019-411595.

Magee, Shane. 2020a. "N.S. Court Reduces Scope of Lawsuit Over Tainted Organigram Cannabis." *CBC News*, May 1, 2020. https://www.cbc.ca/news/canada/new-brun-swick/organigram-class-action-court-decision-1.5552000.

____. 2020b. "Supreme Court Won't Hear Organigram Tainted Marijuana Class Action Case." *CBC News*, November 5, 2020. https://www.cbc.ca/news/canada/new-brun-swick/supreme-court-organigram-class-action-appeal-1.5790837.

Malone, Kelly Geraldine. 2018. "Who Knows Where Bonify Got the Pot It Shipped Out to Meet Demand? Not Investigators." *National Post*, December 28, 2018. https://na-tionalpost.com/news/canada/who-knows-where-bonify-got-the-pot-it-shipped-out-to-meet-demand-not-investigators.

Marijuana Business Daily. 2021. "Cannabis Firm Canntrust Reaches Agreement to Settle Shareholder Claims." January 20, 2021. https://mjbizdaily.com/restructuring-can-nabis-firm-canntrust-reaches-agreement-to-settle-shareholder-claims/.

McArthur, Greg. 2020. Court Freezes Tree of Knowledge's Assets for Selling Faulty Masks to Quebec Hospitals. *The Globe and Mail*, December 23, 2020. https://www.theglobeandmail.com/business/article-court-freezes-tree-of-knowledges-assets-for-selling-faulty-masks-to/.

Michael G. Degroote Centre for Medicinal Cannabis Research. 2021. "Knowledge Synthesis: Contamination of Cannabis Products for Human Consumption." September 2013. https://cannabisresearch.mcmaster.ca/docs/default-source/knowledge-syntheses/mgdcmcr_cannabiscontamination.pdf.

Miller, Jacquie. 2018. "Trailer Park Buds? Cannabis Companies Devise Catchy Brand Names Amid Strict Health Canada Rules." *Ottawa Citizen*, October 15, 2018. https://ottawacitizen.com/cannabis/cannabis-business/pot-names#click=https://t.co/0KeKObrzms.

Milstead, David and Mark Rendell. 2019. "Two CannTrust Officials Sold $6-Million of Stock After the Chair Was Informed of Unlicensed Cannabis Growing." *The Globe and Mail*, July 30, 2019. https://www.theglobeandmail.com/cannabis/article-two-canntrust-officials-sold-6-million-of-stock-after-the-chair-was/.

Nair, Shanti S. and Roy Debroop. 2019. "CannTrust Slumps After Health Canada Finds Unlicensed Pot Cultivation." *Saltwire*, July 8, 2019. https://www.saltwire.com/prince-edward-island/lifestyles/canntrust-slumps-after-health-canada-finds-unlicensed-pot-cultivation-330773/.

North40Cannabis (@40Cannabis). 2020. "Well, it happened. More powdery mildew." Twitter, November 13, 2020. https://twitter.com/40Cannabis/status/1327418886807977985.

O'Cannabiz Conference & Expo. 2019. "Schedule." Toronto, April 25-27, 2019. Accessed online April 25, 2019; no longer available May 30, 2022.

Office of the Commissioner of Lobbying of Canada. 2021. "Registry of Lobbyists". September 30, 2021. https://lobbycanada.gc.ca/app/secure/ocl/lrs/do/advSrch.

Ontario Cannabis Store. n.d. "Featured Flower: Blue Dream." Accessed October 13, 2020. https://ocs.ca/blogs/featured-flower/featured-flower-blue-dream.

Ontario Securities Commission. 2021. "Former Officers and Directors of CannTrust Charged with Securities Act Offences." June 22, 2021. https://www.osc.ca/en/news-events/news/former-officers-and-directors-canntrust-charged-securities-act-offences.

Parry, Chris. 2020. "Ravenquest (RQB.V) CEO George Robinson Resigns, Company Alleges He's Holding Records Hostage." *Equity Guru*, May 2, 2020. https://equity.guru/2020/05/02/ravenquest-rqb-v-ceo-george-robinson-resigns-company-alleges-hes-holding-records-hostage/.

Pfeffer, Amanda and Guillaume Dumont. 2017. "Police Warn Organized Crime, Including the Hells Angels, Has Infiltrated the Medical Marijuana Market." *CBC News*, April 13, 2017. https://www.cbc.ca/news/canada/ottawa/police-warn-organized-crime-including-the-hells-angels-has-infiltrated-the-medical-marijuana-market-1.4067112.

Phoena. 2022. "CannTrust Introduces Phoena, the Company's New Corporate Name." *Cision*, May 3, 2022. https://www.prnewswire.com/news-releases/canntrust-introduces-phoena-the-companys-new-corporate-name-301538740.html.

Rendell, Mark. 2019a. "Cannabis Firm Beleave Acknowledges Participation in Securities Scam." *The Globe and Mail*, June 7, 2019. https://www.theglobeandmail.com/cannabis/article-cannabis-firm-beleave-acknowledges-participation-in-securities-scam/.

___. 2019b. "CannTrust Allegedly Used Fake Walls to Hide Pot from Health Canada. *The Globe and Mail*, July 18, 2019. https://www.theglobeandmail.com/cannabis/article-canntrust-allegedly-used-fake-walls-to-hide-pot-from-health-canada/.

REFERENCES

Reuters. 2019. "Cannabis Producer Canntrust to Destroy $77M Worth of Plants, Inventory to Regain Compliance." *CBC News*, October 14, 2019. https://www.cbc.ca/amp/1.5320585.

Robertson, Kate. 2020. "Regulatory Infraction or Criminal Charge? Licensed Companies and Individuals Are Treated Very Differently When It Comes to Cannabis Laws in Canada." *The GrowthOp*, June 10, 2020. https://www.thegrowthop.com/cannabis-news/cannabis-legalization/regulatory-infraction-or-criminal-charge-licensed-companies-and-individuals-are-treated-very-differently-when-it-comes-to-cannabis-laws-in-canada.

Robertson, Morton. 2020. "OPP Says Criminal Enterprises Exploiting the Health Canada Medical, Personal and Designate Cannabis Production Regime." *Stratcann*, October 22, 2020. https://stratcann.com/2020/10/22/opp-says-criminal-enterprises-exploiting-the-health-canada-medical-personal-and-designate-cannabis-production-regime/.

Royal Canadian Mounted Police. 2021. "Cannabis Seized from Unlicensed Online Cannabis Store, Two Arrested." January 29, 2021. https://www.grc-rcmp.gc.ca/en/news/2021/cannabis-seized-unlicensed-online-cannabis-store-two-arrested.

Sarkar, Arundhati and Taru Jain. 2019. 2nd CannTrust Marijuana Facility Deemed Non-Compliant by Health Canada. *Global News*, August 12, 2019. https://globalnews.ca/news/5754805/canntrust-2nd-facility-cannabis-health-canada-investigation/amp/.

Shecter, Barbara. 2022. "Former CannTrust Officials Acquitted on All Charges in Quasi-criminal Case." *Financial Post*, December 15, 2022. https://financialpost.com/fp-finance/former-canntrust-officials-acquitted.

Skapinker, Michael. 2012. "The Odd Ways We Calibrate Our Outrage." *Financial Times*, July 25, 2012. https://www.ft.com/content/f90bbd50-d4b7-11e1-9444-00144feabdc0.

Stratcann. 2021. "Bonify Is "Winding Down" Operations in the Coming Weeks." August 13, 2021. https://stratcann.com/2021/08/13/bonify-is-winding-down-operations-in-the-coming-weeks/.

Subramaniam, Vanmala. 2019. "Namaste Technologies Plunges 21% After it Fires CEO and Launches Strategic Review." *Financial Post*, February 4, 2019. https://business.financialpost.com/cannabis/cannabis-business/namaste-technologies-plunges-21-after-it-fires-ceo-and-launches-strategic-review.

_____. 2020. "Marie Henein's Law Firm Part of Class-Action Consortium Against CannTrust." *Financial Post*, February 3, 2020. https://business.financialpost.com/cannabis/marie-heneins-law-firm-part-of-class-action-consortium-against-canntrust.

Swaby, Nickeesha. 2018. "Canadian Cannabis Company Faces Class Action After Damning Research Report Calls US Listing Plan 'Fake'." *Courthouse News Service*, October 30, 2018. https://Www.Courthousenews.Com/Canadian-Cannabis-Company-Faces-Class-Action-After-Damning-Research-Report-Calls-U-S-Listing-Plan-Fake/.

Tilray Inc. 2021. "(TLRY) Q1 2022 Earnings Call Transcript." *The Motley Fool*. October 8, 2021. https://www.fool.com/earnings/call-transcripts/2021/10/08/tilray-inc-tlry-q1-2022-earnings-call-transcript/.

Top Class Actions. 2021. "CannTrust $83M Securities Class Action Settlement." October 11, 2021. https://topclassactions.com/lawsuit-settlements/open-lawsuit-settlements/canntrust-83m-securities-class-action-settlement/.

Underwood, Colleen. 2019. "Calgary-Based Cannabis Producer Sundial Growers Facing Class-Action Lawsuit for Allegedly Misleading Investors." *CBC News*, October 7, 2019. https://www.cbc.ca/news/canada/calgary/sundial-growers-class-action-lawsuit-1.5309947.

VOCM Local News. 2020. "Julia Mullaley Leaving Role as Auditor General to Become CEO of NL Housing Corp." March 11, 2020. https://vocm.com/2020/03/11/julia-mullaley-career-shift/.

Windowswear. 2018. "Consumers Have Been Finding Bugs in Bud Purchased from the Ontario Cannabis Store." December 5, 2018. https://www.windowswear.com/consumers-have-been-finding-bugs-in-bud-purchased-from-the-ontario-cannabis-store-straight-com/.

8. Green Rush in the Red

Ball, David P. 2022. "End of an Era as Cannabis Giant Tilray Sells Land and Leaves Nanaimo." CBC News, March 21, 2022. https://www.cbc.ca/news/canada/british-columbia/cannabis-company-tilray-finds-land-buyer-leaves-nanaimo-1.6391681#:~:text=The%20pioneering%20Nanaimo%20cannabis%20company,with%20it%20roughly%20170%20jobs.

Ballard, Joel. 2021. "Cannabis Has Been Legal Almost 3 Years, Yet Retailers Say Banks Are Shutting Them Out." *CBC News*, October 12, 2021. https://www.cbc.ca/news/canada/british-columbia/cannabis-banks-credit-unions-1.6205932.

BBC News. 2021. "Cannabis Part of the Future Says Tobacco Giant." July 28, 2021. https://www.bbc.com/news/business-57995285.

Canada. 2022. "Cannabis Market Data". Modified April 1, 2022. https://www.canada.ca/en/health-canada/services/drugs-medication/cannabis/research-data/market.html.

Canadian Press. 2019. "Tweed Cofounder Chuck Rifici's Cannabis Firm Auxly Lands $123M From Tobacco Giant." *Ottawa Business Journal*, July 25, 2019. https://obj.ca/article/tweed-co-founder-chuck-rificis-cannabis-firm-auxly-lands-123m-tobacco-giant.

Cannabis Council of Canada. 2021. "Not Done Yet Report Card." October 19, 2021. https://cannabis-council.ca/files/Not-Done-Yet-Report-Card-Rationale-10.19.21.pdf.

Canopy Growth Corporation. n.d. "Governance." Accessed April 11, 2022. https://www.canopygrowth.com/investors/governance/board-of-directors/.

Carrigg, David. 2020. "Blaze in Delta Destroys Unused Cannabis Greenhouse." *Vancouver Sun*, November 1, 2020. https://vancouversun.com/news/local-news/smoke-from-delta-greenhouse-fire-visible-from-across-the-region.

Castaldo, Joe. 2018. "Canadian Weed Stocks Have a Serious Accounting Problem." *Maclean's*, January 23, 2018. https://www.macleans.ca/economy/canadian-weed-stocks-have-a-serious-accounting-problem/.

Chan, Margaret. 2013. "WHO Director-General Addresses Health Promotion Conference. Opening Address at the 8th Global Conference on Health Promotion, Helsinki Finland." World Health Organization. June 10, 2013. https://www.foodpolitics.com/wp-content/uploads/DG-WHO-speech-to-Health-Promotion-Conference.pdf.

Deloitte. 2021. "An industry Makes its Mark: The Economic and Social Impact of Canada's Cannabis Sector." January 2021. https://www2.deloitte.com/content/dam/Deloitte/ca/Documents/consumer-business/ca_cannabis_annual_report-en-aoda.pdf.

REFERENCES

Deschamps, Tara. 2020. "Canopy Growth to Close Five Facilities Across Canada, Lay Off 220 Workers." *Toronto Star*, December 9, 2020. https://www.thestar.com/business/2020/12/09/canopy-growth-to-close-five-facilities-across-canada-lay-off-220-workers.html.

____. 2022. "Pot Shop Sales Data Was 'Misappropriated,' Ontario Cannabis Distributor Says." *CBC News*, May 11, 2022. https://www.cbc.ca/news/canada/toronto/pot-shop-sales-data-misappropriated-ontario-1.6448936.

Fernholz, Tim. 2016. "America's Weed Industry is Going to be Massive. Is Big Marijuana a Good Thing?" *Quartz*, April 20, 2016. https://qz.com/664956/americas-weed-industry-is-going-to-be-massive-is-big-marijuana-a-good-thing/.

Fox D Consulting (@FoxDConsulting). 2021. "Cannabis Licence Holders Update: Displaying THC and CBD Content on Dried Cannabis Product Labels and Kief." Twitter, August 10, 2021. https://twitter.com/FoxDConsulting/status/1425159209637851137/photo/1.

Gallant, Collin. 2021. "Aurora Lists Unused Facility for Sale." *Medicine Hat News*, March 5, 2021. https://medicinehatnews.com/news/local-news/2021/03/05/aurora-lists-unused-facility-for-sale/.

Gaviola, Anne. 2019. "Major Weed Companies Are Cutting Hundreds of Jobs as the Industry Struggles." *VICE*, October 25, 2019. https://www.vice.com/en_ca/article/zmjk7w/major-canadian-weed-companies-are-cutting-hundreds-of-jobs-as-the-industry-struggles.

George-Cosh, David. 2021. "Health Canada Probing Cannabis Labelling Amid Canopy Growth Potency Complaint." *BNN Bloomberg*, March 8, 2021. https://www.bnnbloomberg.ca/health-canada-probing-cannabis-labelling-amid-canopy-growth-potency-complaint-1.1574091.

Global Newswire. 2022. "BC Craft Has Filed Notice of Intention to Make a Proposal Under the Bankruptcy and Insolvency Act (Canada)." January 25, 2022. https://www.globenewswire.com/news-release/2022/01/25/2373047/0/en/BC-Craft-Has-Filed-Notice-of-Intention-to-Make-a-Proposal-Under-the-Bankruptcy-Insolvency-Act-Canada.html.

Hathaway, Andrew D., Greggory Cullen, and David Walters. 2021. "How Well Is Cannabis Legalization Curtailing the Illegal Market? A Multi-wave Analysis of Canada's National Cannabis Survey." *Journal of Canadian Studies* 55 (2): 307-36. https://utpjournals.press/doi/abs/10.3138/jcs-2020-0056?journalCode=jcs.

HEXO. 2020. "HEXO Virtually Unveils Belleville Manufacturing Centre of Excellence, Truss Bottling Facility." Global Newswire, December 10, 2020. https://www.globenewswire.com/news-release/2020/12/10/2142897/0/en/HEXO-virtually-unveils-Belleville-manufacturing-centre-of-Excellence-Truss-bottling-facility.html.

____. 2022. "HEXO Provides Update on Strategic Plan; Announces Changes to Further Streamline Operations on Path to Becoming Cash Flow Positive from Operations." Global Newswire, April 21, 2022. https://www.globenewswire.com/en/news-release/2022/04/21/2426912/0/en/HEXO-Provides-Update-on-Strategic-Plan-Announces-Changes-to-Further-Streamline-Operations-on-Path-to-Becoming-Cash-Flow-Positive-From-Operations.html.

Israel, Solomon. 2020a. "As Consolidation Hits Canadian Cannabis Retail, More Mergers and Acquisitions Expected." *Marijuana Business Daily*, November 26, 2020. https://mjbizdaily.com/canadian-cannabis-retail-consolidation-could-spur-more-mergers-and-acquisitions/.

____. 2020b. "The Lay of the Land." *Marijuana Business Magazine*, 7 (8): 50-56. https://mjbizmagazine.com/digital-issues/september-2020/40/.

___. 2021a. "Cannabis Growing Competition May Result in Store Closures." *Marijuana Business Daily*, June 29, 2021. https://mjbizdaily.com/ontario-cannabis-store-growing-competition-may-cause-store-closures/.

___. 2021b. "Retail Shakeout Expected as Ontario Heads Toward 1000 Cannabis Stores." *Marijuana Business Daily*, May 28, 2021. https://mjbizdaily.com/retail-shakeout-expected-as-ontario-heads-toward-1000-cannabis-stores/.

Khan, Shariq and Siddharth Cavale. 2021. "BAT Looks Beyond Tobacco to Canadian Marijuana." *Reuters Business News*, March 11, 2021. https://www.reuters.com/article/us-bat-agreement-organigram-hldg-idUSKBN2B31GG.

Konyukhova, Maria and Nicholas Avis. 2020. "The Crash After the High: Managing Insolvency in the Cannabis Sector, 2020." In 18th *Annual Review of Insolvency Law* 433. CanLIIDocs 3610. https://canlii.ca/t/t1x1.

Krane, Kris. 2018. "Cannabis Attracts Big Tobacco, Alcohol, and Pharma. Which Big Industries Will Join Next?" *Forbes*, December 19, 2018. https://www.forbes.com/sites/kriskrane/2018/12/19/cannabis-attracts-big-tobacco-alcohol-and-pharma-which-big-industries-will-join-next/#4b44ac118daf29.

Lamers, Matt. 2020a. "Aurora Cannabis Execs Saw Raises, Bonuses Despite Multibillion-Dollar Loss." *Marijuana Business Daily*, October 2, 2020. https://mjbizdaily.com/aurora-cannabis-execs-saw-raises-bonuses-despite-multibillion-dollar-loss.

___. 2020b. "Aurora Cannabis leads Canada in Market Share Decline While Smaller Companies Gain, Report Says." *Marijuana Business Daily*, April 13, 2020. https://mjbizdaily.com/aurora-cannabis-leads-canada-in-market-share-decline-while-smaller-companies-gain.

___. 2020c. "Foreign Affairs." *Marijuana Business Magazine*, 7 (8): 41-42. https://mjbizmagazine.com/digital-issues/september-2020/40/.

___. 2020d. "Green Organic Dutchman Removes CEO After Reporting CA$76 Million Loss." *Marijuana Business Daily*, November 12, 2020. https://mjbizdaily.com/green-organic-dutchman-removes-ceo-after-reporting-ca76-million-loss/.

___. 2020e. "How Canadian Cannabis Firms Lost Millions on Bad Greenhouse Deals." *Marijuana Business Daily*, November 2, 2020. https://mjbizdaily.com/how-canadian-cannabis-firms-lost-millions-on-bad-greenhouse-deals/.

___. 2020f. "MediPharm CFO Resigns Days Before 88% Revenue Plunge." *Marijuana Business Daily*, November 16, 2020. https://mjbizdaily.com/medipharm-cfo-resigns-days-before-88-revenue-plunge/.

___. 2020g. "Shoppers Drug Mart Seeks Cannabis Sales in Pharmacies: Q&A with Exec Ken Weisbrod." *Marijuana Business Daily*, October 27, 2020. https://mjbizdaily.com/shoppers-drug-mart-exec-ken-weisbrod-discusses-medical-marijuana-in-canada.

___. 2021a. "Aurora Cannabis Cutting 8% of Workforce, Closing Facility in Edmonton." *Marijuana Business Daily*, September 23, 2021. https://mjbizdaily.com/aurora-cannabis-cutting-8-of-workforce-losing-facility-in-edmonton/.

___. 2021b. "Canada's Legal Cannabis Market Continues to Erode Illicit Market's Share." *Marijuana Business Daily*, May 19, 2021. https://mjbizdaily.com/canadas-legal-cannabis-market-continues-to-erode-illicit-markets-share/.

___. 2021c. "Canada's Unsold Cannabis Inventory Levels Off at 1.1 Billion Grams." *Marijuana Business Daily*, April 26, 2021. https://mjbizdaily.com/canadas-unsold-cannabis-inventory-levels-off-at-1-1-billion-grams/.

___. 2021d. "Canadian Cannabis Firm Aphria Gave CEO $8.1 Million to Become Full-Time Employee." *Marijuana Business Daily*, June 30, 2021. https://mjbizdaily.com/canadian-cannabis-firm-aphria-gave-ceo-8-1m-to-be-full-time-employee/.

REFERENCES

___. 2021e. "Canadian Cannabis Industry 'Increasingly Fragmented' Despite M&A." *Marijuana Business Daily*, September 9, 2021. https://mjbizdaily.com/canadian-can-nabis-industry-increasingly-fragmented-despite-ma/.

___. 2021f. "Canadian Cannabis Producers Have Sold Less Than 20% of Output Since Adult-Use Legalization." *Marijuana Business Daily*, July 28, 2021. https://mjb-izdaily.com/canadian-cannabis-producers-have-sold-less-than-20-percent-of-out-put-since-2018/.

___. 2021g. "Canadian Marijuana Industry Employment Tumbled ss Producers Drew Federal COVID-19 Cash, Analysis Shows." *Marijuana Business Daily*, November 17, 2021. https://mjbizdaily.com/canadian-cannabis-employment-tumbled-as-produ-cers-received-federal-covid-19-cash/.

___. 2021h. "Canadian Producers Destroyed Over 500 Tons of Cannabis Since 2018." *Marijuana Business Daily*, July 13, 2021. https://mjbizdaily.com/canadian-producers-destroyed-over-500-tons-of-cannabis-since-2018/.

___. 2021i. "Canopy Execs Earn Raises, Bonuses After Cannabis Giant Loses CA$1.7 Bil-lion." *Marijuana Business Daily*, August 3, 2021. https://mjbizdaily.com/canopy-ex-ecs-earn-raises-bonuses-after-cannabis-giant-loses-ca1-7-billion/.

___. 2021j. "Canopy Growth, Others Formed JV 'Solely' to Pump Marijuana Stock, Re-filed CA$500 Million Lawsuit Alleges." *Marijuana Business Daily*, March 9, 2021. ht-tps://mjbizdaily.com/canopy-growth-others-formed-jv-solely-to-pump-cannabis-st ock-lawsuit-alleges/.

___. 2021k. "CEO Compensation at Marijuana Producer HEXO Rises to CA$11 million." *Marijuana Business Daily*, January 6, 2021. https://mjbizdaily.com/ceo-compensa-tion-at-marijuana-producer-HEXO-rises-to-ca11-million/.

___. 2021l. "'Craft Absolutely Surprised Us,' HEXO CEO Says as Cannabis Sales Plunge." December 17, 2021. https://mjbizdaily.com/craft-absolutely-surprised-us-HEXO-ceo-says-as-cannabis-sales-plunge/.

___. 2021m. "HEXO Shutting Marijuana Facilities It Recently Acquired, Laying Off 155." *Marijuana Business Daily*, November 9, 2021. https://mjbizdaily.com/HEXO-shutting-cannabis-facilities-it-recently-acquired-affecting-155-workers/.

___. 2021n. "More Canadian Cannabis Firms Filing Complaints About Rival Businesses." *Marijuana Business Daily*, May 19, 2021. https://mjbizdaily.com/more-canadian-can-nabis-firms-filing-complaints-about-rival-businesses/.

___. 2021o. "Ontario Cannabis Store Appoints Sixth President in Three Years, Raising In-dustry Concern." *Marijuana Business Daily*, March 18, 2021. https://mjb-izdaily.com/ontario-cannabis-store-appoints-sixth-president-in-three-years/.

___. 2021p. "Why WeedMD Sold a Cannabis Subsidiary for CA$2.5 Million After Buying It for CA$55 Million." *Marijuana Business Daily*, June 16, 2021. https://mjb-izdaily.com/weedmd-sells-starseed-medicinal-at-a-loss-to-final-bell-canada/.

___. 2022a. "Aurora Cannabis Sets More Closures, Selling Sun Greenhouse at Fraction of Cost." *Marijuana Business Daily*, May 18, 2022. https://mjbizdaily.com/aurora-can-nabis-sets-more-closures-sells-sun-greenhouse/.

___. 2022b. "Cannabis Producer Canopy Growth Sheds 8% of Workforce, Eyes CA$150 Million More in Savings." *Marijuana Business Daily*, April 28, 2022. https://mjb-izdaily.com/cannabis-producer-canopy-growth-cuts-8-percent-of-workforce/.

Lundy, Matt and Irene Galea. 2022. "Why Cannabis Prices Are Plunging—Unlike Just About Everything Else." *The Globe and Mail*, May 2, 2022. https://www.theglobeand-mail.com/business/article-canada-inflation-prices-marijuana-cannabis-industry/.

Macdonald, David. 2021. "The Golden Cushion: CEO Compensation in Canada." The Canadian Centre for Policy Alternatives. January 2021. https://www.policyalternatives.ca/sites/default/files/uploads/publications/National%20Office/2021/01/Golden%20cushion.pdf.

Marijuana Business Daily. 2020a. "Canadian Cannabis Producer Zenabis Gets Fourth CEO in Two Years." September 15, 2020. https://mjbizdaily.com/cannabis-producer-zenabis-gets-4th-ceo-in-2-years/.

___. 2020b. "Cannabis Firm Weedmd Borrows CA$30M from Canadian Pension Fund." September 25, 2020. https://mjbizdaily.com/cash-strapped-weedmd-borrows-ca30-million-from-canadian-union-pension-fund/.

___. 2020c. "Ontario Cannabis Firm HEXO Announces Fourth Chief Financial Officer in Two Years." September 15, 2020. https://mjbizdaily.com/HEXO-to-get-fourth-chief-financial-officer-in-two-years/.

___. 2020d. "Two Canadian Cannabis Retail Chains Report Sales Growth, Net Losses." September 25, 2020. https://mjbizdaily.com/canadian-cannabis-retailers-meta-fire-flower-report-sales-growth-net-losses/.

___. 2021a. "Aurora Cannabis Continues Board Revamp, Installs Ex-Pfizer Executive." July 25, 2021. https://mjbizdaily.com/aurora-continues-board-revamp-installs-former-pfizer-exec-firestone/.

___. 2021b. "Auxly Cannabis Reports CA$13.5 Million Loss on Record Revenue." December 17, 2021. https://mjbizdaily.com/auxly-cannabis-reports-ca15-million-loss-on-record-revenue/.

___. 2021c. "Cannabis Producer Tilray Shutting 'Flagship' Facility in Nanaimo." September 16, 2021. https://mjbizdaily.com/cannabis-producer-tilray-shutting-flagship-facility-in-nanaimo/.

___. 2021d. "Canopy to Buy Supreme for CA$435 Million as Cannabis M&A Heats Up." April 8, 2021. https://mjbizdaily.com/canopy-to-buy-supreme-for-ca435-million-as-cannabis-ma-heats-up/.

___. 2021e. "Pure Sunfarms Posts Quarterly Profit on Surging Marijuana Revenue." August 9, 2021. https://mjbizdaily.com/pure-sunfarms-posts-quarterly-profit-on-surging-cannabis-revenue/.

___. 2021f. "Tilray, Aphria Complete Blockbuster Marijuana Merger." May 3, 2021. https://mjbizdaily.com/tilray-aphria-complete-blockbuster-marijuana-merger/.

___. 2022a. "2 Canadian Cannabis Firms Get Nasdaq Extensions to Regain Compliance." March 3, 2022. https://mjbizdaily.com/2-canadian-cannabis-firms-get-nasdaq-extensions-to-regain-compliance/. Accessed April 12 2022.

___. 2022b. "Canadian Cannabis Producer Eve & Co Receives Creditor Protection." March 29, 2022. https://mjbizdaily.com/canadian-cannabis-producer-eve-co-receives-creditor-protection/.

___. 2022c. "Canadian Cannabis Retailer Choom Granted Creditor Protection." April 27, 2022. https://mjbizdaily.com/canadian-cannabis-retailer-choom-granted-creditor-protection/.

___. 2022d. "Canadian Producer Aurora Cannabis Loses Another CA$1 Billion." May 16, 2022. https://mjbizdaily.com/canadian-producer-aurora-cannabis-loses-another-ca1-billion/.

___. 2022e. "Cannabis Retailer Fire & Flower Posts Revenue Decline, Cites Competition." April 26, 2022. https://mjbizdaily.com/marijuana-retailer-fire-flower-posts-revenue-decline-cites-competition/.

___. 2022f. "Ontario Making Cannabis Retail Delivery, Curbside Pickup Permanent March 15." March 3, 2022. https://mjbizdaily.com/ontario-making-cannabis-retail-delivery-curbside-pickup-permanent-march-15/.

REFERENCES

McBride, Stephen. 2019. "Aurora Cannabis is Dumping its Pot, Which May Be a Sign it's All Over." *Forbes*, October 21, 2019. https://www.forbes.com/sites/stephenmcbride1/2019/10/21/aurora-cannabis-is-dumping-its-pot-which-may-be-a-sign-its-all-over/#329811305775.

Milstead, David. 2020. "Two Years in, Most Pot Stocks Are in the Pits." *The Globe and Mail*, October 18, 2020. https://www.theglobeandmail.com/investing/markets/inside-the-market/article-two-years-in-most-pot-stocks-are-in-the-pits/.

Mouallem, Omar. 2022. "'It's Easier to Sell a Dream Than Reality': Inside Canada's Cannabis Crash." *Canadian Business*. April 14, 2022. https://www.canadianbusiness.com/ideas/canada-cannabis-stocks-crashing/?utm_source=citynews%20kitchener&utm_campaign=citynews%20kitchener%3A%20outbound&utm_medium=referral.

NASDAQ. 2020. "Aphria Inc. Announces Strategic Entry into the United States with an Agreement to Acquire Sweetwater Brewing Company." November 4, 2020. https://www.nasdaq.com/press-release/aphria-inc.-announces-strategic-entry-into-the-united-states-with-an-agreement-to.

NASDAQ Listing Center. 2022. "Noncompliant Companies." February 16, 2022. https://listingcenter.nasdaq.com/noncompliantcompanylist.aspx.

Neptune Wellness Solutions. 2020. "Management Information Circular". July 14, 2020. https://www.sec.gov/Archives/edgar/data/1401395/000156459020032496/neptex992_7.htm?utm_medium=email&utm_source=newsletter&utm_campaign=INTL_20211029_NEWS_Weekly.

Office of the Auditor General of Ontario. 2020. "Value-for-Money Audit: Alcohol and Gaming Commission of Ontario." December 2020. https://www.auditor.on.ca/en/content/annualreports/arreports/en20/20VFM_01AGCO.pdf.

___. 2021. "Value-for-Money Audit: Ontario Cannabis Retail Corporation." December 2021. https://www.auditor.on.ca/en/content/annualreports/arreports/en21/AR_OCRC_en21.pdf.

Ontario Cannabis Store. 2021. "Ontario Now Has 1,000 Legal Cannabis Stores! Let's Celebrate Some Milestones Along the Way." August 20, 2021. https://learn.ocswholesale.ca/blog/ontario-now-has-1000-legal-cannabis-stores-lets-celebrate-some-milestones-along-the-way/.

Porter, Ryan. 2020. "Highs and Lows of 2 Years of Legal Cannabis in Canada." *Leafly*. October 15, 2020. https://www.leafly.ca/news/canada/2-years-legal-cannabis-canada.

S&P Dow Jones Indices LLC. 2022. "S&P Dow Jones Indices Announces Changes to the S&P/TSX Composite Index and S&P/TSX 60 Index." *Cision*, March 4, 2022. https://www.newswire.ca/news-releases/s-amp-p-dow-jones-indices-announces-changes-to-the-s-amp-p-tsx-composite-index-and-s-amp-p-tsx-60-index-863785400.html.

Schmidt, Doug. 2020. "Leamington Loses 120 Jobs as Tilray Kills Cannabis Facility." *Windsor Star*, May 27, 2020. https://windsorstar.com/news/local-news/leamington-loses-120-jobs-as-tilray-kills-cannabis-facility.

Smith, Jeff. 2021a. "10 US Marijuana Ceos Get Million-Dollar Pay in 2020 as Disclosure Practices Questioned." *Marijuana Business Daily*, July 7, 2021. https://mjbizdaily.com/10-us-marijuana-ceos-get-million-dollar-pay-in-2020/.

___. 2021b. "Canadian Cannabis Producers Speed Entry into US Via High-Stakes Wagers." *Marijuana Business Daily*, October 1, 2021. https://mjbizdaily.com/canadian-cannabis-producers-speed-entry-into-us-via-high-stakes-wagers/.

St Anthony. 2020. "Former Vancouver Cannabis Company CEO Collected More Than $1 Million in Compensation for Six Months' Work." *Canada News & Travel*, June 20, 2020. https://stanthonysvancouver.org/former-vancouver-cannabis-company-ceo-collected-more-than-1-million-in-compensation-for-six-months-work/.

Statistics Canada. 2022. "Table 20-10-0008-01 Retail Trade Sales by Province and Territory (x 1,000)." Cannabis Stores, Unadjusted. Modified June 25, 2022. https://t.co/o2Jfxal9nU.

Subramaniam, Vanmala. 2019. "Aurora Cannabis Facility That Was Beacon of Hope for Failing Alberta Town Now Faces Uncertainty Amid Pot Oversupply Woes." *Financial Post*, December 20, 2019. https://financialpost.com/cannabis/aurora-cannabis-facility-that-was-beacon-of-hope-for-ailing-alberta-town-now-faces-uncertainty-amid-pot-oversupply-woes.

____. 2021. "Canadian Cannabis Companies Collect Millions in Emergency Wage Subsidies Even as Sector Consolidates." *The Globe and Mail*, January 26, 2021. https://www.theglobeandmail.com/business/article-canadian-cannabis-companies-collected-more-than-40-million-in-wage/.

Tilray Inc. 2021. "(TLRY) Q1 2022 Earnings Call Transcript." *The Motley Fool*. October 8, 2021. https://www.fool.com/earnings/call-transcripts/2021/10/08/tilray-inc-tlry-q1-2022-earnings-call-transcript/.

____. Tilray Inc. 2022. "Tilray Brands Announces Proposed Agreement for Strategic Alliance with HEXO Corp." March 3, 2022. https://www.tilray.com/tilraynews-master/2022/3/3/tilray-brands-announces-proposed-agreement-for-strategic-alliance-with-HEXO-corp.

9. Let's Try Something Different

l'Assemblée nationale du Québec. 2018. "An Act to Establish the Société Québécoise du Québec Cannabis, Enacting the Law Regulating Cannabis and Modifying Various Road Safety Provisions." Chapter III, Article 23.30: Proceeds from the Sale of Cannabis. [Translated from French to English using Google Translate]. June 12, 2018. http://www2.publicationsduquebec.gouv.qc.ca/dynamicSearch/telecharge.php?type=5&file=2018C19F.PDF.

Auriol, Emmanuelle and Pierre-Yves Geoffard. 2019. "Cannabis: How to Resume Control?" [Translated from French to English using Google Translate]. Conseil d'analyse economique. June 2019. https://www.cae-eco.fr/staticfiles/pdf/cae-note052.pdf.

Barry, Rachel Ann and Stanton Glantz. 2016. "A Public Health Framework for Legalized Retail Marijuana Based on the US Experience: Avoiding a New Tobacco Industry." *PLOS Medicine* 13 (9): e1002131. https://pubmed.ncbi.nlm.nih.gov/27676176/.

Callard, Cynthia, Dave Thompson, and Neil Collishaw. 2005a. "Curing the Addiction to Profits: a Supply-Side Approach to Phasing Out Tobacco." Canadian Centre for Policy Alternatives. Modified May 5, 2009. http://www.aerzteinitiative.at/StrategyCan09.pdf.

____. 2005b. "Transforming the Tobacco Market: Why the Supply of Cigarettes Should Be Transferred from For-Profit Corporations to Non-Profit Enterprises with a Public Health Mandate." *Tobacco Control* 14 (4) : 278-83. http://www.ncbi.nlm.nih.gov/pmc/articles/PMC1748051/pdf/v014p00278.pdf.

Canadian Centre on Substance Use and Addiction. 2019. "Policy Brief: Composition of Boards Overseeing Retail Cannabis Sales and Wholesale Distribution Across Canada." October 2019. https://ccsa.ca/sites/default/files/2019-10/CCSA-Composition-of-Boards-Retail-Cannabis-Sales-Distribution-Canada-Policy-Brief-2019-en_0.pdf.

REFERENCES

Caulkins, Jonathan P., Beau Kilmer, Mark A. R. Kleiman, Robert J. MacCoun, Gregory Midgette, Pat Oglesby, Rosalie Liccardo Pacula, and Peter H. Reuter. 2015. "Considering Marijuana Legalization: Insights for Vermont and Other Jurisdictions." The RAND Corporation. January 2015. https://www.rand.org/content/dam/rand/pubs/research_reports/RR800/RR864/RAND_RR864.pdf.

Chapados, Maude, François Gagnon, Geneviève Lapointe, Sébastien Tessier, Nicole April, Richard Coovi Fachehoun, and Onil Samuel. 2016. "Legalization of Non-Medical Cannabis: A Public Health Approach to Regulation." Institut national de santé publique du Québec. October 2016. https://www.inspq.qc.ca/sites/default/files/publications/2233_legalization_non_medical_cannabis_0.pdf.

Chief Medical Officers of Health of Canada and Urban Public Health Network. 2016. "Public Health Perspectives on Cannabis Policy and Regulation." September 26, 2016. http://uphn.ca/wp-content/uploads/2016/10/Chief-MOH-UPHN-Cannabis-Perspectives-Final-Sept-26-2016.pdf.

Decorte, Tom. 2015. "Cannabis Social Clubs in Belgium: Organizational Strengths and Weaknesses, and Threats to the Model." *The International Journal on Drug Policy*. 26 (2): 122-30. https://pubmed.ncbi.nlm.nih.gov/25179934/.

Gagnon, François. 2021. "The Non-Medical Cannabis Regime in Québec: a Public Health Analysis." Institut national de santé publique du Québec, June 2021. https://www.inspq.qc.ca/sites/default/files/publications/2829-non-medical-cannabis-regime-public-health-analysis.pdf.

Giesbrecht, Norman, Ashley Wettlaufer, Tim Stockwell, Kate Vallance, Clifton Chow, Nicole April, Mark Asbridge et al. 2021. "Alcohol Retail Privatisation in Canadian Provinces Between 2012 and 2017. Is Decision Making Oriented to Harm Reduction?" *Drug and Alcohol Review* 40 (3) :459-67. https://pubmed.ncbi.nlm.nih.gov/33319402/.

Marijuana Business Daily. 2022. "DC's Recreational Marijuana Ambitions Blocked in Federal Bill." March 9, 2022. https://mjbizdaily.com/dcs-recreational-marijuana-ambitions-blocked-in-federal-bill/.

Murkin, George. 2015. "Cannabis Social Clubs in Spain: Legalisation Without Commercialisation." Transform Drugs, January 2015. https://transformdrugs.org/assets/files/PDFs/cannabis-in-spain-briefing-2018.pdf.

Myran, Daniel, Jarvis Chen, Norman Giesbrecht, and Vaughan Rees. 2019. "The Association Between Alcohol Access and Alcohol Attributable Emergency Department Visits in Ontario, Canada." *Addiction* 14 (7): 1183-91. https://onlinelibrary.wiley.com/doi/10.1111/add.14597.

Office of the Auditor General of Ontario. 2020. "Value-For-Money Audit: Alcohol and Gaming Commission of Ontario." December 2020. https://www.auditor.on.ca/en/content/annualreports/arreports/en20/20VFM_01AGCO.pdf.

____. 2021. "Value-For-Money Audit: Ontario Cannabis Retail Corporation." December 2021. https://www.auditor.on.ca/en/content/annualreports/arreports/en21/AR_OCRC_en21.pdf.

Pardal, Mafalda, Tom Decorte, Melissa Bone, Òscar Parés, and Julia Johansson (2020). "Mapping Cannabis Social Clubs in Europe." *European Journal of Criminology* July 18, 2020. https://journals.sagepub.com/doi/abs/10.1177/1477370820941392.

Physicians for a Smoke-Free Canada. 2021. "Considerations for Tobacco Control Planning in 2021." November 2021. http://smoke-free.ca/pdf_1/2021/Letter-to-ministers-nov-2021.pdf.

Quesnel, Géraldine T. 2003. "The Evolution of the Commercial Practices of the Société des alcools du Québec." [Translated from French to English using Google Translate]. Institut national de santé publique du Québec. Modified January 18, 2018. https://www.inspq.qc.ca/sites/default/files/publications/161_evolution-pratiquescommercialessaq.pdf.

Rolles, Steve, Mike Barton, Niamh Eastwood, Tom Lloyd, Fiona Measham, David Nutt, and Harry Sumnall. 2016. "A Framework for a Regulated Market for Cannabis in the UK: Recommendations from an Expert Panel." UK Liberal Democrat Party. March 2016. https://d3n8a8pro7vhmx.cloudfront.net/libdems/pages/10794/attach-ments/original/1457398164/A_framework_for_a_regulated_market_for_can-nabis_in_the_UK.pdf?1457398164.

Room, Robin, Benedikt Fischer, Wayne Hall, Simon Lenton, and Peter Reuter. 2010. *Cannabis Policy: Moving Beyond Stalemate*. Oxford: Oxford University Press. https://www.researchgate.net/publication/50996221_Cannabis_Policy_Moving_beyond_stalemate.

Seddon, Toby. 2020. "Immoral in Principle, Unworkable in Practice: Cannabis Law Reform, The Beatles and The Wootton Report." *The British Journal of Criminology*, 60 (6): 1567-84. https://doi.org/10.1093/bjc/azaa042.

Société Québécoise du cannabis. 2021. SQDC Annual Report 2021. July 2021. https://www.sqdc.ca/en-CA/about-the-sqdc/acces-to-information/Publications.

Spithoff, Sheryl, Brian Emerson, and Andrea Spithoff. 2015. "Cannabis Legalization: Adhering to Public Health Best Practice." *Canadian Medical Association Journal* 187 (16): 1211-16. http://www.cmaj.ca/content/187/16/1211.figures-only.

Stanford Network for Addiction Policy. 2020. "Making Legalized Marijuana Production and Sale Non-Profit to Protect Public Health." Stanford University. May 2020. https://addictionpolicy.sites.stanford.edu/sites/g/files/sbiybj25011/files/me-dia/file/snap_marijuana_nonprofitsales.pdf

Title, Shaleen. 2022. "Bigger is Not Better: Preventing Monopolies in the National Cannabis Market." Ohio State Drug Enforcement and Policy Center. January 26, 2022. https://papers.ssrn.com/sol3/papers.cfm?abstract_id=4018493.

Tobacco Endgame Cabinet. 2019. "The Tobacco Endgame Report: Getting to Less Than 5% by 2035." May 28, 2019. https://www.lung.ca/sites/default/files/EndGameRe-port-final.pdf.

10. What's Next in Drug Policy Reform?

Adams, Peter J., Marta Rychert, and Chris Wilkins. 2021. "Policy Influence and the Legalized Cannabis Industry: Learnings from Other Addictive Consumption Industries." *Addiction* 116 (11), 2939-46. https://doi.org/10.1111/add.15483.

Alan Aldous Inc. 2020. "World's First Psychedelics PR Agency Launched by Canadian Cannabis Professionals." *Cision*, February 18, 2020. https://www.newswire.ca/news-releases/world-s-first-psychedelics-pr-agency-launched-by-canadian-cannabis-pro-fessionals-876457839.html.

Allan, G. Michael, Caitlin R. Finley, Joey Ton, Danielle Perry, Jamil Ramji, Karyn Crawford, Adrienne J. Lindblad, Christina Korownyk and Michael R. Kolber. "Systematic Review of Systematic Reviews for Medical Cannabinoids." Canadian Family Physician 64 (2): e78-e94. https://www.cfp.ca/content/64/2/e78.

AP News. 2022. "Germany Moves Ahead with Plan to Legalize Cannabis Sales." June 13, 2022. https://apnews.com/article/health-business-germany-olaf-scholz-74417f8961981b00917eff0b23a4644b.

REFERENCES

Aphria, Aurora Cannabis, Canadian Medical Cannabis Council Cannabis Canada, CannTrust Inc., Canopy Growth, Cresco Pharma, et al. 2017. "Adult Use Cannabis Advertising and Marketing Self-Regulatory Guidelines for Licensed Producers."
   November 2017. https://cannabislaw.report/wp-content/up-
   loads/2017/11/GuidelinesforCannabis-EN-Nov6.pdf.

Arellano, Gaël. 2021. "Work on the Project Is 'Still Ongoing', Says Minister of Health."
   RTL, February 26, 2021. https://today.rtl.lu/news/luxembourg/a/1678814.html.

Associated Press. 2022. "J&J, Distributors Will Pay $26B US to Settle Claims They Fuelled
   the Opioid Crisis." *CBC News*, February 25, 2022. ht-
   tps://www.cbc.ca/news/world/26-billion-dollar-landmark-settlement-opioid-crisis-
   feb-25-1.6364462.

Bauer, Barbara E. 2021. "Hamilton Morris Synthesizes 5-MeO-DMT in 'Pharmacopeia'."
   Psychedelic Science Review, January 5, 2021. https://psychedelicre-
   view.com/hamilton-morris-synthesizes-5-meo-dmt/.

BBC News. 2021. "Malta Becomes First EU Nation to Legalise Cannabis." December 14,
   2021. https://www.bbc.com/news/world-europe-59660856.

Berger, Miriam. 2021. "In First for Europe, Malta to Legalize Recreational Marijuana, with
   Several Other Countries on the Cusp." *The Washington Post*, December 13, 2021. https://www.washingtonpost.com/world/2021/12/13/malta-legalize-marijuana-can-
   nabis-cultivation-europe/.

Betsos, Alex, Jenna Valleriani, Jade Boyd, Geoff Bardwell, Thomas Kerr, and Ryan
   McNeil. 2021. "'I Couldn't Live with Killing One of My Friends or Anybody': a Rapid
   Ethnographic Study of Drug Sellers' Use of Drug Checking." *International Journal of
   Drug Policy* 87 102845. https://doi.org/10.1016/j.drugpo.2020.102845.

Blanchard, Sessi Kuwabara. 2020. "Leaked FBI Report: Drug Sellers Practice Harm Reduction." *Filter*, December 2, 2020. https://filtermag.org/fbi-dealers-harm-reduc-
   tion/.

Bogot, William, Joshua Horn, and Kimberly Kwan. 2021. "Why the Cannabis Industry
   Should Make Room for Mushrooms." *Marijuana Business Daily*, August 17, 2021. https://mjbizdaily.com/why-the-cannabis-industry-should-make-room-for-mush-
   rooms/.

Boseley, Sarah. 2019. "Doctors Not Prescribing Cannabis Because of Lack of Clinical Trials." The Guardian, July 3, 2019. https://www.theguardian.com/soci-
   ety/2019/jul/03/doctors-not-prescribing-medicinal-cannabis-due-to-lack-of-clinical-
   trials.

Bourgeois, Phillipe, 1995, In Search of Respect: Selling Crack in El Barrio, Publisher:
   Cambridge University Press.

Brinkmann, Bernd, Justus Beike, Helga Köhler, A. Heinecke, and Thomas Bajanowski.
   2002. "Incidence of Alcohol Dependence Among Drunken Drivers." *Drug and Alcohol
   Dependence* 66 (1): 7-10. https://www.sciencedirect.com/science/art-
   icle/abs/pii/S0376871601001776#!.

Bryant, Chris. 2022. "Magic Mushrooms Are Giving Investors a Bad Trip." *The Washington
   Post*, April 14, 2022. https://www.washingtonpost.com/business/magic-mush-
   rooms-are-giving-investors-a-bad-trip/2022/04/14/049e86b0-bbc2-11ec-a92d-
   c763de818c21_story.html.

Bryden, Joan. 2021. "Trudeau Urged to Make Decriminalization of Illicit Drugs a Priority." *CTV News*, October 20, 2021. https://www.ctvnews.ca/politics/trudeau-urged-
   to-make-decriminalization-of-illicit-drugs-a-priority-1.5631807.

Callaghan, Russell C., Marcos Sanches, Claire Benny, Tim Stockwell, Adam Sherk and Stephen J. Kish. 2019. "Who Consumes Most of the Cannabis in Canada? Profiles of Cannabis Consumption by Quantity." *Drug and Alcohol Dependence* 205: 107587. https://pubmed.ncbi.nlm.nih.gov/31600617/.

Callaghan, Russell C., Julia Vander Heiden, Marcos Sanches, Mark Asbridge, Andrew Hathaway, Stephen J. Kish. 2021. "Impacts of Canada's Cannabis Legalization on Police-Reported Crime Among Youth: Early Evidence." *Addiction* 116 (12): 3454-62. https://onlinelibrary.wiley.com/doi/10.1111/add.15535.

Campbell, Bruce (Editor). 2022. Corporate Rules: The Real World of Business Regulation in Canada. Toronto: Lorimer Books.

Canada. 2016. "Consumer Information - Cannabis (Marihuana, Marijuana)." Modified August 19, 2016. https://www.canada.ca/en/health-canada/services/drugs-medication/cannabis/licensed-producers/consumer-information-cannabis.html.

___. 2021a. "Canadian Cannabis Survey 2021: Summary." Figure 11. Modified December 23, 2021. https://www.canada.ca/en/health-canada/services/drugs-medication/cannabis/research-data/canadian-cannabis-survey-2021-summary.html.

___. 2021b. "Canadian Cannabis Survey. Data Blog." Modified December 23, 2021. https://health-infobase.canada.ca/cannabis/.

___. 2021c. "Canadian Tobacco, Alcohol and Drugs Survey (CTADS): Summary of Results for 2017." Modified August 12, 2021. https://www.canada.ca/en/health-canada/services/canadian-alcohol-drugs-survey/2017-summary.html#n3.

___. 2022. "Budget 2022: A Plan to Grow Our Economy and Make Life More Affordable." Modified April 7, 2022. https://budget.gc.ca/2022/home-accueil-en.html.

Canadian Centre on Substance Use and Addiction. 2022."Cannabis Legalization: 2021-2022 Observations." June 2022. https://www.ccsa.ca/sites/default/files/2022-06/CCSA-Cannabis-Legalization-2021-2022-Observations-Policy-Brief-2022-en.pdf.

Canadian Press. 2021. "Vancouver Sends Drug Decriminalization Pitch to Health Canada for Federal Review." *Toronto Star*, June 1, 2021. https://www.thestar.com/news/canada/2021/06/01/vancouver-sends-drug-decriminalization-pitch-to-health-canada-for-federal-review.html.

Canadian Public Health Association. 2017. "Decriminalization of Personal Use of Psychoactive Substances." October 2017. https://www.cpha.ca/sites/default/files/uploads/policy/positionstatements/decriminalization-positionstatement-e.pdf.

Canadian Society of Addiction Medicine. 2020. "CSAM-SMCA Policy Statement. Criminalizing Drug Use is Harming Canadians." October 2020. http://csam-smca.org/wp-content/uploads/2020/10/Criminalizing-Drug-Use-is-Harming-Canadians.pdf.

Canadian Substance Use Costs and Harms Scientific Working Group. 2018. "Canadian Substance Use Costs and Harms (2007–2014)." Canadian Centre on Substance Use and Addiction. https://ccsa.ca/sites/default/files/2019-04/CSUCH-Canadian-Substance-Use-Costs-Harms-Report-2018-en.pdf.

___. 2020. "Canadian Substance Use Costs and Harms 2015–2017." Canadian Centre on Substance Use and Addiction. https://csuch.ca/publications/CSUCH-Canadian-Substance-Use-Costs-Harms-Report-2020-en.pdf.

___. n.d. "Canadian Substance Use Costs and Harms." Database Version 2.0.0. Canadian Centre on Substance Use and Addiction. Accessed April 12, 2022. https://csuch.ca/explore-the-data/.

Cannabis Council of Canada. 2021. "Not Done Yet Report Card." October 19, 2021. https://cannabis-council.ca/files/Not-Done-Yet-Report-Card-Rationale-10.19.21.pdf.

Cannabis Digest. 2010. "An Interview with Elizabeth May. The Greens on Mandatory Minimums and Legalization." November 1, 2010. https://cannabisdigest.ca/an-interview-with-elizabeth-may/.

REFERENCES

Castronuovo, Celine. 2020. "Oregon First State to Legalize Hallucinogenic 'Magic' Mushrooms." *The Hill*, November 4, 2020. https://thehill.com/homenews/state-watch/524453-oregon-first-state-to-legalize-hallucinogenic-magic-mushrooms.

Caulkins, Jonathan P. 2016. "The Real Dangers of Marijuana." *National Affairs* Winter 2016. http://www.nationalaffairs.com/publications/detail/the-real-dangers-of-marijuana.

____. 2017. "A Principled Approach to Taxing Marijuana." *National Affairs* Summer 2017. https://nationalaffairs.com/publications/detail/a-principled-approach-to-taxing-marijuana.

CBC News. 2020a. "Decriminalization of Drugs 'Not a Silver Bullet' for Overdose Crisis, Prime Minister Says." September 2, 2020. https://www.cbc.ca/news/canada/british-columbia/justin-trudeau-decriminalization-1.5709124?cmp=rss.

____. 2020b. "Legal Age to Buy Cannabis in Quebec Is Now 21, the Highest in Canada." January 1, 2020. https://www.cbc.ca/news/canada/Montréal/legal-age-cannabis-edibles-1.5399211.

____. 2021. "BC Mayors Lend Support to Vancouver's Drug Decriminalization Plan." June 15, 2021. https://www.cbc.ca/news/canada/british-columbia/bc-mayors-support-vancouver-decriminalization-1.6065847.

Centre for Addiction and Mental Health. 2014. "Cannabis Policy Framework." October 2014. https://www.camh.ca/-/media/files/pdfs---public-policy-submissions/camh-cannabispolicyframework-pdf.pdf.

____. 2018. "Submission to Health Canada: Consultation on Strengthening Canada's Approach to Substance Use Issues." December 21, 2018. https://www.camh.ca//-/media/files/pdfs---public-policy-submissions/camhsubmissioncdss2018-pdf.pdf.

____. 2021. "Statement on the Decriminalization of Substance Use." September 29, 2021. https://www.camh.ca/-/media/files/pdfs---public-policy-submissions/CAMH-Statement-on-decriminalization-sep2021-pdf.pdf.

____. Drug and Alcohol Treatment Information System (DATIS). 2015. "Characteristics of Substance Abuse, Open, Individuals, Calendar Year 2014." Data file sent to author, August 12, 2015.

____. "Characteristics of Substance Abuse, Open, Individuals, Calendar Year 2016." Data file sent to author, October 25, 2017.

____. "Characteristics of Substance Abuse, Open, Individuals, Calendar Year 2021." Data file sent to author, June 14, 2022.

Centre on Drug Policy Evaluation. 2020. "How Diverse is Canada's Legal Cannabis Industry?" University of Toronto. October 2020. https://cdpe.org/wp-content/uploads/dlm_uploads/2020/10/How-Diverse-is-Canada%E2%80%99s-Legal-Cannabis-Industry_CDPE-UofT-Policy-Brief_Final.pdf.

Charlebois, Brieanna. 2022. "Canadian Governments OK Settlement with Purdue Pharma Over Opioid Addictions." *Toronto Star*, June 29, 2022. https://www.thestar.com/politics/2022/06/29/cp-newsalert-bc-reaches-settlement-with-purdue-pharma-over-opioid-addictions.html.

City of Victoria. 2021. "Council Highlights. Council Member Motion: In Response to the National Overdose Crisis: Regulation, Safe Supply and Decriminalization." January 28, 2021. https://www.victoria.ca/EN/main/city/mayor-council-committees/council-highlights/2021-highlights/january-2021.html

Cohen, Neta, Laura Galvis Blanco, Adrienne Davis, Alyssa Kahane, Mathew Mathew, Suzanne Schuh, Inbal Kestenbom et al. 2022. Pediatric Cannabis Intoxication Trends in the Pre and Post-Legalization Era. *Clinical Toxicology (Philadelphia)* 60 (1): 53-58. https://pubmed.ncbi.nlm.nih.gov/34137352/.

Crépault, J.-F. and Jesseman, R. (2022). *Regulating the Legal Cannabis Market: How is Canada Doing?* Centre for Addiction and Mental Health. April 6, 2022. https://www.camh.ca/-/media/files/pdfs---public-policy-submissions/cannabis-regulation-report-april-2022-pdf.pdf.

Criminal Intelligence Service Canada. 2019. "Serious and Organized Crime in Canada." December 18, 2019. https://cisc-scrc.gc.ca/media/2019/2019-12-06-eng.htm.

___. 2021. "2020 Report: Organized Crime in Canada." February 18, 2021. https://cisc-scrc.gc.ca/media/2021/2021-01-27-eng.htm.

___. 2022. "2021 Report: Organized Crime in Canada." January 25, 2022. https://cisc-scrc.gc.ca/media/2022/2022-01-25-eng.htm.

Crockett, Dale. 2021. "Montréal Councillors Call on City Hall to Ask Ottawa to Decriminalize Simple Drug Possession." *CTV News*, January 19, 2021. https://Montréal.ctvnews.ca/Montréal-councillors-call-on-city-hall-to-ask-ottawa-to-decriminalize-simple-drug-possession-1.5273097.

Csete, Joanne, Adeeba Kamarulzaman, Michel Kazatchkine, Frederick Altice, Marek Balicki, Julia Buxton, Javier Cepeda et al. 2016. "Public Health and International Drug Policy." *The Lancet* 387 (10026): 1427-1480. https://pubmed.ncbi.nlm.nih.gov/27021149/.

DeLaire, Megan. 2021. "Ontario's Top Doctor Considering Push for Decriminalization in 'Rejuvenated' Opioid Strategy." *Cambridge Times*, July 30, 2021. https://www.therecord.com/local-cambridge/news/2021/07/30/ontario-s-top-doctor-considering-push-for-decriminalization-in-rejuvenated-opioid-strategy.html.

DeVillaer, Michael. 2017. "Cannabis Law Reform in Canada: Pretense & Perils". McMaster University, The Peter Boris Centre for Addictions Research. https://fhs.mcmaster.ca/pbcar/documents/Pretense%20&%20Perils%20FINAL.PDF.

Dubinski, Kate. 2020. "Some Doctors, Therapists Get Health Canada Permission to Use Magic Mushrooms." *CBC News*, December 10, 2020. https://www.cbc.ca/news/canada/london/some-doctors-therapists-get-health-canada-permission-to-use-magic-mushrooms-1.5834485.

Egan, Kelly. 2021. "Ottawa Board of Health Wants Emergency Declared Over Drug ODs, More Lenient Laws." *Ottawa Citizen*, September 21, 2021. https://ottawacitizen.com/news/local-news/ottawa-board-of-health-wants-emergency-declared-over-drug-ods-more-lenient-laws.

European Monitoring Centre for Drugs and Drug Addiction. 2021. "European Drug Report 2021: Trends and Developments." Publications Office of the European Union. June 2011. https://www.emcdda.europa.eu/system/files/publications/13838/TDAT21001ENN.pdf.

Farah, Troy. 2019. "Inside the Push to Legalize Magic Mushrooms for Depression and PTSD." *Wired Magazine*, February 7, 2019. https://www.wired.com/story/inside-the-push-to-legalize-magic-mushrooms-for-depression-and-ptsd/.

Federal Office of Public Health. 2021. "Pilot Trials with Cannabis." August 13, 2021. https://www.bag.admin.ch/bag/en/home/gesund-leben/sucht-und-gesundheit/cannabis/pilotprojekte.html.

Fernholz, Tim. 2016. "America's Weed Industry Is Going to Be Massive. Is Big Marijuana a Good Thing?" *Quartz*, April 20, 2016. https://qz.com/664956/americas-weed-industry-is-going-to-be-massive-is-big-marijuana-a-good-thing/.

Fickling, David. 2021. "New Zealand Is Banning Tobacco. Will Anyone Follow?" *Bloomberg News*, December 12, 2021. https://www.bloomberg.com/opinion/articles/2021-12-13/new-zealand-is-banning-tobacco-should-the-world-follow.

REFERENCES

Fischer, Benedikt, Sameer Imtiaz, Katherine Rudzinski, and Jürgen Rehm. 2016. "Crude Estimates of Cannabis-Attributable Mortality and Morbidity in Canada—Implications for Public Health Focused Intervention Priorities." *Journal of Public Health* 38 (1): 183-8. http://jpubhealth.oxfordjournals.org/content/early/2015/01/28/pubmed.fdv005.full.pdf+html.

George-Cosh, David. 2022. "Ottawa Bound: Canada's Pot Companies Renew Lobbying Efforts." *BNN Bloomberg*, January 28, 2022. https://www.bnnbloomberg.ca/cannabis-canada-weekly-lobbying-ottawa-ahead-of-the-cannabis-act-review-stocks-suffer-decline-1.1715123.

Gibbs, Blair, Tom Reed, and Seb Wride. 2021. "Cannabis Legalisation - Canada's Experience." Public First. October 2021. http://www.publicfirst.co.uk/wp-content/uploads/2021/10/REPORT-Cannabis-in-Canada-Public-First-October-2021.pdf.

Gilmore, A.B. and A. Rowell. 2018. "The Tobacco Industry's Latest Scam: How Big Tobacco Is Still Facilitating Tobacco Smuggling, While Also Attempting to Control a Global System Designed to Prevent It." *Tobacco Control Blog*, June 19, 2018. https://blogs.bmj.com/tc/2018/06/19/the-tobacco-industrys-latest-scam-how-big-tobacco-is-still-facilitating-tobacco-smuggling-while-also-attempting-to-control-a-global-system-designed-to-prevent-it/?hootPostID=c1037cc1e8a42abb396508eefb3a988f.

Gilmore, Rachel. 2018. "Scheer Won't Commit to Keeping Cannabis Legal if Tories Form Government." *CTV News*, October 19, 2018. https://t.co/mhyySISzPO.

Goldenberg, Matthew, Mark William Reid, Waguih William IsHak, and Itai Danovitch. 2017.

"The Impact of Cannabis and Cannabinoids for Medical Conditions on Health-Related Quality of Life: A Systematic Review and Meta-Analysis." *Drug and Alcohol Dependence* 174: 80-90. https://pubmed.ncbi.nlm.nih.gov/28319753/.

Goulem, Brigid. 2022. "KFL&A Board of Health Calls for Decriminalization, Safe Supply of Drugs." *The Whig Standard*, April 27, 2022. https://www.thewhig.com/news/local-news/kfla-board-of-health-calls-for-decriminalization-safe-supply-of-drugs.

Graveland, Bill. 2021. "Psychedelic Drugs for Treatment of Mental Illness the Focus of University of Calgary Research Chair." *Global News*, June 12, 2021. https://globalnews.ca/news/7934737/calgary-parker-psychedelic-research-chair/.

Greer, Alissa, Matt Bonn, Alison Ritter, Caitlin Shane, and Alex Stevens. 2021. "How to Decriminalize Drugs: the Design Features of a Non-Criminal Response to the Personal Possession of Drugs." *CrimRxiv*. August 13, 2021. https://doi.org/10.21428/cb6ab371.8d4b953c.

Griffiths, Roland R., Matthew W. Johnson, Michael A. Carducci, Annie Umbricht, William A. Richards, Brian D. Richards, Mary P. Cosimano, and Margaret A. Klinedinst. 2016. "Psilocybin Produces Substantial and Sustained Decreases in Depression and Anxiety in Patients with Life-Threatening Cancer: a Randomized Double-Blind Trial." *Journal of Psychopharmacology* 30 (12): 1181-97. https://pubmed.ncbi.nlm.nih.gov/27909165/.

Grochowski, Sarah. 2021. "Cocaine, Heroin and Meth Buyers' Club Gets Vancouver's Approval to Secure a Safe Supply." *Vancouver Sun*, October 7, 2021. https://vancouversun.com/news/local-news/cocaine-heroin-and-meth-buyers-club-seeking-vancouvers-approval-to-secure-a-safe-supply.

Gutman, David. 2022. "E-cigarette Giant Juul to Pay WA $22.5 Million to Settle Lawsuit." *The Seattle Times*, April 13, 2022. https://www.seattletimes.com/seattle-news/e-cigarette-giant-juul-to-pay-wa-22-5-million-to-settle-deceptive-advertising-lawsuit/.

Haridy, Rich. 2020. "Landmark Clinical Trial Exploring LSD-MDMA Combo to Begin Late 2020." *New Atlas*, August 25, 2020. https://newatlas.com/science/landmark-clinical-trial-lsd-mdma-mindmed/.

Harper, Tyler. 2022. "2.5-Gram Threshold for Decriminaliz40ed Drugs 'a Floor Not a Ceiling,' B.C. Minister Pledges." *The Abbotsford News*, June 2, 2022. https://www.abbynews.com/news/2-5-gram-threshold-for-decriminalized-drugs-a-floor-not-a-ceiling-b-c-minister-pledges/.

Health Canada Expert Task Force on Substance Use. 2021a. "Report 1: Recommendations on Alternatives to Criminal Penalties for Simple Possession of Controlled Substances." May 6, 2021. https://www.canada.ca/content/dam/hc-sc/documents/corporate/about-health-canada/public-engagement/external-advisory-bodies/reports/report-1-2021/report-1-HC-expert-task-force-on-substance-use-final-en.pdf.

___. 2021b. "Report 2: Recommendations on the Federal Government's Drug Policy as Articulated in a Draft Canadian Drugs and Substances Strategy (CDSS)." June 11, 2021. https://www.canada.ca/content/dam/hc-sc/documents/corporate/about-health-canada/public-engagement/external-advisory-bodies/reports/report-2-2021/report-2-HC-expert-task-force-on-substance-use-final-en.pdf

Hill, Kevin P. 2019. "Medical Use of Cannabis in 2019." *Journal of the American Medical Association* 322 (10): 974-975. https://jamanetwork.com/journals/jama/article-abstract/2748398.

HIV Legal Network. 2020. "Decriminalizing People Who Use Drugs: A Primer for Municipal and Provincial Governments." November 12, 2020. http://www.hivlegalnetwork.ca/site/decriminalizing-people-who-use-drugs-a-primer-for-municipal-and-provincial-governments/?lang=en.

International Network of People Who Use Drugs. 2021. "Drug Decriminalisation: Progress or Political Red Herring?" April 12, 2021. https://inpud.net/drug-decriminalisation-progress-or-political-red-herring/.

Israel, Solomon. 2022. "Canada's Cannabis Legalization Review Running Late, As Industry Hopes for Reforms." *Marijuana Business Daily*, February 25, 2022. https://mjbizdaily.com/canadas-cannabis-legalization-review-running-late-as-industry-hopes-for-reforms/.

Jaeger, Kyle. 2020. "Company Gets Trademark for the Word 'Psilocybin', Frustrating Decriminalization Advocates." *Marijuana Moment*, January 20, 2020. https://www.marijuanamoment.net/company-gets-trademark-for-the-word-psilocybin-frustrating-decriminalization-advocates/.

___. 2021. "Fourth Massachusetts City Approves Psychedelics Reform as Movement Grows." *Marijuana Moment*, October 21, 2021. https://www.marijuanamoment.net/fourth-massachusetts-city-approves-psychedelics-reform-as-movement-grows/.

Johns Hopkins Centre for Psychedelic and Consciousness Research. 2021. https://hopkinspsychedelic.org/.

Johns Hopkins Medicine Newsroom. 2021. "Johns Hopkins Medicine Receives First Federal Grant for Psychedelic Treatment Research in 50 Years." October 18, 2021. https://www.hopkinsmedicine.org/news/newsroom/news-releases/johns-hopkins-medicine-receives-first-federal-grant-for-psychedelic-treatment-research-in-50-years.

Kaplan, Sheila. 2020. "Juul Bought Ads Appearing on Cartoon Network and Other Youth Sites, Suit Claims." *Chicago Tribune*, February 12, 2020. https://www.chicagotribune.com/featured/sns-nyt-juul-ads-cartoon-network-lawsuit-20200212-4q44e2y4vrbyxfatbxdjf6mbjq-story.html.

REFERENCES

Kindleman, Tricia. 2021. "Edmonton Company to Produce Psychedelic Drugs for Clinical Use." *CBC News*, February 23. https://www.cbc.ca/news/canada/edmonton/mushrooms-drugs-clinic-medical-edmonton-1.5924035.

____. Knauth, Dietrich. 2022. "J&J Settles West Virginia Opioid Litigation for $99 Million." Reuters, April 18, 2022. https://www.reuters.com/legal/litigation/jj-settles-with-west-virginia-opioid-litigation-99-mln-2022-04-18/.

Lagalisse, Erica, 2018, "The Dangers of Health and Safety: Marijuana Legalization as Frontier Capitalism," *The Journal of Ethnobiology*, 2018, Vol. 38, Issue 4, Pages 473-488.

Liberal Party of Canada. 2021. "Forward for Everyone." September 1, 2021. https://liberal.ca/wp-content/uploads/sites/292/2021/09/Platform-Forward-For-Everyone.pdf.

Lim, Jolson. 2020. "Tony Clement Joins Psychedelic Drug Company as Advisor." iPolitics, June 26, 2020. https://ipolitics.ca/2020/06/26/tony-clement-joins-psychedelic-drug-company-as-advisor/.

Lopez, German. 2015. "Ohio's Marijuana Legalization Ballot Measure, Explained." *Vox*, November 3, 2015. https://www.vox.com/2015/8/13/9146471/ohio-marijuana-legalization-vote.

Luoma, Jason B., Christina Chwyl, Geoff J. Bathje, Alan K. Davis, and Rafael Lancelotta. 2020. "A Meta-Analysis of Placebo-Controlled Trials of Psychedelic-Assisted Therapy." *Journal of Psychoactive Drugs* 52 (4): 289-299. https://www.tandfonline.com/doi/full/10.1080/02791072.2020.1769878.

MacMillan, Douglas. 2022. "Congress Urges DOJ, Treasury to Examine Drug Companies Aiming to Turn Opioid Settlements into Tax Breaks." *The Washington Post*, March 14, 2022. https://www.washingtonpost.com/business/2022/03/14/congress-opioid-deductions/.

Mann, Brian. 2021. "The DOJ Moves to Block the Purdue Pharma Bankruptcy Deal That Shields the Sacklers." *NPR*. September 16, 2021. https://www.npr.org/2021/09/16/1037806819/opioids-purdue-pharma-sackler-settlement-bankruptcy-deal.

Mann, Brian and Martha Bebinger. 2022. "Purdue Pharma, Sacklers Reach $6 Billion Deal with State Attorneys General." *NPR*. March 3, 2022. https://www.npr.org/2022/03/03/1084163626/purdue-sacklers-oxycontin-settlement.

Marijuana Doctors. 2019. "Medical Conditions Treatable with Marijuana." January 30, 2019. https://www.marijuanadoctors.com/conditions/.

Marijuana Business Daily. 2022. "DC's Recreational Marijuana Ambitions Blocked in Federal Bill." March 9, 2022. https://mjbizdaily.com/dcs-recreational-marijuana-ambitions-blocked-in-federal-bill/.

McIntyre, Gordon. 2021. "Feds Approve Vancouver Psychedelics Company's Trial Use of Ecstasy to Treat PTSD". *Vancouver Sun*, July 25, 2021. https://vancouversun.com/news/local-news/0715-ecstacy-study.

McMillan, Dexter. 2021. "Drug Possession Charges Dropped Across Ontario at an Unprecedented Rate." *CBC News*, September 7, 2021. https://www.cbc.ca/news/canada/toronto/drug-charges-dropped-unprecedented-rate-ontario-1.6162632.

Millar, Trevor. 2020. "Why Psychedelics Are Not the Next Cannabis." *Inside the Jar*, May 19, 2020. https://www.insidethejar.com/why-psychedelics-are-not-the-next-cannabis.

Mooney, Harrison. 2020. "Vancouver Mayor Proposes Decriminalization of Simple Drug Possession." *Vancouver Sun*, November 18, 2020. https://vancouversun.com/news/local-news/vancouver-mayor-proposes-decriminalization-of-simple-possession-of-drugs.

Moreau, Greg, Brianna Jaffray, and Amelia Armstrong. 2020. "Police-Reported Crime Statistics in Canada, 2019." Statistics Canada, Canadian Centre for Justice and Statistics, October 29, 2020. https://www150.statcan.gc.ca/n1/pub/85-002-x/2020001/article/00010-eng.htm.

Mulvihill, Geoff. 2021. "Judge Conditionally Approves Purdue Pharma Opioid Settlement." *PBS News*, September 1, 2021. https://www.pbs.org/newshour/economy/judge-conditionally-approves-purdue-pharma-opioid-settlement.

Myran, Daniel T., Michael Pugliese, Peter Tanuseputro, Nathan Cantor, Emily Rhodes, and Monica Taljaard. 2022. "The Association Between Recreational Cannabis Legalization, Commercialization and Cannabis-Attributable Emergency Department Visits in Ontario, Canada: An Interrupted Time–Series Analysis." *Addiction* 117 (7): 1952-1960. https://doi.org/10.1111/add.15834.

Numinus Wellness Inc. 2021. "Numinus First Canadian Public Company to Complete Legal Harvest of Psilocybe Mushrooms." *Cision*, October 22, 2021. https://www.newswire.ca/news-releases/numinus-first-canadian-public-company-to-complete-legal-harvest-of-psilocybe-mushrooms-849901430.html.

Office of the Auditor General of Ontario. 2021. "Value-For-Money Audit: Ontario Cannabis Retail Corporation." December 2021. https://www.auditor.on.ca/en/content/annualreports/arreports/en21/AR_OCRC_en21.pdf.

Owen, Brenna. 2021. "Lawsuit Filed in B.C. Court Argues Criminalization of Drugs Is a Charter Violation." *CBC News*. September 3, 2021. https://www.cbc.ca/news/canada/british-columbia/lawsuit-filed-in-b-c-court-argues-criminalization-of-drugs-is-a-charter-violation-1.6163475.

Owram, Kristine. 2020. "Move Over, Pot: Psychedelic Companies Are About to Go Public." *Bloomberg Business*, February 11, 2020. https://www.bloomberg.com/news/articles/2020-02-11/move-over-pot-psychedelic-companies-are-about-to-go-public.

Pagliaro, Jennifer, 2021. "Toronto Should Ask Ottawa to Decriminalize Drug Possession in the City, Says Public Health Report." *Toronto Star*, June 7, 2021. https://www.thestar.com/news/gta/2021/06/07/toronto-should-ask-ottawa-to-decriminalize-drug-possession-in-the-city-says-public-health-report.html.

Paley, Dawn Marie. 2019. "Canada's Cannabis Colonialism." *Toward Freedom*, October 8, 2019. https://towardfreedom.org/front-page-feature/canadas-cannabis-colonialism/.

Pascual, Alfredo. 2020. "Germany Firmly Rejects Recreational Marijuana Legalization Bill as Hope Fades for Reform." *Marijuana Business Daily*, October 30, 2020. https://mjbizdaily.com/germany-rejects-recreational-marijuana-legalization-bill.

___. 2021. "French Consultation on Marijuana Legalization Passes 200,000 Responses." *Marijuana Business Daily*, January 25, 2021. https://mjbizdaily.com/french-consultation-on-marijuana-legalization-passes-200000-responses/.

Passifiume, Bryan. 2020. "Decriminalize Simple Drug Possession, Urges T.O. Top Doc." *Toronto Sun*, November 6, 2020. https://torontosun.com/news/crime/decriminalize-simple-drug-possession-urges-t-o-top-doc.

Peesker, Saira. 2019. "Former Cannabis Executives Betting Psychedelic Drugs Could Be the Next Big Thing." *The Globe and Mail*, November 29, 2019. https://www.theglobeandmail.com/business/small-business/article-former-cannabis-executives-betting-psychedelic-drugs-could-be-the-next/.

Physicians for a Smoke-Free Canada. 2022. "Canada's Tobacco Companies and Their Use of Insolvency Protection." March 2022. http://www.smoke-free.ca/SUAP/2020/Litigation%20update.pdf.

REFERENCES

Prieb, Natalie. 2021. "Seattle City Council Votes to Decriminalize Psilocybin and Similar Substances." *MSN News*, October 6, 2021. https://www.msn.com/en-us/news/politics/seattle-city-council-votes-to-decriminalize-psychedelics/ar-AAPcOc2.

Psychedelic Finance. 2020. Cybin and Clarmin Announce Closing of CDN$45 Million Oversubscribed Private Placement and Provide Update on RTO. October 19, 2020. https://www.psychedelicfinance.com/articles/cybin-and-clarmin-announce-closing-of-cdn-45-million-oversubscribed-private-placement-and-provide-update-on-rto.

Public Prosecution Service of Canada. 2016. "Annual Report 2015–2016." June 30, 2016. https://www.ppsc-sppc.gc.ca/eng/pub/ar-ra/2015_2016/ar16-ra16.pdf.

____. 2017. "Annual Report 2016–2017." August 16, 2017. https://www.ppsc-sppc.gc.ca/eng/pub/ar-ra/2016_2017/index.html.

____. 2018. "Annual Report 2017-2018." August 23, 2018. https://www.ppsc-sppc.gc.ca/eng/pub/ar-ra/2017_2018/index.html.

____. 2019. "Annual Report 2018-2019." December 12, 2019. https://www.ppsc-sppc.gc.ca/eng/pub/ar-ra/2018_2019/index.html.

____. 2020. "Annual Report 2019-2020." September 30, 2020. https://www.ppsc-sppc.gc.ca/eng/pub/ar-ra/2019_2020/index.html#section_3_3.

____. 2021. "Annual Report 2020-2021." December 3, 2021. https://www.ppsc-sppc.gc.ca/eng/pub/ar-ra/2020_2021/index.html.

Rahn, Eric. 2022. "Opinion: The Battle for Directors and Officers Liability Coverage in the Cannabis Industry." *Marijuana Business Daily*, May 26, 2022. https://mjbizdaily.com/the-need-for-directors-and-officers-liability-coverage-in-the-cannabis-industry/.

Rajagopalan, Suchitra. 2017. "United Nations and World Health Organization Call for Drug Decriminalization." Drug Policy Alliance. June 29, 2017. https://drugpolicy.org/blog/united-nations-and-world-health-organization-call-drug-decriminalization.

Reader, Ruth. 2020. "This Company Is Working on a Drug That Will Make LSD Less Trippy." *Fast Company*, April 23, 2020. https://www.fastcompany.com/90494749/this-company-is-working-on-a-drug-that-will-make-lsd-less-trippy.

Rosner, Abbie. 2020. "Psychedelic Drugs Can Improve Quality of Life - and Death - for Older Adults." *Forbes*, May 6, 2020. https://www.forbes.com/sites/abbierosner/2020/05/06/psychedelic-drugs-can-improve-quality-of-lifeand-deathfor-older-adults/?sh=1ee4f2852aa9.

Rotermann, Michelle. 2021. "Looking Back From 2020, How Cannabis Use and Related Behaviours Changed in Canada." Statistics Canada, April 21, 2021. https://www150.statcan.gc.ca/n1/pub/82-003-x/2021004/article/00001-eng.htm.

Roy, Eleanor Ainge. 2020. "New Zealand Narrowly Votes No to Legalising Cannabis in Referendum." *The Guardian*, November 6, 2020. https://www.theguardian.com/world/2020/nov/06/new-zealand-narrowly-votes-no-to-legalising-cannabis-in-referendum.

Shepert, Elana. 2021. "Free Heroin, Cocaine and Meth Will Be Handed Out in Vancouver This Month. Here's Why." *Vancouver is Awesome*. August 24, 2021. https://www.vancouverisawesome.com/video/free-heroin-cocaine-and-meth-will-be-handed-out-in-vancouver-this-month-heres-why-video-4241768.

Shepherd, Jake. 2022. "High Societies: International Experiences of Cannabis Liberalisation." Social Market Foundation. April 2022. https://www.smf.co.uk/wp-content/uploads/2022/04/High-societies-April-2022.pdf.

Smith, Jeff. 2022. "US House Passes Landmark Federal Marijuana Legalization Bill—Again." *Marijuana Business Daily*, April 1, 2022. https://mjbizdaily.com/us-house-again-passes-landmark-federal-marijuana-legalization-bill/.

Steacy, Lisa. 2021. "'We Cannot Do This Anymore': VANDU Withdraws from Decriminaliz- ation Talks with City." *News 1130*, May 10, 2021. ht- tps://www.citynews1130.com/2021/05/10/vanocuver-drug-decriminalization-talks/.

Stevens, Alex, Caitlin Elizabeth Hughes, Shann Hulme, and Rebecca Cassidy. 2019. "De- penalization, Diversion and Decriminalization: a Realist Review and Programme Theory of Alternatives to Criminalization for Simple Drug Possession." *European Journal of Criminology* 19 (1): 29-54. https://journals.sage- pub.com/doi/full/10.1177/1477370819887514.

Stoa, Ryan. 2018. *Craft Weed: Family Farming and the Future of the Marijuana Industry.* Cambridge MA: MIT Press.

Stockings, Emily, Gabrielle Campbell, Wayne D. Hall, Suzanne Nielson, Dino Zagic, Rakin Rahman, Bridin Murnion, Michael Farrell, Megan Weier, and Louisa Degenhardt. 2018. "Cannabis and Cannabinoids for the Treatment of People with Chronic Non- cancer Pain Conditions: a Systematic Review and Meta-Analysis of Controlled and Observational Studies." *Pain* 159 (10): 1932-1954. ht- tps://pubmed.ncbi.nlm.nih.gov/29847469/.

Strassman, Rick. 2001. *DMT the Spirit Molecule. A Doctor's Revolutionary Research into the Biology of Near-Death and Mystical Experience.* Rochester VT: Park Street Press.

Sutton, Matt. 2021. "U.S. House Representatives Bonnie Watson Coleman & Cori Bush Introduce Federal Bill to Decriminalize Drug Possession, Replace with Health- Centreed Approach." Drug Policy Alliance. June 17, 2021. https://drug- policy.org/press-release/2021/06/us-house-representatives-bonnie-watson-cole- man-cori-bush-introduce-federal.

Szigeti, Bala´zs, Laura Kartner, Allan Blemings, Fernando Rosas, Amanda Feilding, Dav- id J. Nutt, Robin L. Carhart-Harris, and David Erritzoe. 2021. "Self-Blinding Citizen Science to Explore Psychedelic Micro Dosing." *eLife*, March 2, 2021. https://elifesci- ences.org/articles/62878.pdf.

Talking Drugs. n.d. "Drug Decriminalization Across the World." Accessed August 15, 2021. https://www.talkingdrugs.org/drug-decriminalisation.

TheraPsil. 2020. "4 Palliative Canadians Approved for End of Life Psilocybin Therapy Through Section 56(1)." August 4, 2020. https://therapsil.ca/4-palliative-canadians- approved-for-end-of-life-psilocybin-therapy-through-section-561-first-legal-medic- al-exemptions-for-psilocybin-in-canada-since-1970s/.

Thomas, Gerald. 2012. "Levels and Patterns of Alcohol Use in Canada." Canadian Centre on Substance Abuse. November 2012. https://ccsa.ca/sites/default/files/2019- 05/CCSA-Patterns-Alcohol-Use-Policy-Canada-2012-en.pdf.

Times of Israel. 2020. "Israel Announces Plan to Legalize Recreational Cannabis Within 9 Months." November 12, 2020. https://www.timesofisrael.com/israel-announces- plan-to-legalize-recreational-cannabis-within-9-months/.

Transform Drug Policy Foundation. 2021. "Cannabis Legalisation: a Global Change." May 11, 2021. https://transformdrugs.org/blog/cannabis-change-is-happening-across- the-world.

Tunney, Catharine. 2020. "Federal Prosecutors Told to Avoid Drug Possession Charges When Possible in New Directive." CBC News, August 19, 2020. ht- tps://www.cbc.ca/news/politics/simple-drug-possession-change-1.5657423.

Tunney, Catharine and Christian Noel. 2021. "Liberals Introduce New Bill to Relax Penal- ties for Drug Offences." *CBC News*, February 19, 2021. https://www.cbc.ca/news/politics/justice-reform-drug-treatment-criminal-code- 1.5917710.

REFERENCES

UHN. 2021. "First-of-Its-Kind Research Centre Will Bring Psychedelic Psychotherapy to UHN." October 20, 2021. https://www.uhn.ca/corporate/News/Pages/First_of_its_-kind_research_centre_will_bring_psychedelic_psychotherapy_to_UHN.aspx.

United Nations. 2021. "World Drug Report 2021." https://www.un-odc.org/res/wdr2021/field/WDR21_Booklet_1.pdf.

Wang, Jing, Yanling Wang, Mengting Tong, Hongming Pan, and Da Li. 2019. "Medical Cannabinoids for Cancer Cachexia: A Systematic Review and Meta-Analysis." *BioMed Research International* June 23, 2019:2864384: 6 pages. https://www.ncbi.nlm.nih.gov/pmc/articles/PMC6612387/.

Washington DC. 2019. "Mayor Bowser Unveils Legislation to Establish Legal Sales of Marijuana to Enhance Safety, Advance Equity, and Provide Clarity." May 2, 2019. https://dc.gov/release/mayor-bowser-unveils-legislation-establish-legal-sales-marijuana-enhance-safety-advance.

Webster, Paul. 2021. "Hundreds of Scientists Sign Letter Arguing That Regulation Is Stifling Cannabis Research." *Nature Medicine.* April 22, 2021. https://www.nature.com/articles/d41591-021-00023-7.

Whiting, Penny F., Robert F. Wolff, Sohan Deshpande, Marcello Di Nisio, Steven Duffy, Adrian V. Hernandez, J. Christiaan Keurentjes et al. 2015. "Cannabinoids for Medical Use: A Systematic Review and Meta-analysis." *Journal of the American Medical Association* 313 (24): 2456-73. https://www.ncbi.nlm.nih.gov/pubmed/26103030.

Wikipedia. 2022. "Legality of Cannabis." March 29, 2022. https://en.wikipe-dia.org/wiki/Legality_of_cannabis.

Woo, Andrea and Marcus Gee. 2022. "B.C. to Decriminalize Possession of Small Amounts of 'Hard' Drugs Such as Cocaine, Fentanyl and Heroin." *The Globe and Mail*, May 31, 2022. https://www.theglobeandmail.com/canada/article-decriminalize-drugs-british-columbia-canada/.

Wright, Pam. 2021. "Municipal Council Urges Drug Decriminalization." *Toronto Star*, September 21, 2021. https://www.thestar.com/news/canada/2021/09/21/municipal-council-urges-drug-decriminalization.html.

Wright, Teresa. 2020. "Talks Needed on Decriminalizing Hard Drugs to Address Opioid Crisis, Tam Says." *Toronto Star*, August 22, 2020. https://www.the-star.com/news/canada/2020/08/22/talks-needed-on-decriminalizing-hard-drugs-to-address-opioid-crisis-tam-says.html.

___. 2022. "NDP Decries Defeat of National Drug Decriminalization Bill: 'Blood on Their Hands'." Global News, June 1, 2022. https://globalnews.ca/news/8885995/bill-criminal-penalties-canada-possession-drugs-defeated/.

Yang, Andrew (@AndrewYang). 2019. "We should explore making psilocybin mushrooms legal for medical and therapeutic use particularly for veterans." Twitter, December 14, 2016. https://twitter.com/AndrewYang/status/1206055111304392704.

Zimonjic, Peter. 2020. "Police Chiefs Call on Ottawa to Decriminalize Possession of Illicit Drugs for Personal Use." *CBC News*, July 9, 2020. https://www.cbc.ca/news/politics/chiefs-police-decriminalize-posession-personal-use-1.5643687.

Zussman, Richard. 2021. "BC Asks Federal Government for Exemption to Decriminalize Illicit Drugs." *Global News,* February 11, 2021. https://global-news.ca/news/7634613/british-columbia-federal-government-exemption-decriminalize-illicit-drugs/.

About the Author

Michael DeVillaer has spent his entire career working in the field of drug use, problems, and solutions. He has been a counsellor, teacher, community developer, research collaborator, policy analyst, advocate and a Director at the Centre for Addiction and Mental Health (CAMH), one of Canada's largest mental health and addiction organizations. He currently maintains a part time faculty appointment in the Department of Psychiatry and Behavioural Neurosciences at McMaster University in Hamilton, Ontario, Canada. Mike is also a faculty associate with the Centre for Medicinal Cannabis Research at McMaster and St. Joseph's Healthcare Hamilton, and the Peter Boris Centre for Addictions Research at McMaster. He is a member of the Canadian Public Health Association and the Canadian Society of Addiction Medicine.

DeVillaer was invited to testify on cannabis legalization before the Canadian House of Commons Standing Committee on Health, as well as the Canadian Standing Senate Committee on Social Affairs, Science and Technology. He has also consulted with the Ontario Legalization of Cannabis Secretariat and the Québec Ministère de la Santé et des Services Sociaux and has presented to municipal councils on cannabis legalization. His presentations have been heard by thousands of people including students, social justice advocates, health and social care providers, policy analysts, and academics at conferences. He has appeared on many media platforms and published in academic journals and books on cannabis legalization. DeVillaer writes about drug policy at Drug Policy Alternatives (drugpolicyalt.ca).

For his educational contributions at McMaster University, DeVillaer was awarded the John C. Sibley Award for Outstanding Contribution to Health Sciences Education and Research.

Ask your local independent bookstore
for these titles or visit blackrosebooks.com